A New Economic View of AMERICAN HISTORY from Colonial Times to 1940

Second Edition

A New Economic View of AMERICAN HISTORY from Colonial Times to 1940

Second Edition

Jeremy Atack
Peter Passell

W. W. Norton & Company
New York London

Printed in the United States of America

The text and display of this book is composed in Baskerville.
Composition by New England Typographic Service.
Manufacturing by Maple-Vail.

Library of Congress Cataloging-in-Publication Data

Atack, Jeremy.
A new economic view of American history : from colonial times to 1940. — 2nd ed. / Jeremy Atack, Peter Passell.
p. cm.
Rev. ed. of: A new economic view of American history / Susan Previant Lee and Peter Passell, 1st ed. © 1979.
Includes bibliographical references.
1. United States—Economic conditions. I. Passell, Peter. II. Lee, Susan, 1943– New economic view of American history. III. Title.
HC103.L34 1994
330.973—dc20 93-29990

ISBN 0-393-96315-2

W. W. Norton & Company, Inc., 500 Fifth Avenue, New York, N.Y. 10110
www.wwnorton.com

W. W. Norton & Company Ltd., Castle House, 75/76 Wells Street, London W1T 3QT

0

Contents

Acknowledgments

Writing up the results of one's own research is much easier than writing a text. Being partisan is easy. Trying to represent fairly all sides in the debate over critical and controversial issues is tough. I have tried, but I probably haven't always been successful. Doubtless colleagues who think that I have skewed, slighted, or ignored their work or interpretations will be quick to point out my errors to their students. I hope so because despite the adoption of scientific method and twenty-twenty hindsight (to the extent that there are records), history remains a matter of interpretation.

The organization and presentation of the material in the second edition of this book owe much to the patience of undergraduates and graduate students at the University of Illinois and at Harvard University who wittingly or unwittingly have served as my guinea pigs. I thank them and trust that those who follow will have benefited from their predecessors' experiences.

This book is not the product of the authors working in a vacuum. The first edition owed much to the criticisms of Robert Fogel and Gavin Wright and the suggestions of William Alpert, Stuart Bruchey, Stephen DeCanio, Donald Dewey, Stanley Engerman, Woody Fleisig, Ron Findlay, Robert Gallman, Claudia Goldin, Kenneth Jackson, Hillel Jaffe, Merrill Jensen, Stanley Lebergott, Peter Lindert, Don McCloskey, Jacob Mincer, Richard B. Morris, Chris Norwood, William Parker, Jane Price, Joe Reid, Lloyd Reynolds, Hugh Rockoff, Maria Schmundt, Richard Sutch, Peter Temin, Jeffrey Williamson, and Kathryn Yatrakis. Likewise, many colleagues have given generously of their advice and encouragement in the development and realization of this second edition, some of them for the second time. Part or all of the manuscript was read and critiqued by Lee Alston, Fred Bateman, Charles Calomiris, Ann Carlos, Stanley Engerman, Mary Eschelbach Gregson, Kyle Kauffman, Donald McCloskey, Robert Margo, David Mitch, Matha Olney, Jonathan Pritchett, and Gavin Wright. Of these, three deserve special mention: David Mitch and Gavin Wright suffered through two rewrites and contributed valuable insights and corrections, while Mary Gregson not only read, reread, and critiqued the manuscript along the way but then had the "pleasure" of helping fix what needed fixing. I am deeply indebted to all of them for their advice, their help, and, above all, their encouragement. Others (not mentioned above) have contributed as yet unpublished results or helped me understand their own work better, including Claudia Goldin, Farley Grubb, Charles Kahn, Richard Steckel, Peter Temin, Thomas Weiss, and David Wheelock. Last, but certainly not least, I want to acknowledge the deep debt that I owe to my colleague of seventeen years, Larry Neal, whose constant encouragement and unflagging faith gave me the strength to finish the task and who organized the weekly Economic History Workshops at the University of Illinois that did so much to broaden my education and maintain and stimulate my interest in the field. Not all these persons may wish to be identified with particular interpretations for which the authors take full responsibility, but they may take credit for the best parts—whatever those may be.

I also thank Ed Barber, Drake McFeely, and Cathy Wick, my editors at Norton for putting up with my procrastinations. Ed, with whom I began this project almost a decade ago, in particular, showed great faith in his judgment when I suffered a protracted writer's block. Lastly, I thank my family for putting up with my moods and absences (both physical and mental) as this book took shape.

Jeremy Atack
Vanderbilt University

Preface

When Susan Lee and Peter Passell embarked upon the first edition of *A New Economic View of American History* in the mid-1970s, the "new economic history" was still relatively new. Since then the field—like many of its practitioners—has matured considerably. It has, however, retained much of its vitality. New and novel data sources are continually being developed, and advances in theory offer fresh insights and tools to tackle questions old and new. Moreover, the field has grown enormously as the students of the students of the pioneers have begun to make their own contributions to our understanding of American economic growth and development. The tools of the new economic approach—the explicit use of a theoretical framework and application of quantitative methods—have also spread to other disciplines, such as political science and social history.

The first edition made no claims to being encyclopedic in its coverage of American economic history. Instead it tried to present the results of significant contemporaneous research into controversial issues in American economic history. Slavery dominated the book as it dominated the field in the 1970s. Fully one-third of the book was devoted to the analysis of the "peculiar institution" and its aftermath.

No single issue dominates the field today in the way that American slavery did twenty years ago. Scholarly research has broadened. This revision mirrors that trend. The basic tools of the trade—explicit economic modeling and the use of quantitative methods—remain the same, but as economic theory and econometric methods have advanced, so, too, has their use in economic history, and this has inevitably found its way into the revision. However, despite the increasing sophistication of economic theory, the analysis in this book provides striking testimony to the power of simple supply and demand analysis, which remains the central economic concept for most of the historical economic questions addressed here. Economic theory is a tool, not an end in itself. Its role is to provide the crucial insight into the workings of the economic system, not just historically but today and, one might venture, tomorrow since the basic human motivation that underlies all economic behavior has proved remarkably invariant over time and across space and cultures.

As before, we have made every effort to explain the underlying economic theory and interpret the quantitative results in straightforward terms.

Where technical jargon and particularly powerful concepts could not, or should not, be avoided we have defined them in the text as well as in a glossary at the end of the book. A number of chapter appendices deal with particular theoretical or applied questions, such as the measurement and interpretation of total factor productivity or the IS-LM approach to the determination of national income, at a level of detail which would have intruded if included directly into the text.

Topical coverage in this new edition is still not comprehensive although coverage has been expanded considerably. Nor does this new edition cover the last fifty years or so of American history. Whereas the first edition ignored those issues where the new economic historians had not yet trod, the new edition recognizes that some issues are important even if new economic historians haven't found much to fault or elaborate in the more traditional treatments of economic history. Migration and immigration, for example, were not mentioned in the first edition, and population growth was virtually ignored, but in this new edition population growth and migration get full treatment in their own chapter. Moreover, a separate chapter examines the operation of the nineteenth-century labor market. Another chapter deals with the philosophy of tariff policy and its impact upon regional and industrial development. Although the focus of the tariff chapter is America's trade relationship with Great Britain in the seventy-five years or so following independence, the themes are familiar to anyone following the debate over America's trading relationship with Asia, especially Japan, today. Late-nineteenth- and early-twentieth-century development, all but ignored in the first edition, receives coverage comparable to that of events between independence and the Civil War. New chapters examine the changing structure of American industry and finance, including the emergence of the modern business corporation, the development of antitrust, the growth of financial intermediaries and financial markets, and the establishment of the Federal Reserve. Other new chapters deal with the evolution of interventionist government policies and the development of federal fiscal and monetary policy to regulate the level of aggregate economic activity. The decision not to cover the period since the Second World War in this revision reflects our view that the new economic history has not yet developed a perspective on the period.

Even where new chapters have not been added, much that is new, such as the long-term perspective provided by data on height, the role and contribution of indentured servitude, the economics of the U.S. Constitution, and a comparison of the many different explanations for the Great Depression, has been included in the text. Where the original text has been preserved, it has been reorganized and restructured to develop a more coherent narrative theme while retaining the topical approach of the first edition and focusing upon specific, sometimes controversial issues. Some underlying historical background and narrative are introduced to set these issues in context. This new edition preserves and extends the use of analytical graphs as an integral part of the exposition. It also relies more upon the graphical presentation of data than does its predecessor. By the end of the book the student not only should know more about American history and growth and development in the American economy but also should be more appreciative of the power of economic theory as an aid to our understanding of events and their motivation.

Introduction: What's New about the "New View" of American Economic History?

OK, it's confession time: Not much. What was called "the New Economic History" when jeans had bell-bottoms is no longer very new. But it certainly is improved, in large part because it's been around now for almost forty years—long enough for three generations of ambitious scholars to have added their own contributions and to have scored a few points at the expense of their elders. Long enough, too, for related disciplines—social and political history, for example—to have incorporated many of the methods of the new economic history and call it their own.

When the new economic history was truly new, its hallmark was the application of economic theory and statistical methods to problems in history, as opposed to the study of historical questions that had some economic content. Thus, when two Harvard economists, Alfred Conrad and John Meyer, set out in 1958 to answer the question of whether southerners in the first half of the nineteenth century were rational to buy and breed slaves, they chose to approach the question as a standard investment problem—as if it were GM deciding to buy new robots for the production line. If one assumes markets worked, the price that a sensible investor would pay for an economic asset just equals the discounted value of expected future income on the asset. That the "asset" in this case was a person rather than a new machine tool was irrelevant to the theoretical construct of the question.

Conrad and Meyer ended up not only answering the question—slavery was indeed profitable to the whole South—but also revolutionizing the discipline of economic history.[1]

In the years that followed, first a trickle, then a flood of books and articles adopted this approach to economic history. These early practitioners were dubbed oh-so-cutely "cliometricians"—Clio being the muse of history—though it was soon apparent that it was more than an interest in numbers and measurement that made them different from brand X historians.

[1] Others—W. W. Rostow (1948) and J. R. T. Hughes and Stanley Reiter (1958)—also have legitimate claims to primacy on the new methodology.

However, the label stuck, perpetuated in the Conference on the Application of Economic Theory and Quantitative Methods to Problems in History, popularly known as the Cliometric Conference, and in the Cliometric Society. The phrase "New Economic History" was later coined by Jonathan R. T. Hughes, and Donald McCloskey now talks of "historical economics." Although not all economic historians identify with this approach or are even on speaking terms with its practice, it is fair to say that no one with the remotest interest in economic history can ignore the "new view."

The techniques pioneered by Conrad and Meyer are no longer novel, and they no longer shock, but they have not lost their power to illuminate. Nor has the economic history been static. Rather, as new tools and insights have been added to the economist's toolbox—whether principal-agent problems, human capital theory, computable general equilibrium models, or game theory, to name but a few—economic historians found that they provided better ways to interpret the past. Consequently, they have been quick to adopt them. At the same time economic history has not merely borrowed from economics but also contributed to our understanding of economics. Economists, by training and inclination, typically assume that what is is and rarely question the process by which economic institutions emerged. Time is an inconvenience, or as Joan Robinson, a famous Cambridge economist, may have said, "Time is a device invented by economists to prevent everything from happening at once."

History, however, teaches a different view of time. In the long run we all may be dead, but our descendants can see an evolutionary trend or a revolutionary change. Economic historians therefore can play a vital role by reminding economists that institutions are not fixed and immutable: that they have a beginning and an end and that contrary to one of economics' most cherished assumptions, tastes can and do change.

Beginning with the work of Ronald Coase in the late 1930s (hot stuff, by the way—he got the Nobel Prize for it in 1991), we now recognize that the negotiations to establish rules and to enforce them involve costs. This has led to the view of institutions as compromises, the practical balance between anarchy and gridlock. Coase used this balancing of costs to understand the origin of the firm. And these same considerations also can explain, for example, the choice of sharecropping as the dominant form of tenancy in the South after the demise of slavery.

Economic historians, however, don't just seek to rationalize institutions and outcomes. They also seek to understand how institutions shape the future and how events determine outcomes; call it path dependency, if you want, or historical determinism. Efforts to understand path-dependent processes, whether the adoption of the "QWERTY" typewriter keyboard (so called because this is the arrangement of the first six keys on the top left-hand side of keyboard with which most of us are familiar) or the triumph of alternating current for electricity distribution, also break with the old traditions by trying to understand the dynamics of change—the structure at work. As a result, economists are forced to grapple with the problems of irreversibilities—"lock-in"—that prevent the reconsideration of paths-not-taken.

Consider, for example, what explains the peculiar arrangement of keys on the standard QWERTY keyboard. It certainly bears no relation to logic or linguistics—in English or any other language. Indeed, the Stanford economist Paul David has argued that this was precisely why the keys were arranged that way. The explanation (though it is not universally accepted) is that this pattern, which was but one of a number of competing layouts in the late nineteenth century, solved a technical problem. The action—the mechanical linkage between key and typebar—of early typewriter designs was slower than the speed at which even a modestly accomplished typist could type. The result was a tangle of typebars against the carriage. One possible solution, a speedier typebar return, would have required a stronger spring; that in turn would have required either greater mechanical force upon the key or greater mechanical leverage in the linkage. An alternative was to handicap the typist!

Christopher Sholes, inventor of the first practical typewriter, adopted this latter course, and his machines with the QWERTY layout went into production on machines manufactured by Remington. This arrangement minimized the number of common letter clusters in the English language that were adjacent to one another on the keyboard, it placed more commonly used characters at greater distance from the "home" row and under weaker fingers, and it laid out the keys so that adjacent letters were more likely to come from opposite ends of the typebar, minimizing the risk of typebars' tangling.

What assured the eventual triumph of this layout, however, was the market dominance of the Remington typewriter. This ensured that most typists learned the QWERTY layout. They thus acquired what we call specific human capital, their familiarity with the QWERTY keyboard. They could be retrained, but employers had little incentive to bear these costs so long as the workers were women who were not expected to form lifetime attachments to work outside the home, let alone to a specific employer. As a result, the QWERTY keyboard survives to this day even though the rationale that gave rise to it has long since disappeared. Certainly, computer keyboards can be quickly and simply remapped to whatever configuration one might desire. Instead, most of us stick with the familiar layout even when we complain about lack of standardization over placement of other keys such as <Alt>, <Ctrl>, and <Esc>.

Moreover, economic historians can offer unconventional insights into important questions. Consider, for example, economic growth. Statistics on aggregate and per capita income can make for dutiful, if essential, reading—as the next chapter, alas, shows. The problem with such data, though, goes much deeper than the dryness of the statistics: We want to draw inferences about the quality of life, but an economic measure such as income per person is an imperfect proxy. The economic evidence that is available (and this is increasingly sketchy prior to 1840) suggests that successive generations of Americans have enjoyed almost three centuries of rising real incomes. On the basis of this evidence, it is tempting to assume that the quality of life rose more or less in lockstep. Until recently we had little systematic historical evidence to support or refute such a hypothesis. Recently, however, a team of researchers led by Robert W. Fogel at the University of Chicago have begun working with vast quantities of historical biomedical and biometric information, particularly data on height by age, that shed new light on this question.

Height data were frequently collected as part of induction into the military and these records are available for America from the French and Indian War (1756–63) on. In other countries they go back much earlier. Such data can cast new light upon at least one aspect of the standard of living: how well people ate. Laboratory experiments on animals and scientific observations of human populations have shown that height and weight at given ages, the age at which growth ends, final heights, and the rates of change of height and weight during the growing years are reliable indexes of the average nutritional status. Despite continued scientific debate over the relative importance of environmental (which includes nutrition) and genetic factors in explaining individual variations in height, these data provide invaluable corroborating evidence on living standards, supplementing more conventional measures such as real wages and income. High-income levels are almost always associated with greater height, though we cannot say on the basis of this that higher incomes are the *cause* of the greater height. Moreover, although changes in height during infancy, as well as the prepubescent and pubescent "growth spurt," are sensitive to current nutrition levels, final height reflects not only the accumulated lifetime nutrition of the individual but also that of his or her mother and perhaps even earlier generations.

The earliest height data for America, dating from the French and Indian War, reveal that American recruits aged twenty-four to thirty-five were three to three and a half inches taller than British recruits at the time.[2] Since the colonists were predominantly of English descent, this suggests that accumulated lifetime nutrition for mid-eighteenth-century American recruits was far superior to that of English recruits. Indeed, work on the British data reveals that the short stature of British recruits reflected the deprivations of the lower classes in Britain, since cadets at Sandhurst—the British counterpart to West Point—were just as tall as the Americans.[3] More important for the debate at hand, though, Americans before the Revolution were almost as

[2] Sokoloff and Villaflor (1982).
[3] Floud (1990).

FIGURE 1

Life Expectancy and Final Height of American-Born White Males, 1710–1960

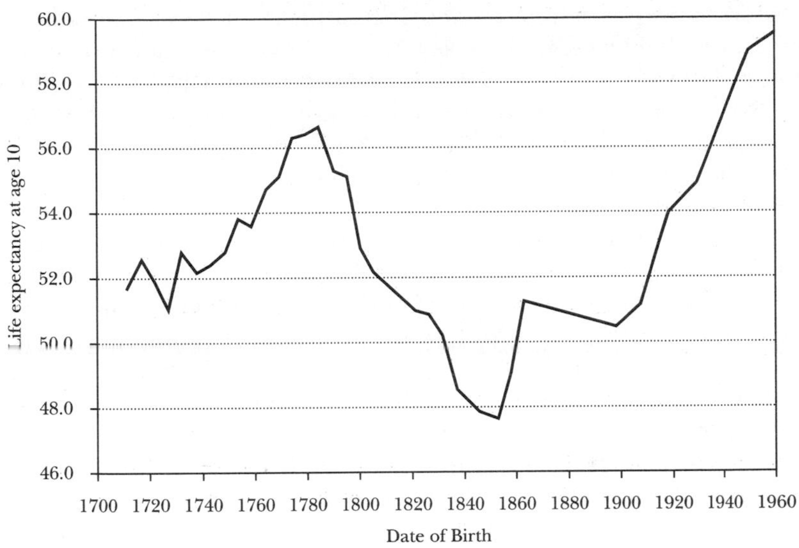

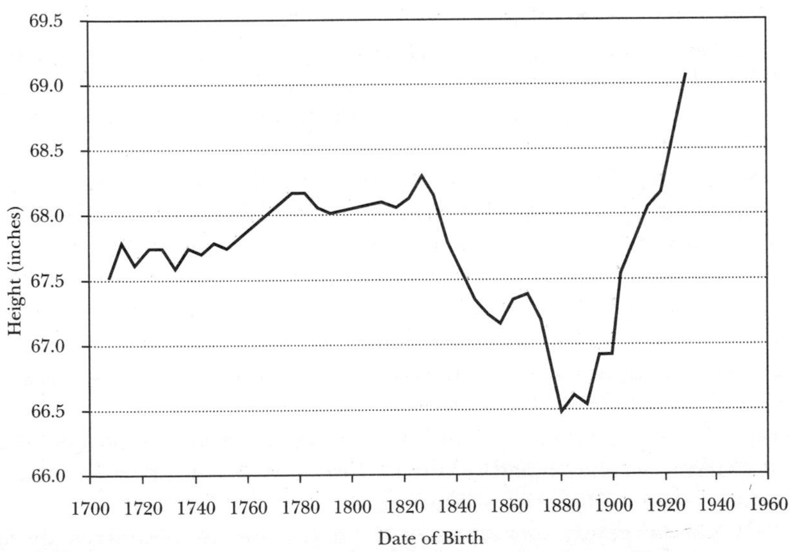

Source: Robert Fogel, "Nutrition and the Decline in Mortality since 1700," in Stanley Engerman and Robert Gallman, eds. *Long-Term Factors in American Economic Growth* (Chicago: University of Chicago Press, 1986), Table 9.A.1.

tall—68.1 inches on average—as American recruits for World War II (Figure 1). Americans thus reached modern stature almost two centuries ago.

Average heights in America were increasing from at least the 1740s, with southerners slightly taller than New Englanders and rural residents taller than urban dwellers. These trends continued in the early antebellum period. By the time of the Civil War, the average height of recruits into the Union army was 68.5 inches.[4] Recruits born before 1820 were somewhat shorter than those born later, but height again began to fall slightly for those born after 1830–35.

There then begins a long secular decline in the height of native-born white male Americans that apparently did not reverse until the early 1890s. During this period the final height of Americans declined by 2 inches to 66.5 inches. Since that time heights have recovered and even exceeded earlier levels. The decline in heights was only briefly interrupted during this period by a slight recovery for that generation of Americans born in the decade following the Civil War.

Does this mean that the quality of life worsened? The answer seems to be a qualified yes, although we are still awaiting the final verdict. Certainly in the period after the Revolution until around 1860 we can say that the *quantity* of life was declining. Life expectancy at age 10 peaked in 1790 at 56.7 years (Figure 1). Thereafter it declined to a low of 47.8 just before the Civil War and has since risen to over 70.

Although the timing of changes in life expectancy and height is not entirely consistent, the patterns are similar, and a single explanation can be given for both even though the decline in life expectancy predates the decline in height and improves before height recovers. The reason may be environmental. Urbanization increased the spread of infectious diseases, contributing to the early decline in life expectancy. Improving public health, particularly in the provision of water supplies, on the other hand, accounts for much of the improvement after 1850. The decline in stature coincides with pollution and declining nutritional quality in urban areas that accompanied industrialization and a lengthening of the food supply chain.

Until very recently historians had a very jaundiced view of the economists' version of economic history and condemned it for attempting to do history without knowing any. Greek letters and regression equations may look great on the printed page, but they make for a rotten literary or oral argument. Moreover, shouldn't we *care* why Andrew Carnegie succeeded and why Populist reformers failed? Historians think so, but it often seemed as if the New Economic Historians didn't.

This is no longer the case. Instead, the historians and cliometricans have found they have much to gain from one another. The dominant theme of

[4] Margo and Steckel (1983).

cliometrics is no longer one of exposing the "errors" of historian colleagues but rather has become a part of the broader reinterpretation of American history through the replacement of one way of thinking with another. Moreover, techniques similar to those used by cliometricans are finding increasing use throughout the social sciences. The New Economic History, the New Social History, the New Political History, and so on complement one another, as well as their parent disciplines. Such complementarity can produce strange bedfellows. A case in point is the reinterpretation of the origins of railroad regulation, as serving the needs of regulated business rather than the interests of consumers, that coincides with Marxian history.

Historical economics also has much to offer the economists who are hooked on the paradigm of the natural sciences—physics, chemistry, and biology. For decades economists have been working to shed their image as "soft" scientists—getting rid of the "social," if you will—by mathematizing every part of the profession and granting extraordinary prestige to the specialty least tainted by subjectivity—mathematical theory. Economic history, however, reminds them of their origins in history and philosophy on the humanities side of the tracks. This may be uncomfortable, but as Robert Heilbroner once remarked, "Mathematics has brought rigor to Economics. Unfortunately, it has also brought *mortis.*"

The New Economic History, while part of the economics profession's trend toward formal theorizing, has retained its contact with the real world. The lesson is that *history really does matter,* not just in path-dependent processes but also in the historical parallels, in recognizing change, and in seeking to understand the underlying processes.

Even for economists who find nothing intrinsically interesting about the past, a good case can still be made for studying historical economics. Understanding economic processes makes it easier to analyze contemporary questions. Contemporary issues, such as foreign competition and protectionism, the funding of large federal deficits, international debt crises, bank failures, stock market crashes, or the geographic relocation of industry and population, all have their historical antecedents. In their history we see events played out. Moreover, to the extent that contemporaneous data were collected, they were gathered for the practical purpose of understanding those events. And these interests and concerns were not too different from those we have today.

In the 1920s and particularly the 1930s, economists gathered data on the business cycle in an effort to understand its origin, its consequences, and how it might be controlled. While study of this topic seemed moribund in the growth and general optimism that prevailed for twenty-five years after the end of World War II, the resurgence of the business cycle in the 1970s and 1980s has resurrected interest in the subject. Economic historians thus find themselves in the happy position of guardians of the accumulated knowledge on this topic now lost to the profession in the mists of time and the minds of a past generation. A list of other subjects with modern relevance might include the determinants of technological change, the returns to public investment in education, the impact of government regulation on transportation, the role of international trade and finance on growth, the costs and benefits of liberal immigration policies, the effects of regional economic specialization, the impact of war on the national economy. We hope to provide an insight into each.

Economists, for all their desire to be objective scientists, are often prisoners of untested theories. Myths about the past become assumptions about the present. As a practical matter such conventions can't be avoided. But good history can give them a critical foundation. We can avoid "stylized" (which all too often is a synonym for "erroneous") facts.

Economic historians offer two other olive branches to economics. First, economic history remains one of the few fields in economics where hypothesis testing is taken seriously. Economists reading economic history are likely to encounter imaginative and creative—and perfectly correct—uses of econometrics. Economic historians are not simply content to report statistical results, noting their (statistical) significance and concordance with the dictates of theory. They actually try to analyze the results, discussing the implications of specific estimates and their independent contributions. Second, although one of the early and leading practitioners of the New Economic History, Lance Davis, once caustically observed that "it will never be literature," economic history remains better written than most economics, perhaps because it has to rely upon persuasion at least as much as differential calculus. Indeed, the work of Robert Fogel has been cited as a prime example of the use of rhetoric in economics.

This book is about events much broader than the keys on computer keyboards or the profitability of slavery. It seeks to provide a perspective on American economic growth and development, presenting the fruits of the New Economic History. Our purpose is to improve our knowledge and understanding of the past in the hope of understanding the present.

The issues dealt with in this text and the attention they receive generally mirror those in the historical economics literature. Some adjustments have been made; otherwise slavery and its aftermath, for example, would constitute perhaps a third of this book—out of line with its importance in the scheme of American development. Most chapters deal with specific topics: What was the basis for pre–Civil War tariff policy? How did slavery affect southern development? What created the Great Depression, and why did it begin in 1929? and so on, arranged in rough chronological order, but the text does not give a complete chronological overview of American economic development. This reflects the dominance of topic-oriented studies in the new economic history. It also permits the in-depth study of some critical issues. Studies using data across time are few in number and are generally limited in time scale, usually twenty to thirty years at most. However, the next chapter dealing with long-term economic growth and the chapter on population embrace the whole sweep of American development.

Students reading this text are expected to be familiar with economic concepts at an introductory level (a glossary of terms and concepts is provided at the back of the book) and be able to interpret simple graphs and arithmetic relationships. Indeed, one of our hopes is that students reading this text will gain a better appreciation of the use of economic theory to illuminate policy issues—whether historical or contemporary.

Bibliography

Coase, Ronald. "The Nature of the Firm." *Economica* 4 (1937): 386–405.

Conrad, Alfred, and John Meyer. "The Economics of Slavery in the Antebellum South." *Journal of Political Economy* 66 (1958): 95–130.

David, Paul. "CLIO and the Economics of QWERTY." *American Economic Review* 75 (1985): 332–37.

Floud, Roderick, Kenneth Wachter, and Annabel Gregory, eds. *Height, Health and History.* New York: Cambridge University Press, 1990.

Fogel, Robert. "Nutrition and the Decline in Mortality since 1700: Some Preliminary Findings." In *Long-Term Factors in American Economic Growth,* Stanley Engerman and Robert Gallman, eds. Chicago: University of Chicago Press, 1986: 439–527.

Hughes, Jonathan R. T., and Stanley Reiter. "The First 1,945 British Steamships." *Journal of the American Statistical Association* 53 (1958): 36–81.

Margo, Robert, and Richard Steckel. "Heights of Native Born Whites during the Antebellum Period." *Journal of Economic History* 43 (1983): 167–74.

Rostow, W. W. *British Economy of the Nineteenth Century.* Oxford: Clarendon Press, 1948.

Sokoloff, Kenneth, and Georgia Villaflor. "The Early Achievement of Modern Stature in America." *Social Science History* 6 (1982): 453–81.

American economic growth: a long-run perspective

1

The economic history of the United States is a success story, one of tremendous growth and development. In 1620 immigrant settlers in what was to become the United States numbered about 2,300, mostly English, but including 20 or so African slaves.[1] This population tottered on the brink of starvation, under the imminent threat of attack, and was ravaged by epidemic diseases. Nevertheless, it survived, was reinforced by waves of immigration, and multiplied. In 1990 the U.S. population was almost 250 million and included persons of almost every race and ethnic origin, including about 30 million of African ancestry, more than 22 million with Hispanic roots, more than 7 million from Asia, and almost 2 million indigenous Americans. Although starvation, the threat of attack, and epidemic diseases have not been completely banished, Americans enjoy a standard of living and quality of life that is the envy of much of the world's population, with the result that it remains the destination of choice for so many emigrants.[2]

This chapter presents the evidence that economic historians have assembled to put U.S. growth into perspective. Estimates of growth during the colonial and early national period are largely conjectural, but they are sup-

[1] The actual numbers are still in dispute. U.S. Bureau of Census (1975): Series Z1–19, lists the population as 2,302 including 20 blacks whose status is not further described but who many argue were not slaves. The number of African-Americans (or more correctly, Africans) apparently derives from a letter by John Rolfe of the arrival in Virginia of an armed Dutch ship in 1619 that landed "twenty and odd Negroes." Whatever their precise number, however, McColley argues that they were almost certainly slaves and that their arrival was no accident. See McColley (1986).

[2] U.S. Bureau of the Census, *Statistical Abstract of the United States: 1992* (Washington, D.C.: GPO, 1992), Table 16.

ported by a growing body of independent corroborating evidence. Those for later in the nineteenth century and early in the twentieth century are based upon interpolations about census-year benchmark estimates. The factors underlying this growth are then elaborated in much of the rest of the book.

It is useful to think of the economy as a "black box" that transforms factor inputs of hours of work, land's bounty, managerial skill, and machine-hours into products and services that people find useful and desirable.[3] The growth of output depends upon the growth of these factor inputs and how efficiently they are used. Growth arising from an increase in inputs is known as extensive growth while an increase in output per unit of input is called intensive growth. Extensive growth occurs, for example, when the labor force grows—whether as a result of immigration or the number of children growing up faster than the old die—when the acres in cultivation grow, or when more machines are used. Intensive growth, on the other hand, occurs when technology changes, when the composition of output changes, or when productivity increases for some other reason. Whereas extensive growth simply describes the size of the economy—"bigger"—intensive growth may be loosely thought of as "better" since with intensive growth each person can consume more with the same effort or expend less energy to enjoy the same consumption levels. The United States has enjoyed both intensive and extensive economic growth.

Such economic growth is conceptually distinct from economic development although we often speak of "growth and development" in the same breath. Development involves fundamental changes in economic and social institutions and attitudes, such as the substitution of a system of secure for uncertain property rights, changes in attitudes toward work, increased reliance upon markets, the development of an infrastructure, and revised expectations about the quality and length of life. Such changes often accompany growth and may even stimulate growth. Thus, for example, many economists and historians view the adoption of the U.S. Constitution in 1789 as crucial to America's success. Consequently, many Eastern European countries today look to U.S. social, economic, legal, and political institutions as they try to chart new courses for their citizens and their economies.

The Colonial Period

Most colonists worked in agriculture, but surprisingly little is known about the rate of growth of output in the century and a half between America's initial settlement and independence beyond the fact that agricultural output at

[3] The measurement and interpretation of intensive and extensive growth are elaborated in the appendix.

least kept pace with population. We know, or can conjecture, more about the factor input side. Land, at least from the narrow perspective of the colonists, was available in virtually limitless supply at the opportunity cost of clearing it and defending it against wild animals, the French, and Indians. Capital, on the other hand, was extremely scarce, both relative to land and in absolute quantity. Considering the small margin above current consumption needs, it must have been accumulated only very slowly, much of it the result of off-season labor spent in clearing land, digging ditches, and building fences and barns. Thanks to various colonial censuses, though, much more is known about population, one of the most important determinants of the dominant factor input, labor. From a modest start in settlements in Virginia and Massachusetts, the colonial population grew rapidly. By the 1660s it exceeded 100,000; by the 1740s it had passed 1 million and, on the eve of the Revolution it numbered about 2.5 million.[4] This is equivalent to an average annual rate of growth of about 3.5 percent per year, a pace at which population doubles every twenty years; whereas population growth today is under 1 percent per year.[5]

As rapid as colonial population growth was, there is no evidence that it reduced the available output per person, in large part because the margin of settlement—the frontier—could be pushed back. Indeed, Thomas Malthus, a noted English economist of the late eighteenth and early nineteenth centuries and the pioneer of modern population economics, drew particular attention to the U.S. case as an example of what might happen if there were no checks on population growth from famine, war, or disease. Population could grow exponentially, and this growth under less favorable circumstances than were found in America could easily outstrip the means of production and precipitate a population crisis. The evidence from colonial America, though, suggests, if anything, that material living standards improved slightly during the period as output grew just fractionally faster than population.

Some early estimates put colonial per capita income as low as $28 for the white population in 1710,[6] but Robert Gallman, a leading figure in early national income estimation, argues that $28 was almost certainly too low.[7] His reasoning is as follows: In terms of purchasing power, $28 would barely cover average expenditures for fuel and food at mid-nineteenth-century levels when prices were not that much different from one hundred years earlier. Since the colonists did not spend all their income on food and fuel, and since it is improbable that per capita expenditures on these items rose markedly over the century, $28 is surely too low. As an alternative, Gallman

[4] U.S. Bureau of the Census (1975): Series Z1–19.

[5] Dividing 72 years by the annual rate of growth gives the number of years that it takes for something to double at that annual rate of growth. This so-called rule of 72 is an extremely useful rule to remember.

[6] Taylor (1964).

[7] Gallman (1972).

suggests that the actual level of income in 1710 was probably somewhere between $28 and English per capita income at the time, which is known to have been about $45. Moreover, per capita income cannot have been much less when settlement began a hundred years earlier.

Sixty years later, on the eve of the Revolution, per capita income was perhaps one-third higher—a very modest increase, certainly, compared with what came later (Table 1.1). After 1839, for example, per capita income in real terms grew at an average annual rate of about 1.6 percent for more than a century. With the fairly solidly based income estimate of $109 per person in 1839, if income had risen this rapidly earlier, then per capita income on the eve of the Revolution would have had to be less than $40 and only about $13 in 1710—less than half of the most pessimistic estimate. Even if one makes the most favorable assumption for rapid growth—that income was very low in 1710 and very high in 1775—late colonial growth rates could not have exceeded 1 percent per year. If, on the other hand, one accepts Gallman's more plausible supposition that per capita income in 1710 was close to $45 and had grown to $60 by 1775, then the implied growth rate is less than one-half of 1 percent per year.

TABLE 1.1

Benchmark Estimates of U.S. Per Capita Income, 1710-1990

Year	Current Dollars	Constant 1989 Dollars[a]	Annual Rate of Growth between Benchmark Dates
1710 (Taylor's estimate)	$28	$350	
1710 (Gallman's estimate)	45	550	
1775	60	750	1.18%[b] 0.48%[c]
1840	109	1,350	0.91
1880	205	2,650	1.70
1929	847	6,150	1.73
1945	1,515	10,450	3.37
1960	2,788	11,100	0.40
1990	22,099	20,950	2.14

[a]Rounded to the nearest $50.

[b]Using Taylor's estimate for 1710.

[c]Using Gallman's estimate for 1710.

Sources: George Rogers Taylor, "American Economic Growth before 1840: An Exploratory Essay," *Journal of Economic History* 24 (December 1964). Reprinted by permission of Cambridge University Press. Robert Gallman, "The Pace and Pattern of American Economic Growth," in *American Economic Growth,* ed. Lance Davis et al. Copyright © 1972 by Harper & Row, Publishers, Inc. Reprinted by permission of HarperCollins Publishers, Inc. U.S. Bureau of the Census, *Historical Statistics of the United States* (Washington, D.C.: Government Printing Office, 1975); U.S. Bureau of the Census, *Statistical Abstract of the United States: 1992* (Washington, D.C.: Government Printing Office, 1992).

Although per capita income grew only modestly between 1710 and 1775, total output increased nearly tenfold, driven largely by the population growth rate of well over 3 percent per year. It was this extensive growth that allowed the colonies the luxury of paying for an army capable of winning independence from Britain and the capacity to supply a hefty percentage of the world's trade in tobacco, rice, and indigo.

Today many economists believe that population growth in low-income countries seriously retards increases in per capita income. Since personal income is determined by labor productivity, more people in these countries virtually always mean less output per person since the amount of land and capital per person correspondingly declines. For such nations as Bangladesh, Indonesia, and Haiti, unchecked population growth—at rates roughly equal to the American colonial rate—has made it all but impossible for them to raise living standards above a level considered inadequate in Europe two hundred years ago. Additional workers in these predominantly agricultural countries reduce the land-labor ratio and labor productivity. In contrast, in the America of two hundred years ago, high-quality land was readily available at the frontier of settlement and labor productivity did not decline. Instead the frontier was pushed westward. Nor did the market value of the average worker's output fall. Elastic international demand for American products supported export prices as output expanded—that is, as supply shifted, the proportionate change in the quantity demanded was greater than the proportionate decline in price—while good water transportation made it possible to deliver goods to port at reasonable cost. As a result, the colonies were able to accommodate a more than sixfold increase in population without a decrease in living standards. It is even possible that extensive growth increased productivity by allowing colonists to take advantage of economies of scale in transportation and distribution. For example, port cities, such as New York and Boston, were probably able to store and distribute goods more cheaply as the frequency of sailings increased.

Even the colonists were never really poor. They might not have been especially rich, but they were not desperately poor in the way that the citizens of Ethiopia, Bangladesh, or Haiti are today. Critical questions such as the extent of the market economy and the cost and composition of a representative "market basket" of goods make historical and international comparisons of price levels and incomes exceedingly troublesome.[8] For example, by one measure, consumer prices in America in 1990 were twelve or thirteen times higher than they were during the colonial period, but other, less conservative indexes suggest a ratio of 20:1 or more. Comparisons can, however, be

[8] A case in point is a recent International Monetary Fund study reported in the *New York Times* (May 20, 1993) calculating China's GNP in terms of what China's currency will buy rather than in terms of U.S. dollars. The recalculation catapults China from the tenth-largest economy with a GNP of about $400 billion to the third-largest with a GNP of about $1.7 trillion in 1992. Such revisions have radical implications for computed growth rates and per capita income estimates.

instructive (Table 1.2). Conservatively measured, a per capita income of $45 in 1710 would be equivalent to an income of about $550 in 1990, but it might have been worth as much as $900 to $1,000, while the nine poorest countries today have per capita incomes under $200 and per capita income in between a quarter and a third of all countries today is less than $550. This 1710 income would thus have placed the American colonies ahead of Indonesia but behind countries as poor as Angola or Bolivia in 1990. By 1840 Americans enjoyed a level of material welfare that would have ranked them among the wealthiest half of nations today, with an income level about equivalent to that enjoyed by the average Turk or the average Jamaican and more than residents of the less prosperous Latin American countries such as Colombia, Equador, Paraguay, or Peru. By 1880 Americans had about the same purchasing power as the average citizen of Uruguay or Yugoslavia (before its recent disintegration into ethnic violence and civil war) more than a hundred years later. Today the United States ranks sixth in terms of per capita income, having been surpassed most recently by Japan in the late 1980s, whereas from World War I until the late 1960s the United States had the world's highest per capita income.

With its large population, the United States nevertheless sustains a gross domestic product (GDP) that is more than double Japan's and perhaps 10 percent larger than the combined economies of the members of the European Economic Community, based upon the most recent International Monetary Fund estimates.

Growth in the Early Antebellum Period

On the eve of the Revolution America was experiencing rapid extensive growth thanks in large part to the impetus supplied by a fast-growing population and virtually limitless land. Further, living standards had gradually improved over the preceding two or three generations, and the population now enjoyed a margin of security above its subsistence needs. Indeed, hundreds of merchants and plantation owners led lives of luxury while thousands of family farmers and skilled artisans, forming the nucleus of a substantial middle class, enjoyed very modest but economically secure lives. The Revolution, however, plunged the country into a new and uncertain political and economic environment both at home and abroad.

Gallman's estimate of 1840 per capita income, $109 (1840 dollars), is almost double the level on the eve of the Revolution. This implies a growth rate for per capita income over the intervening period of almost 1 percent per year or more than double the rate before the Revolution. Moreover, by 1860 per capita income had risen to perhaps $144, or at an annual average rate of 1.5 percent since 1840. Obviously the pattern of economic growth must have changed sometime between the Revolution and the Civil War. The question is when. Opinions have differed wildly.

TABLE 1.2

U.S. Prosperity in Historical Perspective in Today's World

Rank	Country	GNP per Capita (1989 $)	Annual Growth Rate 1965–89	Life Expectancy at Birth in 1989
124	Mozambique	80	n.a.	49
123	Ethiopia	120	-0.1	48
122	Tanzania	130	-0.1	49
121	Somalia	170	0.3	48
120	Bangladesh	180	0.4	51
...	...	...	...	...
	United States in 1710	**550**		
82	Angola	610	n.a.	46
81	Bolivia	620	-0.8	54
...	...	...	...	...
76	Philippines	710	1.6	64
	United States in 1775	**750**		
75	Dominican Republic	790	2.5	67
...	...	...	...	...
60	Thailand	1,220	4.2	66
59	Jamaica	1,260	-1.3	73
	United States in 1840	**1,350**		
57	Turkey	1,370	2.6	66
...	...	...	...	...
38	Hungary	2,590	n.a.	71
37	Uruguay	2,620	1.2	73
34	**United States in 1880**	**2,650**		
36	Yugoslavia	2,920	3.2	72
...	...	...	...	...
24	Saudi Arabia	6,020	2.6	64
	United States in 1929	**6,150**		
23	Ireland	8,710	2.1	74
...	...	...	...	...
19	Singapore	10,450	7.0	74
	United States in 1945	**10,450**		
	United States in 1960	**11,100**		
18	New Zealand	12,070	0.8	75
...	...	...	...	...
7	Denmark	20,450	1.8	75
6	**United States**	**20,910**	**1.6**	**76**
5	Sweden	21,570	1.8	77
4	Finland	22,120	3.2	75
3	Norway	22,290	3.4	77
2	Japan	23,810	4.3	79
1	Switzerland	29,880	4.6	78

Source: *World Development Report 1991* (New York: Oxford University Press, 1991, for World Bank and International Bank for Reconstruction and Development).

The conventional wisdom—pre-1967—went something like this: After 1790 the American economy prospered mightily as a result of the trade boom in the Napoleonic war era. Then the withdrawal of the United States from world trade, as the result of President Jefferson's decision to suspend commerce with the warring parties, produced a sharp drop in per capita income after 1807.

Thereafter stories diverge, but the plot lines remain similar. An early study by Robert Martin published at the end of the 1930s suggested that per capita income might have continued to decline for almost three decades, bottoming out in the 1830s before commencing a period of sustained rapid growth. No one accepted Martin's work without reservations especially after his methods were challenged by a future Nobel laureate and pioneer of national income accounting, Simon Kuznets, and by William Parker and Franklee Whartenby. But then, no one totally bought Kuznets's radical speculation that per capita income might actually have risen during the period. Agricultural historians Marvin Towne and Wayne Rasmussen, for example, argued that rapid geographic expansion represented a serious drag on agricultural labor productivity, depressing per capita income levels in the dominant sector of the economy. The economy, of course, grew extensively under pressure from a rapidly growing population. But the United States had to run hard just to stay in place, as farmers were increasingly burdened by soils depleted through cultivation of tobacco and later cotton. Cost increases in hauling crops to ever more distant markets were barely offset by improving water transportation. Not until sometime in the 1820s did things turn around, thanks to improved farm implements and a spreading transportation network.

Having emphasized the significant productivity growth that accompanied the trade boom between 1790 and 1807, Douglass North, who compiled the early U.S. balance of payments estimates, argued (1961) that the postembargo collapse was so fundamental that significant growth only recommenced in the 1830s. Per capita income was thus less in 1835 than it had been in 1800. Seeking a middle ground between North and Towne and Rasmussen, George Rogers Taylor, writing in 1964, described the whole 1775–1840 period as one of no overall progress; the productivity gains of the late colonial period barely held against the depressing forces of geography and population expansion.

Divergent as these stories might be, they all have one common thread: a turnaround in the 1820s or 1830s marked by an acceleration in the rate of economic growth (Figure 1.1). This acceleration marks what Walt Rostow, one of the pioneers of the new economic history, called the "take-off into self-sustained growth," which he attributed to the expansion of the railroad network in the early 1840s. According to his explanation, railroad demand for inputs and its impact upon the consumers of transportation services created an engine of growth. The development of this leading productive sec-

FIGURE 1.1

Differing Interpretations of American Economic Growth, 1776–1840

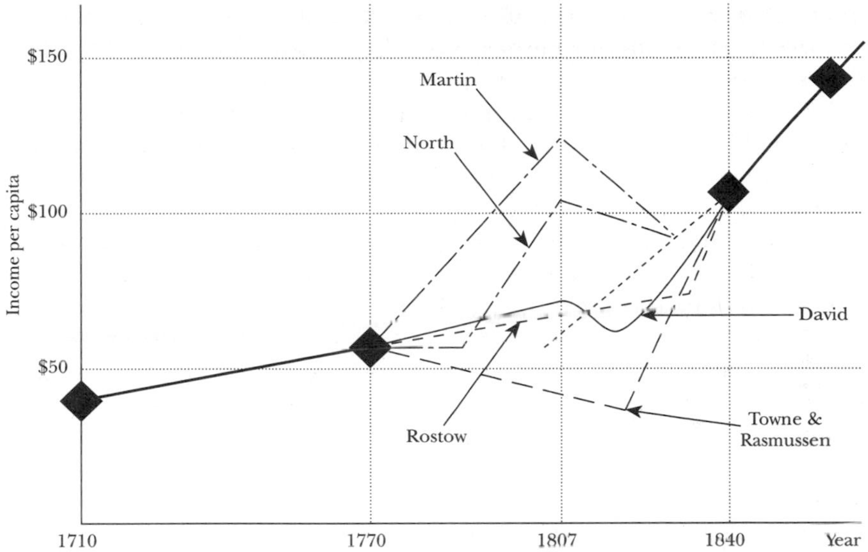

tor in the economy and the emergence of a high national savings rate then stimulated growth in other industries until growth itself became endemic in the economy.

This take-off thesis is particularly enticing because it seems to explain growth spurts in many countries. The Industrial Revolution in Britain, for example, appears to have been led by the cotton textile industry. These growth spurts, however, have differed markedly from country to country. Britain, the first to experience modern economic growth, had the slowest rate, only 1.3 percent per year between 1780 and 1880. Rates in other countries were generally positively correlated with the dating of the take-off. Thus, in the United States growth after 1840 averaged about 1.5 percent a year while in Japan between 1880 and 1960 the economy grew at an annual rate of 2.4 percent. Singapore, which only began its take-off in about 1965, on the other hand, has managed a per capita real income growth of 7.8 percent for the last 20 years. At this rate of growth, income doubles every 9.2 years.

Rostow's take-off, and other theories of economic development that start from the premise of a sharp discontinuity in growth, fit nicely with the conventional wisdom about pre Civil War growth patterns. On closer inspection, however, American history fails to fit these stylized facts. In particular, Paul David's indirect analysis of changes in per capita output, which combines the use of "hard" data with carefully constructed assumptions, suggests a very different picture. Although per capita income before 1840 fluctuated widely, after 1840 the underlying trend was growth at about the same rate.

David's "hard" evidence, and that for many other studies investigating different aspects of nineteenth-century American life, come from the federal decennial census that was mandated by the Constitution for the apportionment of taxation and representation among the people. The census, however, quickly expanded in scope beyond that necessary to fulfill this function. While the first census in 1790 was limited to inquiries regarding the name of the head of the household, color, sex, free or slave, and, if male, whether sixteen or older, in 1810 questions about manufacturing activities were added. In 1820 enumerators began to collect information on occupations. However, agriculture—the dominant economic activity at the time—was not surveyed until 1840. The 1840 census consequently was the first to give a comprehensive view of the nation and its economic activities.

A century later Simon Kuznets extended GNP estimates back to 1870 based upon interpolations around the decennial census benchmarks, but he thought that the censuses before 1880 were too full of errors to use.[9] Other scholars, however, have been more optimistic than Kuznets about the quality of the earlier data. In particular, Robert Gallman, a student of Kuznets's, extended his mentor's series back to 1834, on the basis of extrapolations from 1840. The period before 1834, when Gallman's extrapolations end, however, remains a statistical dark age.

Paul David tried to fill this void using a series of simple arithmetic identities as a framework for careful conjectures about the pattern of growth. Rather than estimate the absolute level of GNP per capita for which the data are nonexistent, David estimated relative levels and rates of change. In the process he produced radically different results from the conventional wisdom of what happened before 1840, yet his analysis when applied to the post-1840 period yields results consistent with the growth rates in Gallman's GNP series.

By definition, output per worker for the economy as a whole is equal to the average output per worker in each sector, weighted by the proportion of workers in each sector. Similarly, output per capita must equal average output per worker times the fraction of the population working. According to estimates by Gallman, manufacturing workers in 1840 were almost twice as productive as workers in agriculture, but there is no information for earlier years to complement the agricultural productivity estimates that can be derived from estimates of total farm output made by Towne and Rasmussen. David therefore assumed that productivity outside agriculture grew no more rapidly than agricultural productivity so that relative productivity was constant over the period. Estimates of the proportion of workers in the agricultural sector were derived from the census for every tenth year between 1800

[9] The GNP estimates for the 1870s are based upon 1880 extrapolations, not the 1870 data.

and 1860 by revising figures derived from the census and originally prepared by the labor economist Stanley Lebergott; the remaining fraction of the work force was assigned to a catchall "nonagricultural" sector. The proportion of the population in the work force—what economists call the labor force participation rate—was also derived from Lebergott's estimates.

Per capita income thus depends upon three variables—the proportion of the population that is in the labor force, productivity growth in agriculture, and the proportion of the labor force in agriculture—and one constant: the productivity of nonagricultural activities relative to agricultural activities. Consequently, per capita income growth depends upon how each of the three variables changes (Appendix A).

What do the computations reveal? Table 1.3 shows an index of David's best estimates per capita income (1840=100) and the average annual rates of growth they imply. For purposes of comparison with the later period, an index of Gallman's direct estimates of output per capita are shown for 1840–60. The decade averages show no particular break in the 1830s or 1840s contrary to the conventional wisdom. Progress, however, is far from uniform—per capita output declined from 1800 to 1810—but the first forty years of the century, taken as a whole, are clearly years of substantial growth.

David distinguished three separate episodes of growth between 1790 and 1860. The first extends from 1790 (although his data do not begin until 1800) through the opening few years of the nineteenth century. During this period, corresponding to the period of rapid growth in foreign trade identified by Douglass North, David speculated that per capita income grew at about 1.6 percent a year until the expansion was interrupted by the trade

TABLE 1.3

Conjectural Estimates of the Growth of Real Product, 1880–1860

	Per Capita Output Index	Annual per Capita Growth (%)
1800	64.4	—
1810	61.9	−0.4
1820	67.6	0.9
1830	84.0	2.2
1840	100.0	1.8
1850	110.4	1.0
1860	137.0	2.2

Source: Paul A. David, "The Growth of Real Product in the United States before 1840: New Evidence, Controlled Conjectures," *Journal of Economic History* 27 (June 1967): 151–97. Reprinted by permission of Cambridge University Press.

embargo of 1807 and the War of 1812. A second growth spurt started in the 1820s and lasted until the mid-1830s, with per capita growth averaging 2.5 percent. The growth rate then slowed to 0.6 percent annually (but remained positive) for the next decade. The third and last pre–Civil War boom, starting roughly in 1845, produced an annual growth rate of 2.1 percent, although in the last few years before the Civil War growth slowed.

Since David's analysis explicitly attributes growth in real per capita output in the period 1800–40 to a combination of increased agricultural productivity, the shift of labor out of agriculture and changes in labor force participation rates, one can apportion that growth among these three factors. The results of this exercise are shown in Table 1.4. Each component of change is estimated on the assumption that all other factors remain unchanged over the decade interval. By this exercise, if the fraction of the labor force in agriculture and average agricultural labor productivity had remained unchanged between 1800 and 1810, then increased labor force participation would have raised per capita output by 0.3 percent. Instead it actually fell by 3.9 percent, principally because agricultural productivity declined during the decade. Similarly, if between 1830 and 1839 labor force participation and agricultural productivity had remained unchanged, the shift of labor out of agriculture would have raised per capita output by 5.5 percent. Notice, however, that this intuitive method of apportioning change does not exactly account for the total change shown in the last column because the factors are not independent of one another. For example, greater emphasis upon dairy farming in the Northeast was an important source of agricultural productivity growth in that region, but it required the active involvement of more of the farm family members, especially women.

TABLE 1.4

The Sources of Change in per Capita Output, 1800–1860

	Percentage Change Attributable to:			
Decade	Shift out of Agriculture	Change in Agricultural Productivity	Labor Force Participation Rate	Total
1800–09	−0.009	−0.032	0.003	−0.038
1810–19	0.039	0.035	0.019	0.095
1820–29	0.066	0.178	−0.012	0.240
1830–39	0.055	0.110	0.025	0.200
1840–49	0.061	0.000	0.066	0.131
1850–59	0.011	0.215	0.000	0.228

Source: Paul A. David, "The Growth of Real Product in the United States before 1840: New Evidence, Controlled Conjectures," *Journal of Economic History*, 27 (June 1967): 151–97. Reprinted by permission of Cambridge University Press.

Apportioned this way, the dramatic decline in the percentage of the population employed in agriculture from 83 percent in 1800 to only 63 percent by 1840 increased per capita income by at least 15 percent as proportionately more workers were employed in higher-productivity sectors of the economy. Robert Gallman suggests two factors that may explain the productivity gap. First, average skill levels—human capital—were probably much higher in manufacturing or service jobs than in agriculture because early-nineteenth-century farmers had relatively little training, while many specialized nonfarm jobs—blacksmithing, clothing manufacture, shoemaking—demanded considerable skill. If so, then the shift away from agriculture was not in itself the cause of increased productivity. Investments in training and capital were also needed before the shift increased overall output per worker. Second, the gap probably reflects the failure of markets to allocate labor to its highest value use. This should not really be surprising. Markets take time to adjust to changing conditions, and when change is particularly rapid, it is almost inevitable that markets will be in disequilibrium.

Changes in labor force participation rates were less important quantitatively, reflecting the divergent influences at work. On the one hand, slave population growth did not keep pace with total population growth—the proportion of slaves in the population fell slightly from 16.9 percent in 1800 to 14.5 percent in 1840—lowering labor force participation, since all slaves, male and female, were put to work as early as possible. On the other hand, a gradual shift in the source of white population growth—from births to the immigration of working-age adults—tended to raise labor force participation. The net result was very little change before 1840.

Changes in average farm labor productivity, which increased more than 30 percent between 1800 and 1840, were much more important. Contrary to the predictions of Towne and Rasmussen, rapid westward expansion did not depress farm productivity. Richard Easterlin's estimate of output per worker in 1840, broken down geographically, shows that the newer farming regions west of the Appalachian Mountains were much more productive than areas close to the Atlantic coast. Transportation was apparently adequate to permit the development of successful specialized commercial farming at great distance from the East, and new studies of midwestern agriculture support this conclusion. Indeed, the regional shift alone accounts for an 8 percent increase in average farm productivity nationwide. The rest of the productivity change thus must be attributed to reduced transport and marketing costs, which allowed specialization, and unappreciated improvements in agricultural technology.

The precise nature of these improvements in agricultural technology before 1840, however, is not clear, and it generates a puzzle: Agricultural productivity growth in the decades before any revolutionary changes in agricultural techniques, such as mechanization, was faster than later, when such changes loomed large. The answer seems to be that agricultural productivity growth was much less than David estimates. New research by Thomas Weiss shows that the occupational switch from agriculture to other activities was much less rapid than previously believed. In particular, Weiss concludes that many of those whom the census described simply as "laborers" (as distinct from those described as "farm laborers") must have worked in agriculture since they lived in rural areas far from alternative sources of employment. His revisions once again push back the spurt in agricultural productivity growth to the Civil War or later. They also reduce pre-1840 growth rates to levels consistent with other estimates of agricultural productivity growth and the growth of real wages in agriculture.[10] In the final analysis, though, pre-1840 growth rates may not be much different from those reported by David. Recent evidence suggests that productivity grew more rapidly in manufacturing than agriculture in the years after 1800.[11]

Still, further revisions are unlikely to produce the sharp growth discontinuity assumed in Rostow's model. The first few decades of the century mark no pause before the great expansion, and the last decades before the Civil War show no "takeoff." As a result, scholars partial to stage theories may be tempted to look for a discontinuity at some other convenient spot—notably the Civil War. This fits well with Marxist development theories, but as we shall see in a later chapter, the evidence is not very convincing. The Civil War appears as an interruption, not as a turning point, in America's long-term economic growth.

The Pattern of Economic Growth after 1840

The pace, timing, and pattern of economic growth after 1840 are not so controversial. Data are more abundant, complete, and similar to those collected by the government today. Moreover, Kuznets's estimates of gross national product since 1869 and Gallman's estimates from 1839 have received a wide degree of acceptance in the profession and link to the official GNP series begun by the Department of Commerce in 1934 for the period from 1929.

During the nineteenth century real GNP grew at over 4 percent per year. In the twentieth century it has averaged a little over 3 percent per year. A number of factors help explain this slowdown. For example, the rate of population growth has slowed because people are choosing to have fewer children. Moreover, despite periodic liberalization for special groups, such as Cuban refugees, Vietnamese, or Soviet Jews, U.S. immigration policy became much more restrictive after 1920. Because of earlier extensive growth, more capital resources are now spent on capital deepening (that is, raising capital per worker) rather than capital widening (that is, expanding the cap-

[10] See, for example, Gallman (1975) and Adams (1986).
[11] Goldin and Sokoloff (1984) and Sokoloff (1986).

ital stock at the same pace as the growth of the labor force), and rates of return have fallen because the most profitable ventures attracted the earliest investment. This, in turn, has slowed the rate of capital accumulation. Lastly, those resources best adapted to their intended use are the first to be employed, and the productivity of successive factors is lower.

These same forces also explain why growth rates differ between countries, in particular why the U.S. growth rate since 1945 has lagged behind that of Germany and Japan, and why Japan has now surpassed the United States in terms of per capita GDP. They also help explain why international per capita income and productivity levels appear to converge in the long run. It's tough to stay ahead of the race when the latecomers can benefit from your experience and expertise.[12] Indeed, we now see Japan experiencing much greater economic difficulties.

Growth, however, has hardly been smooth and uninterrupted (Figure 1.2). The economy has suffered periodic and often sharp fluctuations many times in its past, but the Great Depression of the 1930s in particular stands out. Not only was it unique as the largest and deepest depression in American history, but there was also another serious recession in its midst. Lying behind these economic fluctuations and the underlying long-term economic growth are substantial shifts in regional and sectoral income and employment. Although the shift in the labor force from agriculture to manufacturing was taking place before 1840, not until the 1880s was a majority of the labor force employed outside agriculture. This transition might have occurred sooner and with less political and social disruption had it not been for the federal policy of selling land cheaply or giving it away. The reasons for the shift away from agriculture are not difficult to pinpoint. The income elasticity of demand for food is generally believed to be below one. Hence every 10 percent increase in per capita income results in less than a 10 percent increase in food demand. With per capita income growing at about 2 percent a year and no compensatory reduction in the relative price of food, a slow shift in the share of resources devoted to food production is reasonable. Foreign demand for grain temporarily buoyed agricultural demand growth after the Civil War, but this gain must be balanced against the clear decline in the rate of growth of foreign demand for cotton.

Manufacturing was the principal beneficiary of agriculture's relative employment decline. Indeed, manufacturing grew especially rapidly following both world wars, thanks in large part to foreign demand from the countries whose industries had suffered wartime destruction. Despite all the media attention given deindustrialization and the emergence of a service economy in recent years, history reveals that the service sector, in fact, has also grown fairly steadily following two notable declines, the first immedi-

[12] Denison (1962; 1967; 1979). See also the debate on convergence: Baumol (1986) and DeLong (1988).

FIGURE 1.2 PANEL A

Deviations of Real GNP from Trend, 1790–1840

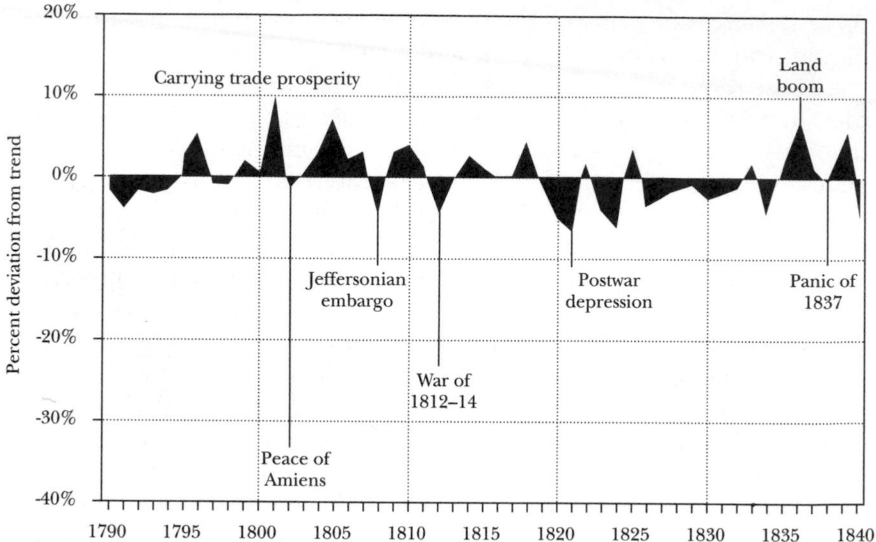

GNP estimates from Thomas S. Berry, "Production and Population since 1789" (Bostwick Paper No. 6, 1988). Trend calculated from overlapping simple trend lines of 40–60 years' duration.

FIGURE 1.2 PANEL B

Deviations of Real GNP from Trend, 1840–1890

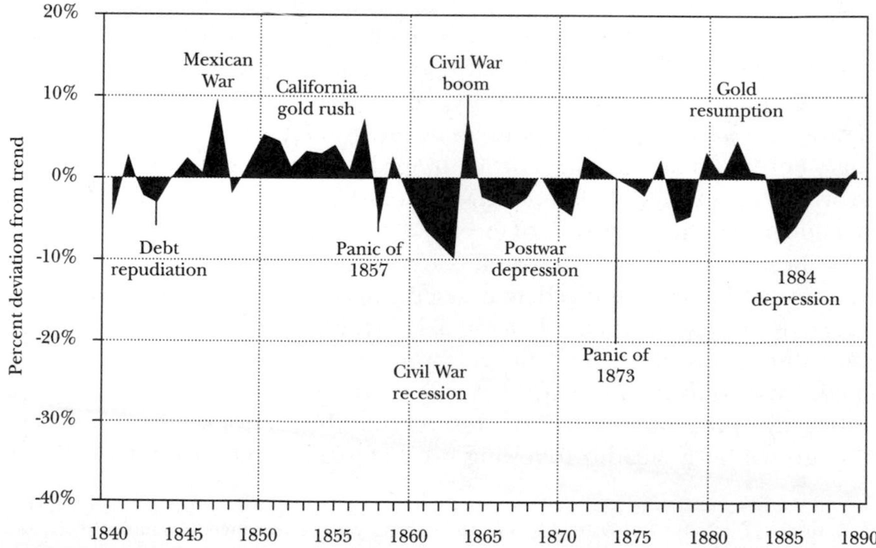

GNP estimates from Thomas S. Berry, "Production and Population since 1789" (Bostwick Paper No. 6, 1988). Trend calculated from overlapping simple trend lines of 40–60 years' duration.

FIGURE 1.2 PANEL C

Deviations of Real GNP from Trend, 1890–1940

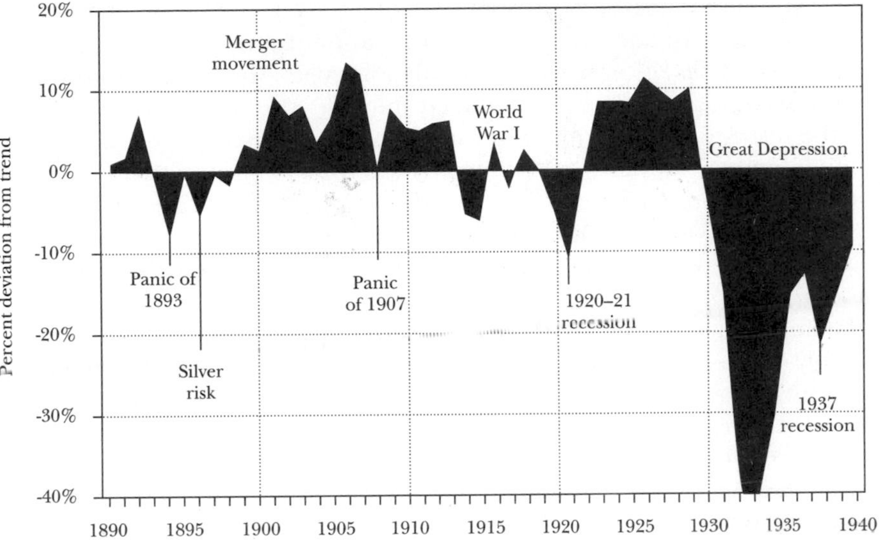

GNP estimates from Thomas S. Berry, "Production and Population since 1789" (Bostwick Paper No. 6, 1988). Trend calculated from overlapping simple trend lines of 40–60 years' duration.

FIGURE 1.2 PANEL D

Deviations of Real GNP from Trend, 1940–1990

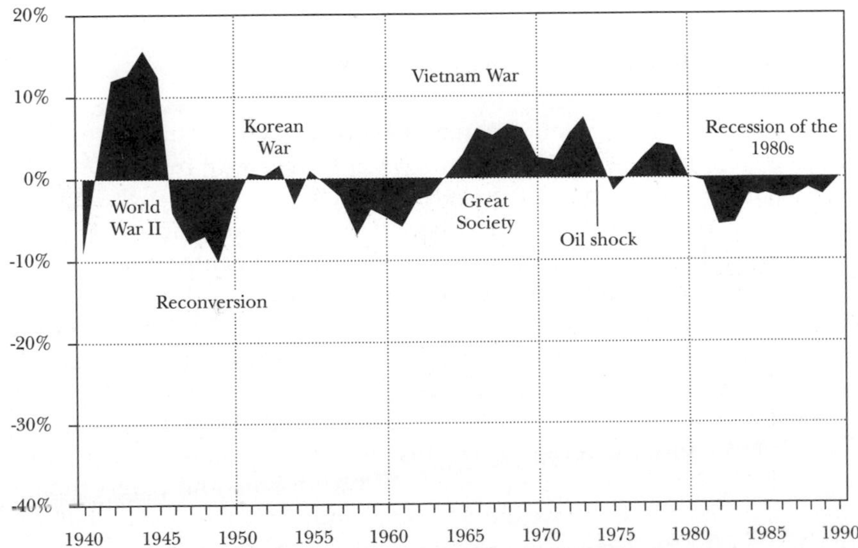

GNP estimates from Thomas S. Berry, "Production and Population since 1789" (Bostwick Paper No. 6, 1988). Trend calculated from overlapping simple trend lines of 40–60 years' duration.

ately following the Revolution, the second following President Jefferson's embargo on foreign trade in 1807. In particular, retail trades, financial services, and the like grew especially rapidly with spreading urbanization, especially from the 1910s.

The nineteenth and twentieth centuries also witnessed dramatic shifts in the geographic distribution of population. With the opening of the Northwest Territory, population flooded into the Midwest. Subsequently, with the discovery of gold in California and then the persistence of high-paying job opportunities out West, tens of thousands pushed ever farther westward to the point where California today is home to about one-eighth of the U.S. population in 1990 and would rank as one of the largest economies in the world today. Pacific coast population growth follows from the obvious economic opportunities for labor, but the Midwest's surge requires further explanation. In the nineteenth century some of the new residents were probably drawn to the Midwest by the availability of inexpensive farmland. Hence it is at least plausible that a good portion of their income was psychic rather than monetary. They may have accepted low nominal returns to their labor in order to have the independence and security of farming their own acreage. It is also likely that migrants to the region expected to do better than they actually did.

Nor is rapid growth in the Sun Belt a recent phenomenon. The South has generally grown more rapidly than the rest of the nation since about 1900, but it has taken a century to catch up from the income loss suffered in the Civil War. Much of the Midwest, on the other hand, has been in relative decline since the 1920s, but only recently has this attracted much notice—just when a resurgence seems under way.

The Sources of Economic Growth since 1840

Between 1840 and the present, net national product (NNP) has increased at an average annual rate of 3.4 percent. This output growth reflects both the growth of factor inputs and the growth of total factor productivity. Among factor inputs, only capital expanded more rapidly than output—3.9 percent per year—while the labor force grew at a rate of 2.1 percent and land at 1.75 percent. These data within a production function framework allow us to partition the growth of output between those factors accounting for extensive growth—capital, labor, and land—and intensive growth (see Appendix B). Rather than treat the entire period as a single epoch, it has been broken into three periods. The first period, 1840–60, is short but encompasses early industrialization and the period of expansion in the agricultural heartland. The second, 1870–1930, excludes the Civil War decade and covers the period of extensive and intensive industrial development. The third, 1940–80, excludes the Great Depression decade and covers the period of recent growth, including the alleged deindustrialization of America and emergence of a service-oriented economy.

In the first half of the nineteenth century almost half of the growth can be attributed to expansion of the labor supply (Table 1.5). Land, despite the dramatic expansion of the area under cultivation and the sale and settlement of hundreds of millions of acres of the public domain, accounted for only about 10 percent of the nation's growth in the first half of the nineteenth century. Productivity growth accounted for somewhat more, about 15 percent. In the sixty years after the Civil War the importance of land decreased dramatically. Expansion into the High Plains and the closing of the frontier accounted for only 15/100 of 1 percent growth over the period, or about 4 percent of the realized growth in net national product. Labor's relative importance also fell during this period. This is consistent with the slowing of the rate of natural increase of population and the decline in the rate of immigration, particularly in the twentieth century. The relative importance of capital, on the other hand, remained almost constant. Productivity almost doubled in relative importance, accounting for more than a quarter of the growth between 1870 and 1930. In the most recent period, 1940 to 1980, productivity is the dominant source of growth. Indeed, but for the very

TABLE 1.5

Accounting for Growth, 1840–1990

PANEL A

Period	Annual Rate of Growth of: Labor	Capital	Land	Net National Product
1840–1860	3.42%	6.57%	3.73%	4.75%
1870–1930	2.24	4.35	2.55	3.75
1940–1990	1.59	3.14	0.34	3.22

PANEL B

Period	Percentage of the Growth in Net National Product Attributable to: Labor	Capital	Land	Productivity (the residual)
1840–1860	49%	26%	10%	15%
1870–1930	43	27	4	27
1940–1990	41	14	0	45

Source: After Edward F. Denison, *Sources of Economic Growth in the United States* (Washington D.C.: Brookings Institution, 1962) and Lance Davis et al., *American Economic Growth* (New York: Harper and Row, 1972): 34–39.

sharp drop in productivity growth during the 1970s, it would have contributed well over half the total growth during the period. Land made virtually no contribution. Capital's contribution also fell dramatically, declining by almost 50 percent to only 14 percent of total growth.

These data present a clear trend: Extensive growth, particularly the growth of land and labor supplies, is of declining importance in the modern economy. Indeed, productivity is now three times as important to the overall rate of growth as it was 150 years ago. The same is also true of other modern economies. Considering this dominant role of productivity growth in overall economic growth, there is little wonder that economic performance in the 1970s was so poor when productivity failed to increase at its usual pace.

Some attribute this remarkable about-face to costly hidden adjustments associated with rapid changes in the cost of energy and environmental regulation. Others associate it with decreased investment in basic research by business and government or argue that confiscatory tax rates act as deterrents to highly productive but extremely risky investment. Still others believe the change is caused by a shift in the opportunities for productive investment. This last explanation is the most depressing because it suggests that no institutional change—tax reduction, government investment in research, deregulation—can bring productivity growth back to its historic growth path. Whatever the cause of current problems, however, there is little doubt about the importance of the intangible productivity factor in nineteenth-century economic maturation.

The decomposition of the growth of output into the fraction attributable to the growth of factor inputs—land, labor, and capital—tells nothing about the sources of productivity change. One possible source is organizational improvement that increases the efficiency of resource allocation, raising the value of output derived from given factor inputs. Capital markets—stock and bond exchanges, banks, and insurance companies, for example—exist because they are better, on average, at allocating savings among the alternative investments. Similarly, improved transport, such as railroads and steamboats, and improved communications, such as newspapers' want ads, channel workers to where they are most needed. The growth of large urban areas reduces the unit cost of distributing goods to consumers. The most important sources of productivity change, however, are thought to be technical improvements embodied in new capital and increased worker skill levels. Labor skills are a sort of "human capital," which many economists prefer to measure as a distinct factor of production like land or machines or structures. The potential impact of technical education—the late nineteenth century, for example, was the era in which formal training of engineers began in earnest—is obvious. Not as obvious, but possibly more important, were more fundamental labor skills like literacy, the ability to follow schematic diagrams, and facility in arithmetic.

Without this long history of productivity growth, incomes would not have risen, life would not have improved, immigrants would not have flocked to these shores, and people could not have moved off the land and into cities. In short, our whole history would have been radically different. It is to an examination of these issues that we now turn.

Appendix A: David's Method of Computing Output per Capita between 1800 and 1840

David makes use of the simple accounting identity

$$V = r\,[S_a P_a + (1 - S_a) P_n] \quad [1]$$

where

V = output per capita
r = fraction of the population in the labor force
S_a = fraction of the labor force in agriculture
P_a = output per worker in agriculture
P_n = output per worker in nonagricultural activities

If the value of each parameter (r, S_a, P_a, P_b) were known for each date, output per capita, V, or an index of output per capita V_t / V_0 for each year t relative to year 0 could easily be calculated.

Unfortunately, P_n is not known before 1840. Instead David assumed that the ratio of output per capita in nonagricultural activities to agricultural activities was constant throughout the period at its 1840 level:

$$Z = \left[\frac{P_n}{P_a}\right]_{1840}$$

Moreover, if Z is constant for all periods, then the index of output per worker in the two sectors must be equal:

$$\frac{(P_a)_t}{(P_a)_0} = \frac{(P_n)_t}{(P_n)_0}$$

Substituting ZPa for P_n in equation [1]:

$$V = r \cdot P_a \cdot \{Z - S_a(Z-1)\}$$

and the index of output per capita:

$$\frac{V_t}{V_0} = \frac{r_t}{r_0} \cdot \frac{(P_a)_t}{(P_a)_0} \cdot \frac{\{Z - (S_a)_t(Z-1)\}}{\{Z - (S_a)_0(Z-1)\}}$$

TABLE 1.A

Values for David's Index of the Growth in Real Product 1800–1860

Year	Z	S_a	$\frac{(P_a)_t}{(P_a)_0}$	$\frac{r_t}{r_{1840}}$	$\frac{V_t}{V_{1840}}$
1800	1.957	0.826	0.764	0.966	0.644
1810	1.957	0.837	0.739	0.970	0.619
1820	1.957	0.790	0.766	0.987	0.676
1830	1.957	0.707	0.900	0.976	0.840
1840	1.957	0.634	1.000	1.000	1.000
1850	1.957	0.548	1.000	1.065	1.130
1860	1.957	0.532	1.215	1.065	1.380

Source: Paul A. David, "The Growth of Real Product in the United States before 1840: New Evidence, Controlled Conjectures," *Journal of Economic History* 27 (June 1967): 151–97. Reprinted by permission of Cambridge University Press.

Appendix B: Economic Growth: A Production Function Viewpoint

Consider the following simple mathematical representation of the production process whereby quantities of labor, land, and capital (L, T, K) are converted into output, Q, using the available technology, organization, etc., as embodied in the functional operator, f:

$$Q = f(L,T,K) \quad [1]$$

$$\frac{dQ}{dL} > 0, \frac{dQ}{dT} > 0, \frac{dQ}{dK} > 0 \quad [2]$$

Economists have found it advantageous to assume particular functional forms for the production function, the most useful of which (and easiest to work with) is known as a Cobb-Douglas production after the economists who developed it. Specifically, the Cobb-Douglas production function is of the form:

$$Q = AL^{\alpha}K^{\beta}T^{\phi} \quad [3]$$

where α, β, and ϕ are the output elasticities with respect to labor, capital, and land. These measure the increase in output that would result from a 1 percent increase in the factor input in question. Thus, for example, if $\alpha = 0.6$, then a 1 percent increase in labor input would increase output by 0.6 percent, all else unchanged. The sum of these output elasticities measures returns to scale, where unity represents a production function with constant returns to scale, a sum greater than unity, increasing return to scale and a sum less than unity, decreasing returns to scale. Under perfectly competitive conditions, $\alpha + \beta + \phi = 1$ and the values of α, β, and ϕ are the same as the factor shares of each input in national income. A is an index of total factor productivity:

$$A = \frac{Q}{L^{\alpha} K^{\beta} T^{\phi}} \quad [4]$$

that is to say, output per unit of composite inputs. Another frequently used productivity concept, labor productivity (Q/L), is related but distinct.

Consider now, equation [3] expressed in terms of rates of growth:

$$\mathring{Q} = \mathring{A} + \alpha \mathring{L} + \beta \mathring{K} + \phi \mathring{T} \quad [5]$$

where $\circ$ denotes rate of growth, Extensive growth, $\mathring{Q}$, may result from increases in L, K, or T. $\mathring{A}$, the rate of growth of total factor productivity, measures intensive growth:

$$\mathring{A} = \mathring{Q} - \{\alpha \mathring{L} + \beta \mathring{K} + \phi \mathring{T}\} \quad [6]$$

In the real world, we can observe $\mathring{Q}, \mathring{L}, \mathring{K}$, and $\mathring{T}$ and the output elasticities, but A is unknown. Consequently, it is computed as the residual fraction of the growth of output not accounted for by the growth of factor inputs. This notion of productivity as the residual was first proposed by Moses Abramovitz and is an extremely powerful concept, not least of which because it represents those factors for which we cannot account. In Abramovitz's words, it is a measure of our ignorance.

Bibliography

Abramovitz, Moses. "Economic Growth in the United States: A Review Article." *American Economic Review* 52 (1962): 762–82.

Adams, Donald R. J. "Prices and Wages in Maryland, 1750–1860." *Journal of Economic History* 46 (1986): 625–45.

Baumol, William J. "Productivity Growth, Convergence and Welfare: What the Long-Run Data Show." *American Econmic Review* 76 (1986): 1072–85.

Berry, Thomas S. "Production and Population Since 1789" (Bostwick Paper No. 6, 1988).

David, Paul, "The Growth of Real Production in the United States before 1840: New Evidence, Controlled Conjectures," *Journal of Economic History* 27 (1967): 151–97.

DeLong, J. Bradford. "Productivity Growth, Convergence and Welfare: Comment." *American Economic Review* 78 (1988): 1138–54.

Denison, Edward F. *Sources of Economic Growth in the United States.* Washington, D.C.: Brookings Institution, 1962.

——— *Why Growth Rates Differ.* Washington, D.C.: Brookings Institution, 1967.

———. *Accounting for Slower Growth in the United States in the 1970s.* Washington, D.C.: Brookings Institution, 1979.

Easterlin, Richard. "Regional Income Trends, 1840–1950." In *The Reinterpretation of American Economic History,* ed. Robert Fogel and Stanley Engerman. New York: Harper & Row, 1971: 38–49.

Floud, Roderick, Kenneth Wachter, and Annabel Gregory, eds., *Height, Health and History*. New York: Cambridge University Press, 1990.

Fogel, Robert. "Nutrition and the Decline in Mortality since 1700: Some Preliminary Findings." In *Long-Term Factors in American Economic Growth,* ed. Stanley Engerman and Robert Gallman. Chicago: University of Chicago Press, 1986: 439–527.

Gallman, Robert. "Gross National Product in the United States, 1834–1909." In National Bureau of Economic Research, *Output, Employment and Productivity in the United States after 1800.* Studies in Income and Wealth Series, vol. 30. New York: Columbia University Press, 1966: 3–76.

———. "The Pace and Pattern of American Economic Growth." In *American Economic Growth,* ed. Lance Davis, Richard Easterlin, et al. New York: Harper & Row, 1972: 15–60.

———. "The Agricultural Sector and the Pace of Economic Growth: U.S. Experience in the 19th Century." In *Essays in Nineteenth Century History* (Athens: Ohio University Press, 1975: 35–76.

Goldin, Claudia, and Kenneth C. Sokoloff. "The Relative Productivity Hypothesis of Industrialization: The American Case, 1820 to 1850." *Quarterly Journal of Economics* 99 (1984): 461–88.

Goldsmith, Raymond. "Long Period Growth in Income and Product, 1839–1860." In *New Views in American Economic Development,* ed. Ralph Andreano. Cambridge: Harvard University Press, 1966: 337–61.

Kuznets, Simon. *Income and Wealth of the United States.* Cambridge, England: Bowes and Bowes, 1952.

Lebergott, Stanley. "Labor Force and Employment 1800–1960." In National Bureau of Economic Research, *Output, Employment and Productivity in the United States after 1800.* Studies in Income and Wealth Series, vol. 30. New York: Columbia University Press, 1966:117–204.

Margo, Robert, and Richard Steckel. "Heights of Native Born Whites during the Antebellum Period." *Journal of Economic History* 43. (1983): 167–74.

Martin, Robert. *National Income in the United States 1799–1938.* National Industrial Conference Board Study #241. New York: National Industrial Conference Board, 1939.

McColley, Robert. "Slavery in Virginia, 1619–1660: A Reexamination." In *New Perspectives on Race and Slavery in America: Essays in Honor of Kenneth M. Stampp,* ed. Robert Abzug and Stephen Maizlich. Lexington: University of Kentucky Press, 1986: 11–24.

North, Douglass C. "The United States Balance of Payments, 1790–1860." In National Bureau of Economic Research, *Trends in the American Economy in the Nineteenth Century.* Studies in Income and Wealth Series, vol. 24 (Princeton: Princeton University Press, 1960).

———. *The Economic Growth of the United States, 1790–1860.* Englewood Cliffs, NJ: Prentice-Hall, 1961.

———. *Growth and Welfare in the American Past: A New Economic History*. Englewood Cliffs, NJ: Prentice-Hall, 1974.

Parker, William, and Franklee Whartenby. "The Growth of Output before 1840." In National Bureau of Economic Research, *Trends in the American Economy in the 19th Century.* Studies in Income and Wealth Series, vol. 24. Princeton: Princeton University Press, 1960: 191–212.

Rostow, Walter. *The Stages of Economic Growth.* Cambridge, England: Cambridge University Press, 1960.

Sokoloff, Kenneth. "Productivity Growth in Manufacturing during Early Industrialization: Evidence from the American Northeast, 1820–1860." In *Long-Term Factors in American Economic Growth,* ed. Stanley Engerman and Robert

Gallman. National Bureau of Economic Research, Studies in Income and Wealth Series, vol. 51. Chicago: University of Chicago Press, 1986: 679–736.

———, and Georgia Villaflor. "The Early Achievement of Modern Stature in America." *Social Science History* (1982): 453–81.

Taylor, George Rogers. "American Economic Growth before 1840: An Exploratory Essay." *Journal of Economic History* (1964): 427–44.

Towne, Marvin, and Wayne Rasmussen. "Farm Gross Product and Gross Investment in the 19th Century." In National Bureau of Economic Research, *Trends in the American Economy in the 19th Century*. Studies in Income and Wealth Series, vol. 24. Princeton: Princeton University Press, 1960: 255–312.

U.S. Bureau of the Census. *Historical Statistics of the United States. Colonial Times to 1970.* Washington, D.C.: Government Printing Office, 1975. 2 vols.

———. *Statistical Abstract of the United States: 1992.* Washington, D.C.: Government Printing Office, 1992.

Weiss, Thomas. "Economic Growth before 1860: Revised Conjectures." Working Paper No. 7 in National Bureau of Economic Research Working Paper Series on Historical Factors in Long Run Growth, 1989.

———. "Long Term Changes in U.S. Agricultural Output per Worker, 1800 to 1900." Working Paper No. 23 in National Bureau of Economic Research Working Paper Series on Historical Factors in Long Run Growth, 1991.

The colonial economy

2

The European Background

Archaeological evidence, maps, and legend confirm Viking visits to North America a thousand years or more ago. But the Vikings failed to establish permanent presence here, so most of their knowledge of this continent was lost in the intervening years. The European rediscovery and settlement of the New World more than four hundred years later were the result of fierce rivalry among the emerging nation-states of western Europe and their efforts to break the Italian city-states' monopoly on the lucrative spice trade with the East. These spices—cinnamon, cloves, ginger, nutmeg, and pepper—were eagerly sought to enliven an otherwise bland diet and to disguise the smell and taste of spoiling food. Pepper, which also served as a meat preservative, was especially prized. Although the profits from the trade were already high, they would have been even higher but for the costs of overland transportation between the Indian Ocean and Mediterranean Sea and the bribes and taxes that the Arab traders had to pay for safe passage.

In particular, Portugal, under Prince Henry the Navigator (1394–1460), embarked upon a systematic program of exploration down the west coast of Africa to find an alternative route to the Orient. The Portuguese reasoned, correctly, that an all-water route would be cheaper than the existing overland routes, and if successful, they would be able to undercut the Italians and capture their business. Thanks to the adoption of the lateen sail, which permitted a boat to push farther southward down the coast of Africa against adverse winds, the Portuguese were close to realizing this goal on the eve of Columbus's voyage. In 1488 the Portuguese court received word that Bartolomeu Dias had reached the Cape of Good Hope and the way to the Indian Ocean and Orient lay open. Little wonder, then, that the Portuguese had no interest in the audacious proposal of an Italian adventurer, Christopher Columbus, to reach the Orient by a western route. Nor is it surprising that Spain, jealous of its neighbor's successes and fearful of its growing economic power, was willing to consider the proposal. Instead of finding the East Indies, though, Columbus discovered the West Indies on his first voyage in 1492. It was only after repeated voyages of discovery by British, French, and Spanish explorers that the dimensions of the New World became apparent.

At first the rewards of this discovery seemed small beside the gains that Portugal reaped from its successes to the East. In 1498 Vasco da Gama, returning from the first successful voyage to India, sold his cargo and realized about 6,000 percent return on the capital invested in that voyage. However, the discovery of large hoards of gold and silver among the native Americans and rich mines changed the calculus and along with it the course of European development. The import of treasure from the Americas over the course of the ensuing century and a half drove up European prices. Wages, however, adjusted less quickly than other prices. As a result, the real wage rate fell, and relative returns to other factors of production rose.

Since gold and silver served as money, the American treasure gave the Spanish crown unparalleled command over resources. Other nations felt threatened. Jealousies were roused. The British and French, in particular, sought redress through the outright theft of Spain's newfound treasure whenever possible and, where that failed, by trading for it. Thus was born one of the principles of national policy that was to guide economic relations between nations throughout the colonial period and beyond—mercantilism. It was within this framework that the British foothold in North America was established.

Mercantilism

Mercantilism was a collection of vague, amorphous ideas that were continually being refined, elaborated, and modified. The central feature, however, was the equation of money to power. A wealthy prince was a strong prince, and therefore, whatever was done to enhance the wealth of a nation, as measured by the stocks of gold and silver, increased its political and military power. It was a theory that provided an economic rationale for the political process of nation building.[1] The prime objective was the acquisition and retention of as much money—gold and silver—possible.

For Spain, thanks to the bounty of American treasure, the problem was largely reduced to the bureaucratic one of accounting for the gold and silver stolen from the indigenous peoples or mined in the Americas and en-

[1] See Schmoller (1896).

suring its safe passage back to the mother country. For the other European nations the problem was more difficult and required greater effort. As they established each new colony, there was always considerable optimism that rich gold and silver deposits would be found, though they were generally disappointed.

There was, however, an alternative means of securing gold and silver and thereby increasing the wealth of the nation: trade. If only a country could maintain a favorable balance of payments—that is, earn more from its exports than it paid for its imports—its stock of gold or silver would increase. But each export is another country's import. Trade therefore balances worldwide and, in the context of this theory, is a zero-sum game. One country's gain was another country's loss. Viewed this way, mercantilist trade policy inevitably led to trade disputes, which in turn often degenerated into military struggles.

Moreover, such an important element of national policy could not be left to the whim of the market. Active intervention and bureaucratic oversight were necessary to guarantee a favorable balance of payments. Exports were "good" and to be encouraged even if it required financial underwriting; imports were "bad"—to be actively discouraged by taxes, bureaucratic impediments, and, if all else failed, outright prohibition. Furthermore, if imports met some critical need, then efforts should be made to generate a domestic supply source even at greater cost. As we will see, these were all elements of British policy toward their American colonies.

The mercantilist view of the economic system is at variance with the modern neoclassical economic theory in two areas. First, mercantilism denies the proposition of mutual gains from trade. Second, the wealth of a nation is measured by a stock—the quantity of gold and silver at its disposal—rather than by the flow from the productive capacity of the country and its people. Nevertheless, elements of the mercantilist view find ready parallels in the contemporary world—for example, in the focus upon the trade balance and the growth of customs unions.

Colonies fit into this mercantilist model by providing alternative "domestic" sources of supply for goods that otherwise would have to be imported from "foreigners" or produced at home at even greater cost. By expanding and altering the resource base of the mother country, colonies might also give rise to new and lucrative exports. The ideal colony therefore was one that was as different from the mother country and other colonies as possible. Thus it was that after the French and Indian War the British gave serious consideration to accepting the island of Guadeloupe in the Caribbean as the spoil of victory instead of Canada. The former produced sugar, a commodity that Britain and the colonies still had to import from outside the empire despite the sugar plantations of the British West Indies, whereas the latter simply duplicated the trade and resource base of the northern colonies.

English Settlement of North America

The first British attempt to establish a permanent settlement in North America, however, did not fit the mercantilist trade model. Rather, Sir Walter Raleigh established an outpost on Roanoke Island, just off the coast of North Carolina in 1584 for the purpose of harassing Spanish treasure ships taking advantage of the Gulf Stream just offshore to speed passage to Spain. The colony never became self-sufficient and failed, its settlers disappearing without trace sometime between 1587 and 1591.

A permanent British presence was not established in North America until 1607, when the London Company (subsequently renamed the Virginia Company), a crown-chartered joint-stock company with monopoly trading rights, established a settlement at Jamestown. Dreams of gold and hopes of establishing silk and winemaking (Virginia is on the same latitude as southern Spain and Italy) were soon dashed. Conditions were harsh. Of the original 105 settlers, 67 died the first year from disease, misadventure, and starvation. New settlers sent out by the reorganized and refinanced Virginia Company in 1609 fared even worse, and the colony probably would have failed but for the discovery that tobacco flourished in the climate.

Like Jamestown, the earliest New England colonies were also financed by English commercial interests with profits foremost in mind. Many of the actual settlers, however, were religious dissenters eager to put three thousand miles of ocean between their homes and a capricious, intolerant government. Plymouth, the original Pilgrim settlement founded in 1620, suffered a casualty rate almost as high as Jamestown's. It was eventually absorbed by the larger, better-organized Massachusetts Bay Colony, which had been started a few years later by business-minded Puritans. Massachusetts prospered, anchoring its economy to subsistence agriculture and port services for the growing American trade with Europe.

Virginia and Massachusetts were by far the most important mainland colonies in the mid-seventeenth century; they were home to two out of three English-speaking Europeans in North America. Maine and New Hampshire, on the other hand, were nothing more than conglomerations of small fishing villages of uncertain colonial ownership. Indeed, Massachusetts managed to annex Maine in 1652 and did not relinquish control until the 1820s. New Hampshire, also coveted by expansionist Massachusetts, was luckier; it was granted independent status by the British government in 1679. Connecticut and Rhode Island were first settled in the 1630s—the former by Massachusetts farmers in search of land, the latter by religious dissenters driven from their Massachusetts homes by Puritan orthodoxy.

Of the Middle Atlantic colonies, only New York has any history to speak of before 1680. New Amsterdam—what is now the New York City area—was colonized by the Dutch in the 1620s with the goal of providing logistic support to Dutch commercial ventures in Latin America. From there population spread out along Long Island and up the Hudson Valley. The settlements were loosely governed by the Dutch until England wrested control over the region in a series of wars ending in 1674. Thereafter the region grew quickly; fertile grainland and good water transportation along the river valleys attracted thousands of immigrants to New York, New Jersey, and Pennsylvania.

Maryland, granted by Charles I as a proprietorship to Lord Baltimore, served as a refuge for Catholic dissenters and shared with Virginia the dramatic expansion of the Chesapeake Bay economy founded upon trade and tobacco. Development of the lower South began later during the last quarter of the seventeenth century. Virginia tobacco farmers, for instance, pressed by increased European demand and the depletion of suitable soils for growing the noxious weed, expanded into the northern coastal region of North Carolina. The development of South Carolina depended upon two specialized export crops. Inland swamplands proved ideal for growing rice, while better-drained upland areas specialized in indigo, the plant used to make blue textile dyes. This latter crop could be raised profitably only when the market was shielded by means of trade restrictions or domestic production bounties from Latin American and Caribbean competition.

In the meantime, French settlements in Canada, the Great Lakes, and the Ohio and Mississippi valleys encroached on the western margins while Spanish settlements in the Gulf pushed up from the south. These twin threats led Britain to encourage as rapid a western settlement by English-speaking settlers as possible to establish the English claim over the largest possible territory.

Colonial Development

The issue of population growth is dealt with at length in Chapter 8. Here the focus is upon population growth as an indicator of extensive and intensive growth during the colonial period. Between 1610 and 1620 and again between 1630 and 1640, the colonial population grew 20 percent per year (Figure 2.1), doubling every three and half years, reflecting the impact of boatloads of new settlers—many of them indentured servants and slaves—on a small population.[2] Colonial population growth abruptly slowed after 1640 to between 2.5 percent and 4 percent per year in the years after 1650. Even at these rates, though, population still doubled about every generation. Birthrates were high—forty-five to fifty-five births per thousand population, compared with perhaps thirty-five to forty per thousand in England at the time—and death rates, after the grim, starving years following first settlement, were relatively low, perhaps twenty to twenty-five per thousand,

[2] Remember the so-called rule of 72: At a constant growth rate (x percent), it takes $72/x$ years for the base year level to double.

FIGURE 2.1

Population of Colonial America

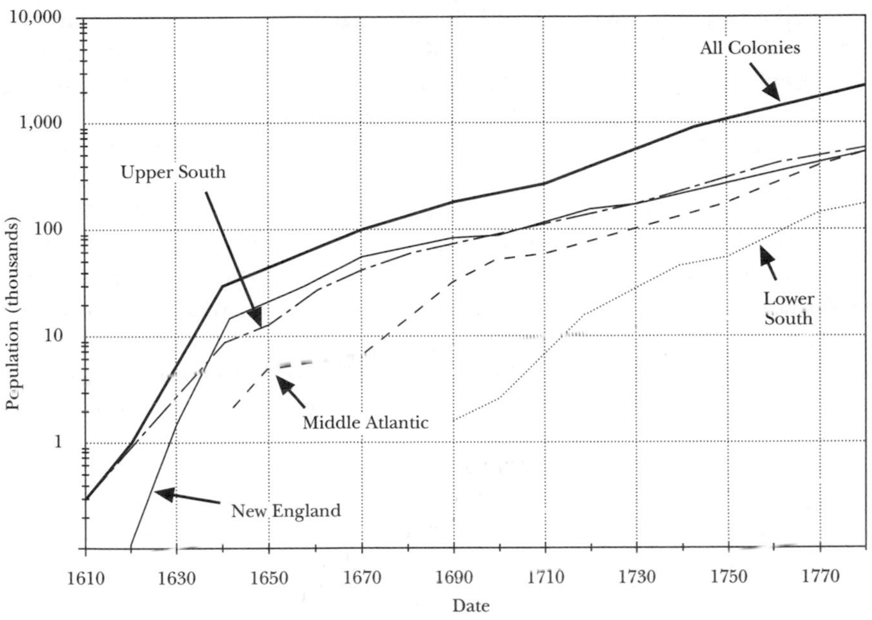

Source: U.S. Bureau of the Census, *Historical Statistics of the United States* (Washington, D.C.: Government Printing Office, 1975): Series Z1–219.

compared with twenty-five to thirty-five per thousand in England. Consequently, the natural rate of increase of the population was high, probably between 2 and 3 percent per year, to which immigration added about one percentage point per year. These high birthrates, low death rates, and high immigration rates testify to the comparatively favorable conditions that settlers found in America.

The native Indian population, however, fared badly. When English settlement began, there may have been as many as three hundred thousand indigenous people in the eastern half of the country. By the time of the Revolution the Indian population had shrunk to one hundred thousand or less, mainly as a result of the ravages of European diseases, such as measles and smallpox, to which the native population had no natural immunities.

Despite the rapid growth of the European population in America, there is no evidence of serious Malthusian crises—war, famine, or disease—ravaging that population. True, there were periods of relatively greater adversity, such as around the turn of the eighteenth century, that had an impact upon population growth visible both in the macro data (as in Figure 2.1) and in individual communities. For example, in Hingham, Massachusetts, historian Daniel Scott Smith found that completed families had an average of "only" 4.61 children between 1691 and 1715, while families both earlier and later had an average of 6 or 7 children. He blames increased economic adversity for the decline in fertility. Such episodes, however, exerted no lasting check upon population and its well-being. On the contrary, the growing colonial population was able to maintain and perhaps even slightly improve its standard of living and quality of life during the seventeenth and eighteenth centuries.

Living standards in colonial America were maintained despite rapid population growth because of the availability of abundant land—the principal resource and source of wealth at the time—at the margin of current settlement. The forest slowly retreated to be replaced by fields and farms and a scattering of towns. Most of the growth, however, was extensive rather than intensive. The reason was, as Thomas Jefferson observed, "We can buy an acre of new land cheaper than we can manure an old acre." This competition from new, more productive land inevitably exerted an impact upon agriculture in older, more settled areas, which were forced increasingly to rely upon their sole immutable advantage, location—that is to say, proximity to markets.

Agriculture was far and away the dominant occupation, employing perhaps 85 percent of the labor force. More people in the South and on the frontier were farmers, and fewer in the Middle Atlantic colonies, and fewer still in New England, where poor, thin soils and a harsh climate made agriculture most difficult. A traditional interpretation of New England farming is that it was subsistence agriculture, incapable of producing substantial marketable surpluses and barely able to sustain even a marginal standard of living for the farm family. Support for this view is to be found in the shorter stature of New England farmers (though, of course, they were still taller than urban residents), in the migration of farmers out of the region as new lands became available, and in the development of manufacturing as an alternative livelihood to farming. The argument, championed primarily by historians, goes beyond mere inability to produce surpluses as a result of physical constraints. It contends that colonial farmers had a psychological predisposition—a mentality—that eschewed profit maximization in favor of "satisficing"—that is, of maintaining the security of farm tenure and minimizing risk. As a result, farmers supposedly consciously, carefully, and deliberately limited market involvement and were reluctant to adopt new practices and new crops. Exchanges, when and where they took place, involved "use values," not market values.[3]

If farmers in the seventeenth and eighteenth centuries had such atti-

[3] The argument that New England farmers deliberately limited their market involvement was first proposed by Percy Bidwell in 1916 and has most recently been resurrected in the work of James Henretta (1978), Robert Mutch (1977), Michael Merrill (1977), and numerous other historians.

tudes and behaved in these ways, then they were very different from their nineteenth-century successors and heirs. But it's not clear that they were so different. Eighteenth-century farmers of southeastern Pennsylvania were certainly commercially oriented toward supplying the Philadelphia market and even markets beyond.[4] Similarly, some Massachusetts farmers were increasingly involved in the market.[5] Data drawn by Winifred Rothenberg from farm account books show farmers who purposefully and consistently produced more than their families could consume and engaged in long-distance and complex searches for markets in which to sell their surpluses. Indeed, the very fact that they kept account books is testimony to their commercial attitudes. Moreover, it would have been surprising if these settlers, coming as they did from a land where commercial traditions embodied in market days, itinerant peddlers, and fairs were long established, had turned their backs upon the market whatever its short-term disadvantages.

In the years before the Revolution, Massachusetts farmers were traveling an average of a day's journey—about twenty-five miles to sell their produce. A few ranged over a hundred miles from home in search of markets. Their collective action in seeking the best market for their produce had the effect of reducing local and regional price variations. Markets thus became integrated and regional rather than separate and local. In short, these farmers made the market work. Growing commercialism among these farmers gave rise to a capital market. Rothenberg reports that even before the Revolution, probated estates contained endorsed promissory notes of unrelated and physically distant debtors. The endorsements in particular are indicative of an active market in credit instruments and evidence of the liquidity of such obligations.

As the dominant sector of the colonial economy, agricultural performance was crucial for aggregate economic growth, yet as the most traditional sector in the economy, agriculture is often viewed as an impediment to, rather than a vehicle for, economic growth. Such is especially likely to be true in a period when technological change was minimal. In Chester County, Pennsylvania (southwest of Philadelphia), though, farming was becoming more capital-intensive and less labor-intensive over the course of the eighteenth century. Farms used much more capital and a little more land but less labor and the weighted quantity of all inputs used on the average farm declined over time (Table 2.1). Despite the decline in factor inputs, though, output per farm was growing in the period up to the Revolution. Consequently, total factor productivity—that is, output per unit of inputs—was growing by about 0.1 to 0.2 percent per year.[6]

No doubts or questions are raised about the commercial mentality of southern planters of tobacco, rice, indigo, or cotton. Theirs were crops

[4] Lemon (1972).
[5] Rothenberg (1992).
[6] Ball and Walton (1976).

TABLE 2.1

Indexes of Inputs, Outputs, and Productivity in Pennsylvania Agriculture, 1714–1790

	Individual inputs					
Years	Land (T)	Capital (K)	Labor (L)	Combined Input[a] (I)	Total Output[b] (Q)	Total Factor Productivity $\frac{\text{Output}}{\text{Inputs}} = \frac{Q}{I}$
1714–31	100	100	100	100	100	100
1734–34	100	114	91	95	101	106
1750–70	106	126	91	97	107	110
1775–90	106	121	88	97	106	109

[a] The combined inputs index is the geometric average of the inputs weighted by their factor shares: $I = T^{0.14} \cdot K^{0.10} \cdot L^{0.76}$.

[b] Total output is adjusted to include some nonagricultural outputs after 1750, increasing the total output index slightly in the last two periods and thus raising productivity growth 1734–45 and 1750–70.

Source: Adapted from Duane Ball and Gary M. Walton, "Agricultural Productivity Change in Eighteenth Century Pennsylvania," *Journal of Economic History* 26 (1976): Table 4, 5, and 7 (column a). Reprinted by permission of Cambridge University Press.

whose markets lay an ocean away, and they depended upon a complex web of middlemen—such as agents, packers, shippers, bankers, and creditors—standing between them and the consumer. Tobacco was far and away the dominant crop during the colonial period, especially in the Chesapeake Bay area. From a few thousand pounds before 1620, production exceeded a hundred million pounds by the time of the Revolution and generating the equivalent of about four million dollars in export earnings (Figure 2.2). It proved an ideal crop for the colonies: Demand was growing rapidly, the British Empire was a protected market, no elaborate and expensive field preparation was necessary, and though it quickly exhausted the soil, new land was always available at the current margin of cultivation.

Although there is no evidence of change in the technology of tobacco production, price data indicate that tobacco farming productivity must have increased rapidly.[7] Despite a drop in tobacco prices from twenty-seven pennies per pound in 1616–19 to one penny per pound or less by 1660 and constant or rising land and labor prices, tobacco farmers stayed in business, and exports of what one contemporary described as that "filthie weede" rose. Consequently, the collapse of prices must be attributed to the rapid expansion of supply rather than to reductions in demand.

In New England, however, the scarcity of cultivable land led to a sharply declining marginal product of farm labor. Additional labor was induced to seek alternative, high-paying activities as soon as possible. Manufacturing

[7] Egnal (1975).

FIGURE 2.2

British Imports of American Tobacco and the Price Received by American Farmers

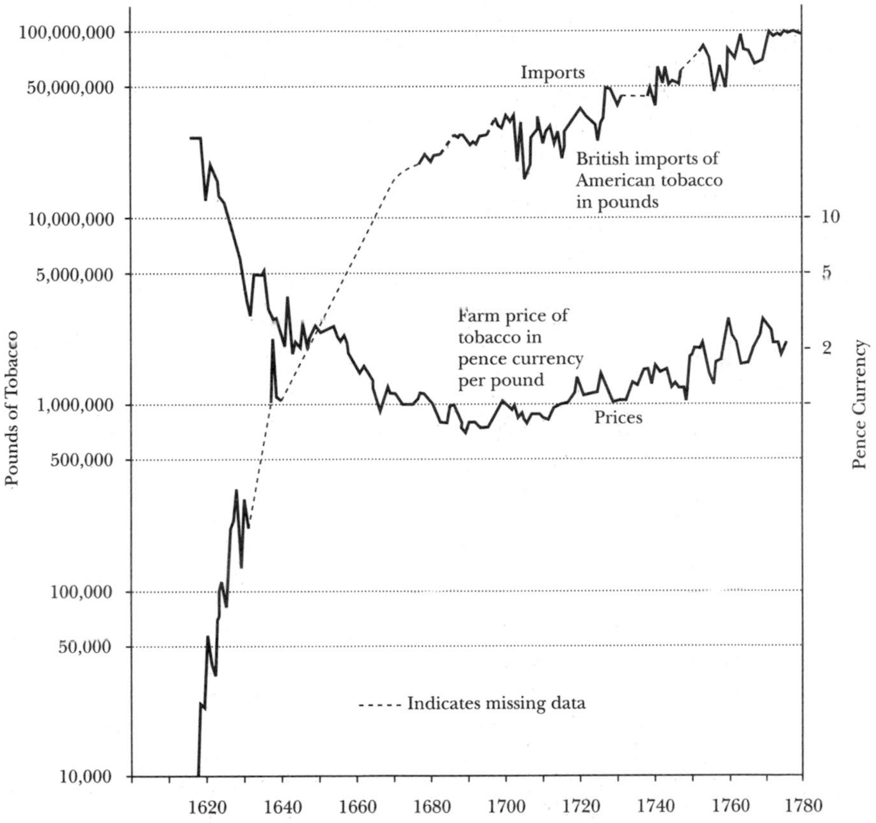

Source: Reprinted from *The Economy of British America, 1607–1789,* by John McCusker and Russell R. Menard. Published for the Institute of Early American History and Culture, Williamsburg, Virginia. Copyright © 1985 by the University of North Carolina Press. Used by permission of the publisher.

opportunities were limited by British mercantilist policy designed to restrict competition with British-produced goods. The colonies were supposed to supply those commodities that were unavailable in the mother country and were to serve as a captive market for the products of its industry. Thus, for example, the colonies were prevented from producing finished iron products, and intercolonial trade in domestically produced textiles was prohibited. As a result, markets were limited, colonial firms couldn't specialize, and potential scale economies were lost. There was, however, one industry—shipbuilding—that enjoyed a substantial cost advantage over the British industry because of the abundant timber resources of the colonies. The same British mercantilist restrictions that limited the development of colonial manufactures protected American merchant shipping from foreign competition. This both increased the demand for new ships and increased the size of the American commercial sector.

During the colonial period, ocean shipping employed perhaps 5 to 10 percent of the labor force—more than any sector besides agriculture. In the decade before the Revolution, exports and related services accounted for about one-sixth of colonial income. The performance of the shipping industry was very important to the overall economy. Indeed, Gary Walton and James Shepherd argue that ocean shipping was a major source of the modest growth in per capita income during the colonial period. Productivity gains in the industry averaged between 0.6 and 1.2 percent per year throughout the colonial period, depending upon the commodity and route, and averaging at least 0.8 percent per year overall (Table 2.2). Put another way, the real resources required to ship goods across the Atlantic were cut by more than half over the period.

This was a remarkable performance. Yet it apparently occurred without any change in the existing technology. How was this possible? Shepherd and Walton offer a variety of explanations. One of most important factors, particularly before the mid-eighteenth century, was an increase in the average number of voyages each ship made in a year. Speed under sail did not increase; in fact, average speed shows no secular trend over the entire period. Rather, a ship was able to make more voyages per year because in-port time declined dramatically. Ships spent less time loading and unloading or await-

TABLE 2.2

Productivity Change in Ocean Shipping by Commodity and Route, 1620–1776

Route	Commodity	Period	Annual Rates of Increase per Annum (%)
Virginia–London	Tobacco	1630–1675	1.2
New York–London	Bullion	1700–1789	1.0
Boston–London	Oil	1700–1774	0.9
Barbados–London	Sugar	1678–1717	0.9
Jamaica–London	Sugar	1678–1717	0.9
New York–Jamaica	Flour	1699–1768	0.8
Maryland–London	Tobacco	1676–1776	0.7
So. Europe–London	Wine	1650–1770	0.6

Source: James F. Shepherd and Gary M. Walton, *Shipping, Maritime Trade and the Economic Development of Colonial North America* (Cambridge, England: Cambridge University Press, 1972): 69. Reprinted by permission of Cambridge University Press.

ing a cargo because of improved organization and coordination. For example, ships sailing out of Maryland and Virginia ports in the 1680s spent an average of 90 to 108 days in port a year. By the 1760s days in port averaged fewer than 50 days per year.

The sheer volume of trade allowed ships and ships' officers to specialize in specific cargoes and routes. The complex "triangular trade" mythologized in history textbooks (New England rum to Africa, African slaves to the Caribbean, Caribbean molasses to New England) was the exception rather than the rule in the late colonial period. By simply shuttling back and forth across the Atlantic or between northern ports and the Caribbean, shipowners cut waiting time in ports, reducing labor and overhead costs. A high volume of trade also reduced the unit cost of port services. More ship traffic meant cargoes spent fewer days in warehouses waiting for transport to the right place. Accumulated experience in trade—what economists call learning-by-doing—meant fewer mistakes in packaging, handling, and storage.

The productivity change in the transportation sector is often the result of economies of scale; some given increase in output requires a less than proportionate increase in inputs with the result that unit costs of production fall. For example, while large ships require more crew members, doubling ship size does not require a crew twice as large. As a result, the ratio of tons of cargo to each crew member rises for larger vessels, and labor productivity is increased. Such scale economies were particularly important later in other transportation media as well. However, they played little or no role in the productivity gains in ocean shipping during the colonial period. Ship size did not change very much because of the nature of the trade.

Nevertheless, substantial reductions in crew size were made, and labor productivity rose for vessels of approximately constant size. The secret? The removal of guns from merchant ships. This permitted the construction of lighter vessels without the special reinforcement needed to withstand the weight and recoil of guns and allowed for the easier and more efficient storage of cargo without interference from special gundecks. In addition, fewer men were needed to operate such a vessel since crews were no longer assigned to manning the guns. Such ships did not represent new technology; the Dutch first introduced these so-called flyboats in 1595. Their belated adoption by the colonists probably resulted in considerable savings toward the end of the colonial era.

Flyboats could not, however, have been adopted earlier because of the dangers of the waters where the colonists traded. Pirates were a constant threat, and England's almost constant involvement in wars put colonial shipping at risk from its adversaries. After the French and Indian War, however, conditions were more settled, and the Royal Navy had secured the sea-lanes from pirates and privateers. Shipping costs were further reduced by the lowering of insurance rates as risks of loss declined by about 20 percent.

Since shipping and distribution expenses amounted to about half the total wholesale price of goods at their final destination, the impact of these gains on colonial income and living standards was quite significant. Narrowing the gap between the price at which farmers sold their crops and the price consumers paid made it profitable for regions—and individual farmers—to specialize in more productive activities. Thousands of farmers, who would otherwise have simply grown food for themselves, instead produced grain, rice, tobacco, and indigo for others. These were ultimately exchanged for manufactured goods from Europe, rum, sugar, and molasses from the Caribbean, and shipping, banking, and insurance services from colonial port cities.

Shipbuilding and overseas commerce flourished in the colonies, and these activities made a major contribution to the colonial balance of payments with the mother country. Records maintained by the British colonial administration and reconstructed by Shepherd and Walton provide a detailed picture of the economic relationship between the colonies and the rest of the world. New England and the Middle Atlantic colonies had very substantial deficits with Great Britain on visible trade (Table 2.3). Aside from lumber, naval supplies, and salted fish, these colonies produced little that the mother country wanted or could reexport. Indeed, except for exports of wheat, flour, and other foodstuffs to southern Europe (Spain, Portugal, and the Mediterranean countries) from the Middle Atlantic colonies, trade surpluses with the rest of the world did little to offset the huge trade deficit with Great Britain. By contrast, the southern colonies had more balanced trade with Great Britain, and they even had small surpluses overall based on their exports of rice, corn, and other foodstuffs to southern Europe.

Sales of ships and shipping services, including insurance, went a long

TABLE 2.3

Average Annual Commodity Trade Balance of the 13 Colonies, 1768–1772 (thousands of pounds sterling)

	Great Britain and Ireland	Southern Europe	West Indies	Africa	All Trades
New England	–609	+48	–36	+19	–577
Middle colonies	–786	+153	–10	+1	–643
Upper South	–50	+90	–9	0	+30
Lower South	–23	+48	+44	*	+69
Total colonies	–1,468	+339	–11	+20	–1.121

Note: A plus sign (+) signifies a surplus, with exports exceeding imports in value. A minus sign (–) denotes a deficit. (*) denotes amounts less than £500. Regional balances may not add to totals as a result of rounding.

Values are expressed in prices in the mainland colonies. Therefore, import values include shipping costs, commissions, and other handling costs. Export values do not include these distribution costs.

Source: Gary M. Walton, and James F. Shepherd, *The Economic Rise of Early America* (Cambridge, England: Cambridge University Press, 1979). Reprinted by permission of Cambridge University Press.

way toward closing the commodity trade deficit of the colonies of £1,121,000 (Table 2.4) and balancing the trade position of the different colonies as New England and the Middle Atlantic colonies specialized in these services. The trade surplus of the southern colonies was, however, more than wiped out by their import of slaves, estimated by Shepherd and Walton at £200,000 a year in the late colonial period. By contrast, the declining trade in white inden-

TABLE 2.4

A Balance of Payments for the 13 Colonies, 1768–72 (thousands of pounds sterling)[a]

	Debit	Credit
Commodities		
Exports[b]		2,800
Imports[c]	3,920	
Balance of trade	1,120	
Ship sales		140
Invisible earnings		
Shipping earnings		600
Merchant commissions, risk, and insurance		220
Balance on current account from trade	160	
Payments for human beings		
Indentured servants	80	
Slaves	200	
British collections and expenditures in colonies		
Taxes and duties	40	
Salaries of British civil servants		40
Military expenditures		230
Naval expenditures		170
Capital and monetary flows		
Specie / Indebtedness		40

[a] All calculations are rounded to the nearest 1,000. Note that the figures in this table differ somewhat from those given in J. F. Shepherd and G. M. Walton, *Shipping, Maritime Trade and the Economic Development of Colonial North America* (Cambridge, England: Cambridge University Press, 1972), Chapters 6, 7, and 8. Because Newfoundland, Quebec, Nova Scotia, Florida, Bermuda, and the Bahamas were included in the source but excluded here, the primary aggregate estimates of exports, imports and shipping earnings have been adjusted downward by £210,000, £420,000, and £10,000, respectively.

[b] Exports are valued FOB exclusive of ocean transport costs and other merchandising costs.

[c] Imports are valued CIF—that is, including ocean transportation costs, insurance, interest, and commission charges.

Source: Gary M. Walton, and James F. Shepherd, *The Economic Rise of Early America* (Cambridge, England: Cambridge University Press, 1979). Reprinted by permission of Cambridge University Press.

tured servants—most of whom were redemptioners by this time and went primarily to the Middle Atlantic states—imposed a much smaller burden.

The international financial position of the colonies in the late colonial period was thus only assured by British military and naval expenditures in America. Taxes and duties that the British collected just offset the administrative cost of the colonies. In addition, there was a small net capital inflow into the colonies, probably in the pockets of immigrants.

Labor Scarcity in the Colonial Economy

While per capita incomes do not begin to show a marked and sustained rise until early in the eighteenth century, the economies of the colonies were growing extensively during the first century after settlement.[8] Such growth was sustainable for an agricultural economy so long as more land was available just a little farther west. All that was needed to fit this new land for production was hard work—clearing the vegetation and tree cover, digging ditches, and making fences. Labor thus created capital. It was labor more than anything else that was the binding constraint on the speed and extent of colonial development. Where these settlers came into conflict with the indigenous people, the Indians were forced to yield to superior force. From the Crown's standpoint, western settlement before 1763 was desirable because every area settled by an Englishman could not be settled by a Frenchman moving down from Canada or a Spaniard moving up from the Gulf. Thereafter, though, it was not the French and Spanish who posed a threat to British hegemony but rather the increasingly independent-minded western settlers.

Those who originally settled Jamestown came as bound servants owning no land, farming collectively, and subject to the will of the company. They were housed in barracks, poorly fed, worked in gangs, and subject to summary punishment and had little incentive to give of their best. Within a decade, however, sweeping changes were instituted, amounting to nothing less than a social revolution. The Virginia Company had envisaged paying the settlers little more than the prevailing English wage while they produced substantially more, thanks to the abundant land that raised their productivity. The difference between the low labor wage and the high labor productivity was intended to compensate the company for the costs of transportation across the Atlantic and provide a more than ample return to its stockholders. The ability and willingness of workers to run away and start their own settlements if ill treated and their failure to give of their best even when they stayed, however, eventually forced the company to modify its policies.

The solution was a system of free labor in combination with leased con-

[8] Taylor (1964); Gallman (1972).

tract labor. The impact was dramatic and immediate. As Captain John Smith put it, "when our people were fed out of the common store and laboured jointly together, glad was he who could slip from his labour, or slumber over his taske, he cared not how; say, the most honest among them would hardly take so much true paines in a week, as now for themselves they will do in a day." This system of leased, contract labor was known as indentured servitude after the name of the contracts, or indentures, that the servants signed.

David Galenson of the University of Chicago has pioneered much of the quantitative work on indenture contracts. In his view, indentured servitude was a credit system financing intercontinental transportation, providing a link between the English labor supply and colonial demand to the colonies. This system successfully overcame capital market imperfections that otherwise would have made emigration to the colonies infeasible for those who could not afford the high cost of passage of £5 to £10—an amount equal to or greater than annual per capita income at the time. Through this mechanism the servant borrowed against the future returns to his or her labor. The indenture was thus a promise to repay a loan, for which the servant was the security. The agreement between the indentured servant and the shipper was a barter transaction of a forward labor contract for freight space. Contracts for labor services were negotiated and fixed before departure and began upon arrival in America, where the contract was sold by the shipper to extinguish the debt for transportation. All risks thus fell on the shipper in the event of unforeseen circumstances—such as debilitating illness, accident, or poor markets—that reduced the price of the indentures contract below the costs of passage.

The traditional descriptions of the typical indentured servant raise serious questions about quality of this labor force. In an often-cited quote, historian Abbot Emerson Smith describes them as follows: "Many . . . were convicts from jails, transported instead of being hanged; a few were political and military prisoners taken in war or rebellion. There were rogues, vagabonds, whores, cheats, and rabble of all description, raked from the gutter and kicked out of the country."[9] Hardly a desirable labor force on which to base the future of a nation, yet as many as half to two-thirds of all white immigrants to the colonies between 1630 and the Revolution came under indentures.

Galenson's empirical work with the indentures contracts themselves, however, casts serious doubt upon this negative description of the quality of the labor force. Indentures were legally binding contracts duly sworn before a magistrate, and these records have been preserved by the courts. Since the trade quite quickly became extensive, regular, and habitual, there emerged standard contract forms in which the principal and agent could fill in the blanks with particulars such as name, age, occupation, destination, and length of service (Figure 2.3). Galenson has drawn samples of thousands of

[9] Smith (1947): 3.

FIGURE 2.3

An Indenture Contract: Middlesex County Court
January 1683–May 1684

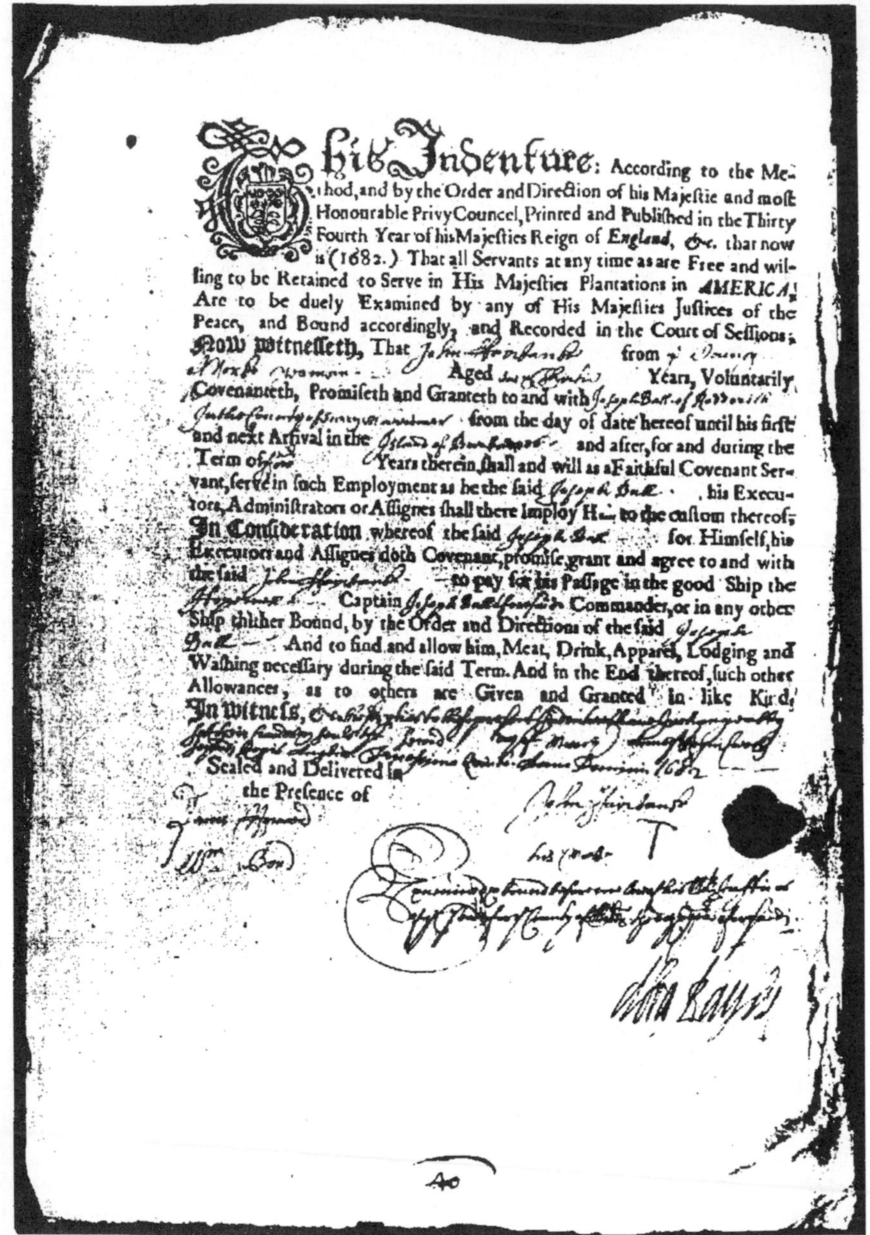

This Indenture: According to the Method, and by the Order and Direction of his Majestie and most Honourable Privy Councel, Printed and Published in the Thirty Fourth Year of his Majesties Reign of *England, &c.* that now is (1682.) That all Servants at any time as are Free and willing to be Retained to Serve in His Majesties Plantations in *AMERICA*, Are to be duely Examined by any of His Majesties Justices of the Peace, and Bound accordingly, and Recorded in the Court of Sessions; Now witnesseth, That [illegible] from [illegible] Aged [illegible] Years, Voluntarily Covenanteth, Promiseth and Granteth to and with [illegible] from the day of date hereof until his first and next Arrival in the [illegible] and after, for and during the Term of [illegible] Years therein, shall and will as a Faithful Covenant Servant, serve in such Employment as he the said Joseph Ball his Executors, Administrators or Assignes shall there Imploy H[illegible] to the custom thereof; In Consideration whereof the said Joseph Ball for Himself, his Executors and Assignes doth Covenant, promise, grant and agree to and with the said [illegible] to pay for his Passage in the good Ship the [illegible] Captain [illegible] Commander, or in any other Ship thither Bound, by the Order and Directions of the said Joseph Ball And to find and allow him, Meat, Drink, Apparel, Lodging and Washing necessary during the said Term. And in the End thereof, such other Allowances, as to others are Given and Granted in like Kind. In witness, [illegible]

Sealed and Delivered in the Presence of

[illegible]

40

Source: David W. Galenson, *White Servitude in Colonial America* (Cambridge, England: Cambridge University Press, 1981): 42. Reprinted by permission of Cambridge University Press.

FIGURE 2.4

The Value of Indentures

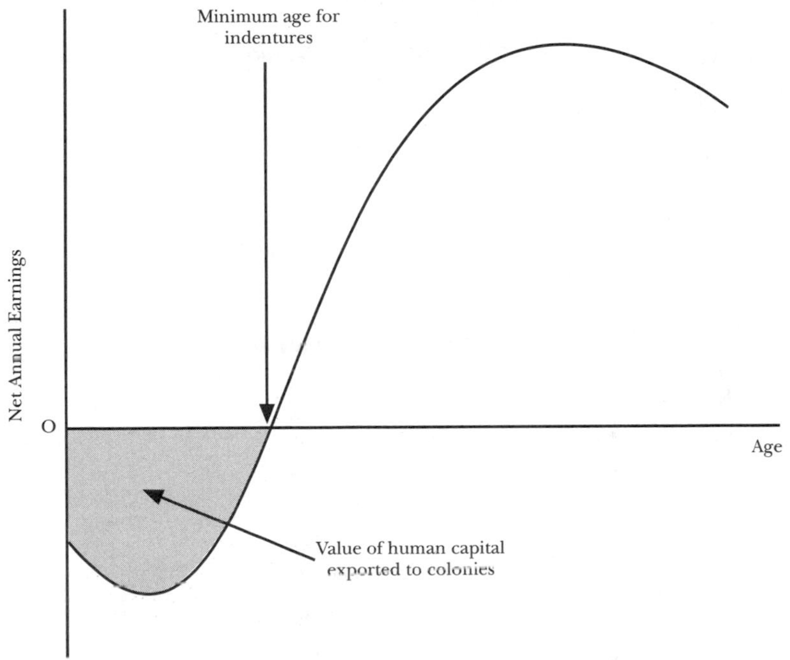

these contracts from courts in Bristol, London, Liverpool, and Middlesex as the basis for his revisionist interpretations of the institution.

An analysis of the characteristics of indentured servants reveals that the vast majority were males (by a better than four to one ratio, and the proportion of males increasing over time) in their late teens and early twenties. They were at the peak of their productive ability, representing a significant capital export from the mother country, which had met their rearing costs from infancy to productive adult and borne the costs of early mortality of nonsurvivors (Figure 2.4). Presumably no servant who could not earn a surplus above and beyond his or her maintenance cost would be bound. On the basis of ability to sign, evidenced by those contracts that have survived, Galenson concludes that about 41 percent of those who were bound in the 1680s were literate, while in the eighteenth century perhaps 69 percent of indentured servants were literate (Table 2.5). These fractions compare favorably with estimates of the literacy rate among the British population as a whole at the time. Finally, the data on occupations show a shift over time away from agriculture and away from unskilled labor toward a trade or craft. All in all, then, this hardly seems to fit Smith's description of indentured servants as "rabble of all description." Instead they appear to be a highly desir-

TABLE 2.5

Some Characteristics of Indentured Servants In the 1680s and 1700s

Characteristic	1680s[a]	1770s[b]
Average age, men	22.8	24.3
Average age, women	21.4	22.8
Percent male	80.7	90.6
Percent literate, male	40.5	68.8[c]
Percent literate, female	10.8	34.9[c]
Percent males skilled	35.0	85.0
Percent males destined for mainland	47.3	99.6
Percent females destined for mainland	58.4	100.0

[a] Middlesex County sample, 1683–84.

[b] London sample, 1773–75.

[c] 1718–59.

Source: David W. Galenson, *White Servitude in Colonial America* (Cambridge, England: Cambridge University Press, 1981). Reprinted by permission of Cambridge University Press.

able labor force that was at least as good as the average British worker. Moreover, quality was improving over time.

The data also provide an insight into value of different kinds of human capital, such as skill levels and literacy, and other factors affecting labor productivity. The indentures contracts were sold in America to cover the cost of passage. This cost was virtually constant across all servants over the period. The size of the debt was thus fixed for all servants, and the question was how long it would take for the surplus value of the servant's labor to extinguish that debt (see Figure 2.4). Galenson argues that competition between recruiters led to the adjustment of the length of indentures such that the expected sale price of the contract at auction in America was just equal to the cost of transportation across the Atlantic. Since this was constant for all servants, the term of indentures would thus be inversely related to the market valuation of the servant's stock of human capital.

Consequently, Galenson tries to explain variations in the length of individual indentures in terms of the observable characteristics of each servant that are crude measures of the servant's human capital, such as age, occupation, and literacy, and the servant's destination. He estimates that the average indenture for a twenty-year-old illiterate male with no occupation bound for Pennsylvania was fifty-six months (Table 2.6). An otherwise similar fifteen-year-old, on the other hand, could be expected to serve eighty-two

TABLE 2.6

Differential Value (in months of service) of Various Characteristics of Indentured Servants and Their Contracts: Servants Indentured in London, 1718–1759

Characteristic	Months' More or Less Indentured Service
Under 15 years old	33
15 years old	26
16 years old	16
17 years old	9
18 years old	4
19 years old	2
Female	−2
Literate	−1
Farmer	−4
Metalworker	−4
Textile worker	−4
Bound for Antigua	−5
Other West Indies	−6
Maryland	4
Virginia	2

Note: Months' more or less service are added to or subtracted from the 56 months' average service for 20-year-old illiterate male with no recorded occupation bound for Pennsylvania (months rounded to nearest whole month).

Source: Computed from David W. Galenson, *White Servitude in Colonial America* (Cambridge, England: Cambridge University Press, 1981): Table 7.1. Reprinted by permission of Cambridge University Press.

months (= fifty-six months + twenty-six months). The additional twenty-six months of service represent a penalty for the lower earnings capacity of a 15-year-old, compared with a twenty-year-old, and the extra service is an estimate of how much longer it took a fifteen-year-old to generate the income above his or her consumption needs to extinguish the debt of his or her transportation to the Americas. In the context of Figure 2.4, this additional servitude represents the necessary increment along the age axis such that the area under the curve for a fifteen-year-old serving eighty-two months is the same as the area under the curve for a twenty-year-old serving fifty-six months. Women served a couple of months less than a man with otherwise identical human capital and destination preferences, while someone who could sign his or her own name served less than someone without that skill. The reduction in the terms of service for those with specific human capital attributes may be thought of as the prices or values (in terms of months of service) of those characteristics and are the products of both supply and demand forces. For example, although a male servant may have been physically more productive than a female servant, if female servants were in greater demand, then, other things being equal, her services would be more highly valued, and her period of service correspondingly shorter.

Further analysis by Galenson, however, shows that only women under eighteen years of age received shorter periods of service. This result is consistent with evidence assembled by Robert Fogel and Stanley Engerman that suggests net earnings of female slaves, exclusive of the value of childbearing, were higher than for men to age eighteen which they attributed to the earlier physical maturation of girls.[10] Various occupational categories, such as textile worker, also reduced the period of indentured service.

Servants willing to be bound for the West Indies received substantially shorter indentures than those destined for the mainland. By choosing Antigua as a destination over Maryland, a servant might reduce the period of indenture by ten months. Galenson interprets the shorter terms for those going to the West Indies as compensating differentials for poorer working conditions, greater risk of disease and death, and poorer opportunities for the freedman or woman after working out his or her contract.

In Galenson's model, the indentured servant market functions through the adjustment of the period of service to compensate for differences between servants and destinations. If this market functioned perfectly and was efficient, then all servant contracts should have sold for the same price in the colonies, and this price should have been just sufficient to keep the shippers in business. Unfortunately the evidence does not, at first glance, seem to support Galenson's assumptions. Contract prices in Philadelphia—the largest and most active of the indentures markets—varied considerably. Indeed, Farley Grubb, a former student of Galenson's, has concluded that the contract sale price was not very well explained by factors, such as sex, literacy, or occupation, known at the time of recruitment. In fact, these explained only 2 percent of the variance in contract prices—an insignificant amount. Where profit opportunities could be foreseen, they were successfully arbitraged and disappeared through adjustments in the period of service, as Galenson showed. The indentures business, however, was inherently speculative, and mistakes were made. The labor demand was in America; the labor supply was in Europe, thousands of miles and many weeks of travel time away. Consequently, there were significant lags between the expression of demand and the supply response appearing on the American market. Grubb concludes that unforeseen and unforeseeable events in this interval account for the large variance in contract prices.

[10] See Chapter 12.

FIGURE 2.5

Segmented Labor Markets and the Supply of Labor in Colonial America

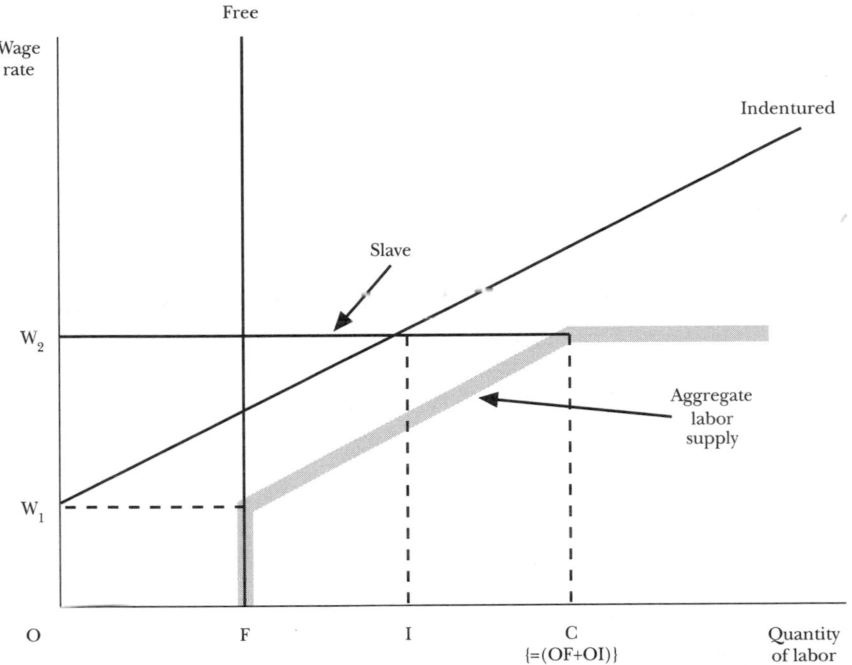

Although indentured servants were a major factor in the early colonial labor supply, they were gradually displaced by black slave labor, especially on southern plantations. Why? In particular, why didn't contract terms for indentured servants adjust to compensate for this competition from slave labor? Galenson offers an elegant and compelling explanation. Initially there were three distinct sources of labor for the colonies: those already in the colonies (who included free whites, indentured servants, and slaves), European workers willing to take out indentures for passage to the colonies, and Africans who could be enslaved. At any moment of time the supply of labor already in the colonies was perfectly inelastic—a stock—though, of course, the entire curve would shift rightward in response to population growth (Figure 2.5). At wage rates below w_1, the labor force consisted solely of people already in the colonies. However, when the colonial wage rose to w_1 (the reservation price of potential emigrant labor) or above, the colonies became attractive to indentured servants willing to be bound for a period of years so they could take advantage of the superior opportunities offered in America. The aggregate supply of labor at each wage rate is thus the (fixed) stock of labor already in the colonies plus the number of indentured servants willing to risk passage. The higher the American wage, the greater the number of indentured servants willing to commit. The elasticity of supply of indentured servants depends upon conditions in America relative to those at home. The better things look in America relative to conditions at home, the more responsive will be the supply of indentured servants. If the wage rises to w_2—the cost of securing and importing slaves—then slave labor will be imported. The supply of slave labor is perfectly elastic at any rate above the cost of importation—that is, from the slavers' perspective, there was a limitless supply of potential slaves in Africa, theirs for the taking, subject only to the costs of transportation. Consequently, at wages between w_1 and w_2 the demand for labor in America will be met by a combination of free white and indentured labor, but once the wage rate rises to w_2, ll new labor is supplied by slaves.

Suppose now that w_1 rises relative to the supply price of slaves so that it is now more expensive to import servants (at a cost of w_1*) than slaves (at a cost of w_2*). As a result, for all wages below w_2* the colonial labor force consists only of free domestic labor while any additional labor demand that raises the wage to w_2* is met by slaves (Figure 2.6). In the transition, as w_1 rises relative

FIGURE 2.6

The Disappearance of Indentured Servants

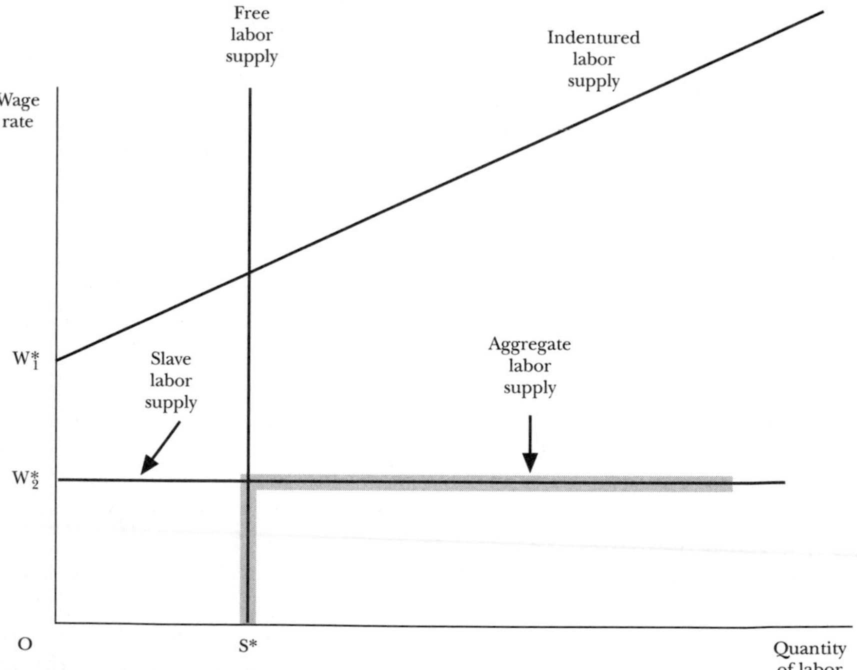

to w_2, the proportion of labor supplied by servants falls and that supplied by slaves rises, until servants disappear when $w_1 > w_2$.

What is particularly satisfying about this explanation is that w_1 rises and w_2 falls for the same reason: the decline in the costs of ocean shipping as ocean shipping productivity increased. The effect of this, however, was different for the supply of indentured servants and the supply of slaves. For the indentured servant, the lower costs of passage to the colonies reduced the need to borrow in order to pay for the cost of passage. The capital market imperfection that had stimulated the emergence of the institution became less necessary, and the supply of indentured servants shifted to the left. At the same time, the same reduction in shipping costs reduced the supply price of slaves. Rising real incomes in Britain, caused by industrialization, both raised the reservation price for indentured servants and simultaneously reduced the need to resort to credit for passage to America and the incentives to migrate.

Before the system of bound white labor in America passed into history, one important variation deserves special mention. The system of indentures we have described was a forward labor market in which the risks were borne by the shipper since the contract terms were fixed in advance but the price was uncertain. In the late colonial period, however, an alternative spot market developed. Servants opting for this method of paying passage were called redemptioners. It persisted well into the nineteenth century and became the universal means of financing German migration to America, though it was adopted only slowly and never completely by the British. Under this system, immigrants borrowed the cost of passage plus extra money for provisions and other expenses from the shipper before leaving Europe and agreed to repay the loan within days or weeks of arrival in America usually through negotiation of a labor contract that would extinguish the debt. The size of the debt was thus known beforehand and the risk of a change in the value of labor fell upon the redemptioner. Why would individuals prefer this system?

According to Farley Grubb, there must have existed benefits that compensated the redemptioner for assuming the risks borne by the shipper under indentures. The most obvious benefit was that redemptioners were free to negotiate their own contracts in America and thus had some choice of masters. Subject to paying off their debt, they could also consider nonpecuniary benefits. This seems to have been particularly important for those who sought urban employment. It also enabled families to stick together either through negotiation of a joint contract or through the selection of masters who were located nearby.

By comparing the cash fare for free immigrants with the credit fare charged redemptioners, Grubb estimated that shippers earned an average return per voyage of 11 to 15 percent on redemptioners over and above that earned on free immigrants. Because voyages averaged two months, annual returns seem to have been extraordinarily high—on the order of 45 to 60 percent, compared with returns on safe investments of around 5 percent. Nevertheless, few captains seem to have specialized in the trade. The high return was offset by high risk. A default rate of 12 to 13 percent per voyage would be sufficient to eliminate any excess profit. Passage mortality averaged about 4 percent, and the probability of shipwreck was about 1.5 percent. Defaults also occurred upon arrival. Debarkation morbidity averaged 3.5 percent, and postvoyage mortality another 2.6 percent among German immigrants. As a result, "excess profits" on the trade evaporated. Rising incomes in Europe and declining costs of ocean passage eventually eliminated the need for this market, and it too disappeared. Thereafter immigrants paid their passages in Europe and kept the fruits of their labor in the United States.

By the time of the Revolution the American economy was at least ten times larger than it had been in 1690 and a hundred times larger than in the 1630s. Moreover, colonists in 1775 enjoyed a measurably higher material standard of living than their grandparents and great-grandparents. A per capita income averaging about $60—equivalent to perhaps $750 or so today—made them among the richest in the world at the time and provided some modest cushion against adversity. This is borne out in the estimates of the height of Americans fighting in the French and Indian War. At five feet eight inches, colonists were much taller than those in the lower classes who had stayed behind in England rather than risk all in a transatlantic adventure, suggesting few, if any, serious dietary and nutritional deficiencies. Moreover, probate records indicate that many Americans had managed to accumulate significant wealth holdings, further testimony to an excess of income over consumption in the long run (Table 2.7), although we do not know what percentage of the population had no wealth and therefore left no probate record. Southerners, who were also the tallest, were on average the wealthiest with almost $2,000 in physical wealth at the prevailing exchange rate around the time of the Revolution.[11] With a large slave population, however, wealth was more unequally distributed in the South than in the northern colonies, and proportionately less wealth was invested in land. For example, when Peter Manigault, a South Carolina planter and lawyer, died, his estate was valued at almost £28,000, certainly making him a millionaire in terms of today's purchasing power.

These data pose an implicit question: If material conditions for the colonists were improving steadily and if colonists were well off, why, then, did they rebel and seek their independence from Great Britain? What prompted them to "dissolve the political bands which have connected them with another"? Was it "Life, Liberty and the pursuit of Happiness" that pulled the colonists toward independence or a "long train of abuses and usurpations"

[11] Jones (1978).

TABLE 2.7

Total Physical Wealth of Free Wealth Holders in 1774 (£)

	New England	Middle Atlantic	South	All Colonies
Average physical wealth	£161.20	£189.20	£394.70	£252.00
of gentlemen	313.40	1,233.00	1,281.30	572.40
of merchants	563.10	858.00	314.00	497.10
of farmers with outside income	144.20	257.30	801.70	410.50
of professionals	270.60	240.60	512.20	341.00
of artisans	114.50	144.50	137.80	122.50
Distribution of wealth				
Botton 20%	1.0%	1.2%	0.7%	0.8%
Top 20%	65.9%	52.7%	69.6%	67.3%
Composition of wealth (all wealth holders)				
Land	71.4%	60.5%	45.9%	53.0%
Slaves and servants	0.5%	4.1%	33.6%	21.2%
Livestock	7.5%	11.3%	8.8%	9.2%
Personal	11.2%	8.4%	5.1%	6.7%

Source: Edwin J. Perkins, *The Economy of Colonial America* (1980, Tables 8.1 and 8.4), adapted from Alice Hanson Jones, *American Colonial Wealth: Documents and Methods* (New York: Arno Press, 1978) and Alice Hanson Jones, *Wealth of a Nation to Be* (New York: Columbia University Press, 1980).

that drove them toward it? The next chapter examines the economic impact of some of the abuses that might have driven the colonists to seek their independence, particularly British efforts to regulate colonial trade with the rest of the world, cited in the bill of indictment against British rule in the American Declaration of Independence.

BIBLIOGRAPHY

Ball, Duane, and Gary M. Walton. "Agricultural Productivity Change in Eighteenth Century Pennsylvania." *Journal of Economic History* 36(1976): 102–17.

Bidwell, Percy Wells. "The Rural Runaway in New England at the Beginning of the Nineteenth Century." *Transactions of the Connecticut Academy of Arts and Sciences* 20 (1916): 241–399.

Bidwell, Percy, and John Falconer. *History of Agriculture in the Northern United States 1620–1860.* New York: Carnegie Institution, 1925.

Egnal, Marc. "The Economic Development of the Thirteen Colonies, 1720–1775. *William and Mary Quarterly* 32 (1975): 191–222.

Galenson, David W. "Immigration and the Colonial Labor System: An Analysis of the Length of Indenture." *Explorations in Economic History* 14 (1977): 361–77.

———. "British Servants and the Colonial Indenture System in the Eighteenth Century." *Journal of Southern History* 44 (1978): 41–66.

———. "The Market Evaluation of Human Capital: The Case of Indentured Servitude." *Journal of Political Economy* 89 (1981): 446–67.

———. *White Servitude in Colonial America.* New York: Cambridge University Press, 1981.

———. "The Rise and Fall of Indentured Servitude in the Americas: An Economic Analysis." *Journal of Economic History* 44 (1984): 1–26.

Gallman, Robert. "The Pace and Pattern of American Economic Growth." In *American Economic Growth,* ed. Lance Davis et al. New York: Harper & Row, 1972.

Gray, Lewis. *History of Agriculture in the Southern United States to 1860.* New York: Carnegie Institution, 1933.

Grubb, Farley. "The Market for Indentured Immigrants: Evidence on the Efficiency of Forward Labor Contracting in Philadelphia, 1745–1773." *Journal of Economic History* 45 (1985): 855–68.

———. "The Incidence of Servitude in Trans-Atlantic Migration, 1771–1804." *Explorations in Economic History* 22 (1985): 316–39.

———. "Immigrant Servant Labor: Their Occupational and Geographic Distribution in the Late Eighteenth-Century Mid-Atlantic Economy." *Social Science History* 9 (1985): 249–75.

———. "Redemptioner Immigration to Pennsylvania: Evidence on Contract Choice and Profitability." *Journal of Economic History* 46 (1986): 407–18.

———. "Colonial Labor Markets and the Length of Indenture: Further Evidence." *Explorations in Economic History* 24 (1987): 101–06.

Heavener, Robert. "Indentured Servitude: The Philadelphia Market, 1771–1773." *Journal of Economic History* 38 (1978): 701–13.

Henretta, James. *The Evolution of American Society 1700–1815: An Interdisciplinary Analysis.* Lexington: D. C. Heath, 1973.

———. "Families and Farms: Mentalite in Pre-Industrial America." *William and Mary Quarterly* 35 (1978): 3–32.

Jones, Alice Hanson. *Wealth of a Nation to Be.* New York: Columbia University Press, 1980.

Lemon, James. *The Best Poor Man's Country: A Geographical Study of Early Southeastern Pennsylvania.* Baltimore: Johns Hopkins University Press, 1972.

———. "Comment on James A. Henretta's 'Families and Farms: Mentalite in Pre-Industrial America.'" *William and Mary Quarterly* 37 (1980): 688–96.

McCusker, John. "The Rum Trade and the Balance of Payments of the Thirteen Continental Colonies, 1650–1775." *Journal of Economic History* 30 (1970): 244–47.

———, and R. R. Menard. *The Economy of British America, 1607–1789.* Chapel Hill: University of North Carolina Press, 1985.

Merrill, Michael. "Cash Is Good to Eat: Self-Sufficiency and Exchange in the Rural Economy of the United States." *Radical History Review* 3 (1977): 42–71.

Mutch, Robert E. "Yeomen and Merchant in Pre-Industrial America: Eighteenth Century Massachusetts as a Case Study." *Societas* 7 (1977): 279–302.

———. "The Cutting Edge: Colonial America and the Debate about the Transition to Capitalism." *Theory and Society* 9 (1980): 847–63.

Perkins, Edwin J. *The Economy of Colonial America,* 2d ed. New York: Columbia University Press, 1988.

Rothenberg, Winifred. *From Market-Places to a Market Economy: The Transformation of Rural Massachusetts, 1750–1850.* Chicago: University of Chicago Press, 1992.

Schmoller, Gustav. *The Mercantile System and Its Historical Significance Illustrated Chiefly from Prussian History*. New York: Macmillan, 1896.

Shepherd, J.F.F., and Gary M. Walton. *Shipping, Maritime Trade and the Economic Development of Colonial North America*. Cambridge, England: Cambridge University Press, 1972.

Smith, Abbot E. *Colonists in Bondage: White Servitude and Convict Labor in America, 1607–1776*. Chapel Hill: University of North Carolina Press, 1947.

Taylor, George. "American Economic Growth before 1840: An Exploratory Essay." *Journal of Economic History* 24 (1964) 427–44.

Walton, Gary M., and James F. Shepherd. *The Economic Rise of Early America*. New York: Cambridge University Press, 1979.

The american revolution: some causes and consequences

3

As an integral part of the British Empire, the American colonies were subject to a wide variety of British mercantilist regulations. For example, the British restricted the rights of colonies to issue their own money; they prohibited colonial manufacture of specific goods, and some goods for which production was permitted nonetheless were excluded from intercolonial trade; and they imposed wide-ranging regulations governing colonial trade relations with the rest of the world. These latter regulations, known collectively as the Navigation Acts, were the cement that bound the British Empire together. To the extent that any of these rules and regulations were binding upon the colonists and were enforced by the British, they reshaped colonial development and affected the rate of economic growth. Consequently they offer an alternative—or additional—economic explanation to colonists united in their love of liberty against the tyranny of King and Parliament. In short, the Revolution may have been sparked by economic concerns as much as by the broader political issues of the British treatment of colonial legislatures, courts, and sensibilities.

The Navigation Acts

In the mercantilist system, colonies were expected to play a vital role in assisting the mother country achieve a favorable balance of trade and specie inflow by (1) helping achieve imperial self-sufficiency through the supply of products that otherwise would have to be imported from outside the empire, (2) generating export earnings by the production and sale of a product in high demand outside the empire, and (3) providing a market for the mother country's exports. The American colonies were especially valuable to Britain because they fulfilled all three roles, though not necessarily voluntarily. For example, the colonies were a major producer of iron, producing about 15 percent of world output at the time of the Revolution and exporting much of it to Britain. Similarly, the colonies provided strategically important naval supplies, such as tar, pitch, turpentine, and rope, as well as tall timbers suitable for masts. The colonists also produced tobacco to which Europeans were increasingly addicted, exporting more than one hundred million pounds a year to England by the early 1770s, although most of it ended up on the European continent. The development of American manufacturing industry prompted various English efforts to restrict colonial industrial development in products that might compete at home or abroad with products already being produced in Britain. After 1750, for example, the British prohibited the construction of new iron foundries in America, although the colonists largely ignored the ban.

To help ensure a favorable trade balance, Parliament passed a series of laws in the 1630s excluding foreigners from trade with America. These rules were not initially enforced because of British preoccupation with internal affairs during its civil war. But when the war ended, Parliament moved to reaffirm and strengthen its control. To this end, rules were codified and consolidated into new legislation—the Acts of Trade and Navigation—beginning in 1651. This legislation was continually expanded and modified as circumstances changed until its final repeal in the 1840s. The laws passed in 1660, 1662, and 1663 were especially pertinent to the colonies. Three provisions were critical:

1. All trade of the colonies was to be carried in vessels built, owned, and commanded by English or colonialists and manned by a crew that was at least three-quarters English or colonial.

2. All foreign (i.e., not from parts of the British Empire) trade with the colonies had to be conducted through England.

3. Certain colonial commodities, enumerated in special schedules (and thus known as enumerated goods), could be exported only to England. Initially the list of enumerated goods was limited to tobacco, sugar, cotton, dyewoods, and indigo, but early in the eighteenth century other goods, such as rice, molasses, and naval stores, were added.

The intent of the prohibition on the use of foreign shipping was twofold. First, it ensured that the substantial earnings from the carrying trade (see Table 2.4) remained within the empire. This was especially important since the Dutch were able to offer shipping services at lower rates, thanks to their earlier adoption of the unarmed flyboat with its superior efficiency in carrying freight. Second, it was intended to strengthen British naval power. So long as merchant ships were armed against pirates and foreign predations, the distinction between naval and merchant vessels was minimal. By reserving the imperial carrying trade to imperial ships and crew, the Royal Navy hoped to ensure a larger number of potential naval vessels and a larger pool of skilled seamen to man them.

But the system does not appear to have worked that way, at least during the French and Indian War (1756–63). Although the Royal Navy grew dramatically from 8,346 men in 1753 to 85,658 men in 1760, it is unlikely that this increase in manpower was met by conscripting merchant seamen because the size of the merchant marine also increased. In 1753 there were 40,565 men in the British merchant marine. By 1760 there were 45,075 men in the merchant navy, while another 71,276 men worked aboard privateers. The increase in the size of the merchant navy can be explained by the increased demand for shipping services to supply the military overseas, while the sharp increase in privateers reflects the potential profits from the seizure of foreign shipping.[1]

The restrictions on colonial direct foreign trade allowed the mother country to adjudicate which consumption desires of the colonists would be satisfied. Was colonial demand for a particular nonimperial product of sufficient merit to warrant its purchase outside the empire, thus reducing imperial gold and silver stocks? The indirect routing of goods through England also provided employment and profits for English dock workers and merchants although the colonists were permitted some limited direct trade with southern Europe.

Enumerated goods were in a separate category because of their economic or strategic importance to the British economy. Naval stores, for example, were vital to British sea power since the country had few trees left. Tobacco, on the other hand, was the single most important colonial export, worth over £3 million a year between 1768 and 1772 and accounting for about a quarter of all colonial exports by value. Most of it—over 90 percent by the 1770s—was reexported from Britain to the European continent, particularly Amsterdam, and had to bear extra freight and handling charges as a result of this indirect shipment. These added charges lowered the price that American tobacco farmers received for their product while simultaneously increasing the prices paid by consumers of tobacco products.

Economic historians care about British mercantilist trade regulations because the laws further increased the already high costs of transportation

[1] Neal (1977).

in the eighteenth century. From 1725 to 1729, for example, the price of tobacco in Amsterdam was more than four times the price of tobacco in Philadelphia, primarily reflecting the handling and shipping charges between the two markets. Although productivity growth in ocean shipping reduced this differential over time, the gap remained substantial. On the eve of the Revolution the price of tobacco in Amsterdam was still at least double the price in America.

Although freight was the largest single shipping expense, it was far from the only cost (Table 3.1). There were innumerable handling charges and recording fees to be paid as well. Primage, for example, was paid by the shipper to the captain and crew for taking care of the freight while the henneken

TABLE 3.1

Gross Receipts and Net Proceeds from the Sale of a Cargo of 252 Barrels of American Pitch Shipped to London in 1775

	£	s.	d.
Gross sales	203	9	6
Freight	71	17	6
Primage	2	1	8
Pierage	1	3	5
Duty	11	9	0
Sufferance and duplicate	0	3	6
Landwaiters and weighters	1	10	0
Oath	0	1	0
Weighers and hennekens	0	2	0
Post entry on two barrels	0	3	0
Land surveyors for certificate	1	5	0
Passing certificate in the customhouse	1	1	0
Clerk at the navy office	0	2	6
Henneken for wharfage	4	4	0
$\frac{1}{4}$ discount allowed as per agreement and custom	2	10	10
Brokerage for attendance at weighing and making entries at 1%	2	6	0
Commission on gross sales at $2\frac{1}{2}$%	5	1	8
Total charges	105	2	1
Net proceeds	98	7	5

SOURCE: Gary M. Walton and James F. Shepherd, *The Economic Rise of Early America* (New York: Cambridge University Press, 1979): 116. Reprinted by permission of Cambridge University Press. Data from Account and Invoice Book, Wallace, Davidson and Johnson, Maryland Hall of Records, Annapolis, Maryland.

for wharfage covered the cost of ropes used for tying up at the dockside. Shippers of cargoes that were reexported paid many of these charges, such as primage, pierage, and loading and warehousing, twice.

Economic Impact on the American Colonies

Not all colonists lost as a result of the Navigation Acts. On the benefit side, protection against non-British competition boosted the size of New England's shipbuilding and shipping industries. Massachusetts shipyards—close to the forests of upper New England—had low costs compared with those of British shipyards and thus built many ships for British merchants. Once built, these ships also fared well in the competition for imperial trade, particularly between New England and the West Indies. Colonial crews could be paid off and dismissed at home ports; British ships were forced to bear the expense of frequently idle deckhands in the same ports.[2]

A number of colonies also benefited from the British policy of subsidizing some colonial production. For example, the sixpence-per-pound bounty on indigo after 1748 must have been decisive in the growth of South Carolina's industry, for when the bounty disappeared with the Revolution, so did the industry. Bounties on other products—notably tar, pitch, turpentine, and lumber from North Carolina's forests—generated cash payments somewhat in excess of the indigo bounty but did not determine the viability of those industries. Lastly, even colonial exporters of unsubsidized goods benefited indirectly from mercantilist policies because of the protection afforded them in the British domestic market. Colonial exports realized higher prices in Britain because competing nonimperial products bore special, high tariffs.

Balanced against these benefits, though, were the burdens of the Navigation Acts. The colonists had to pay higher prices for most goods imported from nonimperial sources because these imports bore the incremental costs of indirect routing through England. About 15 percent of colonial imports suffered from this import burden. Americans were also forced to pay premium prices for protected English manufactures, such as lace and linen, instead of buying from lower-cost Continental sources.

Analogous to the import burden was the export burden generated by the Navigation Acts. Most of the tobacco and rice produced in the colonies were reexported from Britain, and a large portion of the reexport cost was borne by southern planters, who received lower prices because of the higher transport costs. Colonial exporters paid higher prices for shipping services than they might otherwise, owing to the exclusion of foreign vessels from

[2] Walton and Shepherd (1972).

the trade. Part of the burden fell on foreign consumers forced to pay higher prices, but unless the supply of colonial exports and the demand for colonial imports were utterly unresponsive to price changes—an unlikely notion—colonists shared that burden. Americans paid higher prices and earned smaller incomes than would have been the case if they had been free to use the cheapest shipping service and ship by the most direct routing.

How much lower prices would have been and how much more income the colonists would have earned have been the subject of long and sometimes acrimonious debate. The first quantitative estimates of the burdens and benefits by Lawrence Harper included only the estimated direct costs of rerouting exports and imports through England, minus the subsidies received for colonial exports of indigo, naval stores (tar, pitch, turpentine), and lumber. The resulting net burden upon the colonists was estimated at between $2.5 million and $7 million. Writing two decades later (1965), Robert Paul Thomas recomputed the impact of colonial regulation, working from an explicit counterfactual model of what economic life would have been like without the British presence. He argued that it was unrealistic to speak of a burden from membership in the British Empire before 1763. Separation before then would only have led to domination by another, less benign power—France or Spain. After 1763, however, France had lost Canada in the French and Indian War and Spain had lost Florida, spelling the end of significant continental European influence over the lives of North American residents.

Thomas measured the burden of the Acts of Navigation by analyzing their effect on what economists call the producer surplus (or rent) and the consumer surplus for the year 1770 and for the average year between 1763 and 1772. The producer surplus is the difference between the added resource cost from more output and the increase in the producer from the sale of those additional units of output. The consumer surplus is defined as the difference between what consumers are willing and able to pay for a product and what they actually have to pay for the product.

Consider first the case of American exports, specifically tobacco (Figure 3.1). As an enumerated good, all American tobacco had, by law, to be exported in the first instance to Great Britain, although ultimately the bulk of American tobacco (well over 90 percent by the late colonial period) was actually consumed on the European continent. The demand of European consumers for American tobacco, represented by the demand curve D_x in the figure, is the demand that American tobacco producers seek to satisfy. The supply of tobacco in America is modeled by the supply curve S_{xfob}, where the subscript "fob" stands for "free on board" and may be thought of as representing the supply of American tobacco at the dockside in the colonies. The cost of transporting a pound of tobacco from America to Europe by way of Great Britain (including all the miscellaneous handling charges) is £T_x.

FIGURE 3.1

Measuring the Burden of the Navigation Acts on American Exports

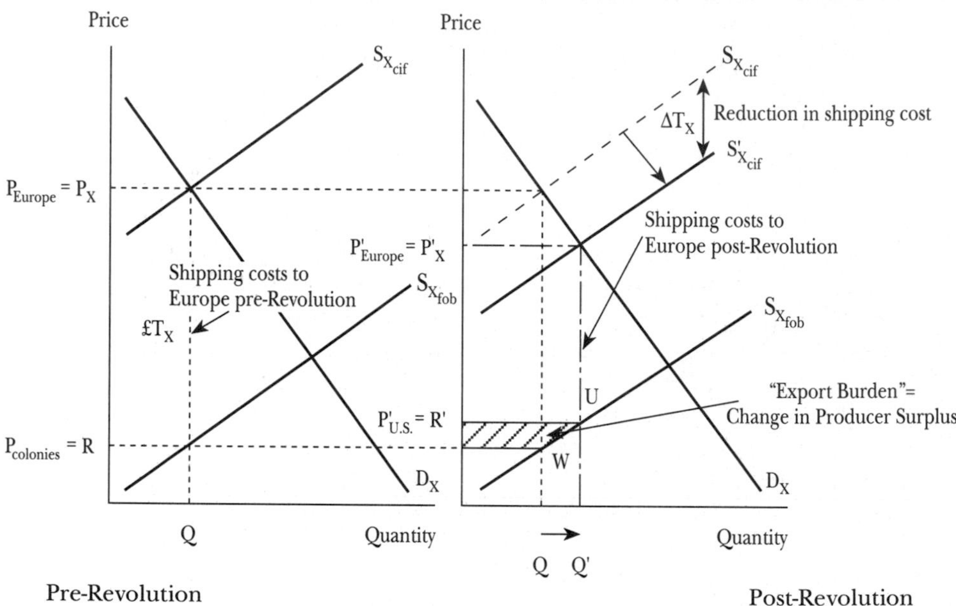

These transportation costs must be added to the production costs. Thus the supply of American tobacco in Europe, delivered by way of Great Britain, is represented by the supply curve $S_{x_{cif}}$, where the subscript "cif" stands for "cost, insurance, and freight." This cif-supply curve lies above the fob-supply curve by the amount of the unit transport costs, £T_x. Market price (that is, the price in Europe), P_x, is then determined by the intersection of the European demand with American supply. Quantity Q of American tobacco is sold in Europe. Of price P_x, the American producer receives only R, with the difference ($P_x - R = T_x$) going to pay the costs of transportation.

Suppose, however, that the colonists had been free to ship directly to their customers instead of routing the tobacco through Britain. This would have reduced transportation and handling charges by ΔT_x, effectively increasing the supply of American tobacco in Europe by shifting the cif-supply curve downward and to the right to $S_{x_{cif}}$. As a result, the price paid by the European consumer falls to P_x'. More important from the American perspective, more American tobacco is sold, Q_x' rather than Q_x. And the American tobacco farmer receives a higher price, R' rather than R. The in-

FIGURE 3.2

Measuring the Burden of the Navigation Acts on American Imports

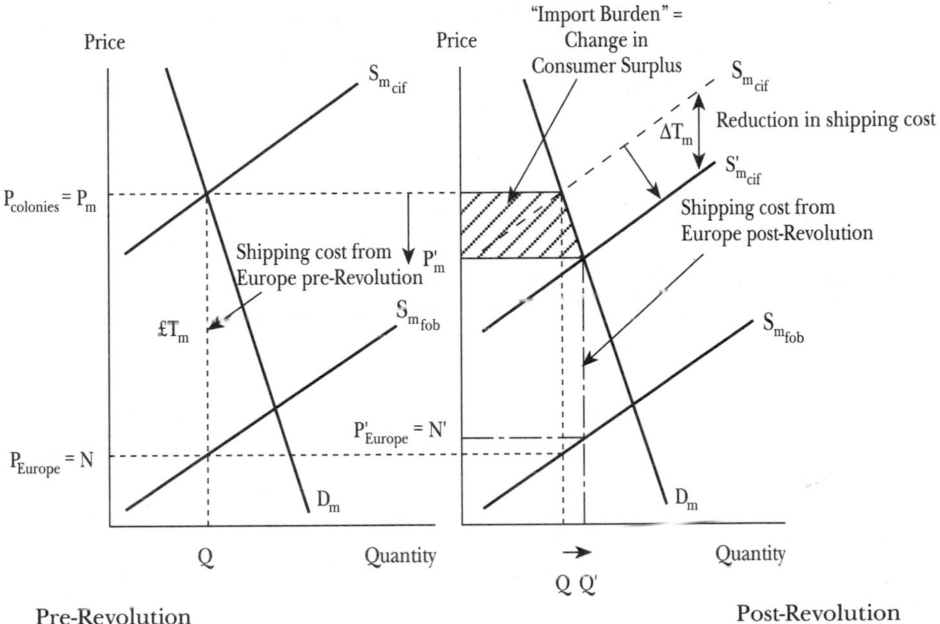

come of colonial tobacco producers increases, but a part of that income goes to paying for additional resources drawn into tobacco cultivation. What's left over, represented by the shaded area, is the increase in the producer surplus in America. This represents what the American tobacco producers were losing as a result of the burden of added transport costs on their exports of tobacco.[3]

The Navigation Acts also imposed a burden on American imports because all nonimperial imports had to be shipped to America by way of Great Britain (Figure 3.2). The American demand curve for nonimperial goods is

[3] Income is measured by price multiplied by quantity. When American tobacco exports were shipped to the European continent by way of Great Britain, American tobacco farmers earned an income R_xQ_x, equal to the area of the rectangle $ORUQ_x$. If tobacco were shipped directly to Europe, farmers' income would have been R'_xQ_x', equal to the area of the rectangle $OR'WQ_x'$. Increasing production from Q_x to Q_x', however, involves an added resource cost, equal to the increment in the area under the supply curve, the trapezoid Q_xUWQ_x', leaving American tobacco farmers with a net increase in their surplus—the excess over and above the cost of the resources—equal to the area of the trapezoid $RR'WU$.

represented by D_m, while the foreign supply of imported goods in the country of origin is represented by the supply curve S_{mfob}. In the absence of transportation and distribution costs or such taxes as import duties, the market price of nonimperial goods in America would have been determined where colonial demand D_m was equal to the foreign supply S_{mfob}. Instead, suppose it costs £T_m per unit to deliver nonimperial goods to the American colonies by way of Great Britain. Then the supply of nonimperial imports in America is represented by the supply curve S_{mcif}. Consequently, the goods sell in America for P_m per unit, of which T_m is transportation and other charges and N is the price received by the foreign producer. If, however, the American colonists had been able to import nonimperial goods directly, they might have saved ΔT_m per unit, so that the supply of the goods in the colonies would have been S_{mcif}' instead of S_{mcif}. The American price would have been P_m' rather than P_m. This would have increased Americans' consumer surplus by the amount of the shaded area.

In short, the Navigation Acts forced Americans to pay more and consume fewer imports and earn less and sell fewer exports. Two additional points should be noted. First, the Navigation Acts reduced the welfare of consumers and producers outside the British Empire. Second, the benefit from a reduction in transport costs is divided between consumers and producers depending upon the elasticities of supply and demand: The more elastic the supply, the greater the quantity effect and the smaller the price effect for producers.

Thomas estimated the gross burden on imports and exports at \$3.1 million in 1770 (Table 3.2). This burden was partially compensated by some benefits accorded the colonists by the mercantilist system. American exports to Britain were protected against competition from nonempire sources. Moreover, Britain made cash payments to the colonies for the production of certain goods, such as indigo, naval stores, and lumber. In addition, the Navigation Acts tended to increase the earnings of colonial shipowners by blocking direct competition from nonempire vessels, but these were offset by the reduction in the total volume of foreign commerce that resulted from the trade restrictions.

Reduced to a per capita burden, British mercantilist restrictions cost an average of approximately \$1.24 per person in 1770, or about 2 percent of colonial per capita income. Furthermore, the colonists did receive one clear benefit from their link with Britain: military (including naval) protection. Thomas estimates that this was worth \$1.775 million, a bit less than \$1 per person. Set against the net burden on commerce, this reduces the net cost to the colonists to less than \$1 million, or about 41 cents per person in 1770—well under 1 percent of income. As a result, it can be concluded that the British presence was not a serious financial hardship to the colonists.

The burden of the Navigation Acts was not shared equally by regions in

TABLE 3.2

The Costs and Benefits of Colonial Membership in the British Empire ($5 = £1)

	1770	Average 1763–72
Burden on Colonial Commerce:		
Exports:		
Tobacco	$1,630,000	$1,035,000
Rice	600,000	695,000
Other	265,000	175,000
Export Burden	2,495,000	1,905,000
Imports:	605,000	720,000
Import Burden	605,000	720,000
Gross Trade Burden	3,100,000	2,625,000
less:		
Preferences	275,000	195,000
Bounties	165,000	175,000
Net Trade Burden	$2,660,000	$2,255,000
Net burden per capital	$1.24	$1.20
Benefits of British Protection	$1,775,000	$1,775,000
Net Trade Burden less Benefit of Protection	**$885,000**	**$480,000**
Per capita	$0.41	$0.26

Source: Adapted from Robert P. Thomas, "A Quantitative Approach to the Study of the Effects British Imperial Policy on Colonial Welfare," *Journal of Economic History* 25 (1965): 626 and 637. Reprinted by permission of Cambridge University Press.

proportion to regional income. The South bore most of the impact, suffering losses on tobacco and rice exports. The burden is even more concentrated because not all individuals had equal stakes in foreign trade. If, in fact, just a few percent of the population—plantation owners—bore the lion's share of the burden, the political impact of the Navigation Acts might have been significant indeed. However, one should not make too much of this specific argument; agitation against mercantile restrictions was actually stronger in New England than in the South. On the other hand, it is simplistic to argue that a small per capita burden meant that the Navigation Acts were unimportant.

Other economists have questioned a yet more fundamental aspect of

Thomas's computation. Thomas used Philadelphia and Amsterdam data to measure American-European price differences. Unfortunately it is doubtful that the sample prices from these individual cities are representative of import and export prices generally. The issue is not a trivial one. As Peter McClelland noted, Philadelphia rice prices rose 28 percent between 1760 and 1789, implying an increase in the rice producers' surplus, while Charleston rice prices fell by 72 percent, reducing the producer surplus if the price decline was due to a reduction in demand for rice. And of course, rice was exported from Charleston, not Philadelphia.

McClelland has offered an alternative, more direct estimate of the burden as a percent of GNP. By definition, the fraction of national income lost as the result of trade route distortions depends upon the proportion of imports and exports bearing those extra costs, multiplied by the extra costs involved with the result expressed as a fraction of GNP. Since more exports were affected than imports and the extra costs that they bore were greater than those on imports, McClelland applies these factors to the entire colonial trade to derive an upper-bound measure of the burden.[4] He estimates the upper-bound burden to be 3 percent of national income—more than Thomas's estimate but in the context of the debate still relatively small.

For the first half of the eighteenth century Britain and the American colonies coexisted on satisfactory, if somewhat uneasy, terms. Trade restraints probably had only a modest impact on colonial incomes, and most of the burden was borne by tobacco and rice planters. The burden would have been greater and rested more heavily on Middle Atlantic and northern colonists if the trade laws had been uniformly enforced. But Britain did not have the will to intervene in illegal—though flourishing—trade between New England and the non–British West Indian sugar islands. High tariffs, embodied in the Molasses Act of 1733, were never paid on the bulk of imported sugar because it suited the Crown to avoid a confrontation with the

[4] McClelland computed the upper-bound measure of the burden as:

$$Z < \delta s \cdot p \cdot \left\{ \frac{X + M}{GNP} \right\}$$

where:
Z = the burden as a fraction of GNP
δs = fractional increase in shipping costs
p = proportion of trade bearing these extra shipping costs
X = value of colonial exports
M = value of colonial imports
GNP = gross national product of the colonies

This relationship is now expressed in terms of variables about which something is known. The incremental shipping costs, for example, were probably on the order of 40 percent, and this was borne by perhaps as much as half of all colonial trade. Furthermore, McClelland estimates that foreign trade amounted to as much as 15 percent (which Walton argues is an underestimate).

colonies. The obvious benefits to the colonies of empire membership—bounties, tariff preferences, naval protection—also helped smooth over inherent conflicts.

The Colonial Money Supply Question

There were persistent complaints throughout the colonies about a scarcity of money, particularly specie, restricting trade and depressing prices. A number of factors could explain such a scarcity: the colonial balance of trade deficit and balance of payments position (see Tables 2.3 and 2.4 on pages 38 and 39); British mercantilist prohibitions on the export of specie from the mother country; a tariff structure that biased the terms of trade against the colonies; prohibitions on the colonial manufacture of goods competing with British products and restrictions upon the colonies' trade with countries outside the British Empire. Moreover, the supply of paper money was restricted by colonial prohibitions on private issues and British parliamentary restrictions on colonial issues, especially if they were accorded legal tender status in payment of private (as opposed to public—that is to say, colonial government) debt. These shortages were further aggravated by the absence of commercial banks and organized capital markets in colonial America. On the other hand, after 1705 Parliament allowed the colonists to overvalue foreign coins by one-third to attract foreign specie so that the official rate of exchange was 133 colonial "pounds" for 100 English pounds.

The complaints about a shortage of money, though, should not necessarily be taken at face value. Although there were no commercial banks or organized capital markets in colonial America, book credit was supplied by merchants, and there was a wide variety of circulating media—foreign coin, specie (that is, gold or silver), some domestic coin, bills of exchange, and private and colonial notes—which served as money. Moreover, in some colonies, commodities were even accepted in payment. Tobacco is probably the best such example. It was received in payment of taxes and other governmental obligations in both Virginia and Maryland. Additionally, many of those complaining about the lack of coin were also apologizing to their creditors for not paying their debts on time.[5] Instead there seems to have been a relative dearth of "sound" money—that is to say, undepreciated currency. Between 1720 and 1774, for example, the price of wheat in paper money in Boston rose almost 700 percent, while the silver price of wheat rose only 62 percent. Experiences, however, differed widely among the colonies. In Rhode Island, which was notorious for its unrestrained issue of paper currency (where there was £31½ per person outstanding in 1760, or about

[5] Weiss (1970).

TABLE 3.3

Indexes of Exchange Rates with London (1720 = 100)

Year	Boston	Rhode Island	Philadelphia	New York	Virginia
1720	100	100	100	100	100
1725	143	143	100	103	100
1730	170	170	114	103	102
1735	223	223	122	103	—
1740	231	231	123	100	107
1745	292	292	132	122	113
1750	430	430	128	112	111
1755	430	785	128	114	116
1760	430	1110	120	115	124
1765	430	1270	129	115	141
1770	430	1440	115	112	104
1774	430	1440	127	112	113

Note: Massachusetts adopted a strict specie standard in 1749.

Source: Roger W. Weiss, "The Issue of Paper Money in the American Colonies, 1720–1774," *Journal of Economic History* 30 (1970): Table 2. Reprinted by permission of Cambridge University Press.

three times per capita income at the time), the exchange rate for local currency on London rose more than 1,400 percent. Certainly Rhode Island seems to have suffered from a surfeit rather than a dearth of money. Where issues were more restrained, however, as in New York (which had only £3½ per person outstanding in 1760), the exchange rate rose only 12 percent between 1720 and 1774 (Table 3.3).

Colonial government paper money was emitted as a result of fiscal crises faced by the governments, particularly in times of war, of which the French and Indian War was the most serious. All governments face a budget constraint requiring that deficits be financed through some combination of taxes, debt, and money creation. Given the simple tax structure, the ease with which taxes could be evaded, and the absence of capital markets, however, colonial governments had little choice but to resort to money creation through the issue of notes to their creditors. What distinguished the colonies one from another, though, were the provisions for retiring this debt. Where governments were able to reassure creditors that the debt would be retired through specific tax obligations, whether current or future, even large issues of paper money did not prove inflationary or cause exchange rates to depreciate.[6] New York, for example, issued £535,000 of

[6] Wicker (1985).

paper money during the French and Indian War but made a credible commitment for their redemption out of future taxes. Indeed, roughly 70 percent of the notes had been redeemed by the war's end, and the rest were withdrawn by 1768. Consequently, despite the large increase in the supply of money, prices in New York rose by less than 20 percent during the course of the war and were only about 10 percent higher in 1765 than 1755. In this regard, New York's experience was perhaps marginally better than that of Massachusetts, which, in 1749, had abandoned earlier inflationary paper currency issues in favor of a pure specie standard (see Table 3.3).

Paper money came to fill a crucial need in many colonies for small-denomination notes to meet everyday transactions. In Philadelphia in the 1740s, for example, the smallest coin in general circulation was worth 7½ shillings, or the equivalent of three days' wages for an unskilled laborer. Paper money, on the other hand, was frequently issued in denominations as small as a shilling. Indeed, 40 percent of the paper money issued by New York was in denominations under 5 shillings, while 81 percent of the paper issued by Rhode Island was in bills as small or smaller.[7]

In the wake of New England currency depreciations, Parliament acted to restrict colonial paper money issues beginning in 1751. It directed that the notes of the New England colonies be retired within two years of issue and prohibited their designation as legal tender in the settlement of private (but not public) debt. Further, in 1764, in the wake of the French and Indian War, Parliament extended the Currency Act to the rest of the colonies and prohibited any legal tender status whatsoever. To the colonists, this was just another case of growing parliamentary interference in their affairs. The law, however, was often flouted, and in 1773 Parliament repealed the prohibition on legal tender status for public, but not private, debt, providing yet another example of British vacillation and willingness to yield to colonial pressure.

A Turning Point in Anglo-Colonial Relations

The year 1763 marked a turning point in the British-colonial relationship. Before then the perceived benefits of empire membership probably dominated perceived costs. After 1763, however, colonial arrangements became increasingly unsatisfactory for both sides. Britain had emerged victorious from the long war with France. But the war had left Britain with an enormous public debt—all the larger because Parliament had reimbursed over 40 percent (£1.069 million) of colonial government contributions to the war effort—and a growing conviction that the colonies must bear a greater

[7] Hanson (1980).

TABLE 3.4

Index of Per Capita Tax Burdens in 1765 (Great Britain = 100)

Great Britain	100
Ireland	26
Pennsylvania	4
Maryland	4
Massachusetts	4
New York	3
Connecticut	2
Virginia	2

Source: Gerald A Gunderson, *A New Economic History of America* (New York: McGraw-Hill, 1976): 89.

share of the cost of maintaining the empire. As Table 3.4 shows, effective rates of taxation in England were already many times higher than tax rates in the colonies and since the war had benefited the colonists, too, the decision was made to shift some of the costs to the colonists. Therefore, the Crown imposed a series of new taxes and reformed colonial administrative practices to enforce new and existing taxes better in order to generate additional revenues.

For their part, the colonists saw the destruction of French power in North America as one less reason to suffer the restrictions of membership in the empire. With the French gone from Quebec and the Great Lakes region, the colonists had much less to fear from external military power. The British victory actually created a new source of conflict: Americans wanted access to Indian lands formerly protected by the French, while the British wanted only peace with the natives so that military expenditures could be reduced. British efforts to prevent colonial encroachment on Indian territory never amounted to much, but the division over land policy hardly strengthened the bond between Britain and America. Further, the Quebec Act of 1774, which ceded the territory between the Ohio and Mississippi rivers to Quebec, played right into the hands of the revolutionaries since Connecticut, Massachusetts, and Virginia all laid claim to that land.

British attempts to raise revenues both broadened the base of hostility to the home country and provided valuable lessons to the colonists in the art of collective resistance. A succession of revenue-related measures—the Sugar Act of 1764, the Stamp and Quartering Acts of 1765, the Townshend Acts of 1767, the Tea Act of 1773—were passed by Parliament. Colonial administrators were given increased power and personal financial incentives to enforce the laws. Whereas before 1763 only southerners had much reason to chafe under empire regulations, enforcement of the Sugar Act alienated articulate northern merchants, and the highly visible Stamp Act tax on documents irritated just about everyone in business. The colonial response was active resistance. The Sugar Act sparked a boycott on imports from Britain. It succeeded in part because "patriotic" gangs called the Sons of Liberty were able to coerce unsympathetic local merchants. Parliament bowed to colonial sentiment but tried again in 1767 by passing a flock of revenue measures known collectively as the Townshend Acts. As might be expected, the colonists responded with another nonimportation agreement, one that this time around received the official backing of the increasingly radicalized colonial legislatures. Imports were cut by one-third in 1768, and once again Parliament's will faltered. The Townshend Acts were repealed in 1770.

The net impact of these skirmishes was to polarize opinion over the right of Great Britain to govern the colonies. The colonists learned that resistance worked, and they gradually developed a popular philosophical rationale for that resistance. The British learned that decentralized rule would no longer work. They responded by increasing the legal authority of colonial administrators and by sending troops to back up that authority.

By 1773 the psychology of conflict had escalated to the point that both sides were just as willing to do battle over the symbols of British authority as they had been earlier to contest actual attempts to raise revenue. Thus, in response to a comparatively innocuous attempt by Parliament to grant a monopoly on the colonial tea trade to the East India Company, merchants organized the famous Boston Tea Party, at which a group of patriots disguised as Mohawk Indians boarded tea ships in Boston Harbor and dumped the tea overboard rather than permit it to enter the country. Parliament responded by closing Boston Harbor. Renewed British attempts to block further settlement of Indian lands with the Quebec Act evoked a third import boycott from the First Continental Congress and a virtual declaration of economic autonomy. Last-minute attempts by Lord North in March 1775 to compromise on basic issues crumbled under the weight of revolutionary rhetoric and mutual preparations for war.

What part did mercantile restrictions play on the road to rebellion? As noted before, they had only modest direct effect on the lives of most colonists. Nevertheless, a basic premise of mercantilism was that the colonies were to enhance the well-being of the home country, and the colonists correctly perceived that the Navigation Acts were a potential vehicle for economic exploitation. They probably also perceived that Parliament would not neglect that opportunity for exploitation indefinitely. Certainly, after 1763 attitudes, in both Britain and the colonies, were beginning to change, and while the Navigation Acts and other mercantilist restrictions did not precipitate the Revolution, they were a potent symbol of the economic differences that underlay the conflict.

The Revolutionary War

Although the Revolution disrupted the lives of many and destroyed a great deal of property, it never placed huge demands on the country's economic resources the way the American Civil War or World War II did. The colonial population numbered about 2.5 million in 1775. Perhaps one-third of that number were men of fighting age. Thus, in theory, the colonial military could have drawn volunteers from a pool of about 800,000. In fact, the Continental army never exceeded 20,000. Another 10,000 may also have served at any one time in the small American navy or the much larger fleet of quasi-military privateers. But the vast majority of colonial males either performed only temporary services or were never involved at all in the patriot cause.

The explanation for this restraint is that the war effort had comparatively few ideologically committed supporters. On one side were the patriots, an articulate group of middle-class lawyers, merchants, and planters who led an underclass of farmers and urbanites enticed by radical ideas regarding the evils of aristocratic privilege. On the other were the loyalists—civil servants of the Crown, northern landed wealth, and Anglican clergy—who strongly opposed the break with Britain. Caught in the middle was the majority with no preference based on perceived economic interest or political theory. This group could not be called on to make great sacrifices. It acted as a buffer during the war, maintaining production out of purely private economic self-interest and preventing "total" war.

The war on the land spanned seven years, from Lexington, Massachusetts, in April 1775 to the last skirmish at Combahee, South Carolina, in August 1782. But little of that time was spent fighting. The British were mostly content to control a few major ports. General Washington was usually too busy keeping together his illfed, poorly paid army to be able to threaten the passive redcoats.

By contrast, the war at sea was pursued aggressively and successfully by colonial privateers, who got to keep what they captured. The Royal Navy was spread too thin and operating too far from home port to offer much protection to its merchant fleet. The war loss in British ships and cargo is estimated at about $18 million, although some have put the figure much higher.[8] Whatever the true figure, though, the redistribution of wealth from British to American pockets was considerable.

What happened to the colonial economy in the meantime? Predictably the small farmers living out of the range of battle and producing only food for local markets were virtually unaffected by the conflict. More surprisingly

[8] Morris (1979).

perhaps, farms in contested regions or in British-occupied territories often prospered, selling their crops to the highest bidder. Attempts by the British to intercept exports of tobacco and rice disrupted the plantation economy of the South, as did seizure of some twenty-five thousand slaves, but exports of major crops remained substantial. Ships bearing tens of millions of pounds of tobacco ran the British blockade and sold their cargoes in Europe. Because British merchants were more interested in profiting than winning the war, much of this tobacco actually ended up in England.

Comprehensive trade statistics are not available for the war period, though it is generally believed that exports were reduced more than imports. The increased trade deficit was at least partially balanced by "invisible earnings" the income of privateers and expenditures by French and British troops on American soil who paid their bills in specie. Late in the war the Continental Congress was able to obtain credit from the French government and private Dutch banks, offsetting the negative impact of the blockade on export earnings.

Not everyone profited from the conflict, of course. Armies, even small armies like Washington's, cost a great deal to keep armed, clothed, fed, housed, and transported. Individual colonies were loath to pay their share of the army's bills through taxation, and the Continental Congress had no power to force them to see their duty. Instead the government resorted to two ancient, if not honorable, methods of war finance: inflation and confiscation.

The Continental Congress printed paper money; a lot of it. Between May 1775 and November 1779 almost a quarter of a billion dollars ($241.5 million) was issued. In addition, the states, acting individually and in defiance of Parliament, issued perhaps another $18 million of bills in 1775 and 1776 while estimates of the stock of specie and bills in the colonies in 1775 range from just $10 million to $30 million. Initially at least, Congress had intended redeeming their paper for specie at a later date, and its promises were believed. Consequently, the first $6 million, issued in 1775, and another $4 million in early 1776 exchanged for specie, dollar for dollar. The colonists were willing to hold much larger real money balances than was possible with the stock of money before the war, in part perhaps because Continental paper money constituted a portable, easily concealed source of wealth. But as the note issues mounted and Congress lacked both the power and the incentive to tax, its promises proved empty and the value of its paper currency depreciated (Figure 3.3). People who sold goods for Continental dollars in lieu of coins were badly burned. By the end of 1776 Continental dollars exchanged two for one against specie, and real Continental paper money balances began a dramatic decline.[9] By early 1777 the Continental

[9] Calomiris (1988).

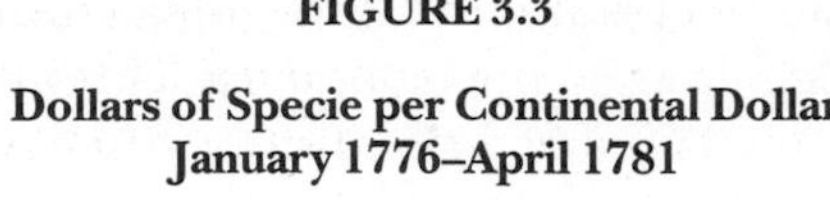

FIGURE 3.3

Dollars of Specie per Continental Dollar
January 1776–April 1781

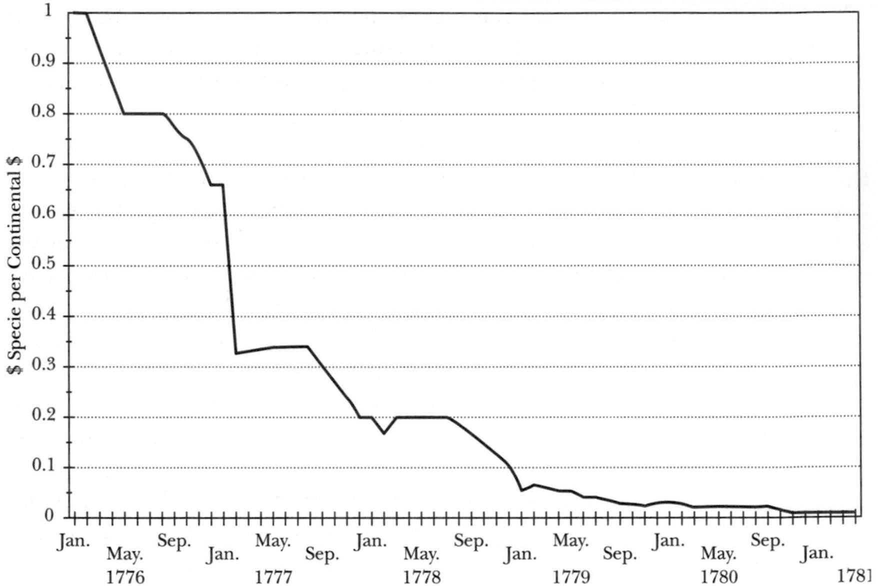

Source: Charles Calomiris, "Institutional Failure, Monetary Scarcity, and the Depreciation of the Continental," *Journal of Economic History* 48 (1988): 47–68. Reprinted by permission of Cambridge University Press.

dollar/specie exchange rate had risen to 3:1. By late 1778 the exchange rate was 10:1, and by 1781 the Continental currency, worth less than 1 percent of its issue value, had ceased to circulate. Hence the expression "not worth a continental."

The alternative to peddling bad debts to unwary merchants was to confiscate goods from the well informed. Loyalists—the first victims—had their lands seized by the state and resold as a source of revenue. After 1781 the army mostly fended for itself, scavenging food and work animals from unlucky farmers in its path.

The Transition to Independence

The period after the Revolution has been portrayed as one of economic decline. In the traditional story, imports exceeded exports and led to a drain of specie from the country. Shortages of money spread the depression beyond export industries into local market economies. This interpretation of the Confederation period endured because it seemed to fit the economic facts. Trade appeared to decline in the post-Revolution years, and shipping interests did indeed complain bitterly about their plight. There was a balance of payments deficit, so presumably specie (gold and silver) was exported. The value of specie did rise as its relative scarcity increased. Reduced trade, however, does not necessarily imply a comparable reduction in output. The export sector, after all, never accounted for more than 10 percent of national income, and the capital and land diverted from the export sector might have been almost as valuable creating goods for domestic consumption. While specie was exported, national wealth was not necessarily reduced since the specie was exchanged for goods of equal value. Nor can we be sure that the specie reduction affected total output or impeded the efficiency of markets for goods or factors of production. Prices fell in terms of specie, but the purchasing power of the remaining coins rose. Other forms of money and what economists call near money—paper notes issued by the states, private warehouse receipts on crops ready for sale, personal IOUs—served then, as they do today, as substitutes for specie.

Nevertheless, times seem to have been hard. The index of total factor productivity in Pennsylvania agriculture (see Table 2.1, p. 34) shows a very small decline between 1775 and 1790.[10] Data collected on the real wages of Maryland agricultural laborers imply a much more precipitous decline—perhaps as much as 40 percent—and commensurately harder times.[11] Estimates of per capita national income show a decline of almost 10 percent between 1774 and 1805.[12] Moreover, price level changes undoubtedly redistributed wealth. A mortgage payable in specie, for example, became more valuable while farms encumbered by such mortgages became less valuable.

As always, adjustment to independence benefited some and hurt others. Losses surely outnumbered gains, but it is hard to go much beyond that qualitative statement, and it is cold comfort for those who lose. The number of people whose lives were altered by independence—for better or worse—provides a clue to why historians looking for signs of serious economic discontent had no trouble finding them. Those who benefit from political and economic events have no particular motive to alert the world to their good fortune. But those who lose are apt to complain, particularly if their expectations were different. Boston merchants did not believe that the fruits of successful revolution should end up in the hands of Philadelphia and New York merchants. Small farmers, once encouraged to identify their troubles

[10] Ball and Walton (1976).
[11] Adams (1986).
[12] Unpublished estimates by Robert E. Gallman.

with arbitrary rule from Britain, did not understand why their debts (which were usually denominated in gold or silver) should become more burdensome after independence had been won.

At least some of the problems stemmed from the flawed system of government under the Articles of Confederation that established a loose confederation of largely independent states with a weak central government. National representatives were unable to negotiate trade treaties with Spain and Britain because the individual states could not agree on necessary concessions. Congress had no powers to tax and thus was poor. And having no money, it had no power. States, however, had few restraints. They were free to pursue their own self-interests even to the detriment of their neighbors. The power to levy tariffs on imports and exports, even between states, lay with the states, not the federal government. Similarly, states controlled the supply of money and credit within their borders. Former colonies openly squabbled with one another over land claims west of the Appalachian Mountains. There was civil unrest, such as Shays's Rebellion in 1786, in which an armed force of impoverished Massachusetts farmers led by Daniel Shays challenged farm and home foreclosures. Although Shays's men were defeated, the state legislature did provide some tax and debt relief.

Under such circumstances, a national economy could not and did not exist. As Alexander Hamilton saw it:

> There is scarcely anything that can wound the pride or degrade the character of an independent nation which we do not experience . . . we owe debts to foreigners and to our own citizens . . . these remain without any proper or satisfactory provision for their discharge. . . . We have neither troops, nor treasury, nor government. . . . Are we entitled by nature and compact to a free participation in the navigation of the Mississippi? Spain excludes us from it. Is public credit an indispensable resource. . . . We seem to have abandoned its cause. . . . Is commerce of importance to national wealth? Ours is at the lowest point of declension. Is respectability in the eyes of foreign powers a safeguard against foreign encroachments? The imbecility of our government even forbids them to treat with us.[13]

Nevertheless, there were also notable successes under the Articles of Confederation—such as the Land Ordinance of 1785 and the Northwest Ordinance of 1787, which are discussed in Chapter 9—that resolved some of the more controversial issues and eased transition to government under the Constitution.

[13] Alexander Hamilton,"The Federalist, No. 15" (December 1, 1787), in *Papers of Alexander Hamilton*, eds. Harold Syrett and Jacob Cooke (New York: Columbia University Press, 1962): vol. 4, 356–64.

The Economics of the Constitution

The Constitution proposed a fundamental restructuring of power and authority. The central government would be drastically strengthened at the expense of states. Among the many fundamental changes, Congress would no longer be dependent upon state largess for money. The new federal system also centralized the authority to print money and to regulate internal and external trade. In effect, the Constitution prepared the way for America to create a mercantile system of its own and thus compete more successfully with European systems organized along similar lines. Given effective power to make foreign policy, President Washington was able to remain free of entanglement in the Napoleonic Wars and was thereby able to develop lucrative European markets for U.S. shipping. At home the Constitution enabled Treasury Secretary Alexander Hamilton to set public finance on a firm footing, with the federal government accepting responsibility for debts of the states and creating confidence in the national fiscal system. In short, adoption of the Constitution, economic historians agree, created a more favorable economic climate in the country as a whole.

In 1913 Charles Beard advanced a radically new interpretation of the debate surrounding the Constitution in which economic self-interest played a role alongside politics and ideology. He argued that "merchants, money lenders, security holders, manufacturers, shippers, capitalists, and financiers" were supporters of the Constitution while farmers and debtors opposed it.[14] The former favored it because they stood to gain from the increased certainty in the rules of the game of commerce, trade, and credit promised under the Constitution. The latter opposed it because proposals to extinguish the public debt relied upon property taxes. Moreover, federal control and restraint of money and credit promised price stability and promoted a well-founded fear that debt repayment might involve a real opportunity cost.

Historians have engaged in heated debate, either embracing or rejecting Beard's interpretation of the Constitution. Historian Forrest McDonald, for example, even quantified the economic interests and voting behavior of delegates to the Philadelphia Constitutional Convention and the state ratifying conventions. On the basis of his analysis of these data, he concluded "anyone wishing to rewrite the history of these proceedings largely or exclusively in terms of the economic interests represented there would find the facts to be insurmountable obstacles."[15]

Economic historians, however, largely ignored the question until the approach of the bicentennial of the adoption of the Constitution. Using the

[14] Beard (1913): 17.
[15] McDonald (1958): 110.

same data that McDonald assembled as the basis for his attack on Beard, Robert McGuire and Robert Ohsfeldt have reappraised the evidence. They conclude that Beard's interpretation is, in fact, substantiated: Delegates to the Constitutional Convention voted in a manner consistent with their economic self-interests. The fundamental proposition in their argument is that the delegates voted so as to maximize their psychic satisfaction—utility, to use the economists' preferred term. Since psychic satisfaction is not cardinally measurable, McGuire and Ohsfeldt assumed that it depended upon each delegate's personal economic interests and ideology. Delegates, however, were not free to vote their own self-interests. They were elected to serve as agents for their constituents—the principals in this principal-agent problem. To ignore completely the interests of those constituents would jeopardize any political future the delegate might have. Moreover, because the Constitution had to be ratified by the states, it had to satisfy at least a majority of the voters in two-thirds of the original thirteen states.

Anyone familiar with politics recognizes the possibility of strategic voting—compromises and logrolling—that may obscure voting patterns. Delegates may vote contrary to their interests on some issues to gain allies on other issues. In their classic study *The Calculus of Consent,* James Buchanan and Gordon Tullock argue such behavior is more likely if the vote leads to decisive action and is not easily reversible and if the delegate trades his vote only in areas where his preferences are weak for allies in areas where his feelings are stronger. Such behavior, insofar as it weakens their model, increases confidence that where patterns are found, they are evidence of a very strong influence on voting behavior.

McGuire and Ohsfeldt use a wide variety of variables to measure economic interest and ideology. The personal interests of delegates, for example, are modeled by their occupations, ownership of slaves, speculation in western lands, ownership of public and private debt, and personal debts. Their ideology was approximated by their ages, whether or not they were of British ancestry, and their service in the revolutionary war. Measuring the interests and ideology of constituents was harder, and McGuire and Ohsfeldt relied upon measures of average per capita wealth and its composition for economic interest while the ideology of constituents was approximated by distance from the sea (those closer were more likely to be commercially oriented), population, and percentage of British ancestry.

Their results for delegate votes on specific issues at the Constitutional Convention show general support for an economic interpretation of the Constitution. Where the economic interests of delegates and constituents were strong, delegates voted those interests. Thus delegates representing coastal areas and large states generally favored increased federal power. Those who represented slaveowners, on the other hand, favored more states' rights. For example, the predicted probability of the average hypothetical delegate who owned no slaves voting for a law providing federal veto power over state laws was 0.439, whereas if the same person had owned one hundred slaves, the probability of his voting yes was only 0.159. If he had two hundred slaves, the probability fell even further, to 0.044. Such results imply that a different mix—perhaps a more representative mix—of delegates would have produced a quite different document. At the same time the evidence of across-the-board rampant economic self-interest is not very strong; delegates did not systematically and uniformly vote their self-interests on every issue.

Similar forces also seem to underlie voting patterns for the ratification of the Constitution. McGuire and Ohsfeldt found that delegates with merchant interests were more likely to vote for ratification than other delegates, all else equal, as were those who owned western lands or had interests in banking or public debt. However, delegates who were in deep personal debt were much more likely to oppose it. They estimate, for example, that owning private securities would raise the probability of a yes vote from 0.59 to 0.84 for a hypothetical delegate with average characteristics in all other respects, while the probability that someone with personal debts would vote for ratification was only 0.37.

Economic conditions certainly improved after ratification of the Constitution although it is clear that much of the revival had little to do with that document. The growth of foreign trade after 1790 was more a result of European wars than the new Constitution. By virtue of American neutrality during the European wars, American ships could trade with both sides. The demand for U.S. products increased substantially, and the demand for American shipping services increased yet more dramatically. A special feature of U.S. trade was the booming new business in reexports. In an ironic reversal of pre-Revolution mercantile roles, British West Indian products were shipped to the United States, relabeled as American, and then shipped to Britain without much risk of confiscation by the French Navy. U.S. reexport trade grew from nothing in 1790 to more than $45 million in 1800, while ordinary exports increased from $19 million to more than $40 million.

With respect to the economic advantages of the Constitution, the burden of proof properly rests on those who see in the document special incentives to growth. A key feature must have been the confirmation of the sanctity of private property, free from the arbitrary predations and intrusions of government and guaranteed by the rule of law. Certainly the Constitution is offered as a model to the former Communist states of Eastern Europe and the Soviet Union, although in the twentieth century we have become dependent on government institutions to regulate the economy. One should not infer from this modern experience, however, that government had an equivalent role to play early in the nineteenth century.

A clear advantage of the new system was that it gave the federal government the right to tax. The Confederation government, dependent on voluntary contributions from the states, was unable to raise revenue for public goods like national defense. It was, after all, in the interest of individual states to resist contributions since they would receive benefits from total national expenditure whether they contributed or not. The quantitative importance of this reform is not certain, though. Revenue requirements of the central government were small by modern standards; discretionary power to tax, short of the blanket authority granted by the Constitution, could have served as well.

The Constitution removed power from the states to tax imports, granting this right only to the federal government. In practice, states within the Confederation couldn't very easily impede imports through tariffs because foreigners could easily transfer their business to competing ports in other states. Under the Constitution, though, only the federal government could restrict imports. Hence the benefit, if any, of this constitutional provision depends upon the debatable returns to protective tariffs and other trade restrictions (see Chapter 5). Another important economic provision of the Constitution was the elimination of state authority to print currency. Centralization of the power to create money is extremely valuable if the government wishes to control the quantity of money in circulation. But the government had no such wish; the very concept of central banking as an instrument of monetary policy had no meaning in the early years of the Republic. In the absence of central banking, the major effect of eliminating state-printed money was to bind the state economies together through a common legal medium of exchange. This sounds more important than it really was. On the plus side, adoption of common currency reduced one cost of doing business in the same way it would be more convenient today to buy and sell goods abroad if foreigners used dollars as money. The common currency meant that businesses did not have to keep track of exchange rates between state currencies or keep special forms of money on hand to buy or sell in other states. On the minus side, however, the common currency probably meant that economic shocks—a fall in the price of tobacco, for example—were transmitted through the national economy more rapidly. On balance, the benefits of economic centralization probably outweighed the costs, but the real benefits from the adoption of the Constitution may well have been in the balance of powers between the executive, legislative, and judiciary that required attention to different constituencies and a diversity of interests.

Bibliography

Adams, Donald R. Jr. "Prices and Wages in Maryland, 1750–1860." *Journal of Economic History* 46 (1986): 625–46.

Ball, Duane, and Gary M. Walton. "Agricultural Productivity Change in 18th Century Pennsylvania." *Journal of Economic History* 36 (1976): 102–17.

Beard, Charles. *An Economic Interpretation of the Constitution.* New York: Macmillan, 1913.

Buchanan, James, and Gordon Tullock. *The Calculus of Consent.* Ann Arbor: University of Michigan Press, 1965.

Calomiris, Charles. "Institutional Failure, Monetary Scarcity, and the Depreciation of the Continental." *Journal of Economic History* 48 (1988): 47–68.

Gunderson, Gerald A. *A New Economic History of America.* New York: McGraw-Hill, 1976.

Hanson, John. "Money in the Colonial American Economy: An Extension." *Economic Inquiry* 17 (1979): 281–86.

———. "Small Notes in the American Colonies." *Explorations in Economic History* 17 (1980): 411–20.

Harper, Lawrence. "Merchantilism and the American Revolution." *Canadian Historical Review* 23 (1942): 1–15.

———. "The Effect of the Navigation Acts on the Thirteen Colonies." In *United States Economic History: Selected Readings*, ed. Harry Scheiber. New York: Knopf, 1964: 42–78.

McClelland, Peter. "The Cost to America of British Imperial Policy." *American Economic Review* 59 (1969): 370–81.

———. "The New Economic History and the Burdens of the Navigation Acts: A Comment." *Economic History Review* 26 (1973): 679–86.

McDonald, Forrest. *We the People: The Economic Origins of the Constitution.* Chicago: University of Chicago Press, 1958.

McGuire, Robert A., and Robert L. Ohsfeldt. "Economic Interests and the American Constitution: A Quantitive Rehabilitation of Charles A. Beard." *Journal of Economic History* 44 (1984): 509–20.

——— and ———. "An Economic Model of Voting Behavior over Specific Issues at the Constitutional Convention of 1787." *Journal of Economic History* 46 (1986): 79–112.

Morris, Richard B. *The American Revolution: A Short History.* New York: R. Krieger, 1979.

Neal, Larry. "Interpreting Power and Profit in Economic History: A Case Study of the Seven Years' War." *Journal of Economic History* 37 (1977): 20–35.

Ransom, Roger. "British Policy and Colonial Growth: Some Implications of the Burden from the Navigation Acts." *Journal of Economic History* 28 (1968): 427–35.

Shepherd, James F., and Gary M. Walton. *Shipping, Maritime Trade and the Economic Development of Colonial North America.* Cambridge, England: Cambridge University Press, 1972.

Thomas, Robert. "A Quantitative Approach to the Study of the Effects of British Imperial Policy on Colonial Welfare: Some Preliminary Findings." *Journal of Economic History* 25 (1965): 615–38.

Walton, Gary. "The New Economic History and the Burdens of the Navigation Acts." *Economic History Review* 24 (1971): 533–42.

———, and James F. Shepherd. *The Economic Rise of Early America.* New York: Cambridge University Press, 1979.

Weiss, Roger W. "The Issue of Paper Money in the American Colonies, 1720–1774." *Journal of Economic History* 30 (1970):770–84.

Wicker, Elmus. "Colonial Monetary Standards Contrasted: Evidence from the Seven Years' War." *Journal of Economic History* 45 (1985): 869–84.

Money and banking before the civil war

4

Depreciation and the eventual repudiation of Continental dollars brought discredit upon the new U.S. central government. The monetary situation only worsened under the Confederation with each state having the power to issue its own currency and very little incentive to use that power conservatively. Little wonder, then, that the Constitution gave the federal government the sole power "To borrow money on the credit of the United States. . . . To coin money, regulate the value thereof, and of foreign coin, and fix the standard of weights and measures." Currency reform loomed large on the national agenda.

What Is Money?

Economists have functionalist definitions of money. Money is whatever is used as a medium of exchange, a store of value, and a unit of account. For our purposes, the definition of money as a medium of exchange is probably the most useful although it encompasses almost anything from promises (such as bank notes, checks, and private promissory notes) to goods (shells, tobacco, furs, gold and silver, and now drugs) or even personal services. The use of such goods as tobacco and furs, services, and personal promissory notes, however, generally reflected a shortage of alternative circulating mediums of exchange. Such barter arrangements were usually short-lived because of the incentive to trade inferior commodities (otherwise known as Gresham's law) and the "double coincidence of wants"—that is to say, both parties desire the product the other offers in trade—implicit in these transactions. Nonetheless, they do have a place in our history. The first governor of the state of Tennessee, for example, was paid 1,000 deerskins for his services while the salary of the Tennessee secretary of the treasury was pegged at 450 otter skins per year. Similarly, research on probated estates in Massachusetts during the eighteenth and early nineteenth centuries has revealed the presence of substantial numbers of personal notes in the portfolios of a wide range of individuals.[1] Many of these notes were endorsed by unrelated and distant third parties, who, by their signatures, were pledging their names and credits to the repayment of the notes. Such endorsements provide clear evidence of the use of the notes in exchanges. The frequent presence of these notes in estates is also evidence of their use as a store of value. In short, they functioned as money. The use of such money, like personal checks in today's economy, increased the monitoring costs of the creditor who generally preferred government-authorized money—legal tender.

Legal Tender and the Bimetallic Standard

During the colonial period the American colonies had used the British pound sterling (£), which, despite its name, was by this time defined in terms of a fixed quantity of both gold and silver and freely convertible into either. As we have seen, it had frequently been in short supply, in part because the colonial trade deficit drained currency overseas. Consequently, the colonists had been forced to rely upon a mix of foreign coin, personal IOUs, commodity money, and colonial paper money that had increased transactions costs and uncertainty and reduced the rate of economic growth. The situation had only deteriorated under the Confederation with each new state issuing its own money and the repudiation of the Continental dollar.

It fell to Alexander Hamilton, the first secretary of the treasury, to create a unified national financial system from this confusion. As a first step Hamilton opted for a bimetallic currency like that in Great Britain and many other countries of the day. Both gold and silver coins, fixed in relative value by law, would be minted and used as money. These coins came in convenient denominations and were of known fineness, eliminating the need to assay the metal prior to acceptance. They were declared "legal tender for all debts, public and private." By the Coinage Act of 1792 both foreign and domestically minted coins were accepted as legal tender (Figure 4.1). Silver coins were valued by the benchmark of the silver content of the Spanish dollar, while the value of gold coins was set at exactly fifteen times as much, by weight, as silver. Hamilton hoped that the use of these two precious metals—the "bimetallic" standard—would increase the total money supply. With both gold and silver money around, he reasoned, commerce otherwise hampered by a lack of an exchange medium would be easier.

In reality, however, only gold *or* silver circulated most of the time.

[1] Rothenberg (1981).

FIGURE 4.1

Two Examples of Legal Tender Coin in the Nineteenth Century

A silver three-cent piece

A Spanish milled dollar

Source: Margaret Myers, *A Financial History of the United States* (New York: Columbia University Press, 1970): 75, 102.

Bimetallism requires the government to fix the relative value of gold and silver and freely exchange gold and silver coins at that fixed rate. But there was no means to ensure that the relative market prices for these metals would remain constant. For example, their supply was subject to the uncertainties of new discoveries of one or the other since they did not generally occur in the same geological formations, while demand depended upon their use not only as money but also in ornamentation and jewelry not just in America but in the rest of the world as well. In short, it would have been nothing short of miraculous if their relative prices had remained constant and equal to the rate at which the mint stood ready to exchange the metals. If, on the other hand, the relative price of the two diverged from the U.S. mint price by just a few percents, only one of the two metals would remain in circulation as money.

Here's why. Suppose the government offers to swap silver for gold (and vice versa) at the ratio of 15:1. Suppose, too, that the rest of the world values gold more highly, requiring fully sixteen times the weight in silver to relinquish a given amount of gold. Americans (or anyone else) could then collect 15 pounds of silver coins and buy 1 pound of gold coins with the silver from the government. They could then ship the pound of gold to, say, London (where world prices prevail) and exchange it for 16 pounds of silver coins. After bringing the silver back home, the arbitrageur could once again visit the government mint, this time walking away with 1.067 pounds of gold (16 pounds of silver = 16/15ths pound of gold = 1.067 pounds of gold). This process would continue as long as it is possible to make a profit buying gold at the mint or until the mint ran out of gold. Thus only the metal that is "overvalued at the mint"—in this case silver—remains in circulation as money. Anyone lucky enough to be paid in gold coins would hoard them or sell them abroad.

That is exactly what happened. Hamilton's original 15:1 mint ratio left gold undervalued and thus unlikely to stay in circulation. The coins that served as money consequently were made of silver. President Andrew Jackson's gold bill of 1834 attempted to restore gold as a medium of exchange by raising the mint ratio to 16:1. This left gold "overvalued" and, naturally, led to the importation of gold from abroad. In some parts of the country, though, the premium on gold was not sufficiently great to drive silver completely out of sight. In the 1850s increased gold production following the 1848–49 California gold rush shifted the relative value of gold downward, widening still further the difference between the U.S. mint ratio and the relative price of gold and silver in world markets. As a consequence, what silver remained in circulation finally disappeared, although it was not officially dropped as legal tender until the United States adopted the gold standard in 1900. Nowadays legal tender is limited to Federal Reserve notes.

Bank Money

There were no banks in colonial America—another reason for the creation and use of private monies such as IOUs and bills of exchange. The three commercial banks chartered during the Confederation—the Bank of North America, the Bank of New York, and the Massachusetts Bank—had the right to print and issue their own bank notes, and they did. So, too, did most banks until 1865. These notes circulated as money. The ability of banks to create money, whether by printing their own bank notes or through the use of checks, accounts for the popularity of bank charters and the government interest in regulating and controlling their activities.

The bank notes issued by commercial banks were, by law, payable to the bearer upon demand in legal tender. These are no longer in circulation, but their closest analogue today would be the cashier's check. Such bank money, though, was a less than perfect substitute for legal tender since it could be redeemed in full in legal tender only upon presentation to the chief cashier of the bank of issue. As a result, bank notes circulated only at a discount (that is, for less than their face value) outside the immediate area served by the bank. The size of the discount reflected the transactions costs associated with conversion—travel expenses and the time value of money in transit—and the risks that an unknown bank might not be able to redeem the note in legal tender as required by law. Such risks were real even where there was partial insurance of notes as under free banking legislation. These risks were

FIGURE 4.2

Bank Money

A One-Dollar Bank Note Issued by the Delaware City Bank in 1854

Source: Margaret Myers, *A Financial History of the United States* (New York: Columbia University Press, 1970): 129.

further compounded by the proliferation of different designs of notes in circulation from the growing number of banks along with the circulation of counterfeits, fraudulent notes, and the notes of banks that had gone out of business. It is estimated that on the eve of the Civil War more than nine thousand kinds of bank notes, issued by the more than sixteen hundred state-chartered banks then operating, were in circulation (Figure 4.2). The existence of mercantile reporting services, such as *Thompson's Bank Note Reporter* and *Counterfeit Detector,* could not eliminate these risks entirely, and the costs of collection still remained.

The personal check, now widely used even for petty transactions, was little used before the Civil War and then only for sizable transactions, typically of hundreds of dollars, equivalent to thousands of dollars today. Although personal checks function as money, they are not universally acceptable or necessarily convertible into legal tender. Rather, a check is a written order to the debtor's banker directing the transfer of a part of the customer's deposits of legal tender in its safekeeping to the creditor. In the event that the customer has less legal tender on deposit than required to cover the check, the order may be refused. And if the check is presented to a bank other than the debtor's bank, payment may be delayed until the order is "cleared"—that is, presented and honored by the issuing bank.

The process of clearing has become much more efficient over time as a result of transportation and communications improvements. The so-called

Suffolk Bank System, begun by the Suffolk Bank in Boston in 1819, was an early attempt to deal with the problem of discounted notes and the difficulties of clearing them outside the immediate area served by the bank of issue. As a service to other banks, the Suffolk Bank offered to debit the discounted value of a bank's notes that it received against the bank's account with the Suffolk Bank instead of presenting the notes for payment in full. The issuing bank was thus able to redeem its notes for less than their face value, while the Suffolk Bank gained deposits from other banks participating in the system. As a result, average discounts fell and the value of country bank notes in the Boston area approached par—that is to say, their face value. The Metropolitan Bank in New York began a similar system in 1851, but a nationwide clearinghouse system emerged only after the Civil War.

Aside from the costs and delay in presenting a note to the bank of issue, there was a very real risk that the bank might not be able to honor its legal obligation to redeem the note in legal tender upon demand. As a result, there were numerous efforts to guarantee payment through insurance. Such schemes generally proved less than perfect in preventing losses to noteholders and depositors. New York State was the pioneer in this regard, passing a bank insurance law in 1829 to protect holders of New York State bank notes in event of bank failure. The so-called Safety Fund required New York banks to pay 3 percent of their capital into a state-administered fund to be used to compensate noteholders in the event of bank failure. The problem, as the larger banks at the time pointed out (and as we all should now realize in the wake of the 1980s savings and loan crisis), was that the holders of insured notes had little incentive to monitor bank soundness. As a result, smaller, less visible banks could free-ride, trading increased profits for increased risk that was shifted to the system as a whole. This situation is known to economists as adverse selection—that is to say, only the unsound and imprudent banks benefited from the system. In the Panic of 1837 bank failures in New York overwhelmed the system, exhausting the insurance fund and obligating New York State taxpayers for the uncovered balance since the legislation had unwisely pledged the "full faith and credit" of the state behind this short-lived, flawed insurance scheme.

What Do Banks Do?

First and foremost, banks are financial intermediaries. They link savers—who want to set aside part of their incomes for later use—with investors—who want to use that surplus income to increase the quantity of capital goods devoted to production. In this role, bankers are brokers and market makers. The standard of performance is measured by how well they match buyers and sellers. To the extent that they are successful, banks have been credited with playing a leading role in economic development and industrialization by, for example, mobilizing capital, substituting bank loans for inadequate equity markets, and facilitating trade by reducing transactions costs.

Though simple in conception, such intermediation is complicated in practice. Banks compete for depositors by offering them higher returns in the form of interest payments, security, and liquidity. They compete for borrowers by charging the lowest interest rate. The difference between what they pay depositors and what they charge investors is the banks' return for the matching service. The banks' profit also includes a return for bearing the risk of illiquidity: Depositors often want instant access to their deposits while borrowers are rarely willing to repay their loans on demand. Banks thus intermediate by standing between short-term lenders and longer-term borrowers.

If market making were the only function banks performed, we could measure their success or failure solely by their impact on the quality of the market for financial capital. But banks inadvertently perform a second function: They create money, a medium of exchange. They perform this miracle by converting an unacceptable medium of exchange—an individual's promise to repay—into a more acceptable medium of exchange—the bank's promise to pay upon demand.

There is nothing inherently wrong with allowing bank liabilities to serve as money, but the ability to create money does put banks in a special position among private enterprises. The quantity of money in circulation has great impact on the economy as a whole by influencing interest rates and thus the demand for goods that are paid for with borrowed funds. It also indirectly affects the level of prices—and, more important, the rate of change of prices. By changing the quantity of money in response to purely private profit motives and competitive pressures, banks have a collective power to influence the composition of output, the rate of growth, and the inflation rate. Consequently, that power has been regulated by governments.

How Does the Financial System Work?

The financial system is thus made up of three economic agents—banks, the public, and the government—that interact. (See Appendix A for a mathematical derivation.) How banks function as financial intermediaries has been described above, but what was not stressed is that banks are constrained in their ability to create money. This constraint may be imposed by the government. But even if the government imposed no regulations, banks would find that the willingness of the general public to hold bank money constrained their money creation powers. In a regulated system, banks can only create bank money up to a maximum of their holdings of legal tender multiplied by the reciprocal of the reserve ratio required of banks (see Appendix A). In an unregulated system a bank can safely create only as much bank money as it can persuade the general public that it can redeem in legal tender upon demand. Banks are driven toward these statutory or prudent limits upon their credit-creation powers by their quest for profits, but they may stop short if they perceive the risk of the marginal loan as being greater than the return.

The government may play an active or a passive role in this system. Government is passive if its role is limited (as for much of the nineteenth century) to defining legal tender and perhaps specifying some minimum reserve ratios. Government is active if it or its agent deliberately enters the market to influence bank behavior by manipulating the quantity of legal tender held by banks or by altering the legal reserve requirements.

The general public enters the financial system on both the supply and the demand sides. On the supply side the public's willingness to borrow and ability to repay provides banks with the means to create money. On the demand side the public holds bank money as part of its portfolio of financial assets of varying liquidity. The currency ratio, defined as the proportion of total monetary assets that the public holds in the form of legal tender, captures the confidence of the public in bank money. The greater its confidence in banks, other things being equal, the higher the proportion of its monetary assets the public will hold in the form of bank money. Bank money is more convenient than gold and silver coin or bullion (unminted gold or silver bars), but for the monetary asset-holding public the issue is the substitutability of bank money for legal tender. Within the public's portfolio, the two exchange dollar for dollar. The mix depends upon convenience, transactions needs, and transactions costs. The willingness of the public to use bank money as a substitute for legal tender is not independent of the reserve ratio, which measures the ability of the banks to convert bank money to legal tender upon demand. For the system as a whole, however, there is an asymmetry. Whereas a dollar in legal tender held by an individual generally represents the same amount of wealth to the holder as a dollar of bank money, that same dollar in legal tender held by the banking system can support many dollars of bank money. Consequently, while the portfolio mix between legal tender and bank money is an individual choice, it has considerable significance for the system as a whole.

In equilibrium, the public's demand for money is equal to the banks' supply of money, which depends upon the quantity of legal tender held by the banks, the reserve ratio, and the currency ratio (see Appendix A).

The Early Banking System

STATE-CHARTERED BANKS

Two kinds of bank emerged in the new federal Republic. The first kind—commercial banks chartered by state legislatures—generally followed the example of the first private commercial banks formed under the Confederation. A group of investors would set aside a reserve of specie from their own assets—the bank's capital—and then solicit deposits and make loans. The loans were generally in the form of engraved bank notes (see Figure 4.2 on page 85)—bank obligations to be redeemed for specie upon demand—in exchange for borrowers' promises to pay back the loan with interest. These notes sometimes found their way into the hands of people who exchanged them for specie at the issuing bank, but the banks hoped the notes would circulate as money. The more the notes that remained in circulation, the larger the sum of interest-bearing loans the bank could maintain and the higher the bank's profits. The loans were typically short-term—60 to 120 days—and were often self-liquidating in that they bridged the gap between production and sale, underwriting trade credit and tiding increasingly commercialized farmers over between planting and harvest.

Sometimes the charters of the banks restricted the kinds of loan the banks could make and set minimum standards for the amount of specie that had to be kept on hand as security against outstanding bank notes. More often such restrictions were self-imposed—not on grounds of altruism but because it made good business sense. A balance sheet with a healthy amount of specie in the assets column increased the confidence of noteholders in the value of their "paper" assets. This private banking system grew by fits and

FIGURE 4.3

The Growth of Commercial Banking 1790–1861

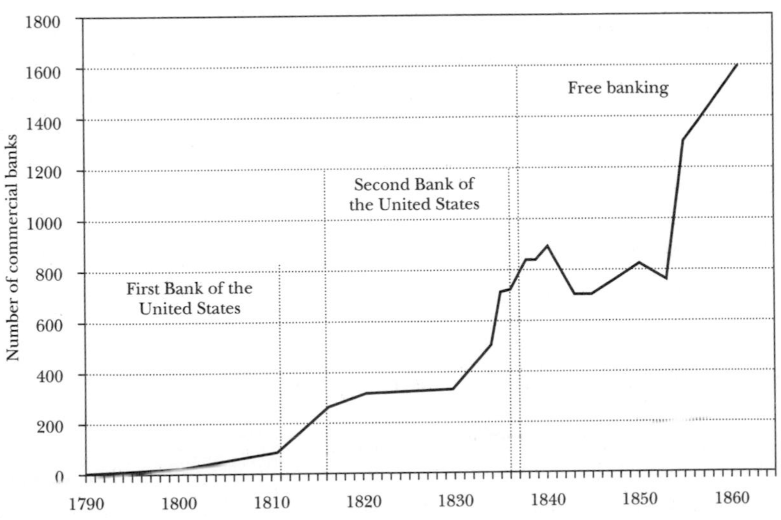

starts (Figure 4.3). The number of banks grew only slowly between 1790 and 1811 and again between 1816 and 1830, largely as a result of the regulatory effects of two large federally chartered banks, the First and the Second Bank of the United States (discussed in the next section). The number of banks actually declined in the wake of two financial panics, one at the end of the 1830s and continuing into the 1840s; the other in 1853.

The network of banks was most dense in the Northeast (Figure 4.4). In New England, for example, there was about one bank per eleven thousand people in 1830 and one bank per six thousand residents by 1860. These are high ratios of banks per customer. In the South and Midwest, on the other hand, the banking market was not nearly so "thick." In Ohio, for example, there was only one bank per eighty-five thousand residents in 1830 and just one bank per forty-five thousand people thirty years later. Today the ratio is about one bank per twenty thousand people. The contribution of the early commercial banks to economic development through the mobilization of capital and the matching of savers to investors, however, cannot necessarily be inferred from these statistics. Many banks apparently simply served as conduits to mobilize local capital for the benefit of bank promoters who had other, nonbanking interests. New England banks, for example, routinely lent the bulk of their funds to insiders, activities that have figured prominently in our most recent banking scandals. The Nahant Bank of Lynn, Massachusetts, for example, apparently lent between one-third and one-half of its funds to its president during the 1830s, while at the Pawtuxet Bank in Warwick, Rhode Island, 47 percent of the discounts were to Rhodes family members who were directors or president of the bank.[2] Such preferential access to funds reduced the social benefits from financial intermediation and may have given insiders an unfair competitive edge over their rivals in nonbank activities. Large loans and discounts to individuals also posed a serious financial risk to the integrity of the bank in the event of default, although the diversity of insider business activities may have provided some measure of insurance against such default. As a result there was a growing tendency by government to regulate such banking practices.

FEDERALLY CHARTERED CENTRAL BANKING

There was one other kind of bank that was simultaneously a commercial bank—but one deriving its authority by act of the U.S. Congress rather than a state legislature—and a quasi-public central bank serving the needs of the government. Its name was the Bank of the United States. The First Bank of the United States, modeled after the Bank of England, owed its existence to Alexander Hamilton. Chartered by Congress in 1791, it operated much like

[2] Lamoreaux (1986)

FIGURE 4.4

The Georgraphic Distribution of Banks
1830

PANEL A

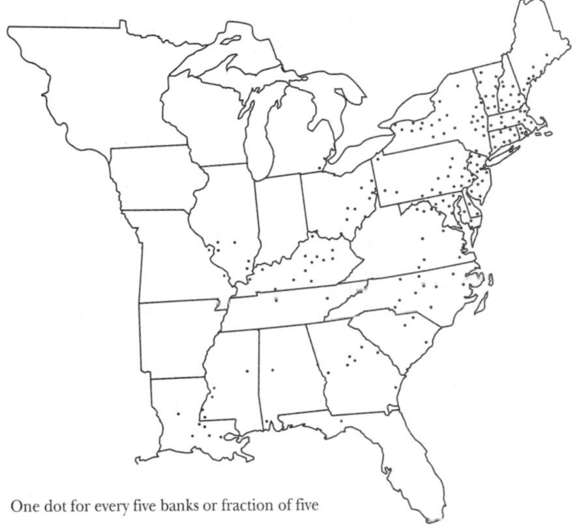

One dot for every five banks or fraction of five

1850

PANEL B

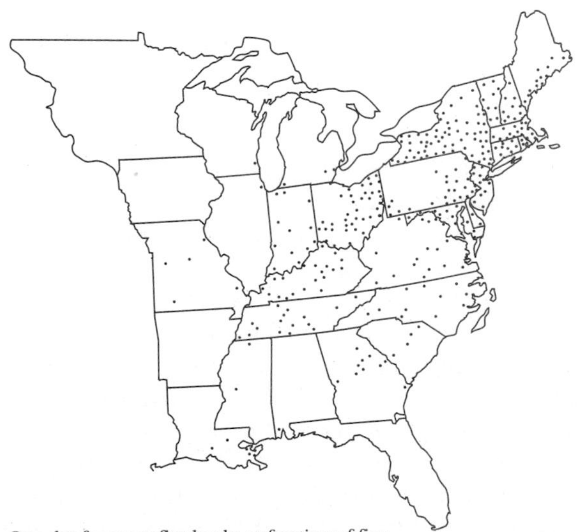

One dot for every five banks or fraction of five

Source: Charles O. Paullin, *Atlas of the Historical Geography of the United States,* (Washington, D.C.: Carnegie Institution, 1932): Plate 154, Panels C and E.

a private bank, printing notes and exchanging them for borrowers' interest-bearing promises to pay. But unlike a regular commercial bank, it had the federal government as a partner and number one customer. One-fifth of the Bank's stock of $10 million was owned by the federal government. The Bank served as the fiscal agent for the government, holding government tax receipts, paying government bills, performing various financial housekeeping tasks. In return, it had privileges unique among commercial banks. The government kept its cash as deposits with the First Bank of the United States, giving it a huge financial base. The government borrowed from the Bank, paying it interest for the use of its notes. The First Bank's federal charter, moreover, allowed it to operate branches in all states, giving it a big competitive edge over regular state-chartered banks, which could operate only in the states that chartered them.

Because of its size, conservative note-issuing policies, and relationship with the federal government, the First Bank of the United States gradually evolved into a sort of banker's bank, gaining the power (if not necessarily the will) to police lesser commercial banks. In general it was a net creditor to other banks, it held more notes issued by commercial banks as assets than commercial banks held of their notes. By using its branch system, the First Bank could speedily redeem commercial bank notes for specie hundreds of miles from where the note had originally been accepted. Though it rarely chose this course, its ability to demand specie for notes at will is thought to have deterred smaller banks that would otherwise have stretched the size of their own note issues, and it may have slowed the rate of growth and spread of commercial banking.

All this changed in 1811, when by a razor-thin margin (the vice president as president of the Senate pro tem casting the deciding vote), Congress decided not to renew the First Bank's charter. Why? In part, opposition to renewal came from Anti-Federalists—notably Thomas Jefferson—who saw the Bank as a bulwark of big government, concentrated economic power, and foreign influence. It is true that British investors did own much of the Bank's stock, but by law they were not permitted to serve as directors. The Bank's policies, no doubt, were influenced by "cosmopolitan" views. Yet it is hard to imagine that any bank run by upper-class city dwellers and dealing largely with the finance of international trade would have escaped such attitudes. Probably as important as these ideological objections to the Bank were the objections of state-chartered banks, which resented its real or imagined regulatory power. Even bankers who might otherwise have supported the need for a conservative overseer of the private banking system were eager to pick up a share of the profitable business the First Bank controlled.

In its five years following the demise of the First Bank, many of the fears of its supporters were realized. The number of state banks almost tripled despite the dislocations caused by war. The quantity of outstanding bank notes rose from $36 million to $76 million. The specie held by the banking system actually declined. As a result, the structure of banking was seriously weakened, and in 1814 a run on banks forced most to renege on their legal obligations to exchange notes for specie. It is possible that a strong central bank with a management devoted to conservative note-issuing practices could have prevented the rapid note expansion, but 1812–15 were war years, and there is no reason to believe that speculative opportunities were any less seductive during the War of 1812 than they were during other wars. The great increase in bank notes was probably due as much to the temptations of financing war-related schemes as to the "cat's-away" effect.

Whatever the explanation, financial instability and the accompanying difficulties of public finance caused Congress to change its mind. In 1816 it chartered the Second Bank of the United States along the same lines as the First Bank. Of the bank's capital of $35 million, 80 percent was private and paid in specie; 20 percent federal, paid in government bonds. With less than $70 million in legal tender in the entire country, this was a *big* bank! Private directors once again controlled the Bank's day-to-day operations. After a rocky start—the first president, William Jones (a Republican politician and secretary of the navy under President Madison), was, apparently, an incompetent manager and a decidedly unconservative leader—the Second Bank recaptured its special position in the banking community under the able hand of prominent Philadelphian Nicholas Biddle.

There followed more than a decade of national financial stability for commodity prices, the money supply, and the stock of specie reserves in the banking system. A traditional school of thought on the period—what banking historian Richard Sylla calls the "quest for soundness" school—attributes this period of stability to the responsible policies of the Second Bank and Biddle. The soundness school saw the Second Bank as a precursor of modern banks that was casually abandoned to the great detriment of the economy.[3]

The central bank today—the Federal Reserve (established at the end of 1913; see Chapter 18)—has two basic functions. It helps, along with other federal agencies, to assure the financial soundness of private banks. In part this is done by banning unsound banking practices. But the Fed's unique role here is as lender of last resort, protecting banks against the embarrassment of insufficient liquid assets to cover the withdrawal demands of their depositors. The Fed's other task is to monitor and control the national money supply. It can order changes in the percentage of bank assets held as reserves; this in turn changes the ability of banks to create money by making loans. More important (at least in practice), the Federal Reserve can change the money supply directly by buying and selling government bonds in the open market.

Under Nicholas Biddle's direction, there is little question that the

[3] Redlich (1968); Hammond (1957); Sylla (1971–72).

Second Bank performed certain control functions. Like the First Bank, the Second limited the note issue of commercial banks by remaining a net creditor to the private banking system. On some occasions it also lent money to commercial banks, in what some observers believe was a deliberate policy to preserve the liquidity of the banking system as a whole. And by virtue of its size, the Second Bank could have changed the money supply by changing its own specie reserve policy. Certainly during the 1820s the number of commercial banks operating in the United States grew only very slowly when compared with the period 1811–16 or the period after 1830.

In fact, the Second Bank did alter the money supply. But unlike the modern-day Federal Reserve, it was not really in the position to exercise this power in a constructive fashion when most needed. When financial crises threaten, the money supply tends to fall as individuals exchange their bank notes for specie anand remove their deposits from banks. A true central bank would try to stem the tide by trading its extremely liquid assets (in this case, specie) for less liquid assets (here the paper liabilities of other banks). The Second Bank, however, had to worry about its own liquidity precisely when a true central bank would have been worrying only about the liquidity positions of other banks. As later banking scholars were to put it, the problem was one of an "inelastic currency"; additional legal tender could not be created at will.

To expand the money supply, the Second Bank could deliberately hold the notes of private banks, rather than redeem them for silver or gold. But this central banking practice would, in effect, have required that the Second Bank make interest-free loans to private banks because while state bank notes were the obligations of those banks, they did not pay interest to their owners. Indeed, Biddle may have held back from cashing in other banks' notes. To the degree that he did, he reduced the profitability of the Second Bank.

The Second Bank could also expand (or control) the money supply by increasing its own note issue. Here, too, though, the Bank's public and private goals were inconsistent. The expansion of its own note issue would have reduced its ability to police the lending policies of other banks. To pose a credible threat to state-chartered banks, the Second Bank had to remain a net creditor. Contracting its own note issue to counteract expansion by the rest of the banking system would have helped stabilize the money supply—but only at the sacrifice of profits to the Second Bank.

The Second Bank War

Like its predecessor, the Second Bank had enemies. It had been embroiled in one of the landmark states' rights cases—*McCulloch v. Maryland* (1819)—over whether or not Maryland could tax notes issued by the Second Bank.

The commercial banks of New York and Boston were jealous of Biddle's special position and covetous of the huge, profitable banking business the Bank attracted to its head offices in Philadelphia. Banks in general resented the Second Bank's privilege of holding government deposits, funds they believed might as easily be part of their own reserve base. Most important, though, the Second Bank had to contend with the bitter opposition of a remarkably effective politician—President Andrew Jackson.

Jackson, elected in 1828, detested the Bank. Just why remains a bit of a mystery and probably always will. Some historians see his opposition as part of a populist ideological opposition to antidemocratic, antifrontier, centrist forces in the nation. Biddle, the Bank's president, was indeed as close as Americans came to aristocracy: wealthy, established, and suspicious of democratic levelers. Jackson was also opposed to the kind of expansionist banking practices that required a strong central banking authority to control.

However one chooses to explain Jackson's desire to torpedo the Second Bank, there is little doubt that he used his political skills extremely effectively to accomplish that end. He announced his goal in 1828, fully seven years before the Ban k would need to be rechartered, and the Bank's existence became an important political issue in the election campaign of 1832. Biddle allowed congressional allies to pass a recharter bill in the summer of 1832, only to see Jackson's expected veto sustained and Jackson returned to office in the fall. Jackson—probably correctly—took his election victory as popular support for his anti-Ban k policy and wasted no time in putting as much distance as was legally possible between the federal Treasury and the national bank. He withdrew government deposits from the Second Bank and placed them in various state-chartered banks around the country. By the end of 1833, 23 so-called pet banks had been selected to serve as federal depositories. Many of the officers of these banks had supported Jackson's reelection and stood to gain from the weakening of the Second Bank's regulatory oversight. At the same time the number of commercial banks operating in the United States exploded, growing from 330 in 1830 to 506 by 1834 and to 704 by 1835 (see Figure 4.3).

Despite its federal charter, the Second Bank was no stronger than its support from the Treasury. This was now gone. Biddle reacted—or was forced to react—to the withdrawal of federal funds by cutting down the volume of outstanding bank loans. It is possible that as some historians contend, Biddle's loan contraction was unnecessarily large in an effort to force Jackson to reconsider. The result was a national financial contraction—albeit a supposedly mild one—because inflows of British specie filled the gap left by the Bank.[4] The Bank itself limped along, mortally wounded, until its federal charter expired in 1836.

After an estimated 6 percent drop in prices in 1834, an inflationary cor-

[4] Temin (1968, 1969).

ner was turned. Commodity prices rose at an average rate of 13 percent a year in 1835 and 1836, and the country seemed gripped by a speculative boom psychology. Land sales—both urban and agricultural—increased enormously, as did the prices of slaves in the South. New canal construction commitments were made on the strength of a huge demand for state bond issues. Two changes in government policy were thought to have had an impact on the boom. In June 1836 Congress (with President Jackson's support) passed a measure authorizing the redistribution of federal revenue surpluses created by land sales revenues; distributions were to be made quarterly, beginning in January 1837. Then, in August 1836, President Jackson, in an apparent effort to check speculative purchases of public lands, issued an executive order, known as the Specie Circular, that the Public Land Office henceforth would accept only specie as payment in land transactions.

In May 1837 a financial panic forced banks to suspend redemption of their notes for gold. The Panic of 1837 was dramatic, though its impact was felt only briefly. In 1838 banks resumed specie payments, and prices began to rise. But a year later, a second financial crisis forced the suspension of specie payments once again. This time the crisis was followed by a prolonged period of falling prices. Numerous banks failed, including Biddle's own bank—the reincarnated Second Bank then operating under state charter as the Bank of the U.S. of Pennsylvania. Recovery from this depression, at least in terms of prices, was to take a decade.

Who Was to Blame?

Everyone agrees on the chronology of events beginning with Jackson's veto and ending with the financial contraction of the early 1840s. Interpretations of why the system failed, however, differ dramatically.

The soundness school sees the events as a morality play: The Bank veto and, more important, the removal of federal funds from the Second Bank eliminated the crucial buttress to the stability of the banking system: a limit on money creation. Without the Bank to police them, state-chartered banks were free to expand their note issues, increasing both the quantity of money in circulation and the vulnerability of the system to liquidity crises. In this view, the inflation of 1834–37 is attributed to this unchecked monetary expansion.

The ensuing panic is thus seen as the inevitable consequence of this unchecked money creation by an undisciplined and unregulated banking system. Like an overfilled balloon, the financial structure gradually weakened until some minor event was sufficient to precipitate the bust. The soundness school cites Andrew Jackson as the proximate cause of the panic. The Specie Circular, they claim, increased the public's demand for precious metal. This drained reserves from a banking system whose reserves were already insufficient to back the existing note issue. The distribution of the Treasury surplus further exacerbated the banking system's shortage of specie as funds on deposit in federal accounts with commercial banks were redistributed between banks and from state to state. The strain proved too great, the reasoning goes, and banks were forced into suspension of specie payments.

The soundness school interpretation endured for decades for two reasons. First, it is internally consistent; there are no obvious logical errors. Second, it appeals powerfully to preconceptions of the inherent instability of unregulated financial institutions. History—including recent history—is filled with examples of how the stupidity and/or the venality of those in charge have brought collective ruin to financial markets, as in the savings and loan crisis of the late 1980s.

A closer look at the evidence, however, reveals the weakness of the soundness school's case. From 1833 to 1836 prices rose 28 percent, and the money in circulation—specie plus bank notes—increased by 64 percent, phenomena the soundness school attributes to the unleashing of the commercial banks (Figure 4.5). If that is true, however, we should observe a de-

FIGURE 4.5

Money and Prices during the Jacksonian Period

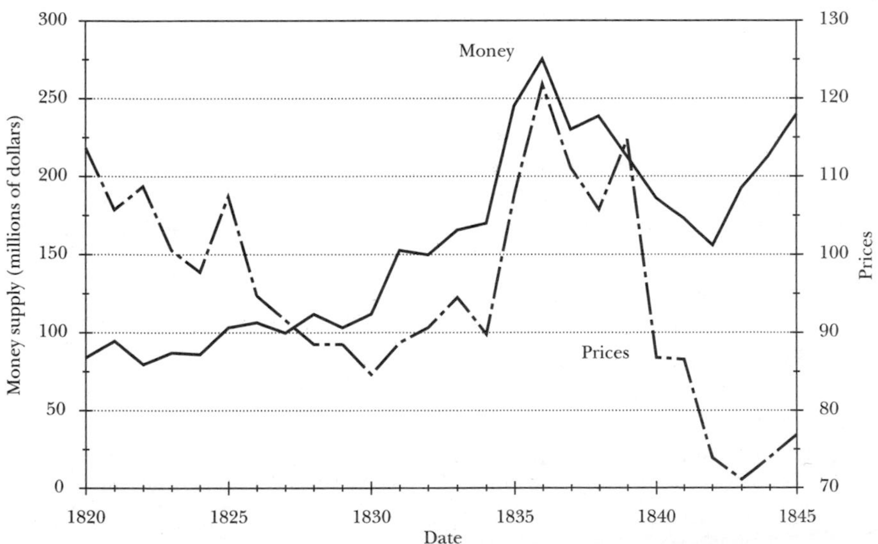

Source: Price data from Ralph C. H. Catterall, *The Second Bank of the United States* (Chicago: University of Chicago Press, 1902): 158. Money supply data from Peter Temin, *The Jacksonian Economy* (New York: W. W. Norton, 1969): 71, 159.

crease in the ratio of bank reserves to bank liabilities (notes and deposits). In fact, very little decrease occurred over the period; banks apparently did not react to the destruction of the Second Bank by embarking on dangerous new loan schemes and running down their cash reserves (Figure 4.6). Reserve ratios certainly rose sharply between 1831 and 1834, though they fell in 1835 and 1836 before rising again.

What, then, caused the increase in the money supply? We have ruled out a change in bank lending policies. That leaves two possibilities: (1) increased public willingness to use paper currency in lieu of coins, thereby leaving more specie on deposit in banks to serve as reserves, and (2) an increase in the total amount of specie held by individuals an d banks as reserves. The first is easily dismissed. A quick check on the data shows that the public *lost* confidence in the banking system and the public willingness to use paper instead of coins actually *decreased* (Figure 4.7). The evidence does, however, show a dramatic increase in the stock of specie in the United States (Figure 4.8).

In the absence of changes in the currency ratio and the reserve ratio, the money supply would have increased by 116 percent because of the increase in the stock of specie in the United States between 1833 and 1836 (Table 4.1).[5] Changes in the currency ratio—reflecting loss of public confidence in

FIGURE 4.6

The Average Reserve Ratio, 1820–1845

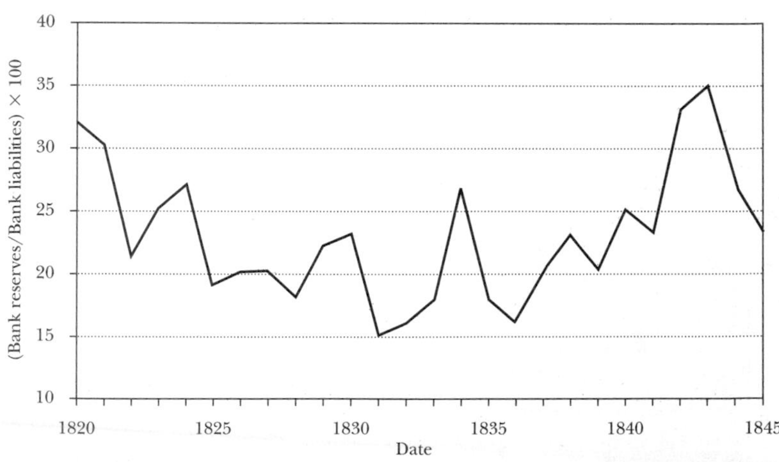

Source: Reserve ratio data from Peter Temin, *The Jacksonian Economy* (New York: W. W. Norton, 1969): 71, 159.

[5] Rockoff (1971)

FIGURE 4.7

The Average Currency Ratio, 1820–1845

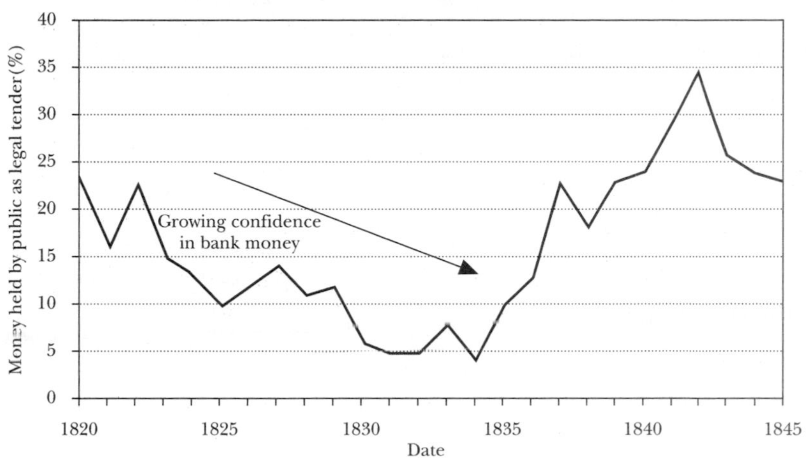

Source: Currency ratio data from Peter Temin, *The Jacksonian Economy* (New York: W. W. Norton, 1969): 71, 159.

FIGURE 4.8

The U.S. Specie Stock, 1820–1845

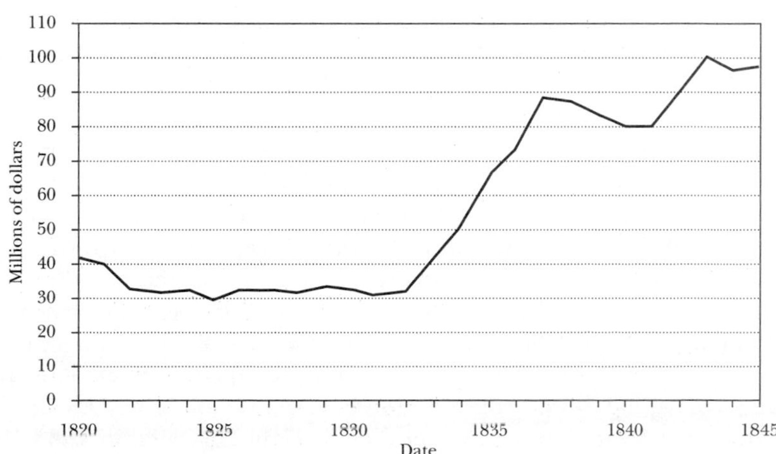

Source: Specie estimates from Peter Temin, *The Jacksonian Economy* (New York: W. W. Norton, 1969): 71, 159.

TABLE 4.1

The Determinants of the Money Supply and the Change in Money Supply during the Jacksonian Inflation, 1833–1836

Annual Rate of Change (%) of: Money Supply and Its Determinants	
Money	16.5%
Specie	19.2
Reserve ratio	2.0
Currency ratio	−5.1
Interaction of currency and reserve ratios	−0.5
Fraction of the Change in the Stock of Money Produced by Each of the Determinants:	
Specie	116%
Reserve ratio	16
Currency ratio	−31
Interaction of currency of reserve ratios	−3
Annual rate of inflation, 1833–36	8.3
Expected annual inflation caused by growth of the money supply in absence of real growth	16.5%

Source: Hugh Rockoff, "Money, Prices and Banks in the Jacksonian Era," in *The Reinterpretation of American Economic History*, ed. Robert W. Fogel and Stanley L. Engerman (New York: Harper & Row, 1971): 452. Copyright © 1971 by Harper & Row Publishers, Inc. Reprinted by permission of HarperCollins Publishers, Inc.

bank money—would have reduced the money supply by 31 percent but for the effects of more specie and lower reserve ratios. The growth in the specie stock thus drove the domestic money supply during this period, and it, in turn, drove prices higher.

The question, of course, is, Why did the U.S. stock of specie increase? There is no single explanation, and the reasons lie beyond American shores. It was due primarily to exogenous events unrelated to Jackson's policies. One source of silver inflow was from Mexico, since some wealthy Mexicans shipped their silver to the United States in search of a safe haven in the wake of political and economic instability.[6] A second source was an indemnity payment by France of $4 million made in 1836 to settle U.S. claims for shipping losses during the French Revolutionary and Napoleonic wars. The third source was a capital inflow from London in response to higher U.S. interest rates. In 1834, $6 million came; another $10 million came in 1838. This

[6] Ibid. Temin explains the silver inflow from Mexico instead as payment for American commodity exports; see Temin (1968, 1969).

money went into American securities, especially canal stock. The fourth source is more complicated and rather sordid. Instead of being an inflow of specie, it was a reduced outflow. Throughout most of its history the United States has run a balance of trade deficit with China that it met by exporting silver to that country. At the same time, growing Chinese demand for a commodity produced outside China—opium from British India—resulted in a derived Chinese demand for a suitable means of payment for this good. Since Americans had balances with London banks, it proved easier and more convenient for all concerned if Americans paid for imports from China with London bills of exchange that the Chinese could in turn use to purchase opium from British India. As a result, America substituted a commodity that was not money in the United States—London bills—for a commodity—silver—that was.

These international events explain the inflation, but what explains the panic? Traditional interpretations pin the blame on the Specie Circular. If the Specie Circular had much impact on the public's demand for coins, then it should show up in flows of specie from East to West (land sales, after all, took place in the West). In fact, there is no evidence of a loss of bank specie reserves from the East following issuance of the circular. Indeed, Peter Temin suggests that Jackson's avowed attempt to stop speculative land sales may have worked by dampening expectations of future demand for land. Like our recent banking history, falling land prices damaged the financial soundness of the holders of land mortgages. But the Specie Circular in itself did not trigger a run on the banks.

The villain—the agent most responsible for the Panic of 1837—was the British government. In 1836 British officials raised interest rates to stem the outward flow of specie, something they had not done in the previous few years. This led to an increase in interest rates on both sides of the Atlantic and, in combination with a fall in the price of the major American export crop, cotton, changed bank-noteholders' views on the security of their assets. The bank panic, then, was largely the result of forces outside the control of Andrew Jackson or anyone else in the federal government. It is true that a stronger banking system might have resisted the shock better, but it is hard to see how Jackson's veto of the Second Bank or his economic measures in 1836 weakened the system significantly. The plain fact is that a small open economy has little control over its own monetary system. Specie served as both bank reserves and international money, and the U.S. financial system was the helpless victim of rapid shifts in the demand for specie at home and abroad.

Temin's analysis thus demotes Jackson to a bit part in the drama. The facts, however, can be interpreted differently. Because the ratio of private bank reserves to liabilities did not change with Jackson's destruction of the Second Bank, he is exonerated from blame for the inflation of the 1830s and the subsequent deflation of the 1840s. In choosing the ratio of reserves to liabilities, however, banks were responding to multiple incentives: their own desire to issue more notes, customers' desire for security, and each banker's personal perception of the stability of the whole system. The reserve ratio, then, is really an "endogenous" variable—the product of causal factors, not the moving force in events. If changes in bank reserve ratios provide an unsatisfactory measure of the impact of the bank war, the only satisfactory measure must come from a model that simultaneously explains the behavior of banks as suppliers of money and the public as demanders of money. Estimates of the supply and demand for money for two separate periods—1823–35 and 1836–39—suggest that after 1836 the public was much less willing to hold money in the form of bank notes; this in turn suggests a basic loss of confidence in the banking system (see Figure 4.7 on page 99).[7] At the same time the banks were far less willing to "stretch" their available specie reserves to make additional loans, despite the high interest rates that made loans exceedingly profitable (see Figure 4.8 on page 99). This loss of confidence may have made the system more vulnerable to the shock of abrupt changes in specie flows by reducing the optimism of bank-noteholders in periods of financial stress. Edgy noteholders might well provoke a run on the banks even when there was little basis for believing that bank policies were fundamentally unsound or bank assets insufficient to cover liabilities. If so, then it is possible that Jackson's policies did have some impact on the financial system. The destruction of the Second Bank did not make the bankers more prone to take risks. Just the opposite: It forced bankers to act more conservatively. This conclusion, however, is sensitive to the choice of 1835–36 as the break between two different banking regimes. Jackson had removed federal deposits from the Second Bank years earlier. It is thus entirely possible that factors other than the bank war caused the changes in banking practices.

How Serious Was the Panic of the 1830s?

By modern criteria, the financial crisis that began in 1837 was extremely severe. The money supply fell by 34 percent from 1838 to 1842. Prices fell 33 percent from 1839 to 1843. By comparison, during the economic catastrophe of 1929–33, now known as the Great Depression, the money stock dipped just 27 percent; the price level just 31 percent. But whereas the depression of the 1930s also cut real GNP by 30 percent, Gallman estimates that real GNP actually *grew* by 16 percent during the 1839–43 slump.

How can we reconcile the most acute price deflation in American history with what was, apparently, not a bad contemporary rate of economic growth? The answer lies in the relative simplicity and institutional flexibility

[7] Sushka (1976).

of the early-nineteenth-century economy. Economic theory tells us that the quantity of money in circulation (M) times the "velocity" (V), or rate of circulation of money, must be identical to the product of real output (T) times the price level (P):

$$MV = PT$$

Today prices and wages are widely regarded as sticky—that is, slow to adjust to changes in the marketplace, especially in a downward direction. Producers in oligopolistic markets, locked into long-term labor contracts and with large fixed debts, are extremely reluctant to lower prices to attract customers. At the same time money velocity, which is determined in part by how much cash businesses and individuals need to support their day-to-day operations, adjusts only slowly to changing business conditions. Hence, if the quantity of money falls dramatically today, the quantity of money equation regains balance today partially through a drop in output. Money—or, rather, the stability of the money supply—matters a great deal in determining national economic output.

By contrast, in the first half of the nineteenth century markets adjusted rather quickly to a fall in demand by lowering prices. Most output was agricultural. Farmers went on planting and harvesting even when prices fell. Industry also apparently reacted briskly to market conditions, trimming costs rather than output. There were no union contracts to contend with, and most manufacturers' debts consisted of short-term borrowings to finance current production. A rapid fall in the money supply was thus balanced primarily by a fall in the price level, not a fall in output.

This is not to say that the deflation of 1839–43 had no impact at all on the "real" economy. The rate of investment fell as foreign investors, alarmed by numerous bond defaults, lost their enthusiasm for canal and railroad building. These virtually ceased for a number of years. Price deflation made foreign goods of all types more expensive and lowered the living standard of the relatively small percentage of the population that consumed large amounts of imports. But twentieth-century experience of the Great Depression provides a misleading perspective on what financial disruption in the nineteenth century could do to the economy.

The Era of Free Banking

If destruction of the Second Bank of the United States was folly, as the soundness school argues, then the price of that folly was several decades of financial instability. Left on its own, or to spotty regulation by state authorities, the banking system, it is argued, was a failure. Unscrupulous entrepreneurs set up "wildcat" banks, deliberately designed to deprive noteholders of their redemption rights and little different in principle from counterfeiting operations. According to historians of the soundness school, such a bank would set up shop with little or no capital, print bank notes, and exchange them for other assets, like specie. The owners would then pay themselves dividends and, when people attempted to redeem their bank notes, declare bankruptcy. It was no accident that such banks were typically located in the West, as far from civilization and intruding noteholders as possible. Wildcat banks, in the view of the soundness school, harmed the economy directly by victimizing unwary patrons and indirectly by reducing public confidence in the entire financial structure. However, a close look at this era of "free banking" presents a different picture.

The "free" in free banking refers to free entry into the banking business, not freedom to conduct business as the banker pleased. Between 1837 and 1860 a majority of states, particularly those in the West, experimented with some form of free banking legislation (see Table 4.2). Typically these laws allowed anyone to set up a bank, provided the issue of notes was backed with securities kept on deposit with the state banking authority. If the bank failed to honor its liabilities, the state could sell the securities and compensate depositors and noteholders.

Some free banking states, like Louisiana, could boast of perfect success in protecting bank customers. Others—notably Michigan—became refuges for wildcatters. Hugh Rockoff, the leading authority on banking history in this period, pins the partial failure of free banking to the type of security required by the state. Michigan allowed banks to use land mortgages at face value, regardless of their true worth.[8] Thus a wildcatter might deposit a $10,000 mortgage on land that the mortgagee had little chance of repaying and then issue $10,000 worth of notes to unwary clients. In Minnesota nearly worthless railroad bonds were accepted as security at 95 percent of their issue value. Much the same thing happened in New Jersey, where the law allowed the use of heavily depreciated bonds issued by other states as security at face value. The fault was thus not in the free banking concept but in the way that it was applied.

In Indiana, Minnesota, New York, and Wisconsin—free banking states for which Minneapolis Federal Reserve Bank researchers Arthur Rolnick and Warren Weber were able to get detailed information—between 36 percent (in New York) and 86 percent (in Indiana) of the free banks closed during the duration of the free banking experiment. Only a fraction of these, though, were failures in the sense that they paid noteholders less than the full (that is, par) value of their notes. In New York only 8 percent of the banks were classified as failures by Rolnick and Weber. In Minnesota, the worst case, as many as 56 percent of the free banks failed.

Despite the failures, the losses were less spectacular than historians have generally believed. Rockoff's computations show a total *cumulative* loss

[8] Rockoff (1974).

TABLE 4.2

The Spread of Free Banking in America

States with Free Banking Laws	Year Free Banking Law Passed	States without Free Banking Laws
Michigan	1837[a]	Arkansas
Georgia	1838[b]	California
New York	1838	Delaware
Alabama	1849[b]	Kentucky
New Jersey	1850	Maine
Illinois	1851	Maryland
Massachusetts	1851[b]	Mississippi
Ohio	1851[c]	Missouri
Vermont	1851[b]	New Hampshire
Connecticut	1852	North Carolina
Indiana	1852	Oregon
Tennessee	1852[b]	Rhode Island
Wisconsin	1852	South Carolina
Florida	1853[b]	Texas
Louisiana	1853	Virginia
Iowa	1858[b]	
Minnesota	1858	
Pennsylvania	1860[b]	

[a] Michigan prohibited free banking after 1839 but passed a new law in 1857.

[b] Very little free banking done under these laws.

[c] In 1845 Ohio had passed a law providing for "Independent Banks" with a bond-secured note issue—that is, essentially free banking.

Source: Arthur J. Rolnick and Warren E. Weber, "New Evidence on the Free Banking Era," *American Economic Review* 73 (1983): 1082, from Hugh Rockoff, *The Free Banking Era: A Reexamination* (New York: Arno Press, 1975): 3, 125—30.

through 1860 from bank failures to be no more than $1.9 million. It might have been a great deal less (Table 4.3). The redistribution of wealth that this implies from noteholder to wildcatter represents less than one one-hundreath of 1 percent of national income during the free banking era. True losses were concentrated in just a few states—Michigan, Indiana, New York—but even so, they hardly represent a significant fraction of wealth.

An alternative measure of the losses to noteholders from bank failures is the expected value of a randomly selected bank note. In New York this expected value never fell below 99 cents and from 1855 onward was $1. The New York experiment was a success. The worst case was Minnesota, where in the year following adoption of free banking the expected value of a $1 note

TABLE 4.3

Cumulative Noteholder Losses under Free Banking to 1860

State	Free Banking Years	Cumulative Losses ($)
Michigan	1837–60	1,000,000
New York	1838–60	394,700
Indiana	1852–60	227,900
Minnesota	1858–60	96,600
Ohio	1851–60	77,600
Vermont	1851–60	24,500
Illinois	1851–60	21,300
New Jersey	1850–60	6,000
Georgia	1838–60	3,000
Alabama	1849–60	0
Massachusetts	1851–60	0
Connecticut	1852–60	0
Tennessee	1852–60	0
Wisconsin	1852–60	0
Florida	1853–60	0
Louisiana	1853–60	0
Iowa	1858–60	0
Pennsylvania	1860	0
TOTAL		$1,851,600

Source: Hugh Rockoff, "The Free Banking Era: A Reexamination," *Journal of Money, Credit, and Banking* 6 no. 2 (May 1974): 150. Reprinted by permission.

was less than 50 cents. However, safety was to improve over time, with expected values exceeding 80 cents in 1860 and achieving par by 1863 as the weak and fraudulent banks were weeded out of the system. The key point here is that the market identified the bad banks relatively quickly, and they went out of business.

True, those unfortunate enough to hold notes from the banks that failed lost, but the losses to noteholders weren't losses to the economy as a whole. The $1.9 million was not destroyed; it simply changed owners. Nevertheless, there were true efficiency losses from wildcatting. People hold money instead of other assets because of its convenience as a medium of exchange. The higher the risk of holding money—say, from inflation or, as in this case, the chance that the issuing bank won't honor its obligation—the less money people will hold and the more inconvenience they will have to put up with in market transactions. Rockoff attempted to measure this true social cost to wildcatting—the inconvenience of not being able to use money—by estimating the determinants of the demand for money. His work suggests that in the states where wildcatting was common, per capita income was lowered by about a $1 a year. Although such a loss is not trivial, it is still less than 1 percent of annual per capita earnings.

So much for the losses of free banking. What about the gains when and where the system worked well? At least in theory the big advantage of free banking was increased competition among banks for business. This should have lowered the cost of financial intermediation. Monopoly profits that arise from restricted entry should have been competed away. Borrowers should have paid lower interest rates, increasing the volume of loans and facilitating investment. What scraps of evidence there are support these arguments. In Philadelphia, a city with few banks and a tightly controlled chartering system, loans outstanding per capita declined in the 1840s and the 1850s. By contrast, in New York, a highly competitive banking city, loans per capita rose sharply over the same period. In Ohio the introduction of free banking in 1851 substantially cut the profits of banks, suggesting, though hardly proving, that banking became more competitive.

Growth and Pre–Civil War Banking

Did banks really matter to antebellum growth? Banks undoubtedly mobilized savings, but as for their value as market makers—efficient allocators of capital to those who could use it most productively—we know relatively little. Certainly loans to insiders limited the public good benefits from banking and restricted market competition and market discipline. Prior to the Panic of 1837 there is evidence that commercial banks were expanding their business from short-term loans financing trade to longer-term loans to manufacturing and agriculture. After the panic banks were less eager to hold assets in such illiquid form, and state regulations often restricted them to short-term loans anyway. The Louisiana free banking law even prohibited banks from renewing short-term commercial loans. It is difficult to know if this withdrawal to a narrow segment of the capital market mattered much, however. For example, other types of financial intermediaries, such as savings banks, life insurance companies, and investment banks, made loans where commercial banks wouldn't or couldn't.[9] And the public market for stocks and bonds in such centers as Boston and New York was becoming increasingly sophisticated.

The thickening web of banks surely sped development by increasing the use of money as an exchange medium and by substituting paper money and checks for commodity money that had alternative, productive uses. From this perspective, the system performed best in the heyday of Biddle's Second Bank. The proportion of money held as specie was 15 percent or less during

[9] Davis (1963).

the entire 1823–37 period; from the panic to the Civil War, specie holding was never below 23 percent.[10] Whether one views the prepanic experience as exceptionally good or the postpanic experience as disappointing, the fact remains that the banking system harbored considerable resources. Gold and silver used as money consumed real resources when a much less resource-intensive medium, paper money, could have been substituted, provided public confidence could be maintained.

Every paper dollar that replaced a silver or gold dollar saved a dollar's investment in precious metals. If we assume that interest rates measure the opportunity cost of holding precious metals, the total interest costs of replacing paper money with specie would have averaged 0.46 percent of GNP in 1825–34, 0.35 percent in 1835–48, 0.43 percent in 1849–58. To the extent that people were more reluctant to hold paper money as a result of the destruction of the Second Bank rather than the panic, the difference between the pre–Second Bank social savings and the post–Bank social savings may be regarded as one clear cost of the destruction of the Second Bank. The other cost—for which we have no measure—is the impact of the reduced use of money as a medium of exchange because of increased uncertainty on the efficiency of commodity and factor markets. To the degree that a scarcity of exchange medium inhibited efficient resource allocation, it reduced income and growth.

From one perspective, the United States was handicapped by the heterogeneity and apparent riskiness of its banking system. Periodic banking panics closed the doors of many banks with substantial losses to noteholders and depositors. The lack of uniformity in banking standards, bank oversight, and bank regulation, together with the profusion of note issues, made bank money a less than perfect substitute for gold and silver. Lack of convertibility of bank money at full face value beyond the immediate vicinity of the bank of issue increased transactions costs and created frictions within the economy that a more centralized banking system might have avoided.

Despite all its obvious flaws, the American banking system seems to have worked. The geographic spread and increasing density of banks and other financial intermediaries were both causes and consequences of the growth of domestic commerce, industry, and agriculture. Diversity within the banking system reflected the diversity of interests and needs between city and countryside, between the industrial Northeast and the agrarian South, West, and frontier. Traditional sources of credit, such as the local merchant, were less well adapted to the increasingly impersonal and geographically diffuse transactions taking place in the economy than the more specialized banks with their ever more complex webs of correspondent banking relationships. Ease of entry, while it might have encouraged fraud, made banks responsive

[10] Engerman (1970).

to local opportunities. It also made for ease of exit as the market quickly sorted the sound from the unsound banks, driving the latter out of business.

All these charges, however, were confined to domestic commerce. In international trade and finance, gold, silver, and the bill of exchange still were supreme. Before exploring the expansion of the domestic economy that took place under this monetary and banking regime, we first turn to a discussion of American foreign trade and commercial policy.

Appendix: The Money Supply and its Proximate Determinants

The money supply (M) consists of bank liabilities (D) and currency (C) held by the public:

$$M = D + C \quad (1)$$

Prior to 1865 bank liabilities consisted primarily of bank notes, although there was some limited use made of checks drawn against bank deposits. These liabilities, however, whether in notes or deposits, were payable in legal tender, generally upon demand.

The government defines what constitutes legal tender (H): gold and silver prior to 1862; gold, silver, and greenbacks between 1862 and 1900; gold, greenbacks, and assorted other government issues, including Federal Reserve notes, from 1900 to 1933; and Federal Reserve notes since then. Government policies affect, though do not necessarily determine, the quantity of legal tender (also called high-powered money or referred to as the monetary base) in the economy. For example, tariff policy affects the external trade balance and determines whether we have to pay foreigners more or less for their imports than they pay us for our exports. The legal tender is in turn held either by the banks where it serves as bank reserves (R) against their liabilities or by the public in the form of currency (C) to meet periodic cash payments and as a hedge against uncertainty about the liquidity of bank liabilities.

$$H = C + R \quad (2)$$

Banks hold legal tender as reserves against their liabilities. The reserve ratio (r) is set by either prudence—what proportion of bank liabilities the bank expects might be presented for redemption in legal tender plus some margin of error—or law. The aggregate holdings of legal tender by the banking system, together with the reserve ratio, then determine the maximum quantity of bank liabilities that can be created:

$$D = \frac{R}{r} \quad (3)$$

The public holds money as a part of its financial portfolio. This money consists of both currency and bank liabilities. The fraction of money held in the form of currency (c) reflects the ease and convenience of holding cash relative to bank liabilities as well as the public's perception of the ability of the banking system to convert those bank liabilities into legal tender. That is, the currency ratio, c, is not independent of the reserve ratio, r, which captures the ability of the banks to meet their obligations to convert their liabilities into legal tender.

$$C = cM \quad (4)$$

Holding reserve ratios and currency ratios constant, we can rewrite the money supply equation (equation [1]) in terms of its determinants: legal tender (H) and the currency (c) and reserve ratio (r). Substituting (3) and (4) into (2):

$$H = cm + rD$$

so

$$D = \frac{H - cM}{r} \quad (5)$$

Substituting (5) and (4) into equation (1) and rearranging terms yields:

$$M = \frac{H}{c + r - cr}$$

which expresses the money supply in terms of its proximate determinants and models the behavior of the three economic agents in the economy: the public, the banks, and the government.

Bibliography

Davis, Lance E. "Capital Immobilities and Finance Capitalism: A Study of Economic Evolution in the United States, 1820–1920. *Explorations in Entrepreneurial History* 1 (1963): 88–105.

Engerman, Stanley. "A Note on the Consequences of the Second Bank of the United States." *Journal of Political Economy* 78 (1970): 725–28.

Hammond, Bray. *Banks and Politics in America from the Revolution to the Civil War.* Princeton: Princeton University Press, 1957.

Lamoreaux, Naomi. "Banks, Kinship, and Economic Development: The New England Case." *Journal of Economic History* 46 (1986): 647–68.

Redlich, Fritz. *The Molding of American Banking: Men and Ideas* (New York: Johnson Reprints, 1968. Originally published as volume 2 of Fritz Redlich, *History of American Business Leaders,* 1951).

Rockoff, Hugh. "Money, Prices and Banks in the Jacksonian Era." In *The Reinterpretation of American Economic History,* ed. Robert Fogel and Stanley L. Engerman. New York: Harper & Row, 1971: 448–58.

———. "The Free Banking Era: A Reexamination." *Journal of Money, Credit and Banking* 6 (1974): 141–67.

———. "Varieties of Banking and Regional Economic Development in the United States: 1840–1860." *Journal of Economic History* 35 (1975): 160–81.

Rolnick, Arthur J., and Warren E. Weber. "New Evidence on the Free Banking Era." *American Economic Review* 73 (1983): 1080–91.

Rothenberg, Winifred. "The Market and Massachusetts Farmers, 1750–1855." *Journal of Economic History* 41 (1981): 283–314.

Sushka, Marie. "The Antebellum Money Market and the Economic Impact of the Bank War." *Journal of Economic History* 36 (1976): 809–35.

Sylla, Richard. "American Banking and Growth in the 19th Century: A Partial View of the Terrain." *Explorations in Economic History* 9 (1971–72):197–227.

Temin, Peter. "The Economic Consequences of the Bank War." *Journal of Political Economy* 76 (1968): 257–74.

———. *The Jacksonian Economy.* New York: Norton, 1969.

Foreign trade and commercial policy in the development of a new nation

5

Independence from British rule did not immediately liberate the United States from mercantilist restrictions. Instead the United States merely switched from the role of active participant within the British imperial system to that of outsider in a world dominated by large mercantilist powers. This change did not bode well for the new nation. British markets were shut to American exporters, unprotected American shipping fell prey to pirates, and Spanish and French mercantilist regulations made it difficult to make up lost trade elsewhere in Europe. One might thus expect that the foreign trade sector that had loomed so large in late colonial development, especially in such port cities as Baltimore, Boston, New York, and Philadelphia, would have been hard hit. If so, it soon recovered.

In the five years from 1784 (just one year after the signing of the Treaty of Paris officially acknowledging American independence) to 1789, the volume of American trade with Britain is estimated at almost 95 percent of its level in the five years immediately preceding the Revolution—a period that had marked the high point in colonial trade. Moreover, trade with the French West Indies, which was no longer subject to British mercantilist restrictions, increased substantially, while the now-illegal American trade with the British West Indies is thought to have flourished despite British efforts to stop it. Certainly by the early 1790s the export trade of the United States exceeded levels of the late colonial period by perhaps 30 percent (Table 5.1).

The years after the Revolution saw important shifts in the composition

TABLE 5.1

Average Annual Exports of Selected Commodities from the 13 Colonies, 1768–1772 and from the United States, 1790–1792* (valued in thousands of 1790–1792 dollars)

	Thirteen Colonies, 1768–72		United States, 1790–92	
Commodity	Quantity	Value	Quantity	Value
Beef and pork	26,036 bbl	209	90,198 bbl	652
Bread and flour	38,634 tons	2,534	67,079 tons	4,399
Cotton	29,425 lb	7	163,822 lb	41
Fish, dried	308,993 quintals	740	375,619 quintals	900
Flaxseed	233,065 bu	189	352,079 bu	286
Grain				
Indian corn	839,314 bu	424	1,926,784 bu	974
Rice	140,254 bbl	1,971	129,367 bbl	1,818
Wheat	599,127 bu	654	998,862 bu	1,090
Indigo	547,649 lb	567	493,760 lb	511
Iron				
Bar	2,416 tons	195	300 tons	24
Pig	4,468 tons	116	3,667 tons	95
Livestock				
Cattle	3,433	63	4,861	89
Horses	6,048	240	7,086	282
Naval stores				
Pitch	11,384 bbl	21	7,297 bbl	13
Tar	90,472 bbl	135	68,463 bbl	102
Turpentine	19,870 bbl	42	51,194 bbl	108
Oil, whale	3,841 tons	212	1,826 tons	101
Potash	1,381 tons	134	4,872 tons	472
Rum, American	342,366 gal	132	441,782 gal	170
Tobacco	87,986 hhd	3,093	110,687 hhd	3,891
Wood products				
Pine boards	38,991 M ft	228	45,118 M ft	264
Slaves and headings	21,585 M	275	31,554 M	401
Total, above commodities		12,181		16,683
All exports				19,465

*For the extensive notes to this table, see the original article.

Source: James F. Shepherd and Gary M. Walton, "Economic Change after the American Revolution," *Explorations in Economic History* 13 (1976): 408–09.

of U.S. exports. Tobacco, which had been the dominant export crop throughout the colonial period, was displaced by flour as the single largest source of export earnings in the early 1790s. Wheat, corn, and meat—primarily products of Middle Atlantic farms—also recorded substantial trade gains, while foreign demand for southern products other than tobacco and cotton, such as rice, indigo, and naval stores, was at best stagnant. Cotton exports grew better than fivefold between the late colonial and the early national period, but cotton remained a very minor crop until after the adoption of Eli Whitney's cotton gin in 1793.

The trade data in Table 5.1 are in terms of constant 1790–92 prices and understate the growth of export earnings between the late colonial and early national periods. The prices of U.S. exports, led by tobacco, were sharply higher. In part the higher prices for American exports reflected the benefit of being able to sell abroad without diverting the trade through Great Britain. High tobacco prices also reflected a slow upward shift in the supply curve for the crop, as soil exhaustion in the Chesapeake Bay area pushed tobacco farther inland and onto the piedmont, where soils were poorer and transport costs were higher. Import prices, on the other hand, tended to fall, thanks to the ongoing British industrialization, which passed along the benefits of British productivity gains to American consumers. As a result, the U.S. terms of trade—defined as the ratio of American export prices to import prices paid by the United States—improved during the early years of nationhood. America could buy more imports with its export earnings.

Although the aggregate trade volume more than recovered, it failed to keep pace with population growth in the two decades following the Revolution. With population growing at over 3 percent per year, 83 percent more people lived in the United States in 1790 than in 1770. Consequently, despite the modest export growth, export earnings per capita fell by almost a third. Unless this earnings decline was made up elsewhere, it implies a small—but probably noticeable—reduction in income per capita of perhaps 5 percent.

Nor were the losses distributed evenly. The decline was particularly precipitous in New Hampshire, where per capita exports fell by two-thirds, and in the South (except Maryland), where declines in per capita exports were typically 50 percent or more (Table 5.2). Export earnings for 1768–72 in South Carolina, for example, had averaged £3.66 ($18.01) per person but for 1791–92 averaged only £1.75 ($8.61) per person. This is equivalent to perhaps a 15 percent reduction in per capita income if we assume that output was not made up elsewhere. Certainly South Carolina's indigo industry never recovered from the loss of the British bounty payments. Even Virginia, despite high tobacco prices, saw its export trade decline and its per capita export income cut in half. In contrast, New England's exports almost doubled

TABLE 5.2

Average Annual Exports from the 13 Colonies and Regions, 1768–1772, and from States and Regions of the United States, 1791–1792*

Origin	1768–72: Total Exports ($)	Per Capita Exports	1791–92: Total Exports ($)	Per Capita Exports	Percentage Change 1791–92/1768–72
New England					
New Hampshire	226	3.64	162	1.13	31%
Massachusetts	1,269	4.77	2,667	5.61	118
Rhode Island	399	6.84	585	8.46	124
Connecticut	453	2.46	728	3.05	124
Total	2,347	4.03	4,143	4.08	101
Middle Atlantic					
New York	920	5.66	2,519	7.43	131
New Jersey	10	0.10	25	0.15	150
Pennsylvania	1,737	7.23	2,873	6.59	91
Delaware	89	2.51	128	2.16	86
Total	2,750	4.97	5,545	5.46	110
Upper South					
Maryland	1,929	9.50	2,371	7.43	78
Virginia	3,788	8.46	3,336	4.48	53
Total	5,717	8.81	5,707	5.36	61
Lower South					
North Carolina	369	1.87	512	1.33	71
South Carolina	2,239	18.01	2,145	8.61	48
Georgia	364	15.60	477	5.76	37
Total	2,967	8.61	3,134	4.33	50
Total, all regions	13,786	6.45	18,529	4.87	76

*See the source for detailed notes on problems of comparisons, valuations, and measurement. Pound sterling values given by Shepherd and Walton are converted to 1790–92 dollars at the rate of £1 = $4.92.

Source: James F. Shepherd and Gary M. Walton, "Economic Change after the American Revolution," *Explorations in Economic History* 13 (1976): 413

and those of the Middle Atlantic colonies, the source of many of the high-demand agricultural exports, increased more than twofold while population grew somewhat less rapidly so that income per person originating in the foreign trade sector increased in these regions.

American Neutrality 1793–1807

About 1789 America's position in the world economy began to change as growing domestic turmoil within France preceding and following the French Revolution disrupted French trade. America's situation was to change dramatically over the ensuing years. In 1793 Britain went to war with France. This conflict, interrupted only by brief truces, was to occupy and drain both nations' energies for the next twenty-two years as the French Revolution became the Napoleonic Wars and eventually involved virtually all Europe. With the two leading world economic powers out of contention, America was free to develop its own potential.

Phase one—a period of rapid growth in the foreign trade sector—began with the American declaration of neutrality in the conflict, reflecting the divergent interests of the Federalists, who favored Britain, and the Republicans, who favored France. As a neutral country the United States claimed the right to unfettered trade with all countries, including Britain and France. The mercantilist restrictions of the European nations evaporated almost overnight. Suddenly American ships were welcomed with open arms as they brought commodities from all over the world and carried away Europe's manufactures for distribution worldwide. Freight earnings boomed. In 1792 American shippers earned an estimated $7.4 million. By 1796 these earnings had risen almost threefold to $21.6 million, eventually peaking in 1807 at $42.1 million.[1]

The country experienced export-led growth as the income from the trade boom diffused throughout the economy. Exports doubled between 1792 and 1795. They doubled again by 1801 and, by 1807, were five times what they had been just fifteen years earlier (Figure 5.1). The rate of growth of foreign trade far outstripped that of population. In 1792 per capita earnings from exports, shipping services, and ship sales had averaged $6.77—about 10 percent of per capita income. At their zenith in 1807 earnings were $22.76 per person. The boom in the American export trade reflected European demand for reexports—foreign goods repackaged in American ports—as well as for American cotton to supply the rapidly growing British textile industry and American food to meet European shortages.

With exports accounting for between 10 and 15 percent of GNP at the time, the increased export earnings must have stimulated domestic de-

[1] North (1960).

FIGURE 5.1

U.S. Merchandise Exports and Imports, 1790–1860

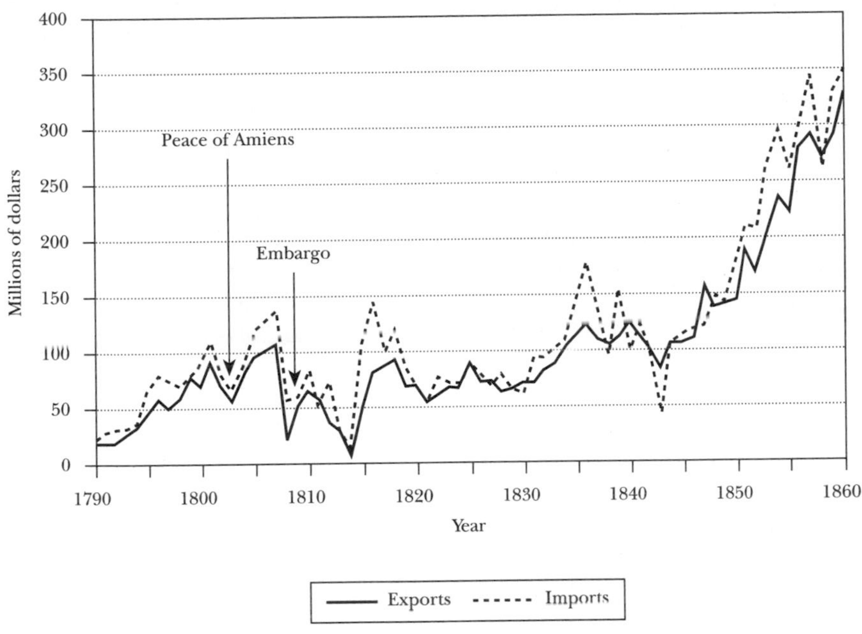

Source: U.S. Bureau of the Census, *Historical Statistics of the United States* (Washington, D.C.: Government Printing Office, 1975): Series U2 and U9.

mand, some of which would have spilled over to domestically produced goods. Moreover, increased foreign demand, much of it for agricultural commodities and raw materials, probably mitigated price declines caused by supply expansion from rapid westward expansion. The result of export-led growth, according to Douglass North, was "years of unparalleled prosperity—this period was a high water mark in individual well being which was to stand for many years, and laid important foundations for the growth of the economy after 1815."

The trade expansion was not, however, without interruption. In 1797 and 1798 an undeclared sea war with France produced a brief dip in export earnings. The most serious interruption, however, was the temporary outbreak of peace between France and Britain from 1801 to 1803 with the signing of the Peace of Amiens. Export earnings fell 40 percent. This slump was followed by another period of rapidly expanding trade.

Imports also increased—often faster than exports—and were only partially offset by invisible earnings from the carrying trade and ship sales. As a result, in most years America ran a balance of payments deficit (Figure 5.2). This deficit was paid by an inflow of foreign investment rather than an ex-

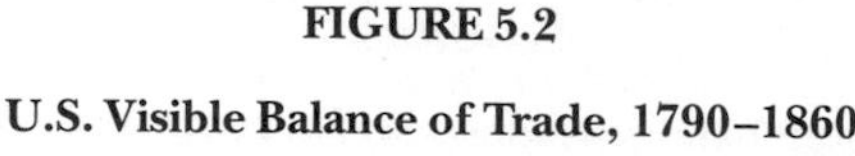

FIGURE 5.2

U.S. Visible Balance of Trade, 1790–1860

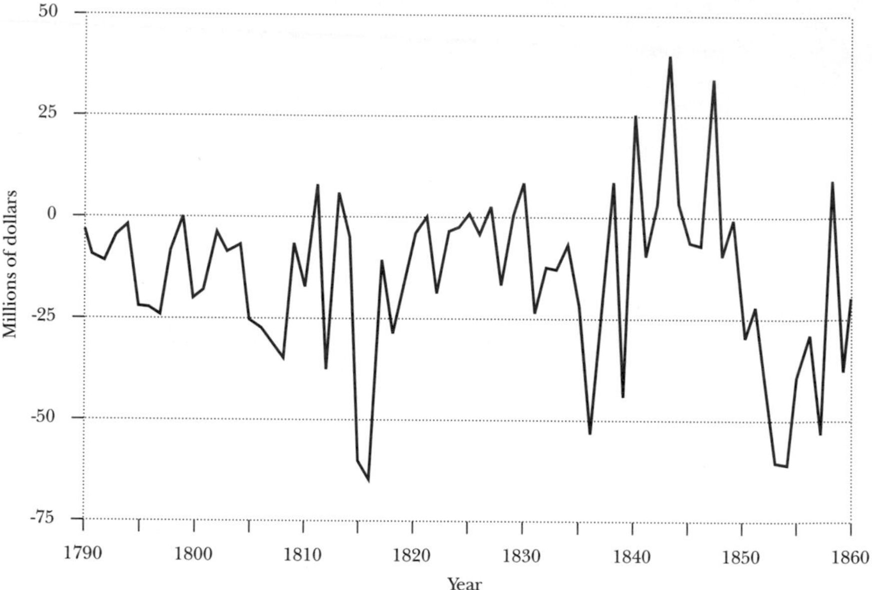

Source: U.S. Bureau of the Census, *Historical Statistics of the United States* (Washington, D.C.: Government Printing Office, 1975): Series U196.

port of specie. These funds mark the start of private commercial investment in the United States by foreigners. By 1807 the cumulative balance was $102.5 million invested in America.

The increased demand for American exports further boosted America's terms of trade, which grew every year between 1795 and 1807, and peaked in 1799 at 180 (1793 = 100). As a result, Americans could buy more imports with the proceeds of a given *volume* of exports. In other words, Americans had to give up fewer of their own resources to gain control over the products of foreign resources. This raised American welfare.

Claudia Goldin and Frank Lewis have tried to measure the income gain from this improvement in the terms of trade, comparing the actual state of the economy between 1796 and 1807 with a counterfactual alternative assuming that the terms of trade remained unchanged from 1793. Their calculations (Table 5.3) indicate incomes would have been between 2.27 percent and 5.20 percent below the level actually achieved if the terms of trade had remained constant at their 1793 level. The additional income generated by the improved terms of trade during this period probably increased

TABLE 5.3

The Effect on Income of No Change in Terms of Trade from 1793 for Selected Years, 1796–1807

Year	Terms of Trade (1793 = 100) North	Effect on Income* (Negative Percentage) Using North's Terms of Trade	Terms of Trade (1793 = 100) Philadelphia
1796	144.1	4.94	111.4
1798	180.2	5.20	105.7
1800	129.8	2.48	99.1
1803	124.7	2.76	104.7
1805	124.3	2.27	113.6
1807	121.1	2.52	111.2

$$* \frac{\partial Y}{Y_i} = \left(\frac{p_{x_i} Q_{x_i}}{Y_i}\right)\left(\frac{\dfrac{P_{x_{1793}}}{P_{m_{1793}}}}{\dfrac{P_{x_i}}{P_{m_m}}} - 1\right)$$

Source: Columns 2 and 3: Claudia Goldin and Frank Lewis, "The Role of Exports in American Economic Growth during the Napoleonic Wars, 1793–1807," *Explorations in Economic History* 17 (1980): 11. Column 4: computed from Donald R. Adams, "American Neutrality and Prosperity, 1793–1808: A Reconsideration," *Journal of Economic History* 40 (1980): Table 1, column 3, 717.

per capita income growth from 1.07 to 1.32 percent. That is, the buoyant foreign sector of the economy contributed about a quarter of a percentage point to the growth rate, or slightly more than 25 percent of the growth (about $2), with per capita income growing from about $57 in 1793 to $65 in 1805 (in 1840 dollars). This income estimate for 1793 implies a decline of about 0.34 percent a year between 1774 and 1793 to be consistent with Gallman's income estimate of the eve of the Revolution and is consistent with the perception of economic adversity during the period of Confederation.

Much of the "kick" in North's export-led growth hypothesis for the period 1793 to 1807 is provided by the terms of trade effect, but some serious doubts have been raised about how these terms of trade were calculated. The import price index, in particular, gives a large weight to foodstuffs, which even North admitted "can hardly be considered representative of American imports." Substituting the prices of exports and imports in Philadelphia, for example, produces an improvement of only 8.5 percent in the terms of trade at best, and in about half the years between 1790 and 1807 the terms of trade were worse than in 1790. As a result, the estimated income gains disappear.

Furthermore, the costs associated with neutrality and the export sector expansion have been understated while the benefits have been overstated. Reexports, for example, might have "crowded out"—that is, displaced—domestic exports by bidding up freight rates and shipbuilding costs. Similarly, the benefits realized by such industries as banking, insurance, and shipbuilding may have been smaller than previously supposed and were concentrated in the northeastern seaports.[2] Nevertheless, there seems little doubt that the period from the early 1790s to 1807 was one of growing prosperity for the majority of the population even if the export trade played a smaller role.

The Jeffersonian Embargo

In the second phase, which began with President Jefferson's embargo on all trade with the warring nations in 1807, America's foreign trade collapsed. Neither the British nor the French were entirely happy with America's role under the claim of neutrality. In Jay's Treaty in 1794 America had recognized the right of the British to intercept and seize even neutral shipping trading with France. In retaliation, the French seized American ships in both 1797 and 1798. As a result, exports dropped and marine insurance rates rose sharply. For example, in 1796 the insurance rate between Philadelphia and France had fluctuated between 3.0 and 7.5 percent of the value of the cargo; between Philadelphia and Britain, the range was 2.5 to 8.0 percent. In 1798 rates to both countries were 15 percent. Ignoring administrative costs and insurance profits, these insurance rates imply expectations that perhaps one cargo in seven would be lost.

The rules of the game were changing to America's disadvantage. Britain's policy of tolerance toward trading with its enemies changed with the readoption of rules from the French and Indian War in the *Essex* (1805) case that neutral shipping was restricted to carrying those cargoes that the neutral ships had traditionally carried. Unable to defeat Napoleon on land, the British adopted a series of orders-in-council in 1806 and 1807 declaring a blockade of continental European ports and requiring that neutral shipping continuing to trade with Europe had to dock in British ports for inspection and licensing or be subject to seizure. Napoleon's responses in the Berlin Decree of 1806 and the Milan Decree of 1807 setting up his "Continental System" was to declare any shipping complying with British regulations liable to capture. America was caught in the middle, philosophically unwilling to fight and militarily incapable of insisting on free passage of the seas.

[2] Adams (1980).

Jefferson's solution was to resort to "peaceable coercion," embargoing all trade with Great Britain and continental Europe in December 1807. A key premise of Jefferson's policy was that Europeans, especially the British, were more dependent upon American exports, especially grains and cotton, than America was upon imports. America's foreign trade fell precipitously. Although trade recovered somewhat in the succeeding years, it was not to reach its former levels until the late 1840s. Indeed, with the British blockade of U.S. ports in the War of 1812–14 America's export trade almost died. This blockade was accompanied by a general worsening in the terms of trade for America, which declined by almost one-fifth between 1807 and 1809.

The embargo was abandoned in March 1809 without achieving its goal of forcing a reversal of British policy. It has been argued that this failure was inevitable since the United States lacked the economic power to make the embargo effective. But this does not seem to have been the case. The goal of the embargo was to deny Britain the benefits that it gained through trade with America, though it simultaneously cost Americans the gains that they had realized through their trade with Britain (see Appendix A). The hope was that losses (that is, the reductions in consumer utility and well-being) to Britain would be greater than those to the United States. All this would have been irrelevant if the trade restrictions could not be enforced. A survey of the quantitative and anecdotal evidence, however, suggests that the embargo was quite effective in cutting off trade. Few American products, particularly cotton and grain, seem to have reached Britain during the embargo either through direct smuggling or by routing through a third party, and their prices rose sharply. The Liverpool price of Sea Island cotton, for example, rose more than 70 percent, while its price in America fell by a third. The prices of manufactured goods in Britain (products that the British usually exported) fell about 10 percent. The price of these goods (which the United States generally imported from Britain) in the United States should, however, have risen. Instead the prices of many manufactured goods in America fell.[3]

Even though Jefferson's embargo was unsuccessful in forcing a reversal of restrictive British trade policy, it may have been a blessing in disguise. While the unemployment and economic distress in coastal areas, especially the port cities, are undeniable, and doubtless many suffered severe income losses (this was no small reason behind Jefferson's defeat by Madison), domestic industry began to grow. Hard, consistent data are virtually impossible to find, but logic indicates that the embargo and blockade meant not only that the United States couldn't trade with foreigners but also that foreigners could not trade with the United States. As a result, if Americans wished to go on consuming certain products, they would have to produce them. Thus America began to develop import substituting industries—especially textiles. These industries attracted mercantile capital denied its traditional use

[3] Frankel (1982).

TABLE 5.4

Factory Incorporations before, during, and after the Jeffersonian Embargo and War of 1812

	Industry:			
	Metal and Machinery	Chemicals	Textiles	Total
1800	1			1
1801				
1802				
1803	1			2
1804				
1805	2		1	3
1806				
1807	4			4
1808	1		5	7
1809	1	5	18	26
1810	3	7	17	30
1811	5	5	30	41
1812	11	3	35	48
1813	5	1	57	66
1814	12	5	105	128
1815	5	1	64	78
1816	6		18	26
1817	3		5	8
1818	2	1	10	12
1819	2	1	6	8

Source: From *18th Cong., I Sess., Senate Document 45, Report of the Secretary of State.* (January 27, 1824), quoted by Stanley Lebergott, *The Americans* (New York: W. W. Norton, 1984): 128.

in foreign trade. According to a report by the secretary of state, seven new factory enterprises were incorporated in 1808 (Table 5.4). The next year twenty-six were chartered, eighteen of them textile firms. Incorporations continued at an accelerated pace through the War of 1812–14, peaking in the last year of the war at 128—105 of them textile mills. The embargo thus achieved what Alexander Hamilton had desired and Jefferson had feared: the beginnings of industrialization.

This pace of industrial expansion was not, however, maintained in the intermediate run. Many of the mills went bankrupt when trade resumed in 1815. Workers lost their jobs, the value of investment in mills plummeted, and new incorporations slipped to seventy-eight (sixty-four textile mills) in 1815. In 1816 new incorporations numbered only twenty-six. Even fewer, eight, were chartered the next year. As a result, both industrial labor and capital sought relief from the government through tariffs on imports.

The Economics of Tariffs

Tariffs are a tax upon imports. Their effects are easily demonstrated. Consider the case of autarky. In the absence of international trade, market equilibrium for a good—say, cotton textiles—is attained when domestic supply, S_{US}, is equal to domestic demand, D—that is, at price P_{US}, where quantity Q_{US} is demanded and supplied (Figure 5.3). Suppose now—for reasons to be elaborated later—that cotton textiles are also available on the world market at a price below the domestic equilibrium price—say, at price P_I. We have assumed for simplicity that the international supply is perfectly elastic at this price. This is tantamount to assuming that potential U.S. de-

FIGURE 5.3

The Impact of International Trade on Domestic Prices and Production

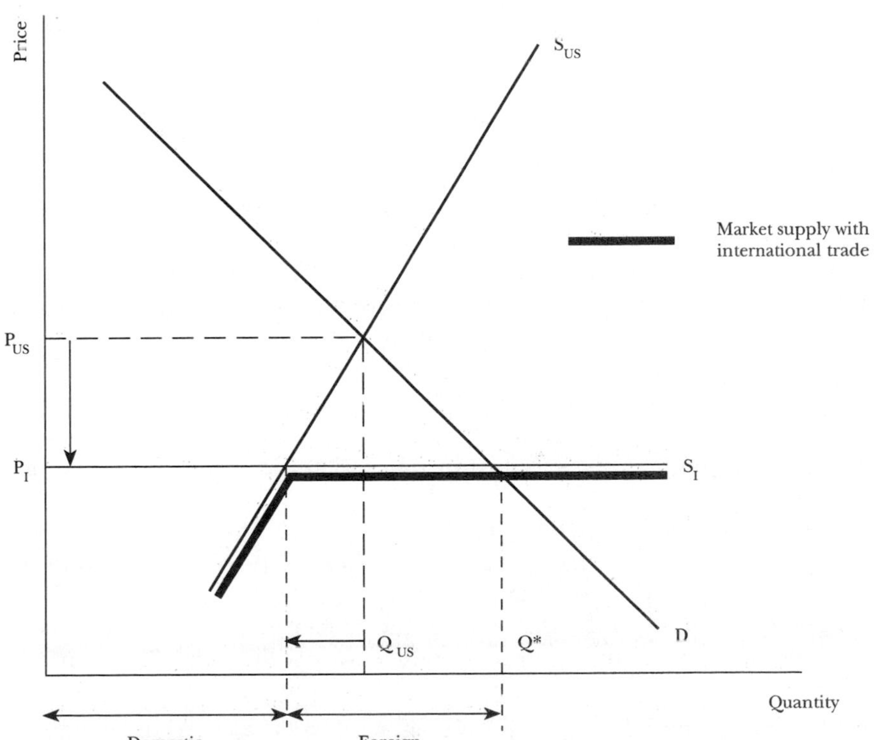

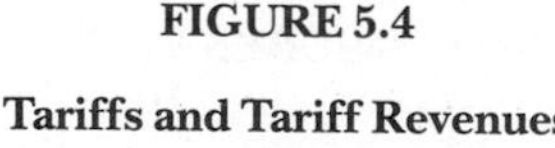

FIGURE 5.4

Tariffs and Tariff Revenues

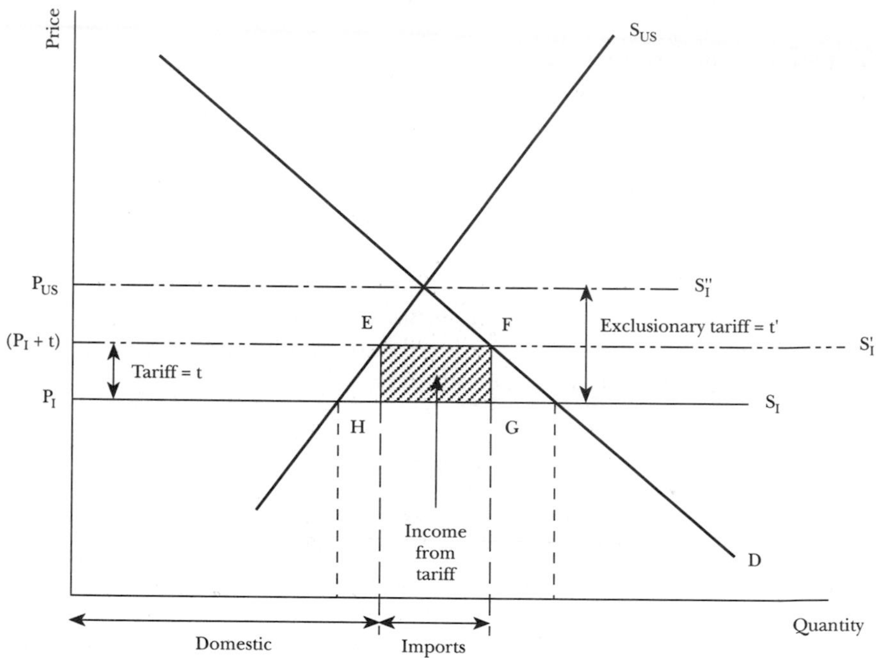

mand is small relative to world demand and production so that the United States is a price taker on world markets.[4]

The relevant supply curve for American consumers is thus made up of those portions of the domestic supply curve S_{US} that lie below the international supply curve—indicating that domestic producers are willing and able to accept lower prices than foreign suppliers—plus those portions of the international supply curve that lie below the domestic supply curve. This supply curve is "kinked" at the price where foreigners enter the market. As a result, the domestic equilibrium price for cotton textiles is driven down from P_{US} to P_I by the opening of the country to international trade. Total sales expand to Q*, some supplied by domestic producers, some from imports.

Imposing a tariff of $t, on this product now raises the international supply price to $(P_I + t)$, raising the domestic equilibrium price to $(P_I + t)$ and reducing the quantity of textiles demanded (Figure 5.4). Although the total market for textiles shrinks as a result of the higher price, sales by domestic producers expand. More domestic producers are willing and able to supply

[4] This is not necessarily true. The United States was the largest market for British textiles until well into the nineteenth century, but so long as the international supply elasticity exceeded domestic supply elasticity (as it almost certainly did), the analysis remains valid.

FIGURE 5.5

Trade-off between Protection and Revenue

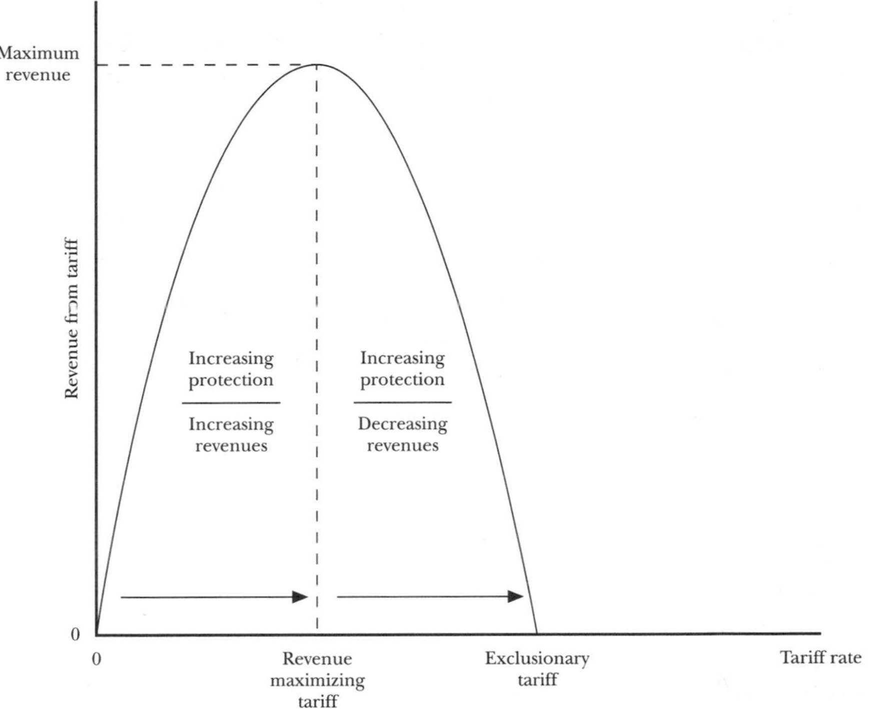

more textiles at a price equal to or less than the new, higher international supply price that includes the tariff. The domestic producers' share of the domestic market expands rapidly as imports shrink and overall market size shrinks.

With each unit of imports paying a tariff of \$t, the government realizes revenues from this tariff equal to the area of the shaded rectangle, EFGH. Even higher duties, however, do not necessarily result in increased revenues for the federal government. Consider what happens if the government raises the tariff on this product to t'. This shifts the international supply curve to S'' as that it intersects the demand curve at the point where domestic supply, S_{US}, is just equal to domestic demand at price P_{US}. As a result, domestic suppliers are willing and able to meet the entire U.S. demand for textiles at a price less than or equal to that at which foreigners can supply the market after paying the tariff. Imports thus fall to zero. Government income from this higher tariff consequently also falls to zero. Higher tariffs than t' would produce the same result. Such tariffs are known as exclusionary tariffs for the obvious reason that they effectively exclude imports from the domestic market.

TABLE 5.5

Some Estimates of Nominal and Effective Tariff Rates in 1845

Commodity or Activity	Nominal Tariff Rate	Effective Rate for Labor and Capital in Activity
Cotton textiles		40
Raw	66	
Manufactured	47	
Bar iron		30
Pig	49	
Bar	36	
Refined sugar		41
Clayed	105	
Refined	92	
Cordage		186
Hemp	39	
Untarred	84	
Shipbuilding		−11 to −12
Materials	18–23	
Ships	0	
Cotton growing		66
Purchased items	22	
Raw cotton	62	
Hemp growing	39	
Sugarcane growing	63	

Source: Stanley Lebergott, *The Americans* (New York: W. W. Norton, 1984): 152.

Government receipts from a tariff thus vary from zero when the tariff rate is zero, to zero with an exclusionary tariff and are positive for all values between these extremes (Figure 5.5). Over some range, increasing tariff rates generate higher revenues for the government, but beyond some point, depending upon the price elasticities of supply and demand, increasing tariff rates realize ever-smaller revenues. This same proposition has most recently found life as the so-called Laffer curve.

The ultimate objective of tariff protection is to preserve, protect, and enhance the contribution of American labor and American capital to the value of the final product. The impact of the tariff thus depends in part upon the domestic component in the product. The protection given these domestic factor services is termed the effective protection. This can differ markedly from the nominal tariff rates (Table 5.5).

A Very Brief History of U.S. Tariffs, 1789–1860

The Constitution vested Congress with the power to "lay and collect taxes, duties, imposts and excises" and "to regulate commerce with foreign nations." Accordingly, in 1789 Alexander Hamilton, the secretary of the treasury, asked Congress to enact a tariff for:

1. the support of the government
2. the discharge of debts of the United States
3. the encouragement of manufactures

Today tariffs are viewed almost exclusively in terms of stimulating domestic industry or protecting it from the rigors of foreign competition; not so in 1789—in part, of course, because there was so little industry to protect. Indeed, the tariff was initially seen almost purely as a revenue source for the federal government, although Hamilton did express the hope that it might encourage manufacturing.

The emphasis on the budgetary implications of the tariff reflected the fiscal constraints imposed upon the federal government by the Constitution, which specifies that taxes have to be proportional to population. This was interpreted as prohibiting income taxes while permitting consumption, or excise, taxes. A second source of revenue open to the government since before the ratification of the Constitution was the sale of public land. The third revenue source until the introduction of the income tax was the tariff, and it was by far the most important, generating at least 80 percent of federal receipts during most of the pre–Civil War period (Figure 5.6).

Two periods of sharply reduced dependence upon the tariff stand out. In each, income from the tariff fell to only about one-half of federal government receipts though they reflect radically different circumstances. The first from 1812–14 reflects the dislocation of war, especially the British blockade of American ports that cut off trade. The second in the late 1830s coincides with the speculative land boom generated by internal improvements and high prices for agricultural commodities when tens of millions of acres of land were sold.

Hamilton's original tariff in 1789 established a uniform ad valorem tariff rate (that is, based on the value of the imported good) of 5 percent. Higher ad valorem rates were placed on some luxuries, and specific duties (which set a dollar tax regardless of the price of the good) were placed on particular goods deemed worthy of domestic encouragement, such as iron, rope, glass, and nails. The highest rate, 15 percent, was on carriages. Rates were generally and progressively raised thereafter. Between 1794 and 1816, for example, twenty-four acts modifying tariffs were passed by Congress, and by 1804 the usual tariff rate had increased to 17.5 percent. The resulting maze of ad valorem and specific duties and temporary surcharges makes it

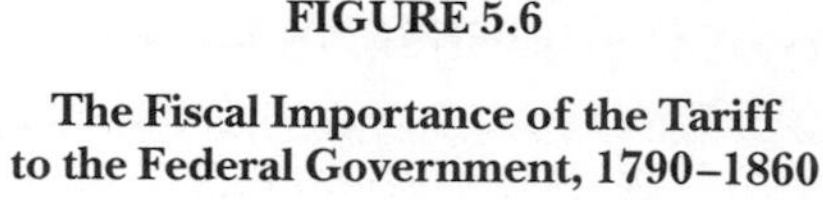

FIGURE 5.6

The Fiscal Importance of the Tariff to the Federal Government, 1790–1860

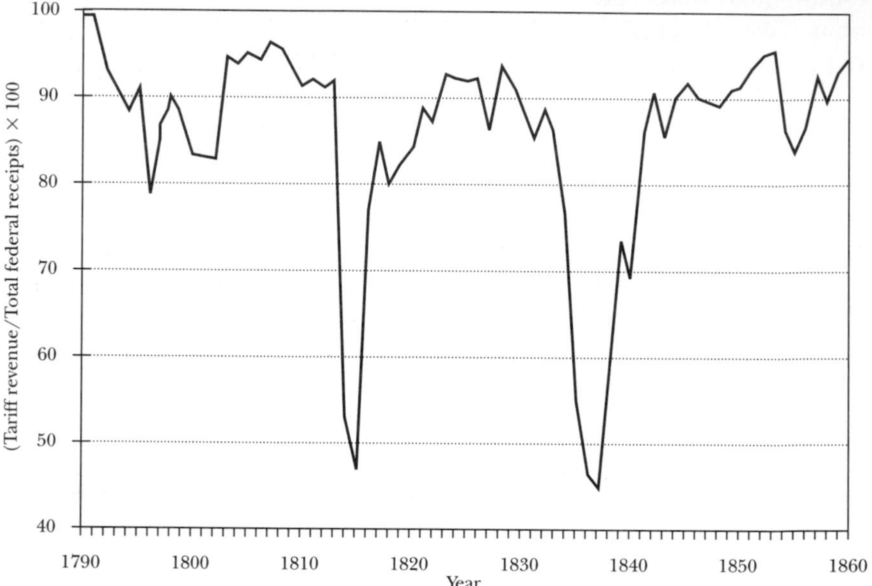

Source: U.S. Bureau of the Census, *Historical Statistics of the United States* (Washington, D.C.: Government Printing Office, 1975): Series Y352 and Y353.

difficult to determine the average tariff rate. For example, the Tariff Act of 1816 set the tariff on cotton cloth at 25 percent of value, but an attached rider allowed rates to go much, much higher. Cloth priced below 25 cents a yard, for example, was to be taxed as if it were worth 25 cents, leaving an effective minimum duty of 6.25 cents a yard, regardless of the actual selling price. This minimum was raised in 1824 and again in 1828. Consequently, without a detailed description of the particular goods and the volume of each kind imported, it is difficult to determine the average tariff rate, although the ratio of customs duties to imports provides a crude measure while the ratio of duties paid to the value of free and dutiable imports, available from 1821, probably provides a somewhat better measure (Figure 5.7).

Important tariff bills that were passed in 1816 and 1824 resulted in sharp increases in average duties, culminating in the so-called Tariff of Abominations in 1828, which raised average duties well above 50 percent and represents the high tide of American tariffs. The sharp protectionist increases in rates in the 1820s raises the question of whether or not tariffs exceeded the revenue maximizing rates. If so, the increasing clamor for

FIGURE 5.7

Government Receipts from the Tariff and the Average Tariff Rate

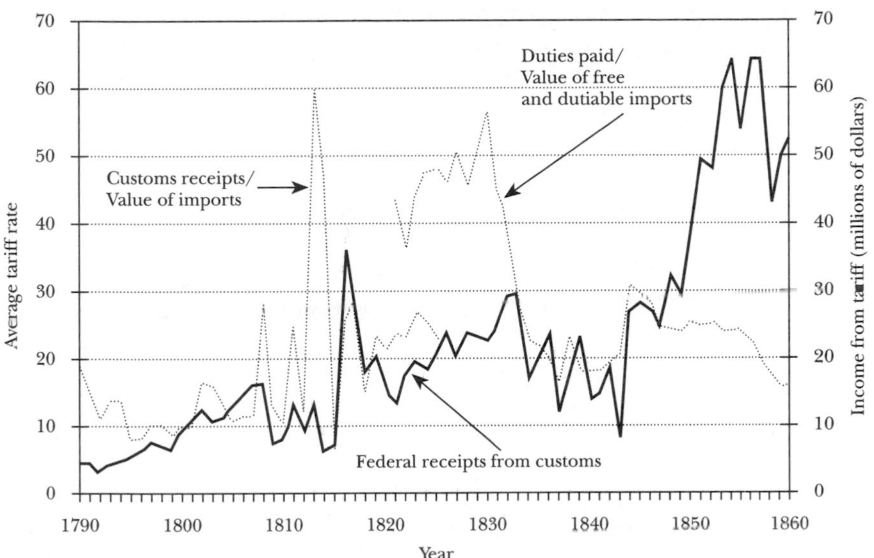

Source: U.S. Bureau of the Census, *Historical Statistics of the United States* (Washington, D.C.: Government Printing Office, 1975): Series U9, U211, and Y353.

protectionism from the manufacturing sector could than be met only by trading away these government projects financed by the forgone revenue. On the other hand, if the tariff was currently below the revenue maximizing rate, then the government not only could satisfy the demand but could also indulge additional spending programs. The evidence is far from decisive. The data in Figure 5.7 suggest that during the 1820s higher federal revenues from the tariff were in fact associated with higher tariff rates. It is possible that in this period the government could satisfy the demands for increased protection without compromising the federal spending plans. Rates were lowered substantially in 1833 under a compromise negotiated by Henry Clay that reduced tariffs to a uniform rate of 20 percent, and this reduction in tariff rates seems to be associated with falling revenues from the tariff. Both findings imply that the United States was at some point to the left of the revenue-maximizing tariff rate (see Figure 5.5) during this period.

Booming land sales during the 1830s and the virtual extinction of the national debt kept the Treasury in surplus despite declining revenues, but the honeymoon ended in the Panic of 1837. The collapse of land sales eliminated the budget surplus and forced consideration of the tariff once again as a revenue measure. President John Tyler signed into law a simplified, albeit higher, schedule of duties, ranging from as little as 5 percent on raw materials and semimanufactures to 100 percent on liquor. Most manufacturers were taxed at 20 to 30 percent. During the late 1850s rates were reduced further, primarily by reassigning goods among the different rate schedules. As a result, on the eve of the Civil War American trade was as free as it was to be during the nineteenth century.

The Politics and Political Economy of Tariffs

Although the leading authority on U.S. tariff history, Frank Taussig, classified the 1816 tariff among the earlier revenue-motivated tariff acts, others see the beginnings of a fundamental shift in American policy toward protecting and encouraging manufactures.[5] Certainly, with the end of hostilities in Europe in 1815, the whole domestic and international environment for American industry changed. European producers moved aggressively to regain the markets that they had lost. American exports encountered vigorous competition in foreign markets, and the domestic market was suddenly flooded with low-priced European imports. In 1815, for example, seventy-one million yards of British cotton textiles—an amount equal to more than three-quarters of U.S. domestic production at the time—were offered on the American market. As a result, textile prices fell sharply. Other prices fell, too, particularly import prices, which fell 15 percent from 1814 to 1815, 20 percent from 1815 to 1816, and another 15 percent from 1816 to 1817. In contrast, domestic prices fell less than 9 percent during these years, but as a result, domestic goods faced serious competition from imports, particularly in the coastal cities and rural areas.

While lower prices may have reflected the production cost advantages enjoyed by many of the European producers that resulted from their exploitation of economies of scale and lower labor costs as well as the sudden increase in supply, there is also evidence of dumping—that is, selling at below the costs of production. The purpose, as the British chancellor of the exchequer (the equivalent of the American secretary of the treasury) declared in 1816, was "to incur a loss upon the first exportation (after the war) in order, by the glut, to stifle in the cradle these risky manufactures in the United States, which the war had forced into existence contrary to the natural cause of things."[6] Similarly, another authority in testimony before Parliament declared "the inundation of British goods . . . have been sold under prime cost."[7] Such actions today are contrary to international trade

[5] See, for example, Dewey (1902).
[6] *Edinburgh Review or Critical Journal* (1916): 264, quoted by Lebergott (1984): 129.
[7] G. A. Lee, testimony in 1816 before a parliamentary committee. Reprinted in *Parliamentary Papers,* Cmd. 397, quoted by Lebergott (1984): 129.

agreements such as the General Agreement on Trade and Tariffs (GATT) and are met with countervailing—that is, offsetting—duties. Then, as now, domestic manufacturers protested and demanded increased tariff protection. This was granted in the 1824, if not the 1816, Tariff Act.

We have already seen (Figure 5.4) how a tariff protects domestic industry, increasing the domestic industry's share of the domestic market and encouraging an expansion of domestic production. But why were American production costs higher than those of foreign suppliers, especially when foreigners had to foot the bill for transatlantic shipment? The explanation usually given is that some American industries, such as textiles, were still in their infancy. That is to say, Americans were still learning the business and hence were probably *temporarily* inefficient. Furthermore, just starting out, American firms had not yet attained sufficient size to realize all economies of scale.

The situation is shown in Figure 5.8. Suppose that long-run average costs in an industry—say, the textile industry—were U-shaped, with substantial economies of scale realizable over the range OQ_{UK} or OQ_{US}. British firms by virtue of their longer experience might have had lower average costs at any level of output than American firms just learning the business:

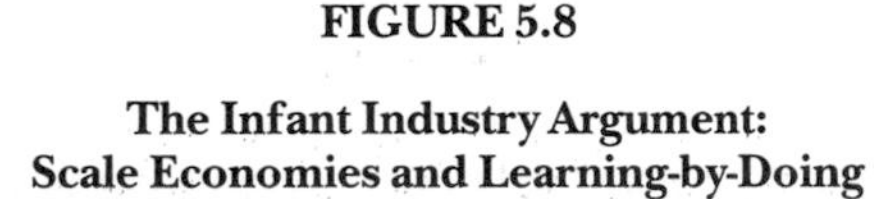

FIGURE 5.8

The Infant Industry Argument: Scale Economies and Learning-by-Doing

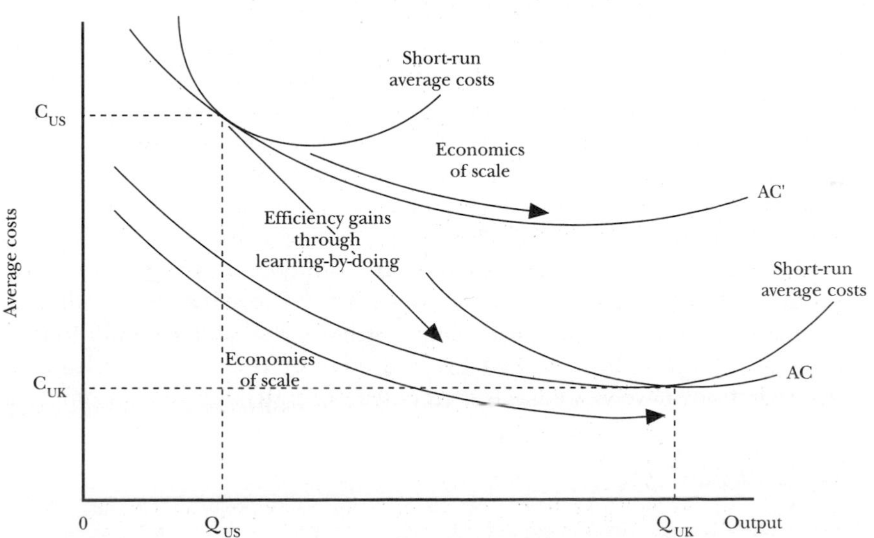

$AC<AC'$ for any given output level. The British companies certainly had access to larger markets; in 1815, for example, the British domestic market had 10.5 million consumers with the highest per capita income in the world. They were able to produce at Q_{UK}—that is, at minimum long-run average cost. American firms, as new entrants and with a smaller domestic market, on the other hand, had to produce at Q_{US}, using an inefficient plant (costs above the long-run costs). Under these conditions, so long as there was free trade between the countries and transport costs from Britain to America were less than the cost differential between firms in the two countries ($C_{us} - C_{UK}$), American firms would be undersold in the domestic marketplace by the British. This would effectively deny to Americans the opportunity to learn the trade and expand their markets so that they could compete with the British on equal terms.

Alexander Hamilton was cogently aware of these problems and, in his 1792 *Report on Manufactures,* argued:

> The superiority antecedently enjoyed by nations who have preoccupied and perfected a branch of industry, constitutes a more formidable obstacle than either of those which have been mentioned, to the introduction of the same branch into a country in which it did not before exist. To maintain, between the recent establishments of one country, and the long matured establishments of another country, a competition upon equal terms, both as to quality and price, is, in most cases, impracticable. The disparity, in the one, or in the other, or in both, must necessarily be so considerable, as to forbid a successful rivalship, without the extraordinary aid and protection of government.[8]

The idea behind a tariff to protect "infant industries" was to make the British production costs plus the tariff and transportation costs greater than the cost difference between firms in the two countries. Or, as Hamilton put it, "To be enabled to contend with success, it is evident that the interference and aid of their own governments are indispensable."[9] Correctly implemented, such a tariff would encourage domestic manufacturers by raising profitability in the protected industry, stimulating new entry and expanded production, shifting domestic costs downward along the long-run average cost curve, and reaping scale economies until domestic industry could compete on equal terms with the British.

The margin between domestic and foreign costs implicit in the tariff plus transatlantic transport costs was quite large. There is a debate whether this margin was justified by real, temporarily unavoidable cost differences (Table 5.6). Most of the attention has focused upon the cotton textile industry, which many have viewed as the archetypal "infant industry" in America.

[8] Hamilton (1850) 3: 218
[9] Ibid.

TABLE 5.6

International Freight and Insurance Charges Compared with U.S. Import Duties in Various Years, 1815–1841

	Freight and Insurance to United States (dollars)	U.S. Duty
Northern products		
Cotton (India), 1816	0.12	
Nankeens (per yard), 1819	0.014	0.025
Iron (Sweden, per ton), 1824	8.00	15.00
Iron (pig, United Kingdom, per ton), 1828	3.60	13.30
Iron (bar, United Kingdom, per ton), 1832	7.00	22.40
Rum (West Indies, per gallon), 1824	0.42	
Calicoes, 1830	0.15	0.45
Salt (Turks Island), 1833	0.08	0.11
Southern products		
Raw cotton (per pound), 1824	0.01	0.03
Hemp (St. Petersburg, per ton), 1824	30.00	30.00
Hemp (St. Petersburg, per ton), 1841	16.58	35.00
Bagging (Scotland, per yard), 1824	0.015	0.03

Source: Stanley Lebergott, *The Americans* (New York: W. W. Norton, 1984): 141.

Although there were numerous early efforts to establish the industry in America, the most famous being the mill of Samuel Slater at Pawtucket, Rhode Island, expansion of the industry in America really began after Jefferson's embargo. Textiles was certainly one of the main industries to feel the pinch of foreign competition, experiencing high levels of unemployment and plant closings, and to campaign vigorously for tariff protection in 1816. Nevertheless, Taussig thought that the industry quickly achieved maturity and was able to meet foreign competition probably as early as 1824 and certainly by 1832. Even so, it continued to enjoy substantial protection. From 1830 to 1832 the real tariff on cotton textiles was 71 percent.[10] In 1833 the tariff per yard of cloth was cut sharply (from 8.75 cents to 8.4 cents), but the price of simple cotton sheeting fell much more, leaving the tariff rate at an average of 82 percent! High as these rates were, they were by no means the high tide for cotton tariffs. Although the duty per yard was pared to 7.53 cents in 1842, sheeting prices slipped below 7 cents so that the tariff exceeded 100 percent. Only after 1846 did tariffs on cotton textiles fall. The

[10] Baack and Ray (1983).

minimum valuation provision was dropped, thereby equalizing the real and nominal—ad valorem—rate at 25 percent. And in 1857 the rate was cut to 24 percent in line with general manufactured goods duties.

If Taussig was right, then the cotton textile industry enjoyed monopoly rents in the years that followed at the expense of American consumers. Others are not so sure. The question is complicated because the British generally specialized in finer-quality textiles with which the American industry made little effort to compete. British cloth exports had an average price of 12.77 cents a yard and paid an import duty of 8.75 cents a yard (69 percent!) in the United States. Consequently, textile imports dominated the market only for cloth priced at 21.52 cents a yard (= 12.77 + 8.75) or higher. On the other hand, plain brown domestic cotton sheeting—the standard American product—sold in New York for 10.17 cents a yard. Given the level of protection, the American industry had an 11.34-cent-a-yard spread for the quality difference between British and American cloth. In the absence of protection, however, the British would only have needed to reduce costs by 2.60 cents a yard—perhaps by a small reduction in the thread count of their traditionally high-quality cottons—to undersell the Americans. The key question is how British costs varied with quality. We really don't know, but it has been estimated that the American cost advantage would have been eliminated and imports would have begun with textiles costing as little as 7.05 cents a yard in the absence of protection. If so, the impact would have been catastrophic for the American industry. It would have reduced the American textile value added by at least three-quarters, bankrupting half the New England textile industry and throwing out of work a large fraction of the industrial labor force. Early protection of textiles probably was thus an important plus for the American economy.[11]

One ex post justification for protection of the textile industry that has been made is its record of "learning-by-doing"—the process of continued productivity growth through subtle improvements in organization and efficiency as the result of accumulated experience—during the early nineteenth century. Such learning shifts the long-run average cost curve to a new, lower level. Labor productivity growth in this industry during the 1830s averaged 6.67 percent per year, 39 percent of which may be attributable to technical progress. Fully three-quarters of this technical progress (that is, 30 percent of total labor productivity growth) was attributable to learning-by-doing.[12] Further, the agglomeration of textile mills in the area around Lowell, Massachusetts, is also credited with sparking the development of the American machinery industry, of which the Saco-Lowell Machine Shops are just the most famous example.

At first glance it would seem that protective tariffs must have played an

[11] Bils (1984).
[12] David (1970).

important role in early-nineteenth-century American economic growth. Certainly the debate over the virtues and vices of tariffs is an old one. Ever since the great British economist David Ricardo wrote more than a century ago on the value of importing grain rather than growing it at home, Anglo-American economists have seen free international trade as a way of improving the lot of all parties concerned. Trade, unfettered by tariffs and quotas, allows each country to specialize in what each does best and then to export the surplus at advantageous terms. But as modern economists point out, the gains from trade can be outweighed by the losses. A young and potentially efficient industry may need time to grow, but foreign competition denies it that opportunity. If in the first stages of development it is allowed no breathing space, the "infant" industry may be stillborn. As a result, the economy will go on importing goods that could have been produced more cheaply at home. Applied to the American cotton textile industry of the 1820s and 1830s, the argument has some appeal. With protection from competition—and the protection was considerable—manufacturers had a chance to "learn" to produce efficiently. Once trained, mechanics and managers could (and did) leave their employers and start new factories, taking with them the accumulated experience of the old factories. If these infant factories hadn't been protected after 1820, the American industry would have grown less rapidly (or not at all), and the experience gained by individual producers and by their suppliers would have been lost to the economy as a whole.

The justification for protection declined as the American industry matured, and later learning-by-doing added only marginally to productivity. Thus it may be hard to make the case for continuing tariffs in the 1840s or 1850s.

The protection of domestic industry is not a free good. It comes at the expense of consumers who pay higher prices and whose choice is constrained. How can favoring one group—manufacturers—over the interests of another, larger group—consumers—be justified, and how were the winnings and losses distributed?

The existence and level of tariffs reflect in part the outcome of the political process that favors vocal, well-funded, cohesive, and concentrated special-interest groups—even if they represent only a small minority—over the more diffuse general interest. The potential gain to each member of the small pressure group from a successful rent-seeking activity is large, while the welfare loss to each individual member of society is small (thus not worth fighting for) even if the aggregate loss is very large.

This certainly seems to have been the case with the 1824 tariff. An analysis of the political economy underlying the tariff act by Jonathan Pincus suggests that the structural characteristics of particular industries determined the levels of protection each received. The highest levels of tariff protection were afforded to these industries with lower total proprietorial incomes (and hence presumably fewer proprietors), greater industrial concentration, and less geographic dispersion. These results are consistent with the model of pressure group behavior in which small, well-identified, and cohesive groups are able to engage in effective rent-seeking behavior. At the same time the pressure from these groups was more effective, the larger the number of states represented—thereby increasing the number of representatives upon whom pressure might be brought—and the greater the total number of establishments affected. Moreover, Congress compensated industries adversely affected by duties on their inputs that increased their costs by according their products even greater protection and thus allowing higher prices.

Ever since economists worked out the theory of comparative advantage (which states that even when one country is absolutely more efficient in the production of all goods than another country, both can gain from trade if each specializes in the production of those goods in which its comparative advantage is more marked), free trade has generally been regarded as one step toward maximizing collective welfare. Did these tariffs therefore mean that welfare in the United States was adversely affected? Not necessarily. Several decades ago the economist Lloyd Metzler showed that contrary to the claims of Ricardo and the other classical economists, free trade is not always optimal. In particular, if a country has a monopoly in international trade, it can raise its income relative to the free trade equilibrium through the judicious use of tariffs. The national income-maximizing tariff is called the optimum tariff.

In the antebellum period the United States was the dominant world producer of raw cotton and supplied about 80 percent of the cotton used by the British cotton textile industry. As a result, potential profits could be made from the judicious application of tariffs. Here is how the "Metzler effect" might work for cotton: Higher tariffs raise the profitability of textile production, drawing labor away from raw cotton production. As a consequence, the raw cotton supply is reduced, raising the world price for the commodity. If this price effect is sufficiently large, cotton farmers more than make up for the fact that the price of protected manufactured goods has also risen. National income could thus go up—with the foreign cotton buyers bearing the burden. The problem in the United States case, though, is that raw cotton was an input in the protected American manufacturing sector as well as an export good.[13]

[13] Estimates made by John James (1978) imply that a tariff rate of 35 to 40 percent in 1859–60 would have maximized GNP, increasing real GNP some 3 percent above free trade levels, primarily as a result of terms of trade effects. At the time the tariff was about 15 percent on all trade and averaged about 20 percent on dutiable goods. Switching to the optimal tariff rate might have raised GNP by 1.75 percent, or about $72 million. These estimates, however, have been criticized in an as yet unpublished working paper by C. Knick Harley (1990), who concludes that the tariff lacked any significant terms of trade effect and thus that the country would have been better off with free trade rather than protectionism. The debate is not yet settled.

While doubts may surround the aggregate effect of tariffs, there is considerable agreement about their distributional effects. These effects were correctly perceived by contemporaries. Owners of northern factories and skilled manufacturing workers benefited from protection since the higher prices the tariff allowed manufacturers to charge would be partially reflected in higher profits and higher wages. On the other hand, producers of unprotected goods—including virtually all southerners—would foot the bill by getting fewer manufactures for each unit of exported and nontraded goods they sold. Thus the increasing tariff rates during the 1820s raised

TABLE 5.7

Nominal Ad Valorem Import Duties on Specific Commodities, 1816 and 1824

Item	1816	1824	% Change 1816–24
Manufactured Products			
Acid, sulfuric	15	71	373
Glass bottles	20	61	205
Iron rods	20	53	165
Paper, folio	30	70	133
Carpets, Brussels	25	52	108
Vinegar	15	31	106
Anvils	20	35	75
Cotton bagging	15	26	73
Candles, tallow	45	75	67
Chocolate	15	20	33
Ale	18	23	28
Alum	64	80	25
Candles, wax	90	90	0
Cards, playing	309	309	0
Agricultural Commodities and Raw Materials			
Wheat	16	20	33
Coal	35	42	20
Coffee	25	25	0
Cotton, raw	19	19	0
Hemp	16	16	0
Molasses	24	24	0
Pimento	26	26	0
Sugar, lump	68	68	0
Sugar, brown	51	51	0
Tobacco	23	23	0

Source: Jonathan J. Pincus, *Pressure Groups and Politics in Antebellum Tariffs* (New York: Columbia University Press, 1977): Table B.3.

strong sectional opposition from the South, which saw them as benefiting the North at its expense.

The evidence presented in Table 5.7 would appear to provide strong support for the southerners' case. Tariffs were raised most sharply on industrial intermediate and final products—products produced almost exclusively in the North, using northern labor and capital, that were also consumed in the South. Further, where tariffs were increased on agricultural commodities and raw materials, it was the products of northerners—wheat and coal—not cotton, hemp, molasses, or tobacco, that benefited from increased protection.

This is certainly how contemporary northerners and southerners perceived the tariff issue. The division of economic interest is usually cited as a major source of political friction between the two regions leading up to the Civil War. The southern champion of states' rights John C. Calhoun even went so far as to estimate the redistribution impact of the tariff. He calculated that southerners lost $15 million—almost $4 per person annually in the form of higher prices. His method was hopelessly inaccurate, but there is little doubt that in the 1830s southerners typically perceived themselves as victims of a northern conspiracy. Increased tariffs adversely affected landowners generally and slaveholders in particular. At the optimum tariff, landowners would have received perhaps 4 percent less than under free trade and about 1 percent less than they were actually receiving in 1859 (Figure 5.9). Slaveholders, on the other hand, already had their incomes reduced perhaps 13 percent by the tariff in 1859 and would have seen another 7 percentage point drop as a result of the adoption of the optimum tariff. Little wonder, then, that the tariff was opposed by farmers in general and southern plantation operators in particular. In contrast, both capitalists and laborers benefited from the tariff. The tariff in 1859 raised capitalist incomes one-half of 1 percent above their free trade levels. Labor benefited by perhaps 1.5 percent higher incomes. Adoption of the optimum tariff would have raised their incomes 3.5 and 4 percent respectively above the free trade levels.

New estimates reinforce these general conclusions but suggest that the impact upon landowners was much greater than that upon slaveowners. In particular, the tariff constrained the expansion of western agriculture where food production might have been 10 to 25 percent higher without the tariff, reducing the welfare of landowners by perhaps as much as 25 percent.[14] However, if western interests stood to gain so much from removal of the tariff, why were they not more vocal in their opposition? Certainly in the postbellum economy they proved themselves more than capable of political organization and agitation to secure beneficial legislative action.

Manufacturers, particularly owners of the textile firms, on the other

[14] Harley (1990).

FIGURE 5.9

Impact of Different Tariff Rates in 1859 on the Real Incomes of Different Groups

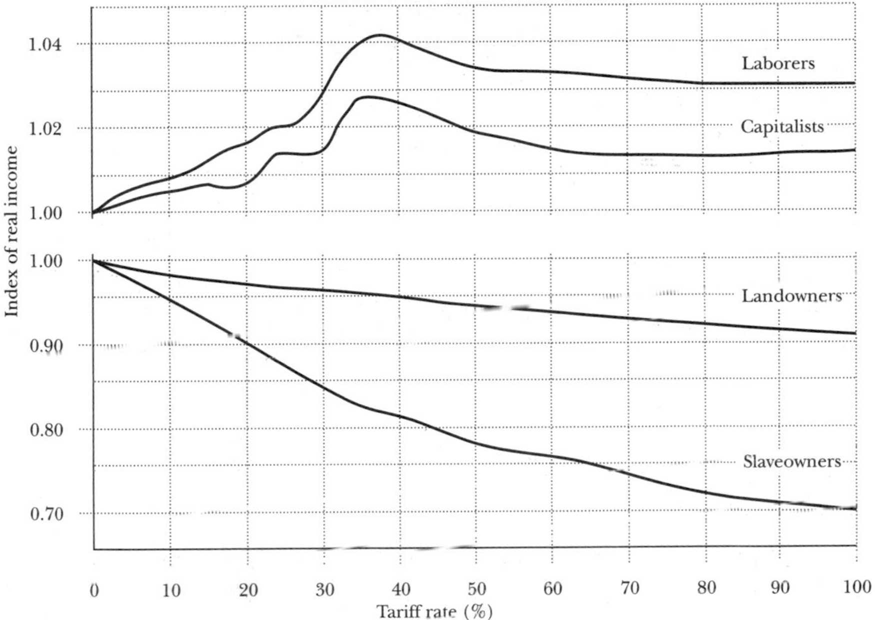

Source: John A. James, "The Optimal Tariff in the Antebellum United States," *American Economic Review* 71 (1981): 732, Figure 2.

hand, gained substantially from the tariff. Removal of the tariff would have devastated the domestic cotton textile industry, where output would have declined by 55 percent, but other manufacturing would also have been hard hit, with output shrinking by 22 percent. Not surprisingly, then, industrial labor—heavily concentrated in eastern urban areas—had a strong interest in preserving the tariff; their incomes were perhaps as much as 15 percent higher. However, the welfare of all other workers was perhaps 2 or 3 percent lower. Consequently, labor in aggregate also stood to gain from removal of the tariff.

Economists offer mixed support for the conventional view that the tariff created a clear division of interest between the North and South. But it is hard to hang the Civil War on such slender threads, particularly since the West did not secede. After the reform of 1846 the odious minimum valuation provision was struck from the tariff law, reducing duties as a percentage of import value. In pushing this reform through Congress, the South showed that it was capable of defending its interests effectively within the Union. Why, then, did the South see in the tariff a source of such conflict, irresolvable except through secession?

Appendix: Production, Consumption, and Welfare Under Free Trade and Autarky

Consider the standard international trade model in which countries produce two goods: manufactures and agricultural commodities.[15] Under autarky—no international trade—each country produces that bundle of goods on its production possibilities curve that corresponds to the highest

FIGURE A.1

Production, Consumption, and Welfare under Free Trade and Autarky

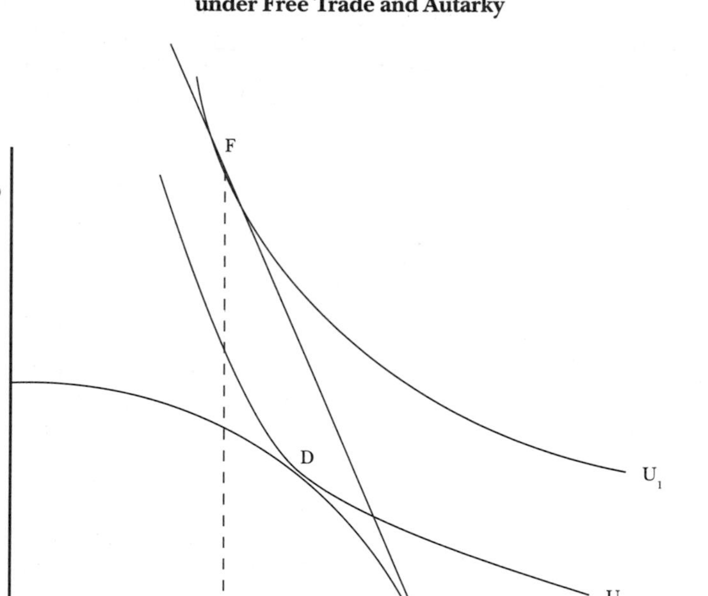

[15] See, for example, Caves and Jones (1990).

possible level of consumer satisfaction, represented by the indifference curve, U_1, say, the bundle D in Figure A.1. This simultaneously determines the relative prices of agricultural commodities which is given by the slope of the production possibilities curve where it is tangent to the aggregate indifference curve at D. If factor endowments, tastes, or other factors result in different relative prices, then trade is possible and potentially beneficial to both parties. In particular, suppose that agricultural commodities were relatively less expensive in the United States than in Britain. This implies that under free trade the United States would export agricultural commodities to Britain and import manufactured goods from Britain. U.S. agricultural prices would thus tend to rise and manufactured goods prices would fall until relative prices in both countries were the same at some level between the initial relative prices in each country. As a result, the United States would now *produce* the bundle of goods represented by E and *consume* that bundle represented by F which results in a higher aggregate level of satisfaction in the United States represented by $U_1 > U_0$. It achieves this by exporting EG of agricultural goods in exchange for GF imports of manufactured goods. The situation in Britain is such as to produce a mirror image of the U.S. trade triangle EFG in that country. This was the situation prior to the embargo.

The purpose of the embargo was to then force a return to autarky—to point E if the resources were temporarily locked into their current uses and eventually to point D when factors could be reallocated—causing, it was hoped, a greater loss of welfare in Britain than America.

BIBLIOGRAPHY

Adams, Donald R. "American Neutrality and Prosperity, 1793–1808: A Reconsideration." *Journal of Economic History* 40 (1980): 713–38.

Baack, Bennett, and Edward Ray. "The Political Economy of Tariff Policy: A Case Study of the United States." *Explorations in Economic History* 30 (1983): 73–93.

Bezanson, Anne. *Wholesale Prices in Philadelphia 1852–1896:* Philadelphia: University of Pennsylvania Press, 1954.

Bils, Mark. "Tariff Protection and Production in the Early U.S. Cotton Textile Industry." *Journal of Economic History* 44 (1984): 1033–46.

Bjork, Gordon. "The Weaning of the American Economy: Independence, Market Changes, and Economic Development." *Journal of Economic History* 24 (1964): 541–60.

Caves, Richard E., and Ronald W. Jones. *World Trade and Payments: An Introduction.* Boston: Little, Brown, 1990.

David, Paul A. "Learning by Doing and Tariff Protection: A Reconsideration of the Case of the Ante-Bellum United States Cotton Textile Industry." *Journal of Economic History* 30 (1970): 521–601.

———. "The Horndal Effect in Lowell, 1834–1856: A Short-Run Learning Curve for Integrated Cotton Textile Mills." *Explorations in Economic History* 10 (1973): 131–150.

Dewey, D. R. *Financial History of the United States.* New York: Longmans, Green and Co., 12th ed. 1934; first published 1902.

Frankel, Jeffrey A. "The 1807–1809 Embargo against Great Britain." *Journal of Economic History* 42 (1982): 291–308.

Goldin, Claudia, and Frank Lewis. "The Role of Exports in American Economic Growth during the Napoleonic Wars, 1793–1807. *Explorations in Economic History* 17 (1980): 6–25.

Harley, C. Knick. "The Antebellum American Tariff: Structure and Welfare." University of Western Ontario working paper, 1990.

James, John C. "The Welfare Effects of the Antebellum Tariff: A General Equilibrium Analysis." *Explorations in Economic History* 15 (1978): 231–56.

Lebergott, Stanley. *The Americans: An Economic Record.* New York: Norton, 1984.

Metzler, Lloyd. "Tariffs, the Terms of Trade, and the Distribution of National Incomes." *Journal of Political Economy* 57 (1949): 1–29.

North, Douglass C. "The United States Balance of Payments, 1790–1860." In National Bureau of Economic Research, *Trends in the American Economy in the 19th Century,* Studies in Income and Wealth, vol. 24. Princeton: Princeton University Press, 1960: 573–627.

Pincus, Jonathan J. *Pressure Groups and Politics in Antebellum Tariffs.* New York: Columbia University Press, 1977.

Pope, Clayne. "The Impact of the Ante-Bellum Tariff on Income Distribution." *Explorations in Economic History* 9 (1972): 375–421.

Ricardo, David. *The Principles of Political Economy and Taxation.* New York: Aldine Press, 1965; first published 1817.

Shepherd, James, and Gary Walton. "Economic Change after the American Revolution: Pre and Post War Comparisons of Maritime Shipping and Trade." *Explorations in Economic History* 13 (1976): 397–422.

Taussig, Frank. *Tariff History of the United States.* New York: A. Kelly, 1967, reprint of 8th ed. 1931; first published 1888.

The transportation revolution and domestic commerce

6

Poor and expensive transportation during the eighteenth and early nineteenth centuries limited competition, protected the inefficient, and raised prices paid by consumers. In this way the colonial and early national transportation system acted like a tariff. Unlike a tariff, though, its burden was borne by domestic as well as foreign trade. Indeed, Daniel Webster, in the congressional debate over the 1824 tariff argued that "Stockholm [Sweden], therefore, for the purposes of the argument may be considered as within fifty miles of Philadelphia," his point being that manufacturers located fifty miles inland from Philadelphia enjoyed the same degree of natural protection that Philadelphia merchants enjoyed from Swedish merchants as a result of the high costs of inland transportation. Improved transportation was essential to the expansion of domestic commerce and to the development of the country. Consequently, transportation attracted the attention of government as well as the interest of private investors and potential beneficiaries.

Early transportation suffered three serious handicaps: Costs were high, often prohibitively so; speed was slow, to the detriment of perishables; and service was irregular, because of local weather conditions and seasonality. In addition, overland wagon transportation was extremely punishing to the cargo and so was unsuited to fragile goods. As a result, western settlement and development proceeded slowly so long as it was difficult, time-consuming, and expensive for labor to move in and to ship products out. Certainly, the Middle West would never have become the industrial heartland of the nation without the development of cheap and convenient transportation. The desire for cheaper access to markets and expectations of appreciated land values from contingent local development and enhanced agricultural profitability were powerful inducements to invest in transportation improvements. They were even more powerful motives for potential beneficiaries to free-ride, engage in boosterism, and solicit public investment.

Thanks in large part to the stimulus provided by British mercantilist policy, ocean transportation, whether international or coastal, was already well developed when the nation achieved its independence. It was cheap and reliable but inaccessible except to those close to the coast or within easy reach of a navigable river. Nevertheless, ocean shipping gave rise to the economic prosperity that the nation enjoyed between 1789 and 1807. Transportation into the interior had, however, languished. The larger East Coast rivers—the Connecticut, the Hudson, the Susquehanna, the Potomac, the James, and so on—were navigable as far inland as the Fall Line of the Appalachian Mountains. In New England this limited river commerce to a narrow coastal plain. Farther south extensive river navigation was possible. The most extensive river navigation was, of course, provided by the Mississippi and Ohio river systems. This network of some ten thousand miles, including the navigable tributaries, was to play a crucial role in the development of the Midwest in the years after 1815.

Roads were virtually useless as avenues of commerce. In wet weather, deep mud made them all but impassable. Indeed, in the South conditions were often so bad that farmers used "mud boats" instead of wagons to haul goods to the nearest navigable river's bank. In dry weather, deep ruts made for a bone-breaking ride, and dust choked human and beast alike. Obstacles, such as rocks and stumps, were moved only when absolutely necessary; an early Ohio law, for example, required merely that tree stumps left in the roadway when first "constructed" be under one foot high. They soon loomed much higher above the road as it eroded around them. Even these crude roads disappeared as population thinned westward, leaving just a few marked trails into the interior. Travel on these roads was painfully slow (in all senses). A wagon loaded with cotton cards, drawn by four horses, took seventy-five days to cover the distance between Worcester, Massachusetts, and Charleston, South Carolina.[1] New York to Washington was a four-day journey, and from New York to eastern Ohio was a two-week trek (Figure 6.1). Such travel time necessarily limited commercial intercourse. Moreover, the condition of public roads was to remain poor until the public authorities abandoned labor services in favor of taxes for repair and maintenance.

So long as the focus of the nation was on international trade, the shortcomings of internal transportation could be ignored. However, President Jefferson's embargo of foreign trade in 1807 changed all that. The resulting decline of foreign trade forced a reappraisal of domestic commerce. It was

[1] Taylor (1962).

FIGURE 6.1

Rates of Travel, 1800

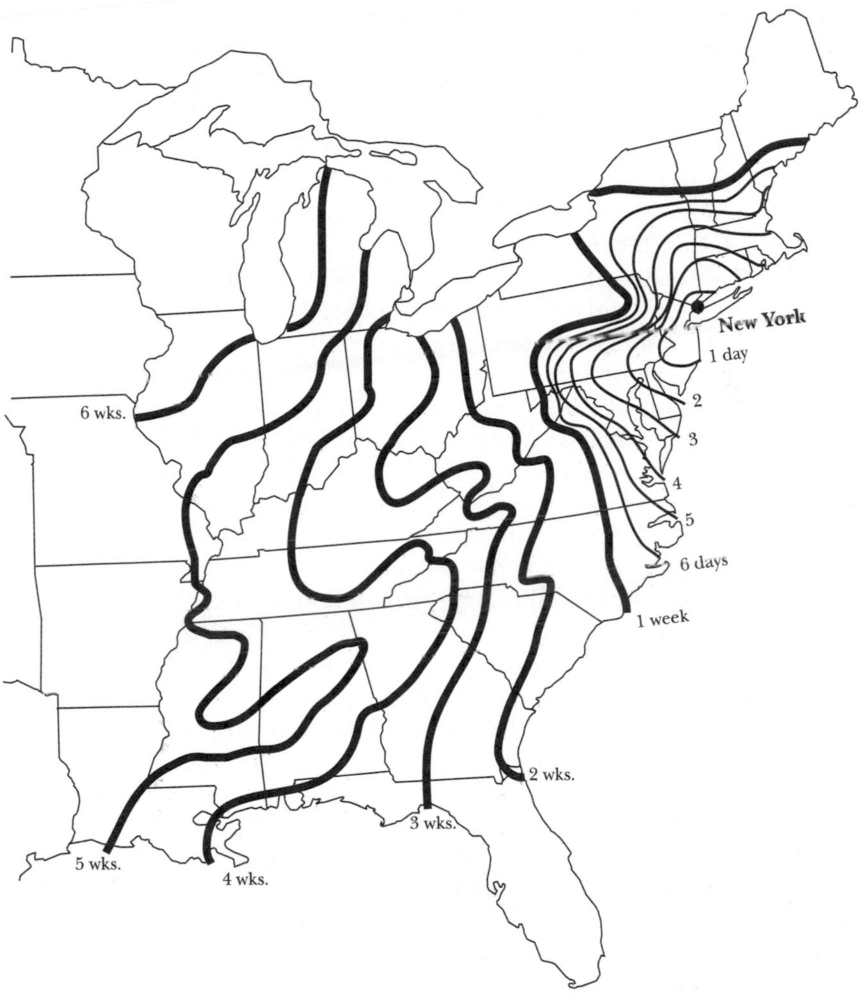

Source: Charles O. Paullin, *Atlas of the Historical Geography of the United States* (Washington, D.C.: Carnegie Institution, 1932): Plate 138A.

no accident that in 1808 the secretary of the treasury, Albert Gallatin, presented a proposal to Congress for federal funding of highway improvements. His plan was not adopted. Indeed, it was not until the twentieth century that the spirit of Gallatin's plan was realized in the interstate highway system.

The Economics of Transportation

The cost of transportation limits the market for commodities. Consider the case of a city located on a featureless plain, such as a midwestern prairie. In the absence of natural features such as hills, rivers, and forests, overland wagon transportation is possible in any direction at a uniform cost, t. The distance from which farmers can ship their surplus goods to market and still earn a normal profit then depends upon their costs of production (which are equal for all farmers on the plain), the price of their goods in the city, and the distance of their farms from that market, given the costs of transportation. In markets where there is perfect information—that is to say, complete knowledge about prices, costs, and opportunities—the cost of shipping products from one market to another establishes an upper bound upon price differences between the two markets. Indeed, this is one measure for market integration.

At the end of the colonial period, transport costs accounted for about half the market price of American tobacco on the Amsterdam market. If we take this as an upper-bound measure of the ability of commodities to bear transport costs, then we can use the information on price, P, and transport costs, t, to establish the margin around our hypothetical city within which farmers can ship their goods to market and still make a normal profit. In this case the area of commercial market production for sale in the city is enclosed by a circle of radius $\frac{1}{2}$P/t miles about the city (Figure 6.2). Farms located outside this area cannot earn at least normal profit on goods shipped to the city because the high cost of transport eats up all the margin between their costs of production and the market price of the commodity. They therefore engage only in self-sufficient production, although they may market unplanned surpluses caused, say, by bountiful harvests, if they live within P/t miles of the city.

Wagon haulage was particularly expensive, and its costs were hard to predict because of the wide variation in road conditions, weather, and other incidentals. Moreover, considerable resources were required for wagon transportation, and the opportunity costs were often highest when the need for transport was greatest—especially around harvesttime. A wagonload—about a ton or so—required the services of a teamster, a wagon, and a team of four to six draft animals but rarely traveled more than twenty miles in a day. A round trip to market could therefore easily take a week, during which time food and lodging had to be provided for the teamster and feed for the draft animals. Such trips were not undertaken lightly or on a whim. Slow speed and rough roads also increased the risk of spoilage, thereby further raising costs.

Within the area of feasible commercial production, land values vary inversely with distance to the city because if production costs and transport costs are uniform for all farmers, the farms located closest to the city will pay

FIGURE 6.2

Land Value and Market Proximity

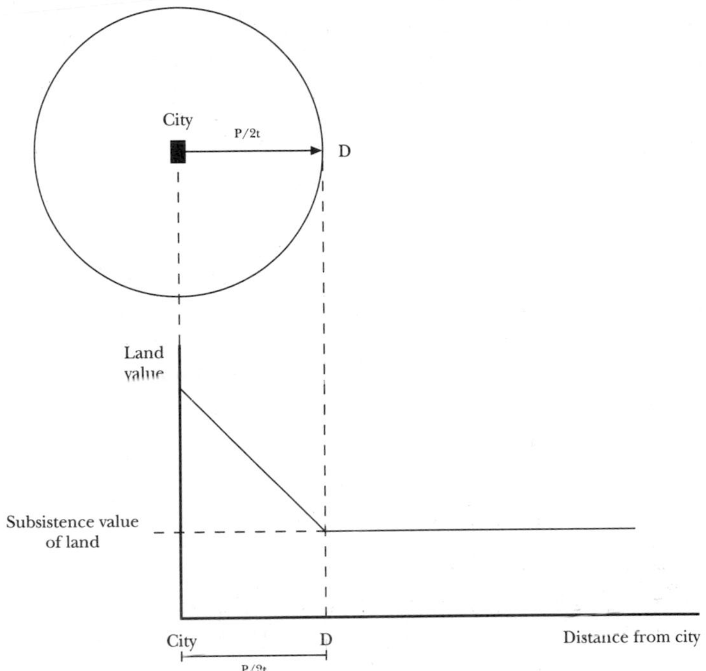

least in transport costs and thus realize the highest profits (see Figure 6.2). If the markets work perfectly, farmers buying these lands will find that the price they have to pay is such that their production costs are raised by a sufficient amount to eliminate any supernormal profits. Transport costs thus define the areas of commercial and subsistence farming and determine land values and the rate of return to farming.

Overland wagon transportation in 1815 cost about 30 cents per ton-mile—that is, it cost 30 cents to carry one ton of goods a distance of one mile (Table 6.1). In New England, where roads were perhaps better maintained, wagon haulage costs are estimated at somewhat less: 15 to 20 cents per ton-mile.[2] Where water transport was available, it was much cheaper. Using the rule of thumb that transport costs could make up no more than 50 percent of the market price of goods, farmers relying solely upon wagon transporta-

[2] Rothenberg (1981).

TABLE 6.1

Transport Costs circa 1815

Transportation Mode	Cost per Ton-Mile (Cents)
Road	30.00 or more
River	
Boat upstream	6.00
Raft downstream	1.30
Ocean	1.00 or less

Source: George Rogers Taylor, *The Transportation Revolution* (New York: Holt, Rinehart, 1962): Appendix A, Table 2.

tion could not ship corn more than about 40 miles beyond the farm gate (Table 6.2). Wheat had a higher value to weight ratio and could be shipped about 80 miles, which is about the upper-bound distance that farmers actually shipped it. Processing commodities to increase the value to weight ratio increased the distances they could be shipped. Thus flour could be shipped perhaps 130 miles. Manufactured goods could generally be shipped even farther, and valuable commodities, such as tea, experienced little or no restriction on the distance they could be transported even when transportation was expensive and of very poor quality. Farms located close to navigable rivers could ship much farther, especially if the markets were downstream, as they invariably were since the country developed from the coast inland. Thus wheat grown on a farm on the banks of the Ohio around Cincinnati could be shipped upriver as far as Pittsburgh or downstream to New Orleans. If the wheat was milled into flour, East Coast markets via the river and coastwise shipping fell within the market sphere. So, too, did Europe. Other refined foodstuffs, such as butter, and important commodities, such as tobacco and cotton, also found markets worldwide, provided they had easy access to ocean shipping.

Turnpikes

Change in transportation came in several forms. The first, and probably least important, innovation was the turnpike, which appeared in the years following the Revolution. Like common roads, most turnpikes were generally poorly surfaced. But unlike common roads, tolls provided funds for more ambitious grading and more frequent maintenance. A good estimate is that they cut the resource cost—the labor and capital input—of moving heavy freight by half.

TABLE 6.2

Shipping Distances for Various Commodities by Different Media before Transport Costs Exceed 50 Percent of Market Price, circa 1815 (miles, rounded to the nearest 10)

Commodity	Road	River Upstream	River Downstream	Ocean
Farm Products				
Corn	40	200	910	1,180
Wheat	80	410	1,900	2,300
Flour	130	670	3,080	4,000
Tobacco	300	1,500	6,920	9,000
Butter	780	3,900	18,080	23,500
Cotton	870	4,330	20,000	Anywhere
Tea	3,000	15,000	Anywhere	Anywhere
Manufactured Products				
Pig iron	90	460	2,120	2,760
Iron bar	230	1,170	5,380	6,990
Nails	420	2,080	9,620	12,510

Notes: Market prices from U.S. Bureau of the Census, *Historical Statistics of the United States* (Washington, D.C.: Government Printing Office, 1975): Series E123–E134. Transport costs from Table 6.1.

Construction on turnpikes seems to have followed distinct building cycles. In the first decade of the nineteenth century most roads were built in New England, where there were more than twenty-eight hundred miles of turnpikes by 1810—about 60 percent of the total nationwide.[3] Construction was interrupted by the War of 1812 but resumed after peace, primarily in the Middle Atlantic states. By 1820 mileage had doubled to almost ten thousand miles. Thereafter turnpikes fell out of favor. Virtually none was built in the South, although the nation's first turnpike had been built in Virginia in 1785.

As much as $30 million was invested in turnpike construction, but the returns were disappointing. Few made money for their sponsors—usually private corporations. Most probably did not. Only 5 or 6 of New England's 230 turnpikes clearly operated in the black, yet turnpikes in that region were considered among the most successful.[4] Data for the most successful Massachusetts road, the Salem Turnpike, show that it averaged dividends of 3.1 percent over sixty years—sufficient to repay construction but probably well below the opportunity cost on capital. Profitability, however, is an inaccurate measure of the net benefits to society provided by improved roads.

[3] Fishlow (1972).

[4] Taylor (1962).

Most of the benefits were captured by users in the form of reduced transport costs and by landowners through appreciated property values rather than by the owners of the turnpike. However, evidence on just how substantial the total benefits to society might have been is impossible to obtain since records of construction costs and freight hauled exist for only a few road segments.

Canals

The construction of canals in the United States was seriously contemplated in the 1790s; two were even built: the Santee in South Carolina and the Middlesex in Massachusetts. Not until 1825, though, was the first major route, the Erie Canal, completed. The lag was probably due not to a lack of technical knowledge—canals were in widespread use in England by the late eighteenth century—but to the uncertain economic conditions. Canals dramatically cut the variable costs of heavy freight transport because one work animal could haul as much tonnage by water as fifty animals hauled by turnpike. But there was no practical way to build a canal with a small capacity, and trade at the time was limited. Long canals were massive undertakings, the largest capital projects of their time. Hence they were only economically justifiable on routes where the burden of huge fixed construction costs could be spread over a great deal of freight traffic.

By the time it was built, the Erie Canal, linking the Hudson River to Lake Erie, certainly qualified. It was an immediate success, opening up a vast interregional trade between the port of New York City and the upper Midwest. Even prior to its completion the canal collected almost $1 million in tolls. Volume surge with completion as the Erie Canal tapped the nascent agricultural surpluses and trade of the Great Lakes area. Its sponsor—the state of New York—was able to recoup the original $9 million investment quickly since the net return over the canal's first ten years of operation was about 8 percent.[5] The social rate of return, which included both the internal financial return to the backers and the advantage to shippers, was many times greater.

The astounding success of the Erie Canal brought forth a wave of imitators. Other states saw the tremendous benefits to the state and city of New York from the Erie and overcame previous reluctance to put their own residents in debt. In part their motives were based on underlying competition among eastern cities for western trade. Boosterism ran rampant. Philadelphia, eager to sustain its position as the premier East Coast port, pushed construction of a canal across the Appalachians to Pittsburgh—the Pennsylvania Main Line. This would have allowed midwestern farmers to send their goods east via the Ohio River rather than via Lake Erie. Maryland entrepreneurs, equally eager to make the Potomac River an outlet for mid-

[5] Fishlow (1972).

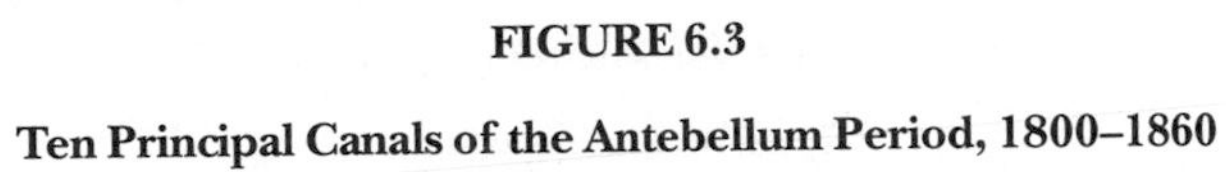

FIGURE 6.3

Ten Principal Canals of the Antebellum Period, 1800–1860

Source: Carter Goodrich, *Canals and American Economic Development* (New York: Columbia University Press, 1961): 184–85.

western freight traffic, received federal and state support for a canal link through Cumberland, Maryland, to the Ohio Valley. By 1860, when canal construction all but ceased, 4,254 miles had been completed—virtually all in the Northeast and Midwest (Figure 6.3).

Neither the Pennsylvania nor the Chesapeake and Ohio (C&O) Canal lived up to the expectations of its promoters. The Pennsylvania Main Line Canal—perhaps the most daring engineering design of the early nineteenth century—was very expensive to build. Moreover, because its middle link over the Appalachians was actually by cog railroad, shippers had to pay the added cost of unloading and reloading their barges in the eastern and western mountain foothills. The C&O Canal, long delayed by construction problems and cost overruns, never even made it to the Ohio River. It finally was completed as far west as Cumberland, Maryland, in 1850. By that time the railroad was a serious competitor, luring traffic away from the canal. Canals,

FIGURE 6.4

Rates of Travel 1830

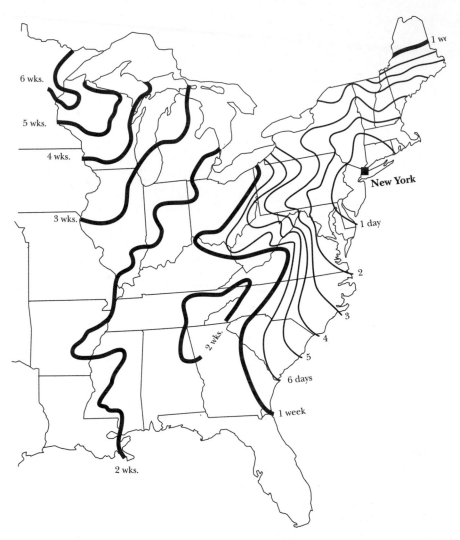

Source: Charles O. Paullin, *Atlas of the Historical Geography of the United States* (Washington, D.C.: Carnegie Institution, 1932): Plate 138B.

western river steamboats, and Great Lakes shipping, however, had a tremendous impact upon travel times, cutting travel times by half (Figure 6.4).

The availability of canal transportation led to a shift away from agriculture and toward manufacturing and commerce. In 1840, for example, canal counties in the western half of New York and Pennsylvania and in Ohio had almost twice as large a fraction of their manufacturing population engaged in textiles and clothing and three times the proportion engaged in metals as did noncanal counties in the same area. At the same time they had less than half the proportion engaged in food and lumber processing. Indeed, the canal counties in the West looked more like the eastern seaboard in their industrial composition than the rest of the Midwest, but the industrial sector in the West was very small, so while it may have looked like the East Coast in terms of its composition, it was one-tenth the scale.[6]

Canal construction proceeded in three distinct waves (Figure 6.5), determined by the different technical complexities, commercial rivalries, and the availability of financing. The first phase (1815–34) saw construction of the New York and Pennsylvania systems and work begun on the Ohio system with the Ohio and Erie; the second (1834–44), construction in the Midwest; the third cycle (1844–60) concentrated on the construction of feeder lines to the existing network. In all, perhaps $188 million was invested in American canals during these three cycles. Of this investment, almost three-quarters ($136.5 million) came from public coffers as state and local governments were sold on the potential social benefits. Rather than tax to pay the cost, states borrowed as much as $127 million of it from foreigners.[7]

Congress also promoted canal construction through a policy of land grants to midwestern states. Beginning in 1827, states were given one-half of the land in a five-mile-wide band along the right-of-way. Alternate sections of land, each one mile square, were reserved to the federal government. In return, Congress demanded freedom from tolls for government use. This legislation established the basic policy for later land grants to the nation's railroads. As will be discussed later, the donation of public lands to encourage, promote, and support local internal improvements was justified by Congress in anticipation of a rise in the value of remaining public lands in the vicinity. In all, midwestern states received more than 4.5 million acres of federal land for canal construction, with almost 1.5 million acres going to Indiana while Ohio and Michigan each received over 1.2 million acres.

At the peak, 1839–40, investment in canals accounted for about 10 percent of the total value of construction nationwide and about 1 percent of the total value added in commodity production. Canal construction also provided full- or part-time employment for about thirty thousand men—5.5 percent of the nonagricultural labor force in the canal-building states. Even so, it has been claimed that canal building did not play a decisive role in the economic fluctuations of the time.[8] Instead the major contribution of the canals may have been the financial development of bond markets and the

[6] Ransom (1967), Neimi (1970).
[7] Segal (1961).
[8] Ibid.

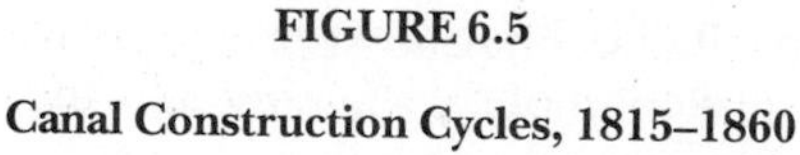

FIGURE 6.5

Canal Construction Cycles, 1815–1860

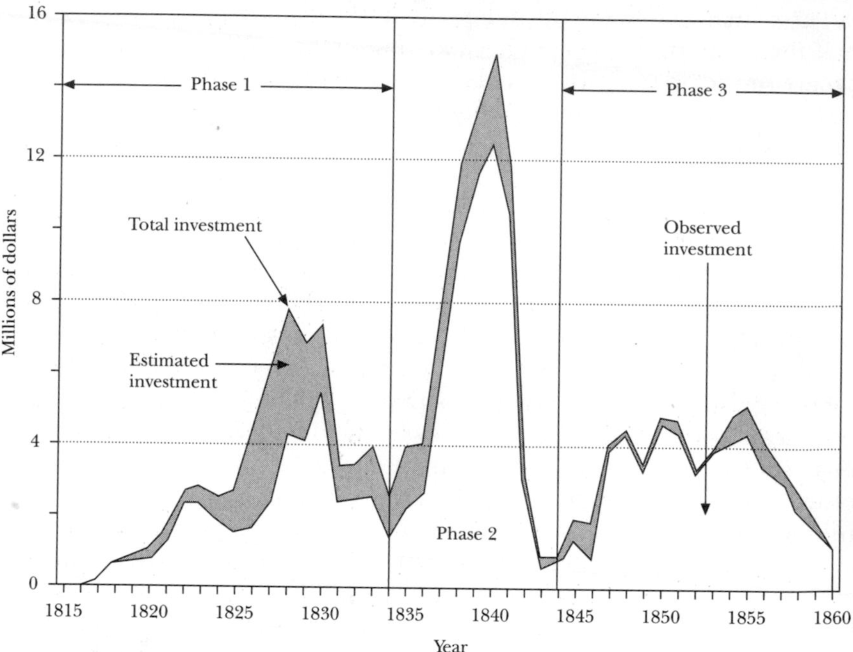

Source: After Segal in Carter Goodrich, *Canals and American Economic Development* (New York: Columbia University Press, 1961): 208–09.

tapping of foreign capital markets. Those financial networks were to prove crucial for financing America's railroads in later years. Foreign loans, primarily British, accounted for about a third of the investment in American canals—and a much higher percentage during the critical second phase—before defaults temporarily spoiled the market.

The narrow private and broader social fortunes of other canals present a mixed picture. The Erie, of course, was an immense success. So, too, were the less ambitious intraregional canals built very early (in the 1820s) to haul coal from the mines of eastern Pennsylvania. Canals built during the second wave were generally financial failures. It seems likely that their social rate of return, including the benefits to shippers, exceeded the cost of capital. The third wave of construction, begun after the economic downturn of the early 1840s, was very obviously a financial disaster for the state governments and private backers that supported and underwrote them. In general these later, shorter canals were of little economic importance. Nevertheless, many of them operated in competition with the railroads for a few decades after their completion.

Although canals required enormous initial fixed investments to construct, they functioned with low variable operating costs. It thus paid to keep a canal operating as long as it could recover a small fraction of the average cost of moving freight. In the late 1850s no one with any sense would have invested in a new canal rather than a new railroad. By virtue of already being there, however, canals were able to match the fares charged by railroads and still cover operating costs. For high-bulk commodities moving long distances—coal and iron ore, for example—the actual resource cost involved in water transport remained lower than rail costs into the twentieth century. Thus it should not be surprising that while canals continuously lost ground to railroads, they shared in the absolute growth of interregional traffic until the 1880s.

During the antebellum period an increasing percentage of the commodity trade of the Midwest was siphoned from the Mississippi and Ohio rivers by the Great Lakes and Erie Canal route (Figure 6.6). In 1836 the Great Lakes and Erie Canal accounted for about 11 percent of all freight from the trans-Appalachian West. The bulk of the traffic (86 percent) was carried by steamboats through New Orleans. By 1860 the northern gateway had supplanted the southern as the preferred route, and the Erie was carrying almost as much trade as the rivers. The progressive trade gains of the northern gateway at the expense of the South probably reflect rising productivity in Great Lakes steamboating and continued improvements to widen and deepen the Erie Canal that allowed the realization of economies of scale.

The failure of the later canals tends to be given too much weight in historical analyses of the canal era. The economic achievements of the canals, considered as a group, were considerable. Canals drove down the cost of shipping from about 20 cents per ton-mile in the 1810s and 1820s to 2 or 3 cents per ton-mile in the 1830s. However, the total transportation cost of shipment to market still remained considerable, as the estimates in Table 6.3 show. Later, costs per ton-mile fell even further to as little as a penny. The social (shipper, consumer, owner) rate of return on all canal construction, based on the very conservative estimate that canals cut freight rates from an average 17 cents before 1846 to 2 cents thereafter, exceeds 50 percent.[9] Much of their collective success was of course due to the spectacular fortunes of the Erie. But even a noted financial failure like the Ohio Canal yielded a respectable 10 percent social rate of return.[10]

[9] Fishlow (1965).
[10] Ransom (1970).

FIGURE 6.6

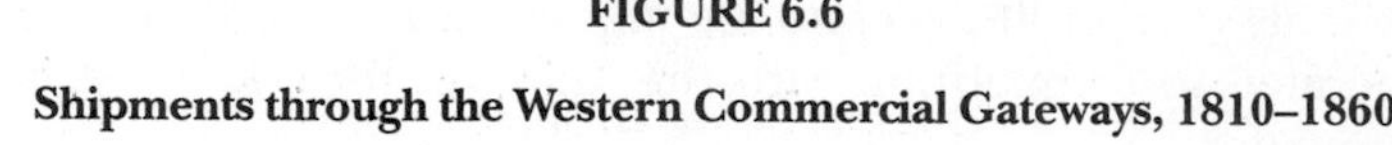

Shipments through the Western Commercial Gateways, 1810–1860

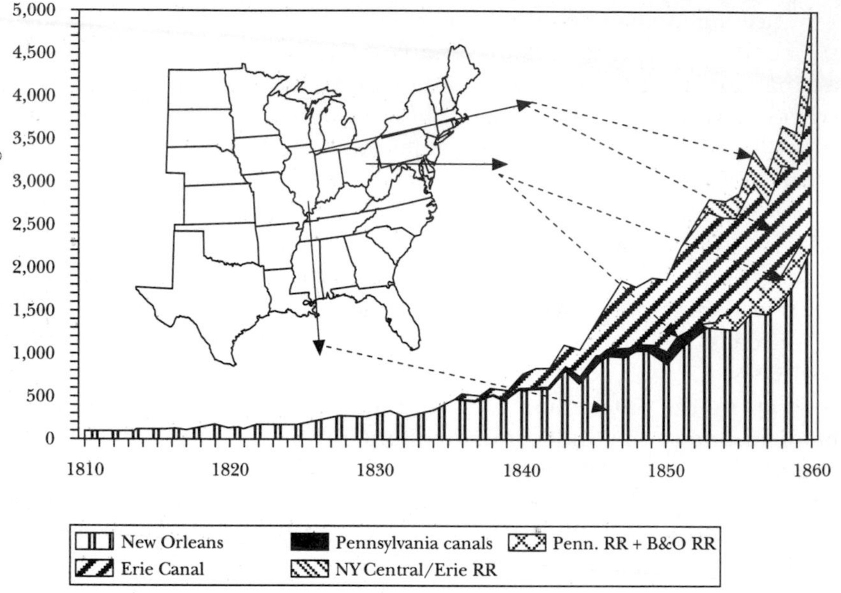

Source: Erik Haites, James Mak, and Gary Walton, *Western River Transportation* (Baltimore: Johns Hopkins University Press, 1975): Appendix A.

Steamboats

Canals were not the only advance in water transportation during the antebellum era. Even after the completion of the major inter- and intraregional canals, most cargo still depended on transport by river, lake, or sheltered coastal waters. At the beginning of the nineteenth century, western river vessels consisted of keelboats—substantial craft steered by rudders—or cruder, raftlike flatboats. They served well enough taking freight downstream but were a wildly inefficient means of hauling goods back upstream. Goods carried downstream by flatboat paid about $16.55 per ton from Louisville to New Orleans between 1810 and 1819. These rafts served only one voyage. They were then broken up for lumber in New Orleans. Keelboats provided upstream passage at a cost of perhaps $100 per ton. Costs were extremely high because these boats were actually hauled upstream by human muscle power—poled along the river, dragged by lines by men on the riverbanks, or pulled hand over hand past overhanging branches and brush—and made but one round trip a year. The amount of trade sustained this way was limited.

TABLE 6.3

Transport Costs circa 1860

Transportation Mode	Cost per Ton-Mile (cents)
Road	15.00 or more
River	
Mississippi	0.37
Illinois	1.20
Canal	
Erie	0.99
Pennsylvania Main Line	2.40
Great Lakes	0.10
Railroad:	
New York Central	2.06
Erie	1.84
Ocean	0.05 or less

Source: George Rogers Taylor, *The Transportation Revolution* (New York: Holt, Rinehart, 1962): Appendix A, Table 2.

The advent of steam power made an enormous difference. First demonstrated on the Hudson River by Robert Fulton in 1807, the steamboat proved its feasibility carrying cargo upstream on the Mississippi in 1815. Early designs were relatively primitive and, in terms of freight-hauling capacity, were inefficient. Advances in steam technology soon thereafter allowed for the use of small, light, high-pressure steam engines. Steamboat designers were then able by trial and error to design a boat that provided more space for freight and greater speed. Complementing these major increases in payload and speed were improvements in engine safety that cut insurance costs and reduced maintenance time. Increased navigation experience by river pilots, plus a considerable investment in the elimination of navigation hazards, also made it possible for steamboats to operate at night. The learning-by-doing of the steamboat designers led as well to drastic reductions in the draft of vessels of a given tonnage. As a result, it was possible to use larger ships and realize economies of scale, navigate in safety at lower water levels more months of the year, and serve more communities along the smaller tributary rivers. The life expectancy of steamboats was short, perhaps five years, because of the hazards of navigation, flimsy construction, and hard use. As a result, technological advances were quickly embedded in the capital stock. The explosion of boilers that contributed to this process also led to the reemergence of regulation in an independent America.

Improvements in hull design, steam engines, and the rivers themselves led to rapid total factor productivity growth on the western rivers (see Chapter 1, Appendix A). From 1817 to 1848 the ratio of the value of transport services to a weighted average of factor inputs increased at an average annual rate between 6 and 7 percent (Figure 6.7). Part of this productivity growth reflects scale economies that are not accounted for separately. By comparison, ocean shipping productivity increased by just 3.5 percent annually (1815–60), canal and turnpike transport hardly at all. As with ocean shipping, reduced port times reflecting extensive local market development were an important factor. Far more important were technological changes in steamboat design that reduced vessel draft, increased carrying capacity on a vessel of given size, and increased speed from more efficient and powerful engines. For example, in 1820 a vessel of 150 tons had a draft when unladen of 42 inches. By 1857 vessels of 777 tons were being built with the same draft. Increased speed and shallower draft translated into more round trips per year—up from three round trips per year between Louisville and New Orleans in the 1820s to twelve round trips by the 1850s—spreading high fixed costs over more units.[11]

Competition among steamboat operators also meant that productivity gains would be translated into declining rates. Freight that cost 5 cents per pound delivered upstream from New Orleans to Louisville in 1816 cost only $\frac{1}{2}$ cent per pound in the 1830s and perhaps as little as $\frac{1}{4}$ cent per pound in the 1850s. Productivity growth would have been even higher but for the emergence of a backhaulage problem in the late 1830s and early 1840s. Demand for upstream shipments did not keep pace with downstream freight volume, with the result that average utilization rates of the steamboats tended to fall. Steamboat operators responded by lowering upstream rates to marginal cost and charging whatever the market would bear on downstream shipments. Consequently, from 1840 or so on upstream freight paid lower rates than downstream despite greater operating costs.[12]

Steamboats naturally drove keelboats off the waterways that were deep enough to support steam-powered craft. Curiously, though, steamboats apparently had no adverse impact on flatboat commerce. More than twice as many flatboats reached New Orleans in 1846 than in 1816. The explanation for this persistence of a seemingly obsolete technology is simple. Flatboats were able to match the cost of steamboats downstream: They were slow but required little capital investment and utilized cheap, abundant off-season farm labor both to build and to operate. And once downstream, flatboats were dismantled, leaving the return of the crew upstream as the remaining expense. But this critical bottleneck in flatboat operation was actually solved by the rival steamboat technology. A trip for the flatboat crew from New Orleans to Ohio that had taken several months in 1815 took just ten days by

[11] Mak and Walton (1972).
[12] Haites and Mak (1970), Haites, Mak, and Walton (1975).

FIGURE 6.7

Productivity Growth in Western River Steamboating, 1815–1860

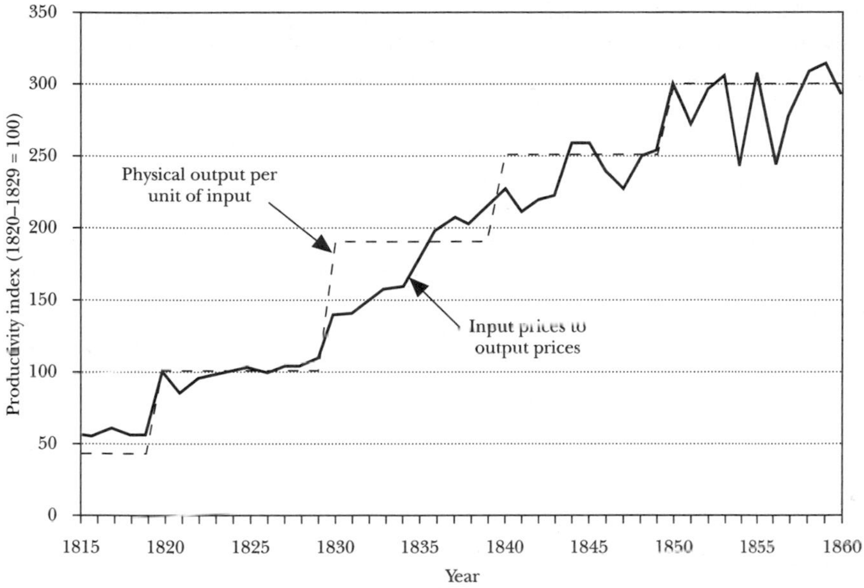

Source: James Mak and Gary M. Walton, "Steamboats and the Great Productivity Surge in River Transportation, *Journal of Economic History* 32 (1972): Appendix Tables 1 and 2. Reprinted by permission of Cambridge University Press.

steamboat in 1840. In fact, in large part because of this technical complementarity with steamboats, total factor productivity for flatboats rose at an average annual rate of about 2 percent from 1815 to 1850.[13]

Great Lakes and Ocean Shipping

Steam technology gave the steamboat a huge advantage over traditional keelboats in river transportation as early as the 1820s. Sailing ships on the Great Lakes and on ocean routes, however, proved more difficult to displace. As late as 1850 steamboats represented just one-third the tonnage working the Great Lakes, one-tenth the tonnage on coastal routes, and barely 4 percent on international routes. Sail power held its own against steam in these areas for a number of reasons. The construction costs of sailing ships were much lower than steamships, and the ratio of cargo space to total ship tonnage was much higher. The high-pressure steam engines on

[13] Mak and Walton (1972).

western river steamboats had a voracious appetite for fuel and fresh water. They could—and did—stop for fuel frequently, and a constant supply of fresh water, albeit full of silt, was constantly at hand. By contrast, space set aside for fuel on lake and oceangoing steamships necessarily depressed productivity. Steamboats were faster than sailing vessels, but the difference was not nearly as great on open water as it was fighting the current of a river. For that matter, specially designed sailing ships—the famous clipper ships—could beat steam-powered boats and still match their cargo-carrying capacity. Steam-powered ships gradually were to narrow these productivity differences after the Civil War as steam engines became yet lighter, cheaper, more dependable, and fuel-efficient. Moreover, the development of the compound marine steam engine conserved fresh water, a precious commodity on long ocean voyages. But it would take the rest of the nineteenth century to make oceangoing sailing ships obsolete.[14]

Railroads

The last and most celebrated change in antebellum transportation was the railroad. Railroads had enormous technical advantages over water transport alternatives. They were faster and more flexible and could deliver cargo from the point of production to market without multiple loading and unloading. They could be built through rugged terrain at a fraction of the cost of canals and could deliver cargo year-round, even in cold climates. In retrospect, then, it might seem surprising that it took at least a quarter of a century from the initial rail construction for railroads to dominate water in interregional transportation. In 1860, of the 2.6 million tons of freight from the trans-Appalachian West via the northern gateway, less than 30 percent came by railroad. Even in 1870 half the grain reaching New York still arrived by water. The advent of the railroad, however, had a profound impact upon travel times. In 1857 eastern Ohio was within a day's journey of New York, southern Wisconsin and most of Illinois were but two days away, and the frontier of settlement in Minnesota, Nebraska, or Kansas was less than a week away from New York (Figure 6.8). Moreover, information could travel much, much more quickly, limited only by the ability of the telegraph operator to tap out the message and decipher the pattern of dots and dashes. Further discussion of the railroad is deferred until Chapter 16.

The Expansion of Interregional Trade after 1815

After 1815 much of the nation's growth was generated by increased British

[14] Fishlow (1972).

FIGURE 6.8

Rates of Travel, 1857

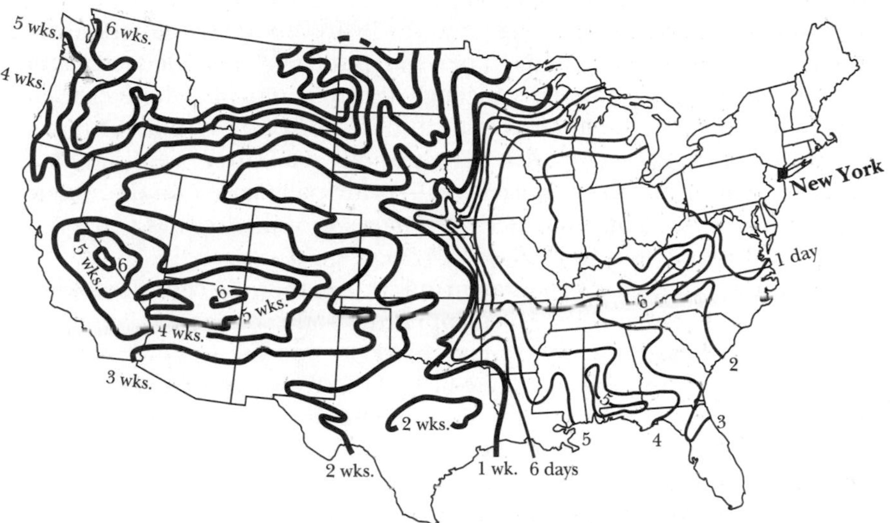

Source: Charles O. Paullin, *Atlas of the Historical Geography of the United States* (Washington, D.C.: Carnegie Institution, 1932): Plate 138C.

demand for raw cotton and midwestern settlement that created opportunities for regional specialization and trade. This argument is now generally associated with Douglass North, but Louis Schmidt and Guy Callender advanced a similar argument decades ago: "The rise of internal commerce after 1815 made possible a territorial division of labor between the three great sections of the Union—the West, the South, and the East. . . . Each section tended to devote itself more exclusively to the production of those commodities for which it was best able to provide."[15]

The model is simple yet powerful, internally consistent, and apparently supported by contemporary evidence. It's also probably wrong. Although supply factors (for example, lower production costs) can't be ignored, North's thesis is that the demand for King Cotton to feed the booming British mills allowed the South to specialize in the production of cotton creating a regional food deficit, which, in turn, created a demand for western grain and livestock. Farmers from Ohio, Indiana, and Illinois were encouraged to produce less for themselves and more for the market towns on the Ohio and Mississippi rivers. From there the food was sent south to New

[15] Schmidt (1939).

Orleans for sale within the Cotton South. Cotton income stimulated economic growth in the Northeast, both directly through sales of manufactures to the South and indirectly by providing purchasing power to the food-exporting West.

Improved transportation stands at the heart of this model. Midwestern population grew at over 5 percent per year, but trade expanded even more rapidly. Midwestern shipments through the northern, northeastern, and southern gateways grew at an average annual rate of over 10 percent from the 1830s as production was increasingly oriented toward more distant markets. Shipments from the western states—principally agricultural commodities—via the Erie Canal increased even more, growing from 54,000 tons in 1836 to 1.9 million tons by 1860, or by 16 percent per year.

Attractive though the argument might be, there is considerable evidence against it. Much of the Mississippi River traffic in food was largely destined for northeastern cities, foreign markets, and the urban population around New Orleans. Less than one-fifth of the West's exports ended up on the dining tables of cotton plantations.[16] The disposition of western food can be traced from trade statistics. The upper South—Kentucky, Tennessee, Virginia, and North Carolina—was a major producer of grain, exporting much of its product to other parts of the South, while the middle South—interior portions of Louisiana, Mississippi, Alabama, South Carolina, and Georgia—was largely self-sufficient in food until after the construction of rail lines, when it began shipping food to the Atlantic and Gulf coasts. Only the lower South—the dense cotton and sugar regions around New Orleans, plus a strip of Atlantic and Gulf coasts from the Carolinas south—was a net food importer. In the early 1840s only about half the corn and flour sent downriver to New Orleans remained in the South (see Table 6.4). About two-thirds of the corn plus one-third of the flour received at New Orleans came from the upper South rather than the West. By the late 1840s New Orleans receipts of corn and flour had roughly tripled, but almost all the additional shipments were exported to foreign countries. Consequently, it was the poor harvests in Europe (in particular, the Irish potato famine), not the needs of the cotton economy, that produced the surge of western grain exports.

Trends reversed sharply in the 1850s. More of the Mississippi grain traffic originated in the West, and more of the grain that made it down to New Orleans remained within the South. Western grain shipments to the South, however, grew at a rate far slower than total western production. Instead most of the increased western output went to meet the demands of the growing western population and to rail and lake shipments direct to the East Coast.[17]

If the South was an important customer for western grain, then one

[16] Fishlow (1964).
[17] Lindstrom (1970); also Callahan and Hutchinson (1980).

TABLE 6.4

Disposition of Corn Traffic through New Orleans

Year	Annual Average Traffic (1,000 sacks)	% Exported East	% Exported Abroad	% Consumed in South
1842–45	529	36	16	48
1846–49	1,920	20	55	25
1850–53	1,309	17	21	62
1854–57	1,592	9	43	48
1858–61	1,831	3	20	78

Disposition of Flour Traffic through New Orleans

Year	Annual Average Traffic (1,000 barrels)	% Exported East	% Exported Abroad	% Consumed in South
1842–45	499	31	21	48
1846–49	1,044	29	41	30
1850–53	817	15	23	63
1854–57	991	24	30	47
1858–61	1,146	17	20	63

Source: Diane Lindstrom, "Southern Dependence upon Interregional Grain Supplies," *Agricultural History* 44 (1970): 104. Reprinted in William N. Parker, ed., *The Structure of the Cotton Economy of the Antebellum South* (Washington, D.C: Agricultural History Society, 1970): 104.

should also find evidence that the regions specializing in cotton production were unable to feed themselves from local production. Instead, on average, farms and plantations in the Cotton Belt produced a food *surplus* sufficient to supply all the slaves and one-sixth of the free people living in non-cotton-producing southern counties, many of which presumably had their own food surpluses.[18]

Consequently, western growth could not have been dependent on nonexistent southern demand for western food. The East, however, had a substantial food deficit. In the Northeast the average farm surplus of grains was very small—about enough to feed only four nonfarmers per farm—and more than half the farms produced less grain than they needed to meet their own needs. Imports from the Midwest could, however, have satisfied the eastern excess demand for grain. Midwestern farms produced enough

[18] Gallman (1970).

to feed more than twenty nonfarmers—more than enough to meet the needs of local nonfarm and urban midwestern consumers. The residual could be, and was, shipped East, where it fed the factory and urban service workers. Some—indeed a growing percentage—was exported to Europe and the Caribbean. At the same time northeastern farmers taking advantage of local transportation improvements produced large surpluses of perishable dairy products. These dairy products found a ready market in the nearby urban areas of the East Coast and were not subject to the same vigorous competition from the Midwest.[19]

The Impact of the Transportation Revolution

The impact of these changes was profound. Midwestern land sales boomed. Settlement and agricultural development proceeded rapidly, just as the promoters had hoped. As a result, midwestern farmers were now brought into direct competition with those back East, forcing changes in eastern crop mixes and accelerating the trend toward industry and city. transport costs, thanks to the development of new transportation media and the extension of the transportation network, fell sharply. If we use the change in transport costs per ton-mile between 1815 and 1860 as a crude measure of productivity change over the period, productivity in road transportation doubled—primarily the result of better road surfaces—and productivity in ocean shipping rose fivefold, while western river steamboating experienced as much as a ten- to twelvefold rise in productivity.

The impact of these reductions in transport costs was to reduce the burden of insurance and freight in the selling price of goods, shifting the supply curve for the product delivered to consumers from S_{cif} to, say, $S_{cif'}$ (Figure 6.9). As a result, the price paid by consumers declines from P to P' while the price received by producers increases from R to R', sharing the reduction in transport costs between consumers and producers depending upon the elasticities of supply and demand. As a result, both the consumer and producer surpluses increase and sales expand to Q'.

The reduction in the burden of transport costs dramatically increased the area of feasible commercial production and the distances over which most commodities could be shipped (Table 6.5). Reliance upon road transportation still limited markets to local or regional areas. Access to rails gave producers nationwide markets, and water transport made many markets worldwide (Table 6.6). It was not coincidence that led to the emergence of an international market for American wheat in the late antebellum period.

The effect of introducing a new lower-cost transport medium such as a railroad, a canal, or even a properly surfaced road, upon economic oppor-

[19] Atack and Bateman (1987).

FIGURE 6.9

The Effect of Transportation Improvements upon Prices Paid by Consumers and Received by Producers

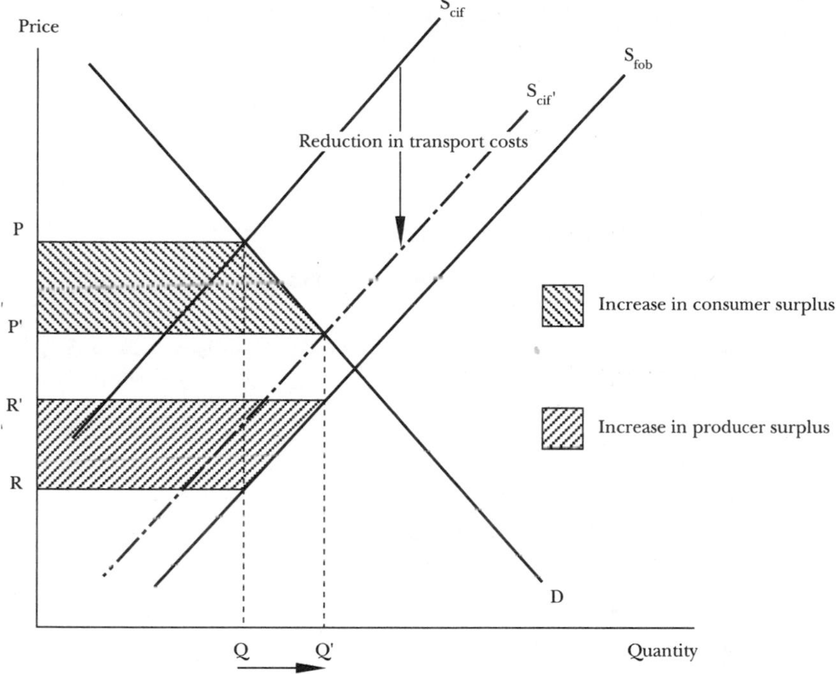

tunity and activity in the immediate area is shown in Figure 6.10, which depicts a city on a featureless plain, as in Figure 6.2, but now goods can also be shipped by canal or rail from farms along the right-of-way. Shipping costs by canal or rail were much lower than those by wagon—perhaps as little as one-tenth as much (see Table 6.3), so farms as far away as $\frac{1}{2}P/t_n$ miles, where t_n is the ton-mile freight rate for shipping via the new medium, can now ship to the city for a cost equal to half the market price of the good.

Farms located some distance off the canal or railroad right-of-way could also ship to the city, provided the sum of the wagon haulage to the canal or railroad and canal or rail freight to the city did not reduce their profits below the normal rate of return. Under the assumptions we have made, the new area of feasible commercial production includes not only the original area that depends solely upon wagon haulage but also a new area bounded by two straight lines starting at the boundary between commercial and subsistence farming and converging on the railroad at the point $\frac{1}{2}P/t_n$ distant from the city. Economic activity within this area thus shifts from self-sufficiency and subsistence to market production.

TABLE 6.5

Western and Upper Southern Grain Exports

Year	Flour Million Barrels	Flour % Shipped East	Corn Million Bushels	Corn % Shipped East
1835	0.4	30	1.0	2
1839	0.8	47	1.0	2
1844	1.5	70	1.5	10
1849	3.0	69	6.0	61
1853	3.0	73	8.0	63
1857	4.0	66	12.0	68
1860	5.0	78	24.0	81

Sources: A. L. Kohlmeier, *The Old Northwest as the Keystone of the Arch to the Federal Union* (Bloomington: Principia Press, 1938) and Albert Fishlow, *American Railroads and the Transformation of the Antebellum Economy* (Cambridge: Harvard, 1965). Both cited in Diane Lindstrom, "Southern Dependence upon Interregional Grain Supplies," *Agricultural History* 44 (1970): 112. Reprinted in William N. Parker, ed., *The Structure of the Cotton Economy of the Antebellum South* (Washington, D.C.: Agricultural History Society, 1970): 112.

TABLE 6.6

Shipping Distances for Various Commodities by Different Media before Transport Costs exceed 50 Percent of Market Price, Circa 1860 (miles, rounded to the nearest 10)

Commodity	Road	Mississippi River	Erie Canal	Great Lakes	New York Railroad
Farm Products					
Corn	90	3,670	1,370	13,750	660
Wheat	150	5,990	2,240	Anywhere	1,080
Flour	180	7,350	2,750	Anywhere	1,320
Tobacco	400	16,220	6,060	Anywhere	2,910
Butter	770	Anywhere	11,610	Anywhere	5,580
Cotton	730	Anywhere	11,110	Anywhere	5,340
Tea	4,000	Anywhere	Anywhere	Anywhere	Anywhere
Manufactured Products					
Pig iron	80	3,310	1,240	12,250	590
Iron bar	190	7,590	2,840	Anywhere	1,360
Nails	240	9,730	3,640	Anywhere	1,750

Notes: Market prices from U.S. Bureau of the Census, *Historical Statistics of the United States* (Washington, D.C.: Government Printing Office, 1975): Series E123–E134. Transport costs from Table 6.3.

FIGURE 6.10

The Impact of Improved Transportation on Economic Activity on a Featureless Plain

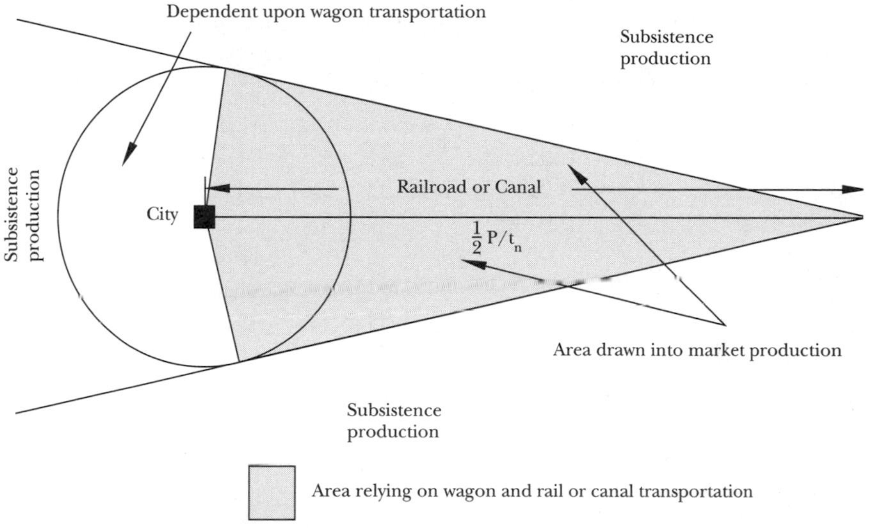

The introduction of the steamboat on the western rivers greatly reduced the costs of interregional trade and induced early midwestern farmers to switch from self-sufficient to market production. In 1818, for example, pork cost $7.50 a barrel more in New Orleans than at the packinghouse in Cincinnati. Ten years later that figure had fallen to about $2.40, and by the late 1850s the differential was only about $1.25 (see Table 6.7).[20] The differential for wheat flour over the same period was cut by about 70 percent. Cost reductions for upstream transport were even greater. Upstream rates in 1860 were only 5 to 10 percent as high as they had been before the steamboat.[21]

The effect of the canal system was almost as startling. After 1825 the Erie Canal made it possible to ship grain and meat by water from lake ports in Ohio all the way to New York City. Western canal construction in the 1830s extended water routes into the interior of Ohio and Indiana. Pork that might have cost as much as $10 a barrel to wrestle over the Appalachians from Cincinnati to New York in 1820 could be transported by water for about $3.50 a barrel in the 1830s (see Table 6.8). Over the same period the differential in the price of flour was cut roughly in half.

Improved transportation also increased land values along and adjacent

[20] North 1961).
[21] Taylor (1962).

TABLE 6.7

Difference between Wholesale Commodity Prices in Cincinnati and New Orleans

Period	Lard ($/lb)	Pork ($/barrel)	Flour ($/barrel)	Corn ($/barrel)
1816–20	0.051	7.57	2.16	NA
1821–25	0.027	2.81	2.37	0.59
1826–30	0.024	2.41	1.75	0.59
1831–35	0.017	2.03	1.29	0.64
1836–40	0.014	2.67	1.66	0.49
1841–45	0.006	1.66	0.61	0.14
1846–50	0.005	1.31	0.60	0.20
1851–55	0.006	1.24	0.59	0.16
1856–60	0.007	1.27	0.63	0.21
1856–60 difference as % of 1816–20 difference	14%	17%	29%	35%

Source: Thomas Berry, *Western Prices before 1861* (Cambridge: Harvard University Press, 1943). Copyright © 1943 by the President and Fellows of Harvard College. Reprinted by permission. Cited in Douglass North, *Economic Growth of the United States 1790–1860* (New York: W. W. Norton, 1966): 261.

TABLE 6.8

Difference between Wholesale Commodity Prices in Cincinnati and New York

Period	Lard ($/lb.)	Pork ($/barrel)	Flour ($/barrel)	Corn ($/barrel)
1816–20	0.048	9.53	2.48	0.48
1821–25	0.031	4.46	2.81	0.39
1826–30	0.026	4.18	1.78	0.36
1831–35	0.025	3.48	1.43	0.38
1836–40	0.020	3.11	1.02	0.42
1841–45	0.011	2.25	1.37	0.30
1846–50	0.010	1.06	1.68	0.36
1851–55	0.007	1.56	1.36	0.31
1856–60	0.004	1.18	0.28	0.27
1856–60 difference as a % of 1816–20 difference	11%	14%	33%	60%

Source: Thomas Berry, *Western Prices before 1861* (Cambridge: Harvard University Press, 1943). Copyright © 1943 by the President and Fellows of Harvard College. Reprinted by permission. Cited in Douglass North, *Economic Growth of the United States 1790–1860* (New York: W. W. Norton, 1966): 261.

FIGURE 6.11

Transportation Improvements and Land Values

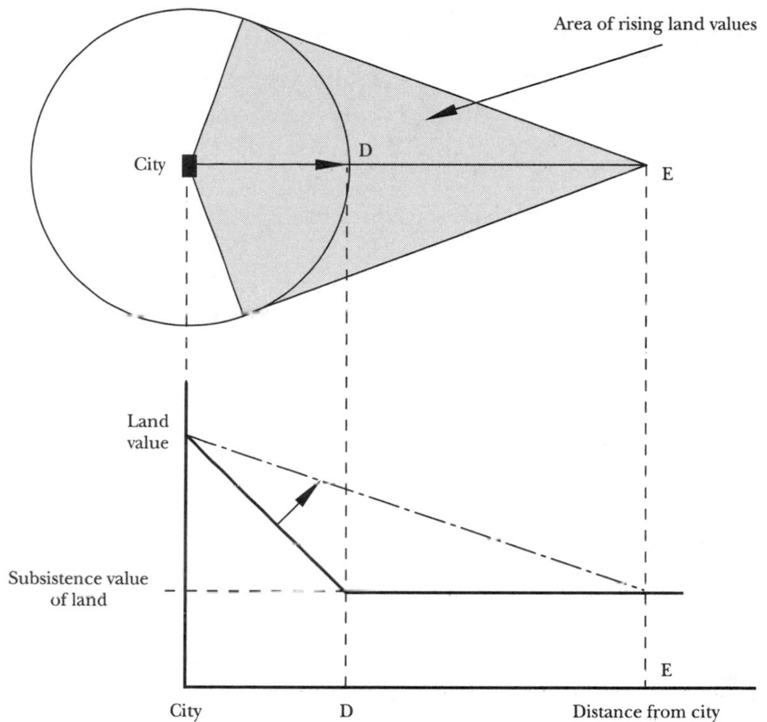

to the right-of-way in the area (Figure 6.11) because the land could now earn at least normal profit from commercial production. If one assumes a perfect market for land, competition among buyers would drive up land values by the amount just sufficient to eliminate any supernormal profit for a new entrant. Existing owners capture this one-time capital gain from their secure property rights in this scarce resource—land with profitable market access.

And landowners were very well aware of the possibilities. For instance, Colonel Busey, a leading citizen and banker in Urbana, Illinois, purchased an eighty-acre tract for $100 in what is now the adjacent city of Champaign. He sold it for $1,600 once the Illinois Central Railroad was built through the property. Nor was he unusually farsighted and aware of the economic possibilities to be generated by improved transportation. One of the leading commercial magazines in the antebellum period, *De Bow's Review,* published a diagram (Figure 6.12) that virtually duplicates Figure 6.10, except that the magazine actually attached dollar values to the anticipated rise in land value at different points along the railroad line.

FIGURE 6.12

Railroad Results Illustrated in the Case of a Railroad of 35 Miles

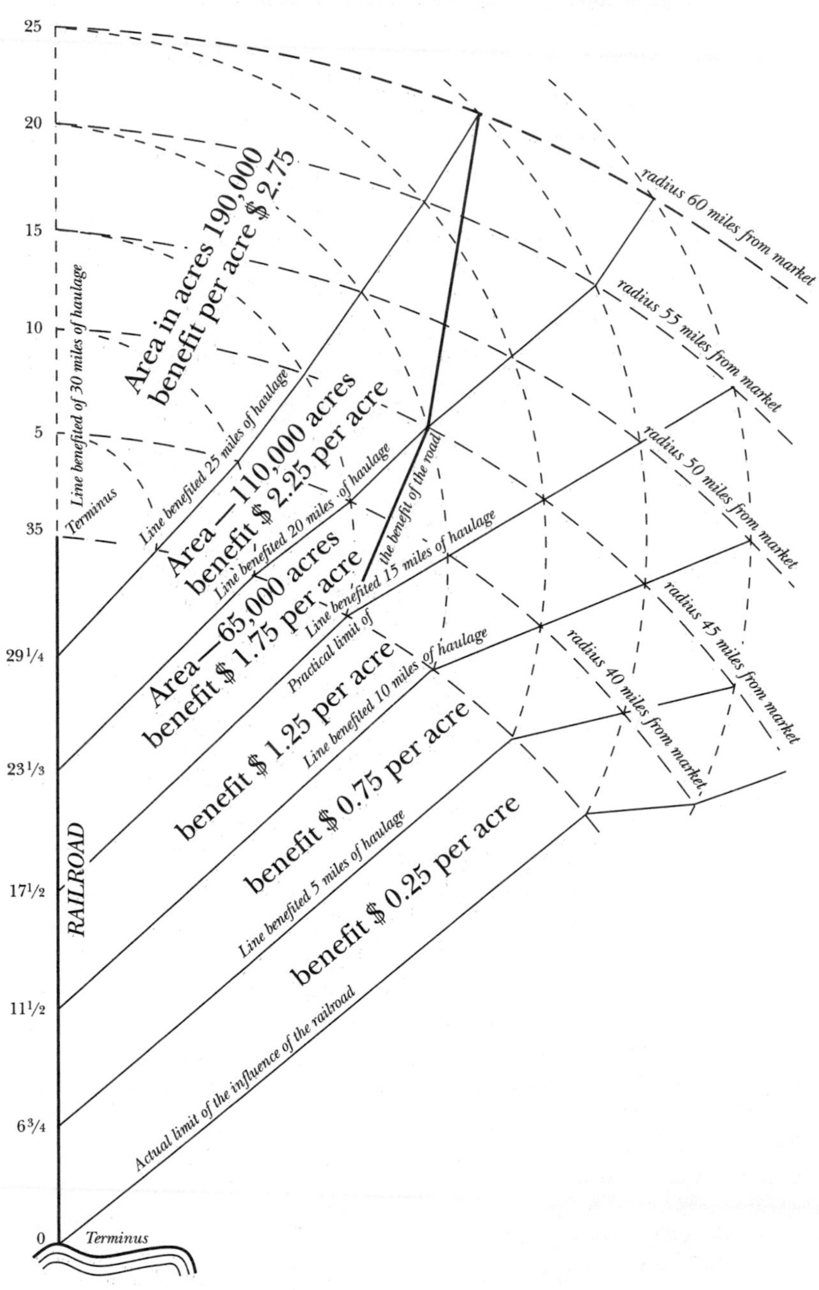

Source: "Railroad Influence on Landed Property," *De Bow's Review* 11 (1851): facing 590.

The rise in land values, contingent upon construction of a new and cheaper transport media, is a perfect example of what is called a positive externality. Landowners along the projected right-of-way stand to reap substantial capital gains from completion of the project and benefit independent of their participation and sponsorship of the project. There is, therefore, also a free rider problem. Security of property rights means that these landowners cannot be denied the profits of land value appreciation even if they do nothing to promote it. Indeed, there is even an economic incentive to oppose it. If voluntary agreement is required to secure the right-of-way, there is the distinct possibility that an intransigent landowner astride the projected right-of-way might hold up construction unless bought off by the other beneficiaries. In this way a shrewd operator could capture virtually the entire private gain. For this reason courts and legislatures often enter the picture through the use of their powers of eminent domain—the right to take private property for public purposes without consent, provided "fair" compensation is paid, with the courts determining what is fair.

Government and Internal Improvements

Legislatures, both state and federal, became involved in the debate over internal improvements, particularly improved transportation, because of the tremendous social importance of these changes. The potential social benefits from the development of unsettled areas seemed to be large. This provided a rationale for direct state sponsorship of internal improvement. States also underwrote privately funded projects, often by pledging the taxing powers of a sovereign body as a guarantee on bond redemption. Such state involvement often reduced the private costs without a compensating reduction in benefits and was therefore eagerly sought by rent-seeking entrepreneurs. States became particularly active in those projects rejected by the private sector—that is, those improvements in which the private cost was thought to exceed the private gain.

In all too many cases the private-sector appraisal proved correct. By 1860 total canal investment was approximately $188 million, of which states had provided almost 73 percent one way or another.[22] Rates of return were typically low and often negative. State guarantees brought financial ruin upon many of the states in the wake of the 1839–43 depression. Among those defaulting were Illinois, Indiana, Ohio, and Pennsylvania.

The federal government was also involved in financing internal improvements amid fierce and continuing debates over constitutionality and because of differing sectional interests. The immediate motivation behind the early federal sponsorship was the woeful inadequacy of the nation's in-

[22] Goodrich (1961); Segal (1961).

ternal transportation system, which had been painfully obvious during the War of 1812–14. The response was the same as after the world wars: Build more roads.

The principal federal road project was the National Road, now U.S. 40, which stretched from Cumberland, Maryland, to Wheeling, (West) Virginia, on the Ohio River. The road was first proposed in the Gallatin plan, but construction was delayed until 1811. Support for federally underwritten roads, however, was sporadic. While President James Madison in 1815 had urged the building of roads and canals under "national authority," two years later he vetoed the congressional plan to implement the proposals. Similarly his successor, President James Monroe, vetoed a bill to raise funds for construction of the National Road by levying tolls, arguing that federally sponsored internal improvements were unconstitutional. Perhaps the most famous (or infamous) presidential veto of internal improvements was Andrew Jackson's veto of the Maysville Road in 1830, though in this case, since the road lay wholly within the state of Kentucky, its constitutionality really was questionable.

Organized sectional opposition came from New England and the South. Both saw internal improvements as benefiting the western territories and recognized that federally funded improvements could be financed only by additional federal taxes. New England already had a comprehensive network of state-financed roads and stood to gain little in the way of new projects. Indeed, better roads to the West would only make outmigration easier and flood the market with a return flow of cheap western foodstuffs that would undercut New England's own farmers with their marginal lands. Opposition from the South reflected the fear that speedier western development would upset the fragile balance between anti- and proslavery forces in Congress.

Some projects could be undertaken only under federal aegis. The western rivers, by virtue of being navigable, fell under federal control. Moreover, these rivers were generally the boundaries between states. Yet even here the federal government was reluctant to make a decisive commitment to improve navigation. Most critical was the removal of obstructions, particularly snags and sawyers—the waterlogged trees embedded in the river bottom that served as spears lying just below the water surface. Snags and sawyers accounted for 419 of the 736 steamboats lost on the rivers between 1815 and 1850—perhaps 15 to 20 percent of all tonnage built over the period—substantially increasing the costs of shipping and insurance premiums. Costs of snag removal were fairly modest—about $4 a snag—but even this small cost exceeded the benefit that any private person could expect to reap from removing a snag. The potential benefits to society through lower freight and insurance charges accelerated midwestern development, and reduced loss of life, however, far outweighed the opportunity cost and may have yielded a higher rate of return than many other investments. The problem was who should pay and how. Because the rivers were federal interstate highways, tolls could not be levied by the states or private agencies to support this activity. Only the federal government could collect tolls, but it was unwilling to do so.

The debate over federal funding of improvements did not end here. It continued, as we shall see in Chapter 16, with the railroads through federal land grants, a policy begun first as a means of financing roads and canals. It is a policy still hotly debated today whenever new highways are built, locks and dams on the Mississippi are improved, or airport facilities are upgraded. As such, federal support for transportation improvements is one of the longest continuing public policy debates in our history.

Bibliography

Atack, Jeremy, and Fred Bateman. *To Their Own Soil: Agriculture in the Antebellum North.* Ames: Iowa State University Press, 1987.

Berry, Thomas. *Western Prices before 1861.* Cambridge: Harvard University Press, 1943.

Callahan, Colleen, and William Hutchinson. "Antebellum Interregional Trade in Agricultural Goods: Preliminary Results." *Journal of Economic History* 40 (1980): 25–32.

Callender, Guy S. "The Early Transportation and Banking Enterprises of the States in Relation to the Growth of the Corporation." *Quarterly Journal of Economics* 17 (1902): 111–62.

Fishlow, Albert. *American Railroads and the Transformation of the Ante-Bellum Economy.* Cambridge: Harvard University Press, 1965.

———. "Antebellum Interregional Trade Reconsidered." *American Economic Review* 54 (1964): 352–64. Reprinted in Ralph Andreano, ed., *New Views in American Economic Development.* Cambridge: Harvard University Press, 1966: 187–200.

———. "Discussion." *Journal of Economic History* 27 (1964): 561–66.

———. "Internal Transportation." In *American Economic Growth,* ed. Lance Davis et al. New York: Harper & Row, 1972: 468–547.

Gallman, Robert. "Self-Sufficiency of the Cotton Economy of the Antebellum South." *Agricultural History* 44 (1970): 5–24. Reprinted in William Parker, ed. *The Structure of the Cotton Economy of the Antebellum South.* Washington D.C.: Agricultural History Society, 1970: 5–24.

Goodrich, Carter. *Canals and American Economic Development.* New York: Columbia University Press, 1961.

Haites, Erik, and James Mak. "Ohio and Mississippi River Transportation 1810–1860." *Explorations in Economic History* 8 (1970): 153–80.

———, ———, and Gary Walton. *Western River Transportation: The Era of Early Internal Development 1810–1860.* Baltimore: Johns Hopkins University Press, 1975.

Hunter, Louis. *Steamboats on the Western Rivers.* Cambridge: Harvard University Press, 1949.

Hutchinson, William, and Samuel H. Williamson. "The Self-Sufficiency of the Antebellum South: Estimates of the Food Supply." *Journal of Economic History* 31 (1971): 591–612.

Lindstrom, Diane. "Southern Dependence upon Interregional Grain Supplies." *Agricultural History* 44 (1970): 101–14. Reprinted in William Parker, ed., *The Structure of the Cotton Economy of the Antebellum South.* Washington, D.C.: Agricultural History Society, 1970: 101–13.

Mak, James, and Gary Walton. "The Persistence of Old Technologies: The Case of Flatboats." *Journal of Economic History* 33 (1973): 444–51.

———, and ———. "Steamboats and the Great Productivity Surge in River Transportation." *Journal of Economic History* 32 (1972): 619–40.

Neimi, Albert. "A Further Look at Interregional Canals and Economic Specialization 1820–1840." *Explorations in Economic History* 7 (1970): 499–522.

North, Douglass C. *The Economic Growth of the United States, 1790–1860.* (Englewood Cliffs, N.J.: Prentice-Hall, 1961.

Ransom, Roger. "Social Returns from Public Transport Investment: A Case Study of the Ohio Canal." *Journal of Political Economy* 78 (1970): 1041–64.

———. "Interregional Canals and Economic Specialization in the Antebellum United States." *Explorations in Entrepreneurial History* 5 (1967): 12–35.

Rothenberg, Winifred. "The Market and Massachusetts Farmers, 1750–1855." *Journal of Economic History* 41 (1981): 283–314.

Schmidt, Louis B. "Internal Commerce and the Development of a National Economy before 1860." *Journal of Political Economy* 47 (1939): 798–822.

Segal, Harvey. "Canals and Economic Development." In *Canals and American Economic Development,* ed. Carter Goodrich. New York: Columbia University Press, 1961: 216–48.

———. "Cycles of Canal Construction." Ibid.: 169–215.

Taylor, George Rogers. *The Transportation Revolution 1815–1860.* New York: Holt Rinehart, 1962.

The beginnings of industrialization

7

Although British mercantilist policy restricted the development of a domestic colonial manufacturing sector in favor of imports from the mother country, the colonists developed several successful industries. Flour mills, lumber mills, leather tanneries, and the like were ubiquitous, and America was the world's leading producer of pig iron. More sophisticated, higher value-added manufactured products, however, were generally imported until President Jefferson's trade embargo in 1807 interrupted the flow of imported substitutes. Then domestic industry expanded rapidly. The new manufactures that emerged were different from those which had existed earlier. They involved new products, new technologies, new forms of organization, made new demands upon traditional sources of power, and required new levels of labor commitment.

Early Industrialization in New England

Industrialization began in New England. Why? Consider the following simple model: Suppose there are two sectors in the economy—agriculture and nonagriculture—and three factors of production—land, labor, and capital. Land is specific to agriculture, but labor and capital can be employed in either sector and can flow between them. In New England, land—especially good, fertile land—was also limited in supply. Once the land in the river bottoms, especially the Connecticut river valley, and along the narrow coastal plain had been taken up, only marginal rocky upland areas with thin, acidic, and unproductive soils remained. Farms in the favored locations were highly productive, thanks to nature's bounty and proximity to markets. As a result, the marginal product of labor—the additional output resulting from the employment of one more person—in New England agriculture was high for those fortunate enough to have good land in a good location but declined sharply as the additional labor was forced to work on less and less productive and more remote land. The marginal product of labor is represented by the curve $MP_{ag\text{-}Northeast}$ in Figure 7.1, Panel A. This curve is the derived demand for agricultural labor in the Northeast. Returns to manufacturing, on the other hand, decline much less rapidly than in agriculture, as shown by the curve MP_{mfg}. Injections of capital or improvements in technology in a sector shift the marginal product curve for that sector upward. In the absence of restrictions on factor mobility, such as cultural norms and prejudices, licensing requirements, and the like, resources, including labor, tend to flow to their highest valued use. Thus labor is employed first in agriculture on the best land, but as the labor force grows, new workers are forced to work on land of progressively lower quality. Both the marginal product of labor and the wage decline. So long as the labor force is smaller than N*, people work only in agriculture because agriculture generates higher incomes. Once the labor force exceeds this critical level, though, some of the additional workers will seek employment outside agriculture where wages and productivity are higher. With a population of N' in the Northeast, for example, N_1 would be employed in agriculture while N_2 would find work in manufactures.

Where land was more abundant and homogeneous, as in the Midwest, the marginal product of labor in agriculture declined much more slowly as sectoral employment increased (Figure 7.1, Panel B). Moreover, continued increases in the quantity of land available for settlement through public land sales maintained or increased the marginal product of labor in the agricultural sector by providing more good land to farm. Consequently, proportionately more persons in that region worked in agriculture and continued to enter agriculture even after industrialization had begun.

The expansion of settlement into the Middle West with its fertile soils and development of transportation routes to the East—initially the Great Lakes and Erie Canal and later the railroads—had a devastating impact upon New England agriculture. The flood of western farm products onto East Coast markets drove down prices, reducing the value of the marginal product of labor in eastern agriculture. At the same time, lower transport costs meant higher farm gate prices in the Midwest, thus increasing the value of the marginal product in the West and stimulating increased agricultural production. As a result, thousands abandoned unproductive and marginal agriculture in the East. Instead of heading west toward the frontier and reestablishing themselves as midwestern farmers, though, some of the disillusioned eastern agricultural laborers sought alternative employment in manufacturing.[1]

[1] Field (1978).

FIGURE 7.1

Occupational Choice between Agriculture and Manufacturing in the Northeast and Midwest

Panel A

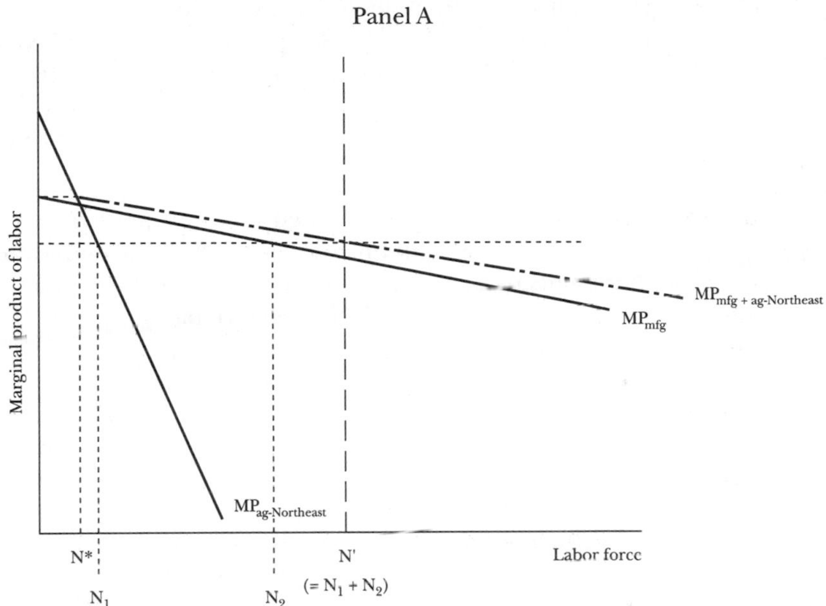

Panel B

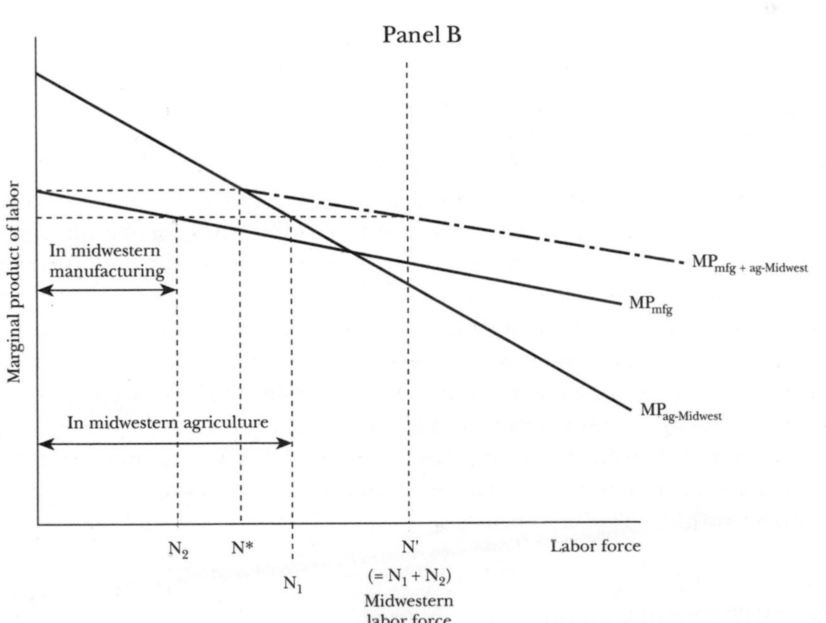

As a Massachusetts House Report remarked:

> the ruggedness of the soil, reluctantly yielding but moderate crops to the most skillful and persevering industry . . . [and] the increased and rapidly increasing facilities of intercommunication with cheaper and more productive lands than are to be found in this region . . . all conspire to produce conviction that the sons and daughters of New England are presented . . . with the alternative of becoming essentially a manufacturing people, or of bidding adieu to their native hills, the land, the home, and the graves of their forefathers and following the rising glories of the west.[2]

In 1820 agricultural workers accounted for 58 percent of the Massachusetts labor force. By 1840, when absolute agricultural employment in Massachusetts was at its peak, the share of labor in agriculture had fallen to only 40 percent. In the next decade farm employment fell precipitously from 87,800 to 55,700, or only 15 percent of the labor force. This precipitous decline coincided with the opening of rail links to the West.

Not everyone was pushed out of agriculture. Massachusetts farming was not so backward and demoralized that farmers quit wholesale rather than adapt their crop mix to new market conditions. The successful New England farmers switched to more intensive animal husbandry, especially dairying, in which they continued to enjoy a comparative advantage by virtue of their location and product perishability, and that evened out labor demand over the year.[3] On the other hand, the "pull" from manufacturing intensified as a result of rapid and widespread productivity growth in the manufacturing sector.[4] Industrialization in New England was well under way before transportation improvements opened eastern markets to western farm products.

In 1790 the textile mill of Almy and Brown opened in Pawtucket, Rhode Island, using British technology pirated by Samuel Slater. This venture was financed out of the merchant capital accumulated by the partners and was dependent for its success upon the ability to imitate and improve the British water frames for spinning many threads at once. The labor was supplied primarily by women and children. Most early manufacturing followed this pattern. The pace of industrialization accelerated when the embargo increased demand for domestically produced goods and forced mercantile capital to seek new outlets. The Lowells of Boston, for example, used their extensive mercantile fortune to establish the nation's first industrial city on the falls of the Merrimack River—Lowell, Massachusetts.

The labor for industry came from the farm sector, but people were not driven out of farming by western agricultural competition lowering the mar-

[2] Massachusetts House Report, Committee on Education, March 17, 1836.
[3] Rothenberg (1981).
[4] Sokoloff (1986).

ginal revenue product in agriculture below subsistence or below that in alternative sectors. Rather, manufacturing offered employment to under- or unutilized sources of labor—women and children. Contemporaries certainly recognized this. Alexander Hamilton, for example, in arguing for federal support of manufactures, wrote "the husbandman himself experiences a new source of profit and support from the increased industry of his wife and daughters . . . women and children are rendered more useful, and the latter more early useful by manufacturing establishments than they otherwise would be."

The potential role of women and children in industrialization has been formalized and expanded by Claudia Goldin and Kenneth Sokoloff. They develop a two-good (agricultural and manufactured), two-factor (men and women), two-region (North and South) general equilibrium model around the well-documented observation that the earnings of women and children in the North relative to those of men were low and employment opportunities for women and children were limited compared with the South. Agriculture was the dominant sector in both economies, but factors—especially labor—did not flow freely between them because of cultural and institutional factors (such as slavery in the South and family ties). As a result, factor prices did not equalize between the regions, and products flowed instead.

The Goldin-Sokoloff hypothesis is that industrialization would begin first in those areas where the marginal products of women and children were the lowest relative to those of men. Further, the greater the productivity gap between factors in agriculture, the faster relative wages would increase when manufacturing was introduced. This well describes the situation in New England at the start of the nineteenth century. Extensive dairy farming and intensive truck farming—that is, fruit and vegetable farming—had not yet emerged in the region to provide productive employment to women and children as well as men. Toward the end of the antebellum period, however, farmers did shift their crop mixes, and agriculture once again began to compete with the mills for the labor services of women.

Suppose now that the domestic price of manufactured goods rises relative to agricultural commodities. This worsening of the agricultural terms of trade might be the result of higher import duties, the effects of the trade embargo, or changes in the costs of transportation as well as increased midwestern agricultural competition. But whatever the source, the effect is to increase the value of the marginal product in manufacturing relative to agriculture. As a result, the northern economy will be induced to switch some of its resources into manufacturing. This will induce labor, especially women and children, into manufacturing and raise relative factor prices in the North. The North begins to industrialize. To induce the same transition in the South would require a much greater economic shock because of the relatively higher ratio of female to male wages. This would delay relative factor price equalization there. Nevertheless, at some point the South will begin to industrialize. The model predicts that the manufacturing sector in the South will be absolutely smaller than that in the North and that the North will produce a higher ratio of manufactured to agricultural goods than the South. Moreover, the model predicts that factor intensities in the North will bound those in the South. Thus, within the context of the two-factor model, northern agriculture will be more male-intensive than the southern, while northern manufacturing will be more female-intensive than southern manufacturing.

Relative wage data suggest that women and children did indeed have very low productivity in agriculture in the North at the start of the nineteenth century. On the basis of scattered data, Goldin and Sokoloff estimate that women's wages were less than 30 percent of the male wage in the North in the early nineteenth century while the child to male wage was even lower—approaching zero according to some estimates. By about 1850, however, the female wage had increased to between 46 and 51 percent of the male wage. This was still less than the range for women in the South, where women earned 57 to 76 percent of the male wage. Labor force participation rates in manufacturing among women under thirty in New England also show a marked rise from virtually zero at the start of the century to at least 10 percent by 1832 and at least 20 percent by 1850.

The increased number of women in the labor force was not a consequence of the growth of a single industry such as textiles, although the rapid rise and blossoming of that industry contributed much to the early growth of industrial job opportunities for women. Rather it was a widespread phenomenon, particularly among larger firms perhaps because the greater mechanization in these firms permitted the use of less skilled labor. Despite the sharp rise in female labor force participation rates, women were a declining fraction of the labor force throughout the nineteenth century as industrialization proceeded rapidly. The reason is still a matter of speculation, but it may reflect the slowdown in the growth of such female-intensive industries as textiles and clothing, technological change, and the rise in female wages relative to male.

The Emergence of the Cotton Textile Industry

Textiles were the first major manufacturing industry to expand rapidly. Several reasons explain why industrialization began with this industry. First, potent new technologies that could increase tenfold the amount of cotton thread that a worker could spin in a day had been developed in Great Britain. Although British law prohibited the export of these new spinning machines, it could not prevent Samuel Slater and his colleagues from emigrating to America, taking their skill in building the machines with them. Second, cloth was expensive relative to its weight and bulk. Consequently, high transportation costs were not a critical barrier to centralized production.

Slater's mill employed water frames—mechanical, water-driven devices for spinning many threads at once. These new spinning techniques, substituting capital for labor, were so clearly superior that the mills soon spread to dozens of New England towns that offered adequate waterpower. Spinning mills, moreover, received a welcome boost of protection from foreign competition during their critical shakedown period. From 1807, the beginning of President Jefferson's embargo against trade, until 1815, the resolution of the War of 1812, imports virtually vanished (see Chapter 5).

Spinning was only the first stage in cloth manufacture. The second more complex step consisted of weaving the thread or yarn into fabric. For a short period in Britain after the introduction of new spinning technology, weaving was a bottleneck in textile production. In the United States, however, power looms were introduced soon after the end of wartime import protection. The cost reduction that the large looms generated was essential for industry survival in the face of the onslaught of cheap British cloth that arrived with the peace treaty in 1815. Despite the presence of the new, technologically superior looms, however, many firms still failed.

Francis Lowell's Boston Manufacturing Company in Waltham, Massachusetts was one of the first to use the power looms. But Lowell's factory is better remembered for organizational rather than technical innovation. His Waltham mill—huge by contemporary standards—was built in 1814 at a cost of $300,000. It was the first to integrate spinning and weaving in one plant, a system that allowed for considerable economies in the use of labor. New questions of inventory handling and distribution were answered with a degree of skill previously unknown in American enterprise. Lowell solved the problem of finding dependable, inexpensive labor both strong enough to operate the machinery and willing to spend endless days in the factory by recruiting young single farm women. They proved ideal. They worked long, hard hours in the mills that left little time or energy for active social lives. Their living arrangements in closely supervised group quarters calmed parental fears about their moral welfare. After a few years the "Lowell girls," as they were called, could return home with tidy dowries.

The price elasticity of demand for cotton cloth (unlike many goods) was high because it presented an attractive alternative to wool. As the new techniques lowered production costs and price, sales expanded rapidly, opening up a huge market capable of supporting large-scale production. Output of cotton cloth grew at an average annual rate of 15.4 percent from 1815 to 1833 (Figure 7.2). Growth slowed to the still-respectable rate of 5.1 percent from 1834 to 1860. On the eve of the Civil War the cotton manufacturing in-

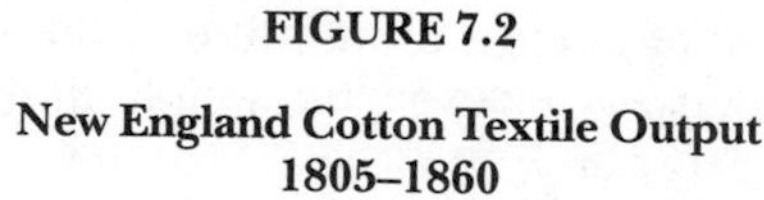

FIGURE 7.2

New England Cotton Textile Output 1805–1860

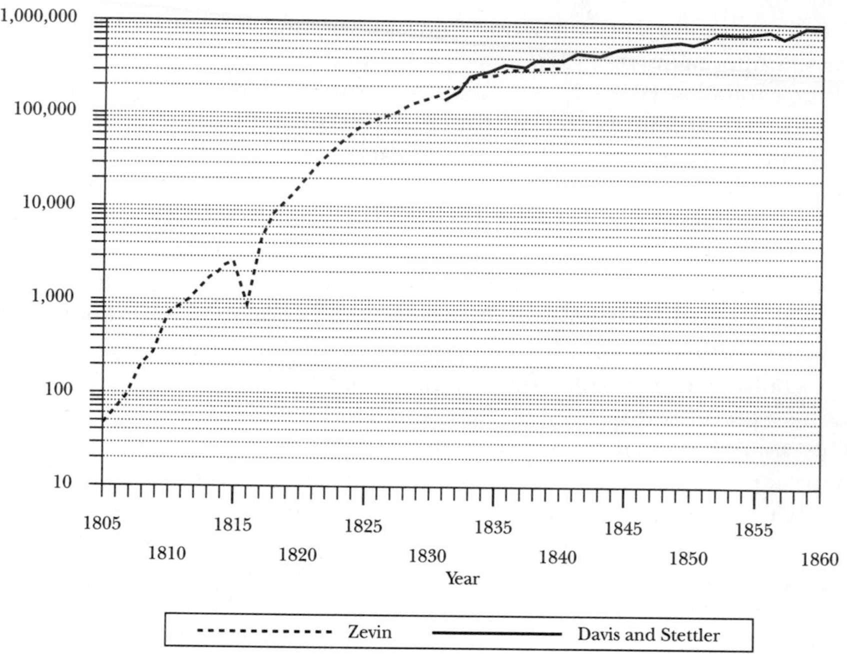

Sources: Lance Davis and Louis Stettler, "The New England Textile Industry, 1825–1860," in National Bureau of Economic Research, *Output, Employment and Productivity in the United States after 1800* (New York: Columbia University Press, 1966): 213–38. Robert B. Zevin, "'The Growth of Cotton Textile Production after 1815," in *The Reinterpretation of American Economic History*, ed. Robert W. Fogel and Stanley L. Engerman (New York: Harper and Row, 1971): 122–147.

dustry employed 115,000 workers, producing about 7 percent of manufacturing income and more than 2 percent of total commodity production in what had become a very large economy.

Cotton textiles, however, were not the only industry to grow in this period. Wool textiles also benefited from some of the same technological and organizational improvements that generated explosive growth in cotton. But after an initial growth spurt wool steadily lost ground to cotton for two reasons. First, the technical problems involved in reducing production costs were inherently harder to solve in the wool industry because animal fibers proved more difficult to handle with machines. Second, sales of wool cloth were less responsive to price reductions; thus the financial incentives for mechanization were less apparent. Wool remained more expensive to manufacture, and wool clothing harder to clean; it could not hope to compete directly with cotton in the great market for cheap, lightweight clothing.

Productivity Change in Cotton Textiles

Technological change in cotton textiles is symbolic of the critical role technology can play in growth. Innovations in textile production, embodied in new machinery and new factories, changed the landscape of Great Britain in the late eighteenth century and performed similar miracles in New England in the early nineteenth. The great technological benchmarks of the American textile industry—Slater's mechanized spinning mill, mechanized weaving, and the big integrated factory at Waltham—all came in the first quarter of the nineteenth century, yet cloth output continued to grow at a dramatic pace after 1825. As a result, some historians have assumed that technology, after the initial surge, must have taken a backseat to other productivity-increasing factors.

Casual historical associations between discrete technical improvements—or lack thereof—and the rate of productivity change are easy enough to understand. Indeed, we generally think of new technology as being embodied in new machines: On day number one the weaver sweats over a hand loom to produce a few yards of cloth. On day two the wily engineer arrives and hooks up a new loom to a waterwheel. As a result, the same weaver (or perhaps even a less skilled worker) now produces three or four or ten times as much cloth in an afternoon. This dramatic increase in output sometimes happens, as it did in the textile industry before 1825, but it isn't the only technological road to higher productivity. Examination of the records of early New England cotton textile mills shows that technical progress apparently continued long after the shiny new machines were in place. The continuing growth in productivity has been attributed to improvements in manufacturing technique gained through experience—a process known as learning-by-doing.[5]

Between 1833 and 1839 labor productivity in cotton textiles was increasing at a rate of 6.67 percent per year (Table 7.1). Paul David estimates that much of this increase took place because each worker tended more machines and processed more raw cotton per hour. Changing the factor proportions within the existing technical know-how raised labor productivity by 4.07 percent per year (=3.33% + 0.74%). Such a result is not surprising. In periods of rapid growth the diffusion of state-of-the-art technology to old facilities can account for great productivity increases. In the case of cotton textiles, diffusion was rapid because the industry was geographically concentrated in New England, especially Massachusetts.

[5] Davis and Stettler (1966).

TABLE 7.1

Sources of Labor Productivity Growth in Cotton Textiles

Source of Productivity Change	1833–39 Average Annual Growth (%)	1833–39 Portion of Total Productivity Increase (%)	1855–59 Average Annual Growth (%)	1855–59 Portion of Total Productivity Increase (%)
Increased capital per unit of labor	0.74	11	0.43	13
Increased raw materials per unit of labor	3.33	50	1.60	50
Improvements in labor force quality	0.33	5	0.33	10
Improvements in machinery technology	0.25	4	0.30	9
Learning-by-doing	2.02	30	0.54	17
TOTAL	6.67	100	3.20	100

Source: Paul A. David, "Learning by Doing and Tariff Protection: A Reconsideration of the Case of the Ante-Bellum United States Cotton Textile Industry," *Journal of Economic History* 30 (1970): 521-601. Reprinted by permission of Cambridge University Press.

What is more surprising about labor productivity growth in the American cotton textile industry is the high rate of technical progress. This is the difference between the 6.67 percent overall productivity gain and the 4.07 percent attributable to increases in raw cotton and machinery per worker. The net 2.60 percent average annual gain is equal to (or better than) the productivity gains achieved by modern industry since World War II. Such a finding hardly conforms to the portrait of a technically stagnant industry. More striking still is the way technology improved. Of the 2.60 percent, David attributes only 0.58 percent to improvements in labor force quality and in textile machinery. The rest (2.02 percent) he attributes to learning-by-doing—in the form of subtle improvements in organization and efficiency achieved through accumulated experience in operating textile mills. Such learning-by-doing provides a strong ex post justification for tariff protection of the textile industry if we accept the argument that the industry remained dependent upon the tariff in the 1830s.[6] The overall rate of productivity increase (3.20 percent) was much lower in the 1855–59 period,

[6] Bils (1984); see also Chapter 5.

as was the proportion of productivity gain attributable to learning-by-doing. This latter finding can be attributed to the fact that by the 1850s textile output was expanding at a much slower rate, so one would expect that learning, represented by accumulated labor experience in textile production, had slowed, too.

A part of the increased labor productivity in cotton textiles in the 1830s and 1840s may have resulted from organizational changes that increased the intensity of work.[7] While the cumulative number of days worked by each weaver explains a significant proportion of the variability in output per hour as implied by the learning-by-doing hypothesis, so, too, does the management requirement that each worker oversee more looms. Indeed, demands that workers oversee more looms and other, more subtle changes in the organization of work were accompanied by the substitution of Irish for Yankee workers. These new workers were less willing—or less able—to resist intensification because of poverty and because they had fewer alternatives. Not all efforts to increase work intensity, though, were successful: When closer supervision of the workers was tried, workers often resisted by slowing down rather than speeding up.

The Growth of Cotton Textile Output

The huge increases in cotton textile production came at the same time that the factory system had sharply reduced the cost of making cloth. Consequently, it seems reasonable to assume that the cost reductions were the cause of the increased sales. The inference is simple: In a competitive marketplace, lowered costs are passed on to consumers in the form of lowered prices. If the demand for cotton cloth were price-elastic, then technical improvements would help explain the observed increase in output. The cotton cloth market could thus look like Figure 7.3, output increasing from A to B as supply shifted downward along an elastic demand curve. By the logic of Figure 7.3, productivity change assumes an enormous independent role in economic development by shifting the supply curve and driving the growth of the largest industry in the nation's young industrial sector.

This supply-driven explanation of cotton textile growth is not, however, the only explanation consistent with falling prices and rising output. Theoretically textile expansion could be driven by demand alone, as depicted in Figure 7.4. The declining long-term price of textiles, however, would be possible only if the supply curve for textiles were sloped downward as a result of economies of scale. More realistic is a scenario somewhere in between the all-supply and all-demand explanation; changes in both supply and demand

[7] Lazonick and Brush (1985).

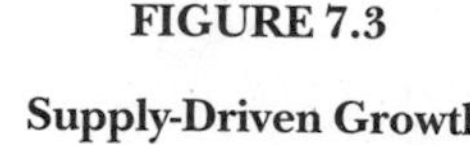
FIGURE 7.3

Supply-Driven Growth

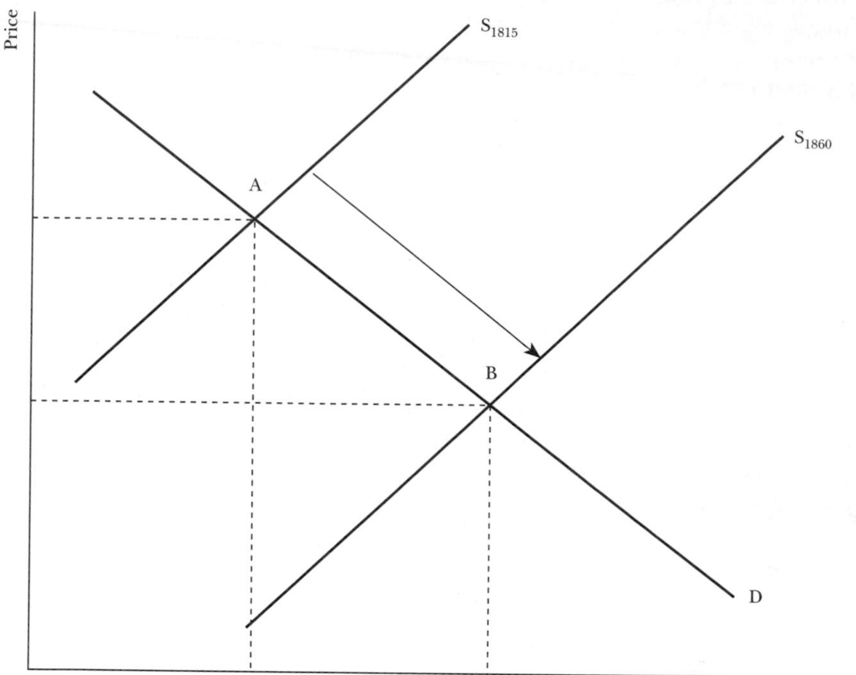

probably contributed to the cotton textile industry's expansion (Figure 7.5).

A variety of factors may explain why Americans demanded more American cloth at a given price. The need to replace imports that were no longer available—import substitution—lay behind the very early growth of the industry in the wake of Jefferson's embargo. The tariff also undoubtedly reduced the competitive position of British producers in the American market in the 1820s and 1830s, effectively shifting the demand for American-made goods outward. Rapid population growth, averaging about 3 percent a year over the 1815–40 period, should also have increased demand at least as rapidly. Actually the impact of the population growth was probably even greater than its numerical value because population grew even more rapidly in urban areas and in the West, where higher opportunity costs meant that people were less likely to make their own cloth. Demographic factors thus probably accounted for substantially more than 3 percent output growth. The growing population enjoyed rising income levels, which also added to the demand for clothing. If we assume an income elasticity for clothing of

FIGURE 7.4

Demand-Driven Growth

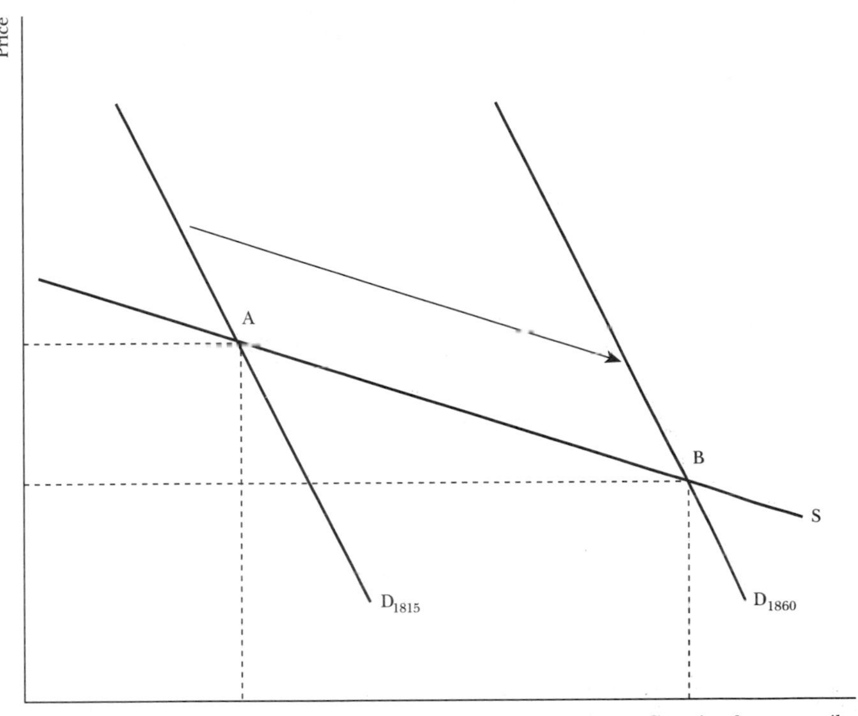

one, higher incomes would have shifted demand outward at a rate of at least 1 percent per year even if we use the most pessimistic estimates of per capital income growth. Some of the increased demand was met by imports because they were superior to (that is, finer than) the domestic product and consequently had a higher income elasticity. Lastly, transportation improvements reduced the difference between what manufacturers received at the factory gate in Massachusetts and what farmers in Michigan or Illinois paid for cloth, effectively increasing the demand for textiles by as much as 1 percent a year between 1815 and 1824, by which time most of the dramatic reductions in transport costs had been realized.[8]

Taken together, these factors may have shifted demand by as much as 9 or 10 percent a year from 1815 to 1824 and 7 to 8 percent from 1825 to 1833. Since total cotton cloth sales increased by a 15.4 percent average rate over

[8] Zevin (1971, 1975).

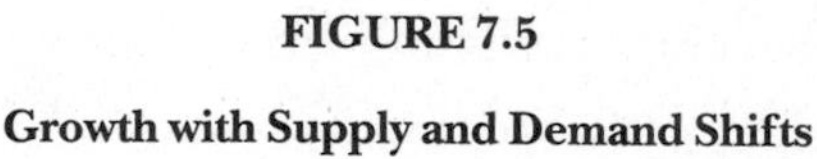

FIGURE 7.5

Growth with Supply and Demand Shifts

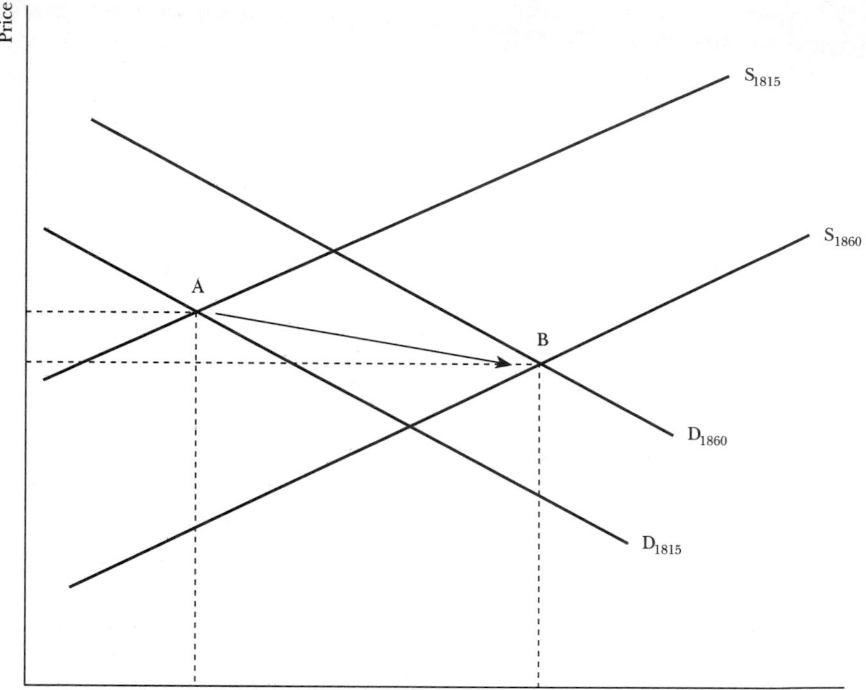

the entire period, it appears that demand changes alone accounted for more than half the expansion of the industry. Later, western and urban areas grew more slowly, and increasingly affluent Americans spent smaller fractions of their income gains on inexpensive cotton clothing. As a result, demand shifted out at just 3 to 4 percent a year after 1834. Nevertheless, because the rate of expansion in the maturing cotton cloth industry declined even more, demand explains an ever-higher proportion of output growth in this period.

Even if the price of cotton cloth had not fallen by three-fourths in the 1815–60 period, the industry would still have expanded enormously in response to national economic growth. By itself the technological revolution in textile manufactures was responsible for only about one-third of the 15 percent annual growth in output in the early years. This conclusion damages the conventional wisdom that technical change was the *single* most important factor setting the stage for economic development.

The Peculiar Case of the American Iron Industry

Iron was the symbol of nineteenth-century industrial development. The shift from labor-intensive manual production was based on iron machinery, steam engines made from iron powered the water pumps that revolutionized coal mining, steamboats opened western rivers, iron pipe allowed the construction of durable water and sewage systems for urban areas, and iron rails made the railroad a practical means of transport. But iron output did not grow anywhere near as rapidly as did cotton textile production—an average of just 6 percent annually in the three decades before the Civil War. Nor did the American iron industry adopt state-of-the-art British production techniques with the aggressiveness of the cotton textile industry. Instead American iron producers continued to smelt iron with charcoal rather than coal until the 1840s. As a result, total factor productivity in the iron industry from 1820 to 1860 grew at an average annual rate of between 1.1 and 1.4 percent—less than one-half that of cotton textiles.

This American failure to adopt new iron technology—in contrast with the rapid transfer of textile technology—is sometimes blamed upon the abundance of charcoal in America, but the principal cost of making charcoal was the cost of labor needed to cut down trees and haul the wood to the charcoal kiln, not the wood itself. The evidence, however, suggests that American labor was more expensive than British labor. Instead one of the reasons why American ironmakers continued to use charcoal was that the kind of coal needed to make coke—bituminous coal—was found in the United States only west of the Appalachians, and the bituminous deposits then known contained too much sulfur to yield high-grade pig iron. However, once a way to use the anthracite coal deposits of eastern Pennsylvania in pig iron production was discovered in the 1840s, coal smelting increased sharply. This switch may well explain the sharp increase in total factor productivity growth in the iron industry between 1850 and 1860. During the 1850s productivity growth in iron averaged between 2.3 and 3.6 percent a year—four or five times faster than earlier, among the fastest of all industries.[9]

At its inception in 1840 the American anthracite pig iron industry was as efficient as any in the world (Figure 7.6). But it failed to grow for the next three decades, so that by 1870 productivity in the industry lagged behind its European counterparts. Thereafter productivity exploded. By World War I the American industry was slightly more efficient than the European. The principal culprit in the American productivity lag was the failure by the pig iron industry to lower fuel consumption per ton of iron at the same rate as the Europeans. Once again this stemmed not from technological backwardness or entrepreneurial failure in the American industry but rather from the

[9] Sokoloff (1986).

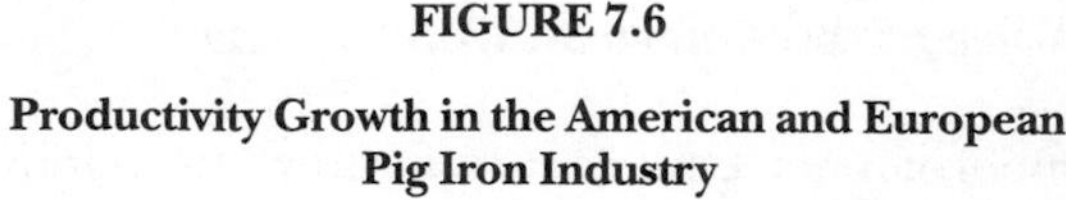

FIGURE 7.6

Productivity Growth in the American and European Pig Iron Industry

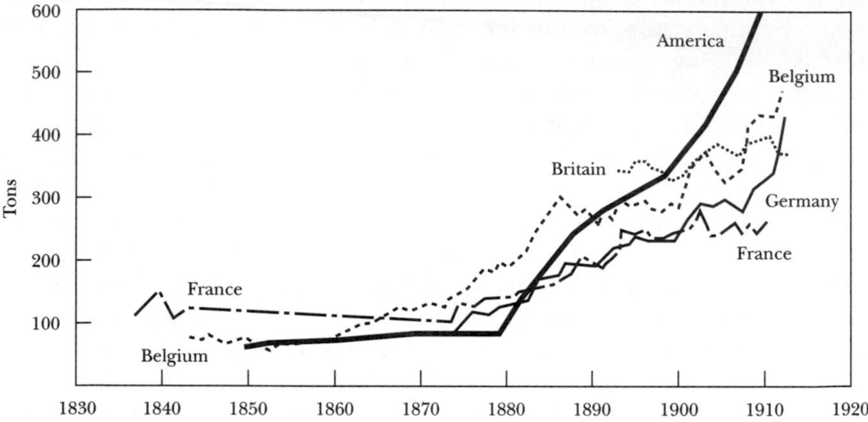

Source: Robert C. Allen, "The Peculiar Productivity History of American Blast Furnaces, 1840–1913," *Journal of Economic History* 37 (1977): 609, Figure 2.

nature of the American iron ore then available, which contained high levels of the mineral silica. The solution—new sources of iron ore—had to await the discovery of the Lake Superior deposits.[10]

The growth of anthracite pig iron at the expense of charcoal pig iron after 1840, however, may not reflect technologically based cost savings. Demand for iron increasingly favored the anthracite form, which was better suited for heavy construction. This demand grew at an average annual rate of 5.5 percent while the demand for charcoal iron actually declined. Without the observed shift in demand, anthracite iron production would have been only half as large by the end of the period. The tariff on pig iron was lowered in 1846, and as a consequence, competition from imports increased. Domestic production of anthracite iron continued to grow rapidly, but production of charcoal iron fell. Historians, influenced by the ideology of free trade, directly connect the decline of charcoal iron to competition from coke-based pig iron—the new modern technology driving out the old. But the truth is more elusive. Foreign competition surely hurt charcoal iron, but even if high tariff barriers had been maintained, slackening demand would have cut into sales. All American producers would have been helped by higher tariffs; however, the biggest beneficiaries would have been anthracite-iron makers, whose product was closer in composition and use to imported coke iron.[11]

[10] Allen (1971).
[11] Fogel and Engerman (1969).

The Spread of Industrialization

By most measures—capital invested, employment, and output—manufacturing in America was developing rapidly across a broad industrial and geographic front during the antebellum years. Census data indicate that this growth was both extensive—more firms—as well as intensive—firm size was growing—but there were substantial regional variations in industry mix, firm size, and extent of manufacturing development. The data in Table 7.2 highlight regional differences in average firm size and extent of industrial development. In the two most industrialized regions, the Middle Atlantic states and especially New England, the number of manufacturing firms declined slightly between 1850 and 1860, while average firm size increased. In the South and Midwest, on the other hand, firm size increased at the same time that the number of firms increased sharply, thanks in part to the more extensive settlement, but firms in these regions remained smaller than those elsewhere. Moreover, manufacturing output per person in the South and Midwest—a key concern of Alexander Hamilton, who equated high personal incomes with the proportion of income originating in manufacturing—was a fraction of that in the more industrialized regions, although productivity per worker compared favorably with that of industrial workers in the Northeast.

Textiles and iron are symbols of the Industrial Revolution, but they were not typical of nineteenth-century manufacturing. Both were geographically concentrated. Of the 1,074 cottons mills enumerated by the 1850 census, more than half (561) were in New England, and only 167 were located in the entire South—about the same number as in Rhode Island. Similarly, 178 of the 404 iron furnaces in the United States in 1850 were in Pennsylvania. Textile mills were also among the industrial giants of the time with an average of ninety-one employees per mill—of whom fifty-eight (over 60 percent) were female. From the start they were typically large-scale integrated joint-stock or corporate enterprises, dependent on inanimate power to drive their machinery, employing a diversified and generally unskilled labor force in narrowly defined tasks for long hours under close supervision. The rest of industry was typically small-scale, unincorporated sole proprietorships or partnerships, using few machines, having little need for power, and employing a relatively small labor force under the direct personal supervision of the entrepreneur, who worked alongside his employees. The archetypal manufacturing establishment in the mid-nineteenth century was a lumber mill (17,895 nationwide), a flour mill (11,891 in the United States in 1850), a boot- and shoemaker (11,305), or a blacksmith (10,373 nationwide). Employment in these firms was highly seasonal, reflecting the rhythms of supply and demand in a predominantly agrarian society where manufacturing activity was secondary to farming. Most were small. As a result, many historians and economists have said, either explicitly or implicitly, that industry before the Civil War must have been competitive, with conditions approach-

TABLE 7.2

Manufacturing in the United States, by Region, 1850–1860

Region	Number of Firms	Capital ($ millions)	Employees (thousands)	Output ($ millions)	Capital per Firm ($)	Number of Employees per Firm	Output per Firm ($)	Output per Employee ($/person)	Output per Capita ($/person)
1850									
New England	22,487	166	313	283	7,364	14	12,594	904	104
Middle Atlantic	54,024	236	421	473	4,363	8	8,757	1,124	71
Midwest	24,921	63	111	146	2,536	4	5,877	1,315	27
South	20,505	67	110	101	3,273	5	4,921	918	12
1860									
New England	20,671	257	392	469	12,456	19	22,669	1,196	149
Middle Atlantic	53,287	435	546	802	8,164	10	15,059	1,469	96
Midwest	33,350	174	189	347	5,216	6	10,395	1,836	38
South	24,081	116	132	193	4,827	6	8,034	1,462	19
Percentage Change 1850–60									
New England	−8	54	25	65	69	35	80	32	43
Middle Atlantic	−1	84	29	69	87	25	71	30	35
Midwest	33	176	70	137	105	50	76	39	40
South	17	73	20	91	47	20	63	59	58

Source: Fred Bateman and Thomas Weiss, *Deplorable Scarcity: The Failure of Industrialization in the Slave Economy* (Chapel Hill: University of North Carolina Press, 1981): 17, Table 1.2.)

ing the economists' notion of perfect competition: large numbers of relatively small producers selling unbranded products with no serious barriers to entry. Others argue that these thousands of small businesses existed solely to meet the needs of local markets isolated from one another by the high costs of transportation. Their numbers and scale of operation reflected the multiplicity and proliferation of markets, not the evolution of a competitive marketplace.[12] This theme will be elaborated upon in Chapter 17.

The Changing Nature and Organization of Industrial Work

As time passed, even small artisan shops operating in traditional industries and markets began to change. The oldest and most pervasive explanations for the change is that there were economies of scale, which required firms either to grow or to leave the industry. The explanation links neatly with the infant industry arguments of Alexander Hamilton and others in favor of tariff protection. The importance of these scale economies was further emphasized by declining transport costs that widened the market and by the new technologies that required heavy capital investments to produce much larger outputs of goods on a continuous basis.[13] This scale argument is also invoked to explain regional differences in industrialization, especially between the slave South and the rest of the country.

A number of authors have tried to measure the importance of scale economies using a variety of different production function forms. Most have concluded that scale economies, if and when they existed, were small and soon exhausted. Firms did not have to be large to be competitive in the first half of the nineteenth century. What advantages to increased scale may have existed were quickly dissipated as firm size increased and firms found that they faced a broad range of outputs over which scale economies were more or less constant. The long-run average cost curve was probably more L-shaped than U-shaped, as studies for the twentieth century also suggest. If so, then we must look elsewhere for explanations of the South's failure to develop a substantial industrial sector and for explanations of the emergence of big business in the second half of the nineteenth century.[14]

There is growing evidence that changes in the organization of production played a major role in the course and pattern of industrialization by raising efficiency. Increased efficiency, like scale economies, raised labor productivity, lowered costs, and made American industry more able to compete with foreign businesses. Efficiency and scale economies are, however, conceptually distinct. Whereas scale economies may be thought of in terms

[12] Bateman and Weiss (1975, 1981).
[13] See Chapter 17 and Chandler (1977).
[14] Atack (1977, 1987); James (1983); Sokoloff (1984).

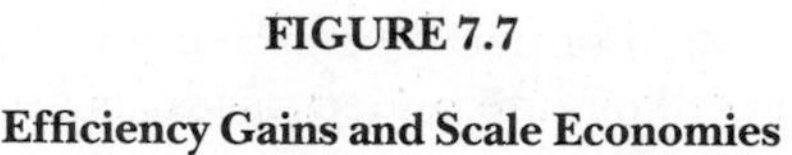

FIGURE 7.7

Efficiency Gains and Scale Economies

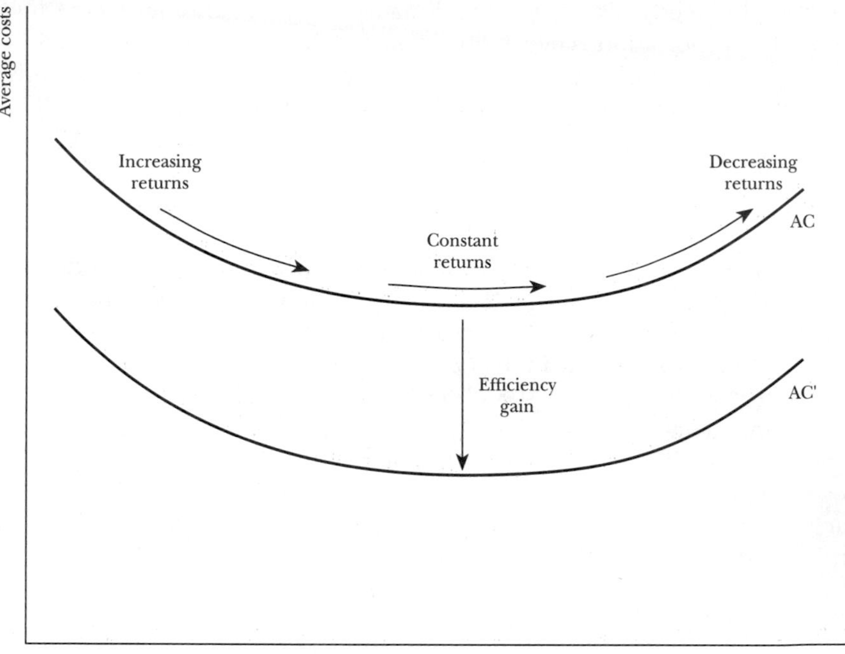

of movement along the long-run average cost curve, efficiency gains are represented by shifts in the long-run average cost curve. With scale economies, the issue is whether one is producing on the downward-sloping portion of the average cost curve. With efficiency, the issue is how the average cost curve shifts in response to input cost, including those for organization and management (Figure 7.7).

Much of the increased efficiency came about through the increased division of labor resulting from the adoption of the factory in place of the artisan shop (Table 7.3). This further reinforced learning-by-doing by increasing repetition, and it increased work intensity through the greater interdependence of workers. Larger establishments had greater opportunities for the subdivision of tasks and increased specialization. And as tasks became more narrowly defined, they became candidates for mechanization. As the size of the labor force increased, so, too, did the need for monitoring and supervision to ensure performance and avoid shirking. The entrepreneur became less likely to work alongside his employees and more involved with

TABLE 7.3

Percentage of Industry Value Added Originating from Different Production Methods in Selected Industries, 1850 and 1870

Industry	Artisan Shops 1850	Artisan Shops 1870	Other Nonmechanized 1850	Other Nonmechanized 1870	Mills 1850	Mills 1870	Factories 1850	Factories 1870
Boots and shoes	39	33	61	45	0	4	0	19
Brewing	41	21	24	0	35	49	0	30
Clothing	13	16	87	66	0	0	0	18
Cotton goods	0	0	4	3	16	1	79	96
Flour milling	7	5	0	0	91	95	2	0
Furniture	50	18	20	14	10	26	19	41
Iron	0	0	33	1	22	10	44	89
Leather	54	20	16	7	26	29	4	43
Liquor	9	4	18	4	73	82	0	10
Lumber milling	3	1	1	2	88	63	8	34
Meat-packing	34	31	29	0	11	69	25	0
Saddlery	62	71	38	28	0	1	0	0
Sheet metal	89	41	6	33	5	2	0	24
Tobacco	24	30	76	68	0	2	0	0
Wagon and carriages	32	33	63	47	3	3	3	18
Woolen goods	0	4	1	12	39	7	60	77

Artisan shops = 1–6 employees; no power
Other nonmechanized = over 6 employees; no power
Mills = 1–25 employees; steam or waterpower
Factories = over 25 employees; steam or waterpower

Source: Adapted from Jeremy Atack, "Economies of Scale and Efficiency Gains in the Rise of the Factory in America, 1820–1900," in *Quantity and Quiddity: Essays in U.S. Economic History* (Middletown, Conn.: Wesleyan University Press, 1987): 296, Table 9.2.

overall management, relinquishing supervisory tasks to other employees and increasing the performance pressure upon workers.

Using quantitative data from the 1820 and 1850 censuses of manufactures, Sokoloff has estimated that factories employing more than five persons were at least 25 percent more efficient—that is to say, given the same factor inputs, they would have produced at least 25 percent more output—than smaller, less specialized artisanal shops. Unfortunately the empirical research does not resolve the debate about the origins of the productivity differences. One theory favors the increased division of labor in larger firms; the other attributes the productivity gain to the intensification of work effort. Both are consistent with the findings. Only one industry deviated markedly from the pattern: In the iron industry smaller firms were consistently more efficient than larger firms until after the Civil War. This may reflect the continued reliance upon charcoal smelting.[15]

In the decades leading up to the Civil War, total factor productivity in manufacturing seems to have grown rapidly, averaging between 1.5 and 2.2 percent per year. It was the dominant factor underlying labor productivity growth (hence rising wages) in American industry, accounting for between one-half and three-quarters of labor productivity growth. Capital deepening (changes in the amount of capital used by each worker), on the other hand, was of less importance. Growth was particularly rapid in the textiles, glass, paper, and woodworking industries, where it averaged between 2 and 4.5 percent per year (Table 7.4). These were also the industries in which there was significant technological progress and mechanization. It was American skill with automatic woodworking machinery, for example, that captured

TABLE 7.4

Annual Growth Rates of Total Factor Productivity in Selected Manufacturing Industries, 1820–1860 (percent)

Industry	1820–32	1820–50	1850–60	1820–60
Boots/shoes		1.3–1.6	2.0–3.0	1.4–2.0
Coaches/harnesses	−0.7	1.9–2.1	1.3–1.5	1.7–1.9
Cotton textiles	5.2	1.8–3.0	2.7–3.6	2.3–2.9
Furniture/woodwork	2.2	2.4–2.9	2.0–3.8	2.7–2.8
Glass	7.7	3.3	−1.0	2.2
Hats	2.4	2.0–2.5	2.3–2.7	2.1–2.5
Iron		0.7–0.8	2.9–3.6	1.4–1.4
Liquors		0.4–1.6	0.5–3.5	1.2–1.2
Flour/gristmills		−0.6–0.2	0.6–2.8	0.2–0.3
Paper	3.6	5.0–5.4	−0.4–3.3	3.9–4.5
Tanning	1.2	1.2–2.4	−2.7–0.8	0.7–1.1
Tobacco		−0.3–0.8	3.1–8.9	1.4–2.0
Wood textiles	3.2	1.0–2.0	3.8–6.4	2.4–2.5
Weighted average	[3.3]	[1.6]–2.1	[2.4]–2.4	[1.8]–2.2

Notes: These total factor productivity growth estimates are computed with value added as output.

Source: Kenneth Sokoloff, "Productivity Growth in Manufacturing during Early Industrialization: Evidence from the American Northeast, 1820–1860," in National Bureau of Economic Research, Long-Term Factors in American Economic Growth, ed. Stanley Engerman and Robert Gallman (Chicago: University of Chicago Press, 1986): 719.

[15] Atack (1987).

British attention at the Crystal Palace Exhibition in 1851 and prompted a parliamentary inquiry into the sources of American technological leadership. Productivity growth was slowest in traditional industries—flour, leather, liquor, and iron—in which production methods were largely unchanged from the eighteenth century. In these industries total factor productivity growth averaged 1 percent or less per year.

Power and Industrialization

The mechanization of production increased demands upon the sources of power in mills and workshops. As a result, human muscle or animal power was increasingly supplemented or replaced by inanimate sources of power—water or steam.

Waterpower had been used in Europe and elsewhere for many centuries, and it probably powered the majority of the nation's flour and lumber mills at the start of the nineteenth century. It also powered the earliest textile mills such as Slater's mill at Pawtucket, Rhode Island. Efforts to exploit the Charles River at Waltham, Massachusetts, however, were soon abandoned, and the industry moved north to the Merrimack River, where the falls at Lowell gave rise to the nation's first industrial city. Many of the earliest waterwheels were inefficient undershot wheels, capable of capturing only 10 to 15 percent of the potential power. This mattered little so long as power needs were limited and water was plentiful, but increased demands from the growing industrial sector and increasingly energy-intensive production processes gradually placed a premium on efficiency. The growth of competing uses for water, especially for drinking water and sanitation in the cities and towns that grew up around the factories, only reinforced the need for greater efficiency. One result was that the Proprietors of the Locks and Canals at Lowell (owners of the water right at the falls), for example, employed a full-time engineer to oversee and police the efficient use of their water resource. By pricing according to water use and time of day (rather than power generated), the Proprietors encouraged the adoption of increasingly efficient prime movers—first huge breast wheels and eventually water turbines in the late 1840s and 1850s. These achieved 90 to 95 percent efficiency, or about as much as today.

Increased hydraulic efficiency temporarily relieved the most serious constraint upon more extensive waterpower use—the site-specific constraint imposed by the water flow—while simultaneously lowering the cost per horsepower for those owning water rights or renting water flows on long-term leases. As a result, waterpower was able to remain competitive with steam power at many locations, especially in New England, until well into the twentieth century, when it was replaced by electric, not steam, power. However, the limited number of waterpower sites, especially in much of the

Midwest, the plains, and the southeastern seaboard meant that spreading industry was increasingly forced to rely upon steam for power.[16]

Each power source had advantages and disadvantages. The use of waterpower meant a large initial investment in building a dam and putting the waterwheel in place. But once these were built, power was almost "free." Steam, on the other hand, required a relatively small initial outlay, but fuel consumption was a continuing expense. Even in areas with plenty of fast-moving streams, waterpower sites were limited, and the raw materials for processing in water-powered mills might need to be hauled dozens of miles and finished products returned the same way. Steam power gave the millowner the freedom to locate near low-cost transportation. But transportation bills might be large nonetheless because fuel would still have to be brought to the factory to feed the boilers. The adoption of steam did reduce the seasonality inherent in waterpower and played a role in the emergence of modern year-round work habits.

Peter Temin's research suggests that early-nineteenth-century manufacturers understood these considerations very well and acted in the way economists would predict, choosing the cheapest power source to suit specific needs.[17] In New England, where textiles dominated manufacturing, water and steam power were sufficiently close in cost (about $50 per horsepower per year) that the choice of power turned on mill location, rather than vice versa. The cotton mills around Lowell, Massachusetts, took advantage of the exceedingly good water sites and accepted the fairly moderate costs of transporting raw cotton to the factories. Along the Atlantic coast, however, mills were driven by steam and fed by coal hauled at relatively low cost from Pennsylvania.

Two industries outside New England, sugar refineries and sawmills, were also major users of steam power, and for good reason. The perishability of raw sugarcane required that refineries be located near the cane fields of southern Louisiana, a region lacking adequate waterpower sites. Sawmills were somewhat less limited in choice of location. They did have to be placed on rivers downstream from a source of timber. Presumably entrepreneurs could choose river sites near waterfalls. But high interest rates in the West, where many mills operated, raised the cost of capital-intensive waterpower above that of steam. This explains, at least in part, why the lumber industry used more steam power than any other in the 1840s.

In 1820 waterwheels outnumbered steam engines by more than a hundred to one, but by 1870 the difference had narrowed to about five to four, and by 1900 steam engines outnumbered waterwheels and turbines by almost four to one. In terms of total power generated, the switch from reliance

[16] Atack (1979).
[17] Temin (1966).

FIGURE 7.8

The Adoption of Steam Power by Manufacturing Firms by Region, 1820–1920

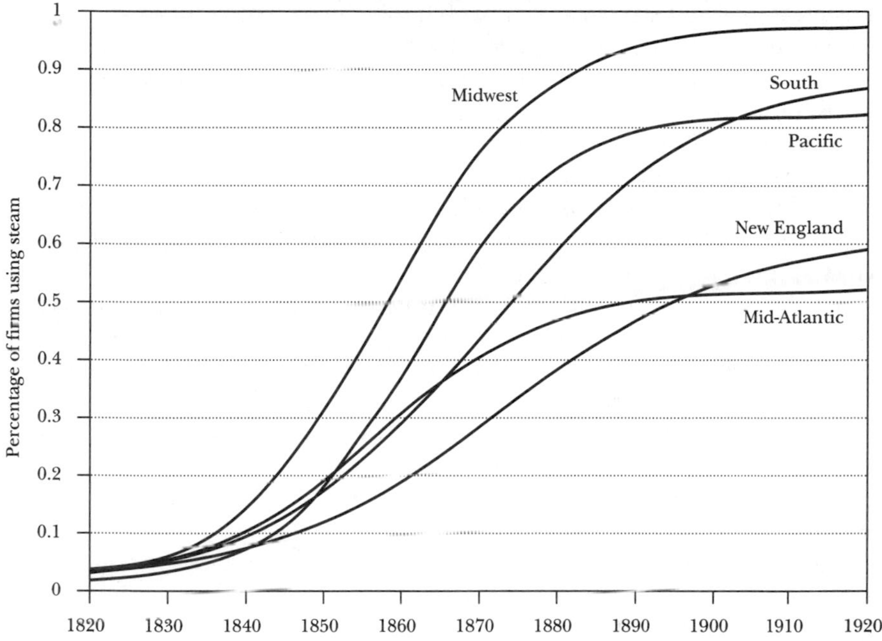

Source: Jeremy Atack, Fred Bateman, and Thomas Weiss, "The Regional Diffusion and Adoption of the Steam Engine in American Manufacturing," *Journal of Economic History* 40 (1980): 287, Figure 1.

upon waterpower to steam took place in the 1860s.[18] As with other inventions, the percentage of firms using steam power is found to follow an S-shaped growth curve (Figure 7.8). Firms in the Midwest, where there were relatively few waterpower sites, adopted steam power earliest and embraced it most enthusiastically. Firms in New England were the slowest to switch from water to steam. Proportionately more New England firms ultimately switched to steam power than in the Middle Atlantic states, where the switch was interrupted in the 1880s by the growing availability of electric power from central generating stations such as the Pearl Street plant in New York and the hydroelectric projects at Niagara.

The iron industry represents an interesting hybrid in which changing manufacturing technology in the 1840s rather than the economics of power generation led to a shift from water to steam. Before the 1840s blast furnaces

[18] Atack, Bateman, and Weiss (1980).

were generally located on streams in heavily wooded areas. Water was needed for cooling, and wood for making charcoal; waterpower was often the bonus for picking a site largely for other reasons. After the 1840s, however, pig iron made with mineral fuel (anthracite, occasionally low-sulfur bituminous coal) began to overtake charcoal iron, and new furnaces were located near coalfields. The availability of suitable waterpower—never an overriding economic priority in the iron industry—thus became even less important, and waterpower quickly gave way to steam in anthracite and bituminous smelting.

Although American hydraulic engineering adapted and improved upon European, American steam technology developed its own unique character in large part because the American Revolution temporarily interrupted the export of technology from Britain at a critical juncture in steam power development. Steam power was used in Britain in the eighteenth century largely to operate water pumps in deep mines prone to flooding. These early steam engines were extremely inefficient, requiring huge amounts of heat to achieve a given amount of physical work. In addition, their action was irregular. As a result, their application to drive machinery was extremely limited. In 1775 the Scottish inventor James Watt made several important technical changes to steam engine design; the most important was the use of a separate condenser. For this invention, Watt was granted a twenty-five-year monopoly on the manufacture of steam engines with a separate condenser, and the firm of Boulton and Watt rose to dominate the British steam engine market. However, it never made much impact upon the American market. A few engines were imported, but they were expensive—if long-lived—pieces of equipment. Instead in 1802 the American inventor Oliver Evans developed a high-pressure steam engine that used the expansive properties of steam to press against a piston—an entirely different principle from that used in the Boulton and Watt engines. The result was a small, compact, and lightweight engine that was easily transported over bad roads, such as abounded in America in the early nineteenth century. Perhaps even more important, the engine was easy and cheap to build. It required no finely machined parts and had few moving parts.

Compared with the low-pressure Boulton and Watt engine, the high-pressure American engine, though cheaper in initial purchase cost, lighter and less complex, was extremely fuel-inefficient and used perhaps five times as much fuel per horsepower per hour as the British engines. Nevertheless, by 1838, 95 percent of the twelve hundred stationary steam engines in the United States were of the high-pressure variety. Fuel efficiency was of little consequence to Americans so long as fuel was cheap compared with the capital and labor savings of the high-pressure American-design engine relative to the British low-pressure engine. High-pressure engines proved uniquely adaptable and were as at home in American factories of all sizes as in American steamboats on the western rivers.

The adoption of the high-pressure engine also had an important impact upon American machine technology. Whereas the low-pressure designs could not achieve more than perhaps sixty cycles per minute, the high-pressure engines typically operated at three to five times this speed. As a result, American machines tended to be driven at higher speeds with consequently greater wear than European. This caused American industry to be closer to the technological frontier at any moment in time as its capital stock was turned over more frequently because of the shorter replacement cycle. High operating speeds also led to an exhaustive search for better lubricants, met first by whaling and then by the petroleum industry.

Labor Scarcity and the Choice of Technology: The American System

The laborsaving aspect of American steam technology is just one example of a more general phenomenon that jolted Victorian Britain—the world's leading industrial power—at mid-century. An American display at the Crystal Palace Exhibition in London in 1851 (the progenitor of the world's fair) demonstrated what came to be known as the American System—the technique of interchangeable parts first adopted in firearm construction. The American System eliminated the need for individual parts to be fitted to one another before the finished product would work properly. In recent years economic historians and historians of technology have become increasingly skeptical of the legend of interchangeable parts as the foundation for the American System of Manufactures. It has been widely accepted that American inventors/entrepreneurs such as Eli Terry (clocks), Simeon North (guns), and Eli Whitney (guns) pioneered extensive mechanization as the means to achieve interchangeable parts and mass production. The evidence, however, suggests that full interchangeability of parts was elusive for a long time and, that where it was achieved, it came only at great cost. David Hounshell, for example, has examined Singer sewing machines in the Smithsonian as well as the products and records of other companies that supposedly achieved large-scale production based upon interchangeable parts. He has found evidence that parts were hand-fitted by trial and error at early stages in the assembly and finishing process. Parts show evidence of hand filing, serial numbers were used to match parts that had to be finished separately, and it was difficult or impossible to reassemble fully functioning devices from mixed-up and randomly selected parts.

True interchangeability of parts demands careful monitoring of the tolerances produced by each machine and was probably not achieved in most consumer goods and producer goods before the 1870s. It came somewhat sooner in the weapons industry, where the federal government was willing to underwrite development costs and guarantee the market for high-priced guns built from parts that were produced under stringent, almost laboratorylike conditions. This important federal role in the development of the American System is just an early example of what President Dwight D. Eisenhower was to call the "military-industrial complex." Still, early experiments with interchangeable parts and the "success" (if not its cost-effectiveness) within one sector of the economy probably accelerated its adoption in the United States. Interchangeable parts became a known technique that probably induced other Americans to experiment with its use as a production technique.

Americans also took an early lead in what is now called the machine tool industry—the production of machines for manufacturing. This specialization of function, in which separate businesses made tools for other industries, allowed for enormous economies in the creation and diffusion of new technology. Mechanics who worked on design problems in one industry—say, handguns—would find broad applications of their engineering solutions in other industries. And as Nathan Rosenberg has pointed out, machinery producers were in an ideal position to provide expertise to emerging industries. The first locomotive manufacturers, for example, cut their technological teeth on textile machinery production. Early-nineteenth-century American manufacturers were also notably advanced in the use of assembly lines. Using the first conveyer belts, Oliver Evans's turn-of-the-century mill processed grain into flour in one continuous process. Slaughterhouses in Cincinnati employed an assembly line strategy in dismembering hogs as they moved from station to station by overhead rail. This permitted specialization of labor and saved human effort in hauling the carcasses.

Following the acclaim accorded the American exhibits at the Crystal Palace Exhibition, the British Parliament appointed a commission to investigate the sources of American technological leadership. The commission reported at length on the number of guns each worker at the Springfield Arsenal could assemble in a day. With the elimination of the "fitting" process—the individual tailoring of metal and wood parts for each musket—assembly time was reduced from a few hours to a few minutes. It seemed as if American manufacturing had suddenly spurted ahead and was more efficiently developed and highly mechanized than the British.

On the basis of these observations, can we then say that American gun manufacture was more laborsaving than British manufacture? Unfortunately the answer is yes and no. There is no doubt that interchangeable parts cut the amount of labor needed to make—or, more important, to repair—the standardized weapon. But the British product not only was made differently but was *different.* British guns were often thought of as fine instruments, handcrafted to the specifications of each buyer. Unless owners were willing to accept muskets exactly like their neighbors', the American System was not practical. Hence it is possible that differing tastes explain different manufacturing techniques in some of the industries that so upset the British. In the United States guns were primarily made for citizen-soldiers and frontierspeople; the emphasis was on plain and cheap. In 1851 much of the British demand was for higher-quality weapons that required labor-intensive processes, no matter where they were made.

To British eyes, though, the American System was more efficient than their own. If so, what was the source of this greater efficiency? One author has attributed the superior efficiency of American industry to "the availability of land and the consequent scarcity of labor [that] have stimulated industry to install laborsaving machinery which has resulted in high efficiency."[19] High wages in manufacturing could be maintained only through increasing the marginal productivity of workers either by employing fewer of them or by providing them with more and "better" capital with which to work. In *American and British Technology in the Nineteenth Century,* H. J. Habakkuk tried to identify the conditions under which such laborsaving technological change might occur, though he failed to distinguish clearly between better machines and more machines, either of which would raise the capital-labor ratio in America. The two are conceptually different (Figure 7.9). "Better machines" give rise to a different production function in the United States from that in Great Britain. With better machines, the "same" output can be produced with less labor and less capital. "More machines," on the other hand, may be nothing more than a response to factor price differences between the two countries. Specifically, if capital were less expensive relative to labor in the United States compared with Great Britain, then American manufacturers would substitute capital for labor. That is, the underlying production technology would be identical between the two countries, but they would use different techniques, represented by different capital-labor ratios, to produce the product.

The argument, however, is more complicated than one might suppose. The conventional argument is that America used more machines because of labor scarcity. Machines were substituted for scarce labor, a condition that was reflected in high wages in America relative to wages in Britain, which was one factor attracting immigrants to American shores. If, however, manufacturing output was a function solely of labor and capital under a given technology, then relative labor scarcity necessarily implies relative capital abundance. But interest rates were higher in America than in Britain, and capital flowed from Britain to the United States. This suggests that capital must also have been relatively scarce in America! The result is a logical inconsistency in the argument: If labor was scarce, then capital was abundant, and America should have used a capital-intensive production technique. But if capital were scarce, as high interest rates implied, then labor must have been relatively abundant, and the United States should not have used capital-intensive production methods.[20]

The resolution of this puzzle requires recognition of the role played by

[19] Rothbarth (1946).
[20] Temin (1966).

FIGURE 7.9

"More" versus "Better" Machines: Labor Scarcity and the Choice of Technology

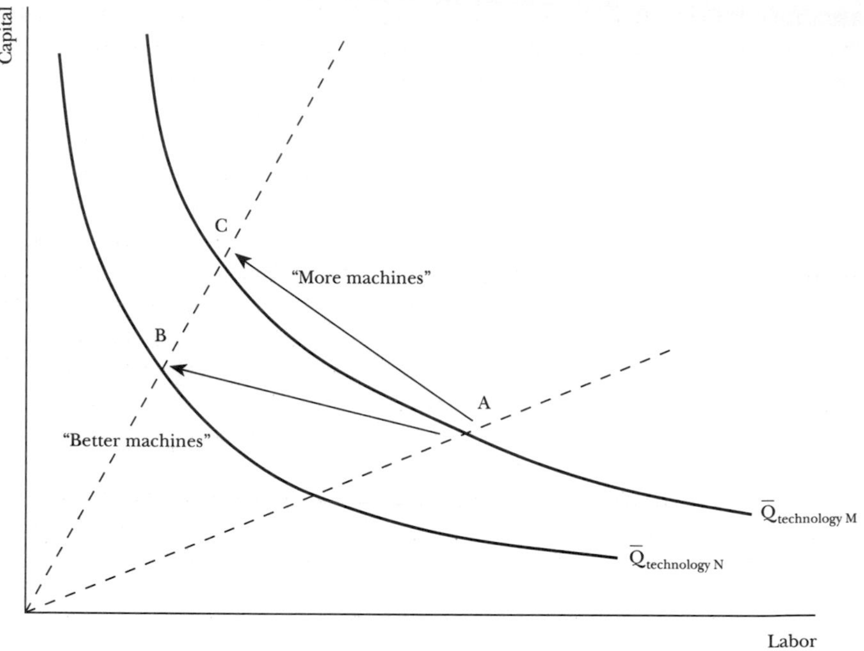

land in American development. American industrial production was resource—land—intensive. Among America's leading industries (in terms of value of output) were flour milling, lumber milling, meat-packing, leather tanning, and cotton textiles. Adding land as an argument of the American industrial production function allows the United States to be both labor- and capital-scarce and land-abundant, with the result that both labor and capital could flow across the Atlantic to America in search of higher returns.[21]

What about the "better machines" argument? Members of Parliament clearly believed that American technology, at least the technology used to

[21] Fogel (1967). A more elaborate model by Clarke and Summers (1980) shows that if agriculture were the land-intensive sector (and this seems reasonable) and if it had a higher capital-labor ratio than manufacturing (this seems more questionable and depends upon precisely how one defines agricultural capital), then an increase in the quantity of land raises the capital intensity of manufacturing. If, however, the demand for agricultural goods is inelastic, then the capital intensity of manufacturing falls as land availability increases.

produce guns, was better than British technology. If so, then why didn't the British simply adopt American technology? There were no American restrictions of the export of technology at the time. If the American System were truly better, then the British should have adopted it, producing their products at lower cost and using less labor than required by their own technology. Since they did not adopt American technology, this would seem to be proof that the "better machines" argument is false. Indeed, one of the few examples of the adoption of American technology by the British in the mid-nineteenth century was in the manufacture of guns, the very area that sparked the whole debate. Even then, the decision to use American technology for guns was not a free market outcome. Instead the British government mandated the use of American technology for the production of guns for its military. As with the early history of interchangeable parts in America, military needs dominated economic considerations. Nevertheless, it is still possible that American technology might have been superior to British technology yet not be used. Economists assume that when a new technology is developed, potential users have full and complete information about the infinite number of potential factor combinations—that is, the different techniques—by which the product might be made using that technology. If, however, the realization of a particular technology is linked to a specific set of factor endowments, then adaptation to other radically different factor endowments requires the expenditure of additional research and development funds, and the activity is indistinguishable from the effort required to develop a new technology.[22]

Lastly, note that there is a simple alternative explanation for Britain's failure to mechanize. If skilled labor is a good substitute for machinery in production, then cheap skilled labor in Britain may have made it unprofitable to adopt capital-intensive methods. In America, by contrast, the relative scarcity of skilled workers may have required the adoption of machines that could be operated by the relatively abundant unskilled workers. This would also be perfectly consistent with the existence of different productive technologies between the two countries.[23]

The Profitability of Nineteenth-Century Manufacturing

Profitability is the ultimate measure of economic success in a capitalist system. By this measure, the average antebellum manufacturing firm seems to have been a success. Industrial firms earned, on average, high rates of profit—high, at least, by comparison with the return on bonds, the rate of return on agriculture, or an assumed competitive return of between 6 and

[22] Rosenberg (1972).
[23] Harley (1974).

12 percent. On the basis of individual firm data from the census, Fred Bateman and Thomas Weiss estimate that nationwide manufacturing profit rates averaged 18.4 percent on capital in 1850. In 1860 the average firm earned even higher returns, 20.2 percent. These high average returns reflect high rates of profit across a wide range of industries, especially in the more traditional local industries where firms, even if they were not large, may have enjoyed some degree of monopoly power (Table 7.5). Indeed, the larger firms which were more likely to be serving regional or national markets had lower rates of return.[24]

Within each industry, however, there was a wide dispersion of rates of return. This variance might be viewed as a proxy for the risk each firm in an industry faced. These risks, particularly the risk of sustaining a loss or going bankrupt, were quite high. One rationalization for the relatively high average returns, therefore, is that they were a compensating payment for the high risks. Modern portfolio analysis suggests that investors would minimize this risk through diversification—that is, investing in a wide range of different activities in different localities. Unfortunately this was not generally possible in manufacturing at mid-century. Few companies enjoyed the privilege of limited liability, joint-stock ownership. General limited liability laws had not yet been passed by most states, and where firms had such a privilege it was by separate act of state legislatures. Most that had such protection were textile firms. As for the rest, they were forced to raise capital from family, friends, neighbors, and suppliers. Those investing directly in such businesses, however, faced unlimited liability for the debts of the firm, and own-

TABLE 7.5

Manufacturing Rates of Return, by Region 1850 and 1860

Region	Rate of Return for All Firms 1850	Rate of Return for All Firms 1860	Rate of Return for "Large" Firms 1850	Rate of Return for "Large" Firms 1860
Northeast	14.7	18.6	12.0	18.4
Midwest	23.8	20.9	24.2	14.4
South	19.8	25.1	16.8	21.1
United States	18.4	20.2	15.8	17.9

Source: Computed from the Bateman-Weiss samples from the manuscript censuses of manufacturers for 1850 and 1860. "Large" firms were defined as firms with $5,000 or more capital invested.

[24] Bateman and Weiss (1975, 1981).

ership could not be divorced from control. As a result, extensive diversification was impossible, so risks remained large. Even where some effort at diversification was made, it may have increased rather than reduced portfolio risk because of inability to diversify away from dependence upon the local economy and because of the loss of control and direct supervision. This hypothesis is consistent with the lower rates of return in those industries, such as cotton textiles, where limited liability and joint-stock ownership were the norm rather than the exception.

Rates of return were generally higher in the South and West than in the Northeast, but the differential was probably not great enough to encourage extensive direct investment by northeasterners in southern and midwestern manufacturing. As a result, equalization of returns across regions was slow in coming, compounded by the ongoing territorial and market expansion, especially in the Midwest. Nor do rates of return appear to have equalized during the antebellum period across industries or sectors even within a region.[25] Comparable estimates of the return to northern and southern agriculture suggest that the returns to manufacturing were often two to three times higher.[26]

Although one must be cautious about inferring marginal returns—the return on the last farm or firm—from average profit estimates, the existence and persistence of such differentials in profits between agriculture and manufacturing imply a loss to society from the misallocation of resources. This can be measured by the Harberger Triangle (Figure 7.10). If resources were perfectly free to flow between sectors, industries, and regions, then returns would be equalized between them. Factor price equalization would occur at B, where factor i is fully employed and the returns—given by the marginal product of the factor in each sector/industry/region—are equal. Instead the rate of return estimates for the nineteenth century suggest that there were high-return activities—paying, say, OM—and low-return activities—paying, say, O'N—with some market imperfection inhibiting the flow of resources from the lower- to the higher-paying activities. As a result, there is a gap equal to the difference between these returns (AC) and a net loss to society shown by the shaded triangle (ABC) that represents the difference between actual total output (measured by the area under the marginal product curves) and what output would have been if resources had been allocated so as to equalize the return in each sector. Too many resources were invested in agriculture—in land in the North and in slaves in the South—and too few flowed into manufacturing, perhaps because of the barriers to entry posed

[25] Bateman and Weiss (1981).

[26] Atack and Bateman (1987), for example, estimate the returns to northern agriculture at 8 to 12 percent, while estimates of the return to southern cotton agriculture averaged about 10 percent. See Fogel and Engerman (1974) and Vedder and Stockdale (1975).

FIGURE 7.10

Factor Price Equalization and Sectoral Factor Allocations: The Harberger Triangle

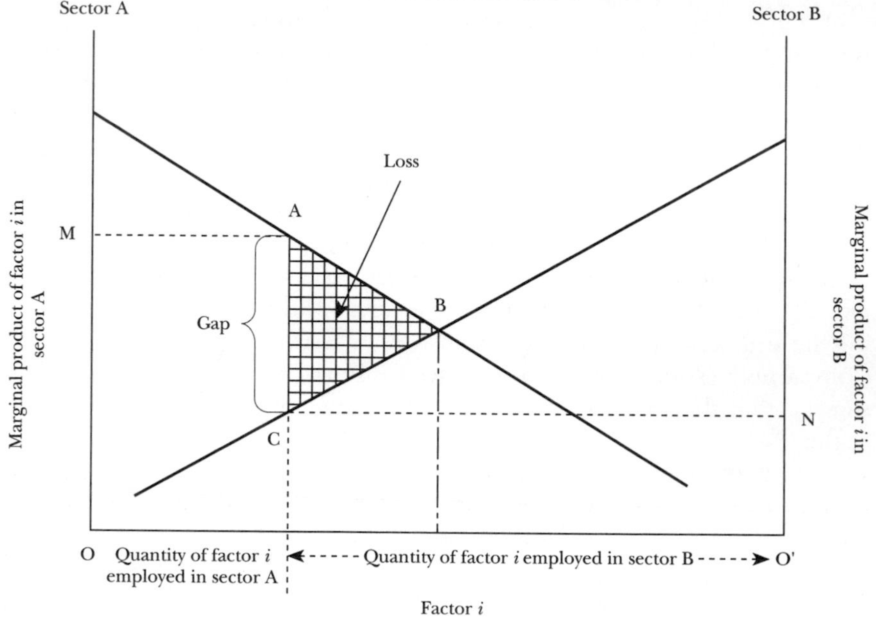

by imperfect capital markets, limited product markets, and lack of familiarity with manufacturing.

By the middle of the nineteenth century American manufacturing had been transformed from the relatively simple processing of raw materials using traditional methods into complex, machine-intensive processes that produced ever more sophisticated goods through an increasingly minute division of labor and specialization. No longer was industry a mere adjunct to agriculture, a secondary source of employment. Instead a growing fraction of the nation's labor force was solely dependent upon industry for its livelihood. An industrial labor force had emerged.

Industry moved from the countryside, becoming increasingly concentrated in urban areas. But existing cities were not industrialized. Industrial towns, such as Lowell, Lynn, Danvers, Fall River, Buffalo, Pittsburgh, Cleveland, and Chicago, became increasingly urbanized.[27] These towns and cities offered large pools of nearby labor with transferable skills, schooled in the need for industrial discipline. They provided a potential market just beyond

[27] Meyer (1989).

the factory gate. And as nodes in the emerging transportation network the industrial cities also provided firms with easier and cheaper access to more distant markets and sources of raw materials. Increasing volumes of trade in turn generated valuable flows of commercial and financial information that lowered transactions costs. Because trade was cheaper, trade expanded. Urban agglomerations were both a cause and a consequence of growing specialization, and they brought with them all the problems that we associate with cities today: crime, pollution, congestion, disease, corruption—everything that Thomas Jefferson had feared from industrialization. For a while, though, America was to remain a predominantly agrarian economy. Industry would not triumph until after the Civil War.

Bibliography

Allen, Robert C. "The Peculiar Productivity History of American Blast Furnaces 1840–1913." *Journal of Economic History* 37 (1977): 605–33.

Atack, Jeremy. "Fact in Fiction? The Relative Costs of Steam and Water Power: A Simulation Approach." *Explorations in Economic History* 16 (1979): 409–37.

———. "Economies of Scale and Efficiency Gains in the Rise of the Factory in America, 1820–1900." In *Quantity and Quiddity: Essays in U.S. Economic History,* ed. Peter Kilby. Middletown, Conn.: Wesleyan University Press, 1987: 286–335.

———, Fred Bateman, and Thomas Weiss. "The Regional Diffusion and Adoption of the Steam Engine in American Manufacturing." *Journal of Economic History* 40(1980): 281–308.

Bateman, Fred, James Foust, and Thomas Weiss. "Profitability in Southern Manufacturing." *Explorations in Economic History* 12 (1975): 211–31.

Bateman, Fred, and Thomas Weiss. "Comparative Regional Development in Antebellum Manufacturing." *Journal of Economic History* 35 (1975): 182–208.

——— and ———. *A Deplorable Scarcity: The Failure of Industrialization in the Slave Economy.* Chapel Hill: University of North Carolina Press, 1981.

Bils, Mark. "Tariff Protection and Production in the Early U.S. Cotton Textile Industry." *Journal of Economic History* 44 (1984): 1033-46.

Chandler, Alfred. *The Visible Hand: The Managerial Revolution in American Business.* Cambridge: Belknap Press of Harvard University Press, 1977.

David, Paul A. "Learning by Doing and Tariff Protection: A Reconsideration of the Case of the Ante-Bellum United States Cotton Textile Industry." *Journal of Economic History* 30 (1970): 521–601.

———. "The Horndal Effect in Lowell, 1834–1856: A Short-Run Learning Curve for Integrated Cotton Textile Mills." *Explorations in Economic History* 10 (1973): 131–50.

Davis, Lance, and Louis Stettler. "The New England Textile Industry 1825–1860." In National Bureau of Economic Research, *Output, Employment, and Productivity in the United States after 1800.* Studies in Income and Wealth, vol. 30. New York: Columbia University Press, 1966: 213–38.

Field, Alexander James. "Sectoral Shifts in Antebellum Massachusetts: A Reconsideration." *Explorations in Economic History* 15 (1978): 146–71.

Fogel, Robert W. "The Specification Problem in Economic History." *Journal of Economic History* 27 (1967): 283–308.

——— and Stanley Engerman. "A Model for the Explanation of Industrial

Expansion during the 19th Century: With an Application to the American Iron Industry." *Journal of Political Economy* 77 (1969): 306–28.
——— and ———. *Time on the Cross.* Boston: Little, Brown, 1974. Reprinted W. W. Norton, 1989.
Goldin, Claudia, and Kenneth Sokoloff. "Women, Children, and Industrialization in the Early Republic: Evidence from the Manufacturing Censuses." *Journal of Economic History* 42 (1982): 741–74.
——— and ———. "The Relative Productivity Hypothesis of Industrialization: The American Case, 1820 to 1850." *Quarterly Journal of Economics* 99 (1984): 461–88.
Habakkuk, H. J. *American and British Technology in the Nineteenth Century.* Cambridge, England: Cambridge University Press, 1962.
Harley, C. Knick. "Skilled Labor and the Choice of Technique in Edwardian Industry." *Explorations in Economic History* 11 (1974): 391–414.
Hounshell, David. *From American System to Mass Production.* Baltimore: Johns Hopkins University Press, 1986.
James, John A. "Structural Change in American Manufacturing, 1850–1890." *Journal of Economic History* 43 (1983): 433–60.
Lazonick, William, and Thomas Brush. "The 'Horndal Effect' in Early U.S. Manufacturing." *Explorations in Economic History* 22 (1985): 53–96.
McGouldrick, Paul. *New England Textiles in the 19th Century: Profits and Investment.* Cambridge: Harvard University Press, 1968.
Meyer, David R. "Midwestern Industrialization and the American Manufacturing Belt in the Nineteenth Century." *Journal of Economic History* 49 (1989): 921–38.
Neimi, Albert W. "Industrial Profits and Market Forces: The Antebellum South." *Social Science History* 13 (1989): 89–107.
Rosenberg, Nathan. "Technology." In *American Economic Growth,* ed. Lance Davis et al. New York: Harper & Row, 1972.
———. *Technology and American Economic Growth.* New York: Harper & Row, 1972.
Rothbarth, Edwin. "Causes of the Superior Efficiency of U.S.A. Industry as Compared to British Industry." *Economic Journal* 56 (1946): 383–90.
Rothenberg, Winifred. "The Market and Massachusetts Farmers, 1750–1855." *Journal of Economic History* 41 (1981): 283–314.
Sokoloff, Kenneth L. "Was the Transition from the Artisanal Shop to the Nonmechanized Factory Associated with Gains in Efficiency? Evidence from the U.S. Manufactures Censuses of 1820 and 1850." *Explorations in Economic History* 21 (1984): 351–82.
———. "Productivity Growth in Manufacturing during Early Industrialization: Evidence from the American Northeast, 1820–1860." In National Bureau of Economic Research, *Long-Term Factors in American Economic Growth,* Studies in Income and Wealth, vol. 51, ed. Stanley Engerman and Robert Gallman. Chicago: University of Chicago Press, 1986: 679–736.
Summers, L. H., and R. N Clarke. "The Labour Scarcity Controversy Reconsidered." *Economic Journal* 90 (1980): 129–139.
Temin, Peter. *Iron and Steel in Nineteenth Century America: An Economic Study.* Cambridge: MIT Press, 1964.
———. "Labor Scarcity and the Problem of American Industrial Efficiency in the 1850's." *Journal of Economic History* 26 (1966): 277–98.
———. "Steam and Water Power in the Early Nineteenth Century." *Journal of Economic History* 26 (1966): 187–205. Reprinted in Robert Fogel and Stanley Engerman, eds. *The Reinterpretation of American Economic History.* New York: Harper & Row, 1971: 228–37.
———. "Labor Scarcity in America." *Journal of Interdisciplinary History* 1 (1971): 251–64.

———. "Manufacturing." In *American Economic Growth,* ed. Lance Davis et al. New York: Harper & Row, 1972: 418–67.

Vedder, Richard, and Lowell Gallaway. "The Profitability of Antebellum Manufacturing: Some New Estimates." *Business History Review* 54 (1980): 92–103.

Vedder, Richard, and David Stockdale. "The Profitability of Slavery Revisited." *Agricultural History* 49 (1975): 392–404.

Zevin, Robert Brooke. "The Growth of Cotton Textile Production after 1815." In *The Reinterpretation of American Economic History,* eds. Robert Fogel and Stanley Engerman. New York: Harper & Row, 1971: 122–47.

———. *The Growth of Manufacturing in Early Nineteenth Century New England.* New York: Arno Press, 1975.

Population growth and redistribution

8

Population growth has been the driving force behind much of America's economic growth from colonial times to the present. The factors that underlie population rate of growth—the birthrate, death rate, and immigration rate—imply much about economic conditions in this country. As a former French consular official to the United States, Chevalier Félix de Beaujour, observed in 1814:

> Everything in the United States favours the progress of population; the emigrations from Europe, the disasters of the European colonies, but, above all, the abundance of the means of subsistence. Marriages are there easier than in Europe, births more multiplied, and deaths relatively less frequent. It is calculated that out of sixty individuals, two are married annually, that one is born out of every twenty, and that the proportion of deaths is only one in forty. This last report, founded on careful observations, seems incredible in a country so recently cleared and naturally not healthy; but it is nonetheless true, because it accords with the number of births, which there is greater than in Europe. In the United States, more children are necessarily born than among us, because the inhabitants, in such an extent of country, finding the means of subsistence more abundant, marry at an earlier age. No human consideration there operates as a hindrance to reproduction, and the children swarm on the rich land in the same manner as do insects.[1]

Since the early nineteenth century America's rate of population growth has slowed markedly. The birthrate, in particular, has fallen dramatically, and the waves of immigration, now regulated, are but shadows of their former

[1] Beaujour (1814).

selves. This chapter documents and interprets these changes and examines how the population has spatially redistributed itself across the face of the North American continent since 1607.

Population Growth

The American population exploded with the beginnings of white settlement. An immigrant population of just 2,302 in 1620 had grown to about 250,000 by 1700, 500,000 by the 1720s, 1 million by the 1740s and was probably about 2.5 million at the time of the Revolution. By the 1820s there were more than 10 million Americans. By the time World War I broke out, population totaled more than 100 million, and the latest estimates put the U.S. population at over 250 million (Figure 8.1).

The native Indian population, however, fared badly. When British settlement began, there may have been as many as 300,000 indigenous peoples in the eastern half of the country. By the time of the Revolution the Indian population had shrunk to 100,000 or less. European diseases, such as measles and smallpox, to which the native population had no natural immunities,

FIGURE 8.1

Rate of Growth and Size of the American Population, 1620–1990

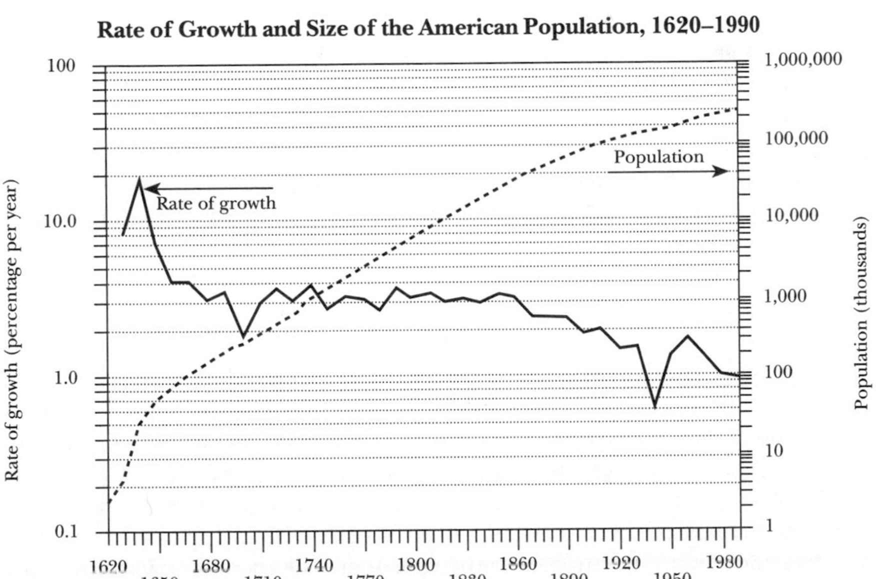

Source: U.S. Bureau of the Census, *Historical Statistics of the United States* (Washington, D.C.: Government Printing Office, 1975): Series A2 and Z1.

ravaged the indigenous population. Moreover, growing pressure on their resource base from encroaching settlers forced fundamental and destructive changes in Indian culture and life-style.

Population growth averaged over 5 percent per year during the seventeenth century, at which rate population doubles in less than fifteen years. Growth slowed abruptly after the initial burst of optimism but still averaged about 3 percent per year during the eighteenth and nineteenth centuries, a rate that leads to a doubling about every generation. Twentieth-century growth has been much slower and has exhibited periodic sharp fluctuations. Growth was particularly slow during the depression decade of the 1930s (when population grew at about 0.7 percent per year) and significantly more rapid during the 1950s, when growth averaged over 1.75 percent per year—the post–World War II baby boom. Since then the rate of growth has fallen and is currently about 1 percent per year, with a small rise in the 1980s as the baby boom generation had children of its own.

This pattern of population growth is the outcome of changes in the rate of natural increase—itself determined by the birth and death rates—and immigration. Let's consider each in turn.

Birthrate

Beaujour explained the "swarm" of children in America as the result of people marrying at an earlier age than customary in Europe and the absence of incentives to limit human reproduction. He was not the first, nor the last, to make this observation. In 1751 Benjamin Franklin observed: "Marriages in *America* are more general and more generally early, than in *Europe*. And if it is reckoned there, that there is but one marriage per annum among one hundred persons, perhaps we may here reckon two; and if in *Europe* they have but four Births to a marriage (many of their marriages being late) we may here reckon eight. . . ."[2]

At the start of the nineteenth century the birthrate was about fifty-five per thousand (Figure 8.2). Nor can it have been much higher earlier since the maximum biological potential for Homo sapiens is reckoned to be about sixty per thousand. During the course of the nineteenth century the birthrate was almost halved, falling to thirty per thousand by 1909 and dipping below twenty per thousand in the 1930s and in recent times. The pattern of long-run decline in the birthrate during the nineteenth century contrasts sharply with the fluctuations that have occurred in the twentieth century. In view of these radically differing patterns in birthrates between the nineteenth and twentieth centuries, it seems likely that different factors were at work in each century.

[2] Franklin (1755).

FIGURE 8.2

The Birthrate, 1800–1970

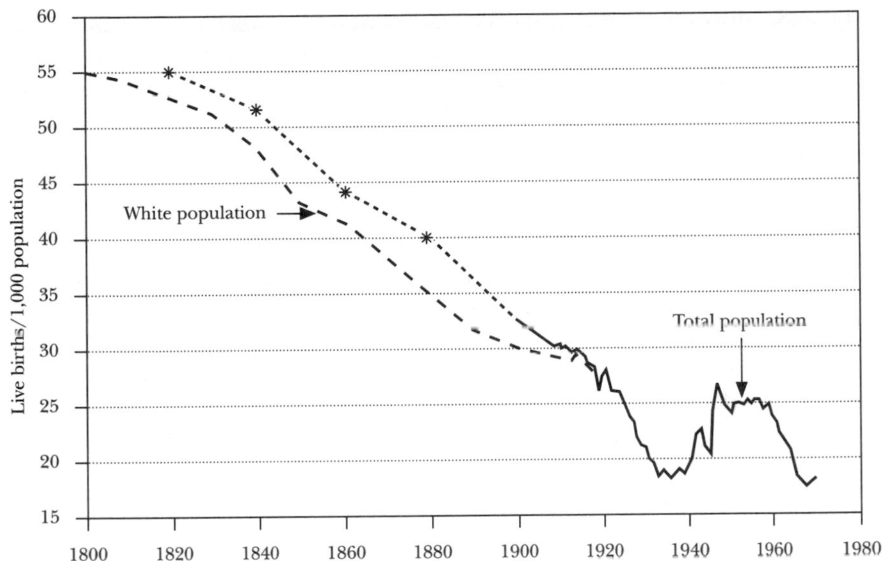

Source: U.S. Bureau of the Census, *Historical Statistics of the United States* (Washington, D.C.: Government Printing Office, 1975): Series B5 and B6.

The usual explanation for the secular decline in birthrates during the nineteenth century dates back even earlier, to the work of Franklin, who attributed the difference between America and Europe to differences in how and where people lived: "[I]n the cities . . . many live single during life, and continue servants to families, journeymen to Trades, &c., hence cities do not by natural generation supply themselves with inhabitants. . . . In countries full settled, the case must be nearly the same . . . those who cannot get land must labor for others that have it; when laborers are plenty, their wages will be low; by low wages a family is supported with difficulty; this difficulty deters many from marriage. . . ."[3] Almost half a century later Thomas Jefferson, in a letter to Jean Baptiste Say, the famed French economist, noted that "here the immense extent of uncultivated and fertile lands enables every one who will labor, to marry young, and to raise a family of any size."[4] This theme has been repeated and elaborated by generations of scholars since then from Ezra Seaman and George Tucker in the 1840s and 1850s to Richard Easterlin and others in the 1970s and 1980s.

[3] Ibid.

[4] Jefferson (February 1, 1804).

The key to these explanations of the birthrate is access to land. With agriculture the dominant source of employment and real estate the major source of wealth in America during the first three-quarters of the nineteenth century, land constituted the principal economic opportunity for most people. Residential crowding in urban areas, on the other hand, discouraged large families, while industrialization and the growth of the service sector created job opportunities for women outside the home, raising the opportunity cost of having children. Thus, other things being equal, economic opportunity and fertility are positively correlated; fertility and urbanization or industrialization are negatively related (Table 8.1).

The argument is as follows: On the expanding frontier (wherever that happened to be at any moment) land was abundant and entry costs were low. The land clearing necessary to make a farm on the frontier required large inputs of labor over a number of years, and the pattern crop cultivation and animal husbandry created myriad employment opportunities for family members of all ages. Demand for labor was therefore high on the frontier. This was reflected in the high wages and frequent complaints of labor scarcity at the time. One solution was for the farm family to produce its own labor force, just as it produced its own workstock and livestock. Such labor could be held captive at least until reaching its majority and maybe even beyond if the farmer used the threat and promise of inheritance judiciously. In the Northeast the relative scarcity of land by the start of the nineteenth century restricted entry. In the South economic opportunities were less readily available because slavery created a barrier to entry into the most profitable southern farming—plantation agriculture.

Although the relationship between land availability and economic opportunity seems clearly established, a universally acceptable measure of land availability has proved more elusive. Among the measures used have been cropland in 1949—a questionable measure of land availability in pre–Civil War America!—and the number of farms in 1880.[5] Richard Easterlin has used the ratio of improved acreage in a particular year to the maximum ever improved. The latter measure has proved quite successful and forms the basis of Easterlin's analysis of the relationship between land availability and fertility decline (measured by the ratio of children to women) in the United States.[6] His analysis of both aggregate state time series data and more microlevel cross-sectional data for 1860 suggests that fertility decline begins

[5] Respectively Yasuba (1961) and Forster and Tucker (1972).

[6] As an alternative to Easterlin's "settlement class" measure of land availability, Donald Leet (see Leet, 1975), one of Easterlin's students, has tried to measure the excess demand for land, approximating the potential supply of farm sites by the number of farms of average size that could be formed out of the available unimproved but cultivable land plus existing farms coming on the market as the result of mortality. This is then compared with the potential demand for farm sites represented by the number of unmarried males' coming of age. The resulting estimates of excess demand can explain much of the variation in fertility rates between townships. See Atack and Bateman (1987).

TABLE 8.1

Number of Children under 5 Years Old per 1,000 White Women Age 20–44 in the United States and Various Geographic Regions and in Urban and Rural Areas, 1800–1940

Region	1800	1810	1820	1830	1840	1910	1920	1930	1940
United States	1,281	1,290	1,236	1,134	1,070	609	581	485	400
Urban	845	900	831	708	701	469	471	388	311
Rural	1,319	1,329	1,276	1,189	1,134	782	744	658	551
New England	1,098	1,052	930	812	752	482	518	441	347
Urban	827	845	764	614	592	468	500	417	321
Rural	1,126	1,079	952	851	800	566	602	541	443
Middle Atlantic	1,279	1,289	1,183	1,036	940	533	539	424	320
Urban	852	924	842	722	711	495	501	386	286
Rural	1,339	1,344	1,235	1,100	1,006	650	680	590	457
East North-Central	1,840	1,702	1,608	1,467	1,270	555	548	458	388
Urban	...	1,256	1,059	910	841	470	485	400	326
Rural	1,840	1,706	1,616	1,484	1,291	672	668	605	533
West North-Central	...	1,810	1,685	1,678	1,445	630	584	495	431
Urban	...	...	...	1,181	705	426	416	365	324
Rural	...	1,810	1,685	1,703	1,481	760	711	614	538
South Atlantic	1,345	1,325	1,280	1,174	1,140	760	694	593	464
Urban	861	936	881	767	770	485	458	401	305
Rural	1,365	1,347	1,310	1,209	1,185	894	851	744	596
East South-Central	1,799	1,700	1,631	1,519	1,408	817	734	655	539
Urban	...	1,348	1,089	863	859	469	441	414	33
Rural	1,799	1,701	1,635	1,529	1,424	922	846	781	648
West South-Central	...	1,383	1,418	1,359	1,297	845	686	584	474
Urban	...	727	866	877	846	504	445	410	342
Rural	...	1,557	1,522	1,463	1,495	977	823	723	591

Source: Donald Bogue, *The Population of the United States* (Glencoe, Ill.: Free Press, 1959): 307.

not long after intensive settlement has begun, when perhaps as little as 20 to 40 percent of the cultivable farmland has been settled, when the land is far from "full settled" (Figure 8.3). Fertility decline is especially marked when less than 40 percent of the potential cultivable land remains.

Population trends in the South have tended to be ignored in the debate over differences between eastern and midwestern fertility rates. The data for

FIGURE 8.3

Child-Woman Ratio and Stage of Settlement for Five Settlement Classes and Six States, 1860

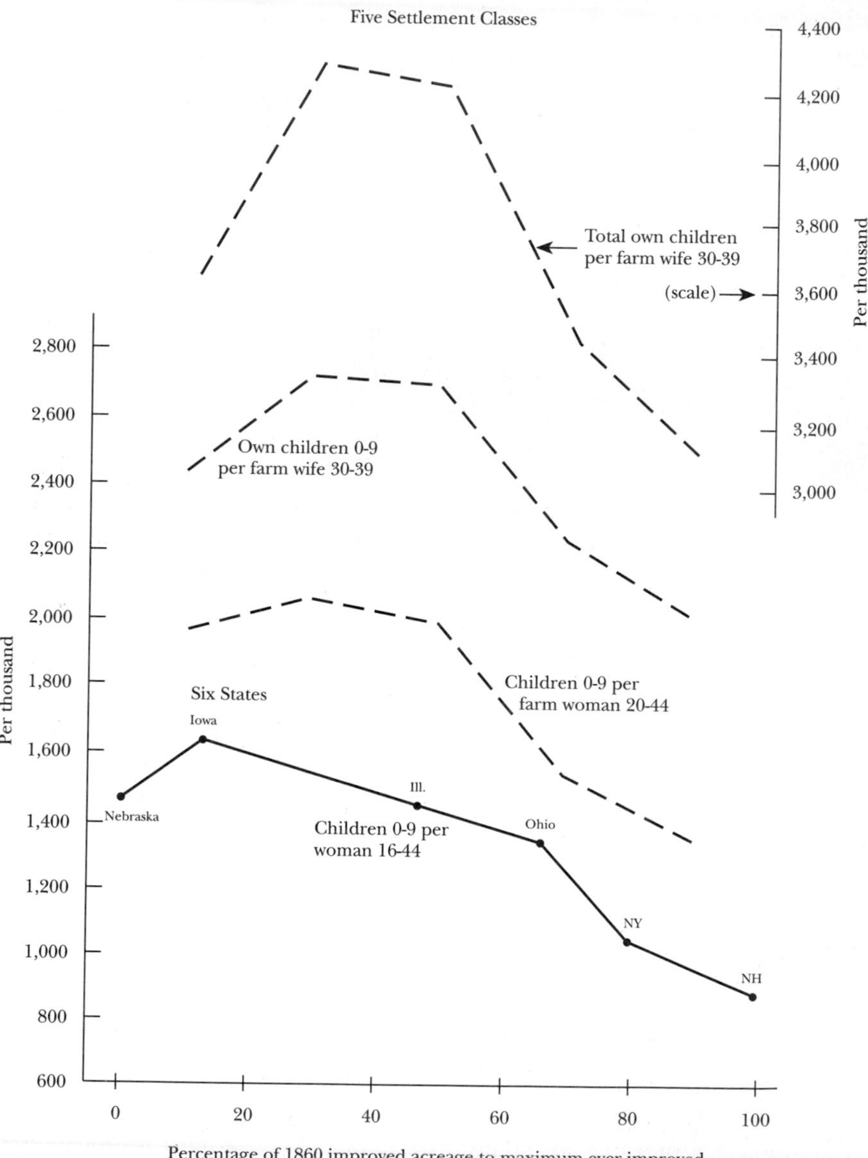

Sources: Richard Easterlin, "Population Change and Farm Settlement in the Northern United States," *Journal of Economic History* 36 (1976): 56. Reprinted by permission of Cambridge University Press. State data from Yasukicki Yasuba, *Birth Rates of the White Population in the United States 1800–1860* (Baltimore: Johns Hopkins University Press, 1961): 61, Table II-7; settlement class data from manuscript census samples).

the South, however, show the same pattern of declining child-woman ratios found for the nation as a whole and the subregions of the Northeast and Midwest.[7] Furthermore, when the southern data are split between the old South (coastal states as far south as Georgia) and the new South (Alabama southward and the interior southern states), fertility was lower in the old South than the New, but the difference narrowed over time (see also Table 8.1).

Underlying these interpretations of American fertility decline is the so-called target bequest model. Nineteenth-century farmers, for the most part, were relatively well-to-do; ownership of a farm almost certainly placed one in the upper half of the contemporary wealth distribution. Like most people who had accumulated wealth, farmers were interested in preserving and, if possible, increasing that wealth rather than in dissipating it. However, the typical farm was a family farm, and multigeniture—equal inheritance by all of equal blood tie—was the norm. In the target bequest model, parents are concerned about the division of their wealth among surviving children with the goal of passing along at least as much as the parents had inherited from their parents. Since the farm could be subdivided only so far before the units became uneconomically small, the farmer preferred to pass down the farm undivided but with an equal share of wealth to the other children, financed perhaps by a mortgage on the farm. If returns to farming were higher in the West than the East, then two farmers starting out with equal wealth—one in the East, one in the West—would choose to have different numbers of children. The farmer in the West, thanks to more rapid accumulation of wealth, would choose to have more children than his contemporary back East.

One implication of this story is that children should be more valuable on the frontier, where there were all these opportunities. Not so, if we accept recent estimates of the value of children in different parts of the country in 1860 (Table 8.2). On the basis of household-level census data, the very young children (six or younger) had little or no value on farms in the mid-nineteenth century. Indeed, a northeastern farm household must have derived consumption utility—satisfaction from the patter of one more set of little feet and the joy of perpetuating one's genetic endowment—equal to \$20.82. From age seven on, though, children did contribute to farm production. Children aged seven to twelve and teenage males were just as valuable in the more settled areas of the Midwest as on the frontier, while teenage females were much more valuable in settled than unsettled areas. Notice that adult women on the frontier contributed almost as much as they did on northeastern dairy farms and much more than women in the Midwest, where extensive grain cultivation rather than intensive animal husbandry was well established.[8]

[7] Steckel (1980).
[8] Craig (1991).

TABLE 8.2

Stage of Life Contributions to Farm Family Income by Men, Women, and Children by Region, 1860

Family Group	Northeast	Midwest	Frontier
Children, age 0–6	$ -20.82	$ 8.59	$ -6.41
Children, age 7–12	22.81	27.76	27.12
Teenage females	22.95	39.75	17.53
Teenage males	111.03	47.45	49.03
Adult women	154.08	70.25	147.28
Adult men	294.77	186.44	193.66

Source: Lee Craig, "The Value of Household Labor in Antebellun Northern Agriculture," *Journal of Economic History* 51 (1991): 74, Table 3. Reprinted by permission of Cambridge University Press.

The target bequest model is not the only explanation for the observed decline in fertility in the nineteenth century. An alternative strategic bequest model has been suggested.[9] In this model the promise of an inheritance is used as an incentive for children to behave a certain way. Specifically there is an implicit agreement between children and parents that children will care for their parents in old age in return for a share of family wealth, through either inheritance or a transfer to heirs prior to death. However, as labor markets in the high-productivity nonagricultural sector improved, the bargaining power shifted in favor of children who could point to the opportunity cost of remaining on the family farm. Each child could expect and demand more in compensation for these forgone alternatives. As a result, the probability that a child would stay around to care for aging parents declined—a process which has been termed child default.[10] As the risk of child default increases, the value that parents place on children as a source of security in old age decreases. Under such circumstances, rational parents would reduce their fertility—that is, have fewer children.

Implicit in both models of fertility decline is the argument that the number of children was a decision variable for nineteenth-century parents. Children were not accidents; rather fertility was part of an overall family strategy. Certainly for the late nineteenth and early twentieth centuries, survey data exist in which women describe their strategies for avoiding unwanted pregnancy, including infrequent intercourse, the use of barriers, withdrawal, the rhythm method, and douching, as well as abortion.[11] But what about earlier? Considering that the birthrate at the beginning of the

[9] Sundstrom and David (1988). Ransom and Sutch (1986, 1989).
[10] Williamson (1985).
[11] David and Sanderson (1986).

nineteenth century was close to the maximum biological potential, the use of family planning seems unlikely. By mid-century, however, average birth intervals of 2.5 to 3 years fall in the gray area between no contraception (or complete contraceptive failure) and planned (that is, contracepted) pregnancies. There is also some indirect evidence of a change in behavior right about this time. Family histories reveal a marked decline in age-specific marital fertility rates beginning about the time of the civil War and perhaps as early as 1850. Women in their mid to late thirties stopped having children.[12] The most likely explanation for this sudden change is a switch in parental preferences for children, presumably accompanied by some change in behavior (for example, abstinence).

Fertility—the number of children born to a woman over her lifetime—is the product of several factors: the age at which the woman first starts having children (generally associated with marriage in traditional societies), the average interval between children (which may be associated with deliberate family planning), the age at which childbearing ceases, and the probability that a woman is at risk—that is, that she marries. Even when contraceptive devices were absolutely unavailable, societies were able to regulate fertility through cultural norms about the frequency of intercourse and when to engage in sexual activity during the woman's menstrual cycle, as well as by postponing marriage and encouraging spinsterhood. For example, women can avoid marriage if there are job opportunities outside the home that offer financial independence, and the existence of such opportunities also makes it easier to avoid early marriage.

During the nineteenth century the marriage rate was fairly stable (Figure 8.4), though there is evidence that more women postponed marriage until later in life. Thus fertility rates were reduced by limiting the number of children a women could bear. In the twentieth century, on the other hand, the marriage rate has fluctuated sharply, reflecting changing societal norms, the effects of wars, depressions, and economic opportunities for women.

Death Rates

There was no systematic nationwide registration of births and deaths in the United States until the 1930s. This is much less of a problem for estimating birthrates than death rates since successful birthing outcomes resulted in the definite presence of a new person, whereas deaths were simply marked by the unexplained absence of an individual. As a result, much less is known about crude death rates than about crude birthrates. The death rate in 1700 was about forty per thousand, so that the natural rate of increase of popula-

[12] Wahl (1986).

FIGURE 8.4

Marriage and Divorce Rates, 1870–1960

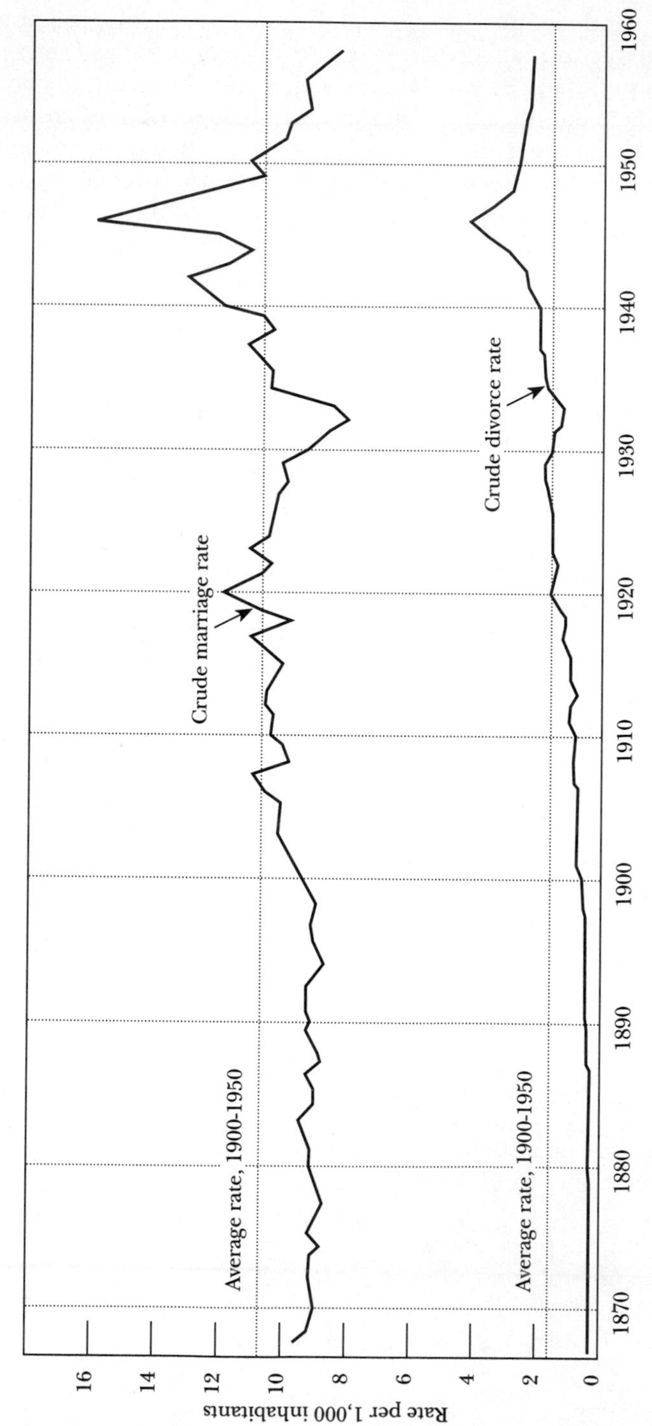

Source: Donald Bogue, *The Population of the United States* (Glencoe, Ill.: Free Press, 1959): 237.

tion was about 1.5 percent.[13] By 1850 death rates had fallen more than 40 percent to about twenty-three per thousand for the white population.[14] With white birthrates of about forty-three per thousand, these estimates imply an increase of perhaps one-third in the natural rate of growth of population to about 2 percent per year. In 1900 the death rate had declined to about seventeen per thousand, but because the birthrate declined faster, the rate of natural increase of population fell to about 1.3 percent. By 1970 it had fallen to only about 0.8 percent per year with a crude death rate of under ten per thousand.

This drop in mortality occurred despite a general aging of the population, especially from the late nineteenth century onward. Such a shift can markedly affect the crude death rate because persons in each age-group have a differential risk of dying, whether from aging, disease, childbirth, or accident. In 1860, for example, about 16 percent of the rural population in the North was less than five years old, while about 6 percent was in its early thirties and only 2 percent of the population was in its early sixties (Figure 8.5). Ninety years later, in 1950, despite the baby boom after World War II, only about 11 percent of the population was under five years old, while almost 9 percent was in its early thirties and over 5 percent was in its early sixties (Figure 8.6). The age pyramid for the United States in 1860 has the characteristic shape of a population growing rapidly through natural increase with a broad base and progressively smaller older age cohorts. By 1950, however, the American population was aging; some older age cohorts were larger than younger age cohorts. The deficit is particularly marked among those born during the depression, who would have been between nine and twenty-one years old in 1950. Adjusting the crude death rate for the changing age structure of the population can have a significant effect. For example, if America had as young a population in 1980 as it had in 1700, the death rate (the standardized death rate) would have been only about five per thousand, or only about half of what it actually was.[15]

The dependence of crude death rates upon the age structure of the population has led many scholars to rely upon estimates of life expectancy for a particular age-group rather than the probability of death in the population at large. Depending upon which age-group is chosen, the data tell somewhat different stories. Life expectancy at birth (e_0) is heavily influenced by infant mortality (the probability of dying between birth and age one). The risks faced by the newborn are many; few were more deadly than waterborne diarrheal diseases to which many succumbed. As a result, life expectancy at birth may be short (Figure 8.7), be subject to sharp fluctuations, and show sharp improvement as a result of modest improvements in sanitation and

[13] Fogel (1986).
[14] Haines (1979).
[15] Fogel (1986).

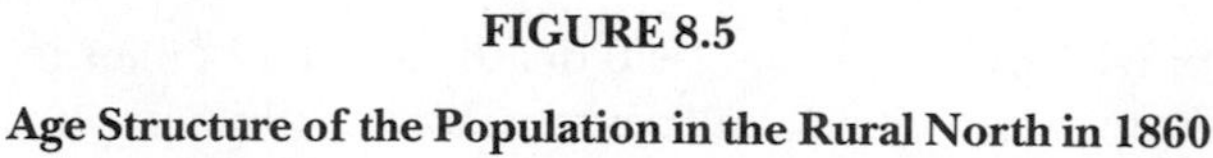

FIGURE 8.5

Age Structure of the Population in the Rural North in 1860

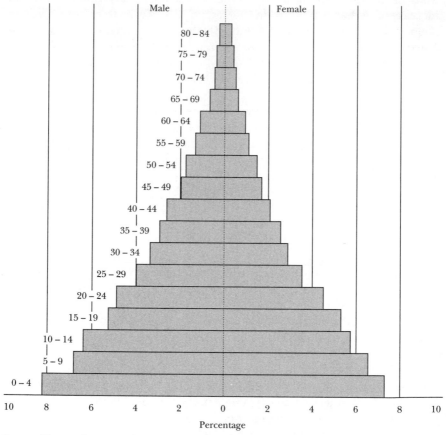

Source: Manuscript census data from the Bateman-Foust sample.

the provision of a safe water and safe milk supply. By age ten, on the other hand, most infant and childhood diseases no longer pose so great a threat to life, and therefore, life expectancy at age 10 (e_{10}) is often preferred as an index of mortality. Data show rising life expectancy (implying falling mortality) throughout most of the eighteenth century.[16] But life expectancy seems to have declined during the first half of the nineteenth century, falling below levels at the start of the eighteenth century by the 1830s. This trend reversed itself about the time of the Civil War; since then life expectancy has generally increased, and by implication, mortality has decreased.[17]

[16] Ibid.
[17] Ibid.

FIGURE 8.6

Age Structure in 1950

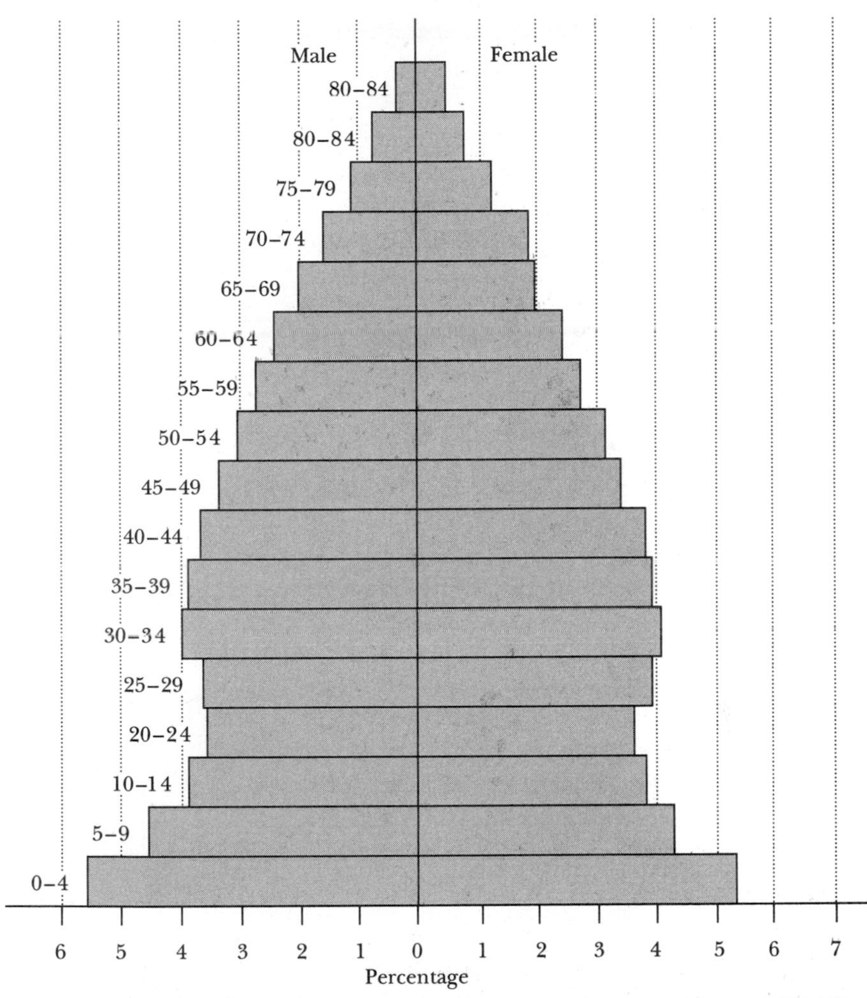

Source: Donald Bogue, *The Population of the United States* (Glencoe, Ill.: Free Press, 1959): 107.

The decline in the birthrate during the nineteenth and twentieth centuries reflects changes in society's preferences and the need for children. However, since few people wish to die, the change in death rates must be explained by other factors. For many years, the conventional wisdom has attributed declining death rates to improved medical care and medical knowledge, reduced virulence of diseases through mutation in the disease organism or human immunity, improvements in personal hygiene, and the provision of public sanitation.

FIGURE 8.7

Life Expectancy in America, 1720–1982

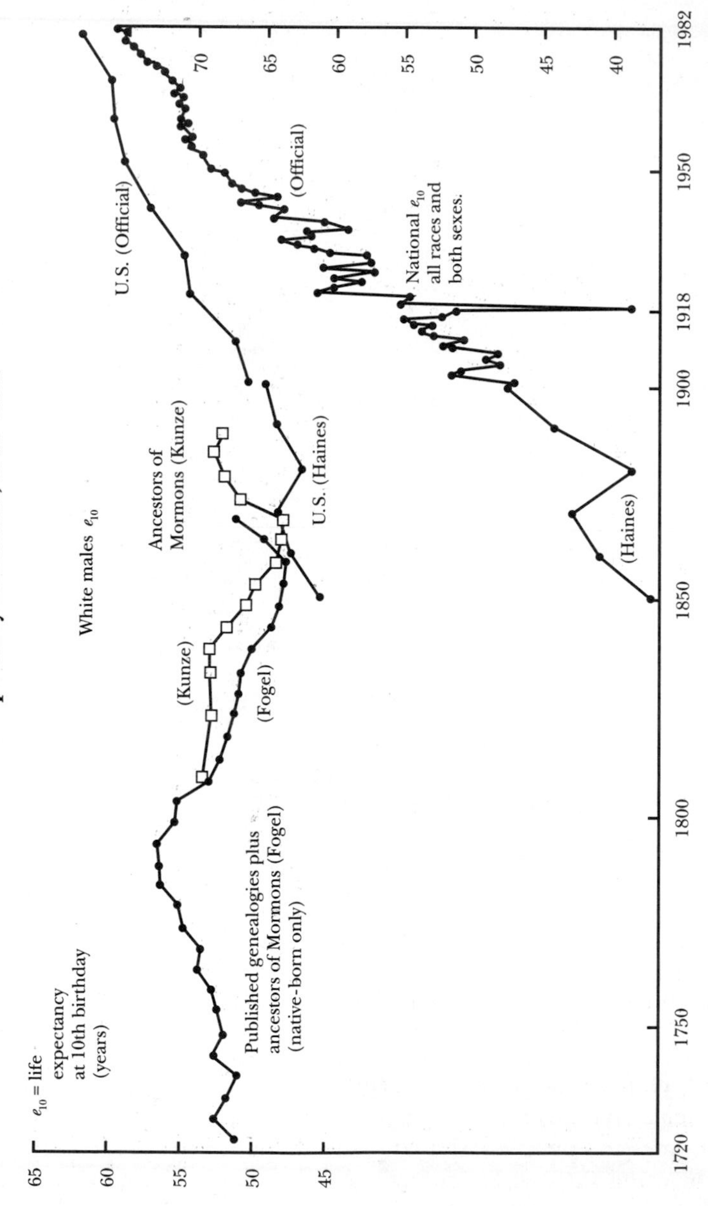

Source: Peter Lindert, "Comment," in National Bureau of Economic Research, *Long Term Factors in American Economic Growth*,, vol. 51, ed. Stanley L. Engerman and Robert E. Gallman (Chicago: University of Chicago Press, 1986): 530.

Epidemiologist Thomas McKeown, however, finds little historical evidence to support these claims in Great Britain. For example, hospitalization actually increased the risk of death; improved personal hygiene through washing hands not only was ineffective but may have actually spread disease so long as water supplies remained polluted; urban crowding increased the spread of infectious diseases. The rate of decline in mortality is too great to be explained by natural selection. Instead McKeown argues that the decline in mortality is most likely explained by increases in the quality and quantity of food available to each person, which improved nutrition and increased human resistance to disease, particularly among children and adolescents. The same argument has been applied to the United States, though there is clearly an anomaly in the first half of the nineteenth century.[18] During this period, and certainly after about 1820, per capita income was growing. So, too, was the available domestic food supply per person. Nevertheless, mortality increased and life expectancy fell until the 1870s. The reasons for the decline are not yet clearly identified; certainly there is no reason to suspect increased virulence from disease pathogens, retrogression in medical knowledge, or a genetic weakening of the population through, for example, increased immigration. Rather it is suspected that urban disamenities—crowding, poor sanitation, and unsafe water supplies—may play a role. So, too, might the lengthening food supply line between progressively more distant farms and growing cities in an era of poor transportation, resulting in a reduction in the nutritional quality of food at a time when the quantity of food was increasing.

This latter hypothesis gains additional credibility from estimates of antebellum mortality in Massachusetts. Life expectancy in rural areas during the seventeenth and eighteenth centuries was significantly higher than in the major urban areas, such as Boston. The urban-rural difference narrowed substantially during the late eighteenth and early nineteenth centuries—a period of considerable improvement in internal transportation in New England.[19] However, none of the public health changes taking place in the cities—pure water, treatment and disposal of sewage, pasteurization of milk, expanded medical care—were taking place in the countryside at this time. Country folk still drew water from shallow wells or cisterns, used outdoor privies, drank raw milk, and trusted nature for healing. Consequently, it is unlikely that the elimination of these possible disease vectors were the source of increased longevity in cities. During the same period, though, real incomes were rising, and those higher incomes probably went into better food and better housing. Indeed, there is a statistically significant negative relationship between crude death rates and personal income per capita: Areas where income was higher had markedly lower crude death rates, all

[18] Ibid.
[19] Vinovskis (1978); Higgs (1973).

FIGURE 8.8

A Schematic of Demographic Transition

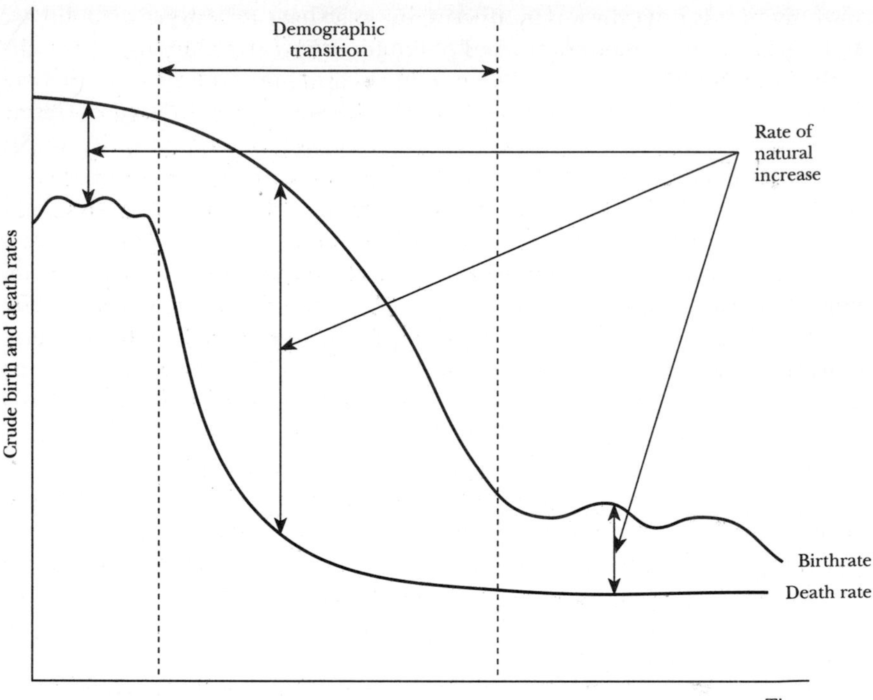

else being equal.[20] Urban living and illiteracy are also associated with significantly higher death rates. Even so, the impact of public sanitation should not be underestimated. For example, deaths from typhoid fever fell 85 percent in Pittsburgh after the city began filtering its water supply.

The widening spread between crude birthrates and crude death rates described above marks what demographers refer to as the demographic transition. This is represented by a shift from a regime of high birthrates and high death rates to low birthrates and low death rates. During the transition, however, the death rate declines more rapidly than the birthrate (Figure 8.8). The result is rapid population growth during the transit from one regime to the other. It may last a number of generations, as in the United States, or it may occur in less than a generation, as in some Latin American and Asian countries in the twentieth century.

[20] Meeker (1974).

Population Growth: The African-American Experience

Our discussion of birthrates and death rates above focuses upon the experiences of white Americans. The African-American experience was different, although the data exhibit the same overall pattern of declining birthrates and rising longevity. However, the decline in, and levels of, African-American crude birthrates lagged those of the white population by forty or fifty years, although the lag seems to have narrowed over time. Whereas the crude birthrate among whites had fallen to under forty per thousand by 1870, African-American birthrates remained above this level until after 1900 (Table 8.3). Black life expectancy has also lagged behind that of the white population. By 1930 a newborn white could expect to live to age 60.8, whereas a black infant had a life expectancy of only 48.5 years. Not until 1950 could an African-American infant expect to live more than 60 years. By then, though, life expectancy among whites was almost 70 years. A major factor behind the much shorter life expectancy of African-Americans (as well as a partial explanation of the higher birthrate) is their significantly higher infant mortality rate, which has been at least 50 percent higher than among the infants born of white parents. Indeed, in more recent times the infant mortality rate for African-Americans has been almost double that for whites. The high rate of death in infancy reflects the effects of poverty, which produces more low-birth-weight infants that are at risk medically, and poorer medical care both during pregnancy and postpartum.

Immigration

American population growth in the nineteenth century was rapid not only because of high rates of natural increase but also because millions of immigrants landed on these shores. The "official" statistics show that between 1820 and 1860, for example, more than 5 million immigrants came—most from Western Europe. More recent estimates put the level of immigration as high as 7 million during this time period; the actual number is probably even higher.[21] Even less is known about immigration prior to 1820, when the U.S. government began requiring ships' captains to deliver manifests of passengers to customs at the ports of entry. Estimates put the flow at 110,000 between 1700 and 1730, 115,000 between 1730 and 1760, 444,000 from 1760 to 1790, and 673,000 from 1790 to 1820.[22]

Regardless of what the "true" totals are, immigrants were not a cross section of the European population in any year. Rather during specific periods one country or another tended to dominate the flow (Figure 8.9). For ex-

[21] McClelland and Zeckhauser (1982); Boyle and O'Grada (1982).
[22] Gemery (1984).

TABLE 8.3

Fertility and Mortality in the United States, 1800–1980

Date	Birthrate[a]		Child-Woman Ratio[b]		Total Fertility Rate[c]		Expectation of Life[d]		Infant Mortality Rate[e]	
	White	Black[f]	White	Black[f]	White	Black[f]	White	Black[f]	White	Black[f]
1800	55.0		1342		7.04					
1810	54.3		1358		6.92					
1820	52.8		1295		6.73					
1830	51.4		1145		6.55					
1840	48.3		1085		6.14					
1850	43.3	58.6[g]	892	1087	5.42	7.90[g]	38.9		217.4	
1860	41.4	55.0[h]	905	1072	5.21	7.58[h]	40.9[k]		196.9[k]	
1870	38.3	55.4[i]	814	997	4.55	7.69[i]	44.1		176.0	
1880	35.2	51.9[j]	780	1090	4.24	7.26[j]	39.6		214.8	
1890	31.5	48.1	685	930	3.87	6.56	45.7		150.9	
1900	30.1	44.4	666	845	3.56	5.61	49.6		120.1	
1910	29.2	38.5	631	736	3.42	4.61	51.9		113.0	
1920	26.9	35.0	604	608	3.17	3.64	57.4	47.0	82.1	131.7
1930	20.6	27.5	506	554	2.45	2.98	60.8	48.5	60.1	99.9
1940	18.6	26.7	419	513	2.22	2.87	65.0	53.9	43.2	73.8
1950	23.0	33.3	580	663	2.98	3.93	69.1	60.8	26.8	44.5
1960	22.7	32.1	717	895	3.53	4.52	70.7	63.6	22.9	43.2
1970	17.4	25.1	507	689	2.38	3.07	71.7	65.2	17.8	30.9
1980	14.9	22.1			1.75	2.32	74.4	68.1	11.0	19.1

[a] Births per 1,000 population per annum. [b] Children aged 0–4 per 1,000 women aged 20–44. [c] Total number of births per woman if she experienced the current period age-specific fertility rates throughout her life. [d] Expectation of life at birth. [e] Infant deaths per 1,000 live births per annum. [f] Black and other population. [g] Average for 1850–59. [h] Average for 1860–69. [i] Average for 1870–79. [j] Average for 1880–84. [k] For the total population.

Sources: U.S. Bureau of the Census, *Historical Statistics of the United States* (Washington, DC: Government Printing Office, 1975). U.S. Bureau of the Census, *Statistical Abstract of the United States, 1988* (Washington, DC: Government Printing Office, 1987). Ansley J. Coale and Melvin Zelnick, *New Estimates of Fertility and Population in the United States* (Princeton: Princeton University Press, 1963). Ansley J. Coale and Norfleet W. Rives, "A Statistical Reconstruction of the Black Population of the United States, 1880–1970: Estimates of True Numbers by Age and Sex, Birth Rates, and Total Fertility," *Population Index* 39, No. 1 (1973): 3–36. Michael R. Haines, "The Use of Model Life Tables to Estimate Mortality for the United States in the Late Nineteenth Century," *Demography* 16 (1979): 289–312.

FIGURE 8.9

The Sources of European Migrants to the United States, 1841–1910

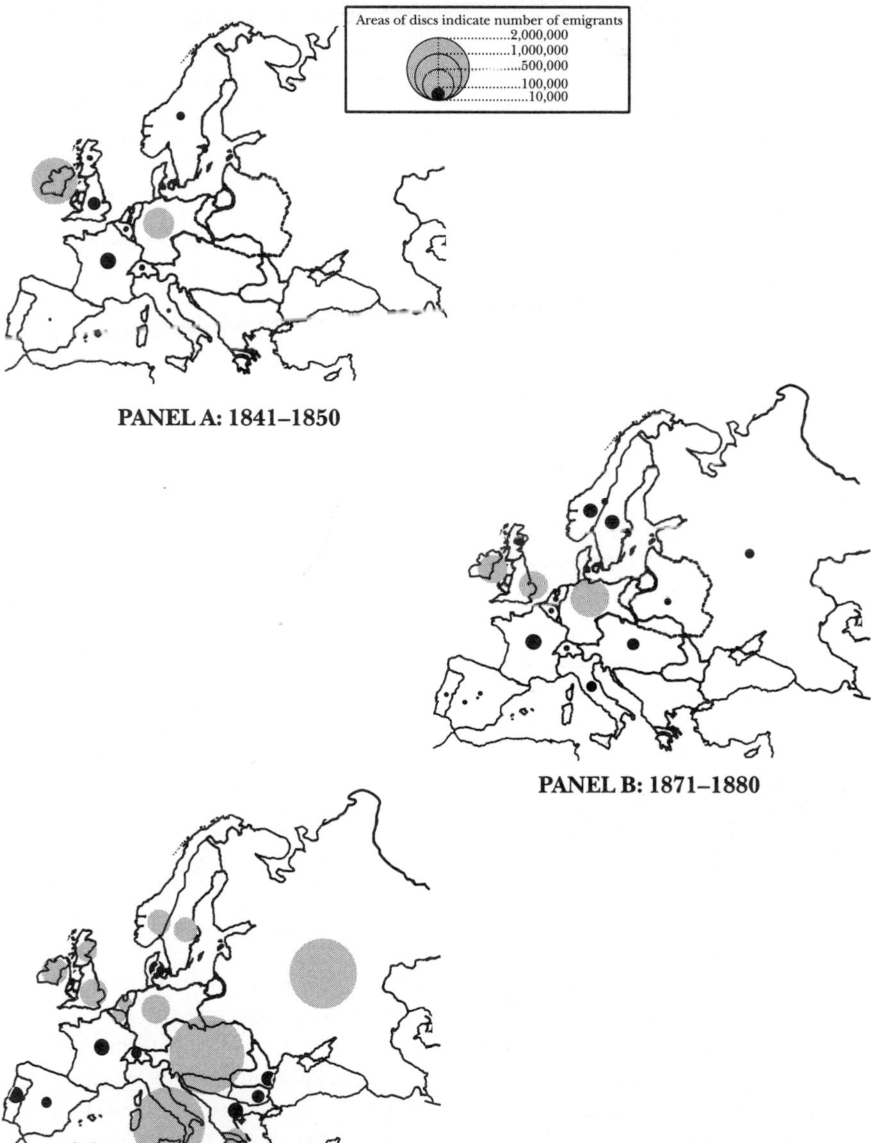

Source: Charles O. Paullin, *Atlas of Historical Geography of the United States* (Washington, D.C.: Carnegie Institution, 1932): Plate 70, Panels F, J, and M.

ample, the Irish flocked to America (as well as England) during and after the potato famine of 1845–46. Germans fled by the thousands in the aftermath of political repression following the unsuccessful 1848 revolution. From 1847 to 1854 more than 100,000 Irish immigrants arrived each year; between 1852 and 1854 German immigrants averaged over 150,000 a year. These flows, however, were small beside the massive inflows from Central Europe, Russia, and Italy at the end of the nineteenth century that mark the so-called New Immigration. Between 1900 and 1914 more than 200,000 Central European immigrants came each year. During the same period migration from Russia averaged over 150,000; another 200,000-plus arrived from Italy each year. In the 1940s refugees fleeing war-torn Europe came to these shores; in the 1960s, Cubans fleeing Castro; in the 1970s it was the turn of the Vietnamese and Soviet Jews. As a result, the vast majority of Americans today count immigrants among their forebears.

Not only have there been significant switches in the sources of immigration during the nineteenth and twentieth centuries, but there have also been sharp year-to-year fluctuations in immigration (Figure 8.10). Why? What was it that brought these waves of people to the United States? Explanations fall into two broad but distinct categories. Some emphasize the "push" factors from the Old World that drove emigrants to seek their fortunes elsewhere. Among those push factors are religious and civil repression (for example, the pogroms against Russian Jews or the repression following the 1848 revolution in Germany), poverty (Italy), hunger (Ireland in the wake of the potato famine), war (Vietnam), and lack of opportunity (working classes from England and Scotland or Haiti). On the other side of the coin are explanations that stress the "pull" that lured immigrants to the New World—cheap land, high wages, social equality, and religious and civil freedom—regardless of whether the new world to which they were drawn was North America, Argentina, or Australia. There is a remarkable lack of consensus about which of these factors were dominant in any particular case at any moment in time.

Was immigration to America in the 1840s and 1850s dominated by push factors in the Old World—the potato famine and political repression—or was it dominated by the pull of high real wages?[23] Differences in opinion may result from viewing multinational migratory movements from the narrow perspective of either the sending country or the receiving country.[24] Viewed from the sending country, the emphasis is upon those factors driving emigrants to seek a life elsewhere; viewed from the receiving country, the focus is upon why they chose one particular country as their destination—why the United States instead of Canada, Argentina, or Australia? Thus, for example,

[23] The push factors, for example, are stressed by Thomas (1973); the pull factors by Williamson (1974).
[24] Neal (1976).

FIGURE 8.10

Immigration, 1820–1970

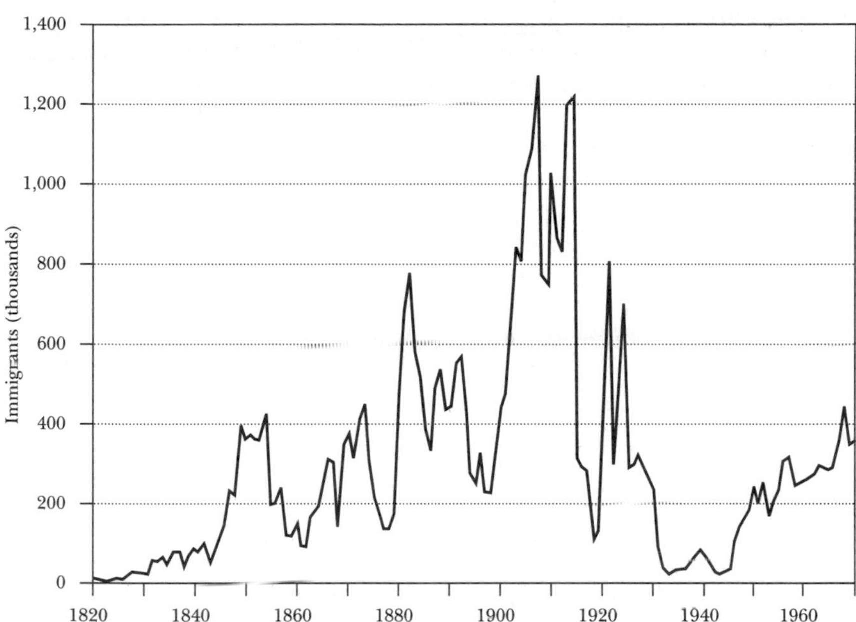

Source: U.S. Bureau of the Census, *Historical Statistics of the United States* (Washington, D.C.: Government Printing Office, 1975): Series C89.

the emigrant flow from the United Kingdom to America can be modeled as a function of high wages and low unemployment in the United States (pull factors) and high unemployment and low wages in Britain (push factors). In addition, measures of emigrant flows from Britain to Australia, Canada, and South Africa (the major alternatives to migrating to the United States) must be included, along with proxies for business cycle downturns in the United States. The results show both push and pull factors at work, but with the pull more important.[25]

Whether driven by push or drawn by pull, more than forty million people moved from Europe to the New World between 1850 and 1914, with every country participating in the outflow to a greater or lesser extent at some time. Secular trends in emigration seem to be systematically related to the rate of natural increase in the source population at any level of income, while for any given rate of natural increase in the sending population, emigration varies inversely with per capita income.[26] However, the shorter-term

[25] Gallaway, Vedder and Shukla (1974).
[26] Easterlin (1971).

fluctuations in emigration seem to be systematically related to the business cycle and to the longer, fifteen- to twenty-year Kuznets cycles in business activity in the principal receiving country, the United States.

By 1870 one-seventh of the U.S. population was foreign-born. This fraction remained more or less constant until World War I, when fighting and then executive and legislative restrictions, such as the quotas imposed in 1921 and 1924, interrupted immigration. The majority of immigrants were young adult men, of prime working age. They participated more fully in the labor market than the native population, making up perhaps one-fifth of the gainfully employed between 1870 and 1910, consistent with the pull of economic opportunity in this country.

The Impact of Immigration on the American Economy

In this spirit, Jeffrey Williamson has modeled the response of immigration to real wages in urban-industrial areas of the East Coast and its impact on the domestic labor market in the United States. He assumes that potential immigrants (emigrants) respond to the real wage in the United States—the pull—represented by the slope of the immigrant supply function, S_i, as well as the push, captured here by the magnitude of the East Coast real wage necessary to induce anyone to emigrate to America, α (Figure 8.11). Thus worsening conditions in the sending country increase the pool of would-be emigrants and shift the supply curve down and to the right (i.e., reduce α), while increased optimism about life in the United States will make the immigrant (emigrant) supply function more elastic (i.e., flatter).

The demand for labor in the urban markets of the East Coast is then represented by D while the aggregate supply of labor is the sum of the domestic labor supply S_d and the immigrant labor attracted to these shores by the American real wage rate. An increase in the demand for labor because of an expanding manufacturing sector will then both increase the real wage rate and increase the inflow of immigrants. Similarly, a reduction in the domestic urban labor supply in response to the opportunities created by cheap land on the western frontier will also raise real wages and lead to increased immigration.

Williamson uses this model to decompose the migrant flow into that portion attributable to increased real wages in America (pull factors)—movements along the supply function—and shifts in the supply curve itself (push factors). His results suggest that for the period 1870–90, migration to the United States would have totaled 4.4 million as a result of the pull factors, but the actual migration was only 3.8 million over the period. As a result, he concludes, push factors must have worked to keep more than half a million would-be immigrants at home. In the next twenty-year period the pull got stronger, but so, too, did forces, such as improving living standards,

FIGURE 8.11

Immigration and East Coast Urban-Industrial Labor Markets

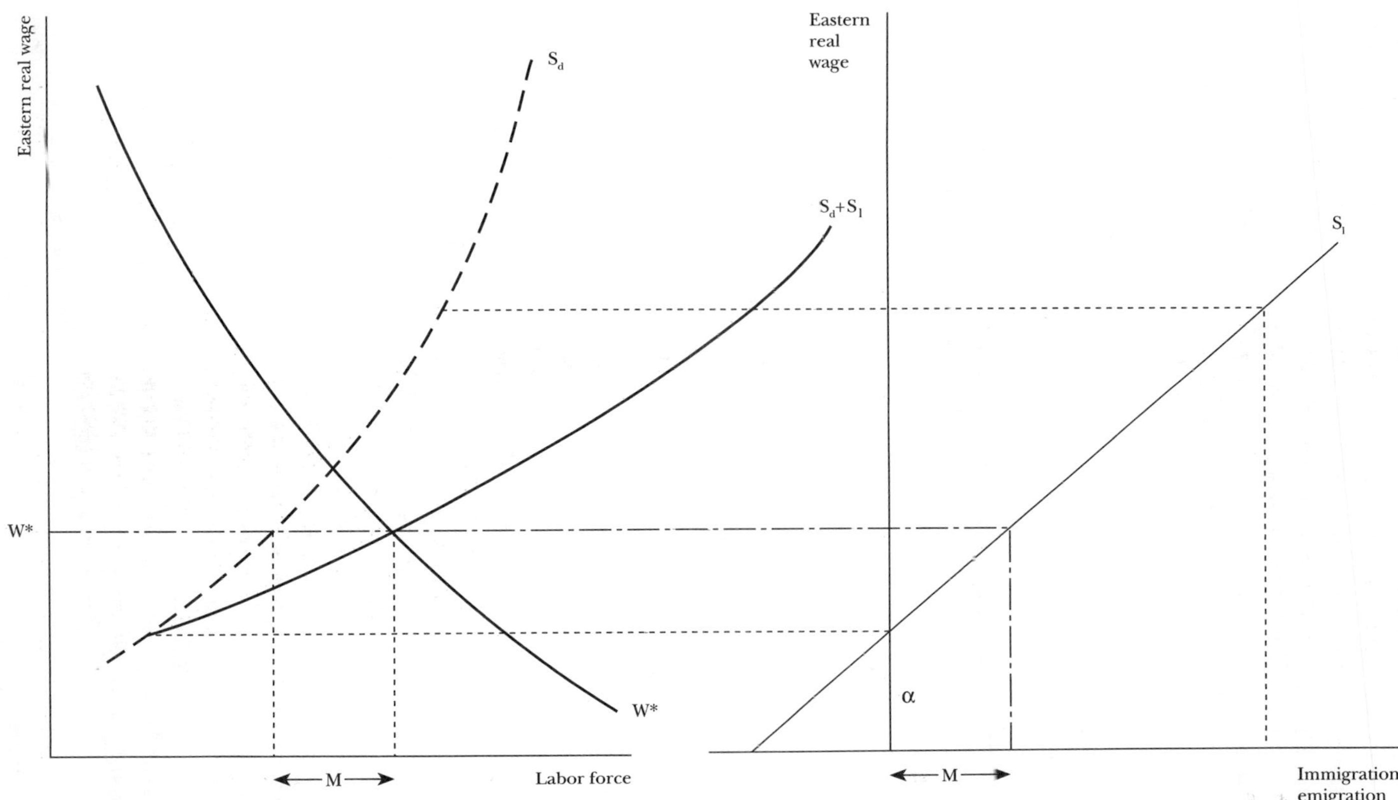

Source: Jeffrey Williamson, "Migration to the New World: Long Term Influences and Impact." *Explorations in Economic History* 2 (1974): 361.

that kept a would-be migrant population home. As a result, Williamson argues that immigration into the United States over the period 1870–1910 would have been some 20 percent greater had European employment and living standards remained at their 1870 levels.

The impact of this immigration upon American wages was minimal. Real eastern wages might have been only about 1 percent lower if immigration had been 20 percent greater. In addition, the effect of cheap western land upon immigration during this period was negligible. If the land stock had remained constant at its 1870 level, net additions to the American foreign-born population would have been only three-tenths of 1 percent below their actual 1910 levels. Immigrants, however, added to urban congestion and constituted a large part of the industrial labor force. Moreover, with different labor traditions from those that grew up in America, immigrant laborers often formed the nucleus of the small but growing labor movement in the late nineteenth century, contributing to the radicalization of the American labor unions.

In our discussion of population growth, we asserted that population growth in the United States was the sum of natural increase and immigration. The view that immigrants were a net addition to the population was, however, challenged by those who argued for controls and limitations on immigration. Francis A. Walker, onetime superintendent of the federal census, noted statistician, and president of MIT, for example, put the case bluntly: "Foreign immigration into this country has . . . amounted not to a reenforcement of our population, but to a replacement of native by foreign stock. . . . If the foreigners had not come, the native element would long have filled the places the foreigners usurped."[27]

Implicit behind this view, of course, is the ugly specter of racial prejudice directed especially against the new immigrants from southern and Eastern Europe. It is therefore pertinent to ask whether immigrants contributed to American economic growth and how their contribution may have changed over time. Were the new immigrants less valuable than the old? Was Walker right? One way to make a lower-bound estimate of the contribution of immigrants is to assume that they simply displaced American-born natives and added nothing to the secular growth of the American labor force. Even so, immigrants would have contributed to the rate of growth of total output since they arrived as full-grown, productive adults. The economy therefore saved those resources that would have been expended in raising a similar number of native-born children. These resources could then be invested in their next best alternative use. Compounded at 3 percent per year, by 1850 approximately 4.7 percent of the total physical capital stock could be attributable to the effects of immigration. By 1880 this figure could have been 10.5

[27] Francis A. Walker, *Discussions in Economics and Statistics* (New York: H. Holt and Company, 1899): 422–25.

percent of the capital stock, and by 1912, 13.2 percent. At 6 percent, a more realistic rate of return, which more closely approximates other rates of return in the economy, immigration might have contributed as much as 9.2 percent of the capital stock by 1850, 18.4 percent by 1880, and 41.9 percent by 1912. At the 3 percent rate of compounding, these estimates imply a five-year retardation in the level of the capital stock; at 6 percent, eighteen years.[28] Clearly, then, immigration had a profound effect upon American growth during the nineteenth century. These estimates make no allowance for the skills and other human capital that the immigrants also contributed. It is likely that their human capital was many times larger than their stock of physical capital.

Two final points deserve to be made about immigration. First, it was but one of the contemporary factor flows. Capital flows—physical, financial, and human—followed. Not only was the United States the largest receiving country for immigration, but it also received the largest share of international foreign investment, beginning with canals and then the railroads. Foreign capital also flowed into American land and American businesses. There was also a smaller return flow of repatriated earnings not just on foreign investments in this country but also from the earnings of immigrants returned to the sending country to support dependents there or to finance further emigration. Second, these factor flows might be regarded as substitutes for the flow of goods. Such factor flows make special sense when transportation is relatively poor and expensive, as it was until the late nineteenth century, although millions more came even after transportation costs had fallen, making the movement of goods more economical.

Population Redistribution

The international movements of labor discussed above are just one part of a broader picture of labor migration both between and within national boundaries. Not only did tens of millions of foreigners choose to emigrate to America, but millions of Americans chose to live somewhere other than where they had been born or where they had been living just a few years earlier. The American population was a restless one, continually uprooting and moving to a new location. As a contemporary European observer remarked, "every day was moving day" in the United States. Like the international migrants, push factors—such as crime, worsening economic opportunities, prejudice, encroachment by groups with different life-styles, reputation, or whatever—may have played a role in the decision of native-born Americans to move. So, too, did pull factors, such as the opportunity of cheap land on which to start a farm or the attraction of high(er)-paying, more glamorous

[28] Neal and Uselding (1972).

jobs in the towns and cities. In particular, throughout much of the nineteenth century, the "frontier" (defined as that area where population density was between two and six persons—i.e., less than one family—per square mile) had great allure. As Frederick Jackson Turner, the great American historian of the frontier, put it, "[W]henever social conditions tended to crystallize in the East, whenever capital tended to press upon labor or political restraints to impede the freedom of the mass, there was this gate of escape to the free conditions of the frontier. These free lands promoted individualism, economic equality, freedom to rise, democracy. . . ."[29] Not everyone, of course, was moved to take advantage of these opportunities. Despite the potential returns to migration, for many of those who stayed behind, place had special meaning: family, friends, memories, and associations.[30]

In 1790 the population of the new United States of America clustered along the eastern seaboard from Maine to Georgia. A few hardier souls had settled in the Ohio and Cumberland river valleys in the Midwest and had pushed toward Lake Ontario up the Mohawk river valley (Figure 8.12). By 1850 settlement had moved across the Mississippi River into Minnesota, Iowa, Missouri, Arkansas, and eastern Texas. By 1900 the American population stretched somewhat discontinuously from East Coast to West, though large uninhabited pockets, such as most of Nevada, Arizona, and Colorado, remained essentially unsettled, with fewer than two persons per square mile. This pattern of progressive settlement was far from random or haphazard. Transportation played a crucial role in channeling the redistribution of that population along particular routes and determining its eventual location and distribution. At first the population settled along the coast and within a few miles of navigable rivers. As the population grew, it pushed westward. Crude trails, then better roads, canals, and railroads maintained contact with the areas of older settlement. These transportation media then channeled subsequent migrations along these lines of least resistance.

Much of what is known about this internal migration is derived from federal census data. Beginning in 1850, the government began to collect information on place of birth as part of the federal population census. These data were eventually published in the census compendiums in the form of place of birth by place of residency matrices. Economic historians have used these data to investigate the push and pull factors underlying the migration patterns of Americans between 1850 and 1960. Using estimates of per capita income by state (as a proxy for the financial lure to migrate), distances between states (to represent information flows and uncertainty), job opportunity data and population density (to proxy land availability) plus a host of noneconomic variables, such as climate, one can try to estimate the elasticities of migration with respect to these factors. The results confirm the wisdom of common sense as well as predictions based upon labor market

[29] Turner (1920): 259.
[30] Barron (1984).

theory. People moved where there were job opportunities and incomes were higher. They were also more likely to move to similar states and to places where land was available. Distance, however, discouraged migration. Studies done by economic historians also suggest that the relative importance of these variables in explaining migration changed over time. The quantitative importance of income differentials was increasing over time, while the importance of distance decreased. Similarly, while income, job opportunities, and distance steadily explained ever more of the migration flows, land availability explained progressively less.[31] The census state-of-birth data have limitations. They provide no evidence on intrastate moves, and the data record only one move for any individual. They do not reflect lifetime mobility.

Growing numbers of people made cities their home. New towns and cities sprang up everywhere, but especially in the North and Midwest (Figure 8.13). The South had relatively few towns until after the Civil War, for reasons discussed later. In 1790 only about 5 percent of the population lived in urban areas, defined as towns and cities over 2,500 (Figure 8.14). By 1850 the urban population had grown to about 15 percent of the population, and by 1900 about 40 percent of the population lived in towns and cities. Today more than 75 percent of Americans live in urban places. However, not until 1920 was a majority of the population classified as urban. Towns and cities thus grew faster than the population as a whole, reflecting the value added from population concentration—the concentration of economic activities—broadly referred to as economies of agglomeration. Such population concentrations permitted firms to realize economies of scale. Initially the largest cities—those over 250,000 or 1 million in Figure 8.14—grew most rapidly, but the fraction of the urban population living in places with more than 1 million people quickly stabilized while the relative share of urban dwellers in cities over 250,000 continued to grow rapidly. Since 1940 most urban growth has been in cities under 250,000, and the share of urban population in cities over 250,000 has fallen.

Immigrants in particular increasingly settled in cities, often their ports of entry.[32] At the 1850 census immigrants made up less than 10 percent of the nation's population, but about 46 percent of New York's population, 34 percent of Boston's, 30 percent of Philadelphia's, 53 percent of Chicago's, and 64 percent of Milwaukee's. Not only did immigrants tend to congregate in the urban centers of America, but the evidence also suggests that they avoided the South. This pattern was so pronounced and pervasive that it has been dubbed the avoidance of the South syndrome. Evidence in support of this hypothesis is to be found in the published census data. In 1860, for example, the foreign-born made up 13 percent of the general population but only 5.4 percent of the population of the South. In 1890 the situation was

[31] See, for example, Gallaway and Vedder (1971).
[32] Ferrie (1992).

FIGURE 8.12

Population Density, 1790–1900

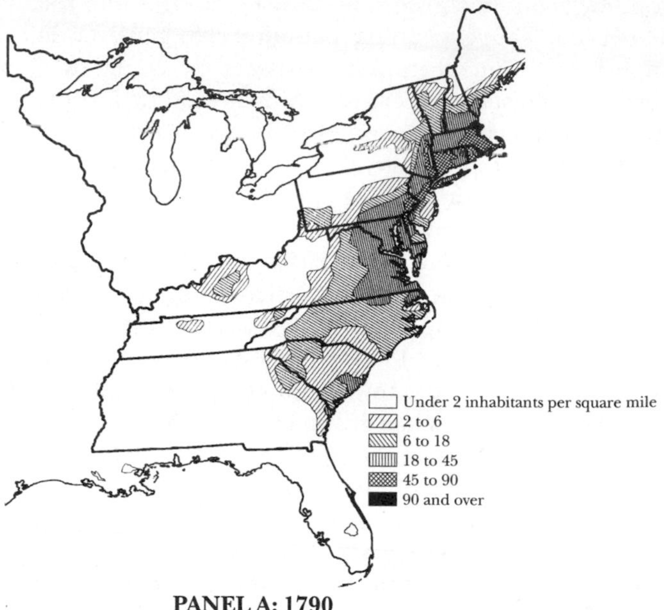

PANEL A: 1790

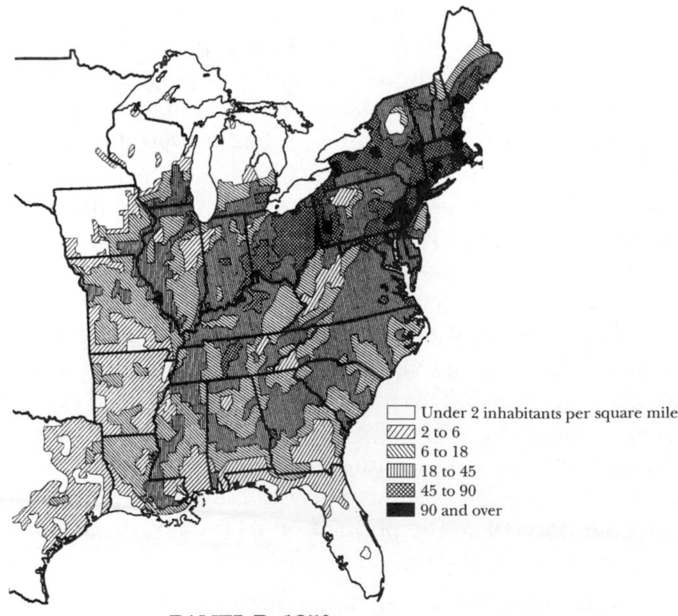

PANEL B: 1850

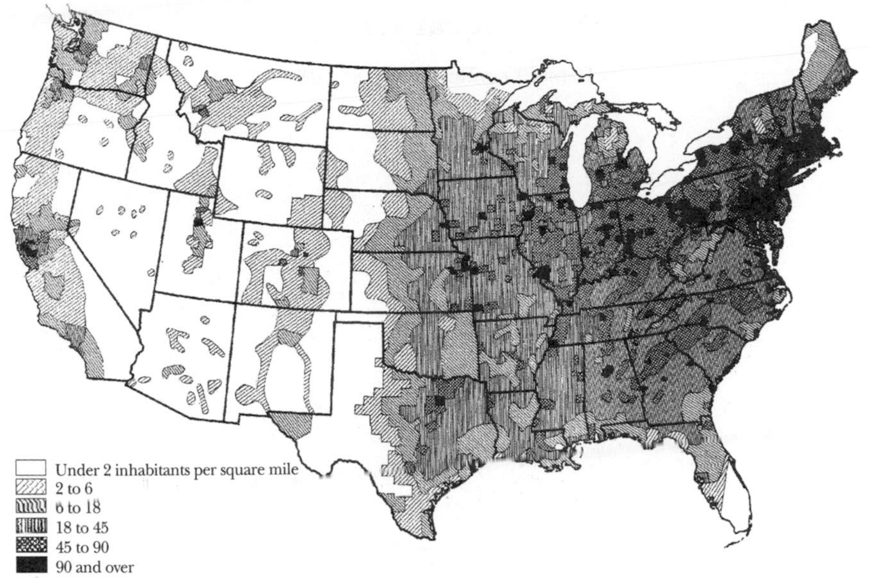

PANEL C: 1900

Source: Charles O. Paullin, *Atlas of the Historical Geography of the United States* (Washington, D.C.: Carnegie Institution, 1932): Plates 76, 77, and 79.

even more lopsided. The foreign-born made up 14.7 percent of the total U.S. population but only 2.6 percent of the South's population.

The avoidance of the South syndrome also shows up in many of the empirical studies of immigration. Most researchers include a dummy variable among their explanatory variables to represent a state's being *southern.* Even after controlling for factors such as income, population, population density, and distance from New York City (the principal port of entry), this dummy variable still shows a strong systematic inclination for immigrants to avoid the South, independent of those other forces. Why?

The usual explanations stress southern hostility toward immigrants as well as the objections of the immigrants to the "cultural climate" in the South, presumably dominated by race relations. One contemporary observer noted, "There was a notion that Negroes abounded everywhere in the South, that no place was free from them, and that anyone who worked at manual labor, especially if he worked with a Negro, would be socially ostracized."[33] Recent work suggests that the English and Germans, in particular, shunned states where there was a high percentage of African-Americans in the post–Civil War era.[34] Indeed, the variable "Southern" is simply a crude

[33] Fleming (1905): 277.
[34] Dunlevy (1978).

FIGURE 8.13

Urban Locations 1850 and 1900

1850

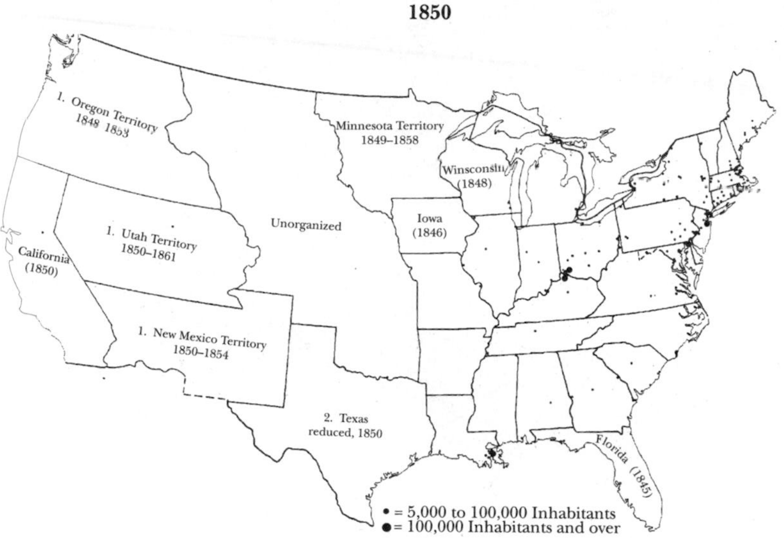

1900

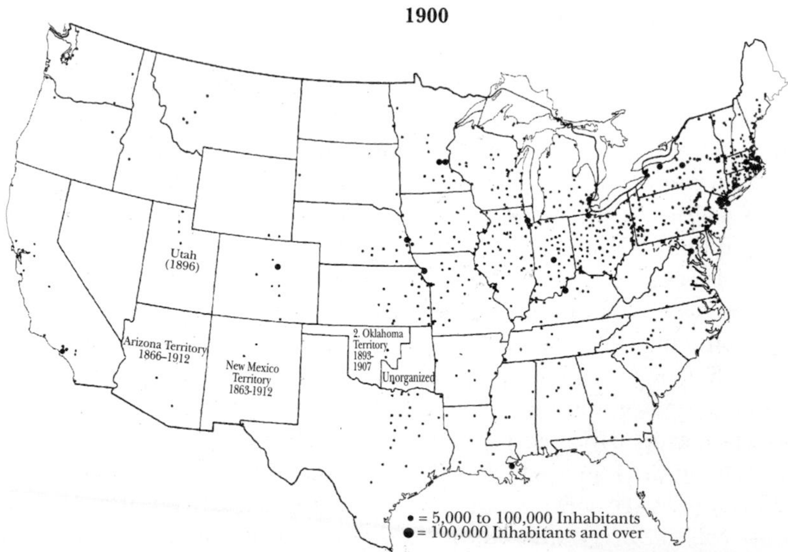

Source: Charles O. Paullin, *Atlas of the Historical Geography of the United States* (Washington, D.C.: Carnegie Institution, 1932): Plates 63 and 65.

FIGURE 8.14

The Growing Concentration of Population in Urban Areas, 1790–1970

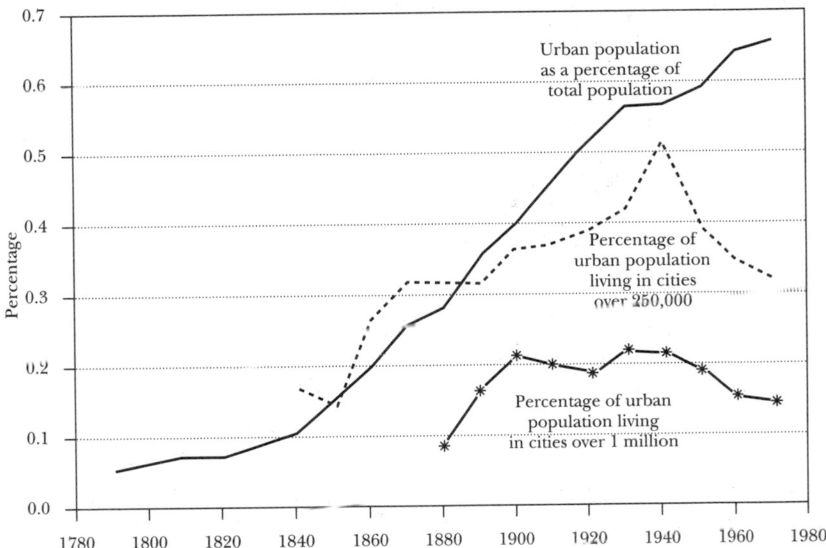

Source: U.S. Bureau of the Census, *Historical Statistics of the United States* (Washington, D.C.: Government Printing Office, 1975): Series A2, A57–A61.

proxy for the fraction of the population of African-American descent. One explanation is racial prejudice; certain immigrant groups objected to living in close proximity to African-Americans. An alternative explanation (and rationalization for any racial prejudice) is that immigrants and blacks competed for essentially the same low-wage jobs. Southerners were well aware that other parts of the country benefited from the steady stream of immigrant labor, and they sought to tap these flows by establishing immigration bureaus. But the welcome did not extend to the new immigrants from southern and Eastern Europe. By the turn of the century southern legislatures were explicitly limiting their appeal to those of Anglo-Saxon origin.

Population redistribution in the nineteenth and twentieth centuries has been more than a simple peopling and filling up of the vast and expanding lands of the public domain on the frontier. The push of population was not just westward; it was almost due west with the population center at any census before World War II lying within a few minutes of the thirty-ninth parallel (Figure 8.15). In 1790 the center of population in the United States was 23 miles east of Baltimore. By 1820 it had moved 16 miles south of Woodstock, Virginia—a westward movement of 127 miles in thirty years. Forty

FIGURE 8.15

Centers of Population

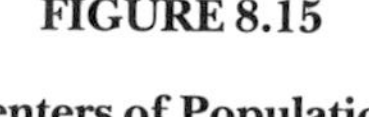

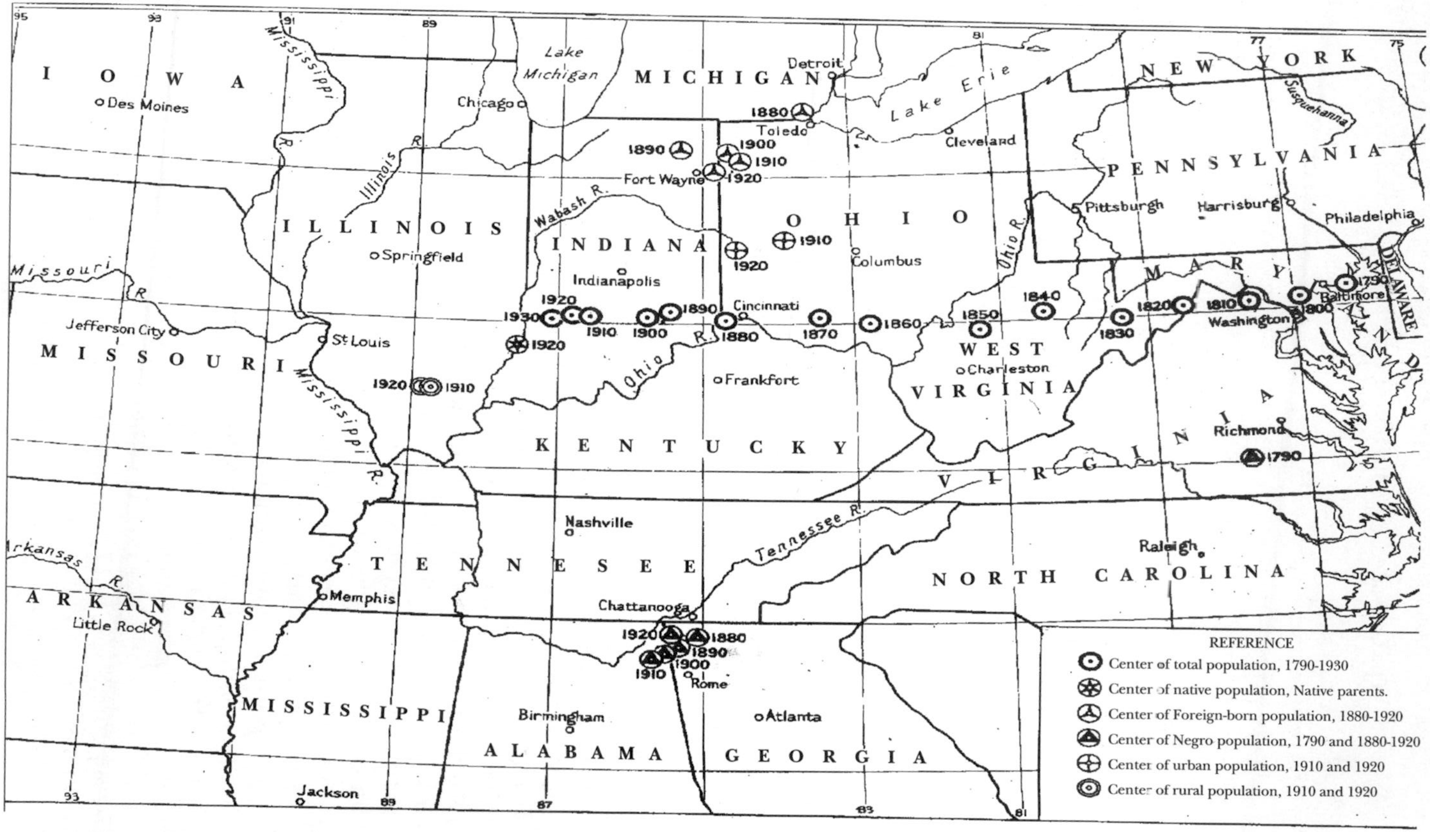

Charles O. Paullin, *Atlas of the Historical Geography of the United States* (Washington, D.C.: Carnegie Institution, 1932): Plate 30, Panel A.

years later it was located 20 miles south of Chillicothe, Ohio, 275 miles farther west. In 1910 the population center was located close to Bloomington, Indiana. Today it lies a few miles east of Rolla, Missouri.

One possible explanation of the dominance of east-west moves over north-south moves was that most early migrants were farmers. These settlers took seeds with them when they moved, but these seeds were adapted to specific latitudes. Agricultural experiment data show marked yield differences in corn adapted to latitudes farther north or south but not much difference east-west. A 250-mile north-south movement could produce a yield decline of perhaps 30 percent, while a similar move east-west would lower yields perhaps 10 percent or less. Moreover, farmers acquired latitude-specific skills. This human capital—familiarity with seasonal patterns, soils, crops, and so on—affected the rate of return to farming, and all were factors strongly influenced by climate, hence by latitude.[35] Letters from those who moved due west should have been more optimistic and glowing than letters from migrants who had moved north. They would thus be more likely to encourage others to migrate due west.

Since the seventeenth century and the beginnings of European settlement in this country, there have been fundamental and dramatic shifts in population size, composition, and location. The U.S. population today is a hundred times larger than it was when America broke away from Britain and a thousand times larger than it was in 1700. From an immigrant population of just twenty-three hundred persons in 1620, most of them English, the American population probably now embraces persons from every ethnic and racial group and country in the world, each contributing its unique culture and perspective. Once concentrated on the East Coast, the American population has pushed westward, settling the Midwest and then the West Coast, almost always in the hope of furthering that illusive dream of economic opportunity that attracted people here in the first place. Originally a mostly rural, agricultural population, few Americans still farm. The vast majority—75 percent—now live in urban areas, where they work at tasks unknown three hundred years ago in ways that were undreamed of then. Contemporary Americans enjoy a material level of consumption that would have been inconceivable without the dramatic changes in the nature and structure of the economy that will be discussed in subsequent chapters.

Bibliography

Atack, Jeremy, and Fred Bateman. *To Their Own Soil: Agriculture in the Antebellum North.* Ames: Iowa State University Press, 1987.

Barron, Hal. *Those Who Stayed Behind: Rural Society in Nineteenth-Century New England.* Cambridge, England: Cambridge University Press, 1984.

[35] Steckel (1983).

Beaujour, Chevalier Félix de. *Sketch of the United States of North America.* Paris: L. G. Michaud, 1814.

Bogue, Donald. *The Population of the United States.* Glencoe, Ill.: Free Press, 1959.

Coale, Ansley, and Melvin Zelnick. *New Estimates of Fertility and Population in the United States.* Princeton: Princeton University Press, 1963.

——— and Norfleet Rives. "A Statistical Reconstruction of the Black Population of the United States, 1880–1970: Estimates of True Numbers by Age and Sex, Birth Rates, and Total Fertility." *Population Index* 39 (1973): 3–36.

Craig, Lee. "The Value of Household Labor in Antebellum Northern Agriculture." *Journal of Economic History* 51 (1991): 67–82.

David, Paul A., and Warren C. Sandersen. "Rudimentary Contraceptive Methods and the American Transition to Marital Fertility Control, 1855–1915." In National Bureau of Economic Research, *Long Term Factors in American Economic Growth,* vol. 51, ed. Stanley L. Engerman and Robert E. Gallman. Chicago: University of Chicago Press, 1986: 307–79.

Dunlevy, James. "Nineteenth-Century European Immigration to the United States: Intended versus Lifetime Settlement Patters." *Economic Development and Cultural Change* 29 (1980): 77–90.

———. "Regional Preferences and Immigrant Settlement." *Research in Economic History* 8 (1983): 217–51.

———. and Henry Gemery. "Economic Opportunity and the Responses of 'Old' and 'New' Migrants to the United States." *Journal of Economic History* 38 (1978): 901–17.

Easterlin, Richard. "Population Change and Farm Settlement in the Northern United States." *Journal of Economic History* 36 (1976): 45–75.

———. "Influences in European Emigration Before World War I." In *The Reinterpretation of American Economic History,* ed. Robert Fogel and Stanley Engerman. New York: Harper & Row, 1971: 384–95.

———, George Alter, and Gretchen Condran. "Farms and Farm Families in Old and New Areas: The Northern States in 1860." In *Family and Population in Nineteenth-Century America,* ed. Tamara Haraven and Maris A. Vinoviskis. Princeton: Princeton University Press, 1978: 22–84.

Ferrie, Joseph. "A Longitudinal Analysis of the Settlement Patterns, Occupation Mobility, and Wealth Accumulation of European Immigrants to the U.S., 1840–1860." Paper presented at the Allied Social Sciences Association Meetings, New Orleans, January 1992.

Fleming, W. L. "Immigration to the Southern States." *Political Science Quarterly* 20 (1905): 276–97.

Fogel, Robert. "Nutrition and Decline in Mortality since 1700: Some Preliminary Findings." In National Bureau of Economic Research, *Long Term Factors in American Economic Growth,* vol. 51, ed. Stanley Engerman and Robert Gallman. Chicago: University of Chicago Press, 1986.

———. *Long-Term Changes in Nutrition and the Standard of Living.* Berne: 9th Congress of the International Economic History Association, 1988.

Forster, Colin, and George Tucker. *Economic Opportunity and White American Fertility Ratios, 1800–1860.* New Haven: Yale University Press, 1972.

Franklin, Benjamin. "Observations Concerning the Increase of Mankind." *Magazine of History,* extra Number 63 (1755).

Gallaway, Lowell E., and Richard K. Vedder. "Mobility of Native Americans." *Journal of Economic History* 31 (1971): 613–49.

———, and Richard K. Vedder. "Geographic Distribution of British and Irish Emigrants to the United States after 1800." *Scottish Journal of Political Economy* 19 (1972): 19–36.

———, and Richard K. Vedder. "Migration and the Old Northwest." In *Essays in 19th Century Economic History,* ed. D. Klingaman and R. Vedder. Athens: Ohio University Press, 1975.

———, and Richard K. Vedder. "Population Transfers and the Post-Bellum Adjustments to Economic Dislocation, 1870–1920." *Journal of Economic History* 40 (1980): 143–50.

———, ———, and Vishwa Shukla. "The Distribution of the Immigrant Population in the United States: An Economic Analysis." *Explorations in Economic History* 11 (1974): 213–26.

Gemery, Henry. "European Emigration to North America, 1700–1820: Numbers and Quasi-Numbers." *Perspectives in American History* 1 (1984): 283–342.

Haines, Michael. "The Use of Model Life Tables to Estimate Mortality for the United States in the Late Nineteenth Century." *Demography* 16 (1979): 289–312.

Higgs, Robert. "Mortality in Rural America, 1870–1920: Estimates and Conjectures." *Explorations in Economic History* 10 (1973): 177–95.

Leet, Donald. "Human Fertility and Agricultural Opportunities in Ohio Counties: From Frontier to Maturity, 1810–60." In *Essays in Nineteenth Century Economic History,* ed. D. Klingaman and R. Vedder. Athens: Ohio University Press 1975: 138–58.

Lindert, Peter. "Comment." In National Bureau of Economic Research, *Long Term Factors in American Economic Growth,* Studies in Income and Wealth, vol. 51, ed. Stanley Engerman and Robert Gallman. Chicago: University of Chicago Press, 1986.

McClelland, Peter, and Richard Zeckhauser. *Demographic Dimensions of the New Republic: American Interregional Migration, Vital Statistics, and Manumissions, 1800–1860.* New York: Cambridge University Press, 1982.

McKeown, Thomas. *The Modern Rise of Population.* New York: Academic Press, 1976.

Meeker, Edward. "The Social Rate of Return on Investment in Public Health, 1880–1910." *Journal of Economic History* 34 (1974): 392–421.

Mokyr, Joel, and Cormac O'Grada. "Emigration and Poverty in Prefamine Ireland." *Explorations in Economic History* 19 (1982): 360–84.

Neal, Larry. "Cross Spectral Analysis of Atlantic Migration." In *Research in Economic History,* ed. Paul Uselding. 1976: 260–97.

———, and Paul Uselding. "Immigration: A Neglected Source of American Economic Growth, 1790 to 1912." *Oxford Economic Papers* 24 (1972): 68–88.

Ransom, Roger, and Richard Sutch. "Did Rising Out-Migration Cause Fertility to Decline in Antebellum New England? A Life-Cycle Perspective on Old-Age Security Motives, Child Default, and Farm-Family Fertility." Working Papers on the History of Saving, No. 5, University of California, April 1986.

——— and ———. "Two Strategies for a More Secure Old Age: Life-cycle Saving by Late-Nineteenth Century American Workers." Paper presented at the NBER Summer Institute on the Development of the American Economy, Cambridge, Massachusetts, July 1989.

Seaman, Ezra. *Essays on the Progress of Nations.* Detroit: M. Geiger, 1846.

Steckel, Richard. "Antebellum Southern White Fertility: A Demographic and Economic Analysis." *Journal of Economic History* 40 (1980): 331–50.

———. "The Economic Foundations of East-West Migration during the Nineteenth Century." *Explorations in Economic History* 20 (1983): 14–36.

Sundstrom, William, and Paul David. "Old-Age Security Motives, Labor Markets, and Farm Family Fertility in Antebellum America." *Explorations in Economic History* 25 (1988): 164–97.

Thomas, Brinley. *Migration and Economic Growth,* 2nd ed. Cambridge, England: Cambridge University Press, 1973.

Tucker, George. *The History of the United States.* Philadelphia: Lippincott, 1856.

Turner, Frederick Jackson. *The Frontier in American History.* New York: Henry Holt, 1920.

Vinovskis, Maris. "The Jacobson Life Table of 1850: A Critical Reexamination from a Massachusetts Perspective." *Journal of Interdisciplinary History* 8 (1978): 703–24.

Wahl, Jenny Bournc. "New Results on the Decline in Household Fertility in the United States, 1750–1900." In National Bureau of Economic Research. *Long Term Factors in American Economic Growth,* vol. 51, ed. Stanley Engerman and Robert Gallman. Chicago: University of Chicago Press, 1986.

Williamson, Jeffrey. "Migration to the New World: Long Term Influences and Impact." *Explorations in Economic History* 11 (1974): 357–89.

———. "Did Rising Emigration Cause Fertility to Decline in 19th Century Rural England? Child Costs, Old-Age Pensions and Child Default." Harvard Institute for Economic Research Discussion Paper No. 1172, August 1985.

Yasuba, Yasukicki. *Birth Rates of the White Population in the United States 1800–1860.* Baltimore: Johns Hopkins University Press, 1961.

Westward expansion and public land policy

9

The Treaty of Paris, signed by Britain in 1783, ceded to the United States all lands south of Canada, east of the Mississippi, and north of Florida, an area that became known as the Northwest Territories. At the time only the eastern third of this land was occupied by European settlers and their descendants. West of the Appalachian Mountains, except for a few isolated settlements—primarily remnants of French exploration and fur trading—the land was largely untouched by European settlement. After 1800 waves of settlers, first easterners, then a mix of easterners and newly arrived immigrants, poured across the Appalachians onto these lands. The population of Ohio rose thirteenfold from 1800 to 1820. Similar growth in the other East North Central states bordering the Great Lakes trailed by only a decade or two. Whereas in 1810 less than 4 percent of Americans lived in what we now call the Midwest, by 1840, 17 percent—three million people—were living there, many of them on land that had not been part of the United States forty years earlier. By 1860 the Midwest had a quarter of the nation's population, and there were more than a hundred thousand new settlers in Kansas. Thousands more were settling Nebraska, and the West Coast population was rapidly approaching half a million. In less than half a century wilderness was converted into one of the world's great agricultural regions—one more than able to keep pace with the food requirements of an emerging urban-industrial power.

Development of this region in the years following the Revolution depended upon the goodwill of other nations. The easiest and cheapest means of transportation and communication from the Northwest Territories to the rest of the country was via the Mississippi River and the Gulf of Mexico. Access to these waters was controlled first by Spain and then briefly by France. Not wishing to trust the economic viability of the West to the good-

FIGURE 9.1

The Territorial Expansion of the United States

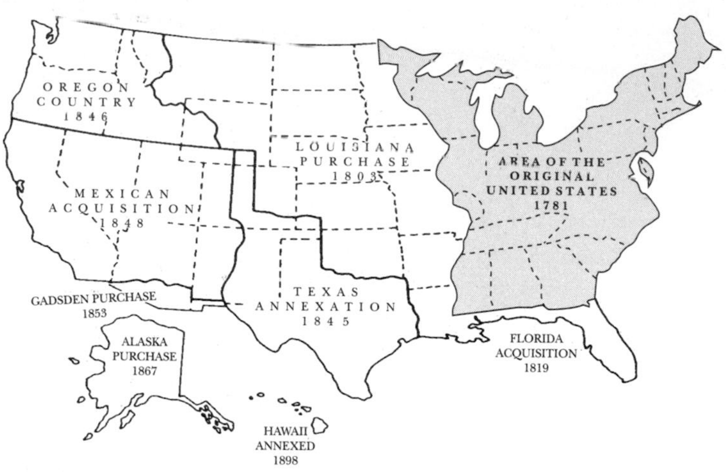

Source: After Ross M. Robertson, *History of the American Economy* (New York: Harcourt Brace Jovanovich, 1973): 106.

will of others, President Jefferson attempted to purchase permanent transit rights along the river and through the port of New Orleans. Instead, he ended up buying the entire Louisiana Territory—a landmass of 828,000 square miles (Figure 9.1).

Jefferson's decision to buy the Louisiana Territory was opposed by the Federalists, led by Alexander Hamilton, who favored a strong central government and who feared that the new territory would eventually guarantee political hegemony for an Anti-Federalist agrarian West. Moreover, while the purchase guaranteed the commercial independence of the Middle West, it did not secure the southern flank of the United States. Spain continued to control what is now Florida and the coasts of Alabama and Mississippi. A revolt by local settlers in 1810 gave President Madison the pretext to occupy the coastal regions of Louisiana and Mississippi. Two years later the U.S. Army seized the rest of West Florida. Spain reluctantly ceded the last remaining chunk of Florida in 1819.

Acquisition of the western third of the continent was not quite so easy. As a part of the agreement over Florida, the United States recognized Spain's ownership of Texas. This foreign control did not stop thousands of Americans from settling in East Texas in the 1820s. Nor did it prevent those settlers from securing their independence from Mexico in 1836. Texas, however, remained a sovereign nation for nine years because of northern opposition to adding another slave state to the Union. This opposition was finally overcome in the great wave of chauvinist sentiment created by the debate over America's "manifest destiny" to rule the continent. Congress annexed Texas in 1845. Relations with Mexico went from bad to worse when Mexico refused to yield to U.S. demands for the quick sale of California and New Mexico and refused to recognize U.S. claims to a disputed chunk of southern Texas.

Mexico's unwillingness to sacrifice territory can probably be explained by its miscalculation that the United States would ultimately be forced to go to war with Britain over Oregon. President James Polk accepted a compromise over Oregon, and Mexico stood alone. Both countries paid dearly for the miscalculation. About thirteen thousand Americans and a far larger number of Mexicans died in the Mexican War (1846–48)—mostly from disease. Direct U.S. military expenditures for the two-year adventure totaled \$97 million, but as part of the peace settlement, Mexico sold California, Nevada, Utah, and the northern tier of Arizona and New Mexico for \$18 million. Five years later Mexico ceded the rest of Arizona and New Mexico for another \$10 million, completing the territory that comprises the first forty-eight states.

The Politics and Economics of Land Policy

The Louisiana Purchase almost doubled the size of the country. The public domain—unsettled land belonging to the federal government—tripled. Subsequent purchases and treaties continually added new land on the western frontier and expanded the size of the public domain faster than land sales diminished it. As a result, by 1850, the federal government held 1.2 billion acres in trust for the American people. In 1880, despite almost twenty years of free land under the Homestead Act, the government still held over 900 million acres (excluding Alaska).

Successive governments all wrestled with the problem of how these lands were to be settled and governed. Before 1763 Great Britain had deliberately encouraged rapid western settlement as a means of consolidating its claim against encroachments by the French from the North and the Spanish from the South. With the defeat of France in the French and Indian War in 1763, however, neither colonial power represented a serious threat to British hegemony in the region. At the same time the seizure of Indian lands by aggressive and independently minded settlers and overlapping claims by many of the original colonies to these lands were a continual source of trouble. The British sought to resolve these problems first by banning new western settlement and then, in 1774, by creating an Indian reservation between the Appalachians and the Ohio River and incorporating the land between the Ohio and Mississippi rivers into Quebec. These decisions had not been popular with the colonists and appear among the list of grievances in the Declaration of Independence. With independence, this hot potato fell into the lap of the Continental Congress, and disputes among the states over competing land claims delayed adoption of the Articles of Confederation. Finally, the cession of claims by New York and Virginia to the federal government paved the way for a settlement, but the issue of how the land was to be settled and governed remained. The first was resolved by the Land Ordinance of 1785; the second by the Northwest Ordinance of 1787.

Land represents wealth, and the question facing Congress was who should derive the benefit. One option was to sell the land at full value, retaining the wealth for the benefit of the nation. Another was to give the land away, thereby distributing the wealth to those deemed worthy. Before the Civil War Congress nominally chose the first option but failed to implement it fully. As a result, the federal government received only a portion of the value while the rest went to purchasers. After 1862 Congress followed the second strategy but again failed to ensure that the policy achieved its goals.

The Federalists viewed the public lands primarily as a source of revenue for the central government. Such revenues would permit the expansion of the role of the federal government, possibly at the expense of state power. Public sale at high prices and in large lots would, Alexander Hamilton argued, secure the maximum advantage for the public treasury and therefore for the public good. He also foresaw that high prices would discourage settlement, limiting agricultural expansion, and indirectly encourage manufactures by forcing labor and capital to seek alternate employment.

The Anti-Federalists led by Thomas Jefferson, on the other hand, saw in the public lands the opportunity to create a nation of small landed farmers. Jefferson believed that these sturdy settlers would be the bulwark of democracy and protection against arbitrary government power. To achieve this goal, the land should be sold (if not given away) at low prices in small lots and on credit so as to be within the financial means of the largest number of people. As Jefferson put it in a letter to James Madison's father:

> Whenever there are in any country uncultivated lands and unemployed poor, it is clear that the laws of property have been so far extended as to violate natural right. The earth is given as a common stock for man to labor and live on. If for the encouragement of industry we allow it to be appropriated, we must take care that other employment be provided to those excluded from the appropriation. If we do not, the fundamental right to labor the earth returns to the unemployed. It is too soon yet in our country to say that every man who cannot find employment, but who can find uncultivated land, shall be at liberty to

> cultivate it, paying a moderate rent. But it is not too soon to provide by every possible means that as few as possible shall be without a little portion of land. The small landholders are the most precious part of a state.[1]

Idealism aside, however, it is clear that the debate on both sides of the issue was dominated by self-interested rent seekers—that is, by those who sought to capture any potential unearned gains for themselves. Cheap land threatened the asset value of all established property owners. If land supply were restricted and prices were kept high, existing landowners stood to gain. On the other hand, if land prices were set low and especially if credit were available, the opportunities for profitable speculation were much greater.

Revenue proved to be a key issue in settling the debate. The Articles of Confederation and the Constitution had deliberately limited the revenue-raising capabilities of the federal government. Congress had authority to levy consumption (excise) taxes, impose import duties, and receive the receipts from land sales, but precious little else. The issue of sale or donation was therefore moot. The land had to be sold; the only question was at what price.

Federalist hopes of vast revenues for the public treasury turned on implicit assumptions about the elasticity of demand for land. If land prices and minimum parcel sizes were set very high, little revenue could be collected. If, by contrast, terms were liberal, a high volume of sales would be offset by low prices. Revenues would be maximized at the point where the volume gain from an additional small reduction in price just equaled the resulting loss in revenue per acre; in economic terms, the price ought to be set where the elasticity of demand equaled one since the cost of the land was zero.

No one, of course, knew what the demand curve for land looked like or really understood the problem in these terms. Conceptually the issue is clouded by the fact that land is not a uniform factor; such characteristics as soil type, climate, and location make every parcel unique. Hence it would have been difficult to talk about the elasticity of demand for land even if the problem had been understood in those terms. Minimum price instead was set and reset by political compromise between the Federalists and Jeffersonians, and the market was allowed to determine the equilibrium.

The *pattern* of settlement also proved a source of debate in Congress. But once settled, this was not tampered with again. Colonial settlement had generally followed one of two models. In New England settlement had proceeded in an orderly manner through the process of township planting. Promoters received permission to establish a new township at the boundary of existing township settlements. These township tracts were commonly six

[1] Thomas Jefferson to the Reverend James Madison, October 28, 1785.

miles square and subdivided into smaller plots for sale at public auction. Title to unsurveyed land could not be secured. It was a system for order upon the land. In the South, on the other hand, the practice had been one of prior settlement. Settlers simply found pieces of unclaimed land that suited them the best and had it marked off by the county surveyor. Settlers thus sought to acquire the most desirable land first and settled it without regard to its relation to other properties. The result was a haphazard patchwork quilt of land claims interspersed with publicly owned tracts of less desirable land.

Public Land Law

THE LAND ORDINANCE, 1785

The principle of orderly systematic settlement on the New England model, as favored by Jefferson as well as by New Englanders such as Nathan Dane, was adopted. The land was to be surveyed prior to sale and settlement. The survey would establish a rectangular grid with respect to east-west base lines and north-south principal meridians and be divided into townships six miles square. Each township in turn was to be subdivided into thirty-six sections, each of one mile square (Figure 9.2), leaving a lasting imprint plainly visible to this day to anyone looking out of an airplane window anywhere over the Midwest.

Parcels of land were surveyed and then offered for sale at public auction subject only to minimum acreages and prices set by the various successive land acts. If no one bid on the land at the initial auction, it remained on sale at the legal minimum price. By auctioning land to the highest bidder, the government could, in theory, have captured the full market value of the land that it sold, but the system didn't work very efficiently for a variety of reasons. Foremost was corruption: Land office officials could be bribed to bypass the auction or misrepresent the land's value; the parcels in question would then pass into private hands at the legal minimum price. Bidders could also conspire among themselves to withhold competitive bids, or they could coerce or bribe potential competitors to refrain from offering higher bids. Equally important, because of imperfect information and imperfect credit markets, the auction system often failed to match the land to those buyers who valued it most highly. As a result, federal land revenues fell short of their potential.

The initial terms of sale represented a victory for the Federalists. Prices were set high, and minimum acreages were large. Alternating townships were to be sold whole; the others by section—640 acres. All sales were to be at public auction so as to ensure that the Treasury obtained the full market price on each sale but subject to a reservation price of $1 per acre. All sales were strictly cash. Under the Ordinance of 1787, section 16 in each township was reserved to underwrite public education. A proposal to reserve similar lands for the maintenance of religious institutions was not passed.

FIGURE 9.2A

The Land Ordinance of 1785

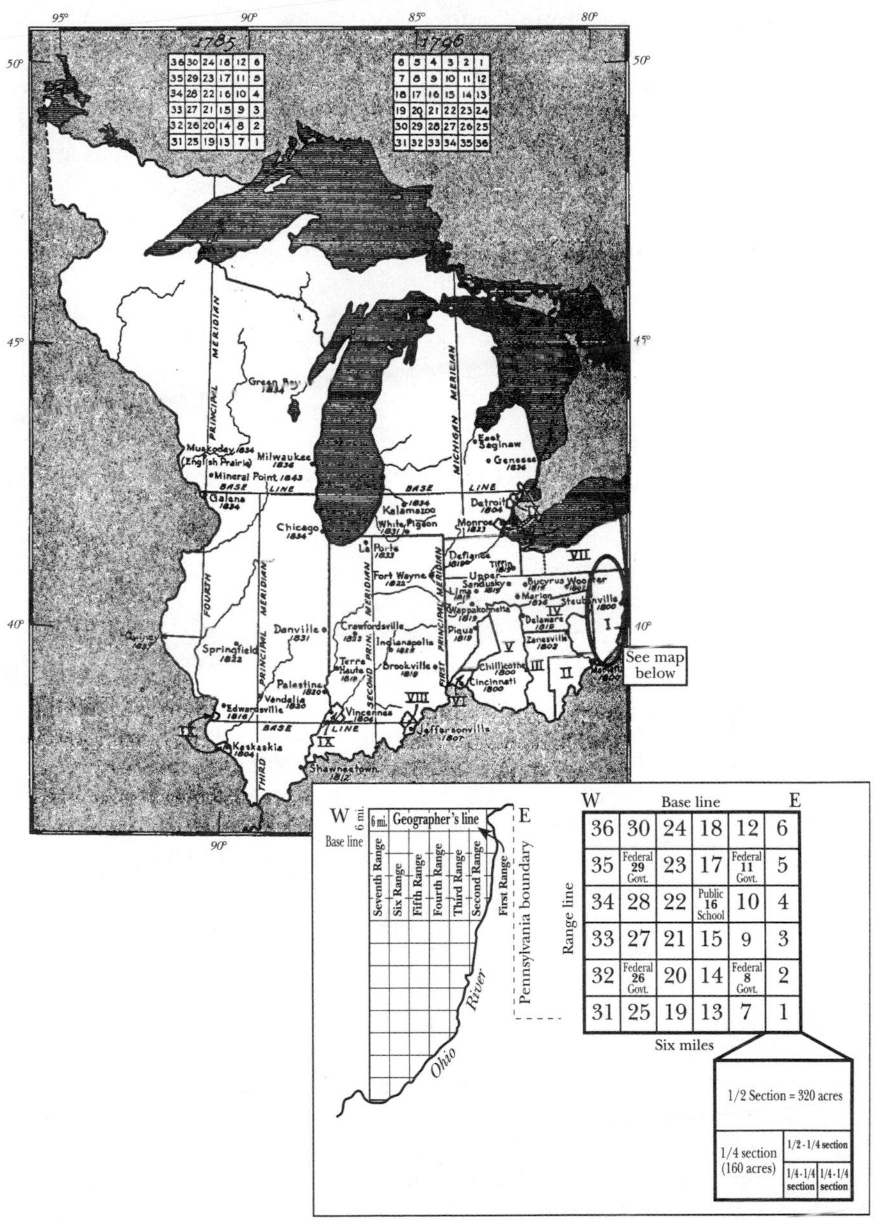

36	30	24	18	12	6
35	Federal 29 Govt.	23	17	Federal 11 Govt.	5
34	28	22	Public 16 School	10	4
33	27	21	15	9	3
32	Federal 26 Govt.	20	14	Federal 8 Govt.	2
31	25	19	13	7	1

Source: Adapted from Ray A. Billington, *Westward Expansion* (New York: Macmillan, 1949): 208 and R. Carlyle Buley, *The Old Northwest* (Bloomington: Indiana University Press, 1951): I: 117.

THE NORTHWEST ORDINANCE, 1787

Two years after passage of the original Land Ordinance, the Continental Congress took up the issue of the terms under which the newly settled land would be incorporated into the political system. The Northwest Ordinance provided that the area be administered by a governor appointed by Congress until such time as the population exceeded five thousand males of voting age. A territorial legislature was then to be elected, and when the population exceeded sixty thousand, the territory was to be accepted as a state on the basis of complete equality with the existing states. This legislation provided for the creation of between three and five states in the area north of the Ohio and east of the Mississippi (five were created), also provided for civil and religious liberty, and prohibited slavery from the territory.

CHANGING LAND POLICY

In 1796 the conservative forces scored yet another triumph when the reservation price was raised to $2 per acre although one year's credit was extended on half the purchase price. Land sales, however, proved disappointing. The anticipated bounty to the public treasury failed to materialize. Thereafter sale terms were progressively liberalized (Table 9.1on pages 258 and 259), although the abolition of credit provisions beginning in 1820 undoubtedly harmed the chances for the poorest potential buyers to become owners. The acreage requirement was halved in 1800 and halved again in 1804. In 1820 the minimum price was slashed to $1.25. Sales, however, remained modest until they exploded under the influence of high crop prices in the 1830s resulting from a series of poor grain harvests caused by rust (a fungus) and the Hessian fly (Figure 9.3). Indeed, land sales (and homestead entries) and grain prices appear to be strongly correlated consistent with the hypothesis that land settlement was driven by the economic opportunity of profitable farming. Not all land was purchased by settlers who planned to farm what they had bought. Some of the land was purchased by speculators, thereby putting a sort of statistical buffer between land sales on the one hand and farm formation on the other, but there is little reason to believe that without speculators, the timing of land sales would have been very different.

Public land issues were often the cutting edge of political conflict in the seventy years before the Civil War. Ideology and sectional politics became increasingly confused. From the perspective of a century, however, one can easily generalize about the trends in policy and their impact. Liberalization of the terms of land sales was virtually continuous after 1800, and revenue considerations decreased in importance as time passed. After the 1820s the price of land was probably a minor barrier to westward expansion. At $1.25 per acre other costs of setting up a farm—clearing land, buying implements and livestock, and maintaining a family until the first crop—dominated. Hence other factors, those determining the profitability of farming and the availability of farm labor, determined the pace of expansion. These are discussed in Chapter 10 below.

FIGURE 9.3

Original Land Entries, 1800–1934

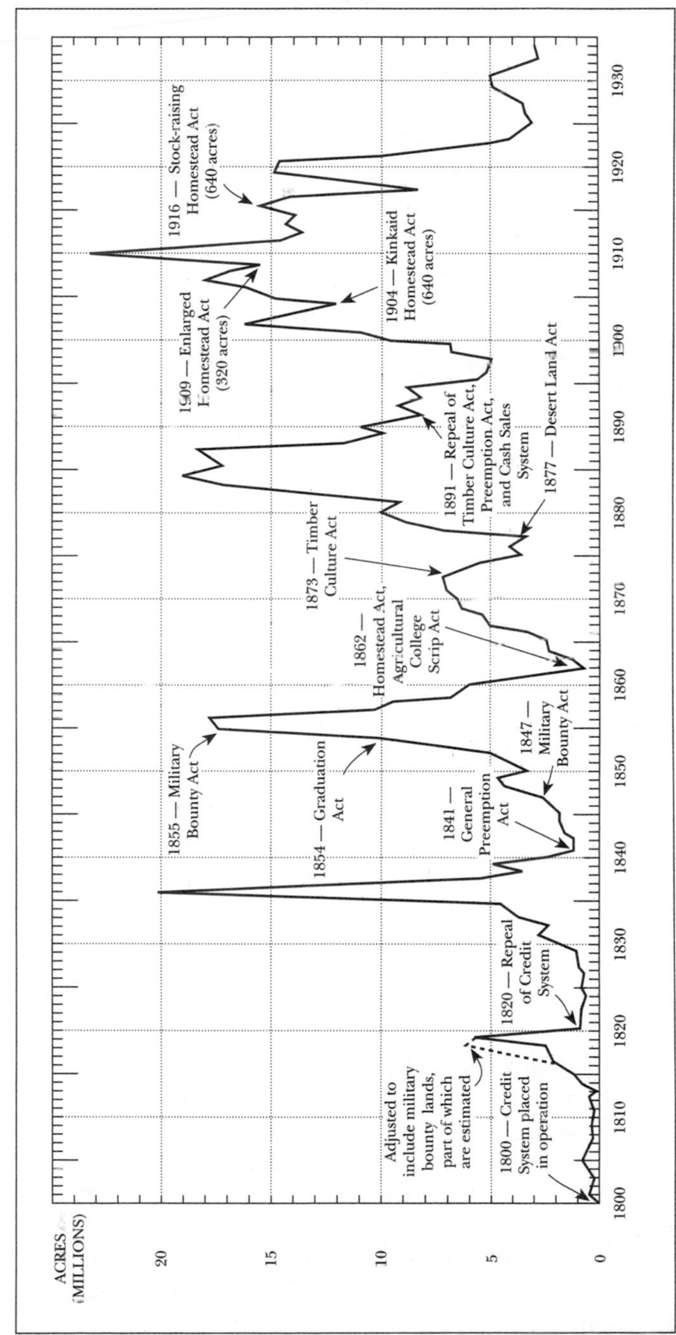

Source: Roy M. Robbins, *Our Landed Heritage* (Princeton: Princeton University Press, 1942): 344.

TABLE 9.1

Significant Public Land Laws, 1785–1916

Year	Legislative Initiative	Minimum Price/Acre	Minimum Acreage	Maximum Acreage	Conditions and Terms of Sale
1785	Land Ordinance of 1785	\$1	640	none	Cash.
1787	Northwest Ordinance of 1787	\$1	640	none	$\frac{1}{3}$ cash; balance in 3 months.
1796	Land Act of 1796	\$2	640	none	$\frac{1}{2}$ in 30 days; balance within a year. First land offices established at Cincinnati and Pittsburgh.
1800	Harrison Land Act (Land Act of 1800)	\$2	320	none	$\frac{1}{4}$ in 30 days; balance in 3 years at 6 percent interest
1804	Land Act of 1804	\$2	160	none	\$1.64/acre for cash. Credit terms as per Land Act of 1800.
1812	General Land Office established				
1820	Land Act of 1820	\$1.25	80	none	Credit system abolished. Cash only.
1830	Preemption Act of 1830	\$1.25		160	Permitted unauthorized settlers—squatters—to purchase up to 160 acres.
1832	Land Act of 1832	\$1.25	40	none	Cash only.
1841	General Preemption Act of 1841	\$1.25	40	160	Preemption only. Cash.

Year	Legislative Initiative	Minimum Price/Acre	Minimum Acreage	Maximum Acreage	Conditions and Terms of Sale
1854	Graduation Act	$12\frac{1}{2}$ cents	40	none	Price progressively reduced on unsold lands to as little as $12\frac{1}{2}$ cents per acre after 30 years
1862	Homestead Act	Free	40	160	$10 registration fee. 5 years' continuous residence on land for full title. Commutation available after 6 months for $1.25/acre.
1873	Timber Culture Act	Free	160	160	Cultivation of trees on $\frac{1}{4}$ of the lot for title. Amended in 1878 to require trees on only $\frac{1}{16}$ of a lot.
1877	Desert Land Act	$1.25		640	Irrigation within 3 years. 25 cents/acre on entry, balance due upon proof of compliance.
1878	Timber and Stone Act	$2.50	40	160	Stipulation that timber and stone be taken for personal use only and not for speculation or other parties.
1909	Enlarged Homestead Act	Free		320	5 years' residence with continuous cultivation. Law for semiarid areas.
1912	Three-Year Homestead Act	Free		160	7 months' residence a year for 3 years with extension for bad weather, etc.
1916	Stock Raising Homestead Act	Free		640	On land suitable only for grazing.

Source: Benjamin Hibbard, *A History of Public Land Policies* (New York: Macmillan, 1924)

The orderly transfer of secure land title from public to private hands envisaged in the land acts was disrupted by overly eager settlers who occupied some of the best lands ahead of the survey teams. These "squatters" posed a dilemma. On the one hand, they contributed to the value of the land by converting it to farmland, an activity viewed as a social good. On the other hand, they often encroached on Indian rights, and by occupying the very best land, they potentially made it unavailable to those who played by the rules. Efforts to sell these lands at public auction to the highest bidder were often frustrated by the appearance of the well-armed settler and friends. The solution was to allow preemption rights, a system formally adopted in 1841. This allowed the settler to purchase up to 160 acres of land at the minimum price of $1.25 per acre.

Despite the reservation price, not all federal lands sold for a price equal to or greater than the minimum. Veterans received land warrants—rights to settle specific acreages of unoccupied land—in partial compensation for their military service. These warrants were transferable and actively traded at prices of about 60 to 85 cents per acre. In addition, the growing problem of pockets of federally owned land worth less than the reservation price and surrounded by private property led Congress in 1854 to pass the Graduation Act. This provided for a progressive reduction in the price of unsold public lands to a minimum of $12\frac{1}{2}$ cents per acre for land unsold more than thirty years.

On May 20, 1862, President Lincoln signed into law the Homestead Act, whereby settlers might acquire full title to 160 acres of land from the public domain, subject only to a $10 registration fee, provided they lived upon it for five years. This ushered in a new era: "free" land for the cultivator, Thomas Jefferson's dream. But the results fell somewhat short of his ideal. Free land did not produce a costless farm, but it may have induced many to enter farming who otherwise would have found alternate, probably more lucrative employment. Moreover, as settlement moved farther west, 160 acres proved inadequate to ensure even farm family self-sufficiency. There followed other, even more liberal homesteading acts (see Table 9.1). Between 1863 and 1900 almost 1.5 million entries were filed for homesteads. Settlement and agriculture expanded, but reality fell short of expectations, and as we shall see in Chapter 15, western farmers ultimately sought political solutions to their economic problems.

Land Sales and Western Settlement

The Land Ordinance of 1785 and the Northwest Ordinance of 1787 provided a basis for the orderly and systematic expansion of the United States through land acquisition and settlement. After its creation in 1812 the General Land Office conveyed vast quantities of land from the public domain to private ownership. In 1836, for example, more than three million acres of public land was sold in Illinois alone. During the 1850s the federal government sold almost fifty million acres—an area approximately one and a half times the size of New York State—while farmland increased by a hundred million acres and six hundred thousand new farms began production.

Public land law had a marked and lasting impact upon the land and the size distribution of farms throughout the territory to which it applied. In 1860 in the Northeast, where public land law did not apply, there was a broad dispersion of farm sizes, as might be expected from sale or subdivision among heirs. Nevertheless, there were clusters of farms of specific sizes—50, 100, 150, and 200 acres—within this broad distribution (Figure 9.4). In the Midwest, on the other hand, there were proportionately fewer farms of "odd" sizes and much greater concentrations of specific farm sizes. In this case, farms were multiples of 40 acres—40, 80, 120, 160, 200, 240, 280, and 320 acres—rather than multiples of 50. They were thus multiples of the land survey section of 640 acres (1 square mile) and the lots under which land was sold at public auction by the Land Office. Indeed, if one focuses upon specific states, the impact of particular land act provisions is apparent in the size distribution data. For example, in Ohio, Indiana, and Illinois, which were being settled when the minimum purchase was 80 acres, 80-acre farms were the modal size, while in Michigan and Wisconsin, which were settled after the revision of 1832 had cut the minimum purchase to 40 acres, 40-acre farms were the modal farms.

The impact of these land sales and transfers has been debated exhaustively. Many scholars have argued that sales increased too rapidly, inducing too much labor and capital into agriculture and starving manufacturing of resources despite its relatively higher rate of return.[2] Others have argued that by establishing minimum acreages rather than maximum, public land policy promoted speculation, concentration of ownership, and tenancy rather than individual small holdings, as Jefferson had hoped.[3] In short, federal land policy has often been criticized as inefficient and growth-inhibiting.

This view has been challenged by Robert Fogel and Jack Rutner. Starting with a theoretical economic model, they show how the release of western land from the public domain induced westward migration and population growth, increased wage rates, affected the size of gross national product, and redistributed income regionally and between different groups in the economy. Their model is a powerful tool for understanding many of the changes in the nineteenth-century economy.

Suppose that land and labor are needed to produce agricultural goods in two geographically separate but contiguous regions, the East and the West. The marginal product of labor in each region—the contribution of

[2] Saloutos (1948).
[3] Gates (1936).

FIGURE 9.4

Size Distribution, Northeastern Farms: 1860

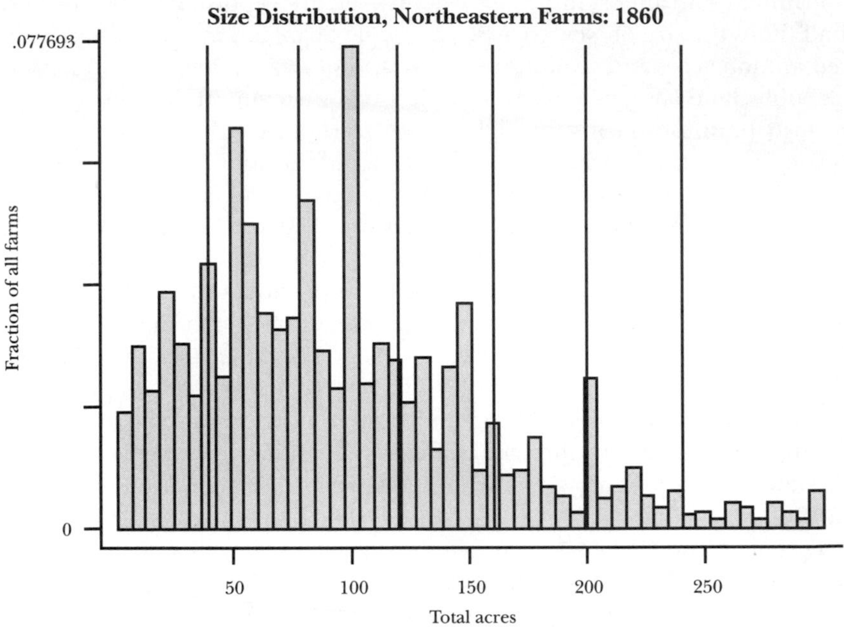

Size Distribution, Midwestern Farms: 1860

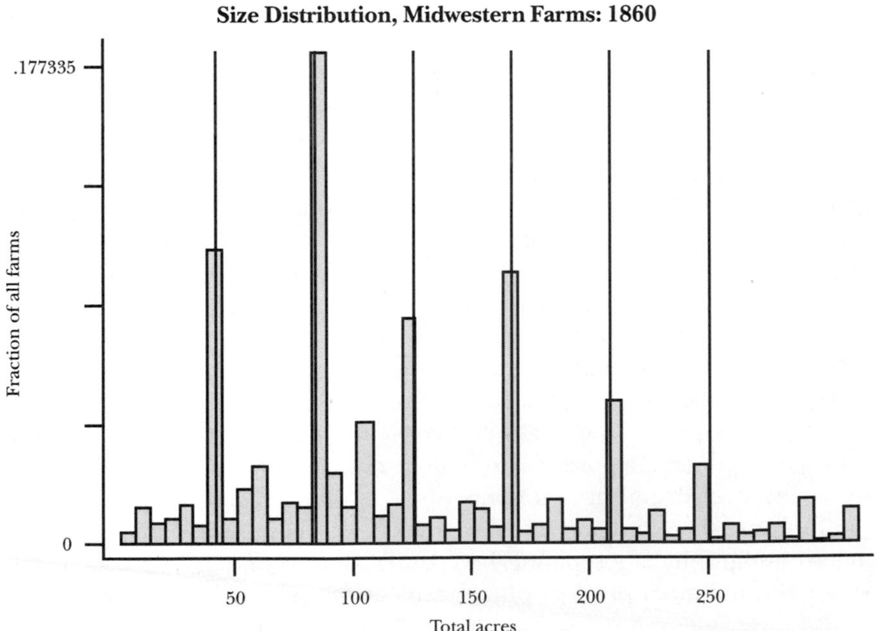

Source: Computed from the Bateman-Foust sample from the manuscript census of agriculture.

FIGURE 9.5

The Determination of Wages, Rents, National Income, and the Geographic Distribution of the Labor Force in an Agrarian Economy

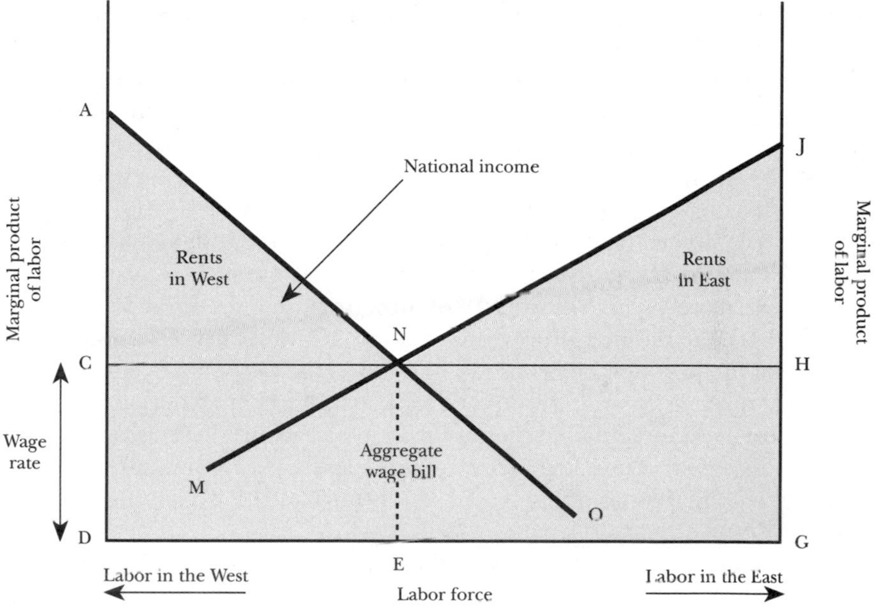

each additional worker to total output—is declining since each new farmer has less land to work with than the earlier settlers and because the best land is farmed first, squeezing newcomers onto more marginal lands. The situation is graphed in Figure 9.5. The horizontal axis, DG, represents the total labor force. This is a function of the size of the population and depends upon the labor force participation rate. The marginal product of western labor, represented by the line AO, is read against the left-hand axis. The marginal product of eastern labor, JM, is read against the right-hand axis. In the absence of transport costs and with perfect information, labor will move between the two regions until everyone is employed and wages—determined by the marginal product of labor—are equalized. This occurs where the two marginal product curves intersect at N and determines the geographic distribution of labor (and population) and the size of national income with its constituent parts—rents and wages—if we assume that the economy produces only agricultural commodities. Labor in both the East and the West is paid a wage equal to DC (= GH), and of the total labor force of DG, those to the left of E (DE) work in the West, while EG people work in the East. The area under the marginal product curves, the polygon DANJG, measures aggregate output—that is, national product—since it is the sum of all marginal increments to total output. The labor force of DG is paid a wage equal to DC. Consequently, the aggregate payments to labor in wages and salary is shown by the rectangle DCHG. The residual national income—the triangles CAN and HJN—is paid as rent on land in the West and on land in the East.

Now suppose that the government releases newly surveyed land for sale from the public domain. This land lies on the western frontier. If we assume that this land has the same distribution of fertility as that already occupied in the region, then the marginal product of labor curve AO will pivot around A to AP since there is now more land of each quality on which labor can work (Figure 9.6). If, on the other hand, we were to assume that at least some of the new land was better than the best of that already under cultivation, then the marginal product curve would shift upward and to the right, lying everywhere above the old marginal product curve AO. Similarly, if we were to assume that the best new land was not as good as the best of the old, then the marginal product curve AO would be kinked at the point where the fertility of the best new land equaled that of the land already under cultivation, and the new marginal product curve would lie above the old thereafter. We will assume that the new land that is sold simply mirrors the distribution of land quality of land already in use.

A number of results follow directly from the sale of new land in the West. National income is increased by ANK since labor now has more good land with which to work (Figure 9.6). Wages rise to DB (= GI), and EF of the labor force migrates from the industrial East to the agrarian West, as Alexander Hamilton had feared. This westward migration in response to the availability of cheap or free land on the western frontier is a crucial element in the "Safety Valve" doctrine discussed below in Chapter 10 and shows up clearly in the migration studies discussed in Chapter 8. The increase in the quantity of good land in the West drives down eastern land rents to the disadvantage and dismay of eastern landowners, and rents decline as a fraction of national income as relative land scarcity decreases while relative labor scarcity increases as reflected in the higher wages. These higher wages may stimulate increased immigration to the United States and higher incomes (and better living standards) may stimulate higher birthrates, at least in the short run.

The gains from the liberal federal land sale and settlement policy may, however, be somewhat less than those shown because of the implicit assumption that labor and the other resources employed in agriculture have no alternative uses. The movement of large numbers of people out of eastern employment and into western farming must have generated considerable dynamic economic dislocation in the East. The shift of the marginal product of labor curve in the West contingent upon the release of public land assumes that virgin land instantly and costlessly becomes productive

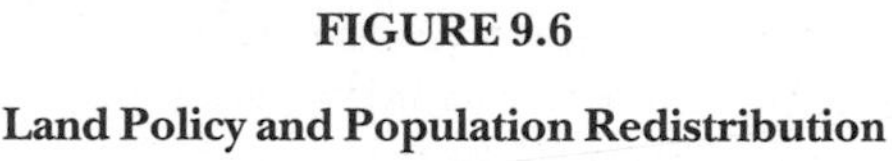

FIGURE 9.6

Land Policy and Population Redistribution

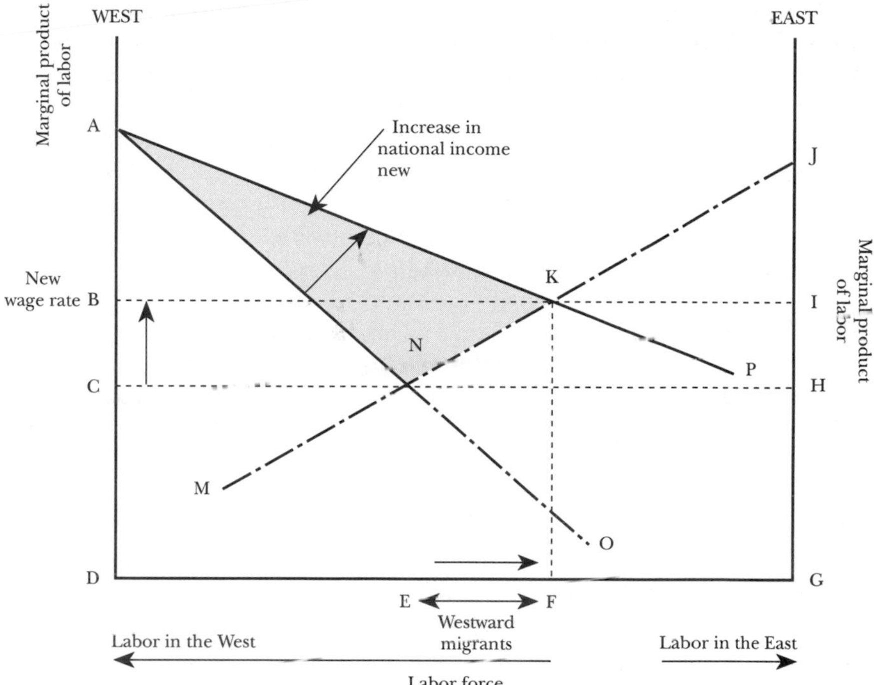

farmland. Rather, substantial human and capital resources—resources that might have been invested elsewhere perhaps at a higher rate of return—were invested in that transformation. The existence of these conversion costs in transforming virgin land to productive farmland means there exists an optimal—output-maximizing—date for the transformation of each plot of land from unsettled territory to settled farmland. By offering land for sale at public auction with competition between cash-paying buyers, federal land policy should have ensured that conversion took place at the "right" time. However, donation of land under the homestead acts may have led to too early a settlement since it misrepresented the true costs of western farming and led to the misallocation of resources.

Certainly, traditional economic historians have generally held the view that federal land policies encouraged rapid agricultural expansion and led directly to overproduction and farm depression. Poor returns to farming created the agricultural distress and loss of ownership that fueled the protest movements of the 1870s and 1880s. The facts marshaled to support this case, however, are limited. True, barely 40 percent of homestead entries were completed, and failure rates among western farms were relatively high. Western farm failures, however, may simply reflect that many farmers were unprepared for the risks of prairie farming, particularly in the West North Central states. Personal bankruptcy, resulting largely from inability to outlast the vagaries of the weather, does not mean that resources were misallocated or that the government should have prevented individuals from voluntarily taking big risks.

Agricultural returns, *on average,* appear to have been adequate. The average return to farming in each decade from 1850 to 1900 was substantial—equal to, if not above, the returns on high-grade bonds, though probably not above the returns now estimated for manufacturing (Table 9.2). Although one cannot infer the return on the marginal investment from these average returns, it is difficult to infer from the numbers any hint of overinvestment in agriculture. Note, moreover, that whereas capital gains on land were thought to be essential to profitability before the Civil War, the current return on farm output dominates the return to capital afterward. Land speculation, however informal, was not the primary source of profit making on the farm after the war. Nor are poor returns in the rapidly developing West masked by the aggregate returns. The return in the North Central (midwestern) states was healthy. Those for the West are downright startling (Table 9.3). One possible explanation for the high returns on land, land improvements, agricultural machinery, and livestock is that they came at the expense of the return to labor—wages actually paid plus the implicit return to self-employed farmers. However, if the South is excluded, Fogel and Rutner show that real wages in agriculture grew at 1.2 percent per year between 1879 and 1899, or about as rapidly as manufacturing wages.

The Federalists had opposed the liberal sales terms for the public land in part on the ground that it would encourage speculation. Government policies, however, only contributed to speculation. After 1820 all land sales were made for cash only, preventing the vast majority of the population from bidding, even when they knew what they wanted. The auctions were thus left to those who had money or access to private credit. With relatively few people in the market for land, speculators were sometimes able to buy large parcels cheaply and then resell the property for much more by accepting mortgages from farmers. For example, between 1870 and 1886 one of the more famous speculator-landlords, William Scully, acquired 220,000 acres in Illinois, Missouri, Kansas, and Nebraska.

To the extent that land speculators were successful, they earned high rates of return and became rich. Iowa land speculators, for example, averaged over 71 percent returns per year on their investments during the 1850s and earned rates of return generally well above those paid by alternate investments until the 1870s.[4] Such profits created jealousies. The speculator

[4] Swierenga (1966).

TABLE 9.2

The Real Return to Agricultural Capital (average annual rate)

Source	1850–59	1860–69	1870–79	1880–89	1890–99
Current production	5.8	11.8	10.6	7.2	8.1
Capital gains on land	2.9	–2.0	3.1	3.0	–1.3
Capital gains on livestock	6.0	2.5	5.4	5.8	2.9
Overall return	8.5	10.1	13.4	10.0	7.7

Interpretation: In each decade the average return to agricultural investment—land improvements, livestock, buildings, farm machinery—was equal to or above contemporary yields on other investments. Note that these yields did not depend on capital gains earned on land, which would partially reflect greater land rents associated with improved transportation.

Source: Robert Fogel and Jack Rutner, "The Efficiency Effects of Federal Land Policy 1850–1900," in *The Dimensions of Quantitative Research in History,* ed. William Aydelotte et al. (Princeton: Princeton University Press, 1972): 398.

TABLE 9.3

Real Return to Agricultural Capital by Region 1880–1899 (average annual rate)

Source	U.S.	North Atlantic	North Central	South Atlantic	South Central	West
Current production	8.1	6.4	5.8	10.9	10.4	20.3
Capital gains on land	0.9	−0.3	1.7	1.8	1.0	0.3
Capital gains on livestock	4.2	1.6	4.6	3.0	5.3	6.3
Overall return	9.3	6.4	7.6	12.4	12.1	21.9

Interpretation: Breaking down returns by region does not suggest overinvestment in the West. The return to investment in the North Central (Midwest) states is relatively low, but higher than in the North Atlantic. Western and South Central investment yields, moreover, are far above the national average.

Source: Robert Fogel and Jack Rutner, "The Efficiency Effects of Federal Land Policy 1850–1900," in *The Dimensions of Quantitative Research in History,* ed. William Aydelotte et al. (Princeton: Princeton University Press, 1972): 398.

was thus almost universally reviled as reaping where he did not sow. The issue, though, is one of distribution. If the speculator had not received these profits they would instead have accrued to the farmer-landowner.

Not all land speculation, though, was a surefire way to riches. Speculator profits suffered wild gyrations in the uncertain land market. For example, the annual return on speculator land sold in Iowa in 1859 was 155.9 percent; two years later the return was only 6.9 percent, or about the same as on government bonds at that time. Sometimes speculators even lost. During the land boom of the 1850s speculators reaped large returns, but in the years after the Civil War they appear to have earned a rate of return comparable to that on good commercial paper (Figure 9.7). This decline in the average returns to speculation is associated with a reduction in turnover and a marked lengthening of the holding period before speculators disposed of their land.

Beyond the simple question of who received the capital gains there lies a more important allegation that the actions of land speculators may have actually reduced national income by withholding land from useful production long after a farmer would have brought it under the plow. Much of this supposed social loss assumes that land speculators pursued a simple "buy and hold" strategy—that is, having bought the land, the speculator simply waited until local development in the vicinity increased land values and sold when the rate of return from (with)holding the land was maximized (see Appendix A). This is a naïve strategy. Speculators could and did make a market in land by generating expectations, whether true or false, about the future course of land values and through boosterism.

Did speculators behave in this way? Yes! There is abundant contemporary evidence of vigorous promotional activities by speculators to sell their lands. They did not just sit back and wait for the market appreciation to take place. For example, Nathan Parker, author of a number of contemporary migrant guides to Iowa and Minnesota (with such tantalizing titles as *Iowa As It Is* and *The Minnesota Handbook*) containing extravagant claims regarding settlement opportunities and the fertility of the soil, was a principal in the Iowa and Minnesota Land Company. Indeed, without revealing his interest, Parker made a vigorous defense of the land speculator: "So far from speculators being a drawback to the settlement of a new country, they are the very men who contribute most to the rapidity of its settlement. Lands would be idle and unimproved for years, were it not for this class of men. They come out here and purchase wild lands in vast bodies, and then make a business of inducing farmers and others in the East to emigrate hither and cultivate them."[5]

If such salesmanship were successful, then the speculator might have earned substantially higher returns from the investment than those offered by the buy and hold strategy. Indeed, the returns from the buy and hold

[5] Parker (1856): 149.

FIGURE 9.7

The Rate of Return to Land Speculation in Iowa Relative to Other Investments

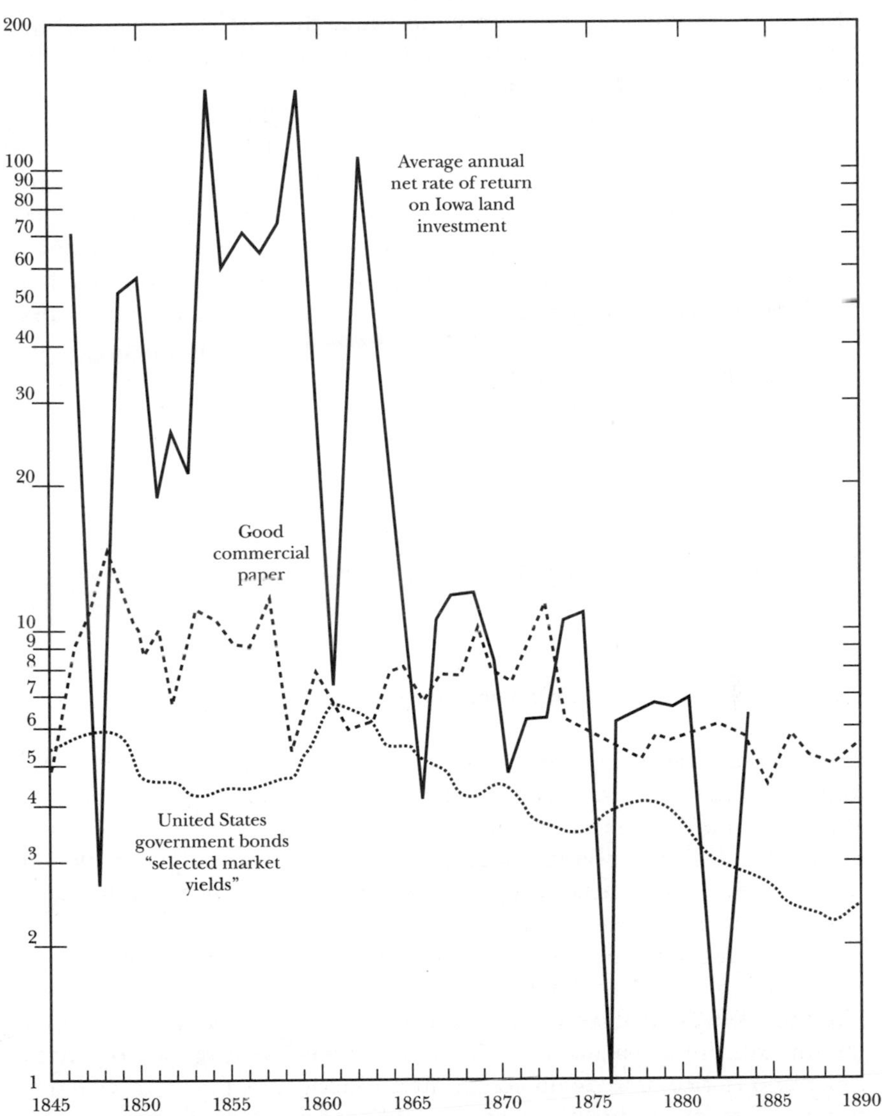

Source: Robert P. Swierenga, "Land Speculator 'Profits' Reconsidered: Central Iowa as a Test Case," *Journal of Economic History* 26 (1966) 25.

strategy represent the lowest returns that the speculator should have earned rather than the maximum that he could have received. Moreover, if the land promotion were successful, then the land would be sold earlier than under the buy and hold strategy, reducing any social cost from speculation in terms of forgone production. It is even conceivable that speculators might have generated a social good by encouraging settlement prior to the time when land would have normally been settled.

Most speculators, though, were not supersalesmen, particularly after the Civil War. The average delay in reselling the land was 32 months, so their activities probably did incur a small social cost.[6] Fogel and Rutner estimate the delay in bringing the land under cultivation at 3.2 years and the loss of GNP at 0.09 percent of 1850 GNP, which, the authors note, "is the amount of national output produced in 1850 during three hours of economic activity." Small potatoes indeed. Or was it? Certainly, as we shall see in Chapter 15 on postwar agriculture in the North, land speculators were a focal point of much of the farm protest movement in the late nineteenth century, blamed for the high price of land, for capturing capital gains that otherwise might have accrued to the farmer, for promoting tenancy, and for various other assorted, real or imagined, ills. These protests challenged the two-party democratic system and wrought fundamental changes in our nation's economic institutions. Still, federal land policy, whatever its faults, played a central role in the settlement of this country, its agricultural development, and its relatively high wages.

Appendix: Modeling Land Speculation Strategies

Consider the situation graphed in Figure 9.A1, which shows the price of a piece of land over time. The price axis is a logarithmic scale so that we can interpret changes in price over time in terms of rates of return. The value of a plot of land rises slowly at first and then accelerates with local settlement, development, and market access. The rate of appreciation subsequently slows as the wave of development moves on.

The essence of successful speculation is that the speculator has information not generally available to the public. In this case, the speculator expects that the price of land will appreciate in value over time in the manner shown, and the speculator buys this land at time S, paying the government reservation price of $1.25 an acre, which is more than the land is currently worth. A farmer, on the other hand, would not buy this land until time T because before then the land is worth less than the $1.25 he would have to pay the government.

Once a farmer has bought the land, it is put to productive use. Thus the land would enter production at time T. The land speculator, on the other

[6] Swierenga (1968).

FIGURE 9.A1

Land Speculation under a "Buy and Hold" Strategy

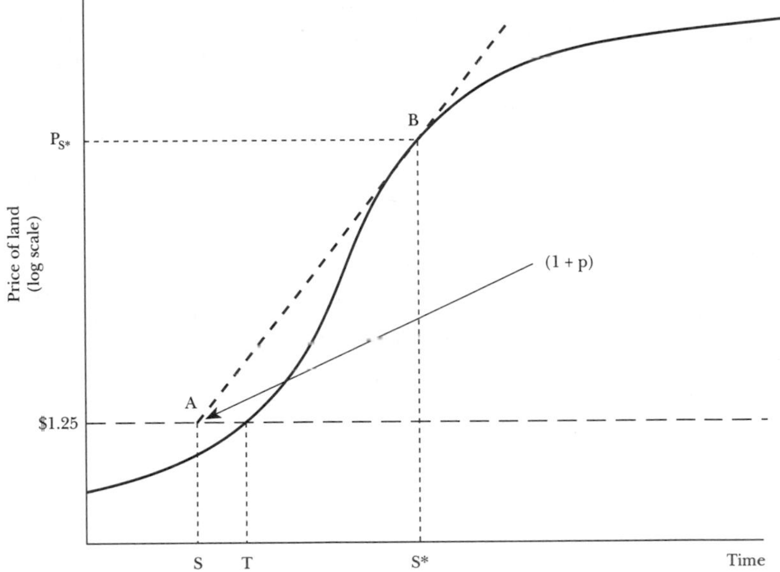

hand, having secured title to the land and pursuing a naïve buy and hold strategy withholds the land until time S*—when it can be resold at price P_s. The speculator thus realizes a return of (P_s − \$1.25) over (S* − S) years. This annual rate of return, p, is the slope of the line from A to B and is the maximum return possible under the buy and hold strategy. Realization of this return to the speculator, however, involves a social cost measured by the forgone production over the time (S* − T) since the farmer would have brought the land under the plow at time T.

Since our legal system provides for a system of secure property rights, the speculator who has bought the land at time S has an economic incentive to reveal his specialist knowledge to the public that land will indeed appreciate in the manner shown. If the speculator is persuasive, then some farmers will be willing to borrow money at the prevailing mortgage interest rate, m, in order to buy some of this land. The line MN traces out all land prices that compounded at the mortgage interest rate m, will, by time M, yield price P_m. These represent the borrowing opportunities that a prudent lender, convinced of the speculator's information, would be willing to offer a qualified buyer, secure in the knowledge that at time T_m, the land will be worth P_m. Indeed, since the speculator often also provided the mortgages, such borrowing opportunities clearly existed.

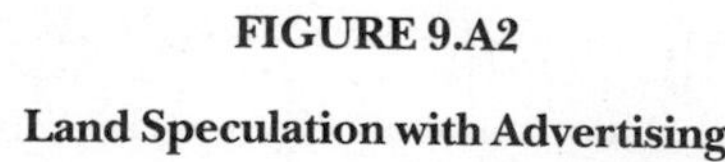

FIGURE 9.A2

Land Speculation with Advertising

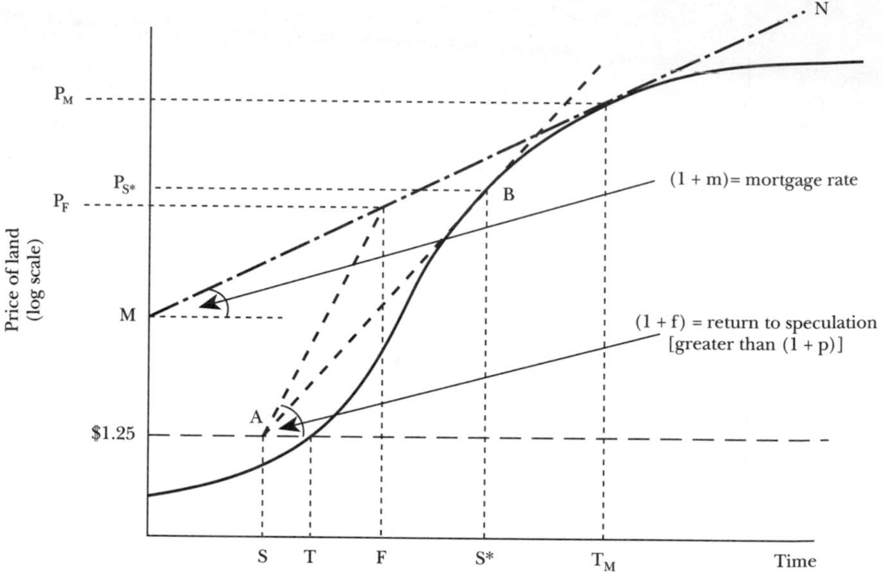

The rate of return earned by the speculator then depends upon how quickly the speculator can convince potential farmers to borrow against the future expected value of the land. If they are convinced at time F, for example, then they can borrow an amount equal to the price P_f against the security of this land. The speculator thus earns the much higher rate of return, f, as a result of this transaction. At worst the speculator might be left to hold the land until time S*, earning a return equivalent to that under the buy and hold strategy. If, however, the speculator is convincing, then his boosterism and promotion activities reduce the social cost of speculation. Indeed, it is even conceivable that time F could come before time T if the speculator is particularly persuasive. In such a case, while the speculator earns a very high rate of return, he also plays a socially beneficial role.

Bibliography

Dennen, A. Taylor. "Some Efficiency Effects of Nineteenth-Century Federal Land Policy: A Dynamic Analysis." *Agricultural History* 51 (1977): 718–36.

Fogel, Robert W., and Jack Rutner. "The Efficiency Effects of Federal Land Policy, 1850–1900." In *Dimensions of Quantitative Research in History,* ed. William Aydelotte et al. Princeton: Princeton University Press, 1972: 390–418.

Gates, Paul W. "The Homestead Law in an Incongruous Land System," *American Historical Review* 41 (1936): 652–81.

Hibbard, Benjamin H. *A History of the Public Land Policies.* New York: Macmillan Co., 1924.

Parker, Nathan. *The Iowa Handbook for 1856.* Boston: John P. Jewett, 1856.

Robbins, Roy M. *Our Landed Heritage.* Princeton: Princeton University Press, 1942.

Saloutos, Theodore. "The Agricultural Problem and Nineteenth-Century Industrialism." *Agricultural History* 22 (1948): 156–74.

Swierenga, Robert P. "Land Speculator 'Profits' Reconsidered: Central Iowa as a Test Case." *Journal of Economic History* 26 (1966): 1–28.

———. *Pioneers and Profits: Land Speculation on the Iowa Frontier.* Ames: Iowa State University Press, 1968.

Northern agricultural development before the civil war

10

In the first half of the nineteenth century American agriculture developed along two separate fronts. In the North there existed what might be called a yeoman democracy—a social and economic order that for a brief instant may have realized some of Thomas Jefferson's vision of a bucolic America as expressed in his *Notes on the State of Virginia* and enshrined in the Northwest ordinances and aspects of the land ordinances. This yeoman democracy was organized about family-owned and family-operated farms that produced a widely diversified crop mix for their own and local consumption but with growing regional and international trade connections. In the South, on the other hand, agriculture was organized around a planter autarky at the center, producing staple crops, especially cotton, for world markets, using slave labor, with a much poorer yeomanry on the periphery, producing food and subsistence crops for its own and local—nonplantation—consumption. The South is dealt with in subsequent chapters. Here we focus on northern agriculture.

Early-nineteenth-century farmers pushed the frontier westward at a stunning rate. The frontier, which the federal census defined as those areas of the country with between two and six persons per square mile (that is, less than one family per square mile), receded rapidly westward. In 1790 much of upstate New York and western Pennsylvania were still beyond the frontier (see Figure 8.12, Panel A). So, too, was most of Ohio except for areas along the Ohio River around Cincinnati, Wheeling, and Marietta. Kentucky also had been settled, albeit thinly, thanks to the Wilderness Road, pioneered by Daniel Boone through the Cumberland Gap. By 1820 Ohio, southern

Indiana, and southern Illinois had been thinly settled. Northern Indiana and Illinois, plus portions of Michigan, Wisconsin, and Iowa, had been opened by 1840. With the railroad in the 1850s the limits of settlement were extended into the rest of Iowa and portions of Minnesota, Kansas, and Nebraska.

Although the migrant flood may bring to mind images of endless lines of hardy pioneers waiting their turns for the ride downstream from Pittsburgh, nothing so simple as the deck space capacity of western river steamboats explains the pace of westward settlement. Instead settlement proceeded in waves that were probably associated with expectations of profit from farming. Peak federal land sales and land entries coincided with peaks in grain prices and progressively lower federal land prices increased the quantity of land demanded.

To Frederick Jackson Turner and a generation or more of historians, this cheap land in the West functioned as a safety valve for economic and social unrest (see Chapter 8). Implicit in this safety valve hypothesis is the notion that an eastern laborer—particularly an unemployed and disaffected laborer—could start a farm on the expanding frontier with little or no capital. Unfortunately this was not true.

Not all unimproved farmland could be bought for $1.25 or less. Settlers who wanted to be close to water or rail transport or within hailing distance of a market town paid much more. The Illinois Central Railroad, for example, offered land obtained by government land grant (see Chapter 16), along its right-of-way in Illinois for $8 to $12 per acre. Even then, land costs represented only a small portion of the costs of setting up a farm.

Farm making meant much more than acquiring title to 40, 80, or 160 acres of arable land. To begin, the land had to be cleared—an extremely arduous task in the forests of Ohio, Michigan, Wisconsin, and Minnesota. The trees had to be cut down and burned or hauled away; then the stumps and any large rocks had to be removed, usually by brute animal force or dynamite. About a month's labor, plus the services of a team of oxen, was required to clear an acre.[1] The fact that the farmer could do this work on his or her own free time doesn't eliminate the cost of the operation; a month of farm labor devoted to land clearing was a month in which the family still had to be fed, sheltered, and clothed. Substantial additional labor was required to build fences capable of keeping livestock out of the crops. Nor did settlement on the treeless prairies avoid these costs. Instead hired help was all the more necessary. Breaking the prairie sod—an almost impenetrable tangle of roots created by millennia of grasses—required special equipment: a heavy plow and a team of four to eight oxen. Because sod breaking had to be done only once, it was almost invariably contracted to specialized crews.

Thus a farmer had two choices, each of which involved considerable in-

[1] Primack (1962).

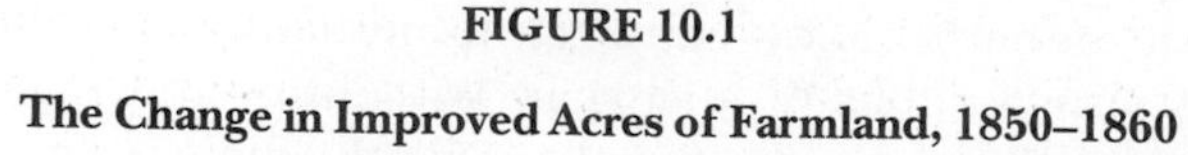

FIGURE 10.1

The Change in Improved Acres of Farmland, 1850–1860

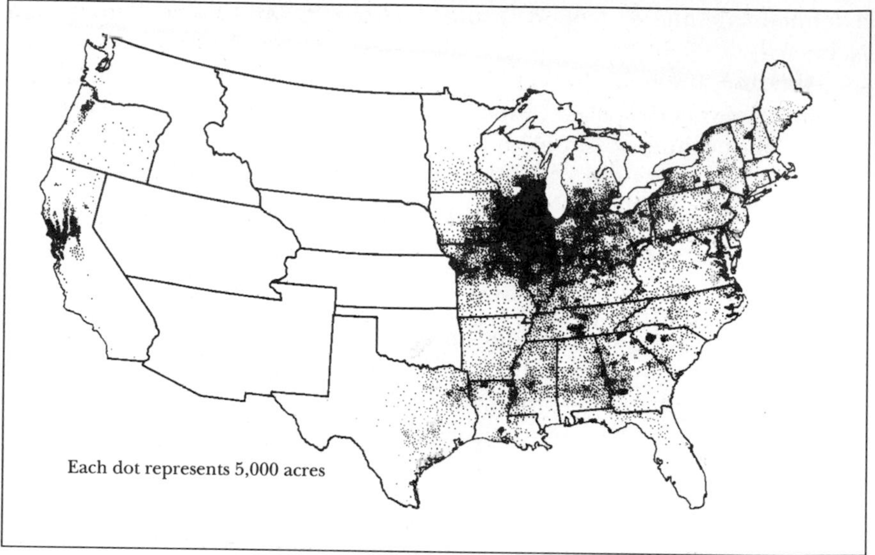

Source: Charles O. Paullin, *Atlas of the Historical Geography of the United States* (Washington, D.C.: Carnegie Institution, 1932): Plate 145D.

vestment. The usual course was for the family to clear five or ten acres each year, planting crops on land as it became available. This meant that it took five or ten years to build a complete farm, five to ten years in which the farmer would be forced to draw down savings, albeit at a decreasing rate (or moonlight as a farm laborer), in order to survive. The alternative was to hire outside labor, a practice that was increasingly common by the 1840s and essential on prairie lands. With outside help, the required investment—about $10 to $12 per acre for clearing woodland and $2 to $5 per acre for prairie—was essentially the same, except the farmer had to have the cash up front.

Despite the effort and expense, millions of acres of land were cleared, representing a vast hidden economic investment, one that at least in part explains the relatively low western commodity output figures. The returns to this investment were a part of the capital gains on land that farmers realized and were an important component in mid-nineteenth-century agricultural profitability. In the forested areas of the Midwest an average of 1.3 million acres were cleared per year in the 1850s (Figure 10.1 and Table 10.1). Whether the $10 to $12 cost of clearing an acre of land was opportunity cost or out-of-pocket expenses, clearing forested land meant an average annual investment of $13 to $16 million, diverting an equivalent amount of resources from commodity production. To put it another way, roughly one-sixth of total midwestern labor force time was engaged in land clearing. This investment eventually paid off in terms of higher output and higher land prices, but in the pre–Civil War era, it was clearly a serious drain on productive labor resources and probably lowered current income.

Although cleared land was the largest single investment needed to make a family farm, it was by no means the only investment. The state of Minnesota, for example, offered would-be settlers the following advice:

> Counting at government price, one hundred and sixty acres is two hundred dollars. The cheapest and best fence, where lumber is cheap . . . is made of boards one inch by six and fourteen feet long, and two posts for every length of boards . . . the cost of fence complete, forty cents per rod. One mile of fence, inclosing forty acres, would cost 320 x 40 = $128; though most have neighbors who help build line fences. . . . A man may build a comfortable house of logs by paying, say fifty dollars for lumber, nails, shingles, windows, &c., and he may make comfortable quarters for stock with poles and straw only, and men seldom put grain in barns when they have them. Horses are worth at present $50 to $100 each; oxen $40 to $50 per yoke; cows $20 each. . . . it is highly desirable that all emigrants should have

The price of their land,	$200.00
team and wagon,	150.00
two cows,	40.00
For building house,	100.00
Breaking twenty acres,	60.00
One steel plow, for crossing,	14.00
One harrow,	6.00
Axes, shovels, spade, forks, scythe, &c.,	25.00
House furniture and provisions for family, which must be bought till they can raise them	200.00
[excluding fencing, ed.]	$795.00

> Some men have started with nothing, and by working out or hiring farms have soon secured homes of comfort, and others will do the same; but to do this requires peculiar material in the man and his wife, and usually families with $500 to $1,000 on their arrival find they have need of the strictest economy.[2]

Fencing, breaking, and the cost of the homestead in Minnesota might be "self-financed" over time with the family's own labor. Even if we assume

[2] Minnesota Commissioner of Statistics, *Minnesota: Its Place among the States Being the First Annual Report of the Commissioner of Statistics* (Hartford: Case and Lockwood, 1860): 88.

TABLE 10.1

Investment in Clearing Farmland, the 1850s

Region	Average Annual Acres Cleared (thousand acres)	% Forested	Average Labor Years Invested (thousands)	% Total Farm Labor Devoted to Clearing
Northeast	570	100	66	7.3
South	1,610	99	175	9.9
Midwest	1,480	90	147	17.7
West	1,230	39	56	16.8
total	4,890	81	445	11.6

Source: Martin Primack, "Land Clearing under 19th Century Techniques," *Journal of Economic History* 22 (1962): 492. Reprinted by permission of Cambridge University Press.

that the land could be mortgaged for the full $200 with no down payment required (typically on a three-to-five-year balloon mortgage), the balance of $595, four times per capita income in the North at the time, would have had to be paid in cash. Thus the prospective farm family would have needed to save a large sum of money and then endure a long period of backbreaking work and subsistence living in order to own a frontier farm that would barely be self-sustaining for many years to come. As a result, there was always an active market in developed farmsteads east of the frontier.

On the basis of his examination of similar contemporary estimates, Clarence Danhof concluded that "the farm-maker's wealth could not fall much short of $1000" for a forty-acre farm. This estimate is very close to what farmers actually had invested in their forty-acre midwestern farms in 1860. The average eighty-acre farm—the most common size of farm—averaged $1,364 for the land, improvements, and buildings, plus $285 for livestock and $67 for implements; that is more than $1,700. In a less settled area, such as Iowa, Minnesota, or Wisconsin, it would cost less, perhaps $800 to $1,300, while farther east, such as in Ohio, it would typically cost much more, perhaps $2,000 or more.[3] At these kinds of costs, only those in the upper one-quarter to one-half of the wealth distribution in 1860 could have afforded to buy their own farms. Farming, thus, was not for the impecunious, and farm makers had either big rainy-day savings or powerful motivations or some combination thereof.

If these capital costs represented a barrier to entry into farming as an owner, there remained the alternative of tenant farming, whether for cash or for shares. This avoided the substantial cash outlay in the farmland, im-

[3] Atack (1982).

TABLE 10.2

Capital Costs of Tenant and Owner-Occupied Farms by Region and Farm Size in 1860

	40-Acre Farm		*80-Acre Farm*		*160-Acre Farm*	
	Owner-Occupied	Tenant	Owner-Occupied	Tenant	Owner-Occupied	Tenant
Midwest						
Farm value	738	969	1,363	1,460	2,490	2,151
Implement value	46	38	67	57	96	87
Livestock value	197	219	285	268	426	335
Total cost to owner-occupier	981		1,715		3,002	
Total cost to tenant		257		325		422
(number)	(494)	(130)	(885)	(232)	(565)	(213)
Northeast						
Farm value	1,599	2,967	2,621	2,772	3,966	3,636
Implement value	65	58	116	80	162	124
Livestock value	256	256	401	277	615	501
Total cost to owner-occupier	1,920		3,138		4,743	
Total cost to tenant		314		357		625
(number)	(85)	(9)	(94)	(23)	(63)	(14)

Source: Jeremy Atack and Fred Bateman, *To Their Own Soil: Agriculture in the Antebellum North* (Ames: Iowa State University Press, 1987): 134, Table 8.2.

provements, and buildings but still required some minimum investment. The average midwestern tenant farmer of eighty-acres had about $325 tied up in the venture, compared with $1,715 for the average owner (Table 10.2). Although the costs for a tenant farmer were substantially lower, they were still out of range for perhaps a third of the population.[4]

Farming Practices and Productivity Growth

The machinery and techniques employed by typical northern farmers in the first third of the nineteenth century were remarkably crude by modern standards. The process of growing wheat and other small grains—the most important antebellum crops—is illustrative. First the soil had to be loosened sufficiently to bury the seed and provide adequate drainage and space for

[4] Atack and Bateman (1987).

root development. This was done with a simple wooden or metal-sheathed wooden plow pulled by a horse or an ox. Then the seeds were scattered by hand and buried under a shallow cover of soil by a light, animal-drawn plow or harrow. When the plants matured, they were cut by a hand-swung scythe and bound together in shocks. The shocks of grain were then stored in a barn until the farmer had time to separate the grain from the straw and remove the remaining chaff and dirt by screening.

Labor productivity—the amount of grain that a farm worker could produce—was limited by (1) by the number of acres that each could plow and harvest, (2) the number of bushels of grain each acre could yield, and (3) the number of bushels each worker could thresh or otherwise prepare for consumption. William Parker and Judith Klein have collected data on each of these variables for three crops—corn, oats, and wheat—in each of three broadly defined regions—the North, Midwest, and South—for two benchmark dates, 1840–60 and 1900–10, that provide an important insight into the sources of productivity change.

In the nineteenth century they estimate that it took, on average nationwide, 1.45 hours to produce a bushel of oats for market, 3.17 hours to produce a bushel of wheat ready for milling, and 3.50 hours to produce a bushel of corn. By 1900–10 the figures had been cut to 0.40, 0.76, and 0.96 hours. As a result, labor productivity increased 363 percent $(= \frac{1.45}{0.40} \times 100)$ in oats production, 417 percent in wheat production, and 365 percent in corn production (Table 10.3).

Parker and Klein's methodology allows them to decompose the observed labor productivity growth into the portions that they attribute to mechanization, the westward movement, and "scientific" farming, broadly defined. They suggest that changes in the time spent plowing, planting, harvesting, and preparing the crop for market reflected changes in mechanization: better plows, the use of seeders, harrows, cultivators, reapers, and mechanical threshers. Changes in yields, on the other hand, reflected "scientific" farming practices, and changes in the regional output shares reflected the regional redistribution of agricultural activities that accompanied the westward movement. Suppose that yields and regional shares had not changed from their 1840–60 levels while the number of hours spent in plowing, planting, cultivating, harvesting, and fitting the crop for market declined as a result of mechanization. It would have taken just 1.29 hours to produce a bushel of wheat in 1910 instead of the 0.76 hours per bushel that it actually took. The reduction in the time that it took to produce a bushel of wheat from 3.17 hours in 1840 to this hypothetical estimate of 1.29 hours in 1910 means that labor productivity would have risen by 246 percent $(= \frac{3.17}{1.29} \times 100)$ in response to mechanization alone (index i_3, Table

TABLE 10.3

The Allocation of Labor Productivity Growth in Corn, Oats, and Wheat Production, 1840-1910

Index	*Period Values for* Regional Weights	Yield per Acre	Hours of Labor Pre-, Harvest, and Post Harvest	Productivity Index ($i_1/i_n \times 100$) Corn	Oats	Wheat
	(1840–60 = 1; 1900–10 = 2)					
i_1	1	1	1	100	100	100
i_2	1	2	1	119	106	118
i_3	1	1	2	227	186	246
i_4	2	1	1	130	123	109
i_5	1	2	2	265	201	302
i_6	2	1	2	330	372	377
i_7	2	2	1	143	118	118
i_8	2	2	2	365	363	417

Source: William N. Parker and Judith L. V. Klein, "Productivity Growth in Grain Production in the United States, 1840–60 and 1900–10," in National Bureau of Economic Research, *Output, Employment and Productivity in the United States after 1800,* Studies in Income and Wealth, vol. 30 (New York: Columbia University Press, 1966): 533.

10.3). Similarly, suppose that the only change to take place between 1840 and 1910 was a change inyields because of scientific farming, selective breeding of seeds, etc. The contribution of this factor in isolation can be measured comparing man-hours per bushel in 1910 (estimated using 1840 weights and labor inputs but 1910 yield estimates) with the number of hours of labor per bushel in 1840 (index i_2, Table 10.3).

The individual contributions of improved yields and the westward movement prove to be fairly modest. These changes in isolation would have raised labor productivity between 6 and 30 percent—far short of the actual observed increases. Little progress was made in raising yields per acre before the Civil War because in large measure yields can be manipulated only by biochemical techniques. Even a basic understanding of genetic principles was insufficient to make seed selection very productive. And "seat-of-the-pants" experimentation with seeds, fertilizers, and other yield-increasing techniques was frustrated by the enormous range of soil and weather conditions farmers faced. Yields might, of course, be raised by farming more productive soil regions. Indeed, just such a change did take place after the Civil War. The share in total output of low-productivity southern grain acreage fell, but the shift of grain production from the Northeast to North Central states before the war left yield levels virtually unchanged. The impact of mechanization—more complete tillage from improved plows, better seed distribution with seed drills, a speedier and more gently handled harvest with a reaper, and a more complete threshing with a steam-powered thresher—on labor productivity was far greater, particularly in wheat production, where it accounted for almost 60 percent of the total labor productivity increase between 1840 and 1910. Such devices not only eased the burden of backbreaking labor but also reduced the number of workers required for each task and the period of employment.

Parker and Klein also examined the contributions of different pairs of factors, such as the westward movement and yield change, and the westward movement and mechanization. As the figures indicate, the westward movement and mechanization (index i_6, Table 10.3) account for virtually the entire growth in labor productivity during the period. Even more significantly, the two factors interacted, mutually reinforcing each other, so that the combined effect was greater than the two could have achieved in isolation. If westward movement and mechanization in wheat production had been independent of each other, then the combined effect should have been to raise labor productivity by 268 percent (109 x 246). Instead it rose 377 percent. Why was there this synergistic interaction? The explanation in this case is probably that the flat land, relatively free of tree stumps and rocks in the Midwest, made for ideal conditions in which to apply farm machinery because there was no danger of overturning or damaging the equipment on an obstacle and less power would be needed to move it.

Agricultural Mechanization: The Reaper as a Case Study

In the absence of mechanization, labor productivity in America would have grown at less than half the actual rate, with potentially serious consequences for late-nineteenth-century industrialization. The factors that underlay adoption of these new technologies is therefore important. Many of the technical improvements in farming came fairly easily, as mechanics adapted techniques invented for the construction of industrial machinery. By the 1820s wooden plows were being rapidly displaced by cast-iron plows of superior durability and design, requiring less animal power. In the 1840s steel plows, pioneered by John Deere in 1837, gradually replaced cast iron, particularly in the West, where they were better suited to turning the heavy prairie soil. In the 1830s and 1840s mechanical threshers greatly reduced labor inputs in removing the grain from the stalk. Prior to mechanization, it took about an hour to hand-thresh a bushel of wheat. Mechanical threshing could cut the time to ten to twelve minutes and the cost of the operation to 3 or 4 cents per bushel, a saving of about half over hand threshing. Unlike other farm equipment of the time, not only were threshers very expensive, but the capacity of a single machine was much greater than that needed by an average farm with fifty or sixty acres in small grains. Nevertheless, the marketplace adapted easily to this economic "indivisibility": Entrepreneurs rented out threshing services to neighboring farmers as their needs required.

As hard work as hand threshing was, it could, at least, be spread out over the long winter months. Planting and harvesting, however, had to be done at specific times and completed within a certain period. Small grain harvesting, in particular, had about a two-week window of opportunity in which the ripe grain could be harvested before it was lost; consequently, the labor available for this task imposed a binding constraint upon the farm. Temporary harvest labor might be used to break the constraint for an individual farmer, but because everyone's wheat in the area needed to be harvested at about the same time, there was a real risk that outside help would be unavailable or available only at very high wages. Consequently, the mechanical, horse-drawn harvester, which effected substantial savings in labor, was a device of considerable economic importance. The first harvesters were patented by Obed Hussey in 1833 and Cyrus McCormick in 1834. At first the machines sold poorly—only thirty-four hundred were manufactured in the years through 1850. But in the early 1850s sales took off: More than seventy thousand of the laborsaving devices were purchased between 1850 and 1858.

If the harvester was so important, why did it take more than twenty years from the invention of the reaper to its general adoption on American farms? The conventional explanation is that high wheat prices in the 1850s raised the profitability of wheat farming. Higher profits encouraged farmers to plant more wheat but made the use of traditional hand-harvesting methods impractical because of the general shortage of labor (Figure 10.2). This explanation, though essentially correct, is unnecessarily ambiguous in meaning. In a famous article Paul David restated the hypothesis in more testable language summarized by Figure 10.3. And, the adoption of the reaper serves as a metaphor for the whole range of technological innovation in industry as well as agriculture.

The figure shows the average cost curve for a grain farmer, relating output to the cost per bushel of producing wheat. C_h is the farmer's cost if he or she chooses to harvest by hand using a device called a grain cradle. This was a prototypical American adaptation of the traditional scythe to which tines or a basket had been attached at the back of the blade. The basket caught the grain as it was cut, relieving labor of the necessity of raking up the cut grain before binding it and stacking it in the field. Grain cradles cost just a few dollars each. The average cost of using one is shown in Figure 10.3 as a perfectly straight line up to a certain point. The shape of the cost curve emphasizes the idea that within the constraints of the family labor supply, an individual farmer could use labor at roughly constant cost per bushel harvested. The curve C_m shows the alternative average cost of producing wheat using a mechanical harvester. For low outputs, costs are very high, but costs fall rapidly

FIGURE 10.2

Wheat Production

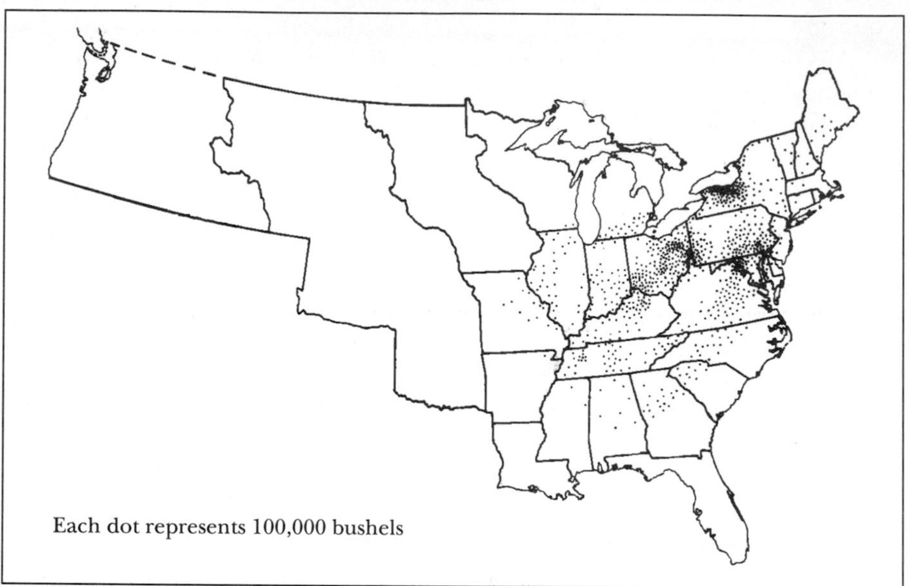

PANEL A: 1839

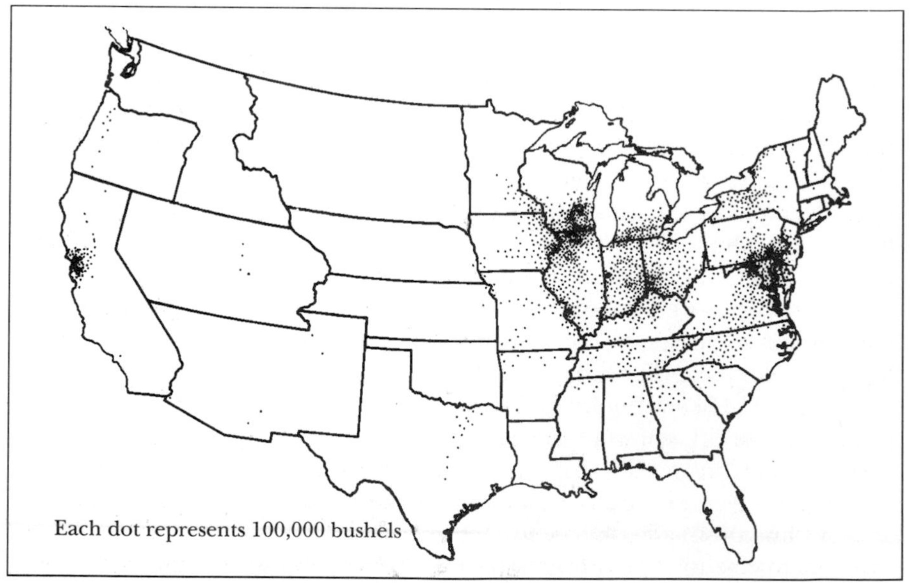

PANEL B: 1859

Source: Charles O. Paullin, *Atlas of the Historical Geography of the United States* (Washington, D.C.: Carnegie Institution, 1932): Plates 143P and 143Q.

FIGURE 10.3

The Threshold for Reaper Adoption

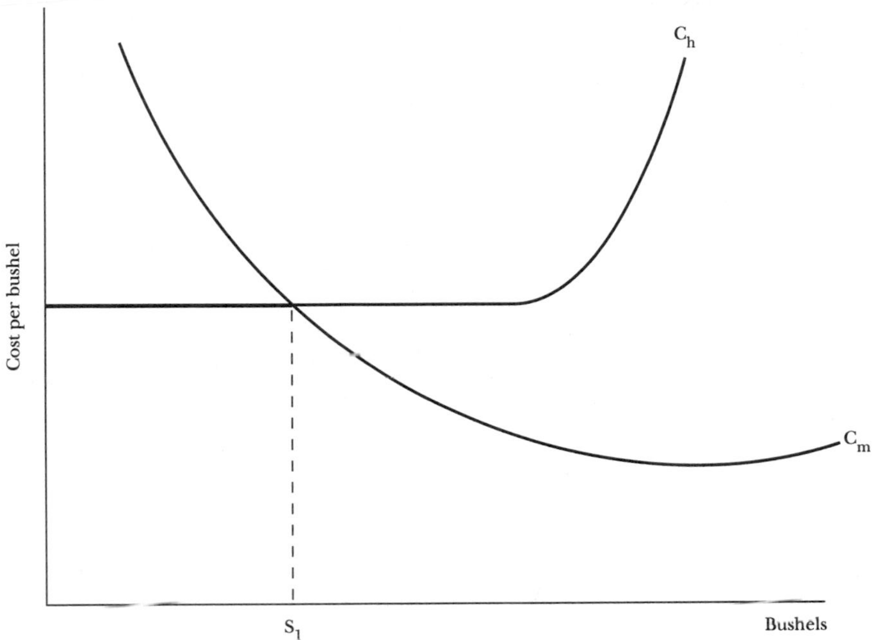

as the scale of farm operation increases. This reflects the fact that much of the cost of operation of a harvesting machine is fixed regardless of output; the farmer has to buy the same piece of equipment whether five acres or fifty acres are to be harvested.

A farmer planting relatively few acres in wheat would naturally prefer to harvest by hand. But now suppose that wheat prices rise and individual farmers wish to plant more land in wheat and less in other crops. Even if the cost of the additional labor remains the same per unit, the more a farmer expands grain output, the less the advantage of using hand labor. When output S_1 is reached, it pays the farmer to buy a mechanical harvester. This point is called the threshold; for any output smaller than S_1, profits will be greater using the cradle than the reaper, and vice versa for all outputs larger than S_1. The threshold thus represents the point at which a farmer switches between the technological alternatives. Actually, by the traditional historical explanation, it may pay to switch at an output below S_1. If the wages needed to hire extra labor rise (or are sacrificed by family members who might otherwise moonlight), reflecting a general upward shift in the demand for labor, the C_h curve shifts upward to C_h' (Figure 10.4). The average cost of hand harvesting now exceeds mechanical harvesting at S_2.

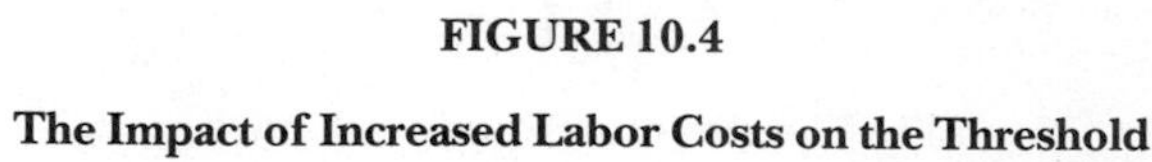

FIGURE 10.4

The Impact of Increased Labor Costs on the Threshold

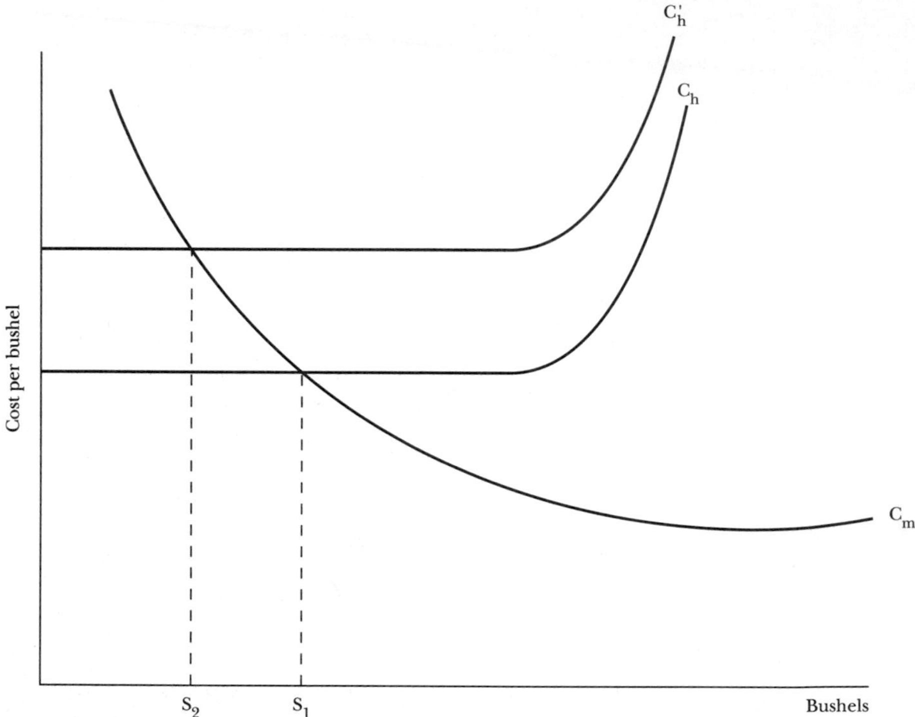

This scenario—connecting the switch from one technology to another to the rising cost of labor and the increased demand for wheat—makes sense. But sense isn't proof. David set out to test the explanation by estimating the acreage threshold (S) at which it would pay to switch to mechanical reaping and then comparing the threshold with actual acreage in grain on Illinois farms. In the 1849–53 period, David found that the delivered purchase price of a standard McCormick reaper was equivalent to 97.6 laborer-days' wages (Figure 10.5). Using estimates of the labor per acre the reaper saved and the annual cost of keeping a reaper, one can show that the hand-machine threshold was 46.5 acres. This was far above the typical Illinois farmer's acreage in small grains, which at the time of the 1850 census averaged just 15–16 acres statewide and 37 acres in the northern Illinois Wheat Belt.[5]

Shortly thereafter the threshold declined to thirty-five acres as wages rose faster than the price of reapers. David can't be certain of a parallel in-

[5] Jones (1977).

FIGURE 10.5

Threshold Functions for Adoption of the Reaper

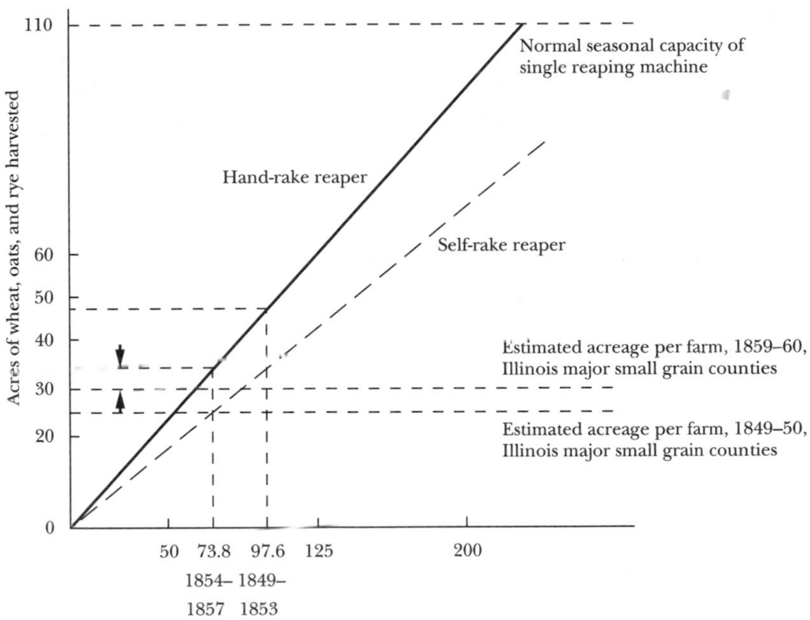

Source: Paul A. David, "The Mechanization of Reaping in the Ante-Bellum Midwest," in *The Reinterpretation of American Economic History*, ed. Robert W. Fogel and Stanley L. Engerman (New York: Harper & Row, 1971): 223. Originally published in *Industrialization in Two Systems: Essays in Honor of Alexander Gershenkron*, ed. Henry Rosovsky (New York: Wiley, 1966).

crease in grain acreage per farm caused by increasing profits in wheat production. The census does not provide enough information to identify what parts of the state showed increases in wheat acreage per farm. But we do know that small grain output per farm for the state as a whole rose by 19 percent over the decade, suggesting that average farm acreage in the wheat counties could easily have pushed across the (reduced) threshold.

Tidy though Paul David's explanation of the rapid transition to mechanical reaping might be, it is not invulnerable to criticism. David's approach implies a perverse causality: Farmers first plant more wheat and then decide to buy a reaper. On the other hand, if the farmer buys the reaper and then plants or plants in anticipation of such a purchase, small grain acreage is no longer an independent variable. David's explanation also ignores the role played by demand in the farmer's decision about what and how much to plant. By his argument, America's farmers responded purely to changes in costs. His argument also falls short of explaining the dramatic increase in the number of farmers who adopted the reaper in the *early* 1850s. Instead it seems likely that profit-maximizing farmers who responded to the higher grain prices by planting more wheat might have suddenly realized that they could earn even higher profits by adopting the reaper *at their existing scale of operation.* Consequently, these farmers switched from using the grain cradle to using the reaper even though they used the reaper at less than its optimal—that is to say, its profit-maximizing—scale (See Appendix).[6] These higher wheat prices in the 1850s reflected two important changes. First, there was an increase in demand for American wheat as a result of the destruction of crops and interruption of the European wheat trade by the Crimean War (1853–56). Ukraine and the Crimean Peninsula in the Black Sea had traditionally supplied much of Western Europe's wheat needs, but these supplies were lost when war broke out between Britain, France, and Turkey, on the one hand, and Russia, on the other. Consequently, Europe had to look elsewhere to satisfy its domestic wheat needs and turned to America. Second, the coming of the railroad to the Midwest reduced transport costs, raising farm gate prices and encouraging farmers to produce more for the market.

Further, David based his estimate of the annual cost of owning a reaper on the assumption that loans to finance the machines could be had at 6 percent interest and that reapers had useful lives of ten years. However, evidence on credit sales from the McCormick papers suggests that the price of credit was 10 percent or more and that the reapers may have lasted as little as five years. These alternative assumptions raise the cost of mechanical harvesting relative to hand harvesting and naturally raise the threshold. David's 1848–53 46.5-acre threshold becomes 810.4 acres, and his 1854–57 35-acre threshold jumps to 67.6 acres.

The threshold itself, however, tells us nothing about how many farmers would find it more cost-effective to harvest using the reaper. Some farmers planted just a few acres in small grains; others planted hundreds. Assuming an average wheat yield of about twelve bushels per acre, Lewis Jones has made some estimates of the number of Illinois farms about the threshold in 1849 and 1859, using census production data. He estimates that about 3,420 farms exceeded forty-six acres of small grains and 836 farms exceeded eighty-nine acres of small grains in 1849. Ten years later, as a result of increased profitability and specialization, the number of farms exceeding David's threshold of thirty-five acres grew 730 percent to more than 28,000, while the number of farms exceeding Alan Olmstead's higher threshold of sixty-eight acres grew even more, 930 percent, to more than 8,000 farms. Over the same period the number of reapers in use grew by more than 1,000 percent. This does not necessarily validate the threshold model, for if

[6] Ankli (1976).

David's estimate of the threshold is correct, then there were far too few American farmers who had adopted the reaper by the late 1850s, while if Olmstead's estimate of the threshold is right, then too many farmers nationwide had made the switch to mechanical harvesting.

As useful as the notion of a threshold—a critical scale of operation—might be, it is based upon a possibly flawed, fundamental assumption that reapers are "indivisible"—that a farmer can't buy the services of a fourth or a half of a reaper. If they can, then the threshold argument becomes meaningless. Mechanized technology would either be cheaper on all farms or none, depending on the relative cost of hand labor and reapers. To see why, check Figure 10.6.

The cost curve for hand harvesting (C_h) remains the same. But if a farmer need not buy a fixed amount of a reaper, the mechanical harvesting cost curve (C_m) loses its downward slope. Now if C_m lies above C_h, hand harvesting is cheaper, regardless of the farm acreage planted in grain. If hand harvesting is more expensive (C_h), all farms, whatever their grain acreage, will use mechanical harvesters. Because David argues that large farms (over forty-six acres) could profit from the use of McCormick's reaper in 1849, by this same logic all farms could have profited from renting the services of a reaper.

Was it feasible to buy less than a whole reaper? David claims that it wasn't, citing the problems of cooperative ownership and rental arrangements (such as who gets to use it when and responsibility for damage) as well as the difficulty of moving such a large, delicate piece of equipment over bad roads. This argument seems a bit strained in view of the thriving contemporary contract market for the services of itinerant threshing crews with their machines. Contracts could be suitably drawn to deal with all possible contingencies. Moreover, Olmstead has unearthed direct evidence in the McCormick archives that neighboring farmers and related farmers often pooled their resources to buy reapers jointly. If so, then David's threshold model of the determinants of reaper use falls apart, although the concept of a threshold scale for technological innovations remains extremely useful.

Once the farmer had adopted a laborsaving device, whether it was the reaper, a self-scouring plow, a mechanical thresher, or whatever, he proved markedly reluctant to return to the old ways of doing things, even when the economic incentives that gave rise to the original adoption were reversed. The farmer became "locked" in to the new technology. Sometimes this was the result of interrelatedness between different technologies. For example, the farmer had to continue planting mechanically if he wished to keep cultivating mechanically. More often, though, technological lock-in on the farm occurred for no other reason than that the labor saved was the farmer's own. Consequently, the structure of farming has to figure prominently in any explanation of crop mixes and technological innovation in American agriculture.

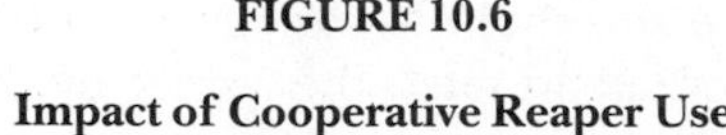

FIGURE 10.6

Impact of Cooperative Reaper Use

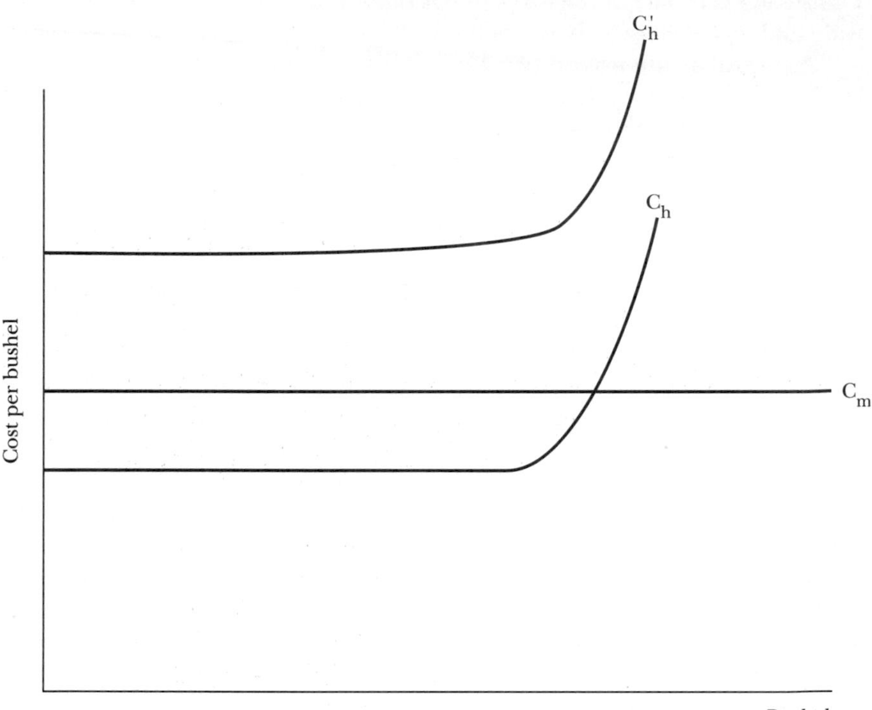

Agriculture and Market Development

The first settlers of Ohio, Indiana, and Illinois had followed the paths of least resistance, settling and cultivating the valleys of the Ohio and Mississippi rivers and their tributaries. They grew grain (mostly corn and wheat) and meat for their own consumption. As one wag put it, "The land would produce nothing but corn. There was no market for the corn so they made it into whiskey. The whiskey market was glutted and the price low, so they drank the whiskey."[7] Thomas Jefferson in his various writings spoke fondly of these small self-sufficient farmers, divorced from the caprices of the marketplace, as "God's chosen people," the ideal, a complete household economy, with economic, moral, and political dimensions. Such a simple life did not last long.

Increasingly, the growing surplus produced on an ever-expanding, improved acreage exceeded local consumption needs and was shipped down

[7] Buley (1950) I: 225.

the rivers to the seaport of New Orleans. From there the surpluses were shipped to other markets, both at home and abroad. Later the railroad carried the goods directly to the East Coast. A crucial question is whether these surpluses were accidental or planned. Were they consistently larger than might be expected from risk-averse behavior? Did farmers choose to trade because they chose not to produce the full range of crops necessary to meet their own consumption needs and that of their farm livestock?

Evidence indicates that farmers were active market participants wherever and whenever possible. Even during the colonial period Massachusetts farmers were making frequent and repeated trips to market with surplus products, and they actively sought those markets with the best prices. As a result, market prices moved together over a wide area, and arbitrage reduced the wedge to the costs of transportation between markets.[8] By the mid-nineteenth century 71 percent of northern farmers had surpluses that could be sold. Those farmers closest to transportation routes generated significantly larger surpluses. These individual sales aggregate to large interregional trade flows in agricultural commodities.[9]

The Impact of Midwestern Settlement on the Northeast

These commodity flows owed much to falling transportation costs—the result of steam navigation on the rivers and Great Lakes and the construction of canals—that sharply narrowed the gap between farm gate and market prices. For example, pork in 1816–20 had cost $9.53 more per barrel in New York than in Cincinnati, but by 1856–60 the price differential, reflecting transport costs between the two markets, had narrowed to only $1.18 a barrel (see Table 6.8). During the same period the price difference on pork between New Orleans and Cincinnati narrowed from $7.57 a barrel to $1.27 (see Table 6.7). One can also infer from these data that pork would not be shipped to New York via the Ohio and Mississippi rivers and coastwise traffic if the cost of coastwise shipment exceeded 9 cents a barrel (as it almost certainly did). Surplus resources and productive capacity in the Midwest resulted in a very elastic supply of goods. Thus much of the gain from improved transportation benefited consumers, especially in the Northeast, via lower market prices, rather than midwestern farmers through higher farm gate prices.

As western grain and livestock began to compete for eastern markets, established northeastern farmers found themselves at a disadvantage with less productive, higher-priced land. One option was to quit farming. Many did, either moving west and further contributing to western competition in east-

[8] Rothenberg (1992).
[9] Atack and Bateman (1987).

ern markets or moving into the cities and towns and taking up new occupations in the growing industrial sector. Eastern farmland in land-extensive grain production was least able to withstand western competition and was either taken out of production entirely or switched to products in which eastern farms still had a comparative advantage. The railroad, which had done much to spur western competition with eastern farms, not only sharply reduced transport costs from upland areas of the rural northeast but also cut the time it took to get fresh foods to market. This improved transport, combined with increased demand for luxury foods, encouraged the growth of the dairy industry that had previously been limited to the fringes of urban areas. By 1860 farms within perhaps a sixty- to seventy-mile radius of such cities as Boston, New York, and Philadelphia were shipping fluid milk to urban consumers, while more distant farms were specializing in butter and cheeses. For the same reasons, Middle Atlantic farmers were induced to switch from their traditional grain crops to the production of fresh fruits and vegetables for urban consumption. Farmers adopted these activities only reluctantly, because they required much more intensive labor effort—that is, labor had to work harder and longer for the same return.

Along with the switch to crops that retained a location advantage over western land, there was also a movement in eastern farming toward more capital-intensive, high-yield-per-acre farming. Some farmers experimented with fertilizer and crop rotation schemes as a means of saving land with declining fertility. One should not make too much of this movement, though. Relatively little was known before the Civil War about capital-intensive, scientific farming, and there is no strong basis for believing that it was profitable to use "land-saving" technology as long as it was easy to open virgin lands in the West. Eastern adaptation to western agricultural expansion was largely based on shifts to crops in which the East had a "comparative advantage." One outcome of all these changes in eastern farm crops and agricultural techniques, however, seems to have been a marked increase in labor productivity of about 15 percent between 1820 and 1850, even in a relatively poor farming area such as Massachusetts.[10]

Trade and the Midwestern Farmer

The fall in transport costs opening up East Coast markets was only one factor making western farming economically more attractive. Rapidly improving industrial technology also resulted in a sharp decrease in the relative price of goods manufactured in the East, compared with the price of western agricultural goods in the Midwest. The purchasing power of western output in

[10] Rothenberg (1992).

interregional trade grew steadily over most of the antebellum years. By the 1840s a composite unit of western output (in western markets) sold for twice as many eastern goods as it did in the 1820s, and by the eve of the Civil War it would buy three times as many eastern goods as in the 1820s (Table 10.4).

The farmers' response to improved terms of trade—the price of the goods they sold relative to the price of the goods they bought—was predictable. Farming became more profitable, making it practical to extend cultivation farther from the waterways. The mix of farm output shifted away from goods for home consumption to goods intended for increasingly distant markets. Douglass North has illustrated this growing market orientation by following the change in population and output in four randomly selected counties in central Illinois. Between 1840 and 1850 the population of these counties increased by 60 percent, but the output of corn grew by 232 percent. This corn, presumably, was sold as feed for hogs raised for export down the Mississippi to New Orleans. These same four counties also responded remarkably quickly to changing incentives during the 1850s. With sharply higher wheat prices, the completion of a rail link between Chicago and the East Coast, and twenty-seven hundred miles of track crisscrossing the state,

TABLE 10.4

Western Terms of Trade, 1816–1860

Years	5-Year Average
1816–20	58
1821–25	59
1826–30	75
1831–35	105
1836–40	125
1841–45	111
1846–50	130
1851–55	160
1856–60	162

Note: Western "terms of trade" are defined as an index of prices received for western goods divided by an index of prices paid for eastern goods where the average terms of trade between 1824 and 1846.

Source: Thomas S. Berry, *Western Prices before 1861: A Study of the Cincinnati Market* (Cambridge: Harvard University Press, 1943), copyright © 1943 by the President and Fellows of Harvard College, cited in Douglass North, *The Economic Growth of the United States,* 1790–1860 (New York: W. W. Norton, 1966): 255.

Illinois farmers switched to wheat production. Wheat production grew by 655 percent; population increased "only" 178 percent.

Farm Income and Profitability

Thanks to the markets provided by an increasingly nonfarm and urban population both near and far, declining transport costs, and adaptation to comparative advantage, farmers in both the Northeast and the Midwest seemed able to have secured adequate, if modest, incomes from their farms. Allowing for capital gains on land through local development, land improvement, and the growth of farm livestock populations, per capita income on midwestern owner-occupied farms averaged $113 a person in 1859–60. Tenants who received none of the capital gains on land earned only $61 per person. Farm families in the Northeast averaged higher per capita incomes. Those on owner-occupied farms received an average of $174 per person; tenant farms generated about $78 income per family member from farming, with much of the difference reflecting the contribution of capital gains on land to the income of the landowner (Table 10.5).

Considering these per capita income figures and the estimates of farm surplus production and net cash flows, it should be no surprise that northern agriculture was profitable. Overall, northern farms generated an average return of 12.1 percent per dollar invested.[11] Average rates of return were somewhat higher in the Northeast than the Midwest, suggesting perhaps that midwestern agriculture was expanding more rapidly than the market, driving down the rate of profit. These returns compare favorably with the return on bonds or from plantation slavery (Chapter 12), but they are small compared with estimated returns in manufacturing (Chapter 7), raising serious questions about mid-nineteenth-century resource allocation. The economy was almost certainly not in equilibrium. But, then, with a rapidly expanding frontier, sharp fluctuations in year-to-year immigration flows, an expanding transportation network, and ongoing industrialization, why should we expect it to be?

The existence of this discrepancy between agricultural returns and manufacturing was not new, and it is not likely to be the result of gross mismeasurement. In 1845 Secretary of the Treasury Robert J. Walker, wrote that "while the profit of agriculture varies from 1 to 8 percent, that of manufactures is more than double."[12] This might explain why on the eve of the Civil War, per capita income in the Midwest had lost still more ground to the Northeast and only narrowed slightly the gap with the South.

[11] Atack and Bateman (1987).

[12] U.S. Congress, Report of the Secretary of the Treasury, *29th Cong., 1st sess. 1846, Senate Document 2.:* 12.

TABLE 10.5

Estimated per Capita Farm Income by State and Tenancy, 1859–1860 ($)

State/Region	Tenants	Owner-Occupiers
Illinois	82	165
Indiana	58	113
Iowa	60	104
Kansas	52	120
Michigan	78	85
Minnesota	61	94
Missouri	21	68
Ohio	99	146
Wisconsin	73	96
Midwest	61	113
Connecticut	68	170
Maryland	19	88
New Hampshire	71	113
New Jersey	100	153
New York	133	221
Pennsylvania	76	128
Vermont	125	177
Northeast	78	174
Entire North	67	135

Source: Jeremy Atack and Fred Bateman, *To Their Own Soil: Agriculture in the Antebellum North* (Ames: Iowa State University Press, 1987): 243, Table 13.8.

Appendix: Reaper Adoption and the Profit-Maximizing Farmer

Most economic treatments of profit maximization employ marginal analysis—that is to say, the profit-maximizing firm produces that output at which its marginal cost of production equals the marginal revenue from the sale of that unit of output. Robert Ankli's model, on the other hand, is most easily explained in terms of total cost and total revenue. Consider Figure 10.A1. Two families of curves are shown. Those for the 1840s are shown as solid lines. Those for the 1850s are represented by dot-dashed lines. The grain cradle cost curves are monotonically increasing, reflecting the impact of local labor scarcity on local wages as all farms in an area try to hire more labor to harvest more acres of wheat. The average and marginal costs of

FIGURE 10.A1

Changes in Reaper Threshold and Desired Scale of Wheat Production in the 1840s and 1850s

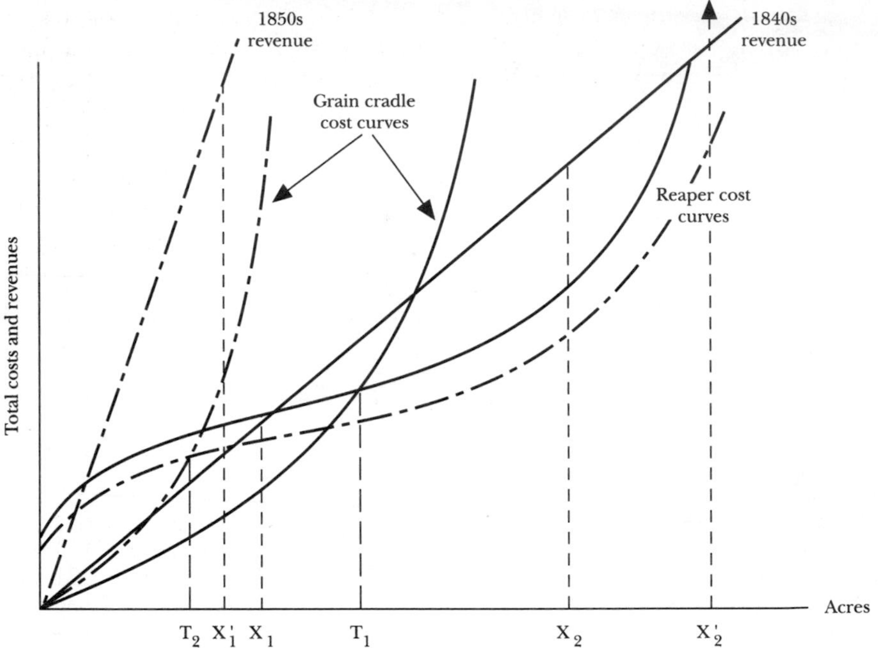

using a grain cradle are thus rising. The total costs of using a reaper are increasing throughout, but first at a decreasing and then at an increasing rate. Consequently, average costs are U-shaped and marginal costs are decreasing, then increasing. The positive y-axis intercept of the reaper total cost curves represents the fixed costs associated with reaper ownership, such as debt servicing. The total revenue curves for the 1840s and the 1850s are linear, reflecting perfectly competitive conditions in the product market. Farmers can sell as much as they can produce at the current market price. The greater slope of the 1850s total revenue line relative to the 1840s reflects the generally higher wheat prices prevailing in the 1850s. During the 1840s, for example, the wholesale price of wheat ranged from 98 cents to $1.37 per bushel. In the 1850s the price ranged from $1.08 to $2.44 per bushel.

The threshold—the scale at which the costs of using the cradle and the reaper are equal—in the 1840s is T_1. The threshold in the 1850s is T_2. The threshold declines for all the reasons suggested by David and Olmstead—namely, higher wages for the reaper are at least partially and perhaps more than offset by falling capital costs and increased reaper longevity, thanks to improved construction.

Faced by these costs and revenue expectations, a profit-maximizing farmer would operate the grain cradle at scale X_1 or the reaper at scale X_2. As drawn, however, it is more profitable to use the reaper than the grain cradle. Consequently, the farmer should have preferred to produce at X_2 using the reaper to producing at X_1 using the cradle. Why didn't he? One explanation is that to do so required time, effort, and expense in clearing more land; in short the farmer was temporarily constrained with respect to scale. Another explanation is that for a small farmer, increasing grain acreage from X_1 to X_2 might raise risks unacceptably high by increasing crop specialization. Higher wheat prices in the 1850s, however, encouraged all farmers to plant more wheat, and the profit-maximizing farmer who was using the cradle planted X_1' acres. This scale lies to the right of the threshold, T_2. As a result, the farmer can now earn even greater profits *at the existing scale of operation* by adopting the reaper, even though the farmer is no longer profit-maximizing once he adopts this new technology.

Bibliography

Ankli, Robert E. "The Coming of the Reaper." In *Business and Economic History: Papers Presented at the Twenty-second Annual Meeting of the Business History Conference,* ed. Paul A.Uselding. Urbana: University of Illinois Press, 1976: 1–24.

Atack, Jeremy, "Farm and Farm-Making Costs Revisited." *Agricultural History* 56 (1982): 663–76.

———, and Fred Bateman. *To Their Own Soil: Agriculture in the Antebellum North.* Ames: Iowa State University Press, 1987.

Bateman, Fred, and James Foust. "A Sample of Rural Households Selected from the 1860 Manuscript Censuses." *Agricultural History* 48 (1974): 75–93.

Berry, Thomas, *Western Prices before 1861.* Cambridge: Harvard University Press, 1943.

Buley, Thomas. *The Old Northwest: Pioneer Period, 1815–1840.* Bloomington: Indiana University Press, 1950.

Callahan, Colleen, and William K. Hutchinson. "Antebellum Interregional Trade in Agricultural Goods: Preliminary Results." *Journal of Economic History* 40 (1980): 25–31.

Danhof, Clarence H. "Farm-Making Costs and the 'Safety Valve': 1850–1860." *Journal of Political Economy* 49 (1941): 317–59.

———. *Change in Agriculture: The Northern United States, 1820–1870.* Cambridge: Harvard University Press, 1969.

David, Paul A. "The Mechanization of Reaping in the Ante-Bellum Midwest." In *Industrialization in Two Systems,* ed. H. Rosovsky. New York: John Wiley, 1966: 3–28.

Easterlin, Richard. "Regional Income Trends 1840–1950." In *The Reinterpretation of American Economic History,* ed. Robert Fogel and Stanley Engerman. New York: Harper & Row, 1971.

Fogel, Robert, and Stanley Engerman. *Time on the Cross.* Boston: Little, Brown, 1974.

Gallman, Robert. "Commodity Output 1839–1899." In National Bureau of Economic Research, *Trends in the American Economy in the 19th Century,* ed. William Parker, Studies in Income and Wealth, vol. 24. Princeton: Princeton University Press, 1960.

Jones, Lewis R. "The Mechanization of Reaping and Mowing in American Agriculture, 1833–1870: Comment." *Journal of Economic History* 37 (1977): 451–55.

Lindstrom, Diane. "Southern Dependence on Interregional Grain Supplies." In *The Structure of the Cotton Economy of the Antebellum South,* ed. William Parker. Washington, D.C.: Agricultural History Society, 1970: 101–13.

North, Douglass C. *The Economic Growth of the United States 1790–1860.* Englewood Cliffs; N.J.: Prentice-Hall, 1961.

Olmstead, Alan L. "The Mechanization of Reaping and Mowing in American Agriculture, 1833–1870." *Journal of Economic History* 35 (1975): 327–52.

Parker, William N., and Judith L. V. Klein. "Productivity Growth in Grain Production in the United States, 1840–60 and 1900–10." In National Bureau of Economic Research, *Output, Employment, and Productivity in the United States after 1800,* Studies in Income and Wealth, vol. 30. New York: Columbia University Press, 1966: 523–80.

Primack, Martin. "Land Clearing under 19th Century Techniques." *Journal of Economic History* 22 (1962): 484–97.

Rothenberg, Winifred. *From Market Places to a Market Economy: The Transformation of Rural Massachusetts, 1750–1850.* Chicago: University of Chicago Press, 1992.

Turner, Frederick Jackson. *The Frontier in American History.* New York: Henry Holt, 1920.

Slavery and southern development

11

Slavery—its moral, political, and economic consequences—has dominated much of American history. It was the foundation of much of the colonial prosperity. It was the source of much of the South's wealth and economic growth before the Civil War. Its continuation in the South after the Revolution made the South different from the rest of the nation since many southerners engaged in an activity, owning human beings, that was illegal elsewhere. Ultimately slavery was the root cause of the greatest calamity to befall this nation, the Civil War. Even 130 years after its abolition, one ugly residue of the institution—racism—continues to plague our society. Little wonder then that so much has been written about the "peculiar institution."

This chapter reviews some of the debate over the economic consequences of slavery for southern economic development before the Civil War. The focus is not on the functioning of the institution itself, which is dealt with in the chapter that follows, but rather on the impact that the institution had upon the structure of the southern economy and the direction in which it developed.

The Emergence of the Cotton Economy

In the eighteenth century, tobacco, not cotton, made the South hum. It had been the principal crop of the Upper South—Maryland, Virginia, North Carolina—since early colonial times. But as intensive cultivation of the "noxious weede" began to deplete the soil of critical minerals and to leave it fit mostly for feed grains and pasture, the tobacco economy gradually receded from northern and coastal areas into the hills of the Appalachian piedmont. Adding to tobacco's economic woes was a decline in export demand after 1790. Farther down the Atlantic coast, in South Carolina and Georgia, the sandy lowland coastal areas were dominated by rice cultivation. And in southern Louisiana, climate and soil made sugar production competitive with the Caribbean sugar islands after 1795.

Cotton was not a serious competitor for resources before the end of the eighteenth century. A variety of cotton was grown along the southern Atlantic coast and on the Sea Islands off the Georgia coast. This Sea Island cotton was much in demand after 1785 as the British cotton textile industry developed, but the plant did not adapt well to the soils and climate inland. An alternative—short-staple green seed cotton—which grew well away from the coast, had one serious drawback: The seeds could not be removed from the picked cotton with the simple roller gin then in use.

Eli Whitney was the first to produce a practical gin for short-staple upland cotton in 1793. This invention removed the greatest technical barrier to cotton expansion. But a unique combination of southern climate and soil made it possible to grow cotton virtually anywhere in the United States south of Virginia and Kentucky (including the southern tip of Illinois and Missouri). Cotton thrived particularly in the deep alluvial topsoil of the Mississippi river valley and its tributaries. But upland cotton also did very nicely in a variety of other southern soil-climate conditions: the hillsides of the Appalachian piedmont, the relatively infertile central plain stretching from Southern Carolina around to Mississippi, the distinctive "black prairie" soil of Alabama, Mississippi, and Tennessee, and the hills of eastern Texas, northern Louisiana, and Arkansas. Moreover, cotton cultivation was less markedly tied to transport innovation than was midwestern agriculture. Navigable rivers served the region well, and cotton, despite its weight and bulk, was a far more valuable crop than midwestern grain. This made it practical to grow cotton considerable distances from the rivers.

Cotton took hold in the piedmont and the western river valleys in the first fifteen years of the century (Figure 11.1). In the 1820s and 1830s there was an almost explosive rush into Alabama, Tennessee, and Mississippi. And then, after the decade-long pause following the Panic of 1837, cotton cultivation expanded rapidly into Texas and Arkansas. Meanwhile, some of the land in Georgia, the Carolinas, and Virginia that was opened to cotton in the first two decades of the century had returned to subsistence food farming, or even been abandoned, by the 1850s.

Abandoned and eroded lands notwithstanding, cotton, unlike tobacco, was not *pushed* west by soil depletion. Instead it was *pulled* west by the attraction of higher yields. Sometimes farmers just walked away from still-adequate farmland because they could make a far better profit exploiting western soils. More typically, farmers didn't try to maintain soil fertility on marginal eastern land because they knew better opportunities awaited them elsewhere.

FIGURE 11.1

Cotton Production in the South

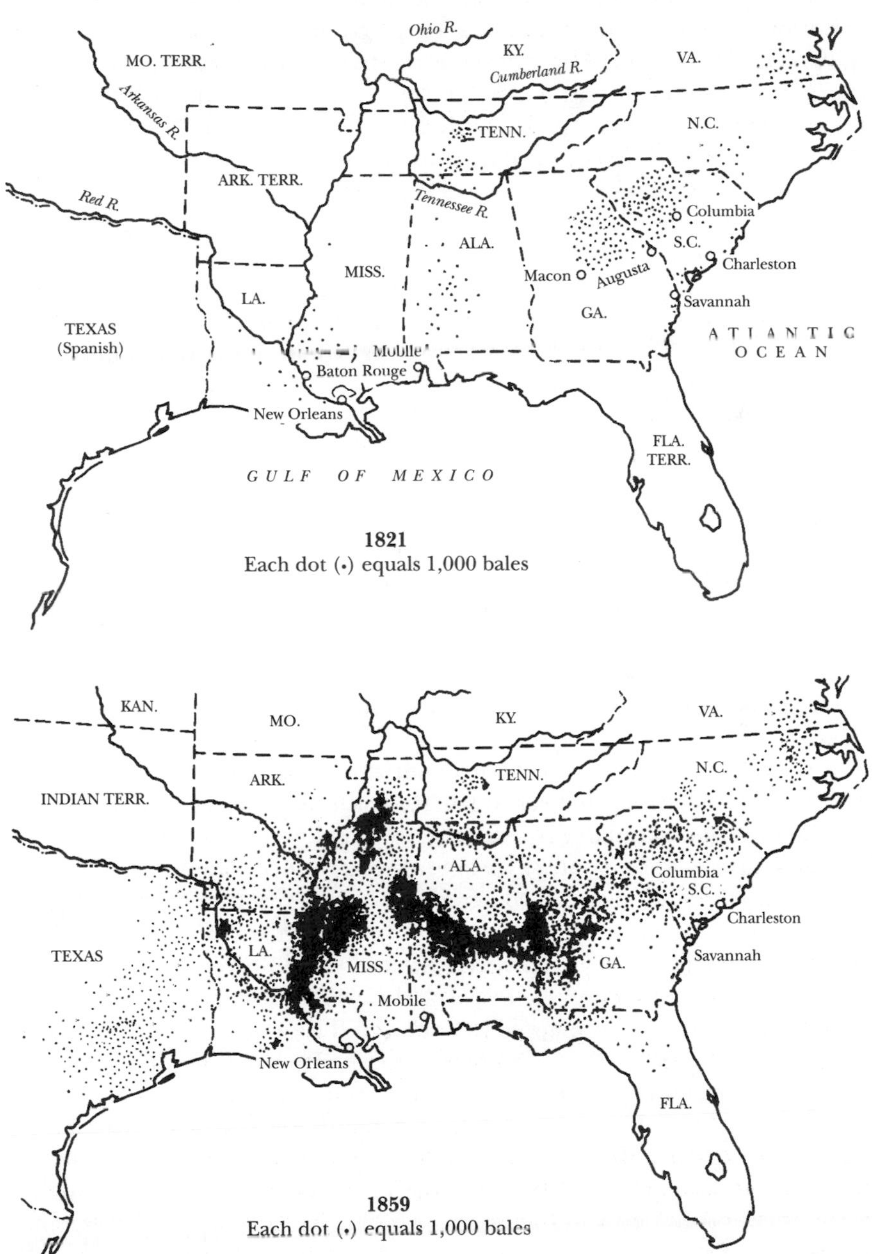

Source: Gavin Wright, *The Political Economy of the Cotton South* (New York: W. W. Norton, 1978): 16, adapted from USDA, *Atlas of Agriculture,* Part V, Advance Sheets (December 15, 1915).

Raw cotton output expanded dramatically. Production exceeded 100,000 bales by 1801, 1 million bales by 1835, and reached 5.4 million bales in 1859, a level of output not attained again until the late 1870s. The growth of cotton production and the spread of the cotton culture were mirrored in the growth and spread of slavery. It was not that cotton needed slave labor or that slaves had no alternative uses. The evidence suggests that the returns to plantation cotton on the newly settled lands in the Lower South drew resources, particularly slaves (who because of their enforced lack of self determination were among the most mobile factors), out of other activities and regions. Still, in the first half of the nineteenth century cotton and slavery went hand in hand.

The dramatic growth of cotton output that was made possible by the availability of fertile land west of the Appalachians spurred southern fears that restrictions on the right to use slave labor would close the frontier to cotton planters and limit the capital appreciation in the value of slaves. The argument goes like this: The more good land available to slaveowners, the higher the productivity of slave labor. Since the value of slaves depended, in part, on expected future labor productivity, securing western land for the slaveocracy helped secure property rights in slaves. Moreover, Alfred Conrad and John Meyer, among others, have suggested that land expansion was the key to profitability for eastern plantations whose major cash crop was young slaves. By closing the West to slavery, the South would be faced with declining land per worker and, inevitably, declining cotton output per slave. Eventually this could reduce labor productivity sufficiently to threaten the survival of the institution and thus the entire southern investment in slave labor.

There are numerous problems with this hypothesis. The rhetoric of "land shortage" aside, the westward rush of the cotton economy had left much of the good land in the South Central region untouched. The annexation of Texas as a slave state subsequently guaranteed to several future generations fertile soil on which to expand. The net result was that improved acreage per capita grew in *every* state in the South prior to the Civil War. Robert Fogel and Stanley Engerman, two of the leading authorities on slavery and authors of much of the research that will be discussed here, estimate that the quantity of land planted in cotton in former slave states *doubled* between 1860 and 1890. One result of this increase in production was that the center of cotton production shifted back eastward after the Civil War.

Indeed, the Old South had little to gain and much to lose from the expansion of slavery and cotton cultivation into the New South.[1] On the surface, it would seem logical that slaveowners stood to benefit from higher slave prices resulting from the greater productivity of western lands, since the price of a slave was just equal to the net present value of the slave's (now

[1] Passell and Wright (1972); Kotlikoff and Pinera (1977); Lee (1978).

FIGURE 11.2

The Course of Cotton Production, 1791–1861

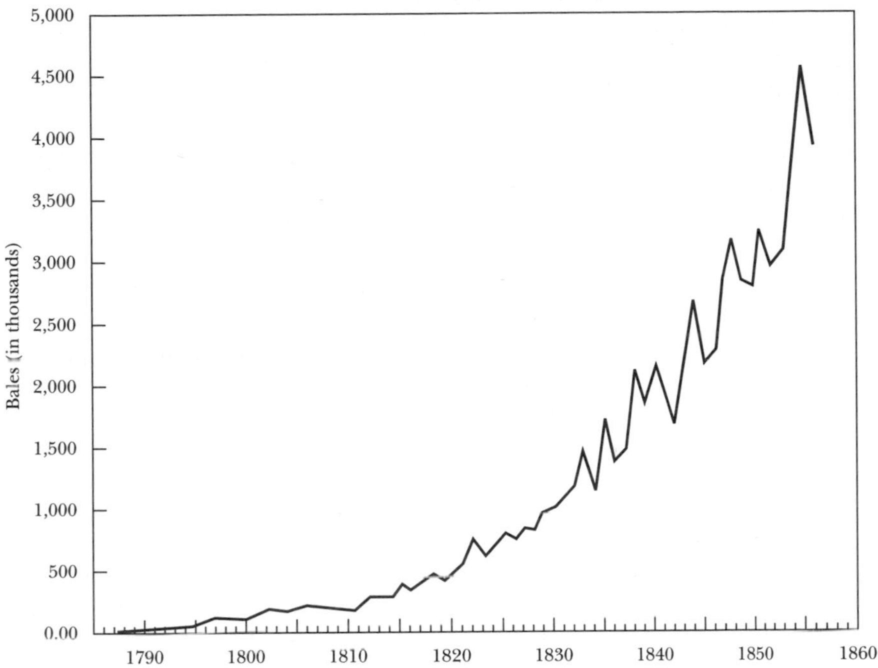

Source: Robert W. Fogel and Stanley L. Engerman, *Time on the Cross: The Economics of American Negro Slavery* (New York: W. W. Norton, 1989; first published 1974): 90, Figure 25.

higher) lifetime marginal productivity. But increased cotton production in the West may have driven down cotton prices. Consequently, slave prices would have risen only if the increased productivity more than offset any tendency for cotton prices to fall as western cotton production rose. In addition, reduced land scarcity and lower product prices lowered the value of eastern land. The potential gains and losses are sensitive to the demand elasticity for cotton but generally support the view that economically at least, the Old South had much to lose and relatively little to gain from the westward expansion of cotton cultivation and slavery. For example, if the output demand elasticity were minus one, a doubling of western land would have reduced eastern wealth by about 20 percent. On the other hand, even if cotton prices had been totally insensitive to increased production, a doubling of western land would have increased eastern wealth by less than 2 percent.[2]

If some southerners misperceived their economic interest, others did not. For example, one South Carolina senator was roundly criticized by the

[2] Kotlikoff and Pinera (1977).

state's press for supporting liberal land expansion policies in 1829. Moreover, southern states' representatives regularly split on congressional votes over public land policy through the 1830s, 1840s, and early 1850s.

The Growth of Southern Slavery

Planters had turned to slaves in the late eighteenth century, when they could no longer meet their needs with white labor. The supply of indentured labor fell with diminished need for immigrants to mortgage their future income for passage to America. Free labor could—and did—grow tobacco on family farms. But it was hard, unpleasant work, and the abundance of land on the frontier (both northern and southern) made it extremely difficult to induce free workers to labor as hired hands. That left slaves as the most promising labor source for any farmer who wanted to expand operations beyond a scale serviceable by family members only.

But northern farmers also faced a labor supply constraint. Why didn't they turn to slavery as a panacea? One argument, since disproved, is that slaves could not profitably be employed producing the kinds of crops that grew in the North. The argument is that there was simply too much seasonal slack in grain farming between planting and harvest and during the long winter months to make it worthwhile investing in a slave when an entire lifetime of labor was embodied in the slave's price. Supposedly it only made sense to employ slaves in highly labor-intensive, year-round activities. Such an argument implicitly denies the proposition that northerners had any special distaste for African-American slavery. It suggests that their rejection of slavery was based not upon moral grounds but rather upon their inability to exploit such labor as effectively as in the South. But slaves were employed in the South growing crops that grew equally well in the North. Most large cotton plantations, for instance, were self-sufficient in food where the emphasis was upon corn and hogs. More significantly, though, farther north in the Virginia piedmont, slaves were employed in large-scale wheat production.[3] Output of wheat per worker on these "wheat plantations" rose as slaveholdings increased. This was not the result of increased specialization. Other crops, particularly tobacco, were not traded off in favor of more wheat. Rather, more wheat resulted from the exploitation of scale economies by larger plantations. As for cotton production in the Lower South, this was possibly due to greater work intensity among interdependent teams of slaves. These economies, however, could not be captured on free farms because the increased output per worker was insufficient to compensate free labor for

[3] Irwin (1986, 1988). Irwin also conjectures that this reliance upon slave labor to grow wheat in Virginia may have been a factor underlying McCormick's decision to leave Virginia and set up shop for his reaper in Illinois since slaves were substituted for machinery in the slave economy.

the increased effort—especially if the effort was one's own labor. Despite the apparent potential for using slaves in more general agriculture, the spread and growth of slavery prior to the Civil War mirrored the spread and growth of cotton production (Figure 11.3).

Why? Economists generally reckon that slaves ended up on southern plantations rather than northern farms because only southern staples were sufficiently lucrative to justify bidding away scarce slave labor from employment in the Caribbean sugar islands. Continued strong demand for southern staples meant that slavery was never in serious danger of dying out in America during the colonial period but that slavery was confined to southern plantations by the high productivity of slaves in the rest of the world rather than by low productivity in America. The rise of cotton was simply a new twist, once again increasing the productivity of slaves in southern agriculture. If we follow this logic, it is possible that without competition from cotton, American slaves would have ended up on wheat plantations in Illinois. Indeed, when the prospects for the profitable use of slaves in grain production seemed promising and the market for cotton was temporarily depressed, many of the free citizen farmers of Illinois (mostly southerners from Kentucky and Tennessee who had settled the southern part of Illinois) sought to enter the Union as a slave state in 1818 and again in 1824. These efforts were rebuffed, and slavery remained confined to the South.

A total of about 661,000 slaves were brought to the United States before further importation was banned by Congress in 1808. This figure represents only about 7 percent of all the Africans who were forcibly transported across the Atlantic. In contrast, 787,000 slaves were imported into Cuba, and more than 4 million were shipped to Brazil. Nevertheless, by 1825 the United States was home to perhaps 36 percent of all slaves in the Western Hemisphere while Brazil had just 31 percent despite importing more than six times as many slaves. This discrepancy between participation in the world slave trade and status as a slave power reflects the high rate of natural increase among the American slave population. Mortality rates were relatively low while fertility rates were high. The life expectancy of American slaves in 1850, thirty-six years, though less than that of the rural free white population, compared favorably with that of continental European countries both earlier and later and exceeded that of many urban populations of the time.[4] In 1830 an African-American slave woman who survived through her childbearing years (defined as age fifteen to age forty-nine) might be expected to bear an average of 9.24 children. In Trinidad, on the other hand, about 1813, the average slave woman bore only 4.44 children.[5] Thus it was that by 1860 the South had a slave population of 3.84 million, more than half the total population of the South.

[4] See Chapter 12.

[5] Fogel et al. (1989).

FIGURE 11.3

The Distribution of the Slave Population in 1790 and 1860

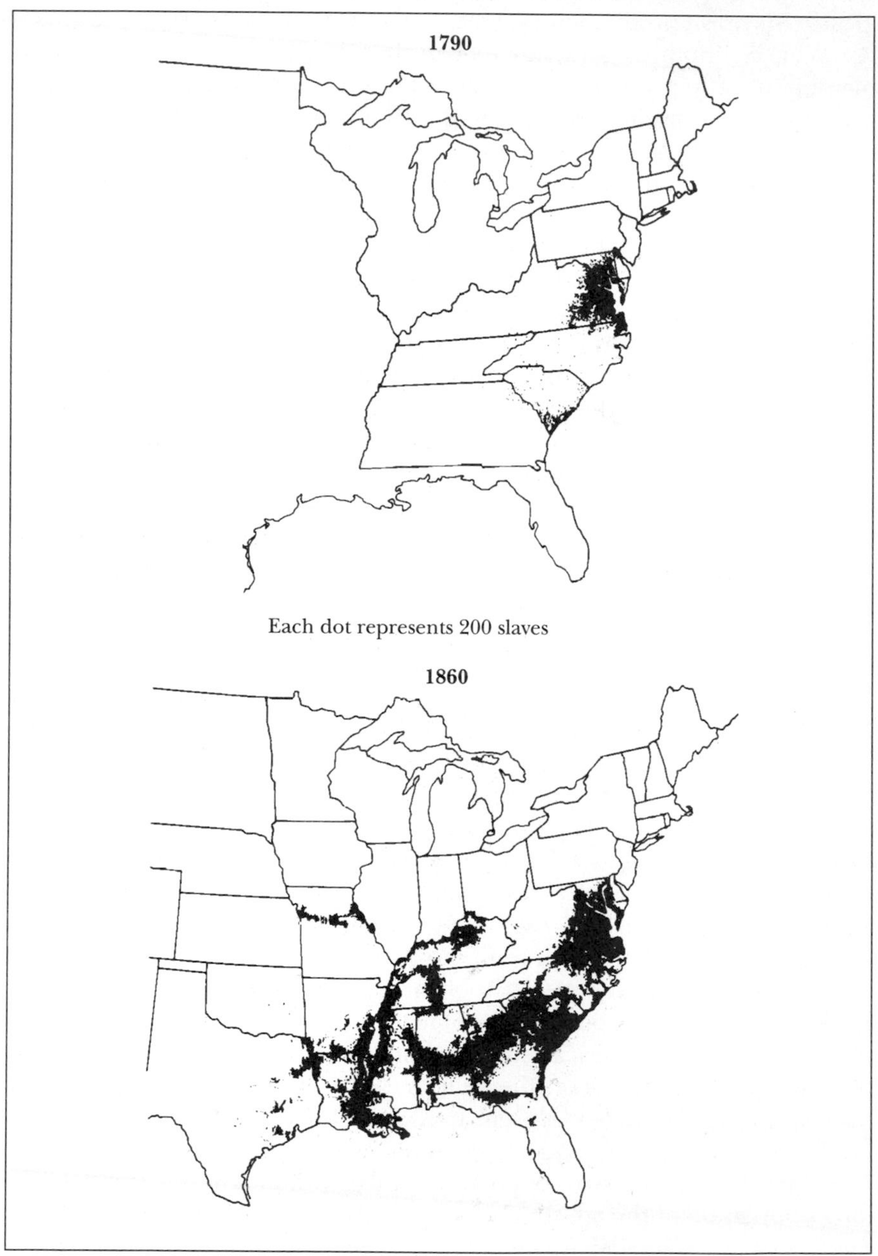

Source: Robert W. Fogel and Stanley L. Engerman, *Time on the Cross: The Economics of American Negro Slavery* (New York: W. W. Norton 1989; first published 1974): 45.

The establishment of property rights in human beings had a profound impact upon the structure of the slave South and the investment strategies of its residents. Almost 60 percent of the agricultural wealth in Alabama, Georgia, Louisiana, Mississippi and South Carolina was in slaves, while land and farm buildings accounted for less than one-third. Consequently, southern slaveowners as owners of a highly mobile factor of production had little economic stake in a particular location and little incentive to invest in permanent improvements, such as urban development and transportation media. As a result, the structure of the southern economy was different from that in the Northeast or Midwest, where the bulk of the population had a major economic stake in local infrastructure and local development.

Yeoman Farming in the Cotton Economy

Although slavery and cotton dominated the southern economy before the Civil War, small family farms operated by yeoman farmers coexisted with medium and large plantations in all parts of the Cotton South.[6] Family farming was not displaced by the slave plantation. Indeed, as many as 50 percent of all farms in the Cotton Belt had no slaves at all in 1860; even in the fertile western alluvial valleys where there was the highest concentration of big commercial plantations, 36 percent of all farms were slaveless. Outside the Cotton Belt, these small freehold farmers dominated, particularly in the piedmont. This group has been largely ignored in the slavery debate. Recently, however, work by David Weiman has begun to provide a quantitative picture of these farmers and their role in the economy.

Weiman's analysis reveals a sharp division between independent farmers in the Cotton Belt and those elsewhere in the South. Although some of the yeomanry owned a few slaves and many grew some cotton, earlier frost, thinner soils, and poorer transportation facilities made dependence upon cotton a riskier proposition, lowered yields, and reduced the price received by farmers. Instead of depending upon distant markets, these farmers depended upon the development of the local economy, grew a wide range of crops, and engaged in substantial home manufacturing as late as 1860, when such practices had all but disappeared elsewhere.

Two prototypical up-country counties in Georgia are the focus of Weiman's analysis. Floyd County, on the western border of the state, was settled by speculators and promoters in the land boom of the 1830s. Because of its location on the Coosa River, it quickly became integrated with wider markets. These ties were reinforced by construction, in the late 1840s, of the Rome Railroad, a feeder line to the Western and Atlantic Railroad. Weiman's other sample county, De Kalb, was settled earlier but developed

[6] See, for example, Owsley (1949).

more slowly in part because it lacked water transportation and in part because local merchants, fearing competition, opposed extension of the Georgia Railroad through the county to Atlanta. Farmers in Floyd County produced larger surpluses beyond their own consumption needs than those in De Kalb. These surpluses could be sold. The surpluses on Floyd County farms were similar to those on Middle Atlantic farms; those in De Kalb were more like the smaller surpluses produced on New England farms. Farmers in Floyd County were more likely than farmers in De Kalb (Table 11.1) to grow cotton and derived approximately double the percentage of gross farm income from cotton sales. However, most farmers in both counties, regardless of their scale of operation, derived the bulk of their income from sources other than cotton. Weiman concludes that farm production in De Kalb was oriented more to the direct satisfaction of household needs because market production was constrained. In Floyd County, on the other hand, most farms (but particularly the medium-size and large farms) were oriented toward market sales both within the local community and in more distant markets. These different orientations reflected differences in attitudes toward the market. Beyond a wealth threshold of about $2,500, farmers in both counties were systematically oriented to market production. However, because local development and transportation improvements increase land values (i.e., wealth), this threshold was surpassed at a much smaller scale of operation in Floyd than De Kalb county.

Lastly, Weiman's analysis points to a substantial difference in the returns to farmmaking between the two counties. The value of farm structures and unimproved acreage in both was about the same, but improved farmland in Floyd was worth more than three times as much as in De Kalb. Thus a family building its farm in De Kalb could expect to accumulate perhaps $330 from farmmaking over five to ten years, while the same effort in Floyd would return $1,275. Little wonder then that land was cleared more rapidly in Floyd than in De Kalb.

Plantation Agriculture

As one might have expected, plantations devoted a higher percentage of available land and labor to the production of cotton than smaller farms. But even the largest and most commercially oriented plantations failed to specialize exclusively in cotton, despite perhaps a 2:1 income per acre differential in favor of cotton over corn. Instead the goal seems to have been self-sufficiency in food, primarily corn, beans, pork, and sweet potatoes. According to estimates, roughly 40 percent of the value of crops on cotton plantations with more than fifty slaves was food. The proportion was even higher, 50 percent, on plantations with sixteen to fifty slaves.[7]

[7] Ransom and Sutch (1977).

TABLE 11.1

Commodity Production on Up-Country Farms by Improved Acreage Class, 1860

	Tenant	1–49 Acres	50–99 Acres	100–199 Acres	200–499 Acres	500+ Acres
De Kalb County						
Percentage producing cotton	45.5%	43.6%	70.5%	73.2%	95.2%	100.0%
(Value of cotton/value of field crops) × 100	15.5%	12.1%	18.9%	16.8%	29.9%	26.9%
Per capita value of						
marketable surpluses	$3.7	$12.1	$11.3	$19.9	$20.4	$19.4
All commodity products	$9.3	$18.3	$23.0	$31.9	$44.8	$43.1
	($17.6)					
Percentage producing for the market	63.6%	74.4%	86.4%	94.6%	100.0%	100.0%
Percentage of output marketed	16.0%	25.8%	28.4%	34.1%	44.9%	40.3%
	(25.1%)					
Floyd County						
Percentage producing cotton	72.1%	62.3%	83.0%	83.3%	85.0%	100.0%
(Value of cotton/value of field crops) × 100	29.1%	29.1%	28.8%	26.6%	46.5%	44.9%
Per capita value of						
marketable surpluses	$6.3	$12.8	$35.4	$37.0	$38.3	$61.7
All commodity products	$19.1	$30.7	$66.0	$63.0	$98.8	$142.5
	($31.7)					
Percentage producing for the market	87.1%	80.0%	98.0%	97.6%	100.0%	100.0%
Percentage of output marketed	27.4%	37.4%	51.1%	52.2%	67.8%	64.8%
	(37.4%)					

Notes: The value of marketable surpluses, cotton, and other farm products is based on wholesale prices. The percentage of farm produce marketed for tenants is estimated in two different ways. The first estimate incorporates rental payments into the calculation of marketable surpluses and cotton revenues and equals the (value of market production/value of farm output less the value of rents) × 100. The second estimate, in parentheses, ignores rental payments and treats tenants like small owner-operators.

Source: David Weiman, "Farmers and the Market in Antebellum America: A View from the Georgia Upcountry," *Journal of Economic History* 47 (1987): 638. Reprinted by permission of Cambridge University Press.

If cotton was more profitable to grow than food, why grow both? The answer, Robert Gallman suggests, lies in the uneven seasonal demands that cotton cultivation placed on labor. If we assume plenty of land was available, a farm that grew cotton alone would be constrained in its total output by the amount of labor available for harvesting the crop in the fall. In other seasons as little as one-eighth the work force could attend to the crop. Rather than let this labor remain idle, farmers looked for ways to utilize it without reducing the farms' capacity to grow cotton. Corn was the natural candidate. Though not particularly suited to southern soils or climate — yields per acre were much higher in the Midwest—it was well suited to the seasonal cotton cycle. Corn placed little demand on workers during the cotton-picking season but kept them busy at times when the cotton plants needed little attention.

Corn, however, was not "free" to cotton farmers in the sense that no additional resources need be expended to generate a corn crop. Land was needed to raise the corn—thus requiring an initial investment in clearing—and some labor was needed year-round also. A plantation growing corn thus sacrificed some potential cotton output, but homegrown corn was probably less expensive than corn bought at market for cash generated solely from cotton production.

This corn was consumed directly as well as indirectly as corn-fattened hogs. Various types of peas and beans, moreover, could be planted between the corn rows without reducing corn yields, as Native Americans had already discovered. These crops were then harvested as food or left for the farm animals to graze. Some foodstuffs still had to be bought from the outside. But virtually all working cotton farms were nearly self-sufficient in food.

Prior to the publication of Fogel and Engerman's landmark book *Time on the Cross* in 1974, slavery was thought to be just efficient enough to make the system viable. Plentiful, fertile land and strong world demand for cotton allowed free white southerners to enjoy a high standard of living—about equal to that of easterners and higher than that of midwesterners—despite the alleged relative inefficiency of involuntary slave labor systems. If, indeed, slavery was inefficient, then presumably output and living standards could have been higher without it. Fogel and Engerman challenged this view. On the basis of census data they figured that the South used just 93 percent as much labor as the North after adjusting for differences in the age and sex composition and occupational mix, only 51 percent as much land after taking account of quality differences, and just 53 percent as much capital, yet it generated an output worth 3 percent more, even after adjusting for North-South quality differences. As a result, Fogel and Engerman estimate that southern agriculture was 41 percent more efficient than northern agriculture (Appendix 11.A). That is to say, the South could have produced 41 percent more output than the North if it had had the North's factor endowment. More important, the superior efficiency of southern agricul-

TABLE 11.2

Indexes of Total Factor Productivity on Southern Farms Relative to Northern Farms by Subregion and Size of Farm, 1860 (Northern Farms = 100)

Farm Size (number of slaves per farm)	Old South (slave-exporting states)	New South (slave-importing states)
0	98.4	112.7
1–15	103.3	127.2
16–50	124.9	176.1
51 or more	135.1	154.7
All slave farms	118.9	153.1
All farms (slave and nonslave) in region	116.2	144.7

Source: Robert W. Fogel and Stanley L. Engerman, "Explaining the Relative Efficiency of Slave Agriculture in the Antebellum South," *Without Consent or Contract: Technical Papers Volume I,* ed. Robert Fogel et al. (New York: W. W. Norton, 1992): 245.

ture only manifested itself on the slave plantations, particularly on the larger plantations (Table 11.2). Free southern farms, by contrast, were little or no more efficient than their northern counterparts. This conclusion ignited a fire storm of protests and efforts to explain away the apparent paradox that forced labor was more efficient than free. The following summarizes some of the more important criticisms and Fogel and Engerman's defense of their methodology and findings.

At the most fundamental level, many of the critics do not accept the idea that Fogel and Engerman really measured efficiency in the usual sense of the term. Total factor productivity indexes have generally been used to compare the efficiency of a single economy at two points in time or to compare the efficiency of two economies with similar choices of product mix. However, the North had no means of producing cotton, the single largest source of southern agricultural income. Climate gave the South an advantage, which shows up in the greater revenue-producing capability of southern farms.

Consider the situation shown in Figure 11.4. The production possibilities curve, AB, shows the production possibilities given resources and technology for producing corn and cotton. Economic theory tells us that the optimal combination is where the marginal rate of substitution between cotton and corn in production, given by the slope of the production possibilities curve, is the same as the rate at which these two commodities can be exchanged in the market, indicated by the price line, MM', which has slope $-(P_{cotton}/P_{corn})$. This is the point S where OE of cotton is grown and OF of corn. However, since the North could not grow cotton, northern farms—as conceptualized by the model—are forced to produce at the corner point, B,

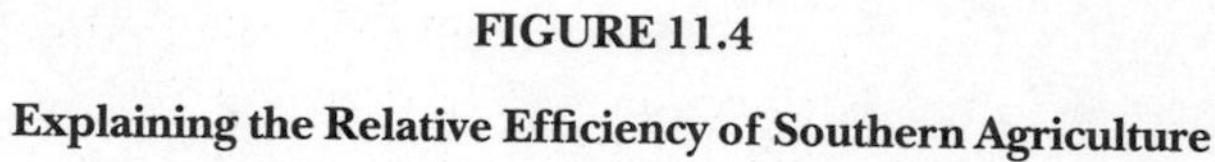

FIGURE 11.4

Explaining the Relative Efficiency of Southern Agriculture

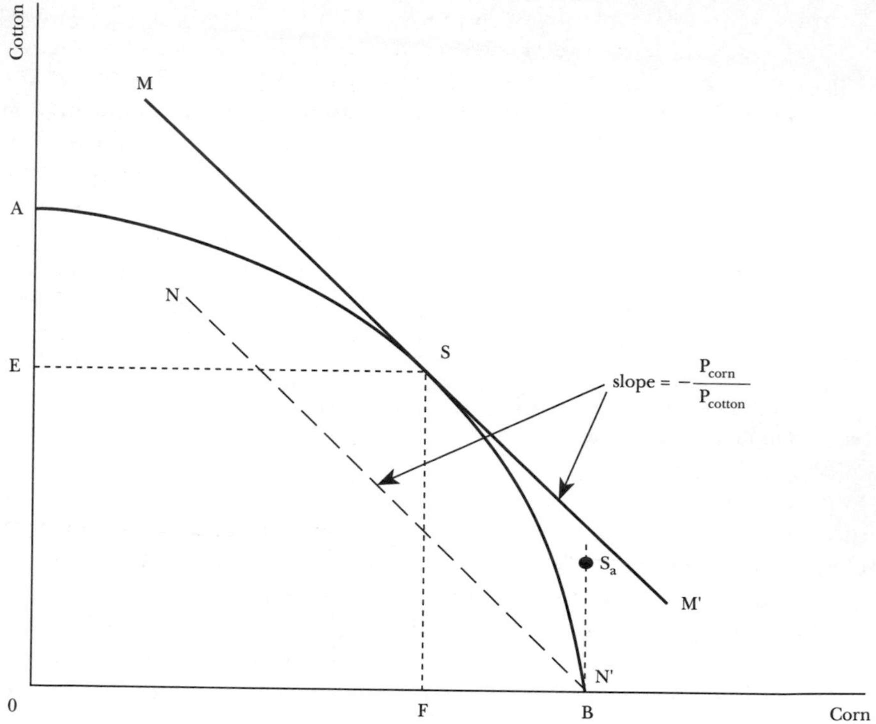

where they grow only corn. By growing only corn, however, northern farms earn lower revenues than southern plantations, shown by the price line/iso-revenue line lying closer to the origin, NN'. Northern farms were thus less *revenue-efficient* than southern farms. Theoretically, of course, productivity is measured as output per unit of input, not dollars per unit of input, but revenues provide a way to aggregate cotton, corn, milk, wheat, and the other myriad products produced on nineteenth-century farms. This aggregation does, however, create difficulties. Suppose southern farms—complete with soil, labor, and capital—had been moved a thousand miles north. Then, in spite of the fact that the farms themselves were physically unchanged, their "efficiency" would plummet because the northern climate would bar the use of any portion of their land and labor to grow cotton. Crops were not perfect substitutes for one another in production. Climate and soils limited the agronomic possibilities so that farmers were unable to respond blindly to the price mechanism.

Fogel and Engerman's response to this criticism, made by Paul David and Peter Temin, was to show that the actual crop mix in the South was in fact much closer to the northern crop mix than implied by Figure 11.4. Rather than produce the output mix represented by the point S, the South actually produced at the point S_a, which lies to the north and somewhat to the west of point B. As a result, these two points could lie on the same production possibilities curve and be tangent to the price line if, and only if, the production frontier were kinked. This seems unlikely since the product mix was different across farms of different sizes and from year to year. Note, however, that Fogel and Engerman make the implicit assumption that both North and South operated on the same production function, forcing any differences to show up as productivity differences as the residual.

Gavin Wright has suggested that 1860 crop values were unusually high in the South and unusually low in the North, biasing upward the relative productivity of the South. Favorable weather conditions produced a bumper cotton crop in 1860, which, thanks to strong world demand, was salable at very good prices. Furthermore, crops were especially good in the New South (Alabama, Mississippi, Arkansas, Louisiana, and Texas).[8] On the other hand, indirect evidence points to a poor crop year in the North in 1860. Exports of wheat, flour, and corn all were below previous years' averages and well below the upward trend expected of a growing export economy. Nor was output loss made up in higher prices, which were no better than average by historical standards. Another confirming indicator is public land sales. Land demand generally followed profit expectations, and in 1859 sales were extremely slow in the midwestern Grain Belt. In the South, by contrast, land sales reached a historic peak. Adjusting for the alleged unusual nature of the crop year drastically reduces the productivity advantage of slavery compared with free agriculture, especially in the New South. Fogel and Engerman, however, show that no plausible reduction of the 1860 crop, whether through reduced yields or lower prices, or both, can eliminate completely the South's advantage. Indeed, the 1860 cotton crop would have to be reduced by 90 percent to eliminate completely the South's relative efficiency.

David and Temin also argue that biases in input measurement, particularly for labor, distort the relative efficiency calculation. Fogel and Engerman assumed that worker-years were the same in the North and South, but the milder climate allowed southerners to work in the fields about sixty additional days each year. It also seems plausible to assume that slaves were worked more hours per day than their free northern counterparts chose to work. Indeed, estimates indicate that once they were given the chance to allocate their own time after the war, ex-slaves cut their average workday by 16 to 22 percent.[9] The antebellum free-slave differential in hours of work may actually have been even greater than these numbers suggest since free whites

[8] See Schaefer (1983).
[9] Ransom and Sutch (1977).

before the war were much richer than free blacks after the war and could thus more easily afford the luxury of leisure. Consequently, David and Temin estimate that taken together, these factors led Fogel and Engerman to underestimate southern labor inputs by 28 to 34 percent and thereby to overestimate relative southern productivity by 15 to 18 percent, though there is some serious doubt about this figure.[10]

The potential biases in land input are much more difficult to analyze. There is no way to estimate the *effective* quantity of land directly. Acreage data are available, but they mask vast differences in land quality. Fogel and Engerman attempt to finesse this problem by substituting land *value* for land *quantity*, assuming that price differences accurately reflect quality differences. But, say David and Temin, this adjustment procedure invites error. Land values reflect not only quality differences in land but location advantages as well. To illustrate the argument, they provide a not-so-hypothetical example. Consider the case in which rail and canal transport greatly increased the amount of land in the North that could be farmed at a profit. This increases the value of both marginal and nonmarginal land and thus, by Fogel and Engerman's argument, increases the "quantity" of land inputs used to create crops, spuriously reducing estimated total factor productivity. The magnitude of the error introduced by using land value as an input measure isn't known, but it could be large. If Fogel and Engerman had simply used acreage — not a recommended procedure either, since land quality varies—relative southern efficiency would have been cut by 25 percent, or more than two-thirds of the identified efficiency advantage. However, it turns out that taking locational advantages into account actually raises the relative efficiency of slave plantations and has relatively little effect upon regional relative efficiency.

Although most of the attention is focused upon slaves, much of the agricultural labor force of the antebellum South consisted of free whites. But few of these worked as hired hands, and none worked in the labor gangs common to large plantations. The rest worked their own farms either as freeholders or as tenant farmers. Some casual farm laborers might be found on occasion, but their presence was hard to guarantee during the critical picking season, and their performance, according to contemporaries, was often lackluster. Slaves, on the other hand, offered the means of extending operations to any desired scale; some plantations were operated with hundreds of slaves, making them among the very largest business enterprises in America at the time and certainly among the most heavily capitalized. Slave plantations thus had a potential advantage over free farms by giving entrepreneurs the opportunity to exploit potential economies of scale. Fogel and

[10] Recent estimates by John Olson (1992) based upon plantation records and time studies by agricultural economists in the early twentieth century, however, suggest that northern farmers worked about 10 percent more hours per year than did slaves in the antebellum South.

Engerman assert that this advantage was critical. It allowed a division of tasks and the assignment of slaves to gangs with collective responsibility for performance that more than overcame any inherent inefficiency in using involuntary labor.

Favoring this hypothesis, Fogel and Engerman found that on average, farms with slaves were 29 percent more productive than those without slaves. There were clear efficiency gains as scale increased, at least up to the sixteen to fifty-slave range. They also argue, although their results don't show it, that the very largest plantations were probably the most efficient of all because of incomplete accounting for their output. Other research has suggested that scale economies were confined to large slave plantations in the pine hills of the Old South and the prairies of the New.[11]

The very existence of scale economies surprised many who have worked with agricultural production functions in the nineteenth century and have invariably found diseconomies of scale. Indeed, Fogel and Engerman reached similar findings when they estimated an unrestricted Cobb-Douglas production function in which they included a dummy variable for the use of gang labor that they defined on plantations employing sixteen or more slaves. The scale parameter was less than one, implying diseconomies of scale, but the shift in the production surface captured by the dummy variable for gang labor was sufficient to compensate for these diseconomies. That is, those large plantations where gang labor was supposedly in use were more efficient—they produced more output with equivalent factor inputs—than small plantations. They were operating on a different, lower-cost family of cost curves than other farms and plantations. These are not strictly scale economies, which are defined within a given technology, but instead represent a different technology available only to larger producers.

Gavin Wright argues that the key to interpreting Fogel and Engerman's total factor productivity comparisons lies in the systematic differences in the mix of crops grown on large and small farms. Family farms devoted a much higher proportion of their land and labor to food production than plantations, a decision Wright attributes to family farmers' unwillingness to bear the risk of unanticipated changes in cotton prices or yields. By taking a "safety-first" approach—growing enough food to maintain the family without resort to markets—they avoided the chance of losing their farms and becoming landless laborers. Risk-averse family farmers might well have chosen to grow more cotton and less corn if they could have cut the inherent risks. In modern economies, efficient market mechanisms make this possible: Farmers borrow money to tide them over bad periods, and they use forward sales contracts to nail down the future price they will receive for crops when they harvest them. Small antebellum farmers had no such alternatives, so they avoided risk at the sacrifice of expected profit. By contrast, slave-using

[11] Schaefer and Schmitz (1979).

farmers did not have to worry about starving or losing their property if they risked all in cotton and lost; their wealth protected them. This doesn't mean that big farms were inherently more efficient than little farms, but it does mean that wealthy entrepreneurs, by virtue of their willingness to take risks and their access to labor beyond the family unit, were able to generate more output value from a given quantity of land and labor.

If gang labor offered opportunities for scale economies, then output per worker (or per acre) should have increased as farm size increased holding crop mix constant. Wright's estimates, however, show no systematic relationship between productivity and scale. Such scale effects are to be found in a more conventional production function approach, and similar results have been reported for slave *wheat* plantations in the Virginia piedmont.[12]

The bottom line of the debate is that Fogel and Engerman's measure of relative efficiency seems to be robust, although many scholars remain troubled by quite how to interpret the estimates. The sources of productivity differences remain a mystery. As pointed out in Chapter 1, if all inputs and outputs were measured perfectly, there would be no unexplained productivity residual. The productivity residual that Fogel and Engerman calculate is therefore a proxy of imperfections in their accounting for inputs and measurement of output. Moreover, these measurement and accounting errors were greater in the South than the North. Beyond such philosophical questions, however, there are other issues that are as yet unresolved. Suppose, for example, that we accept Fogel and Engerman's argument that the primary source of this differential was the use of the gang labor system on slave plantations that increased the speed and intensity of work. Were northern farms and southern plantations on the same production function? Were output elasticities the same in the North and South? Did differences in factor mixes and the nature of those factors, such as the apparent substitution of slaves for mechanization on southern farms, matter? What impact did scale differences have between North and South and between slave and nonslave farms within the South? Unfortunately we still don't know the answers to these questions.

Slavery and Industrialization

Despite the best efforts of numerous industrial promoters such as New Orleans publisher James De Bow, South Carolina industrialist William Gregg, and Governor of South Carolina James Hammond, the primary markets for cotton lay beyond the South's borders in the mills of England and New England. Other manufacturing also failed to develop rapidly in the South. Table 11.3 reveals the large—and growing—differences between

[12] Irwin (1986, 1988).

TABLE 11.3

Manufacturing Investment and Output (\$/Capita)

	Manufacturing Capital		Manufacturing Output	
Region	1850	1860	1850	1860
New England	57.96	82.13	100.71	149.47
Middle states	35.50	52.21	71.24	96.28
South	7.60	10.54	10.88	17.09
Cotton South	5.11	7.20	6.83	10.47

Source: 8th and 9th censuses of manufactures, cited in Gavin Wright, *The Political Economy of the Cotton South* (New York: W. W. Norton, 1978): 110.

North and South. In 1860 the South produced less than one-fifth the value of manufactures per capita as the Middle Atlantic states and only one-eighth that of New England. In the Midwest cities specialized in consumer and producer durables, transportation and intermediate goods that grew with the growth of family agriculture and generated positive externalities. Southern cities, on the other hand, specialized in resource processing, low-wage textiles, and printing and publishing.[13] But even then the industrial sector in southern cities remained small. Southern cities were commercial centers, not manufacturing centers. The local cotton gin, the self-sufficient orientation of most plantations, and the minimal subsistence consumption supplied to slaves failed to provide a nucleus for urban growth and a market for most manufactures.

It does not necessarily follow, however, that slavery blocked efficient division of resources between agriculture and industry. Quite the contrary. Slavery may simply have made it possible for the South to exploit more fully its inherent economic advantage in cotton agriculture. Indeed, efficiency questions hinge on just such distinctions.

Many hypotheses have been advanced to explain "deplorable scarcity" of manufacturing in the South.[14] Fogel and Engerman, for example, stress comparative advantage—that is to say, given relative factor endowments, the South chose to specialize in the production of export staples, particularly cotton but, to a lesser extent, sugar, rice, and tobacco. Many historians have stressed noneconomic barriers to industrialization, including social, political, and legal obstacles. These barriers were created by the planter elite to raise entry costs and discourage competition for resources. The lack of discretionary and surplus income among slaves has been blamed for the failure

[13] Meyer (1989).
[14] Bateman and Wright (1981).

of the South to industrialize by limiting the market for specific products and preventing firms from realizing scale economies, although the empirical evidence fails to support this claim.[15] In the North the constraint of family labor made mechanization necessary for farmers who wanted to expand their profits and acreage. The expansion of this industry played an important role in the development of metalworking and mechanical skills. Southern cotton planters, on the other hand, faced no comparable constraints; farms could expand merely by adding slaves and acreage.[16] The institution of slavery itself has also been cited as an impediment to southern industrialization. Various reasons are given. It is alleged that by monetizing human capital, slaves absorbed capital that would otherwise have gone into the accumulation of nonhuman capital. Large plantations may have lured away the best managerial and entrepreneurial talent.[17] Others have argued that slaves were an unsuitable labor force for industry and that slavery led to the association of manual labor with race and enslavement, causing white labor to eschew physical work. Slavery may also have discouraged immigration into the South, depriving industry of a major source of labor. Lastly, it is claimed that whites fearing slave rebellion opposed concentrations of slaves in urban areas.

Fred Bateman and Thomas Weiss have found each of these hypotheses wanting as explanations for the failure of the South to industrialize. They argue that the planters failed to provide entrepreneurial leadership to manufacturing, that their purchases of slaves denied capital to industry, and that they did not respond as vigorously to market signals reflected in the relatively higher returns in manufacturing as did investors elsewhere. In particular, Bateman and Weiss argue that planters as a group were significantly more risk- averse than potential investors in other regions, their willingness to risk all in war notwithstanding. According to their estimates, average rates of profit of 20 percent or more for manufacturing firms in the South, particularly in the Cotton South, were higher than those elsewhere. These higher returns, however, were apparently insufficient to overcome southerners' risk aversion. Others have made similar points.[18]

The existence and persistence of regional and sectorial profit differentials do not necessarily mean that southerners were economically irrational. Markets were functioning, albeit slowly and perhaps imperfectly. Investment funds did flow—dribble might be a better description—into those activities with the higher returns more rapidly than into activities where returns were lower. Instead southerners were simply different. They had different tastes and preferences. For example, they clung to slavery, an unlawful activity in

[15] Atack (1977).
[16] Wright (1978).
[17] Fleisig (1976).
[18] Linden (1946).

the rest of the country. Moreover, there was minimal North-South migration and only very limited immigration into the South, which kept that region segregated from the rest of the country.[19]

Potential investors outside the South were discouraged from filling the gap by economic, legal, and political obstacles as well as social and cultural barriers. In particular, there existed well-documented capital market imperfections throughout the United States, but especially in the South, Midwest, and West, that were diminishing over time but that persisted through the nineteenth century. Moreover, legal impediments to limited liability reduced the scope for impersonal investment funds. Investors therefore tended to invest only in those activities that they could help oversee or in which they knew the principals. Both were unlikely in interregional commerce. Fundamentally, however, these data do not demonstrate quantitatively significant market failure. To make a convincing case for inefficiency, it must be argued that society's economic interests differed from the interests of the individuals who made the decisions.

While this sort of "externalities" argument does make some sense, it is difficult to measure the actual deviation between social and individual interests. Industrialization may generate benefits greater than those captured by resource owners by increasing the average skill level of the work force through learning-by-doing or by reducing the cost of inventive activity. It may also diversify the fortunes of the economy, protecting it from the rapid income fluctuations that are common when many are dependent on a single export crop.

The case for externalities in this case, though, is far from self-evident. To the degree that northern manufacturing substituted for southern manufacturing, the external benefits were not lost, only transferred to another region of the country. That represents a cost to society only if "society" is narrowly defined to mean the South. Slavery made it possible to capture one important external benefit—investment in human skills—that evades manufacturers operating in a free labor market. A trained crafts worker gets to keep the payoff from the invested skills when he or she changes jobs—unless, that is, the worker is a slave.

Slavery and Urbanization

Only one southerner in ten lived in a city, compared with one New Englander in three (Table 11.4). The reason, it is claimed, was that slavery was incompatible with urban life.[20] The argument is that it was more expen-

[19] Bateman and Weiss (1981).
[20] Wade (1964).

TABLE 11.4

Percentage of Population Living in Urban Areas

Region	1820	1830	1840	1850	1860
New England	10.5	14.0	19.4	28.8	36.6
Mid-Atlantic	11.3	14.2	18.1	25.5	35.4
East North Central	1.2	2.5	3.9	9.0	14.1
West North Central	—	3.5	3.9	10.3	13.4
South	5.5	6.2	7.7	9.8	11.5
East South Central	0.8	1.5	2.1	4.2	5.9

Source: Douglass C. North, *The Economic Growth of the United States, 1790–1860* (New York: W. W. Norton, 1966): 258.

sive to secure the free population against slave revolt in cities because it was harder to isolate slaves and shield them from abolitionist propaganda. Slaves also "upset" the free workers with whom they associated by lowering the self-perceived status of the white working class. Thus urban fears of slaves and the concomitant increased cost of slave security may explain the relative decline of urban slavery after the 1830s and the absolute decline during the 1850s. If true, then the slave labor system was an artificial (and increasingly important) constraint on the allocation of black labor to industry. If free white labor could not substitute perfectly for black slave labor, the cost of manufacturing was raised in the South, and the division of resources between industry and agriculture was inefficient.

Claudia Goldin has offered an alternative explanation for the drop in urban slave population based on the efficiency, not the inefficiency, of the southern labor market. She argues that the demand for all labor was growing in southern cities, but the slaves left because their owners were pulled by opportunities for profit in the cotton fields, not because they were pushed by increasing reluctance to use slaves in manufacturing. Because slave and free labor were fairly close substitutes in cities, where they performed the same tasks in the same ways, the urban demand for slave labor was elastic with respect to price. Consequently, a small increase in slave hire rates, other factors being equal, would lead urbanities to switch to free labor. On cotton plantations, however, slave "willingness" to be driven in labor gangs made slave labor unique. Since there were no close substitutes for their services, the rural demand elasticity for slaves was low. The slave exodus from cities in the 1850s, Goldin claims, was caused by an increase in slave prices associated with the cotton boom. Urban areas did not compete for slave services at higher prices because they did not need to compete.

Slavery and Economic Growth

The aggregate outcome of all these economic decisions is reflected in the growth performance of the southern economy. Although it probably comes as no surprise to find that northerners had higher per capita incomes in both 1840 and 1860, it may surprise those who think of the South as backward that estimates indicate that the South was substantially better off at both dates than the predominantly rural North Central states (Ohio and states west).[21] The South, moreover, grew one-fifth faster than the North and at a rate little different from that of industrializing countries. Fogel and Engerman see these figures as macroeconomic icing on the microeconomic cake of plantation efficiency. How else, they ask, can we interpret such a long period of sustained growth that compares favorably with the American North and with European economies?

Gavin Wright (1978) argues that the South's good fortunes were dependent on factors outside the control of southerners. The relentless increase in the demand for raw cotton (at an average rate of 5 percent annually from 1830 to 1860) provided opportunities for southerners to extend the cotton economy westward without experiencing a long-term decline in cotton prices. Lots of high-quality land in the New South, moreover, made it possible to raise labor productivity with no change in technology or farm organization. More land per worker allowed risk-averse farmers to shift a higher percentage of their output into profitable cotton without sacrificing the benefits of self-sufficiency in food.

The rapid growth of the South also appears paradoxical upon closer inspection. Notice that the rate of growth in each subregion of the South was not only lower than the average growth rate for the region as a whole but also lower than in the North and the subregions of the North (Table 11.5). By this standard, each region of the South was growing more slowly than the rest of the country. Indeed, growth was slowest of all in the highest-income region of the South. How can the South appear to do so well when all its constituent parts do relatively poorly?

The explanation lies in the effect upon average southern incomes of population redistribution from the poorer southern states east of the Mississippi River to the higher-income states west of the Mississippi, especially Texas and Arkansas. In the North, on the other hand, population migrated from the high-income Northeast to the lower-income North Central region. If we ignore the Northeast and West South-Central, then per capita income in the Midwest and rest of the South was approximately equal.

The southern response to growing foreign demand and to the availability of fertile land was surely efficient; cotton was where the profits lay. But

[21] Easterlin (1971).

TABLE 11.5

Regional per Capita Income, 1840 and 1860

Region	1840	1860	% Average Annual Growth
United States	$96	128	1.4
North	109	141	1.3
Northeast	129	181	1.7
North Central	65	89	1.6
South	74	103	1.7
South Atlantic	66	84	1.2
East South Central	69	89	1.3
West South Central	151	184	1.0

Interpretation: Southern incomes were, on average, lower than northern incomes before the Civil War. But note that most parts of the South had a higher living standard than the predominantly rural North Central (Midwest) states. And most important, southern income was growing substantially faster than northern during the two decades before the Civil War.

Source: Robert Fogel and Stanley Engerman, *Time on the Cross* (Boston: Little, Brown, 1974): 248.

the resulting per capita growth must be looked at somewhat differently from, say, the growth record of the North. The South was a modern extractive economy capable of growth because it possessed abundant resources and was blessed by expanding demand from the outside. Growth did take place, but the resulting specialization may have left it unprepared to cope with the changes wrought by decelerating demand for cotton in the late nineteenth century.

Slavery made this extremely rapid economic expansion possible by allowing plantations to achieve economies of scale and by allowing greater market orientation by farmers. However, the attraction of cotton-slave agriculture retarded industrial development, leaving the South vulnerable to the long-term vicissitudes of the world cotton market.

The critical issue, then, is how well the slave South would have coped with demand changes that reduced the return to cotton farming. Indeed, it should be noted that while we have estimates of the return to plantation slavery, we do not have estimates of the return to southern agriculture as a whole. The latter would include potential capital gains on land and livestock. In the North these were quite large, and while they were almost certainly smaller in the South because of more limited local development (including urban growth and transportation) and southern livestock practices, it seems likely that they would add a few percentage points to the returns on slavery. This would only further tip the scales in favor of continued agricultural investment.

If southerners had succeeded in transferring resources to industry, the transition from cotton agriculture would have been cheap in economic terms. The slave society of the antebellum South might have become a sort of precursor to South Africa, operating a diversified economy off the backs of an exploited underclass of workers. If, on the other hand, the commitment to cotton had been difficult to reverse under slavery, losses of missed late nineteenth-century growth opportunities might have outweighed the gains from early growth opportunities. We look at some of these questions in the chapters that follow.

Appendix: A Partially Adjusted Index of the Relative Efficiency of Southern Agriculture, 1860[22]

	South as a Percentage of the North
1. Relative output: $\left(\frac{Q_S}{Q_N}\right)$ corrected for the quality of livestock	102.5
Inputs:	
2. Relative labor input: $\left(\frac{L_S}{L_N}\right)$ corrected for age and sex differences and the occupational mix	93.3
3. Relative land input: $\left(\frac{T_S}{T_N}\right)$ corrected for quality differences	50.5
4. Relative capital input: $\left(\frac{K_S}{K_N}\right)$	53.4
5. Index of factor inputs: $\left[\left(\frac{L_S}{L_N}\right)^{0.58} \cdot \left(\frac{K_S}{K_N}\right)^{0.17} \cdot \left(\frac{T_S}{T_N}\right)^{0.25}\right]$	72.8
Index of relative total factor productivity (line 1 divided by line 5)	140.8

[22] From Robert W. Fogel and Stanley L. Engerman, *Time on the Cross: Evidence and Methods* (Boston: Little, Brown, 1974): 135.

Bibliography

Atack, Jeremy. "Returns to Scale in Antebellum United States Manufacturing." *Explorations in Economic History* 14 (1977): 337–59.

Bateman, Fred, and Thomas Weiss. *A Deplorable Scarcity: The Failure of Industrialization in the Slave Economy.* Chapel Hill: University of North Carolina Press, 1981.

Conrad, Alfred, and John Meyer. "The Economics of Slavery in the Antebellum South." *Journal of Political Economy* 66 (1958): 95–130.

David, Paul, and Peter Temin. "Slavery: The Progressive Institution." *Journal of Economic History* 34 (1974): 739–83.

———. "Explaining the Relative Efficiency of Slave Agriculture in the Antebellum South: Comment." *American Economic Review* 69 (1979): 213-16.

Easterlin, Richard, "Regional Income Trends 1840–1950." In *The Reinterpretation of American Economic History,* ed. Robert Fogel and Stanley Engerman. New York: Harper & Row (1971): 38–49.

Fleisig, Haywood. "Slavery, the Supply of Agricultural Labor, and the Industrialization of the South." *Journal of Economic History* 36 (1976): 572–97.

Fogel, Robert W. et al. *Without Consent or Contract: The Rise and Fall of American Slavery,* vol. 1. New York: W. W. Norton 1989.

———. *Without Consent or Contract: Evidence and Methods,* vol. 2. New York: W. W. Norton, 1992.

———. *Without Consent or Contract: Technical Papers Vol. I,* vol. 3. New York: W. W. Norton, 1992.

———. *Without Consent or Contract: Technical Papers Vol. II,* vol. 4. New York: W. W. Norton, 1992.

———, and Stanley Engerman, *Time on the Cross.* Boston: Little, Brown, 1974. Reprinted, New York: W. W. Norton, 1989.

———. *Time on the Cross II: Evidence and Methods.* Boston: Little, Brown, 1974.

———. "Explaining the Relative Efficiency of Slave Agriculture in the Antebellum South: A Reply." *American Economic Review* (1980): 672–90.

Gallman, Robert. "Self-Sufficiency of the Cotton Economy of the Antebellum South." In *The Structure of the Cotton Economy of the Antebellum South,* ed. William Parker. Washington D.C.: Agricultural History Society, 1970: 5–24.

Genovese, Eugene. *Roll Jordan Roll: The World the Slaves Made.* New York: Pantheon 1974.

Goldin, Claudia. *Urban Slavery in the American South.* Chicago: University of Chicago Press, 1976.

Gunderson, Gerald. "Southern Antebellum Income Reconsidered: A Reply to Gallman." *Explorations in Economic History* 10 (1973): 151–76.

Irwin, James R. "Slave Agriculture and Staple Crops in the Virginia Piedmont." University of Rochester Ph.D. diss., 1986.

———. "Exploring the Affinity of Wheat and Slavery in the Virginia Piedmont," *Explorations in Economic History* 25 (1988): 295–322.

Kotlikoff, Laurence, and Pinera, Sebastian. "The Old South's Stake in the Interregional Movement of Slaves, 1850-1860." *Journal of Economic History* 37 (1977): 434–50.

Lee, Susan. "Antebellum Southern Land Expansion: A Second View." *Agricultural History* 52 (1978): 488–502.

Linden, Fabian. "Economic Democracy in the Slave South: An Appraisal of Some Recent Views." *Journal of Negro History* 31 (1946): 140–89.

Meyer, David. "Midwestern Industrialization and the American Manufacturing Belt in the Nineteenth Century." *Journal of Economic History* 49 (1989): 921–38.

Olson, John F. "Clock Time versus Real Time: A Comparison of the Lengths of the Northern and Southern Agricultural Work Years." In *Without Consent or Contract: Technical Papers I,* ed. Robert Fogel et al. New York: W. W. Norton, 1992: 216–40.

Owsley, Frank. *Plain Folk in the Old South.* Baton Rouge: Louisiana State University, 1949.

Passell, Peter. "The Impact of Cotton Land Distribution on the Antebellum Economy." *Journal of Economic History* 31 (1971): 917–38.

———, and Gavin Wright. "The Effects of Pre-Civil War Territorial Expansion of the Price of Slaves." *Journal of Political Economy* 80 (1972): 1188–1202.

Ransom, Roger, and Richard Sutch. *One Kind of Freedom: The Economic Consequences of Emancipation.* New York: Cambridge University Press, 1977.

Schaefer, Donald F., "The Effect of the 1859 Crop Year upon Relative Productivity in the Antebellum Cotton South." *Journal of Economic History* 43 (1983): 851–66.

———, and Mark Schmitz, "The Relative Efficiency of Slave Agriculture: A Comment." *American Economic Review* 69 (1979): 208–12.

Schmitz, Mark D., and Donald F. Schaefer. "Slavery, Freedom, and the Elasticity of Substitution." *Explorations in Economic History* 15 (1978): 327–37.

Weiman, David. "Farmers and the Market in Antebellum America: A View from the Georgia Upcountry." *Journal of Economic History* 47 (1987): 627–48.

Wright, Gavin. *The Political Economy of the Cotton South.* New York: W. W. Norton, 1978.

———. "The Relative Efficiency of Slave Agriculture: Another Interpretation." *American Economic Review* 69 (1979): 219–26.

Wade, Richard C. *Slavery in the Cities: The South 1820–1860.* New York: Oxford University Press, 1964.

How the southern slave system worked

12

In the late eighteenth century slavery in North America was under siege. Many of the ex-colonies had adopted constitutions banning slavery even when they had no slaves to ban, and slavery was outlawed in the Northwest Territory. Furthermore, demand for tobacco, a leading slave crop, was stagnant. These conditions have led historians to argue that but for the appearance of cotton, slavery might have become economically unsustainable and withered away. Instead three generations later tens of thousands died in the Civil War and billions of dollars were spent in the effort to eradicate slavery from North America. Clearly southerners were not prepared to relinquish their "peculiar institution" willingly. In this chapter we examine the research on the economic motivation that drove southerners to fight to preserve their system and how slaves were treated by their masters. Although surely no one doubts that slavery was morally indefensible, there is substantial disagreement over how well (or badly) African-Americans fared under slavery.

The Profitability of Slavery

Considering the South's willingness to fight over its states' rights to preserve slavery, it should come as no surprise to learn that economists have found that slavery was profitable on the eve of the Civil War. Early efforts to assess profitability generally concluded that the rate of return on invested capital was quite low, although slavery yielded positive net revenues. A contemporary, Frederick Law Olmsted (who designed New York's Central Park), for example, believed that capital gains arising from the ban on importation of new slaves and the income from the sale of children were the chief sources of income but that slaves generally did not produce any surplus income from current production beyond their maintenance costs.

In the 1930s Charles Sydnor published one of the more celebrated—and erroneous—estimates of slave profitability. On the basis of the account books of large Mississippi plantations in the 1850s, Sydnor reconstructed a "typical" profit and loss statement. His figures (Table 12.1) show average net earnings after expenses of just $880 on an investment of $36,000 ($30,000 for fifty slaves, plus $6,000 for six hundred acres of cleared land), or a yield of just 2.4 percent ($880÷$36,000) on capital. Because this rate of return was well below that on secure private bonds, Sydnor concluded that slave labor, though profitable, was not a desirable investment.

A careful look at Sydnor's figures, however, reveals the opposite. As historian Kenneth Stampp first noted, at least two of the expense items—the implicit interest cost of the slaves and of the land investment—really belong as part of the return to the total investment. Sydnor had calculated something closer to what economists would call "supernormal" profits—that is, the return in excess of the opportunity cost of capital. Shuffling the numbers accordingly, the profit becomes $3,040 ($1,800 + $360 + $880), for a return on investment of 8.4 percent ([3,040÷ 36,000] × 100). This return compares favorably with the 5 to 6 percent yield on bonds at the time. In fact, the true return to slave investments might have been considerably higher because Sydnor included a depreciation cost for slaves but failed to include the symmetric profit from slave reproduction and counted only the value of cotton production but nothing for other crops, domestic service, and so forth.

TABLE 12.1

The Profitability of Slavery on a Typical Mississippi Plantation

Income		
63,200 lbs. of cotton @ 10¢ per pound		$6,320
Less Expenses		
Interest cost at $30,000 slave investment @ 6%	$1,800	
Depreciation (death, injury) of slave investment @ 6%	1,800	
Interest cost on $6,000 land investment @ 6%	360	
Depreciation on land investment @ 3%	180	
Overseer's wages	300	
Plantation supplies	1,000	
		−$5,440
Profit		$880

Source: Charles Sydnor, *Slavery in Mississippi* (New York: Appleton-Century, 1933), cited in Robert Fogel and Stanley Engerman, eds. *The Reinterpretation of American Economic History* (New York: Harper & Row, 1971): 321.

Sydnor also may have overcounted true plantation expenditures by adding in some of the owner's expenditures for food and clothing.

A more rigorous attempt to arrive at a rate of return on an investment in slaves was made years later by two Harvard economists, Alfred Conrad and John Meyer. They approached the issue as an analytically simple problem in business economics: Slaves could be treated like any other productive asset that generated income, required maintenance, and eventually wore out. Under these circumstances the appropriate model is the "capital asset pricing model." Assuming well-functioning, competitive markets, this model asserts that a willing buyer would pay a price just equal to the discounted present value of the expected future net revenue stream from the asset over its expected life.

Gross slave income consisted of the market value of the cotton they produced plus, in the case of women, the market value at birth of their offspring. This will understate true revenues to the extent that slaves engaged in home manufactures, produced other crops, cleared land, or performed domestic services in addition to their work in the cotton fields. Maintenance costs consisted of the expenditures to keep slaves alive and healthy—food, clothing, shelter, medical care—plus supervision. The durability of slave assets depended on their longevity.

Conrad and Meyer used traditional sources to make estimates of the cost of purchasing a slave, the average amount of cotton produced per field hand, the price of cotton, out-of-pocket maintenance, and life expectancy. In the case of female slaves, they also estimated the expected number of successful pregnancies and the net cost of raising children to productive age. Then they separately computed the expected yield on hypothetical investments in male and female slaves on lands of differing productivity. Returns for males varied from 2.2 to 5.4 percent (depending on cotton prices and yields) on poor-quality eastern seaboard land, to returns of 10 to 13 percent on fertile western land (Table 12.2). The average return to investors, Conrad and Meyer reckoned, was about 6 percent. For females working on average-quality land, the return varied from 7.1 percent for those having five children to 8.1 percent for those bearing ten. The relatively small difference between these two rates of return reflects the low present value of children to be sold off at some distant future date.

These figures don't necessarily tell us what slaveowners actually earned in the late antebellum years. Consider, for example, the plantation owner who bought young adult slaves in 1850 in anticipation of getting thirty years of labor from them. Just eleven years later the gross income from slave labor would have fallen drastically when the blockade of southern ports made it almost impossible to sell cotton outside the South. And fifteen years after the purchase date the slaveowner would have seen his or her capital confiscated through enforced emancipation. Still, their estimated rates of return do tell us what a plantation owner expected to earn in a stable economic environ-

TABLE 12.2

Realized Rates of Return on Prime Field Hands under Various Hypothetical Conditions

Case	Slave Price	Yield per Acre (bales)	Farm Price of Cotton (cents/lb)	Internal Rate of Return (percent)
1.	$1,350–1,400	3¾	7	4.5
2.	$1,350–1,400	3¾	8	5.2
3.	$1,350–1,400	3¾	9	6.5
4.	$1,600	4½	7	5.0
5.	$1,600	4½	8	7.0
6.	$1,600	4½	9	8.0
7.	$1,250–1,300	3	7	2.2
8.	$1,250–1,300	3	8	3.9
9.	$1,250–1,300	3	9	5.4
10.	$1,700	7	7	10.0
11.	$1,700	7	8	12.0
12.	$1,700	7	9	13.0

Source: Alfred Conrad and John Meyer, "The Economics of Slavery in the Antebellum South," *Journal of Political Economy* 66 (1958): Table 9, 107.

ment. With an average expected return on male slaves of 6 percent and on female slaves of between 7 and 8 percent, slaveowners could reasonably justify their investment in slaves at current market prices. This answers the charge by the noted southern historian at the turn of the century, Ulrich Phillips, that slaves had become highly speculative investments whose price could not be justified by current or expected productivity. Instead Phillips attributed the price increase to (1) a speculative boom based on the unavailability of imported slaves and reinforced by concentration in the ownership of the existing stock and (2) the desire of individual plantation owners for more slaves as a form of conspicuous consumption—that is, for noneconomic purposes.

Conrad and Meyer's estimates have not gone unchallenged. For example, one scholar has suggested downward revisions in the average amount of cotton produced per slave and upward revisions in the market price of the average slave.[1] The net effect of these revisions is to reduce the average rate of return on male slaves from 6 percent to 1.5 percent. Another scholar has criticized Conrad and Meyer's implicit assumption of a 4 percent annual growth rate of the slave population—twice the rate actually recorded in the

[1] Saraydar (1964).

TABLE 12.3

Average Rate of Return on Slaves by Quinquennia, 1830-1860 (percentage)

Period	Upper South	Lower South
1830–35	10.5	12.0
1836–40	9.5	
1841–45	14.3	18.5
1846–50	12.6	17.0
1851–55	13.8	12.0
1856–60	9.5	10.3

Source: Robert Evans, Jr., "The Economics of American Negro Slavery," in National Bureau of Economic Research, *Aspects of Labor Economics* (Princeton: Princeton University Press, 1962): 217.

census.[2] Slower population growth meant fewer slave children to sell, reducing the average rate of return on slaves below 5 percent.

Not all studies, however, find that Conrad and Meyer were overly sanguine about the return to investment in slaves.[3] The average annual rental data for slaves, for example, imply rates of return varying from a low of 9.5 percent in the upper South in the late 1830s and again on the eve of the Civil War to over 18 percent in the lower South during the early 1840s (Table 12.3). Slaves generated a substantial surplus beyond their costs of maintenance.[4] Moreover, despite sharp and sometime acrimonious debate over the nature of slavery and its consequences, Robert Fogel and Stanley Engerman's estimate that slaveowners earned about 10 percent on the market price of their bondsmen and women has gone almost unchallenged for two decades.[5] The issue now seems fairly settled: Slavery was profitable.

The Viability of Slavery

Estimates of sustained slave profitability from at least the 1830s suggests that southern slaveowners were unlikely to have freed their working slaves voluntarily.[6] Profitability studies, however, do not directly address the fundamen-

[2] Butlin (1971).
[3] See, for example. Battalio and Kagel (1970); Evans (1962); and Fogel and Engerman (1974).
[4] Evans (1962).
[5] Greenwald and Glasspiegel (1983), however, suggest that adverse selection, or the fear that adverse selection was operating, reduced the auction market price of slaves (only bad slaves—runaways, troublemakers, shirkers, and the like—were offered at public auction), causing others, including Fogel and Engerman, to overestimate the returns to slavery. This criticism itself has now been questioned by Pritchett and Chamberlain (1993), who argue that if anything, the rate of return to slavery has been understated.
[6] Evans (1962).

tal question of whether slavery was a viable institution—that is, was it worthwhile raising one more slave infant to adulthood? If it was, then slavery could have continued for at least another generation. If not, then it would eventually have withered and died without the upheaval and costs of the Civil War.

The clearest statement of the view that slavery was moribund on the eve of the Civil War was by Charles Ramsdell in an essay entitled "The Natural Limits of Slavery Expansion." Ramsdell argued that the continued viability of slavery depended upon (1) the existence of a large supply of new land suitable for cotton cultivation and (2) the maintenance of high cotton prices. In his view, the westward rush of slavery in the 1850s into Missouri and Texas and expansion of cotton lands elsewhere with the spread of the railroad had exhausted the supply of virgin land suitable for cotton production. Moreover, the long-term trend in cotton prices was downward. Consequently, he viewed it as inevitable that the value of the marginal product of slave labor would eventually fall, reducing the value of a slave. At some point this declining marginal product would no longer cover the cost of subsistence for slaves. There would thus be no surplus for the slaveowners to expropriate, and slavery would be abandoned.

Ramsdell's argument is flawed on many counts. True, cotton prices were declining, but not because of stagnant or sluggish growth in demand. Rather increased productivity had lowered production costs. True, economic theory does predict declining marginal productivity if more and more labor is combined with a fixed quantity of land, *other things being equal.* But there is no reason why farmers should not have adopted more intensive farming techniques and worked to maintain or even improve soil fertility, postponing any tendency for marginal product to decline. Nor had cotton reached its geographic limits by 1860. West Texas, Arizona, and California awaited the twentieth century to become leaders in cotton production, but there was no technological reason why these lands should not have been cultivated earlier. Lastly, slaves could be employed in other activities, including other agricultural crops, such as grains (as in Virginia and to a lesser extent on virtually all cotton plantations), or in manufacturing and craft activities (as earlier in the century). Ramsdell looked at only one margin: cotton production.

Ramsdell's arguments for the imminent demise of slavery on the eve of the Civil War thus make little sense. The work of Yasukichi Yasuba showed that slavery was indeed viable. So long as the productivity of slaves was greater than their subsistence—which most profitability studies and all rental data show to be the case—it paid to keep slaves of working age. It is possible that passive slave resistance (feigned incompetence, abuse of machinery and work animals, malingering) or active slave resistance (slave rebellion) reduced productivity. Even so, it seems unlikely that resistance could have pushed the surplus to zero, considering the generally high levels of labor productivity in nineteenth-century America and the slaveowners' almost absolute power over their chattels. Slaveowners would thus continue to work their existing stock of slaves, and slavery would have continued for at least the current generation of slaves.

What about future generations? Raising children to adulthood involves considerable sunk costs, even if a child can be put to work at a fairly tender age. There is the opportunity cost of the mother in birthing and early child care, and there are the consumption expenses unmatched by any offsetting productive activity during infancy and early childhood. Moreover, the consumption expenses and opportunity costs are incurred long before there is any productive activity to help defray those costs. They thus have a relatively high present cost. If owners were to have an incentive to allow their slaves to reproduce, then the market value of a working slave must have exceeded those costs. Yasuba very conservatively calculated the difference between a slave's market value at maturity (plus the value of childhood labor) and his or her rearing costs and discovered that at no time between 1820 and 1860 did this "capitalized economic rent" in a young adult slave fall below 50 percent of a slave's market value (see Table 12.4). Whether the system would have survived a prolonged depression in cotton prices or a liberation move-

TABLE 12.4

The Gain to the Slaveowner from Enslavement: The Capitalized Rent in an Eighteen-Year-Old Male Slave

Years	Average Price	Gross Rearing Costs	Income from Child Labor	Capitalized* Rent	Capitalized Rent as % of Price
1821–25	736	657	349	428	58
1826–30	792	614	286	464	59
1831–35	974	671	431	734	75
1836–40	1,206	848	497	855	71
1841–45	744	591	379	532	72
1846–50	936	737	546	745	80
1851–55	1,252	807	600	1,045	83
1856–60	1,596	938	922	1,580	99

Interpretation: As long as the capitalized rent—the portion of a slave's value above the investment needed to raise a slave to working age—is positive, it pays to raise more slaves. Note that the capitalized rent per slave was large, and generally rising across the decades.

*Average slave price, less rearing costs, plus child labor income.

Source: Yasukichi Yasuba, "The Profitability and Viability of Plantation Slavery in the United States," reprinted in Robert Fogel and Stanley Engerman, eds., *The Reinterpretation of American Economic History* (New York: Harper & Row, 1971): 367.

ment funded and armed from outside is anyone's guess, but the numbers give us every reason to believe that slavery would have been around for a long while. Indeed, Fogel and Engerman argue that slaveowners were increasingly optimistic about the future right up to the outbreak of war.

The Rate of Exploitation and the Paradox of Forced Labor

An alternative question to how much slaveowners profited from slavery is to ask how much more they gained from using slaves as opposed to free labor. According to the tenets of neoclassical economic theory, in a competitive economy workers are paid the value added by the last worker. Workers are exploited whenever they fail to receive this competitive return. The rate of exploitation can thus be defined as the percentage of the competitive wage that the employer expropriates.

However, a regular employer hires and fires free labor at will, but slaves were different. Once freed (an illegal act in a number of states), they could not be reenslaved. Fogel and Engerman therefore define the expropriated portion of a slave's product as the difference, at birth, between discounted lifetime earnings and discounted lifetime slave income (that is, maintenance costs that the slaveowner supplied). As Yasuba has shown above, this was positive from at least the 1820s; otherwise the slaveholder would have had no motive to raise slaves from birth, and slavery would have disappeared.

The expropriation rate defined this way is much smaller than one might suppose primarily because the annual value of a slave's earnings was less than the cost of their maintenance until age nine (Figure 12.1). Thereafter the exploitation rate—defined as the fraction by which current income falls short of current earnings—was positive, but it took another eighteen years for the excess of earnings over income for a typical slave to pay back the debt accumulated during childhood. From age twenty-seven to death (say, at age seventy) the surplus is substantial, but in terms of present value at birth the surplus barely topped \$32 in 1850. Since the calculated present value of lifetime earnings at birth was about \$265 for the same slave, the rate of expropriation is just 12 percent (\$32 ÷ \$265) and would have been even lower if the subsistence goods and services supplied to slaves were valued at market, as opposed to wholesale, prices.

Three factors help account for this seemingly low rate of expropriation. First, slaves who live full lifetimes must, in effect, pay for those who do not survive to adulthood. Second, the costs of slave rearing are paid early in life in dollars that are more valuable than those received later. Although good field hands could produce about \$100 more per year than they cost to maintain, the present value of those future dollars was small, compared with the immediate costs of child rearing. Third, it has also been suggested that the

FIGURE 12.1

Average Accumulated Value (Discounted to Birth) of Income Appropriated from Slaves (1850 dollars)

The chart shows the cumulative value of the surplus an average slave earned over his or her lifetime. Note that owners begin to get back more than they put into a slave at about age nine. Sometime in the slave's early twenties the owner breaks even on the investment, as the slave's earnings discounted back to birth equal the slave's discounted rearing cost. Fogel and Engerman guess that around age fifty slave earnings again fall to about the level of maintenance costs. By this point, the cumulative value, discounted back to birth, a net slave earnings equals a little more than $30. Hence the argument that at birth a slave is worth about $30.

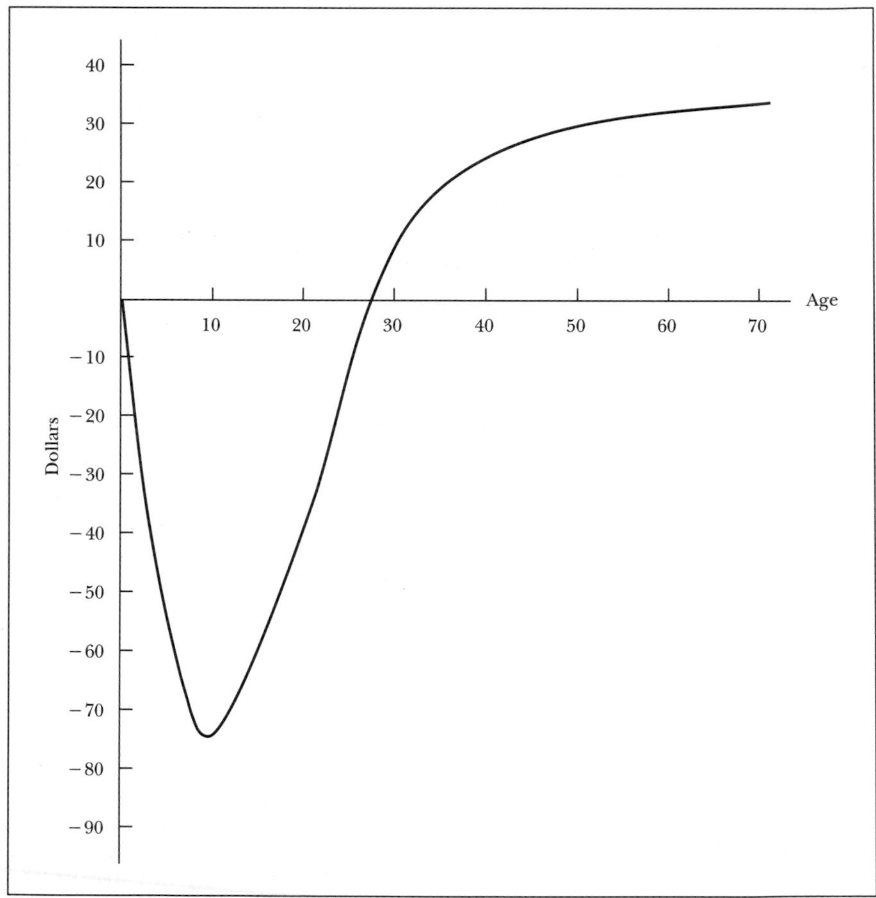

Source: Robert Fogel and Stanley Engerman, *Time on the Cross* (Boston: Little, Brown, 1974): 154.

maintenance costs imputed to young slaves by Fogel and Engerman are too high, averaging $34.13 per slave per year (or $48.12 per adult male), thereby exaggerating the deficit accumulated by slaves before they began work and understating the rate of expropriation.[7]

From the standpoint of the slaveowner, the present value of a slave's lifetime earnings that the slaveowner could expropriate provides an answer to the question of what sum of money could leave the slaveowner indifferent between a lifetime of slave services and purchasing those services on the free market. It is not, however, the only question of interest. One might also ask what portion of a slave's current earnings the slaveowner could capture by virtue of chattel ownership of the slave. That is to say, by what fraction did a slave's income fall short of the value of his or her marginal product? Although the dollar estimates of the amount of income that slaveowners were able to exploit vary, the rates of exploitation are of similar orders of magnitude. Slaveowners were able to extract between 50 and 65 percent of the value of the marginal product from their chattels (Table 12.5).

What should we make of these results? Slaves were not the only workers who were exploited as a result of market imperfections. It is estimated, for example, that northern civilian workers during the Civil War lost at least 47 percent of their wages because of unanticipated inflation.[8] Postbellum southern country stores may have expropriated about 13 percent of the in-

TABLE 12.5

Estimates of the Neoclassical Rate of Exploitations of Slave Workers

	Vedder	Ransom and Sutch		Fogel and Engerman	
		All Slave Farms	Large Plantations	All Slave Farms	Large Plantations
Marginal worker's contribution	$85.76	$62.46	$78.78	$73.98	$85.80
Less value of slave consumption	30.00	28.95	32.12	34.13	42.99
Equals expropriated income	55.76	33.51	46.66	39.85	42.81
Rate of exploitation	65%	54%	59%	54%	50%

Sources: Richard K. Vedder, "The Slave Exploitation (Expropriation) Rate," *Explorations in Economic History* 12 (1975): 455; Roger Ranson and Richard Sutch, *One Kind of Freedom* (Cambridge, England: Cambridge University Press, 1977): 203–12, reprinted by permission of Cambridge University Press; Robert W. Fogel and Stanley L. Engerman, *Time on the Cross: Evidence and Methods* (Boston: Little, Brown, 1974): 159.

[7] David and Temin (1974).

[8] DeCanio and Mokyr (1975).

come of (predominantly black) sharecroppers by charging monopoly interest on small loans.[9] And the wages of antebellum textile workers in the North may have lowered by 20 to 30 percent as a result of monopsonistic labor markets.[10] Still, slaveowners were able to capture a much greater share of slave income, as well as deprive their slaves of their personal liberty and freedom of choice to live and work as they saw fit.

In *Time on the Cross,* Fogel and Engerman estimate that a prime field hand received consumption goods worth approximately 15 percent more than the wage imputed to free farmers tilling their own land. Why? The answer presumably is not because there was any sense of guilt or paternalistic concern about slave welfare but because it paid masters to give slaves positive incentives to work hard. Fogel and Engerman argue that it was possible to sustain this relatively high material living standard for slaves yet still reap a tidy return because plantation agriculture was so much more productive than small-scale family farming. Slaves got to keep roughly one-fifth of the extra value generated by large-scale farm organization. However, the peculiarly productive farm organization made possible by slavery—gang labor—was so repugnant that the intangible "nonpecuniary" losses that the slaves suffered more than offset their tangible material gains. One measure of this is that after the Civil War landowners had to pay wages $75 a year above the going rate for nongang labor to induce free people to work in labor gangs on sugar plantations in Louisiana. The implicit nonpecuniary loss to workers ($75) was far greater than the potential material gain attributable to gang labor scale economies ($23 per year).

Even without our placing an explicit value upon personal freedom, it should be clear from the foregoing that slaves lost more from being slaves than owners gained from enslaving them. Why, then, couldn't they work out a deal in which slaves traded some of their material income for the intangible benefits of freedom? The answer is deceptively simple. It would take an average of $15 (the $23 productivity advantage to gang labor, less the $8 returned to slaves as incentives to work) to compensate slaveowners for their annual net loss of income. But slaves couldn't afford to make the deal. They just weren't rich enough to give up an additional $15 a year and still have enough income to survive.

It is, however, eminently plausible that such a fundamental change in the master-slave relationship might have left both parties better off. Under slavery, owners profited by confiscating the difference between what a slave produced and what a slave consumed. Yasuba and others leave little doubt that this surplus was substantial. But it is also possible that the surplus could have been even larger if slaves had incentives to work as hard and productively as they were capable. Slaves, of course, did have incentives: the threat

[9] Ransom and Sutch (1977).
[10] Vedder (1975).

of punishment and, not unusually, the promise of special treatment for good service. But these incentives did not always work; passive resistance, which cut labor productivity, was probably not uncommon.

Hence, at least in theory, there was the possibility of a rearrangement of the slave-master "contract," leaving workers with more income and privilege and plantation owners with a greater return. For example, an arrangement by which slaves bought their freedom over a period of many years by working as independent contractors would have meant that the harder the slave worked, the faster he or she would have gained freedom. In a small number of recorded cases, slaves were able to buy their freedom. The price they paid was typically above the market value, but it is difficult to infer that self-purchase would have been mutually attractive for the average field hand and master. Most cases of self-purchase involved skilled artisans working in cities. Even if such an arrangement was mutually beneficial, it is unlikely that society would have accepted the change. Large numbers of free African-Americans working alongside those still in bondage would very likely have made slavery infeasible.

Getting the Work Done: Reward Versus Punishment

The optimal balance between force and material rewards needed to maximize the difference between slave production and slave maintenance is not at all obvious. Force—physical coercion, restriction of freedom of movement—usually has the advantage of being cheap. It will not be effective, however, if slaves resist passively, taking opportunities to vandalize equipment and avoid work. Material incentives—better food, clothing, additional leisure, promotion within the slave hierarchy—are expensive in the sense that they raise maintenance costs. If used effectively, though, they might induce the slave to identify with his or her owner's interests and thus raise labor productivity by an amount more than sufficient to offset the increased costs. The problem facing slaveowners was to determine the optimal mix of the carrot and the stick, given slave preferences and reactions to these very different incentives.[11]

Giorgio Cannarella and John Tomaske have argued that the internal logic of slavery should bias owners toward the use of force. First, there is an asymmetry in slave response to positive and negative incentives. Force always works (if applied carefully) up to the point where slaves can do no more. Material reward, by contrast, works only up to the point where the additional income to the slave outweighs the unpleasantness of additional effort. Second, there are positive "externalities" in the use of force that are missing in the use of reward incentives. Punish one slave harshly, and the threat of

[11] Kahn (1992b).

punishment may suffice to keep the others in line. Providing a Christmas ham for a hard worker, on the other hand, may only create resentment among those slaves who don't get hams. However, a reward to one slave can surely induce others to work harder in hope of receiving similar benefits, and punishment may only generate sympathy and slave community solidarity against the master. Does one punish a slave who convincingly feigns stupidity? What if resistance is passive or secretive?

Both force and reward work reasonably well in getting jobs done, and in a perfectly competitive marketplace, where information is obtained costlessly and everybody responds identically to incentives, only the best technique would survive. But the slave labor market was not so perfectly competitive, nor was information cheap. It was expensive to monitor and measure performance. Perhaps more important, plantation agriculture was so lucrative that owners could typically afford to use less than optimal techniques. They might earn less than maximum profits, but with economic rents on slaves so high, they were unlikely to go out of business.

Whipping, along with public humiliation and loss of privileges, was the principal means of punishment on plantations. In the early nineteenth century this was not viewed as particularly cruel or unusual; flogging, for example, was still used in the Royal Navy, and child laborers in British textile mills were subject to corporal punishment. On the basis of the diary of Louisiana planter Bennet H. Barrow, Fogel and Engerman argue that plantation owners used whipping with discretion. Diary entries reveal that over a two-year period, 45 percent of the slaves were never whipped and another 19 percent were whipped just once. In reviewing these data, Fogel and Engerman dispassionately note that the average number of whippings per hand was 0.7 per year. Probably no other statistic in *Time on the Cross*—with its associated interpretation that slavery was not necessary driven by the rod—aroused more outrage (Figure 12.2).

Herbert Gutman and Richard Sutch, however, suggest that the frequency of whippings on the Barrow plantation was actually much higher than Fogel and Engerman report because the number of field slaves on the plantation was lower while the recorded number of whippings higher. By their reckoning, only 22 percent of Barrow's slaves escaped the lash, and whippings per hand per year were 1.2, not 0.7. During the two-year period, Gutman and Sutch point out, Barrow held one public whipping every fourth day and also "jailed, beat with a stick, threatened with death, shot with a gun, raked the heads of, and humiliated" his slaves.

Regardless of the question of whether the actual number of whippings per hand per year was 0.7 or 1.2, it must be recognized that a whipping was not the same as a spanking that an irate parent might administer to a recalcitrant child. Rather a whipping was a public humiliation and brutalization, capable of causing permanent physical (not to mention psychological) scarring with a risk of death from shock or septicemia, a point that Fogel and Engerman make, but their cautionary note has been frequently overlooked.

FIGURE 12.2

Distribution of Whippings on the Bennet H. Barrow Plantation, 1840–1842

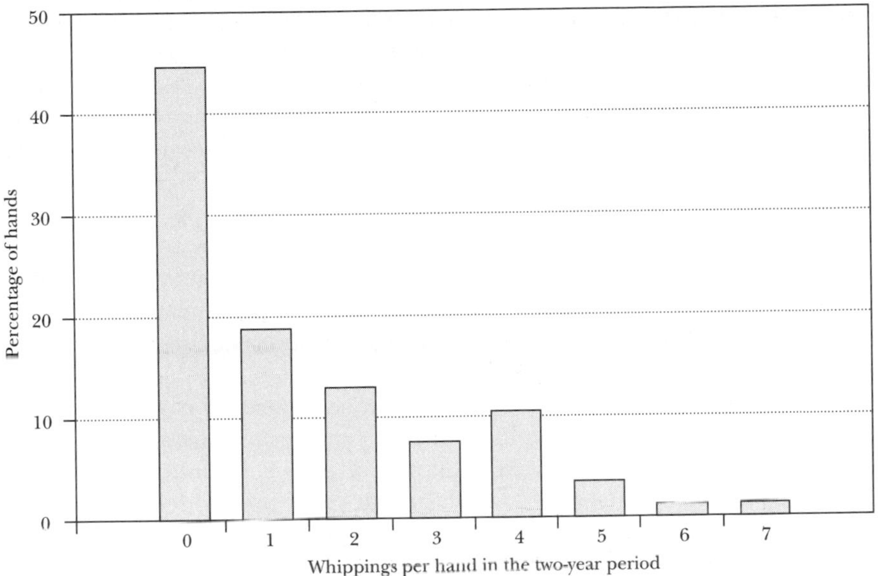

Source: Robert W. Fogel and Stanley L. Engerman, *Time on The Cross: The Economics of American Negro Slavery* (Boston: Little, Brown, 1974): 145, Figure 40.

For this reason alone, if for no other, one might expect that slaveowners would have resorted to the whip only relatively infrequently since it jeopardized their capital and potentially affected the marketability of the slave by providing tangible evidence of adverse selection. Moreover, for most of us such demonstrations of brute power would not need to be made frequently to induce the desired behavior. Thus whether whippings were administered frequently or infrequently is irrelevant to the question of whether or not performance was driven by fear more than reward. A credible threat itself should be sufficient, provided the linkage between behavior and punishment was made clear.

Most discussions of whipping assume that its goal was to motivate labor performance, and it doubtless provided a strong short-term stimulus to meet expectations. A study of the ex-slave narratives, however, suggests that whipping was more likely to be used as a means of maintaining social control over the slave population through the fear and intimidation of a power relationship than to motivate work performance.[12] Rewards, on the other hand, were frequently and systematically employed as work incentives. Good per-

[12] Crawford (1992).

formance in the fields might mean extra days off, luxury goods, or prizes. Barrow distributed substantial gifts at Christmas to this end. On a Texas plantation owned by Julian Devereux, slaves cultivated cotton on special plots in their spare time, earning as much as $100 per family in a good year. Another planter, William Jemison of Alabama, was even more clearly oriented toward material rewards as incentives. Jemison's slaves were, in effect, sharecroppers with lifetime, unbreakable contracts. They were obliged to set aside one-third of the crop for their owner but were allowed to keep the proceeds from the rest after netting out the cost of services provided by Jemison.

Gutman and Sutch's reading of the record is different. Barrow's gift giving was no regular event. Of the ten years' experience recorded in his diary, Barrow made major gifts in only three; the other seven years the slaves had to settle for holiday parties. However, it's hard to say whether these rewards were incentives for hard work or a matter of paternalistic custom. As for the separate land plots, the evidence can be read either way. By setting aside a small amount of land for slaves, owners might be rewarding their chattels for services rendered. Or they might simply be sharing the market and risks associated with farming in a convenient and socially acceptable manner. In good years master and slave ate well; in bad years they suffered together. Unless evidence surfaces showing that the plots were increased or decreased in size according to specific actions by slaves, there is no obvious way of interpreting masters' motives. Only Jemison's slaves were unambiguously motivated by reward.

For free men and women, occupational choice is a matter of personal motivation, aptitude, family wealth, and kinship ties; for slaves, occupation could (if the master wished) be a matter of rational income maximization. If slaveowners had pursued a "human capital" strategy, then they would have singled out bright, young, willing workers and trained them in crafts or as managers. The earlier they gained skills, the greater the return on the investment to the owner. Instead Fogel and Engerman found that younger workers were underrepresented among the skilled, whereas male slaves in their thirties and forties and fifties were overrepresented. They believe the explanation for this lies in the use of occupation as a reward for service. Field hands could get away from odious gang labor only by hard work and docility for a decade or two. Those lucky enough to succeed would have a chance at less monotonous work, greater control over their daily lives, and higher status within slave society. Although slaves were virtually excluded from the professions and from top managerial posts, 7 percent were managers, 7 percent were craftspersons, and 7 percent had semiskilled jobs as personal servants, gardeners, and teamsters. As Gutman and Sutch see it, however, the evidence just does not support Fogel and Engerman's conclusion. The overrepresentation of older workers in skilled jobs may be explained by a reward system, but it is also consistent with the hypothesis that older workers may have been less fit to work as field hands.

In some instances, then, work effort was driven by punishment (or threat thereof); in others, by reward. Stefano Fenoaltea has suggested a simple extension of a transactions cost model that predicts the division of tasks between these two incentive systems. According to his thesis, pain is capable of generating greater worker effort, but less care, than reward. At the same time activities are either effort-intensive or care-intensive. As Fenoaltea puts it, "where the worker's productivity depends overwhelmingly on his brute effort and negligibly on his carefulness . . . a shift to a system that eliminates the supervisor and lets the worker retain his marginal product would *not* yield a reduction in total labor costs, precisely because the attendant shift from pain incentive to ordinary rewards causes a reduction in the worker's effort and productivity. In care-intensive activities, in contrast, the substitution of care for effort does not reduce the worker's productivity."[13]

On the basis of this dichotomy, Fenoaltea characterizes cotton, sugar, and rice production as effort-intensive activities because lack of care does not impair next year's production and performance is fairly easily monitored. On the other hand, urban handicrafts placed a much greater premium upon care. Therefore, the former should be driven more by the whip and closely supervised while the latter should be motivated by reward, including manumissions, and subject to only lax supervision. This, of course, is exactly what we observe, but the observation also fits with the use of the whip to maintain tight social control over a large, concentrated, and potentially hostile force.

Meeting Slave Subsistence Needs

It would never pay the slaveowner to deny slaves basic subsistence and thus impair their current and future productivity and value, but there's a wide margin between subsistence and living well. Corn and pork constituted the bulk of the slave diet, and there is little question that the energy value of the basic ration described in documented instructions to overseers was adequate to keep slaves going. Fogel and Engerman argue, however, that the corn-pork ration obscures the substantial variety and nutritional balance provided by slave masters—presumably as an incentive to good work.

Using data from the Census of Agriculture, Fogel and Engerman count as slave consumption whatever food production remained on large plantations after subtracting for food consumed by free whites, food sold in local markets, and crops used for other uses, such as next year's seed. The diet that they estimate of eleven foodstuffs, including milk, butter, Irish and sweet potatoes, and beef in addition to the ubiquitous pork and corn, provides 4,185 calories per slave per day (Table 12.6). Foods other than corn and pork provide one third the calories. The average slave diet computed

[13] Fenoaltea (1984).

TABLE 12.6

A Comparison of Slave Diets (pounds per day)

	Least-Cost Diet	Fogel & Engerman Estimate	Sutch Estimate	"Standard Ration"
Pork	—	0.31	0.53	0.50
Beef	—	0.15	0.10	—
Mutton	—	0.01	—	—
Butter	—	0.01	0.01	—
Milk	0.60	0.60	0.41	—
Sweet potatoes	0.25	1.12	0.72	—
Irish potatoes	—	0.08	0.06	—
Cowpeas	0.58	0.35	0.12	—
Corn	1.74	1.78	2.23	2.00
Wheat	—	0.12	0.12	—
Cost per day (cents)	4.4	8.2	8.7	5.2

Source: Charles Kahn, "A Linear Programming Solution to the Slave Diet," in *Without Consent or Contract: Technical Papers Volume II,* ed. Robert W. Fogel et al. (New York: W. W. Norton, 1992): 529, Table 25.3.

was high in protein, iron, calcium, vitamins A and C—high enough in fact to meet modern USDA recommended daily allowances—and was probably supplemented by greens, poultry products, wild game, and fish that are not reported by the census. Slaves worked hard but were fed adequately. Indeed, according to Fogel and Engerman, their diet compared favorably in variety and nutritional value with the diet of contemporary free persons and might even have been superior to the free diet insofar as it included more roughage and green leafy vegetables and less fat.

We do not know whether small plantations, which kept less complete or no records, fed their slaves the same way. The residual technique for calculating the available food supply is sensitive to assumptions about other ways in which food may have been used and the question of spoilage. The results are also sensitive to assumptions about such things as how many hogs there were in the average litter and the weight of a dressed carcass of meat. There is thus considerable uncertainty about exactly what slaves actually ate. Corn and pork were certainly ubiquitous components of the slave diet. Richard Sutch has argued that they formed a far greater proportion of the slave diet than Fogel and Engerman suggested. The diet that Sutch proposes contains 25 percent more corn and 70 percent more pork but much less milk and beef and fewer sweet potatoes and cowpeas. Such a diet actually provides more calories—4,206 calories per day—but at the expense of much of the variety—and nutritional value—in the diet. However, such a diet would place annual per capita meat consumption by slaves, 179 pounds, almost on a par with that consumed by Americans in 1879 (186 pounds) and exceeding that of most other populations. Parisians in 1850, for example, consumed only 159 pounds per year; the British in 1890, only 105 pounds, while the Italians ate only 23 pounds. It seems unlikely that slaves would be fed this much meat because meat is generally thought of as an income elastic good and the amount of meat consumed is sometimes taken as an indicator of living standards. Moreover, research reported in *Without Consent or Contract* indicates that neither the diet proposed by Fogel and Engerman nor that suggested by Sutch was the lowest cost means of supplying 4,000 plus calories per day to slaves but that the Fogel and Engerman diet had a lower cost (not to mention greater variety and nutritional value) than that proposed by Sutch.[14]

A diet high in calories and rich in a variety of nutrients is not, however, necessarily nutritionally adequate. Data on the height by age from a variety of sources, including coastwise shipping manifests (required for identification purposes after the ban on importation in 1808), Union army records, slave appraisals, and the registrations of free blacks in Virginia, offer new perspective on the nutrition and general health of American slaves.[15] Such height data are a good measure of net nutrition—that is, actual diet minus demands upon that diet made by maintenance, physical exertion, and disease. The data (Figure 12.3) show that the average height of adult male slaves was between 66.5 and 67 inches—at least an inch shorter than the stature of white American males at the same time. Since well-fed Americans of African origin achieve approximately the same height as Americans of European origin today, it seems unlikely that this difference reflects genetic traits. The implication is that they were less well fed, over their lifetime, than the free white population. The data also indicate that slaves born between 1790 and 1800 were shorter than those born earlier or later, consistent with findings for the free population in the same periods.[16]

Although they were on average shorter than the average white American of the time, U.S. slaves were tall compared with other populations, especially other slave populations. They were taller, for example, than British laborers and Russian factory workers in the late nineteenth century. Adult male slaves achieved an average height equal to or greater than 27 percent of the modern British population, while adult slave women, averaging 62.5 inches tall, were taller than 28 percent of the modern population. More significantly, American slaves were several inches taller than those employed on Caribbean sugar plantations, whose average height achieved only the third centile against modern populations (Figure 12.4).

[14] Kahn (1992a).
[15] Margo and Steckel (1982).
[16] Steckel (1979); Sokoloff and Villaflor (1982).

FIGURE 12.3

Time Profile of Height of Slave Men Aged 23–49

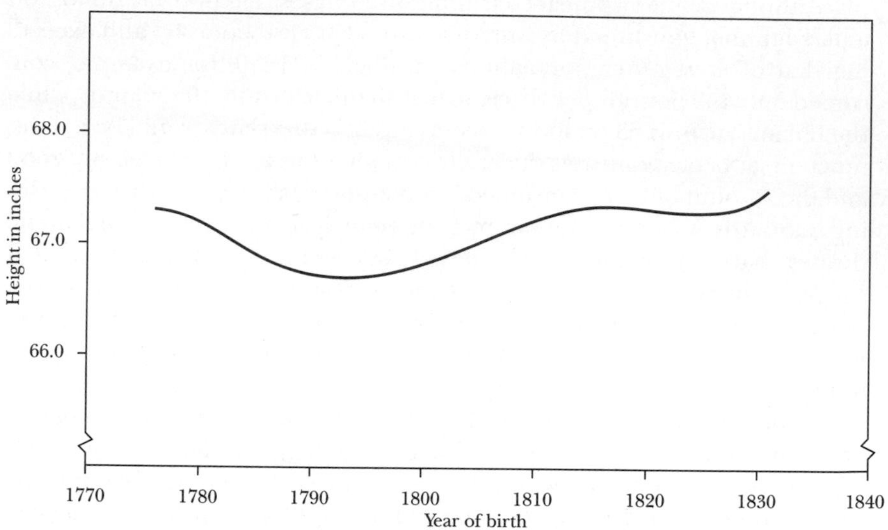

Source: Robert A. Margo and Richard H. Steckel, "The Heights of American Slaves: New Evidence on Slave Nutrition and Health," *Social Science History* 6 (1982): 523.

FIGURE 12.4

Height of Adult Males, Aged 25–45, from Various Populations

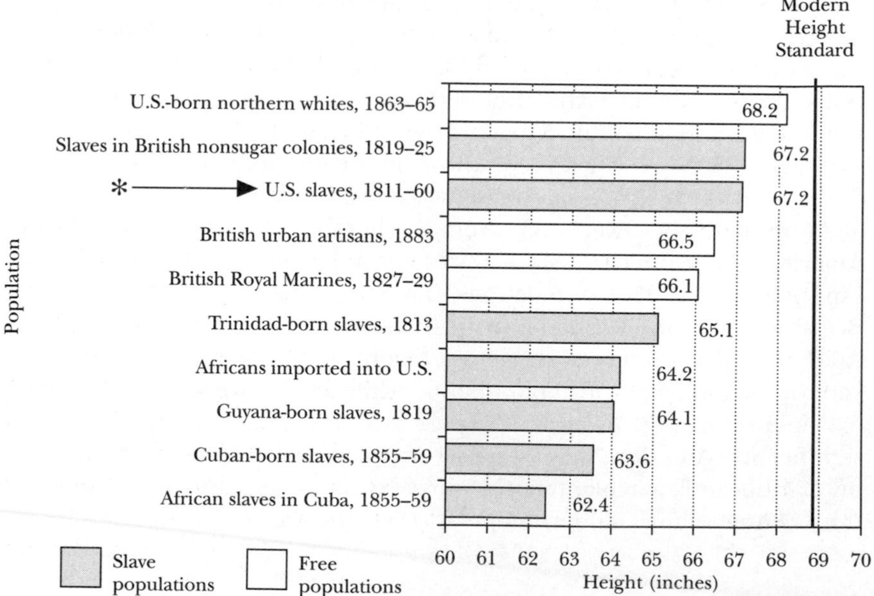

Source: Robert W. Fogel, *Without Consent or Contract: The Rise and Fall of American Slavery* (New York: W. W. Norton, 1989): 141, Figure 24.

Although the American slave heights fell in the range considered normal, Fogel suggests that they are indicative of significant malnutrition during some part of their growing years. Steckel's evidence suggests that slave infants were very small—a point to which we will return—but began to catch up starting at about age seven and particularly in their early to mid-teens. He observes that this catch-up coincided with their participation in the plantation labor force and concludes that once they started to work they were better fed by the slaveowners. Indeed, they were sufficiently well fed while working that they managed to achieve physical maturity earlier than contemporary Europeans, although somewhat later than native-born whites. For example, the average age of menarche among U.S. slave women was probably no more than 14.5—at least two years earlier than for European women in the nineteenth century.

Fogel and Engerman portray the typical slave as housed and clothed in much the same fashion he or she was fed—simply but not badly. Five adults lived in an eighteen- by twenty-foot cabin with one or two rooms, a plank floor, a fireplace, and shuttered windows. This was more space per person than New York's free poor could expect in the late nineteenth century and compares favorably with contemporary descriptions of pioneer accommodations. This conclusion, however, is sensitive to assumptions about occupancy rates and room dimensions.[17] Each individual received four sets of cotton shirts and pants, or dresses, one or two pairs of leather shoes, plus coats and blankets as needed. Not much perhaps, but more than unskilled white urban dwellers had. And in many cases slaves were able to earn money from crops cultivated in small gardens that could be used to supplement the standard clothing issue.

Slave Health and Longevity

Medical care was almost irrelevant to the well-being of antebellum Americans, white or black. Medical knowledge was so primitive that a physician was as likely to hurt as help, and hospitals were merely traps for communicable diseases. General environmental factors—adequate sanitation, clean water, diet—thus largely explained differences in key measures of general health. Here, Fogel and Engerman argue, the record for slaves is reasonably good.

According to their data, only 6 of every 1,000 pregnancies among slave women in 1850 ended in the deaths of the mothers, a figure lower than that of white southern women. However, 183 slave infants out of each 1,000 failed to reach one year of age, as opposed to 146 deaths per 1,000 among white ba-

[17] Sutch, for example, suggests fifteen by fifteen was more common and occupied by six rather than five persons, reducing floor space per person by 50 percent.

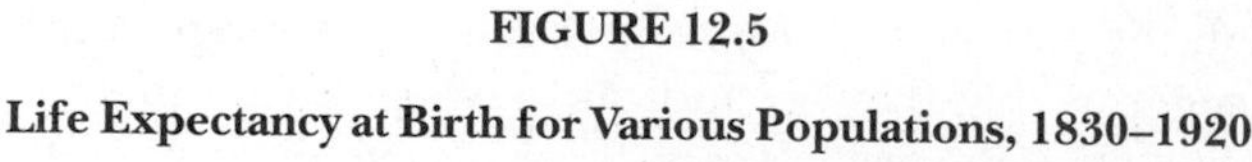

FIGURE 12.5

Life Expectancy at Birth for Various Populations, 1830–1920

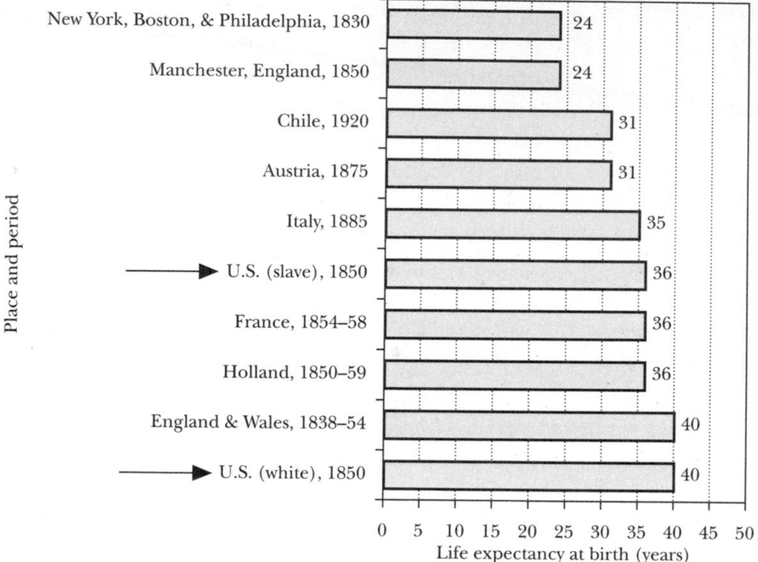

Source: Robert W. Fogel and Stanley L. Engerman, *Time on The Cross: The Economics of American Negro Slavery* (Boston: Little, Brown, 1974): 125, Figure 36.

bies. Moreover, Fogel and Engerman claim slaves had a relatively long life expectancy, thirty-six years, at birth, comparing favorably with life expectancy in many European countries and elsewhere about the same time and much better that urban life expectancy in Britain or the United States (Figure 12.5).

Sutch had criticized Fogel and Engerman for accepting Robert Evans's estimate of slave infant mortality, on the one hand, but arbitrarily rejecting Evans's estimate of white infant mortality (104 per 1,000) in favor of their own much higher calculation (146 per 1,000). There is now serious reason to doubt these figures. Recent work by Richard Steckel, in particular, paints an even more dismal picture of infant mortality and the well-being of slave children than Evans.[18]

Slave children seem to have had a truly dreadful childhood until they entered the work force. On the basis of the coastwise shipping manifest data, Steckel concludes that slave infants were extraordinarily small, even assuming that these infants were "scrunched up" when measured. At age one, Steckel calls them "Lilliputian" by modern standards. Even if we allow for the problems of measuring the length of newborns and infants, by age three,

[18] Steckel (1986a; 1986b; 1986c).

FIGURE 12.6

The Average Height of Male Slaves in the U.S. and Trinidad Compared with Modern Height Standards

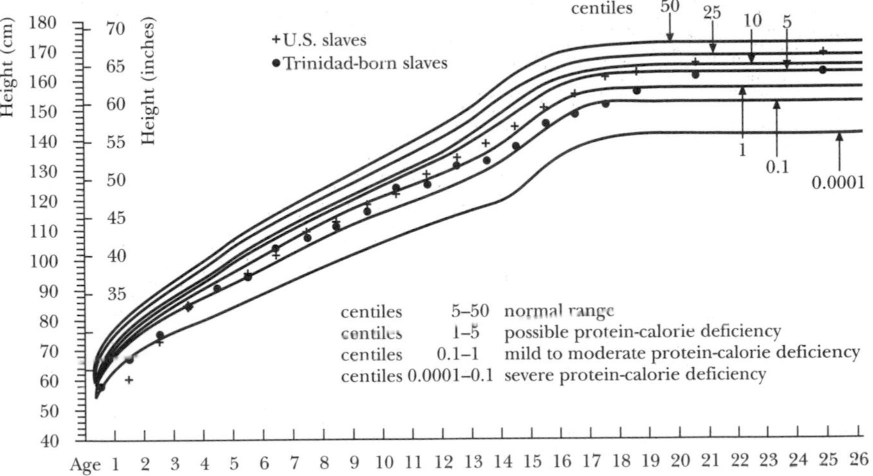

Source: Robert W. Fogel, *Without Consent or Contract: The Rise and Fall of American Slavery* (New York: W. W. Norton, 1989): 143, Figure 25.

when they could be measured standing, males achieved only the 0.2 centile (that is to say, 99.8 percent of three-year-old male children in Britain today are taller), while females fared even worse at the 0.1 centile. This is much worse than slum dwellers in Lagos, Nigeria, or the children of urban Bangladeshis today. At ages three to six slave children were on average 4.5 to 5.8 inches below modern height standards (Figure 12.6).

Using these height data, Steckel (1986a) has estimated that the average slave at birth weighed only 5.1 pounds (2,320 grams), placing slave newborns among the smallest documented for poor populations in developing countries today. Since birth weight is correlated with neonatal mortality rates (probability of dying within the first month after birth), Steckel estimates that neonatal mortality among slave infants averaged about 152 per 1,000 live births—more than 80 percent of the mortality rate for the entire first year of life used by Fogel and Engerman. Indeed, Steckel's estimate of infant mortality (1986b) is 350 per 1,000—more than double the rate among white children. Moreover, the mortality rate among slave children, ages one to four, remained much higher, 201 per 1,000, than for the entire United States—93 per 1,000. The mortality rate declines sharply for five- to nine-year-olds to 54 per 1,000 but remains above that for the entire population until adulthood (Table 12.7).

Why were birth weights so low and infant mortality so high? Slaveowners

TABLE 12.7

Mortality Rates per Thousand for Slaves and the Antebellum Population

Age	Slaves	Entire United States
0	350	179
1–4	201	93
5–9	54	28
10–14	37	19
15–19	35	28
20–24	40	39

Source: Richard H. Steckel, "Dimensions and Determinants of Early Childhood Health and Mortality among American Slaves," *Social Science History* 10 (1986): 428.

often blamed careless and neglectful mothers for infant deaths, but low birth weights point instead to prenatal conditions as the likely explanation for this appalling mortality. Of the possible explanations—maternal malnutrition, specific maternal dietary deficiencies, maternal and fetal infections, ingestion of such toxic substances as alcohol and tobacco, small maternal stature, and the work regimen during pregnancy—Steckel concludes that the most likely explanation was the work demand placed upon slave women during pregnancy. The typical slave workweek was fifty-four hours of usually intense physical labor, particularly during planting and harvesting, requiring that the woman be on her feet continually and often bent over, a position that was harmful for fetal development. As late as the last month before delivery, slave women picked at least 76 percent as much cotton as nonpregnant women and within one week of delivery were still averaging 36 percent of a normal work load. Slave children thus were born to physically exhausted mothers and entered the world in poor condition, less able to survive the rigors and dangers of life.

Nor did their lives improve much before age seven or so. The effects of fetal deprivation persisted during early childhood through sudden infant death syndrome. Low-birth-weight infants were at greater risk from the ill effects of poor nutrition and disease. Steckel argues that slave mothers were given little time to bond with and care for their children. Instead they were expected back in the fields within days or weeks of birthing. As a result, the care and feeding of their children were abandoned to others. Slave infants moved swiftly from breast milk to solids or concocted formulas. This diet often lacked sufficient protein and essential vitamins and minerals. Formula, in particular, was probably prepared from contaminated products under unsanitary conditions, adding the stress of disease and infection to the effects of malnutrition.

One major reason for the protein deficiency was the widespread exclusion of meat from slave children's diets. Steckel speculates that this was because slaveowners had found through trial and error that feeding meat to children was unprofitable. As he puts it, "Feeding meat to slave children can be considered as an investment. The net income was negative during the early years of the investment period because meat was costly and children did not work." Indeed, Steckel calculates that the return from feeding meat to children was –1.7 percent. Since malnourished children are more apathetic, less aggressive, and more dependent, slaveowners may have found this strategy beneficial by reducing planter supervision costs for slave children. The strategy is also consistent with the hypothesis that planters had little interest in the mental development of slaves—most likely to suffer permanent damage from malnutrition—but more interest in their physical development, which is only temporarily affected by malnutrition.

Slavery and the Family

Their experiences under slavery have been blamed for many of the ills that beset African-American families today, such as absent fathers and children having children. Under ordinary circumstances families are vulnerable to involuntary separation created by death, military conscription, and so on, but slave families were faced with an additional threat: separation through sale. Furthermore, with capitalized rents on slaves so high, slaveowners certainly had a economic interest in the fecundity of their slaves.

It has long been assumed that the great westward movement of the cotton economy meant the separation of a high percentage of slave families living in less productive parts of the South. Fogel and Engerman, however, argue that the family was a valuable tool exploited by owners in maintaining the productivity and fertility of slaves. The family hierarchy could be used to discipline the young and to ensure fair distribution of food and clothing, although Steckel's work implies that it did little to protect the interests of the very young. Kinship ties, moreover, helped ensure proper care for the young, sick, and old and discouraged runaways. Thus planters had economic incentives to encourage marriage (even where prohibited by the state), discourage adultery, and avoid relocation that would separate husbands from wives or parents from children.

According to estimates by Fogel and Engerman, 84 percent of slaves who moved west moved with their owners. Extrapolating data from Maryland, Fogel and Engerman estimate that the total slave sales (inter- and intrastate) averaged only 1.92 percent of the slave population per year. Further, data from the New Orleans slave market suggest that only 13 percent of sales resulted in the separation of mates. If so, then just 2 percent of slave marriages $(0.13 \cdot [1.0-0.84])$ were destroyed by the westward push of slavery. These estimates, however, are almost certainly too low. Recent work by Michael Tadman suggests that between 60 and 70 percent of the interregional movement of slaves took place through slave traders as opposed to planter migration. Moreover, whatever incentives that the planters may have had in preserving family units were almost certainly not shared equally by the traders. As a result, the trade resulted in the breakup of perhaps one-fifth of the marriages and the separation of one-third of the children from their parents in the Upper South.[19] But even if the yearly risk of forced migration was relatively low, an annual sale rate of 1.92 percent implies that over a thirty-five-year lifetime, the average slave would have faced a 49.3 percent chance of being sold and a slave with sixteen close relatives (two parents, six siblings, seven children, one spouse) could expect to live to see eleven of them sold.[20] Nonetheless, analysis of the ex-slave narratives collected as part of the Federal Writers Project of the Works Progress Administration in the New Deal reveals that almost two-thirds had lived in nuclear families as slaves.

Slaveowners who stood to earn hundreds, and perhaps thousands, of dollars in capitalized rent from producing new slaves had an incentive to encourage early sexual activity by slave women as a means of maximizing the number of children they bore. However, Fogel and Engerman estimate that the potential return to the slaveowner from such additional children was small while the potential costs from a breakdown in the morale and discipline engendered by tight family structures was high. Consequently, they believe that owners may have discouraged sexual activity among young unmarried slaves. As one might expect, information on something as personal as the extent of sexual activity is largely conjectural, though one product of sexual activity—children—is more readily observed. The data indicate that slave women were on average 20.6 years old at the birth of their first child. This is older than one would have expected among a sexually active population, especially one in which such activity was being encouraged, if we assume that female slaves reached sexual maturity somewhere between ages 13 and 15, as is consistent with data on the pubescent growth spurt. If this indeed had been the case, one might have expected the mean age of first childbearing to be about age 16½ or 17.[21] Still, slave women bore children much earlier than white farm women, who were usually 23 to 25 years old when they bore their first children. Despite the later than expected start to childbearing, high rates of growth for the slave population in the face of these very high infant mortality rates means that new pregnancies must have quickly followed stillbirths and neonatal deaths, while the abbreviated pe-

[19] These figures would imply that 12 percent (= 60% × 20%) or more of slave marriages were broken up by the interregional slave trade; a rate six times greater than that suggested by Fogel and Engerman.

[20] Sutch (1975); Gutman (1975).

[21] Trussell and Steckel (1978).

riod of breast feeding increased the likelihood of pregnancy among those mothers whose infants survived.

The Status of Research on American Slavery

Is it now possible to draw conclusions about the physical or material condition of African-Americans in bondage? Not really. Fogel and Engerman have effectively challenged a priori convictions that because owners had the legal right to brutalize their slaves, they also had the incentive to do so or, in fact, did so. If most slaveowners treated their chattels as they treated other earning assets—an assumption that has not been proved or disproved—it follows that consideration would be given to constructing positive incentives for hard work and obedience. Thus purely economic considerations should have protected slaves from a short, brutish existence. At some margin, however, it probably paid to encourage sexual promiscuity and to sell slaves at will though each owner had to balance the potential financial gain against the potential cost in terms of lost family cohesiveness and general loss of morale. Certainly, there was no uniformity in the treatment of slaves, in either the United States or the rest of the world. Slaves in America may have fared better than those any place else, but that is no justification for American slavery. Moreover there is abundant, if scattered, evidence supporting almost any interpretation of slavery that provided ample material for different interpretations of slavery from that offered by Fogel and Engerman in *Time on the Cross,* ones sometimes more in accord with the conventional wisdom.

Some issues remain unresolved. The debate over the relative efficiency of slave versus free agriculture, for example, still has some play. So, too, do the peculiar demographics of the slave South. Americans, however, have been reluctant to admit that slavery may have had a rational economic basis, reluctant to accept that the Civil War ultimately was about slavery, reluctant to admit that by some measures African-Americans may have been better off under slavery than they were when freed but penalized and ostracized by racism both overt and covert, reluctant to relinquish cherished myths. *Time on the Cross* was not a defense of the slave system, only an attempt to understand and to measure how it worked (as the new afterword in the recently reprinted edition makes clear). The recent publication of *Without Consent or Contract* and its supporting volumes, however, has renewed the challenge to traditional beliefs. *Time on the Cross* may have portrayed the institution of slavery as benign, even benevolent. But the scientific method demanded that the authors put aside their sense of moral outrage. Such concerns, however, now receive full treatment in *Without Consent or Contract.* Moreover, to the extent that a society can be judged by how well—or badly—it treats its poorest and weakest members, the recent research on the care and feeding of slave children, which is reprinted in *Without Consent or Contract,* should dispel any misperception of benevolence in the slave system forever.

Perhaps the greatest contribution of the controversy begun by *Time on the Cross* is the subtle shift away from slavery itself as the sole explanation for the situation in which African-Americans find themselves today. It is surely much more convenient to blame the deep social and economic divisions between blacks and whites on a bunch of morally degenerate and long-dead slave owners than to deal with modern racism.

Bibliography

Battalio, Raymond, and John Kagel. "The Structure of Antebellum Southern Agriculture: South Carolina, A Case Study." *Agricultural History* 44 (1970): 25–38.

Butlin, Noel. *Antebellum Slavery.* Canberra: Australian National University Press, 1971.

Canarella, Giorgio, and John Tomaske. "The Optimal Utilization of Slaves." *Journal of Economic History* 35 (1975): 621–29.

Conrad, Alfred, and John Meyer. "The Economics of Slavery in the Antebellum South." *Journal of Political Economy* 66 (1958): 95–130.

Crawford, Stephen C. "Punishments and Rewards." In *Without Consent or Contract: Technical Papers, Volume II,* ed. Robert W. Fogel and Stanley L. Engerman. New York: W. W. Norton, 1992: 536–50.

David, Paul, and Peter Temin. "Slavery: The Progressive Institution." *Journal of Economic History* 34 (1974): 739–83.

David, Paul, Herbert Gutman, Richard Sutch, and Gavin Wright. *Reckoning with Slavery.* New York: Oxford University Press, 1976.

DeCanio, Stephen, and Joel Mokyr. "Inflation and Wage Lag during the American Civil War." *Explorations in Economic History* 14 (June 1977): 311–36.

Evans, Robert, Jr., "The Economics of American Negro Slavery." In National Bureau for Economic Research. *Aspects of Labor Economics.* Princeton: Princeton University Press, 1962.

Fenoaltea, Stefano. "Slavery and Supervision in Comparative Perspective: A Model." *Journal of Economic History* 44 (1984): 635–68.

———. "The Slavery Debate: A Note from the Sidelines." *Explorations in Economic History* 18 (1981): 304–08.

Fogel, Robert W. et. al. *Without Consent or Contract: The Rise and Fall of American Slavery,* vol. 1. New York: W. W. Norton, 1989.

———. *Without Consent or Contract: Evidence and Methods,* vol. 2. New York: W. W. Norton, 1992.

———. *Without Consent or Contract: Technical Papers Volume I,* vol. 3. New York: W. W. Norton, 1992.

———. *Without Consent or Contract: Technical Papers Volume II,* vol. 4. New York: W. W. Norton, 1992.

———, and Stanley Engerman. "The Economics of Slavery." In *The Reinterpretation of American Economic History.* New York: Harper & Row, 1971: 311–41.

———. *Time on the Cross: The Economics of American Negro Slavery.* Boston: Little, Brown, 1974.

———. *Time on the Cross II: Evidence and Methods.* Boston: Little, Brown, 1974.

Genovese, Eugene. *The Political Economy of Slavery.* New York: Vintage Press, 1967.
———. *Roll Jordan Roll: The World the Slaves Made.* New York: Pantheon, 1974.
Greenwald, Bruce, and Robert Glasspiegel. "Adverse Selection in the Market for Slaves: New Orleans, 1830–1860." *Quarterly Journal of Economics* 98 (1983): 479–99.
Gutman, Herbert. "The World Two Cliometricians Made: A Review Essay." *Journal of Negro History* 60 (1975): 53–227.
———. *The Black Family in Slavery and Freedom.* New York: Pantheon Books, 1976.
Kahn, Charles. "A Linear Programming Solution to the Slave Diet." *Without Consent or Contract: Technical Papers Volume II,* ed. Robert W. Fogel et. al. No. 25 (1992a).
———"An Agency Theory Approach to Slave Punishments and Rewards." *Without Consent or Contract: Technical Papers Volume II,* ed. Robert W. Fogel et. al., No. 27 (1992b).
Margo, Robert, and Richard Steckel. "Height, Health, and Nutrition: Analysis of Evidence for U.S. Slaves." *Social Science History* 6 (1982): pp. 516–38.
Olmsted, Frederick L. *The Cotton Kingdom: A Traveler's Observations on Cotton and Slavery in the American Slave States,* ed. A. M. Schlesinger. New York: Knopf, 1953; first published 1861.
———. *The Slave States.* New York: Capricorn Books, 1959.
Phillips, Ulrich B., "The Economic Cost of Slaveholding in the Cotton Belt." *Political Science Quarterly* 20 (1905): 257–75.
Pritchett, Jonathan B., and Richard Chamberlain. "Selection in the Market for Slaves: New Orleans, 1830–1860," *Quarterly Journal of Economics* (forthcoming, 1993).
Ramsdell, Charles. "The Natural Limits of Slavery Expansion." *Mississippi Valley Historical Review* 16 (1929): 151–71.
Ransom, Roger L. *Conflict and Compromise: The Political Economy of Slavery, Emancipation, and the American Civil War.* New York: Cambridge University Press, 1989.
———, and Richard Sutch. "Capitalists without Capital: The Burden of Slavery and the Impact of Emancipation." *Agricultural History* 62 (1988): 133–60.
———. *One Kind of Freedom: The Economic Consequences of Emancipation.* New York: Cambridge University Press, 1977.
Saraydar, Edward. "A Note of the Profitability of Antebellum Slavery." *Southern Economic Journal* 30 (1964): 325–32.
Sokoloff, Kenneth, and Georgia Villaflor. "The Early Achievement of Modern Stature in America." *Social Science History* 6 (1982): 453–81.
Stampp, Kenneth. *The Peculiar Institution.* New York: Knopf, 1956.
Steckel, Richard H., *The Economics of U.S. Slave and Southern White Fertility.* New York: Arno Press, 1977.
———. "Slave Height Profiles from Coastwise Manifests." *Explorations in Economic History* 16 (1979): 363–80.
———. "Birth Weights and Infant Mortality Among American Slaves." *Exploration in Economic History* 23 (1986a): 173–98.
———. "Dimensions and Determinants of Early Childhood Health and Mortality among American Slaves." *Social Science History* 10 (1986b): 427–65.
———. "A Peculiar Population: The Nutrition, Health, and Mortality of American Slaves from Childhood to Maturity." *Journal of Economic History* 46 (1986c): 721–42.
Sutch, Richard. "The Profitability of Antebellum Slavery Revisited." *Southern Economic Journal* 31 (1965): 365–77.
———. "The Treatment Received by American Slaves." *Explorations in Economic History* 12 (1975): 335–438.

Sydnor, Charles. *Slavery in Mississippi.* New York: Appleton-Century, 1933.

Tadman, Michael. *Speculators and Slaves: Masters, Traders and Slaves in the Old South.* Madison: University of Wisconsin Press, 1989.

Trussell, James, and Richard H. Steckel, "The Age of Slaves at Menarche and Their First Birth." *Journal of Interdisciplinary History* 8 (1978): 477–505. Reprinted in *Without Consent or Contract, Technical Papers Volume II,* ed. Robert W. Fogel et al., No. 20: 435–54.

Vedder, Richard K. "The Slave Exploitation (Expropriation) Rate." *Explorations in Economic History* 12 (1975): 453–58.

Wright Gavin. "New and Old Views on the Economics of Slavery." *Journal of Economic History* 33 (1973): 452–66.

———. "The Efficiency of Slavery: Another Interpretation," *American Economic Review* 69 (1979): 219–26.

———. *The Political Economy of the Cotton South.* New York: W. W. Norton, 1978.

———. "Slavery and the Cotton Boom." *Explorations in Economic History* 12 (1975): 436–51.

Yasuba, Yasukichi. "The Profitability and Viability of Plantation Slavery in the United States." In *The Reinterpretation of American Economic History,* ed. Robert Fogel and Stanley Engerman. New York: Harper & Row, 1971: 362–68.

The economics of the civil war

13

The Civil War was the greatest catastrophe that the United States has ever experienced. For four long years the war dominated the fortunes of Americans as no other armed conflict in our history has. More than six hundred thousand died, and five hundred thousand were wounded—a casualty rate four times the casualty rate for the U.S. armed forces in World War II. The scars from this conflict run deep. Even five generations later many still count it important whether their ancestors wore the blue or the gray; the Confederate flag adorns license plates and state flags; regional hostilities persist. What drove the North and South to such a bloody and costly misadventure?

In the late antebellum years the economies of the North and South were remarkably different. In the North an eastern industrial sector powered by immigrant labor and a western area of family farms were becoming increasingly dependent on each other for markets. The South, on the other hand, was culturally independent of the North and economically oriented more toward Europe, both as a place to sell cotton and as a place to buy manufactures. It would seem that economics provided little for the North and South to fight about, but neither did it give them much reason to cooperate as a nation.

The trouble with this argument is that despite differing cultural orientations, the North was in fact economically dependent on the Cotton South. It even had a stake in the continuation of slavery. While the free farmers of the western territories might fear direct competition from slave labor, northern labor and capital more generally had something to gain and very little to lose from the expansion of the cotton economy and the enslavement of blacks. The bigger the cotton economy, the larger the output of cotton—and the lower the price of the raw material for northern textile mills and the better the terms of trade received by northern sellers of manufactures. The institution of slavery independently contributed to northern living standards by breaking the labor supply constraint on family cotton farming, thereby lowering the competitive market price of raw cotton. A possibly larger—and certainly a more visible—gain to the North from slavery was the reduced competition over industrial jobs and markets resulting from the South's failure to develop a substantial manufacturing sector. Northern labor also had a stake in the continuation of slavery for the very reason that free farmers wanted to keep slaves out of the West: Slavery was an impenetrable barrier for blacks who might otherwise have migrated north to the cities and competed for jobs. While it is unlikely that emancipation would have created chronic white unemployment in the relatively competitive, rapidly growing economy of the antebellum North, it is likely that it would have meant lower competitive wages and living standards for white workers.

The Civil War was thus probably not in the best economic interest of northerners although, as Robert Fogel has documented, abolitionist sentiment gradually gathered steam. What of the South? We have already discussed two important sources of conflict—the tariff and whether newly settled lands would be slave or free. Perhaps more important, though, changes in the national economy posed an increasing threat to southern property rights regarding slaves.

Property Rights and the War

Much of the wealth of the South was tied to slave property rights. Claudia Goldin estimates the capital value of slaves (a measure of their expected future net revenues) in 1860 at $2.7 billion—almost three times as much as invested in all manufacturing activities in America at the time. Others have made even higher estimates. Emancipation without compensation would have deprived slaveowners of these expected future net income streams, reducing white per capita income in eleven cotton states by as much as 23 percent (see Table 13.1). Thus, while abolitionist agitators might not have represented a serious threat to the South in 1860, they sharpened southerners' fears about the long-term security of their property rights. Southerners could see a day when Congress would be dominated by the representatives of family farmers and urbanites whose attachment to slavery was weak and whose votes were potentially available to the abolitionists. Although northern industrialists and the urban working class had a stake in perpetuating slavery, this hardly offered slaveowners the sort of security and legal protection they craved. Indeed, a rising tide of antislavery ideology was taking hold. It threatened the day-to-day value of southern property even if the South had no good reason to believe that it would ever be confiscated by Congress. Why take a chance on the North's common sense and goodwill when secession offered a permanent solution to the problem?

TABLE 13.1

Potential Income Loss to White Southerners from Abolition in 1860

State	Per Capita Income (all persons)	Per Capita Income (free persons)	% Population Enslaved	% Potential Income Loss of Whites Postabolition
Alabama	75	120	45	42
South Carolina	80	159	57	36
Florida	89	143	44	34
Georgia	84	136	44	29
Mississippi	125	253	55	29
Louisiana	131	229	47	24
Texas	100	134	30	24
North Carolina	79	108	33	19
Tennessee	75	93	25	18
Arkansas	95	121	26	17
Virginia	88	120	32	17
Total	91	135	38	23

Source: Gerald Gunderson, "The Origin of the American Civil War," *Journal of Economic History* 34 (1974): 922. Reprinted by permission of Cambridge University Press.

With the value of a slave tied to expectations of future revenues from slave services, abolition was not necessary for slaves to be rendered less valuable to their owners. During the 1840–60 period all those who owned slaves of working age or below should have earned huge capital gains on their property because the average price of an eighteen-year-old male slave rose by 115 percent between 1841–45 and 1856–60. But future increases in value—or even the maintenance of current value—depended upon continued buoyant expectations about both the price of cotton and the security of investments in slave property.

This link to expectations explains the extreme—almost paranoid—reaction of slaveowners to the menace of abolition, their escalating demands for reassurance from the North, their intolerance for dissent on slavery-related issues within the South, and—finally—their decision to risk all in secession.[1]

Rational slaveowners knew that it would be expensive to grow cotton in the deserts of the Southwest and that the number of slaves who managed to escape to the North would be trivial, but they did not know how others might react to symbolic changes in the legal status of slavery. Consequently, it made sense to press for the expansion of slavery to the territories and for the vigorous enforcement of the fugitive slave statutes. Moreover, some south-

[1] Fogel (1989); Wright (1978).

erners actively participated in a movement to permit international trafficking in slaves. In part, they saw it as a gesture, a direct challenge to the charge that slavery was immoral. In part, too, slave importation was seen as a way to protect the political power of the South: More slaves would mean greater representation in the House—each slave counted as three-fifths of a person in apportioning representation—and more rapid westward expansion. But when the issue was actually voted upon, slaveowners rationally perceived that their primary interest lay in the value of existing slave property. Additional slaves, they understood, would undoubtedly lower the market price of slaves, and no southern state voted to reopen the slave trade. Indeed, the Confederate Constitution of 1861 left to Congress the right to prohibit the entry of slaves into the Confederacy from slave states that remained in the Union. This may have been only a bluff designed to press wavering border states into joining the secession, but it should not be dismissed as evidence of southerner rationality about slave property values.

The Economics of Emancipation

Emancipation of slaves in the American South was never discussed as a practical issue before the Civil War. Southern slaveowners had no desire to free their chattels, with or without compensation, and northern politicians didn't have much motive for tackling the issue. When war came, Congress appropriated funds to compensate slaveowners in the District of Columbia and the border states that had stayed loyal to the Union. However, neither Lincoln's 1863 executive order abolishing slavery in enemy territory—the Emancipation Proclamation—nor the Thirteenth Amendment (1865), outlawing slavery in the nation, provided compensation.

As with stolen goods, if no ownership right to property exists, then no compensation for taking is due. This was not the way most property-owning citizens looked at the emancipation question in the nineteenth century. Other countries that had abolished slavery generally accepted the principle that society as a whole should bear the burden of the loss. In the North Vermont's constitution (1777) expressly prohibited slavery. Courts in New Hampshire and Massachusetts (1783) ruled that state constitutional declarations that "all men are born free and equal" effectively banned slavery. The other northern states (Pennsylvania, Connecticut, Rhode Island, New York, and New Jersey), however, adopted proposals for the gradual emancipation of slaves by requiring manumission of the next generation of slaves on reaching their twenty-eighth birthday. According to estimates by Fogel and Engerman (see Figure 12.1), the cumulative net present value of such a slave was approximately zero with the result that slavery disappeared rather more quickly. It is thus both interesting and relevant to ask how slavery might have been abolished in the South without a war.

One option would have been for all slaves to be purchased by the federal government at market prices and then freed. Claudia Goldin estimates the total cost would have been $2.7 billion in 1860—almost two-thirds of the country's GNP of $4.2 billion (Table 13.2). Such a purchase could be financed only by long-term borrowing, and an annual tax of $7.25 per person (excluding former slaves) would have been needed to meet the interest and principal payments on thirty-year 6 percent bonds issued for this purpose. Slaveowners might have been willing to accept such bonds in exchange for their slaves even though the current rate of return on slaves was higher, recognizing that the return on the bonds was less risky. The tax to amortize this loan would have amounted to about 5 percent of national income at the beginning of the period and much less by the time the bonds were discharged in 1890. Moreover, if Congress had offered to emancipate the slaves in 1850 rather than 1860, taxpayers could have avoided the cost of the enormous capital gains earned on slaves during that decade. The cost in 1850 would have been only $1.3 billion, fundable over thirty years at a bargain rate of only $4.80 per person per year.

One objection to this proposal is that it would have required slaveowners to share in the tax burden of the loan amortization. Had southerners as a group, as well as former slaves, been forgiven the tax obligation, the annual per capita cost in 1860 would have gone up to $9.66, or about 7 percent of GNP the first year.

The market price of slaves, however, does not necessarily represent the entire burden of emancipation to white Americans. Once freed, the African-Americans represented an enormous potential problem for a racist society loath to integrate. Many who favored emancipation also believed in repatriation to Africa. Had Congress allocated $100 per ex-slave in resettlement

TABLE 13.2

The Cost of Emancipation in 1860

Plan	Total Cost (million $)	Annual Per Capita Cost: All Free Persons	Northerners	All Persons
Immediate emancipation	2,700	7.25	9.66	6.30
Immediate emancipation + resettlement in Africa	3,084	8.00	10.70	6.90
Emancipation in next generation	210	.56	.75	.49
Abolition in 30 years	550	1.50	2.00	1.30

Source: Claudia Goldin, "The Economics of Emancipation," *Journal of Economic History* 33 (1973): 85. Reprinted by permission of Cambridge University Press.

costs—a figure well below the actual cost of voluntary resettlements earlier in the century to Liberia—the total cost of emancipation in 1860 would have topped $3 billion, or $10.70 annually per northerner.

An alternative—gradual emancipation such as that adopted in Pennsylvania, New York, or New Jersey—would have eliminated slavery in a generation and a half at relatively little cost to owners and no cost to taxpayers. By requiring some years of obligation from the next generation, these states avoided the slaveowners' incentives to abandon slave infants, yet they chose emancipation ages remarkably close to the break-even point, where discounted slave earnings could just compensate for rearing costs. Such a plan, however, still had problems. Slaveowners would still have paid a small price under this scheme because of the loss of that portion of female slave value attributable to potential gains from reproduction. Moreover, it consigned all current slaves to life sentences and encouraged owners to work young slaves more intensively since their continuing productivity after emancipation was a matter of no economic interest to the profit-maximizing owner.

Goldin has computed the cost of two alternative gradual emancipation plans for the South. If only the children of slaves had been freed at the age when they would have fully returned their rearing costs, then the total cost to slaveowners (or the taxpayers) would have been based upon the value of female reproduction. This portion of property rights in female slaves was worth about $210 million in 1860. A more liberal emancipation plan would have freed all present slaves in 1890. This would have had a present value cost of $340 million in 1860 and freeing their children when they had returned rearing costs would have added $210 million to this bill, for a total of $550 million.

The Cost of the War

Wars cause injury, death, and destruction. They also divert resources from nonmilitary uses, where they satisfy various wants, to military uses, where they meet the needs of the moment. Such losses occurred on both sides of the Mason-Dixon line in the Civil War. If slavery was its sole cause, then this war was indeed a most expensive and inefficient solution as estimates of the costs by Claudia Goldin and Frank Lewis show (Table 13.3).

The value of resources diverted to military use are easily measured by government expenditures on war equipment and supplies plus wages and bonuses to those in uniform. These, however, overstate the diversion of resources since a standing army was normally maintained for national defense. Consequently, Goldin and Lewis subtract the estimated cost of the peacetime military. At the same time, though, the government expenditures also understate the true cost of the resources that they diverted. Both armies failed to attract adequate numbers of volunteers, so the respective govern-

TABLE 13.3

Direct Costs of the Civil War (in millions of 1860 dollars, discounted at 6 percent back to June 1861)

	North	South
Government expenditures	2,291	1,011
Undercounted labor costs associated with draft	11	20
Destruction of physical capital	—	1,487
Human capital lost		
Killed	955	684
Wounded	365	261
Less the "risk premium" component of soldier's pay	−256	−178
	3,366	3,286

Source: Claudia Goldin and Frank Lewis, "The Economic Cost of the American Civil War: Estimates and Implications," *Journal of Economic History* 35 (1975): 304-09. Reprinted by permission of Cambridge University Press.

ments resorted to the draft to coerce labor at less than it would have cost to attract volunteers. Normally we have no way of knowing what it would have taken to hire a volunteer wartime army, but in the 1860s those who were drafted could buy substitutes—if, of course, each had $150, which was the typical payment. One result of this policy was the substitution of rural soldiers for urban draftees, which aggravated the growing labor scarcity in American agriculture, hastening mechanization, notably the adoption of the reaper (see Chapter 10).

Goldin and Lewis attribute no losses of physical capital to the North because there are no data on losses from events such as Morgan's raid on southern Indiana and Ohio or even General Robert E. Lee's march to Gettysburg. Most of the capital losses, though, were suffered in the South, where most of the fighting took place. The Union army deliberately pursued a policy of destroying the Confederacy's economic capacity to sustain its military by exploiting the data collected in the census of manufactures and agriculture for 1860. This represents possibly the first strategic military use of economic data. A Senate report estimated these southern war losses in property (exclusive of slave property) at $1.1 billion.[2] This figure includes changes in property values related to lowered expectations of future earnings as well as physical damage. It thus overstates the extent of physical war-related losses.

In addition to the destruction of physical capital, more than a million people died or were wounded in the conflict. This, too, represents significant economic loss. The courts today have relatively little trouble placing a

[2] Sellers (1927).

value on life and limb. A life, for example, can be valued at the discounted present value of expected future income over the individual's anticipated working life; the cost of a handicap can be valued by the reduction in earnings and life expectancy. Within these general principles, however, there is considerable room for disagreement over what future income might be expected, and over what period, and over what the appropriate discount rate should be, with account taken of expected inflation and the "normal" return on assets. Such valuations overstate the economic impact of loss upon the survivors since much of the lost lifetime wages would have been spent on the individual's own consumption. On the other hand, they cannot capture the loss in human welfare although the courts try to establish a value for emotional costs such as "pain and suffering" or "loss of companionship." These caveats notwithstanding, Goldin and Lewis put the human capital losses at almost $2.3 million (of which about $1.3 million was lost by the North), a sum far greater than any estimate of the physical capital losses from the war.

Goldin and Lewis make one final correction to their estimate of the costs of the war to the North and South: They subtract "risk premiums" on soldiers' wages on the ground that if we assume the markets were efficient, then a portion of the military pay (or the fee paid to a substitute) compensated soldiers in advance for the risk of death or injury. Without this adjustment, the same cost is counted twice, once as special combat wages and again in the lost lifetime earnings for the unlucky six hundred thousand who died. Goldin and Lewis assume that the entire difference between civilian and military wages consisted of this risk pay and thus must be subtracted from the actual human capital loss.

Note that, by this logic, soldiers in both armies settled for premium pay equal to less than one-fifth their lost wages; members of the Union army, for example, took only $256 million in compensation for $1,320 million ($955 million + $365 million = value of northern human capital losses discounted back to 1861) in lost future wages. One possible explanation for this is that they systematically underestimated the risks—a common error of those in hazardous occupations. Or perhaps the difference between the actual human capital loss and the required risk premium paid reflected unmeasured nonmaterial benefits the soldiers received in fighting for their cause(s).

Goldin and Lewis's final aggregate estimate of the cost of the war, $6.6 billion, amounts to $206 for every American in 1861—almost twice the average annual per capita consumption before the war. This same amount invested in productive resources at a safe 6 percent return could have provided each of the thirty-two million then-living Americans with an annual bonus of about 10 percent of 1860 consumption expenditures forever.

If this does not impress, consider the following scenario: The amount of $6.6 billion would have been enough to buy the freedom of all the slaves (at 1860 market value), to give each slave family a forty-acre farm and a mule, and still have left $3.5 billion for reparations payments to the ex-slaves in lieu of one hundred years of back wages. The South's losses alone ($3.3 billion) would have been sufficient to cover compensated emancipation, land, and even the mules. Unfortunately no one was sufficiently prescient in 1860 to understand how expensive the war would really be.

The Civil War as a Turning Point in American Development

To historians Charles and Mary Beard and, later, to Louis Hacker, the Civil War was a watershed. By destroying not only slavery but also the slaveocracy, the war shifted the balance of political power to northern industrialists and spurred American industrialization. Never again would those who pursued profit through industrial capital be thwarted by traditional agrarian attitudes. The argument is appealing. Unfortunately it is very difficult to identify the Civil War as the turning point in economic growth or industrialization from the historical data.

The rate of growth in commodity output in the twenty years before the war (4.6 percent average annual rate) was just as rapid as it was in the thirty years following (1870–1900 average annual growth rate = 4.4 percent). More important for the thesis of the Beards and Hacker, though, while value added in manufacturing grew at an average rate of 7.8 percent from 1840 to 1860, it grew at only 6 percent from 1870 to 1900 (Table 13.4).[3] These aggregate statistics, however, might be somewhat misleading, since with a slowdown in population growth, per capita output grew at an annual rate of 2.1

TABLE 13.4

Average Annual Rate of Growth of Commodity Output

Year	U.S. Economy	Manufacturing Sector
1840–59	4.6	7.8
1860–69	2.0	2.3
1870–99	4.4	6.0

Interpretation: Manufacturing growth was as rapid from 1840 to 1859 as it was from 1870 to 1899.

Source: Robert Gallman, "Commodity Output 1839–99," in National Bureau of Economic Research, *Trends in the American Economy in the 19th Century*, vol. 24, Series on Income and Wealth (Princeton: Princeton University Press, 1960).

[3] Gallman (1960).

percent from 1870 to 1900, as opposed to just 1.45 percent from 1840 to 1860, although this acceleration may simply be catch-up from war losses.

Even if growth did not accelerate for the country as a whole, the war may have put the winners in a better position. In this view, growth rates are competitive, and the slower growth of the South may have led to more rapid growth in the North. Certainly southern per capita income fell from 72 percent of the national average in 1860 to just 51 percent of the national average in 1880 and 1900. The share of total personal income going to southerners slipped from 26 percent on the eve of the war to 15 percent 20 years later. In the same period the share going to the North and Midwest climbed from 70 to 78 percent.[4] The North thus fared relatively better than the South.

A more relevant test, however, is the North's absolute growth performance. Here there is some modest tangible evidence of postwar acceleration. Between 1840 and 1860 northern per capita income grew at an average annual rate of 1.3 percent. From 1860 to 1879, however, that rate rose to 1.75 percent, and from 1880 to 1900 it rose again to 1.9 percent. Moreover, the percentage of income devoted to new capital formation—land improvements, factories, buildings, and so on—also shows a similar discontinuity. From 1850 to 1860 the share was 19.4 percent; from 1869 to 1878 it rose to 27.4 percent.

These statistics don't necessarily prove the Beard-Hacker thesis. A closer look at some of the specifics is needed.

The Beards, writing in the wake of World War I, which had stimulated industrial production, thought that the Civil War might have supplied a similar stimulus to industry. But twentieth-century wars have been fought with iron and gasoline, while nineteenth-century wars were fought with mules and salt pork. True, cannon and rifles and ironclad ships were used in the Civil War, but their quantities were probably too small to have had much impact on these industries. Small arms production, for example, used just 1 percent of total U.S. iron output from 1861 to 1865, while the war disrupted the most iron-intensive industry of all—railroad construction. At the 1855–60 track-laying rates, small arms demand made up just one-seventh of the 1861–65 shortfall resulting from the suspension of rail projects.[5]

Although the data between census years are sketchy and cannot provide conclusive proof, what evidence is available hardly supports the Beard-Hacker thesis. The war placed enormous stresses on an economy already going full tilt. With the withdrawal of the services of perhaps one-fifth of the labor force, the disruption of normal channels of supply, and the weakening of foreign exchange earnings by the loss of raw cotton exports, it would, in fact, have been very surprising if the war had not disrupted industrial

[4] Easterlin (1971).
[5] Wacht (1966).

growth. Stanley Engerman notes that Massachusetts boot and shoe production (one-half of the nation's) slipped from forty-five million pairs in 1855 to thirty-two million in 1865.[6] Military demand apparently fell well short of replacing lost markets in the South and the declining demand from urban dwellers suffering the impact of war inflation (more on this later). Labor productivity was virtually unchanged despite mechanization.

The wool textile industry, however, did boom, probably doubling output during the war. Labor productivity in the Massachusetts woolen industry also rose by 12 percent. Much of this gain was due to the decline in the availability of raw cotton, whose sale was embargoed by the Union military; growth in the woolen industry failed to offset the 30 percent decline in cotton textiles production. Indeed, manufacturing value added in the two industrial states with five-year census reports—New York and Massachusetts—declined during the war years.

Unlike clothing manufacturers, midwestern grain farmers did not depend upon the South for raw materials or markets. Instead the war probably stimulated demand since armies eat a lot of food and waste even more. Increased European demand for North American grain in the early 1860s put further pressure on production. With demand for grain high and labor scarce—about one-fourth of the northern adult male population was in uniform—a surge in demand for laborsaving agricultural machinery might have been expected. The numbers, however, show little deviation from the prewar trend. Sales of mowers and reapers had already taken off in the 1850s and manufacturers continued to do well during the war. By 1862 perhaps a quarter of a million reapers had been sold. But there is anecdotal evidence that after an extraordinary year in 1861 sales figures slipped. The unsold inventory of reapers held by the McCormick Company after the 1864 harvest, for example, is reported to have been unusually high.

One reason, however, why industrial activity supposedly boomed during the war is that unanticipated price inflation, resulting from the government's decision to finance at least a part of the costs of the war through money creation, led to an increase in industrial profits. Profits surged because wages, which at the time were renegotiated only infrequently, lagged behind price increases. These high profits then stimulated additional investment in manufacturing. This sort of redistribution figures prominently in the Beard-Hacker explanation of how industrialists managed to gain from the war.

Although one always worries about accounting for such things as skill levels, hours of work, and seasonality that enter into wage determination and about the construction of an appropriate cost of living index, Wesley C. Mitchell's 1903 estimates of real wages have not been seriously challenged. These show that while nominal wages for day laborers rose from $1.03 a day

[6] Engerman (1966).

in 1860 to $1.48 in 1865, real wages (in 1860 dollars) fell from $1.03 to $0.84 in 1865 and were actually even lower, 79 cents, in 1864. Wage lag, however, is not the only reason why real wages may have fallen. One explanation for the lower real wages addressed by Mitchell as well as by later researchers is a deterioration in the quality of the labor force resulting in lower real wages, unadjusted for skill levels, as wartime demands brought marginal workers into the labor force.[7] Unfortunately there are no solid data on labor force quality with which to confirm or refute this argument. While it seems plausible that labor scarcity would pull unskilled and undisciplined workers into the labor market, it also seems logical that workers with substantial skills and earning power would be more likely to avoid military service. They were certainly in the position to buy substitutes. Moreover, labor scarcity should have driven up wages, offsetting at least some of the downward wage pressure from reduced skill and productivity levels.

Instead, Reuben Kessel and Armen Alchian argue that half the decline in real wages can be attributed to the sharp drop in the America's terms of trade with the rest of the world, caused by the disruption of the American export trade. Before the war southern cotton had generated two-thirds of the nation's export revenues. The blockade effectively eliminated these cotton exports, and New England mills were forced to import increasingly scarce foreign raw cotton. Both phenomena helped generate a huge balance of payments deficit for the Union. Given the shaky position of the Union, foreigners were reluctant to finance this deficit in 1862. Indeed, foreigners were eager to repatriate their loans in view of the uncertainties caused by the war. Hence the United States effectively had to do what countries do today in similar circumstances: It devalued its currency.

In the Civil War era this meant going off the gold, or specie, standard. Under this system, foreign exchange rates had been fixed automatically by the relative precious metal content of the coins. Instead, as will be discussed in greater detail in Chapter 18, the Treasury printed paper money—greenbacks. These were not freely exchangeable for gold coins of the same face value, but they were declared legal tender for all debts public and private, except for import duties and interest on the national debt. The greenback issue, $450 million, approximately doubled the size of the 1860 money supply and debased the currency.

By effectively "floating" its currency against others, the United States allowed international supply and demand to determine the exchange value of the paper dollar. As a result, gold (and foreign currency) prices rose relative to the dollar. Imported goods became far more expensive for Americans who paid their bills in dollars (Table 13.5). This reduced the real purchasing power of anyone—wage earner, farmer, capitalist—whose products were

[7] See Kessel and Alchian (1967) and Engerman ((1966).

TABLE 13.5

U.S. Domestic Prices and the Price of Gold in Greenbacks 1860–65

Year	Day Laborers' Daily Wage	Hoover Consumer Price Index (1860=100)	Index of Real Day Laborers' Daily Wage	Price of Gold in Greenbacks
1860	$1.03	100	100	1.00
1861	1.04	101	100	1.00
1862	1.08	113	93	1.02
1863	1.20	139	84	1.37
1864	1.39	176	77	1.56
1865	1.48	175	82	2.02

Sources: Clarence Long, *Wages and Earnings in the United States, 1860–1890* (Princeton: Princeton University Press, 1960): Series A–12; U.S. Bureau of the Census, *Historical Statistics of the United States* (Washington, D.C.: Government Printing Office, 1975): Series E-174; James K. Kindahl, "Economic Factors in Specific Resumption: The United States, 1865–1879," *Journal of Political Economy* 59 (1961): 36.

sold abroad or who consumed goods made abroad. As a result, even if wages had been explicitly tied to the cost of goods made in America, higher foreign prices would explain fully half the observed decline in wage purchasing power from 1860 to 1864.

Most of the remaining deterioration in real wages can be attributed to changes in taxes. Federal expenditures rose from $63 million in 1861 to almost $1.3 billion ($674 million in 1860 dollars) in 1865 (Table 13.6). While most of the increase was financed through borrowing and by payment with freshly minted greenbacks, taxes were also raised. Tariffs were hiked in 1862 and 1864, reversing the trend toward freer trade begun in 1832. By the last year of the war rates averaged 47 percent and customs receipts had risen from $39.6 million in 1861 to $102.3 million in 1864. The total cost to consumers, however, was probably much greater because added tariff protection also allowed domestic manufacturers to raise prices. Specific excise taxes were also placed on many goods, such as tobacco and liquor in 1862, and rates were raised in 1864. By 1865 excise taxes raised more than the tariff. In addition, two new taxes were introduced. In 1862 the nation's first income tax was levied. It had relatively little effect on wage earners because most of them were too poor to be affected by its progressive rate structure. Even so, 2 percent of government receipts in 1863 came from the income tax, and in 1865 it brought in $61 million—18 percent of federal receipts. In 1864 this was supplemented by a 5 to 6 percent turnover tax on manufactured goods (listed under "Miscellaneous" in Table 13.6). This was often collected at more than one stage of production, doubling or tripling the final rate passed on to consumers.

Unfortunately Kessel and Alchian cannot quite prove their point because of the absence of adequate information on the incidence of the war taxes and the impact of international terms-of-trade deterioration on wage earners' cost of living. Moreover, there is evidence that the Civil War labor market failed. Labor does not seem to have been paid the value of its marginal product. Stephen DeCanio and Joel Mokyr have tried to separate the effect of unanticipated inflation (the wage lag) from other forces acting on wages by statistically estimating the determinants of real wages between 1861 and 1900. The estimated wage lag is then the difference between actual wages paid and the wages that the model predicts would have been paid in the absence of inflation. For 1861 they find no evidence of a wage gap, in fact, real wages were slightly higher than would be expected without unanticipated inflation. Thereafter, however, a gap opens up, explaining at least 47 percent of the actual decline in real wages during the war years.

If wages lagged, then profits, which were the residual claimant, should have surged. There is evidence of this. Many companies paid extraordinarily high dividends to their stockholders during the Civil War. For example, the Pepperell Company, a New England textile mill, which had paid a dividend of only 4 percent in 1859, paid a dividend of 90 percent in 1863. Similarly, the Boston Manufacturing Company paid 30 percent in 1862, much more than its customary dividend.

Remarkable as the wage lag and the profit surge may have been, it is difficult to argue that they were the tail that wagged the dog. At the time of the Civil War only about 28 percent of the labor force worked in manufacturing. Even a major "inflation tax" on this small, relatively poorly paid group doesn't add up to much. Average northern capital formation in the late antebellum period was four times the largest estimated average annual wage gap. The gap accounted for (at most) 25 percent of total federal expenditures during the war, 33 percent of the difference between government expenditures and tax revenues.

Taxes played a relatively minor role in paying for the war. Instead the lion's share—74 percent—was financed through the sale of interest-bearing bonds. As a result, the national debt soared from less than $65 million ($2.06 per person) in 1860 to almost $2.7 billion in 1865 ($75.01 per person). This made it possible to pay for the war without cutting personal private consumption very deeply through higher taxes. But there was a cost to this policy. Federal government debt crowded out private investment expenditures by exchanging federal government bonds for the financial resources that private investors would otherwise have made available for purchases of farm machinery, factory construction, housing, and so on. There is no estimate of the quantitative importance of this crowding out, though Jeffrey Williamson

TABLE 13.6

Federal Government Finances
1860–1865
(millions of current dollars)

Receipts by Source:							less	= National		
Year	Tariff +	Land Sales +	Excise Taxes +	Income Tax +	Inheritance Tax +	Miscel-laneous +	= Federal Receipts	Budget Expenditures	Surplus/ Deficit	Debt
1860	$53.2	$1.8	$0	$0	$0	$1.1	$56.1	$63.1	−$7.0	$64.8
	(95%)	(3%)				(2%)				
1861	39.6	0.9	0	0	0	1.0	41.5	66.5	−25.0	90.6
	(95)	(2)				(2)				
1862	49.1	0.2	0	0	0	2.8	52.0	474.8	−422.8	524.2
	(94)	(0)				(5)				
1863	69.1	0.2	35.3	2.7	0.1	5.4	112.7	714.7	−602.0	1,119.8
	(61)	(0)	(31)	(2)	(0)	(5)				
1864	102.3	0.6	90.1	20.3	0.3	51.0	264.6	865.3	−600.7	1,815.8
	(39)	(0)	(34)	(8)	(0)	(19)				
1865	84.9	1.0	149.3	61.0	0.5	37.6	333.7	1,297.6	−963.9	2,677.9
	(25)	(0)	(45)	(18)	(0)	(11)				

Note: Figures in parentheses under Revenue by source indicate share of total federal receipts from particular source.

Source: U.S. Bureau of the Census, *Historical Statistics of the United States* (Washington, D.C.: Government Printing Office, 1975).

notes that increases in the federal debt during the war represented 15.5 percent of northern GNP while gross investment in the last decade before the war was just 19.4 percent of GNP. If just one-fourth of gross investment went toward the replacement of depreciated capital equipment, then bond-financed federal deficit spending may have equaled or exceeded expected net investment! To put it another way, the private non-war-related capital stock of the North may have actually shrunk during the Civil War, as scarce investment resources were channeled into the war machine, though some of the deficit doubtless came out of reduced consumption from the reduction in real wages. This government borrowing certainly drove up interest rates and disrupted private capital markets. It would have been all but impossible if the capital markets had not already expanded to finance America's railroads in the 1850s.

If war financing crowded out private investment and retarded industrial growth during the war, the private sector was able to recoup thanks to postwar government financial policies. Initially the government tried to use the large federal tax revenue surpluses after the war to retire the greenbacks it had printed during the conflict. Congress soon rejected the strategy because of its impact on prices, in favor of a policy of reducing the interest-bearing debt outstanding. Between 1866 and 1893 the stock of greenbacks fell only from $429 million to $374 million, but government bonds held by the private sector declined from $2.33 billion in 1866 to $587 million in 1893. Much of the money for debt retirement came from the tariff, providing a justification for maintaining high tariff rates in the spirit of Alexander Hamilton's original argument.

The decision to retire federal debt rather than lower taxes or redeem greenbacks drove down interest rates and may have led to crowding in, according to John James. Debt retirement might crowd investment indirectly if public and private debt were close substitutes in individual wealth portfolios. As public debt was retired, wealth holders would simply substitute private debt for public. Debt retirement might also crowd in indirectly through its impact upon the money and capital markets. The reduction in public debt reduced the yields on private assets and drove down interest rates, thereby stimulating investment and economic growth. If we assume a dollar-for-dollar shuffle from government bonds to private investment, an additional 1 percent of GNP per year was made available to the private capital market between 1866 and 1872 and 0.8 percent per year between 1872 and 1878 (Table 13.7)[8] The regressive tax structure reinforced this redistribution in favor of investment. Taxes were collected from the poor, who had low savings rates, to pay interest on the war debt held by the rich, who saved higher proportions of their incomes. As a result, the national savings rate increased, and in the immediate postwar years (1866–72), debt repayment

[8] Williamson (1974).

TABLE 13.7

Federal Debt Management and Northern Capital Formation

Years	Federal Bond Change as % of GNP	Net Interest Redistribution Available for Reinvestment as % of GNP	Bonds + Interest as % of GNP
1849–59	0	0	0
1861–66	−15.5	0.7	−14.8
1866–72	1.8	1.0	2.8
1872–78	0.1	0.8	0.9
1869–78	0.8	0.9	1.7

Interpretation: Column 1 shows the change in federal debt as a percentage of national income. A positive percentage indicates that the government was retiring bonds, freeing capital for use in the private sector.
Column 2 shows the impact on savings associated with taxing poor people to pay government bond interest to rich people.
Column 3 shows the combined impact on the percentage of income available for private investment.

Source: Jeffrey Williamson, "Watersheds and Turning Points: Conjectures on the Long Term Impact of Civil War Financing," *Journal of Economic History* 34 (1974): 651. Reprinted by permission of Cambridge University Press.

plus regressive interest transfers allowed a 2.8 percent catch-up in investment.

New estimates of the impact of public debt retirement by John James suggest that direct crowding in was probably not that important.[9] Rather changes in the stock of public debt affected financial markets indirectly through the interest rate. His estimates suggest that if the stock of debt had been held constant between 1865 and 1890, then the real stock of capital would have been 5 percent lower than it actually was and the level of real income would have been 1.6 percent lower. On the other hand, if the government had pursued a policy of extinguishing the debt over a thirty-year period (as was actually suggested by some government officials in 1865), then the capital stock in 1890 would have been 2.16 percent higher, and real income 0.7 percent higher, than it actually was. These results suggest that federal debt management played a significant role in the growth of capital formation in the late nineteenth century. Capital formation also accelerated

[9] James (1984).

TABLE 13.8

Ratio of Capital Goods Prices to the Overall Price Level (index 1929 = 100)

Year	Price Index (Capital Goods/ All Goods)	Year	Price Index (Capital Goods/ All Goods)
1839	111.9	1899–1908	77.2
1849	109.4	1909–18	94.8
1859	103.4	1919–28	100.3
1869–78	86.6	1929–38	107.3
1879–88	89.3	1939–48	108.5
1889–98	81.2	1944–53	111.6

Interpretation: The table shows a strong, continuous price trend favoring buyers of investment goods over all goods through 1909. Williamson associates this trend favoring investment in part with tariffs.

Source: Jeffrey Williamson, "Watersheds and Turning Points: Conjectures on the Long Term Impact of Civil War Financing," *Journal of Economic History* 34 (1974): 654. Reprinted by permission of Cambridge University Press.

as a result of a marked decline in the relative price of capital goods during the Civil War decade (Table 13.8). This increased the expected profitability of postwar investment expenditures and is perhaps the most dramatic evidence yet of a Civil War watershed favoring industrial capitalism. The causes are not completely understood, but Williamson argues that the change was a result of Civil War tariff policy, which had provided relatively more protection for consumer goods than for capital goods.

Southern secession released the logjam in Congress on economic legislation, such as tariffs, railroad land grants, the use of foreign contract labor, and more liberal land policy, that was seen as inimical to southern interests. These legislative initiatives undoubtedly had an effect, but it is difficult to evaluate their overall impact since the connections between industrial growth and institutional change are not very well defined. Nor were the changes necessarily that innovative or fundamental. Contract labor was rarely used after it was legalized, except in California, where thousands of Chinese workers were engaged to help build the state's railroads. Land grants had been used by states to sponsor canal construction and rail construction subsidies, though to the extent that these projects would have generated adequate rates of return even in the absence of land grants, the grants are now thought to have had little effect on national income. The Homestead Act, which gave 160 acres to anyone promising to farm them for at least five years, looks just like a continuation of the progressive liberalization of public land law dating back to 1800. Moreover, with land cost such a minor portion of farm-making costs, it is doubtful that the promise of free land "democratized" landownership or hastened the westward movement to any significant degree. Indeed, if anything, agricultural historians see "free land" as the source of agrarian discontent and the farm "problem." Enough is known, too, about nineteenth-century banking to be skeptical that centralized regulation would have much impact on capital markets.

What, then, is the bottom line on the Beard-Hacker thesis that the Civil War spurred American industrialization and the hegemony of urban-industrial interests over rural-agrarian interests? We are suspicious of the grand theme. The Civil War did not eliminate fundamental impediments to industrial growth since it is hard to find many impediments to be eliminated. Rather the war cost the North dearly, setting back the process of industrialization and retarding the rate of economic growth during the years of struggle.

The Real Civil War Watershed: The Pauperization of Southern Agriculture?

While it is certain that the last word hasn't been written on the Beard-Hacker thesis, one thing is clear: The relatively rapid growth of manufacturing output shown in Table 13.4 reflects the fallacy of composition. True, aggregate output of mining and manufacturing grew from $892 million in 1860 to $1.148 million in 1870, or by 29 percent, whereas agricultural output grew only 15 percent from $1.492 million in 1860 to $1.723 million in 1870. However, if commodity output is divided regionally, a radically different interpretation emerges (Table 13.9). Thanks to high crop prices and liberalized land policy, agricultural production in the North actually grew faster during the Civil War decade than output in the other sectors—46 percent versus 33 percent. In 1860 the values of agricultural output and mining and manufacturing output outside the South were approximately equal, at more than $800 million each. Ten years later agricultural output was more than 10 percent larger, $1.246 million, than that of mining and manufacturing, $1.091 million.

The decline in agriculture's share of total output for the economy as a whole reflects not the rapid growth of manufacturing but rather the pauperization of southern agriculture—a topic that we address in the next chapter. Southern agricultural production fell more than 25 percent from $639 million in 1860 to just $477 million in 1870. In 1860 the value of southern agricultural output was about 75 percent that of the North's. In 1870 southern agricultural output was worth less than 40 percent of the North's. Rapid industrial growth, on the other hand, waited until the decade of the 1870s.

TABLE 13.9

Commodity Output by Region and Sector, 1860–1880 (1879 prices; millions of dollars)

Year	Total[a]	Agriculture	Mining and Manufacturing
Non-South			
1860	$1,674	$853	$821
1870	2,337	1,246	1,091
1880	3,876	1,861	2,015
South			
1860	710	639	71
1870	534	477	57
1880	838	738	100

[a] Excluding construction.

Source: Stanley L. Engerman, "The Economic Impact of the Civil War," *Explorations in Entrepreneurial History* 3 (1966): 180.

Bibliography

Beard, Charles, and Mary Beard. *The Rise of American Civilization.* New York: Macmillan, 1927.

DeCanio, Stephen, and Joel Mokyr. "Inflation and the Wage Lag during the American Civil War." *Explorations in Economic History* 14 (1977): 311–36.

Easterlin, Richard. "Regional Income Trends 1840–1950." In *The Reinterpretation of American Economic History,* ed. Robert Fogel and Stanley Engerman. New York: Harper & Row, 1971: 38–49.

Engerman, Stanley. "The Economic Impact of the Civil War." *Explorations in Economic History* 3 (1966): 176–99.

Fogel, Robert, and Stanley Engerman. *Time on the Cross.* Boston: Little, Brown, 1974.

Fogel, Robert W., et al., *Without Consent or Contract: The Rise and Fall of American Slavery,* vol. 1. New York: W. W. Norton, 1989.

———. *Without Consent or Contract: Evidence and Methods,* vol. 2. New York: W. W. Norton, 1992.

———. *Without Consent or Contract: Technical Papers Volume I,* vol. 4. New York: W. W. Norton, 1992.

———. *Without Consent or Contract: Technical Papers Volume II,* vol. 4. New York: W. W. Norton, 1992.

Gallman, Robert. "Commodity Output 1839–1899." In National Bureau of Economic Research, *Trends in the American Economy in the 19th Century,* Studies in Income and Wealth, vol. 24. Princeton: Princeton University Press, 1960: 13–67.

Goldin, Claudia. "The Economics of Emancipation." *Journal of Economic History* 33 (1973): 66–85.

———, and Frank Lewis. "The Economic Cost of the American Civil War: Estimates and Implications." *Journal of Economic History* 35 (1975): 294–326.

Gunderson, Gerald. "The Origin of the American Civil War." *Journal of Economic History* 34 (1974): 915–50.

Hacker, Louis. *The Triumph of American Capitalism.* New York: Columbia University Press, 1940.

James, John A. "Public Debt Management Policy and Nineteenth-Century American Economic Growth." *Explorations in Economic History 21* (1984): 192–217.

Kessel, Reuben, and Armen Alchian. "Real Wages in the North during the Civil War: Mitchell's Data Reinterpreted." *Journal of Law and Economics 2* (1959): 95–113. Reprinted in *The Reinterpretation of American Economic History,* ed. Robert W. Fogel and Stanley L. Engerman. New York: Harper & Row, 1971: 459–69.

Kindahl, James K. "Economic Factors in Specie Resumption: The United States, 1865–1879." *Journal of Political Economy* 59 (1961): 30–48. Reprinted with omissions in Robert Fogel and Stanley Engerman, eds., *The Reinterpretation of American Economic History.* New York: Harper & Row, 1971: 468–79.

Long, Clarence D. *Wages and Earnings in the United States, 1860–1890.* Princeton: Princeton University Press, 1960.

Mitchell, Wesley. "The Greenbacks and the Cost of the Civil War." Reprinted in Ralph Andreano, ed. *The Economic Impact of the Civil War.* Cambridge, Mass.: Shenkman, 1962: 66–78.

Ransom, Roger. *Conflict and Compromise: The Political Economy of Slavery, Emancipation and the American Civil War.* New York: Cambridge University Press, 1989.

Rose, Louis. "Capital Losses of Southern Slaveholders due to Emancipation." *Western Economic Journal* 3 (1964): 39–51.

Sellers, James. "The Economic Incidence of the Civil War on the South." *Mississippi Valley Historical Review* 14 (1927): 179–91. Reprinted in Ralph Andreano, ed. *The Economic Impact of the Civil War* (Cambridge, Mass.: Shenkman, 1962): 79–89.

Wacht, Richard F. "A Note on the Cochran Thesis and Small Arms Industry in the Civil War." *Explorations in Entrepreneurial History* 4 (1966): 57–62.

Williamson, Jeffrey. "Watersheds and Turning Points: Conjectures on the Long Term Impact of Civil War Financing." *Journal of Economic History* 34 (1974): 631–61.

Wright, Gavin. *The Political Economy of the Cotton South.* New York: Norton, 1978.

The south after the civil war

14

In the North the Civil War resulted in a brief pause in long-run growth and development. In the South it brought a complete restructuring of economic relations as well as military trauma. It was not just that slave and master became freedman or freedwoman and employer. The change was more fundamental. For generations the principal asset in the southern economy had been movable slaves. Overnight the primary asset became immovable land. Before the war southern planters had shown little interest in developing an infrastructure beyond the minimum necessary to facilitate the export of their cotton—some modest river and port improvements, for example—but little support for banks, railroads, and market towns serving local needs. Certainly as individuals southern planters had little or no incentive to maintain and improve their land so long as new and even more productive land lay just a few miles farther south and west.[1] Instead there was a continuous and relentless drift of cotton production into Arkansas, Mississippi, and Texas (see Figure 14.1). Moreover, slaveowners had little incentive to stimulate population growth if it reduced labor scarcity and the value of their capital stock in slaves.

Emancipation radically altered these incentives. Suddenly, overnight, cheap labor became a necessary and desired input and land became the principal source of wealth. As a result, southerners became interested in local development—small towns, roads, and railroads—development that would generate positive externalities that landowners could capture. They also became interested in farm improvement and soil conservation.

[1] In the aggregate, however, the slaveowners had much to fear from the westward migration to more fertile lands undermining the price of slaves and land by driving down cotton prices. See Kotlikoff and Pinera (1977).

FIGURE 14.1

Cotton Production in the United States: 1859 and 1899

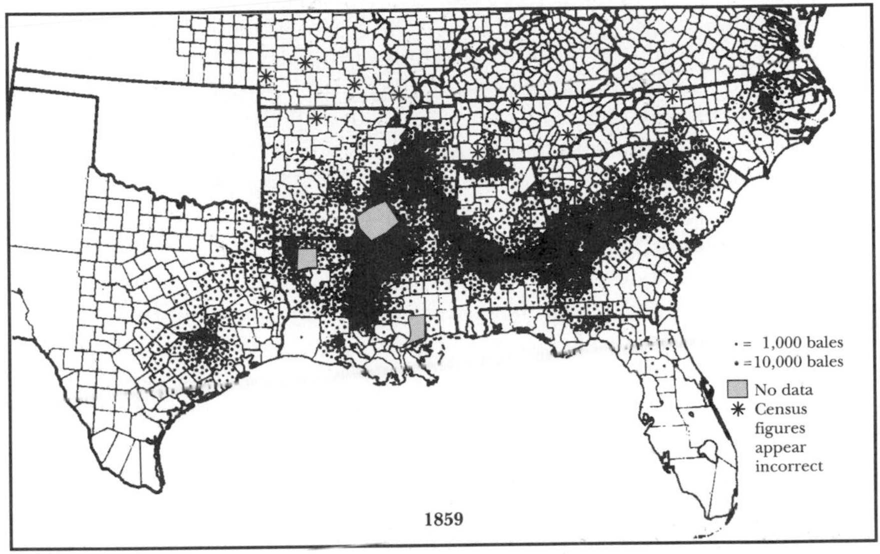

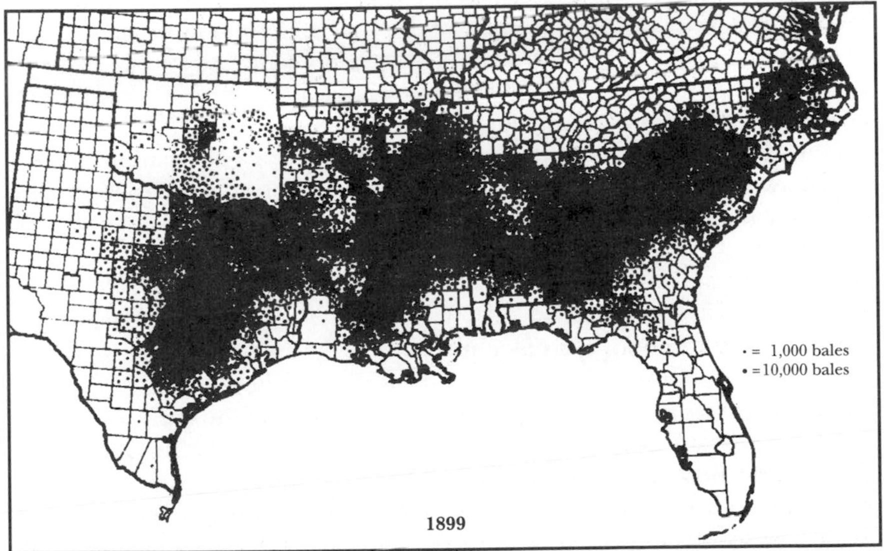

Source: U.S. Department of Agriculture, *Atlas of American Agriculture*, part 5, sec. A (Washington, D.C.: Government Printing Office, 1918), 17.

Southern agriculture became land-intensive and labor-extensive rather than labor-intensive and land-extensive. And the relentless westward push of cotton production ceased. The result was nothing short of a revolution, but it failed to integrate the South into the broader, developing national economy.

In 1860 southern per capita commodity output had been slightly higher than the North's, thanks largely to splendid returns to cotton agriculture on the fertile lands west of the Appalachians. But while the North was recording a 9 percent gain per capita in commodity output during the Civil War decade, southern per capita output slipped by 39 percent. In part this reflected the drastic reversal of fortune for the West South Central region: Arkansas, Louisiana, and Texas. In the antebellum period per capita income in this region had been well above the national average, and a growing fraction of southern population lived there, boosting southern per capita income. In 1880, though, per capita income in this region had fallen much farther and faster than in other regions and stood at only 60 percent of the national average. Income levels fell throughout the South between 1860 and 1880. Although the South grew at about the same pace as the North thereafter, the huge income gap that had opened up during the Civil War decade and the 1870s began to close only around World War II. Whereas southern personal income per capita in 1840 had been more than 10 percent higher than personal income per capita in the Midwest, by 1880 it was barely half the midwestern per capita income (Figure 14.2). Although the gap had narrowed substantially by 1950, it was still over 25 percent.

It is not difficult to come up with explanations for this long-term southern economic distress. In fact, the real problem is to choose among the plausible theories. Here we survey some of the competing explanations for the South's dismal economic performance and then consider a closely related issue: the bitter experience of ex-slaves in the hostile world of the post-Civil War South.

The Southern Economy in Decline

There was extensive physical damage in the South from the war. Much of the war was fought on southern territory, and major cities, including Charleston, Richmond, and Atlanta, were destroyed by the Union army. Moreover, whatever livestock and food supplies in the path of the fighting were not requisitioned by Confederate forces were confiscated by the boys in blue. Still, Claudia Goldin and Frank Lewis's estimate of $1.5 billion in war-related capital destruction or James Seller's estimate of $1.1 billion in property loss (40 percent of total southern property value) may overstate the actual physical damage.

Whatever the damage, though, it was quickly repaired. By 1870 the southern transportation system had been virtually restored to prewar capac-

FIGURE 14.2

Personal Income per Capita in the South as a Percentage of That in the Midwest

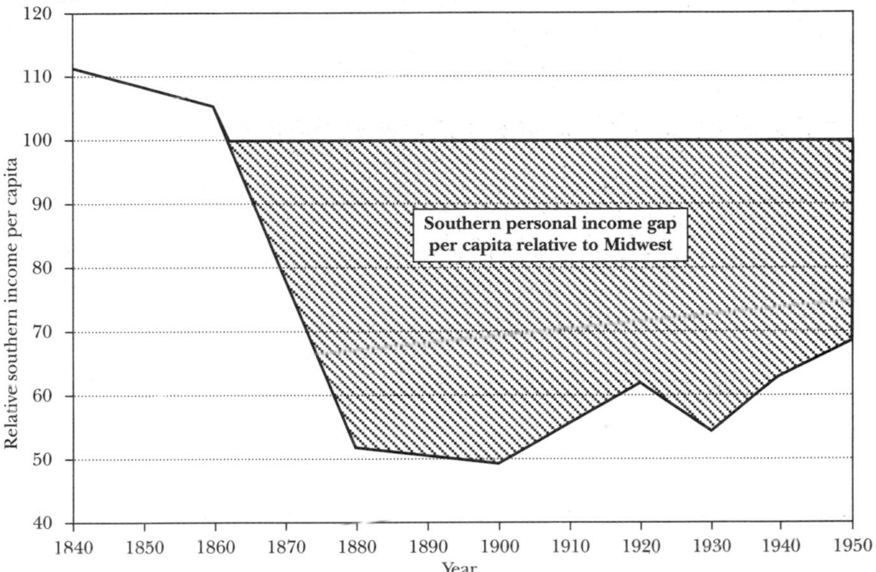

Source: Based upon estimates by Richard Easterlin. "Regional Income Trends, 1840–1950," in *The Reinterpretation of American Economic History,* ed. Robert W. Fogel and Stanley L. Engerman (New York: Harper & Row, 1971): 40, Table 1.

ity. Similarly, although the southern manufacturing sector remained small, manufacturing establishments in the towns and cities of the Cotton Belt—presumably a prime target of the Union forces—were producing about 5 percent more output (with about 5 percent more invested capital) in 1870 than they had produced in 1860. Even agriculture, which dominated the southern economy, seems to have suffered no shortage of capital. True, the census shows a one-third decline in the number of draft animals between 1860 and 1870 but if this had constrained output, one should have seen a corresponding increase in the price of the remaining stock as farmers bid for this scarce resource. Instead, after adjustment for inflation, prices fell. In 1870, a mule colt fetched only about $40 or 0.54 of a bale of cotton whereas in 1859 one had been worth about 1.03 bales of cotton.

Nevertheless, many have accepted war damage as the primary source of the southern economic decline. This interpretation has also suited succeeding generations of southerners who blamed the long postwar malaise on Yankee pillage. There is reason, however, to question whether so great and lasting a decline can be explained so easily. After all, Japan and Germany recovered rapidly from far worse destruction in World War II. Indeed, the modern experience has been that the military victors have often ended up the economic losers while the military losers have wound up the economic winners.

What, then, made the South's experience so different? Why was southern per capita commodity output in 1880 20 percent below 1860 levels?

Some have blamed the South's loss of its export monopoly in raw cotton.[2] During the war European mills had eventually replaced blockaded American supplies with Indian, Brazilian, and Egyptian cotton. Once growers in these countries had invested in cotton production, they were reluctant to switch to other crops. Consequently, it was more than a decade before the South recaptured its market share (Table 14.1). Other forces may also have impeded the South's recovery of its cotton market share. Deflationary federal policies, increased world demand for midwestern grain, and capital inflows from Europe increased the dollar price of goods, including American cotton, improving the U.S. terms of trade but making it harder for American cotton to compete with that from other countries. The argument is twofold. On the one hand, the war shifted foreign supply function for cotton outward; on the other, the appreciation of the dollar, by making cotton priced in dollars relatively more expensive in terms of foreign currency, shifted the foreign demand curve for American cotton inward.

Gavin Wright has tested these propositions by estimating the supply and demand functions for cotton. He concludes that Indian, Brazilian, and Egyptian cotton supply curves were indeed shifting outward, suggesting that competition from these countries was growing over time, but the growth in supply from India—the South's largest competitor—was as fast before the war as during and immediately after. Brazil and Egypt were much smaller producers than India. Hence shifts in their supply functions had less impact on the demand for American cotton. At the same time high cotton prices probably affected exchange rates more than the other way around. Instead Wright explains southern retardation in terms of the fundamental dependence of the southern economy on world demand for cotton. In the three decades before the Civil War the demand for cotton expanded at roughly 5 percent a year. Prices fluctuated from year to year because crop size varied with the weather, but in the long run cotton suppliers responded as textbooks predict firms in a competitive economy would respond: expanding output at constant cost to maintain the real price of cotton at about 11 cents a pound (1880 prices). Now five percent cotton output growth at a stable price meant rapid extensive economic growth for the South throughout the antebellum years. After the war, however, demand changes made price more sensitive to year-to-year fluctuation in crop size, but much more important, between 1860 and the 1870s demand for cotton plunged and then stag-

[2] Conrad et al. (1967).

TABLE 14.1

Average Annual Cotton Imports into Great Britain by Source (thousands of bales)

Years	U.S.A.	India	Brazil	Egypt	U.S. Percentage Share
1850s	1,638	406	132	103	72
1860	2,581	563	103	110	77
1861	1,842	987	100	98	61
1862–65	216	1,418	206	282	10
1866	1,163	1,867	408	200	31
1867	1,226	1,511	437	198	35
1868	1,269	1,452	637	201	35
1869	1,040	1,496	514	227	31
1870–71	1,957	1,150	459	246	50
1872–73	1,651	1,179	595	317	42
1874–75	1,909	1,048	461	291	50
1876–77	2,041	649	324	313	60
1878–79	2,330	469	102	220	73
1880–81	2,688	544	176	256	72
1882–83	2,670	870	291	249	65

Interpretation: The U.S. prewar share of the cotton market was not recovered until the 1870s. India and Brazil, which had picked up the market during the Civil War, gradually lost it again, but the regression took more than fifteen years.

Source: Thomas Ellison, *The Cotton Trade of Great Britain* (New York: Augustus Kelley, 1968), cited in Gavin Wright, "Cotton Competition and the Post Bellum Recovery of the American South," *Journal of Economic History* 34 (1974): 611. Reprinted by permission of Cambridge University Press.

nated. While demand had been growing at 5 percent before the war, it slowed to just 1.3 percent per year for the period 1866-95 and grew at only 2.7 percent, or about half the antebellum average, between 1880 and 1900. Thus, with or without the war, it would have been impossible for the South to sustain its earlier economic success. The long boom in cotton was over. The question is why factors failed to seek alternative employment.

Roger Ransom and Richard Sutch have offered an entirely different explanation for the collapse of the southern economy: the reduction in labor supply associated with emancipation. Their evidence shows that as slaves African-Americans, regardless of gender, had no choice but to begin working earlier in life, work more hours each day and more days each year. Once they were free to choose, they opted to spend some of their potentially greater income on time off. Indeed, Ransom and Sutch estimate that freed

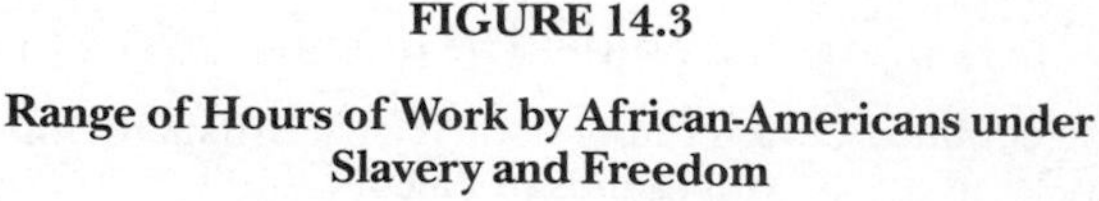

FIGURE 14.3

Range of Hours of Work by African-Americans under Slavery and Freedom

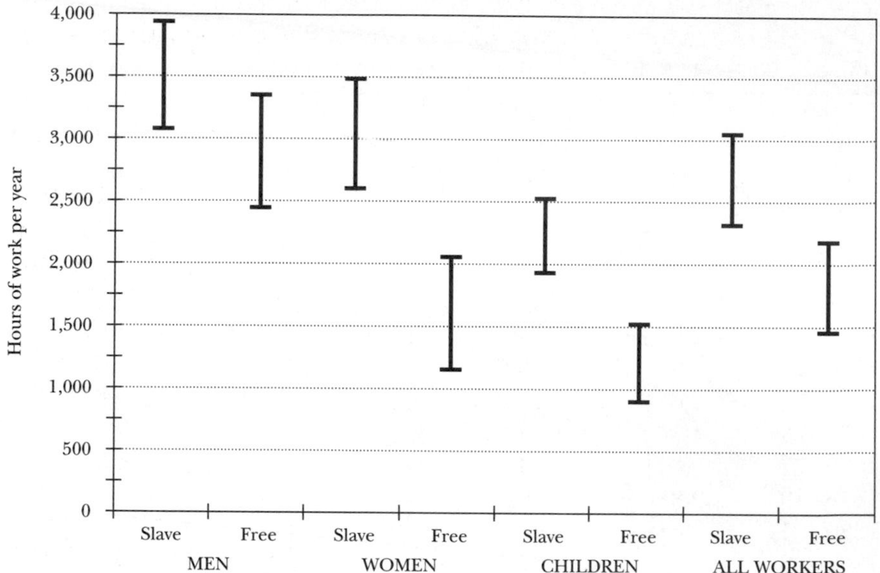

Source: Roger Ransom and Richard Sutch, *One Kind of Freedom* (New York: Cambridge University Press, 1977): 45, Figure 3.1.

African-American children (ages ten to fifteen) and women put in only about half as many hours of work per year (Figure 14.3), while freed men cut their annual hours of work by about one-fifth. Overall, man-hours (weighted for productivity differences) declined from between 2,306 hours and 3,047 hours per year to between 1,448 and 2,187 hours a year, or by perhaps a third. The net effect was to reduce average rural African-American work effort per capita between 28 and 37 percent. These statistics raise some puzzling questions: Why did the female labor supply fall so much? How is such a decline, if true, to be interpreted in terms of a choice between market versus nonmarket work? Why did African-Americans work so much less than northern farmers, who still averaged around 3,000 hours or more per year?[3]

Such a drastic reduction in labor supply could explain much of the shortfall in postwar output. Output per African-American slave on plantations in the Cotton South fell from $147.93 in 1859 to just $74.03 per African-American sharecropper in 1879, a decline of 50 percent. Physical output per labor hour, however, fell much less because of the reduction in work hours. Slaves had supplied about 70 percent of southern labor before

[3] Goldin (1979); Olson (1992)

the war, so a 37 percent reduction in African-American labor could indeed cut total southern labor per capita by as much as 26 percent (=37 percent of 70 percent). With an 1859 cotton crop over 30 percent higher than might have been expected, and other crops also well above normal, the combined effect of a return to expected output per laborer and the reduction in hours worked because of emancipation probably reduced per capita output by 50 to 60 percent. In fact, physical productivity actually fell to 52 percent of the 1859 level. The sharp decline in southern economic fortunes can thus be entirely ascribed to factors other than wartime destruction.

Ransom and Sutch explain the decline purely in supply terms; Wright's explanation centers on demand factors. Can these two radically different views be reconciled? Happily, the answer is yes. In fact, Peter Temin has done precisely that. His argument is elegant, yet simple. Consider Figure 14.4. The supply and demand curves represent the relative positions of antebellum supply and demand (S_0 and D_0) and postbellum supply and demand (S_1 and D_1) for American cotton. In particular, D_0 represents actual prewar demand and the hypothetical relative position of postwar demand if prewar trends had continued unabated. Instead, if demand for cotton grew much less rapidly after the war than before, then postwar demand would be *relatively* less than if the trend had been sustained; that is why D_1 lies to the left of D_0. Evidence suggests that both supply and demand for cotton shifted and the economy moved from a market equilibrium at A before the war to B afterward. The price of cotton (both nominal and real) remained above prewar levels until the late 1870s, gradually returning to prewar levels. Southern per capita income, however, fell to 60 percent or less of the national average.

By focusing solely upon the supply shift from S_0 to S_1, Ransom and Sutch view the change as from A to C. Notice that in a sense Ransom and Sutch are right: The reduction in market sales from Q_0 to Q_1 is attributable solely to the shift in supply. However, the income earned by the South from the sale of cotton depends upon demand as well as supply—that is to say, both price and quantity matter. By emphasizing the role of demand changes, Wright, on the other hand, focuses upon the shift in demand from D_0 to D_1—that is, from A to D.

For southern income, the question is whether a move from A to C that reflects supply shocks results in a larger or smaller income loss than the demand-shock move from A to D. Temin answers this question by first calculating the increase in income from a move from B to C or D. Point C clearly represents a higher income level than B: Sales are unchanged at Q_1, but prices are higher. How much higher? According to Wright's calculations, if we assume no change in demand, prices for the decade centered on 1880 would have been about 80 percent higher than they were. Revenue at C would therefore be 80 percent higher than at B. Since cotton accounted for about half of agricultural income and agricultural income was about 80 percent of total income in the five major cotton states, total income at C would

FIGURE 14.4

The Supply and Demand for Cotton Before and After the Civil War

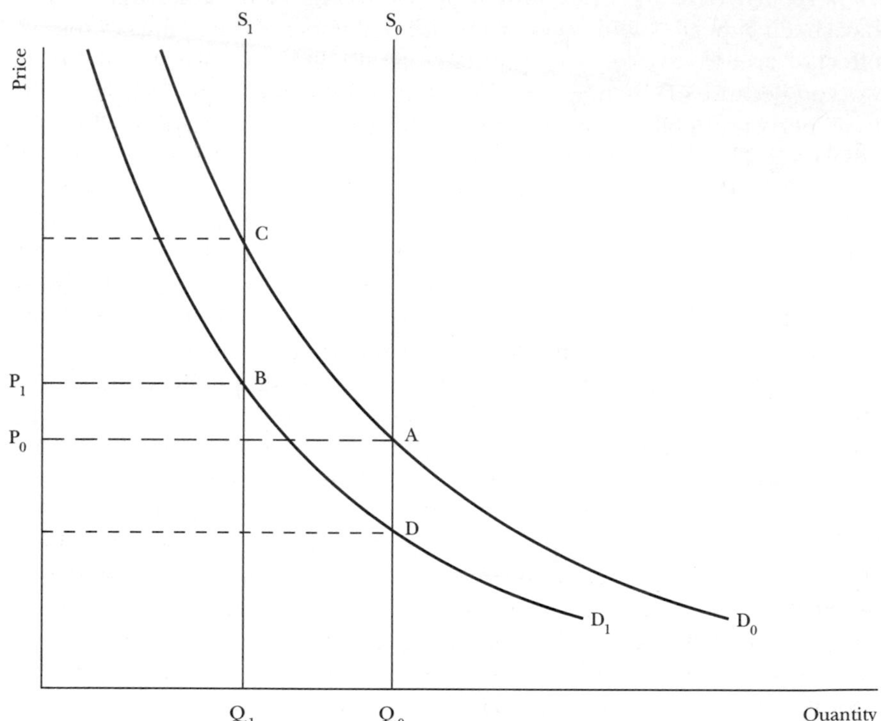

be about a third higher than at B ($0.8 \cdot 0.5 \cdot 0.8 = 0.32$). The effect on income of a move from B to D is more difficult to calculate and depends upon the elasticity of the demand curve D_1. Wright estimates that this increased from unit elasticity before the war to about 1.5 after the war. Ransom and Sutch estimate that per capita agricultural output in 1880 was only two-thirds to three-quarters what it had been in 1860; thus a shift from Q_1 to Q_0 represents an increase of between a half and a third. If we assume a constant elasticity demand curve, a 50 percent increase in output could be sold only if price were reduced by about 24 percent. If, on the other hand, production increased by only one-third, then price would have had to fall by about 17 percent.[4] In the former case, cotton producers' income would have been

[4] The usual formula for elasticity: $\epsilon = (\Delta Q/Q)/(\Delta P/P)$ doesn't work in this case since "ΔQ is not "small." Instead the calculations reported here were made by evaluating a normalized constant elasticity demand curve: $Q = P^{-1.5}$. The prices changes needed to absorb the change in output are much smaller than one might have expected because the change in quantity is not small and because of the concave (to the origin) curvature of the demand curve.

about 14 percent higher; in the latter case, income from cotton would have increased by about 10 percent.[5] It is reasonable to suppose that in the absence of reduced labor effort, output of other crops would also have increased. If one assumes that demand for them was perfectly elastic so that their price did not change in response to increased production, then income from these other commodities would have increased between one-third and one-half. If half of farm income came from cotton and farm income represented 80 percent of total income, then these changes should have increased total income between 17 and 26 percent, where 26 percent = 80 percent of (0.5 · 14% + 0.5 · 50%)

Thus, if the supply curve alone had shifted—that is, by moving from A to C rather than A to B—income would have been about 32 percent higher than it actually was and income per capita could have been as high as 80 percent of the national average instead of 60 percent or less. If, on the other hand, the demand curve had shifted while supply remained unchanged, then income might have reached 70 to 75 percent of the national average. Ransom-Sutch's labor force withdrawal and Wright's demand stagnation are thus of similar orders of magnitude. Note one important difference, though: The stagnation of cotton demand generated a real loss of welfare to the South, while the withdrawal of African-American labor as the result of emancipation merely transformed measured income into unmeasured non-pecuniary income for those who chose to work less.

The Operation and Performance of Postbellum Agriculture

The fact that the sharp drop in southern per capita income following the war can be explained by either external demand forces or the emancipation of the slaves does not necessarily mean that the drop in income was therefore the result of those changes in demand or the reduction in the supply of labor. Nor does it necessarily mean that the economy was otherwise operating efficiently. Emancipation brought with it a fundamental restructuring of relationships between the factors of production, and it took time for other institutions to adapt to these changes. Moreover, if southern slave agriculture had indeed been more efficient than southern farming with free labor, then the switch to an all free labor system should have reduced regional total factor productivity. This alternative supply side explanation, advanced by Robert Fogel and Stanley Engerman, could also explain the decline in southern per capita income after the war.

In the wake of military defeat, southern planters had attempted to retain the basic features of the plantation system by hiring former slaves on *annual*

[5] Temin (1976) reports the income gain at 15 to 25 percent. We have been unable to duplicate this result.

wage contracts. Ex-slaves were hired to work the fields in gangs and were subject to discipline by overseers, including fines and discharge without back pay but not whipping. By working their newly freed labor in gangs on the old plantations, the planters hoped to preserve the efficiencies that had served them so well when the labor had been supplied by slaves: self-monitoring of the gangs through collective responsibility. For the freed slaves, though, this system was too like the slavery from which they had been freed. The faces of the plantation owner and the overseer, the nature of the tasks, and the sometimes abusive, insulting, and demeaning treatment were only too familiar to them. The only major difference in their work lives was the receipt of take-home pay. But even then the wages were not necessarily competitively determined, and ex-slaves probably continued to receive less than the value of their marginal products. The courts and state legislatures, for example, tried to restrict African-American mobility and prevent open competition for their labor services by binding the freedman to particular employers through so-called Black Codes. Planters set up employer cartels and encouraged the use of violence and intimidation to coerce employee acceptance and restrict vocal dissent or complaint. Inevitably this system broke down within a few years, in part because ex-slaves fiercely resisted working in gangs, as they had when enslaved, and partly because the general shortage of labor made it difficult to prevent landowners from breaking ranks and competing with one another by offering labor arrangements more pleasing to their former chattels.[6]

The pure plantation was maintained where its advantages were decisive, such as on sugar and rice plantations in Louisiana,where the planters paid whatever wages were necessary to attract the labor they needed.[7] The answer, however, for many of the larger planters was to subdivide the plantation into plots of 20 to 50 acres, each suitable for cultivation by a single—typically African-American—family under new tenancy arrangements. With this change the labor gangs disappeared along with any efficiencies they had generated. To the extent that the plantation was broken up into smaller operating units, economies of scale were also dissipated. As a result, the postwar southern economy lost the key features that Fogel and Engerman credited as its sources of economic success before the war. After emancipation, for example, at least twenty-five tenant families and others, many of them former Barrow slaves, worked the Barrow Plantation. With similar changes elsewhere throughout most of the South, acres per farm declined dramatically in every southern state except Texas, falling from 149 acres per farm in 1880—slightly more than in the average midwestern farm of the time—to only 70 acres by 1930 (Table 14.2). The decline in the Deep (predominantly cotton) South was even more precipitous. These increasingly

[6] See, for example, Shlomowitz (1992).
[7] Wright (1979, 1986).

TABLE 14.2

Acres per Farm, 1880-1930

	1880	1890	1900	1910	1920	1930
Alabama	139	126	93	79	76	68
Arkansas	128	119	93	81	75	66
Florida	141	107	107	105	112	85
Georgia	188	147	118	93	82	86
Louisiana	171	138	95	87	74	58
Mississippi	156	122	83	66	67	55
North Carolina	142	128	101	88	74	65
South Carolina	143	115	90	77	65	66
Tennessee	125	116	91	82	77	73
Virginia	167	150	119	106	100	98
5 Deep South states	159	130	96	80	73	67
10 southern states	149	128	98	84	77	70
Midwest	122	133	145	158	172	181

Source: Adapted from Gavin Wright, *Old South, New South* (New York: Basic Books, 1986): 54, Table 3.2.

small farms were typically cultivated by tenants and sharecroppers, many of whom were African-American, especially on the smaller farms (Figure 14.5). Indeed, the average African-American–operated farm in the South in 1900 (regardless of tenure) was only about one-third the size of the average farm operated by a white farmer. On the other hand, over the same period, the average farm size in the Midwest grew almost 50 percent to 181 acres.

The breakup of large plantations—hence the dissipation of economies of scale—may be an illusion, since the census identified only farm operators and the farm that each operated. True, those data clearly show a sharp rise in the number of individual farm operators, a decline in average farm size, and a shift in the distribution of farm sizes toward much smaller units after the war. In 1860, for example, 37 percent of farms in the five major cotton-growing states had fewer than fifty acres of improved land, and almost 7 percent exceeded five hundred acres. In 1870 more than 60 percent of farms were smaller than fifty acres while just over 2 percent exceeded five hundred acres. But to the extent that there was still a single landlord who provided the managerial direction and supervision, set lease terms, and so forth, it is not so clear that the activities among the individual farm workers and operators were uncoordinated. Instead plantation landholdings continued to be managed as a single unit even when subdivided.

The typical landlord subdividing a plantation assigned some lots to sharecroppers, others were rented to tenants, and yet others were farmed by

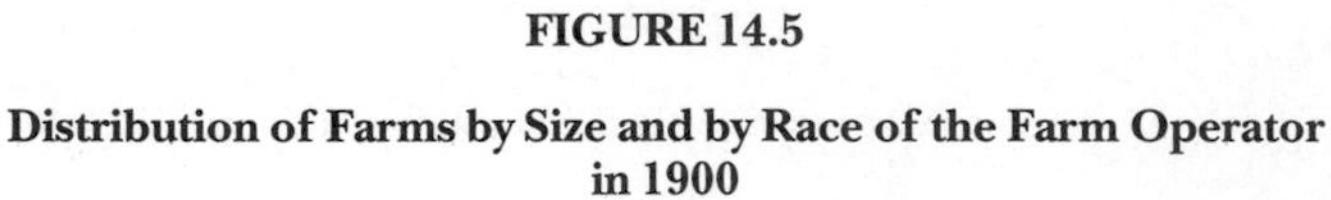

FIGURE 14.5

Distribution of Farms by Size and by Race of the Farm Operator in 1900

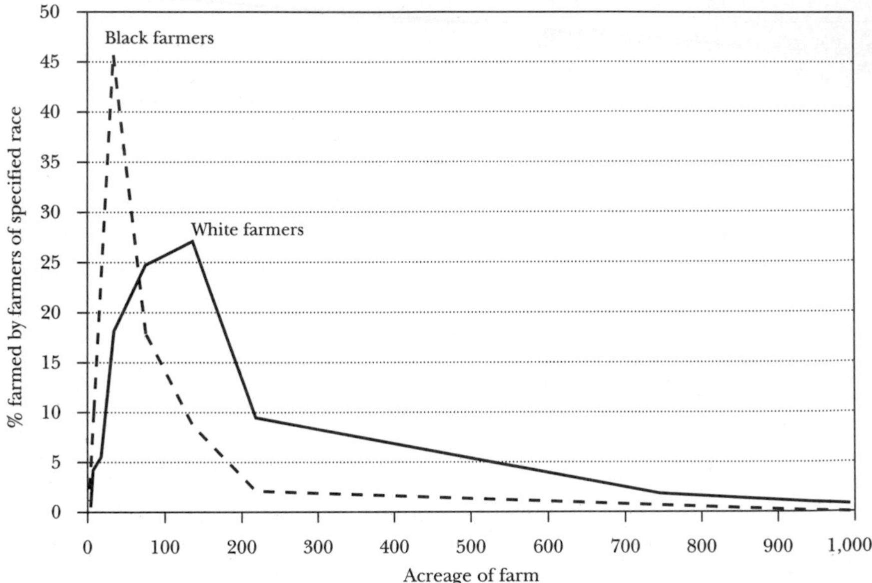

Source: U.S. Bureau of the Census, *Agriculture,* 12th Census (1900), vol. 5 (Washington, D.C.: Government Printing Office, 1902): Table 1.

the planter using wage labor in a systematic, economically rational manner.[8] Monitoring and other enforcement costs played a key role in determining the spatial distribution of different forms of land tenure and farm operation on the plantations. Wage labor, which required daily instructions and constant monitoring, farmed the land closest to the planter's home. Croppers required less close supervision since the landlord's interest was less with the day-to-day cropper's work effort than with the overall well-being of the crops in which the landlord had a vested interest. Consequently, sharecroppers farmed land farther from the owner's house, while the cash tenants farmed the land on the boundaries of the plantation since the only landlord concerns were with the stewardship of the land and the tenant's ability to make the rental payment when due.[9] The mix between these different groups was then determined by the planter's equalizing marginal profitability (after taking account of the different transactions and enforcement costs associated with each) across farm operators, taking into account the wages and other

[8] Alston and Higgs (1981); Virts (1987).

[9] See Thomas J. Wooffer, *Landlord and Tenant on the Cotton Plantation* (Washington, D.C.: Works Progress Administration, 1936).

FIGURE 14.6

Determining the Optimum Allocation of Land between Different Tenure Systems

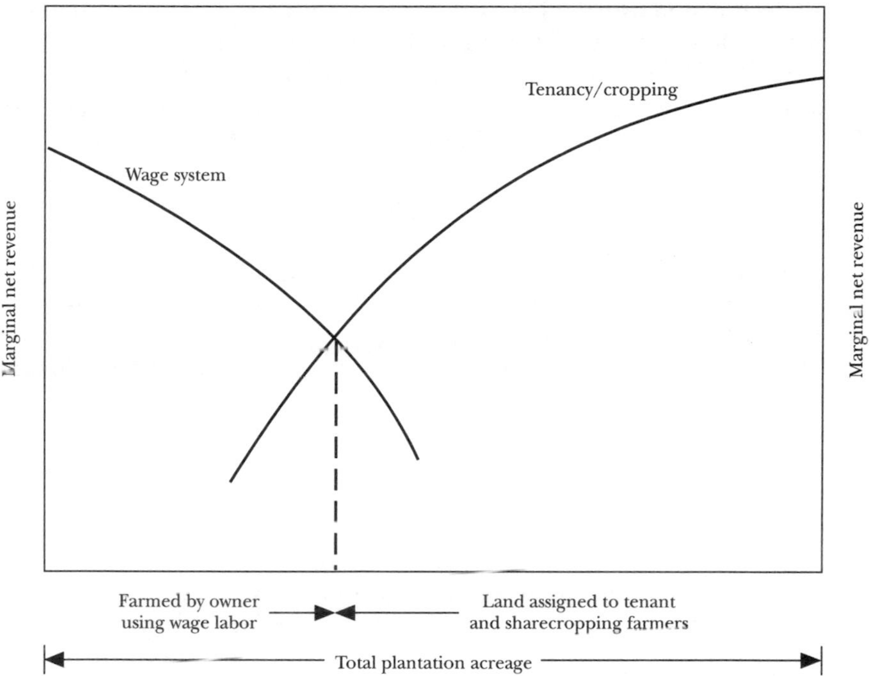

Source: Warren Whatley, "Institutional Change and Mechanization in the Cotton South," unpublished Ph.D. dissertation, Stanford University, 1982: 60.

benefits they would have to offer to attract wage labor—primarily unmarried males—and the terms (especially size of plot) needed to attract sharecroppers and their families (Figure 14.6).

As a result, there was a tremendous diversity of institutional arrangements in the South for combining the planter's land with the freedman's labor and miscellaneous other farming inputs. Wage contracts, for example, might involve time wages per day, week, month, or year. Payment might be made frequently or only after harvest. Additionally, wage contracts might specify piece or task rates, and the contracts might cover groups ("gangs") as well as individuals. Wage contracts went overwhelmingly to young unmarried males, who presumably had few local ties. Just as there was diversity in wage rates, so fixed payment tenancy took two forms: money ("cash rent") or crops ("standing rents"). Moreover, there was sharecropping, in which the landlord provided the land and managerial supervision and some or all of the equipment and workstock in return for a share of the output. As with other tenure arrangements, this broad category encompassed true share tenants who supplied everything but the land. They had secure legal tenure.

There were also croppers who might supply nothing but their labor. Tenant shares might range from perhaps two-thirds for the true share tenant to as little as one-third for the cropper. These contracts typically went to older persons of reputation with families (who might supply additional labor in times of need), while the cash tenants were older, well-established families of reputation with some wealth and resources. In addition, any of these diverse contracts could be modified by innumerable side payments and agreements. The result was a hodgepodge of different contractual arrangements that might be explained by a variety of complementary rather than mutually exclusive hypotheses, such as risk-sharing arrangements and monitoring and supervision costs.[10]

Sharecropping in its various forms emerged as the dominant tenure arrangement in the postbellum South as a compromise. The ex-slaves detested wage work in gangs and wanted some ownership or tenure rights even if these involved some risk. The landlords disliked the idea of arm's-length cash-rental agreements because they did not trust African-Americans to work hard or to maintain property carefully on their own. Sharecropping involved a mix of the two systems, providing some independence to African-Americans, but not so much that landowners could not supervise the day-to-day activities of their tenants.

It is alleged, however, that sharecropping (as opposed to renting) was an inefficient economic solution to the problem of how best to work the land because it reduced production incentives. Consider, for example, the case of a sharecropper who knows that one more day's work in the cotton fields, harvesting the remnants, will increase total crop output by $5 worth. On half shares, the expected gain to the cropper is only $2.50. Consequently, if the casual day labor market wage (or the cropper's shadow price of leisure) is anything over $2.50, the tenant would prefer to let the $5 worth of cotton rot in the fields. As a result, aggregate income (or welfare) is reduced by the difference between the $5 worth of cotton and the day wage (or shadow price of leisure). However, adverse incentives exist under other arrangements as well. Under either a wage contract or straight land rental contract, one of the two parties has a guaranteed income and thus no direct stake in maximizing the value of output.[11] Under a sharecropping arrangement, by contrast, both parties have a clear stake in rapid adjustment to changes in weather or price expectations, and no barrier stands in the way of adjusting work schedules. Sharecropping agreements, moreover, were not lifetime arrangements; they were renegotiated annually. If the landlord suspected that tenants might have produced greater yields through greater diligence, he could always look for a new tenant. Competition among tenants thus

[10] Reid (1973), for example, stresses risk while Alston and Higgs (1981) emphasize the role of transactions costs and the creation of incentive to optimize land use in the absence of continuous monitoring.
[11] Reid (1973).

might force sharecroppers to work as hard as renters, but in general the absolute residual claimancy of one of the parties under either a wage contract or cash tenancy generated stronger incentives to maximize output.[12]

Lack of security in tenure may also have generated adverse incentives with respect to land use. Without some security of tenure or the offer of compensation, effort expended preventing soil erosion, repairing fences, improving breeding stock, and so on was effort wasted from the tenant's perspective. The fruits of any significant productivity improvement would be captured by the landowner. Tenants who shirked on maintenance could always be thrown off the land at the end of the contract year, to be replaced by new tenants who offered a competitive level of service. Cash side payments could also be made to get tenants to finish specific tasks.

Even so, sharecropping was well suited to conditions in the postemancipation South. The ex-slaves had few marketable resources beyond their labor to offer. The owners of the now relatively scarce resource land had an incentive to work it as labor-intensively as possible. With the landowner receiving a fixed share of the total crop, the more intensively the land is worked, the more money the landlord stood to make. Consequently, landowners adopted the strategy of limiting the acreage worked by a single tenant family to induce intensive cultivation. By making land the fixed factor and labor the variable one, as there was less land with which to work, the value of the marginal product of land (and the return to the landlord) rose while labor income fell, although ultimately market forces limited the landlord's ability to reduce labor productivity.

Just as the market limited the ability of tenants to neglect completely the landlord's interest in long-term land investment, the market limited the landlord's ability to exploit his tenants. One measure of how well the market worked is the high degree of geographic mobility among southern farmers. In the early twentieth century more than a third of southern farmers had been on their land less than two years, and more than 60 percent had been there less than five years. Among tenant farmers the five-year persistence rate was less than 20 percent.[13] African-Americans as a group, who were to be found overwhelmingly among the ranks of the sharecropping tenants, were thus much more likely to have moved recently than whites, although whether this was by choice or necessity is not known. Within specific tenure groups, however, African-Americans were less likely to move than others, perhaps because these longer-term residents were the recipients of patronage and paternalism from the landlord. These nonmarket services, which protected the black families from intimidation and an arbitrary criminal and civil justice system in return for deference and subservience, were of substantial value and not lightly relinquished for marginal market gains.[14]

[12] Alston and Higgs (1981).
[13] Pritchett (1987).
[14] Alston and Ferrie (forthcoming).

Emancipation granted the ex-slaves nothing beyond their freedom and the right to the products of their future labor. Slavery had restricted their acquisition of human capital. Most had known little other than unskilled labor, and literacy rates were low. Despite the pernicious influence of racial discrimination, incomes of black Americans grew more rapidly than those of whites, averaging about 2.7 percent per year.[15] Moreover, African-Americans accumulated wealth, including real estate, more rapidly than whites in the late nineteenth and early twentieth centuries. In Georgia, for instance, the value of black property per person increased from just one thirty-sixth that of whites in 1880 to perhaps one-sixteenth of the white per capita property holdings by 1910.[16] This general pattern was repeated across the South.[17] Still, African-Americans achieved farm ownership only slowly. In Georgia, for example, they owned fewer than six hundred thousand acres (about 2 percent of the land in farms in Georgia and an area about the size of a county) by 1880. By 1880 only 9 percent of southern cropland was cultivated by wage laborers on large farms while tenant farmers, both African-American and white, farmed about 40 percent of the land. The remaining acreage was mostly owned and operated by white family farmers.[18]

Although the South had relatively few banks before the Civil War, there seems to have been no shortage of short-term credit for cotton and other staple crop producers. The commodity credit system was shattered by the Civil War. By 1880, though, it had partially recovered. The growth in the number of banks after the war masks a sharp reduction in total bank assets from prewar levels. Nowhere was the resulting lack of bank credit felt more keenly than among small farmers, particularly former slaves. Poor, small farmers had neither the time nor the skills to make a two-day trip to the county seat to negotiate a $100 bank loan against next autumn's crop. Nor would these bankers have had the knowledge of a tenant's reputation and abilities to make a rational and fair appraisal of the risks of such a loan. Thus local merchants became bankers by default, selling food, clothing, and agricultural inputs (on credit) to farmers who pledged their crops as security. These merchants were able to exercise some degree of monopoly power because of (1) location advantages—farmers were naturally reluctant to travel beyond the nearest town to do their provisioning—and (2) high market entry and contract enforcement costs—merchants had to know their credit customers well.[19] One way in which this monopoly power manifested itself was in the alleged high price of rural credit. For example, the credit price for foodstuffs was perhaps 30 percent higher than the cash price (Table 14.3). However, since it is difficult to assert ownership rights over goods that have already been consumed, a good part of this difference may reflect the high risks of

[15] Higgs (1977, 1982).
[16] Higgs (1982).
[17] Margo (1984).
[18] Ransom and Sutch (1977).
[19] Ibid.

TABLE 14.3

Food Prices for Southern Farmers, 1879–1880

Food	Cash	Credit	% Difference
Shelled corn ($/bushel)	.765	.998	30
Bacon ($/lb)	.080	.102	28
Food index (1859 = 100)	79.1	101.5	28
Overall cost of living (1859 = 100)	86.2	99.6*	13

* If 60 percent of family purchases are made on credit.

Source: Roger Ransom and Richard Sutch, *One Kind of Freedom* (Cambridge, England: Cambridge University Press, 1977): 218. Reprinted by permission of Cambridge University Press.

such business. Indeed, despite these high interest rates, local merchants rarely became wealthy. Few had a net worth over $5,000 and there was considerable turnover in the business. There were few barriers to entry other than the potential number of customers, and the actual rapid entry into this business should have kept any potential monopoly profits in check. Equally, many country shopkeepers must have made frequent errors of judgment in extending credit to customers or in the pricing of that credit, for many failed and exited the business.[20]

Suppose, however, that we allow some element of monopoly in rural store credit. Under ordinary circumstances, such monopoly power distorts resource allocation by reducing the output of the product or service monopolized—in this case agricultural credit. Ransom and Sutch, however, claim that country store credit created or at least exacerbated a very different sort of allocative inefficiency: overspecialization in cotton production. Merchants insisted that debtors grow cotton to secure their debts, possibly because this tended to lock in debtors, reducing farm self-sufficiency in food and thereby ensuring that the farmer would be back next year needing food on credit. There is, however, a far less sinister motive for country merchants to have preferred payment in cotton over other crops: There existed a finely developed national and international market in cotton that lowered the transactions cost of dealing in cotton as opposed to, say, corn.

One important consequence of what Ransom and Sutch label "debt peonage" was the marked decline in postbellum southern food production. In the Deep South, where the change was most dramatic, corn production declined from 29 bushels per person in 1860 to only 17.3 bushels per person in 1880. Between 1850 and 1890, on the other hand, the ratio of cotton to corn output more than doubled. With food output per person halved, the South switched from being a net exporter of food to a net importer. This switch from food to staple production was most marked among the smaller farmers

[20] Goldin (1979).

and tenants. Before the war small farmers tended to grow a lot of corn and relatively little cotton, presumably because they had self-sufficiency in food as their primary goal or were too isolated from markets. After the war they devoted a relatively high percentage of their acreage to cotton. Those who rented or sharecropped (the poorest farmers, who needed a cash crop to meet their obligations) devoted an even larger share to cotton as a result of the economic bind in which they found themselves.

Whereas farmers with a potential income above subsistence would plant enough corn to meet their family needs and then plant the remaining acreage in profitable market crops, the only way a small tenant farmer living at the edge of subsistence could be sure of sufficient income to live on was to grow the most lucrative crop:—cotton (Table 14.4). Croppers had little choice but to plant what the landlord ordered. Even other tenants were constrained by lack of suitable security debts other than marketable crops in the field.

Consider the situation depicted in Figure 14.7, which shows the production possibilities of corn and cotton for a small farmer given his land, work-

TABLE 14.4

Value of Output per Acre of Cotton and Corn, 1866–1900

	Yield × Price per Acre		Cotton Yield × Price + Seed − Nonlabor Costs
	Cotton	Corn	
Alabama	$14.39	$7.99	$8.58
Arkansas	22.00	9.80	18.95
Georgia	15.24	6.71	8.88
Louisiana	21.68	9.67	16.20
Mississippi	17.98	8.82	12.52
North Carolina	18.60	6.89	11.16
South Carolina	17.37	6.88	10.39
Tennessee	18.49	8.94	15.07
Texas	21.32	11.01	18.82
Unweighted average	18.52	8.52	13.40
Weighted average	18.25	7.68	11.70

Sources: Table taken from Gavin Wright, *Old South, New South* (New York: Basic Books, 1986): 36, Table 2.6. Data from U.S. Department of Agriculture, Division of Statistics, "The Cost of Cotton Production," Misc. Series, Bulletin no. 16 (Washington, D.C.: Government Printing Office, 1899); U.S. Department of Agriculture, Agricultural Marketing Service, *Cotton and Cotton Seed,* Statistical Bulletin no. 164 (Washington, D.C.: Government Printing Office, 1955); U.S. Department of Agriculture, Bureau of Agricultural Economics, "Revised Estimates of Corn Acreage, Yield and Production 1866–1929" (mimeo, 1934); U.S. Department of Agriculture, *Prices of Farm Products Received by Producers,* Statistical Bulletin no. 16 (Washington, D.C.: Government Printing Office, 1927).

FIGURE 14.7

Crop Mix Choice under Assumptions of Self-Sufficiency and Market Involvement

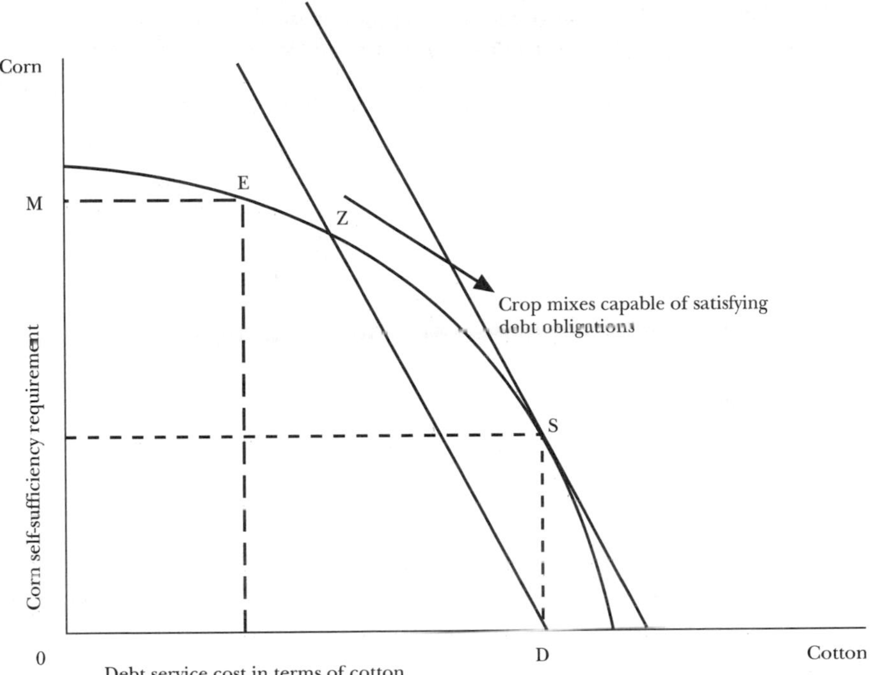

stock, and implements. A farmer who wished to preserve his financial independence and avoid debt with its attendant risks of forced sale or foreclosure might opt for self-sufficiency, what Gavin Wright and Howard Kunreuther call a safety-first strategy. If self-sufficiency requires OM of corn, then the safety-first farmer would produce the basket of goods represented by E even though the expected profit-maximizing set is S. Suppose, however, that the farmer owes a debt that requires a cash income of at least OD to meet the obligation. He cannot now both achieve self-sufficiency and meet his financial obligations. As a result, the farmer is forced to grow more cotton and less corn, producing at least as much cotton as at the point Z since this just generates sufficient cash to meet the debt obligation of OD. Furthermore, since the farmer is now no longer self-sufficient, he probably has to borrow to buy corn at the inflated credit price so the family can eat until harvest. Economic necessity thus dictated crop choice.

Both the Ransom-Sutch lock-in to cotton as a condition for credit and the Wright-Kunreuther hapless-victim theory have provoked vigorous criticism in part because they eschew simple neoclassical economic theory. It seems unlikely that country stores could have exercised much monopoly power over rural credit when entry into the business was so easy or that they were successful in their efforts since exit was so common. High interest rates may indicate the high risk of default and high transactions costs for very small loans just as easily as measuring monopoly power. Relative price shifts rather than changes in attitudes toward risk can explain why farmers chose to plant more cotton and less corn. Moreover, tenant and croppers were not free to choose their own crop mixes. This might well explain why it was these groups rather than the larger owner-operators that changed their crop mixes so dramatically. Whatever the explanation, increasing specialization in a crop with a unit elastic demand resulting in invariant income with changes in price cost the South dearly, at least partially explaining the lag in southern income growth.

Economic Efficiency and Racism in Southern Agriculture

Economists find it useful to distinguish between those kinds of discrimination that affect only personal happiness and those that affect the creation of value. Most aspects of discrimination—the right to sit at the front of the bus or buy a house in a white neighborhood, for example—are largely distributive in the sense that they mainly affect the distribution of personal happiness. Such discrimination allowed African-Americans less personal happiness while, presumably, giving whites more satisfaction. In general such discrimination does not reduce economic efficiency. It is therefore often more difficult to eradicate. There were, however, ways in which the South's denial of equal rights to former slaves may have led to allocative waste and reduced growth rates.

Job discrimination is dealt with in the chapter on labor markets. It was almost certainly an important source of waste, but it is probable that even if there had been no racial discrimination, most African-Americans who remained in the South after the war would have worked in unskilled agricultural jobs since few were literate or possessed marketable skills. Nonetheless, racism blocked the path to personal advancement: landownership. African-Americans could rarely borrow money to buy land, and even when they did amass the necessary cash, whites were often reluctant to sell to them or to tolerate them as neighbors. The failure of African-Americans to buy their own land does not itself prove discrimination, for ex-slaves were starting from the position of owning nothing while landownership is often the product of many generations' accumulated savings. Indeed, African-Americans were able to accumulate real estate rather more rapidly than whites. But whereas elsewhere and among whites tenancy was a stepping-stone to personal independence as an owner, African-Americans found it difficult to advance from cropper to share tenant, let alone to cash tenant or owner, and where African-American farmers were able to buy land, they were often still unable to acquire the necessary capital with which to work the land. Doubtless some of the differences were accounted for by the different types and locations of land. But the value of farm implements per acre in crops on black-owned farms was little more than half that on white-owned farms; whereas 37 percent of white-owned farms purchased fertilizer, only 21 percent of African-American-owned farms did. African-Americans, moreover, had less opportunity to raise productivity by means of land-intensive farming methods. Owner-operated white farms used nearly twice the acreage per worker, allowing them to rest about double the acreage each year.[21]

Compounding this "static" allocative inefficiency was the "dynamic" long-term inefficiency created by racial barriers to investment in education and skill acquisition. The ability to read, write, and do simple arithmetic gave farmers access to information useful in raising productivity. In 1880 more than three-quarters of the black population aged ten and over was illiterate, compared with only about a fifth of the white population. Similarly, in the late nineteenth century school attendance rates among the white school-age population were perhaps 50 percent higher than among black children. The problem was not one of lack of interest in and concern with education, but poverty and the need for many hands to make light work on the black-operated farms of the rural South. Indeed, it is interesting to note that educational expenditures per pupil in the 1880s in many southern states were relatively equal for white and black students.[22] Data show that school expenditures per pupil were equal regardless of race in Alabama and North Carolina in 1890. Even where expenditures were quite different between the two groups, the ratio of expenditures per African-American pupil to expenditures per white student was relatively much more equal than it was to become in the early years of the twentieth century. In Florida, Louisiana, and Mississippi, for example, expenditures per African-American student were about half those for white students in 1890, but by 1910 Florida and Mississippi spent little more than a quarter as much per black student as they spent on white students, while Louisiana spent less than one-fifth as much on a black student as on a white.[23] These differences may overstate the difference in the quantity of education between the two groups because African-American teachers were also the victims of discrimination, being paid less than white teachers with similar qualifications. The switch in policy around the turn of the century was part of a larger movement to deny African-Americans their rights through disenfranchisement. This movement reflected envy at the remarkable gains that African-Americans had made since emancipation and increased economic competition between blacks and whites over jobs and resources.[24]

[21] Ransom and Sutch (1977).
[22] Higgs (1977); Margo (1990).
[23] Margo (1990).
[24] Higgs (1977); Kousser (1974); Margo (1990).

The Plight of the Ex-Slave

In spite of social and legal discrimination, the economic status of African-Americans surely improved with the end of slavery. By assuming that ex-slaves were able to obtain the equivalent of a competitive wage—that is, that ex-slaves were not exploited in the neoclassical sense—Ransom and Sutch calculate that the typical per capita income for an African-American sharecropping family was 43 percent higher than that for slaves. Slaves on large plantations had enjoyed more material benefits; hence they gained less from the transition to freedom—about 30 percent (see Table 14.5). Using Fogel and Engerman's computation of typical slave incomes generates somewhat different results. Their more generous estimates for plantation slaves put the material gains to freedom at a much lower level. Indeed, ex-slaves who had lived on large plantations would seem to have lost ground as a result of emancipation.

However, any possible ambiguity in the direction of change in income disappears by imputing a value to the increase in leisure time freed slaves chose to consume (see Table 14.6). The low estimate, which assumes that African-Americans reduced their average work input by 28 percent, brings per capita income equivalence to $57.75; the high estimate, based on a 37 percent labor time reduction, puts the figure at $65.91. The narrowest margin—the one between Fogel-Engerman's plantation slave and an ex-slave with an income equivalent to $57.75—suggests a gain of at least 34 percent.

Ransom and Sutch simply assume that African-American sharecroppers received the full competitive wage. But there is little doubt that landowners made every effort to strangle competition for labor, barring African-American entry into some occupations and passing vagrancy laws that restricted African-Americans from searching for alternative employment. Landowners were also guilty of behaving paternalistically—that is, dispensing nonmarket goods, such as justice and protection, to those deemed "worthy" while denying them to the "unworthy."[25]

If these policies were successful, then landless African-Americans whose market alternatives were limited by racism and overt racial hostility might have been paid real wages below those dictated by labor productivity. One test of this is to compare the share of output that would accrue to southern agricultural labor in a competitive market with sharecroppers' allotments.[26] If croppers received less than their competitive share, this could be interpreted as evidence of exploitation. The data, however, suggest that labor's share should have been between 21 percent (Texas) and 36 percent (Alabama), with an average predicted share of 31 percent for the South as a whole—well below the 50 percent specified in many sharecropping con-

[25] Alston and Ferrie (forthcoming).
[26] DeCanio (1974).

TABLE 14.5

Black per Capita Income (1859 dollars)

	Fogel-Engerman (1859)	Ransom-Sutch (1859)	Black Sharecroppers (1879)
Large plantations	42.99	32.12	41.39
Average	34.13	28.95	

Sources: Robert Fogel and Stanley Engerman, *Time on the Cross II* (Boston: Little, Brown, 1974): 159; Roger Ransom and Richard Sutch, *One Kind of Freedom* (Cambridge, England: Cambridge University Press, 1977): 3, 5. Reprinted by permission of Cambridge University Press.

TABLE 14.6

Black per Capita Income-Equivalent Welfare (1859 dollars)

	Large Plantations	Sharecroppers (1879)	% Change 1859–79
Material income	32.12	41.39	29
Value of additional leisure time			
Low estimate		16.34	
High estimate		24.52	
Total			
Low estimate	32.12	57.75	80
High estimate	32.12	65.91	105

Source: Roger Ransom and Richard Sutch, *One Kind of Freedom* (Cambridge, England: Cambridge University Press, 1977): 7. Reprinted by permission of Cambridge University Press.

tracts. Thus it seems that landlords were unable to exploit their tenants by paying an implicit wage below the competitive market wage. Exploitation, however, may still have been possible if tenants were forced to farm very small plots of land, thus constraining labor productivity rather than pushing wage payments below their competitive level.[27]

Overall, with a century's hindsight, it seems that markets performed reasonably well, at least when they were given a chance. White political control—maintained by restrictive voting laws and terror—which limited access to education and the provision of other local services and public goods, seriously handicapped a large fraction of the population. The South's unimpressive economic performance in the first few postwar decades was almost

[27] Wright (1986).

inevitable: Free African-Americans could not be expected to work like slaves. Nor could the South control the declining fortunes of cotton in the world economy. The real failing of the southern economic system was its lack of flexibility. Land and labor remained locked into staple production, but per capita economic growth depended upon diversification and, most probably, substantial movement of labor into manufacturing or out of the region entirely. In part the continuing misery of African-Americans after emancipation is attributable to economic exploitation and to racial discrimination in everyday life. But the great portion of blame must go to the failure to provide ex-slaves with property comparable to that of landed whites or to provide access to the education and jobs vital to social mobility.

Bibliography

Aldrich, Mark. "Flexible Exchange Rates, Northern Expansion and the Market for Southern Cotton." *Journal of Economic History* 33 (1973): 339–416.

Alston, Lee J., and Robert Higgs. "Contractual Mix in Southern Agriculture since the Civil War: Facts, Hypothesis and Tests." *Journal of Economic History* 42 (1981): 327–53.

Alston, Lee J., and Joseph Ferrie. "Paternalism in Agricultural Labor Contract in the U.S. South: Implications for the Growth of the Welfare State." *American Economic Review* (forthcoming).

Brown, William, and Morgan Reynolds. "Debt Peonage Re-examined." *Journal of Economic History* 33 (1973): 862–71.

Conrad, Alfred, et al. "Slavery as an Obstacle to Economic Growth in the United States: A Panel Discussion." *Journal of Economic History* 27 (1967): 518–60.

Decanio, Stephen, "Cotton Overproduction in Late 19th Century Agriculture." *Journal of Economic History* 33 (1973): 608–33.

———. "Productivity and Income Distribution in the Postbellum South." *Journal of Economic History* 34 (1974): 422–46.

Fogel, Robert W., et al. *Without Consent or Contract: The Rise and Fall of Slavery*, vol. 1. New York: W.W. Norton, 1989.

———. *Without Consent or Contract: Evidence and Methods*, vol. 2. New York: W. W. Norton, 1992.

———. *Without Consent or Contract: Technical Papers Volume I*, vol. 3. New York: W.W. Norton, 1992.

———. *Without Consent or Contact: Technical Papers Volume II*, vol. 4. New York: W. W. Norton, 1992.

Fogel, Robert, and Stanley Engerman. *Time on the Cross*, New York: Little, Brown, 1974.

Goldin, Claudia. "'N' Kinds of Freedom." *Explorations in Economic History* 16 (1979): 8–30.

———, and Frank Lewis. "The Economic Cost of the American Civil War: Estimates and Implications." *Journal of Economic History* 35 (1975): 294–326.

Higgs, Robert. "Patterns of Farm Rental in the Georgia Cotton Belt, 1880–1900." *Journal of Economic History* 34 (1974): 468–82.

———. *Competition and Coercion: Blacks in the American Economy, 1865–1914.* New York: Cambridge University Press, 1977.

———. "Accumulation of Property by Southern Blacks before World War I." *American Economic Review* 72 (1982): 725–37.

Kotlikoff, Laurence, and Sebastian Pinera. "The Old South's Stake in the Interregional Movement of Slaves, 1850–1860." *Journal of Economic History* 37 (1977): 434–50.

Kousser, Morgan. *The Shaping of Southern Politics: Sufferage, Restructuring and the Establishment of the One Party South, 1880–1920.* (New Haven: Yale University Press, 1974).

Margo, Robert A. "Accumulation of Property by Southern Blacks before World War I: Comment and Further Evidence." *American Economic Review* 74 (1984): 768–76.

———. *Race and Schooling in the South, 1880–1950* (Chicago: University of Chicago Press, 1990).

McGuire, Robert A., and Robert Higgs. "Cotton, Corn and Risk in the Nineteenth Century: Another View." *Explorations in Economic History* 14 (1979): 167–82.

Olson, John F. "Clock Time versus Real Time: A Comparison of the Lengths of the Northern and Southern Agricultural Work Years." In Robert Fogel, et al. *Without Consent or Contract: Technical Papers Volume I* (New York: W. W. Norton, 1992): 216–40.

Pritchett, Johnathan. "The Term of Occupancy of Southern Farmers in the First Decades of the Twentieth Century." *Historical Methods* 20 (1987): 107–12.

Ransom, Roger, and Richard Sutch, "Debt Peonage in the Cotton South after the Civil War." *Journal of Economic History* 32 (1972): 641–69.

———. "The Ex-Slave in the Postbellum South: A Study of the Impact of Racism in a Market Environment." *Journal of Economic History* 33 (1973): 131–48.

———. "The Impact of the Civil War and of Emancipation on Southern Agriculture." *Explorations in Economic History* 12 (1975): 1–28.

———. *One Kind of Freedom: The Economic Consequences of Emancipation.* Cambridge, England: Cambridge University Press, 1977.

Reid, Joseph. "Sharecropping as an Understandable Market Response: The Postbellum South." *Journal of Economic History* 33 (1973): 106–30.

Schlomowitz, Ralph. "'Bound' or 'Free'? Black Labor in Cotton and Sugar Cane Farming, 1865–1880." In Robert Fogel, et al., *Without Consent or Contract: Technical Papers Volume I* (New York: W. W. Norton, 1992): 665–86.

Sellers, James. " The Economic Incidence of the Civil War on the South." *Mississippi Valley Historical Review* 14 (1927): 179–91.

Temin, Peter. "The Postbellum Recovery of the South and the Cost of the Civil War." *Journal of Economic History* 36 (1976): 898–907.

Virts, Nancy. "Estimating the Importance of the Plantation System to Southern Agriculture in 1880." *Journal of Economic History* 47 (1987): 984–88.

Weiher, Kenneth. "The Cotton Industry and Southern Urbanization." *Explorations in Economic History* 14 (1977): 120–40.

Wright, Gavin. "Cotton Competition and the Post Bellum Recovery of the American South." *Journal of Economic History* 34 (1974): 610–35.

———. *The Political Economy of the Cotton South.* New York: W. W. Norton, 1978.

———. "Freedom and the Southern Economy." *Explorations in Economic History* 16 (1979): 90–108.

———. "The Strange Career of the New Southern Economic History." *Reviews in American History* 10 (1982): 164–80.

———. *Old South, New South: Revolutions in the Southern Economy.* New York: Basic Books, 1986.

———, and Howard Kunreuther. "Cotton, Corn and Risk in the 19th Century." *Journal of Economic History* 35 (1975): 526-51.

Northern agricultural development after the civil war

15

Before the Civil War—and for a short time afterward—agriculture was preeminent in America. In 1860 there were just over 2 million farms in America. Forty years later there were 5.75 million farms, and land in farms had more than doubled to a little over 840 million acres. Nevertheless, agriculture did not grow as rapidly as other sectors of the economy, and productivity was low compared with that in manufacturing. In 1860, for example, agriculture employed six times as much capital as manufacturing and two and one-half times as many people, yet produced just twice as much value added. Before the Civil War, however, northern agriculture contributed more to commodity output than did manufacturing; producing output was valued at $853 million (in 1879 prices), compared with $821 million for manufacturing and mining (see Table 13.9 above). But the lead did not last long. By 1880 the value of manufacturing and mining commodity output in the North, $2.015 million, exceeded that of agriculture, $1.861 million. As agriculture failed to keep pace with other sectors of the economy, the share of population living on farms or in rural areas also declined. In 1860 about 80 percent of the population was living in communities of fewer than 2,500 but by 1900 only 60 percent lived in such places. In 1880, the earliest date for official statistics of the farm population, 43.8 percent of the population—about 22 million persons—lived on farms. Twenty years later the fraction had slipped to only 41.9 percent, and beginning in the late 1930s the absolute number of people in agriculture also began to decline. By 1990 less than 2 percent of the population—about 4.5 million people—still lived on farms.

The transformation of America from a rural, agricultural economy to an urban-industrial economy had a profound and oftentimes traumatic effect upon the farm sector. As one historian has put it, "Perhaps no development of the nineteenth century brought greater disappointment to the American farmers than did their failure to realize the prosperity that they had expected from industrialism."[1] In this chapter the focus is on the changes in agriculture in the northern states and how farmers sought political solutions to their real or imagined economic problems. In subsequent chapters we shall see how some of these political solutions affected the other sectors of the economy and shaped many of our institutions.

Much of agriculture's dramatic post–Civil War expansion took place in the Midwest and West, partly in response to the Homestead Act and other changes in federal land policy. Whereas in the Northeast the number of farms increased by only about 20 percent, in the Midwest the number tripled, and out West the number grew sevenfold. Improved acreage—that is, land planted in crops—expanded particularly rapidly in Missouri, Iowa, Kansas, Nebraska, Minnesota, and the Dakotas and in the Central Valley of California (Figure 15.1). Millions of acres of once-virgin land were brought under the plow, sometimes with disastrous ecological consequences.

As land in farms expanded, agricultural output grew dramatically. Gross farm output increased at an average annual rate of 2.5 percent between 1869 and 1909, with corn production growing 3.1 percent per year and wheat production 2.2 percent per year.[2] Much of this growth, however, was extensive rather than intensive. Western wheat yields, for example, rose only one bushel per acre to fourteen bushels per acre between 1840 and 1910, partly because labor supply problems in northern agriculture encouraged the use of ever more land-extensive farm practices.[3] Despite the rapid growth in output, however, total factor productivity in agriculture lagged well behind that of the rest of the economy. The average annual improvement for the farm sector was only about 0.7 percent, and just 0.6 percent for the midwestern Grain Belt, compared with 1.7 percent for the nonfarm sector between 1889 and 1899.[4] Nonetheless, as we have seen (Chapter 10), massive doses of capital in the form of laborsaving machinery did allow substantial increases in labor productivity.

Federal land policy and improved transportation had opened up vast areas of the continent to farming and settlement, but much of the new land, particularly in the high plains and the Far West, was marginal and ecologically fragile. By 1859 the center of wheat production in the United States was near Indianapolis, and in the years that followed it shifted farther west,

[1] Saloutos (1948)
[2] Kendrick and Peck (1961).
[3] Parker and Klein (1966). In the South, however, emancipation was accompanied by a sharp increase in yield per acre for most crops as southern agriculture switched from land-extensive and (slave) labor-intensive methods toward more land-intensive cropping patterns by croppers and tenants, with the size of the lots being determined by the landlord so as to maximize the rent—that is, the surplus production from the land.
[4] Kendrick and Peck (1961).

FIGURE 15.1
Improved Land

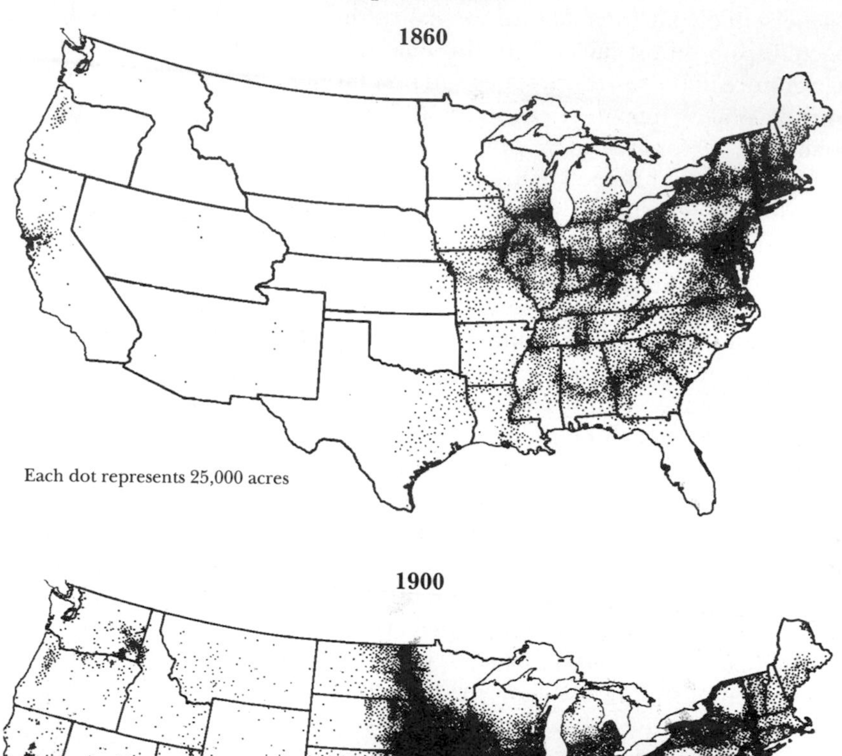

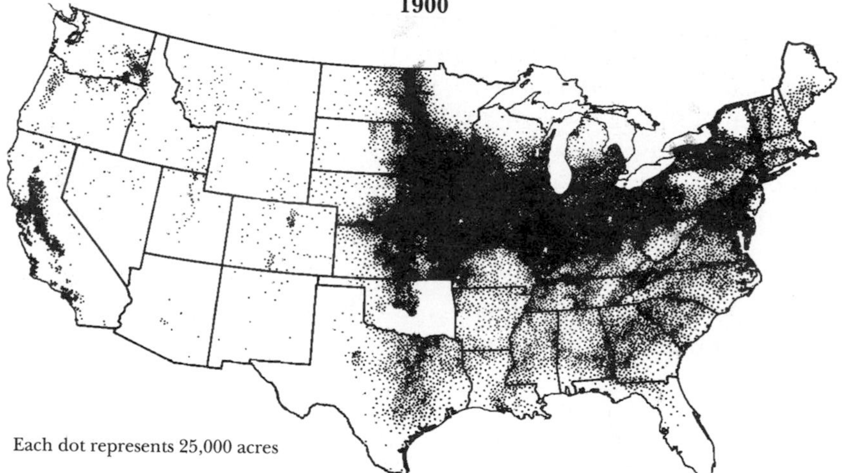

Source: Charles O. Paullin, *Atlas of the Historical Geography of the United States* (Washington, D.C.: Carnegie Institution, 1932): Plates 144D and 144H.

being located in western Iowa by 1919. As the center of wheat production shifted farther west, two distinct wheat-growing areas emerged: hard spring-planted wheat in the northern plains states and Minnesota, winter wheat to the south from southern Illinois through Kansas and Oklahoma (Figure 15.2). Sandwiched between the two was the Corn Belt (Figure 15.3). The

FIGURE 15.2

Wheat Production

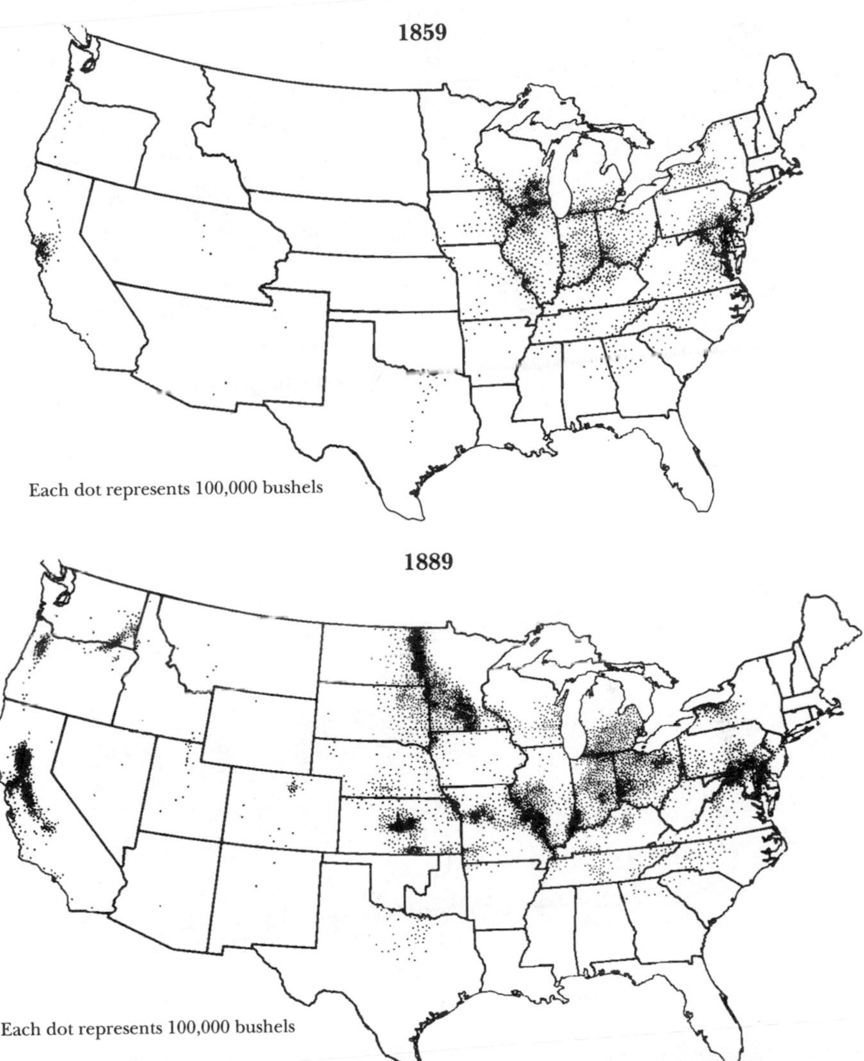

Source: Charles O. Paullin, *Atlas of the Historical Geography of the United States* (Washington, D.C.: Carnegie Institution, 1932): Plates 143Q and 143R.

emergence of the Wheat Belts and the Corn Belt in the North reflect growing regional specialization, defined as the fraction of the nation's output of a crop produced by a particular region, in American agriculture. However, whereas southern cotton farms after emancipation grew more cotton and less of everything else, northern farms remained relatively and absolutely

FIGURE 15.3

Corn Production

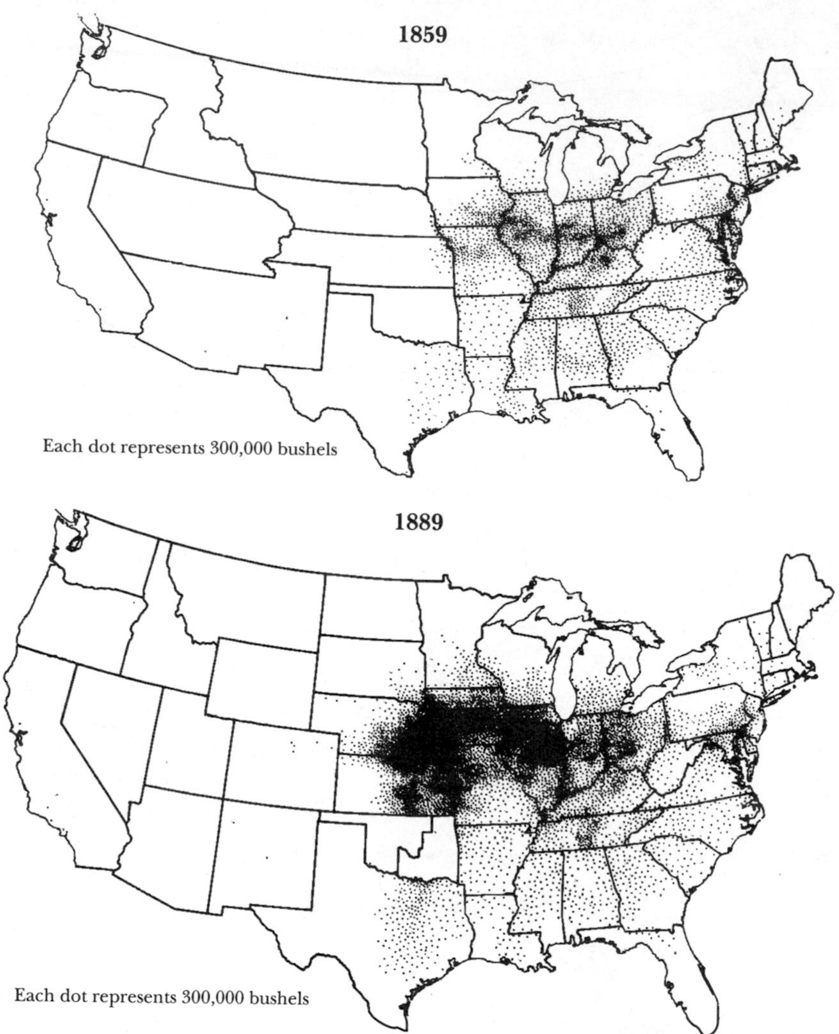

Source: Charles O. Paullin, *Atlas of the Historical Geography of the United States* (Washington, D.C.: Carnegie Institution, 1932): Plates 143L and 143M.

more diversified until the twentieth century. Indeed, recent research has found that farmers in Missouri at least actually became less specialized, growing a greater diversity of crops, in the years before 1880.[5]

[5] Gregson (1993).

Farm Tenancy and the Agricultural Ladder

The progressive liberalization of the terms of transfer of the public lands into private hands must have limited the scarcity value of land in the nineteenth century. Locational advantages, such as proximity to a city or access to cheap transportation, still, of course, carried a premium, but even close to cities, rapid urbanization and the spread of the rail network did much to diffuse those gains over a wide area. Over time, land prices rose, reflecting a myriad of different factors, including improvements made to the land, increased demand, changes in locational advantage, as well as decreased supply (Figure 15.4). Between 1850 and 1915, for example, the real value of land rose at an average annual rate of 2.08 percent, increasing more than fourfold over the period. This rise might have been even faster—2.18 percent a year—had not the drift to poorer-quality land in the West more than offset the 0.29 percent per year quality gain through improvements to fixed sites.[6] Even so, land prices in America were low relative to elsewhere in the developed world of the nineteenth century. Land prices were also undoubtedly lower than they would have been in the absence of the liberal federal land policy. Because land was relatively cheap in America, the dominant view in American history has been that anyone who wanted land in the nineteenth century could have it.

This interpretation did not go unchallenged. Reversing the logic of the traditional argument that free or cheap land promoted ownership, the noted agricultural historian Paul W. Gates claimed that the system instead promoted the growth of tenancy: "The Land Ordinance of 1785 and subsequent laws had placed no restrictions upon the amount of public land that individuals or groups could acquire. . . . The policy of unlimited sales and unrestricted transfer of titles made possible land monopolization by speculators, who acquired most of the choice lands in certain areas. . . . This resulted in the early disappearance of cheap or free land and the emergence of tenancy."[7]

In Gates's view, passage of the Homestead Act in 1862 simply exacerbated the problem as speculators found dummy entrymen to file claims, made fraudulent land entries, and took advantage of the commutation privilege of paying $1.25 an acre to receive title rather than cultivate the land for five years and receive the land for free. As a result, large tracts of land were acquired by speculators, land companies, and the wealthy. Moreover, the railroads were given vast acreages through federal land grants with the result that the market supply of land was reduced and price was bidden up.

Higher land prices meant that would-be farmers were compelled to spend more of their incomes on land since the demand for land was inelas-

[6] Lindert (1988).
[7] Gates (1939): 3.

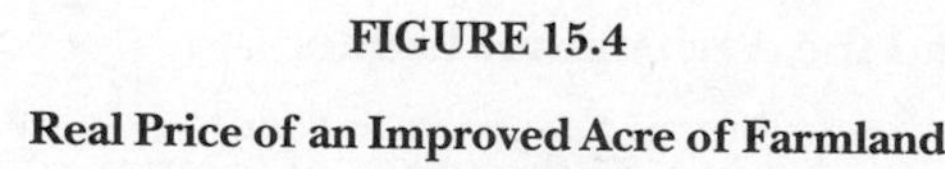

FIGURE 15.4

Real Price of an Improved Acre of Farmland

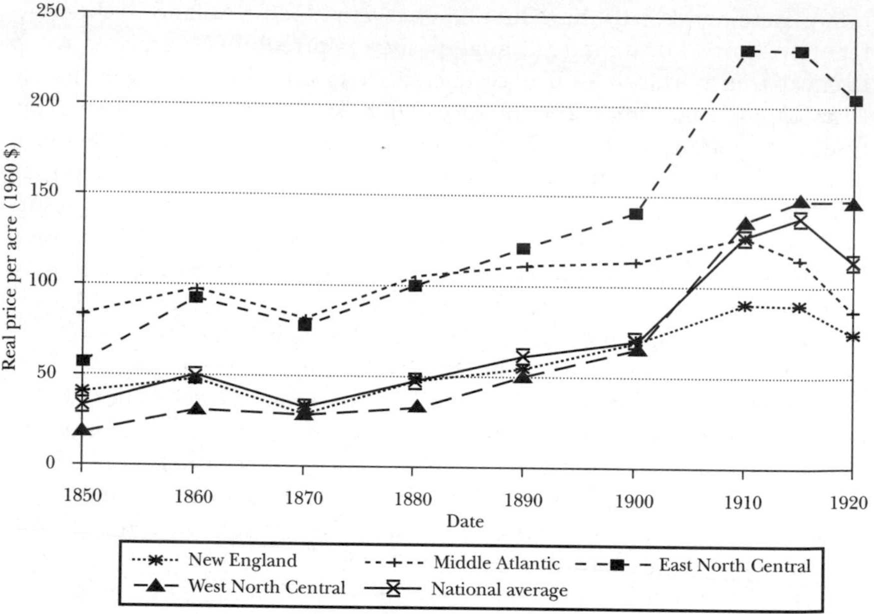

Source: Peter H. Lindert, "Long-run Trends in American Farmland Values," *Agricultural History* 63 (1988): 52–53, Table 2.

tic. Those who could not afford to pay these higher prices and could not borrow were faced with a choice of farming smaller areas or becoming tenants. Some may have been excluded from the land market altogether, forced into farm wage labor or pushed into seeking their livelihoods elsewhere.

When the first statistics on tenancy were collected in 1880, they showed that nationwide a quarter of all farmers did not own the land they farmed. Although tenancy was common almost everywhere, it was most prevalent in the South. Perhaps more surprisingly, tenancy rates in the Midwest—where settlement had taken place most recently and under the supposedly favorable conditions created by federal land policy—were higher than on the East Coast, where factors promoting economic concentration, such as luck, superior ability, and inheritance, not to mention institutional factors, such as the manorial settlement patterns in early New York, had operated longer. Subsequent censuses revealed steady increases in the tenancy rate. In state after state the fraction of farmers who owned their farms shrank. In the western part of the Midwest, for example, tenancy increased 50 percent between 1880 and 1900. Elsewhere in the United States the rate increased about 30 percent over the period. In 1880 almost a quarter of Iowa farmers were ten-

FIGURE 15.5

Relative Size of Tenure Categories in Four States, 1880–1930

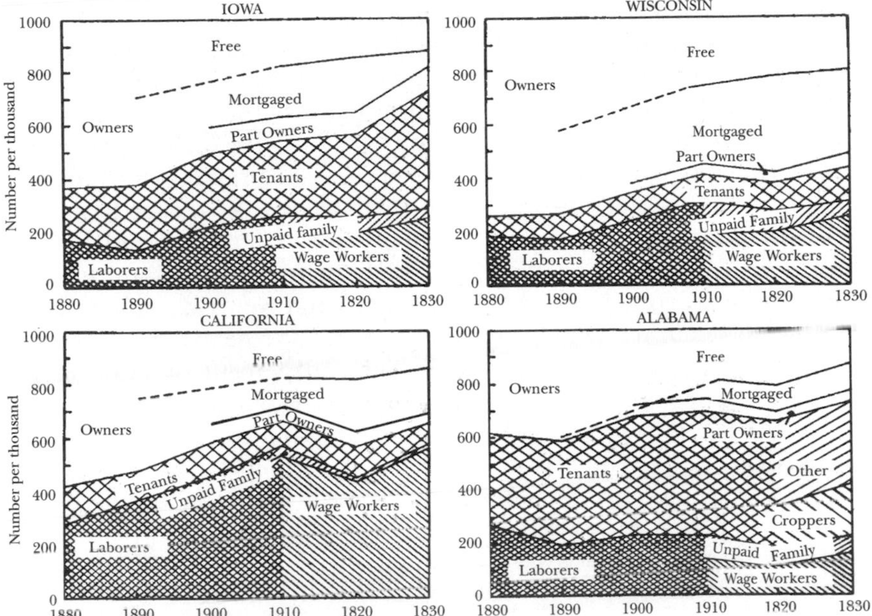

Source: John D. Black and R. H. Allen, "The Growth of Farm Tenancy in the United States," *Quarterly Journal of Economics* (1937): 401.

ants. By 1900 more than a third were tenants, and by 1930 the tenancy rate in Iowa neared one-half. In Wisconsin more farmers owned their land, but even there the trend was the same. In 1880 the tenancy rate in Wisconsin was about 9 percent, by 1900 it was 13.5 percent, and by 1930 it had risen to 18.2 percent (Figure 15.5).

The question that interested agricultural economists and agricultural historians was why tenancy rates were increasing. Some viewed tenancy as "a convenient way of approach to full ownership. It is, in fact, part of the agricultural ladder . . . one step in the process whereby a man starting in life with limited capital, or with nothing but his own energy and enterprise, and after a time acquire the ownership of a farm."[8] Gates and others, however, thought that tenants were yeomen who had fallen on hard times and were slipping back down the agricultural ladder toward landless wage labor. While Gates blamed federal land policy itself, others suggested that the closing of the frontier had cut off the supply of good, cheap public land. Yet others blamed economic adversity. In the farm crisis that began with the

[8] Goldenweisser and Truesdell (1924).

Depression of 1921 and ended with the outbreak of World War II, for example, an average of ninety-six thousand farms per year were foreclosed. At the peak of the crisis in 1933 two hundred thousand farmers lost their farms and were either driven from the land or lapsed into tenancy.[9]

The premise of the agricultural ladder thesis is that there is occupational (and economic) mobility over the life cycle of each individual. This mobility could be up—as assumed by the optimists—or down—as assumed by the pessimists. On the optimists' side, a study conducted as part of the 1920 census found that at least half of all new tenant farmers in the northern half of the United States between 1915 and 1920 had once been farm wage laborers. On average, farm laborers had become tenants by their late twenties in Iowa, Minnesota, and Wisconsin and by their early to mid-thirties elsewhere in the North, except for Massachusetts and New Hampshire, where they had to wait until their late thirties. Tenants also rose to become owners. At least 30 percent outside New England—50 percent or more in the Midwest—of persons who became yeoman farmers during the same period had once been tenants. Upward mobility was thus quite pronounced during the period. It was also quite swift. In Illinois, for example, the truly upwardly mobile—those who had been both laborers and tenants before becoming owners—had spent an average of 6.2 years as laborers and 11.1 years as tenants. In Wisconsin progress was even swifter with an average of only 5.8 years as laborers and 6.1 years as tenants before rising to owners.

However, there was also evidence of some downward mobility. In 1920 about 20 percent of tenants across the northern states farmed land they once had owned. Much of this downward mobility was attributed to inefficiency and misfortune rather than to "the system."[10]

In general, though, it is extremely difficult to document the agricultural ladder because it requires detailed individual life histories. Instead researchers have relied upon cohort analysis—the study of individual groups born within specific time intervals—across successive decennial censuses. The problem with this approach is that cohort membership changes over time, making definitive interpretation risky. Nevertheless, some conclusion can be drawn from the evidence. The data show that more young farmers began as tenants and more remained in each age-group over time.[11] In 1890 more than half of all farmers under twenty-five years old nationwide began as tenants. By 1910 more than three-quarters started out this way (Figure 15.6). The data would thus more than seem to justify the pessimism that movement on the ladder was predominantly one of descent rather than ascent. However, if it is assumed that each age cohort at successive censuses is composed mainly of survivors from the younger cohort at the preceding census (a possibly heroic assumption), then the percentage in any age co-

[9] Alston (1983).
[10] Goldenweisser and Truesdell (1924).
[11] Atack (1988); Wright (1988).

FIGURE 15.6

Tenancy Rates by Age of Farm Operator, 1890–1930

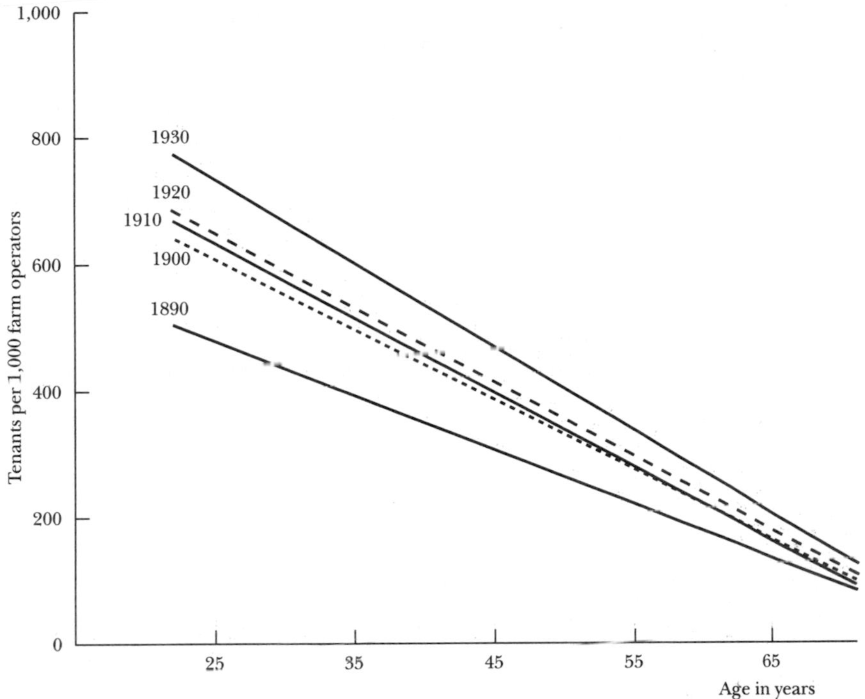

Source: John D. Black and R. H. Allen, "The Growth of Farm Tenancy in the United States," *Quarterly Journal of Economics* 51 (1937): 410.

hort at one census should have exceeded that in the younger age cohort at the preceding census if farmers were backsliding into tenancy. Instead the reverse was true, except between 1890 and 1900, when the agricultural crisis was particularly severe.

The pattern of rising tenancy, particularly among young farmers just embarking upon their careers, is consistent with the view that rising capital costs over time, driven largely by rising land values, posed an increasing barrier to entry. The data also reveal that tenancy rates for different decades tended to converge among the more elderly so that the fraction of septuagenarian farm operators who were tenants was almost a constant. If success is defined as owner occupancy among those who remained in farming, then success was approximately constant over the forty years from 1890 to 1930 and maybe even since 1850. Unfortunately the data provide no clue to whether these people were tenants because they chose to be or whether the economic system generated a more or less constant fraction of aspiring farmers who failed in their bids for owner occupancy yet refused to quit the business.

Farm Mortgages and Foreclosure

Farming became increasingly expensive in the late nineteenth century. The real price of land was rising throughout the period until after World War I.[12] Mechanization further strained the financial resources of farmers. For many, tenancy was the only way to farm, but others chose to borrow. For some, borrowing was a fatal mistake, which resulted in foreclosure and loss of the family farm. Others were successful, but they had to pay close attention to agricultural product markets and the farm cash flow to generate the cash to meet their periodic financial obligations and avoid default. Even for the successful farmer, however, a mortgage in the nineteenth century must have been cause for worry. The only available mortgages were short-term balloon mortgages. Such loans were unamortized—that is, periodic payments met the interest obligations but contributed nothing to the principal, which was payable in full upon expiration of the mortgage. Mortgage terms were typically three years or less and might be renewed, though terms were never certain. Why? One suggestion is that such arrangements were preferred by lenders (since they could be rolled over—an important consideration when interest rates themselves were uncertain) and by creditworthy borrowers (who would signal their creditworthiness by accepting shorter-term mortgages with the expectation of more certain renewal).[13] The long-term, amortized mortgages familiar today did not begin to appear until the 1920s.

Farmers in the late nineteenth century complained that monopoly power allowed the representatives of banks and insurance companies to charge interest above competitive rates. The evidence, however, suggests that the western mortgage industry was immensely competitive, thanks, ironically, to the entry of the hated eastern moneylenders into the western market. Interest rates in the 1850s in Iowa averaged 10 percent, which was the usury limit in many states; true interest rates, after allowances for fees, commissions, and so on, were probably much higher. By the 1890s, though, interest rates had declined to 6.5 to 7.5 percent, still higher than interest rates on gilt-edged securities, but the higher rates on farm mortgages probably only reflected the risks of farming on the Great Plains in the 1880s.

There is a subtler argument against agricultural creditors that, on initial hearing, appeals to economists. Mortgages are fixed obligations in money terms, not in real value terms. Hence in a period of declining prices, like the first three post–Civil War decades, mortgage holders were paid back in increasingly valuable dollars by property owners whose incomes were not necessarily growing apace with their financial obligations. The flaw here is that market interest rates adjust to anticipated price trends. Only if debtors fail to

[12] Lindert (1988).

[13] This point has been forcefully and persuasively made by Kenneth Snowden in recent professional presentations.

anticipate declining prices do they truly lose out. And it is hard to believe that farmers' price expectations could have failed to adjust to a trend that lasted thirty years. Farmers were simply not likely to borrow at interest rates that they knew could not be supported by future crop revenues. Moreover, with a short time to maturity, any losses caused by unanticipated price changes should have quickly worked through the system.

In 1890 only 29 percent of farmers were encumbered by mortgages. Among those who were, the debt averaged only 35 percent of their worth. Debt rates were higher in the troubled plains states (60 percent in Kansas, 54 percent in Nebraska). In the years that followed, the average mortgage debt relative to equity fell but more and more farmers became encumbered (Table 15.1).

TABLE 15.1

Percentage of Owner-Occupied Farms Mortgaged (of those reporting)

	1890	1900	1910	1920
New England	28.3	34.1	34.9	39.8
Middle Atlantic	37.0	40.3	38.3	41.1
East North Central	37.6	39.4	40.9	46.1
West North Central	48.0	44.3	46.1	56.9
South	5.7	17.2	23.5	29.0
Mountain	14.1	14.4	20.8	44.4
Pacific	28.7	27.6	26.8	52.1
U.S.	28.2	31.0	35.6	41.4
Non-South	39.9	39.1	40.1	49.4

Mortgage Debt/Farm Value on Mortgaged Farms

	1890	1910	1920
New England	40.4	31.8	33.8
Middle Atlantic	43.2	34.5	36.3
East North Central	33.2	28.6	31.2
West North Central	33.6	25.8	26.5
South	41.3	26.6	28.6
Mountain	31.8	23.9	30.5
Pacific	30.1	23.4	29.8
U.S.	35.5	27.3	29.1

Sources: Gavin Wright, "American Agriculture and the Labor Market: What Happened to Proletarianization?" *Agricultural History* 62 (1988): 187. Based upon data from 13th Census (1910), Vol. V, *Agriculture* (Washington, D.C.: Government Printing Office, 1913): 159–60; 14th Census (1920), Vol. V, *Agriculture* (Washington, D.C.: Government Printing Office, 1922): 484–86.

TABLE 15.2

Probability of a Neighbor's Suffering Foreclosure at Various Foreclosure Rates

Local Annual Foreclosure Rate[a]	Probability[b] of At Least One Neighbor Suffering Foreclosure after: 1 year	2 years	3 years
1%	13%	26%	36%
2	26	45	60
3	37	60	75
5	54	79	90
10	79	96	99

[a]Annual number of foreclosures/total number of mortgages outstanding.
[b]Computed using the binomial distribution with the assumption that fifteen neighboring farms are under mortgage and that the foreclosure of one farm does not affect the probability of a neighboring farm's being foreclosed.

Source: James Stock, "Real Estate Mortgages, Foreclosures and Midwestern Agrarian Unrest, 1865–1920," *Journal of Economic History* 44 (1984): 95. Reprinted by permission of Cambridge University Press.

The risk of individual foreclosure was quite small; the 1890 census quotes foreclosure rates of 0.61 percent in Illinois in 1880 and 1.55 percent in Minnesota in 1891, or between 2.4 percent and 6.1 percent of all mortgages, if we assume an average term of four years. Moreover, the average debt was small. As a result, Robert Fogel and Jack Rutner calculate that the overall wealth loss to farmers caused by foreclosures could not have been large. Even so, farmers probably had good reason to worry. Balloon mortgages, as many borrowers in the late 1970s and early 1980s can attest, carry substantial risk and fear of mortgage foreclosure in the face of repeated bad luck. Statewide foreclosure rates also may seriously understate the risk of foreclosure since it appears that mortgages were particularly heavily concentrated in just a few counties in each state. Indeed, estimates of the probability that a farmer had a neighbor who had been foreclosed are quite high (Table 15.2). Farmers were probably right to worry about foreclosure, particularly during some of the longer lasting periods of low farm prices or repeated harvest failures, such as the 1880s and the 1890s.[14]

The Integration of Northern Agriculture into the World Economy

The integration of markets—the bringing together of suppliers and demanders—is essential for economic efficiency. Although the Civil War appears to have interrupted this process, there is considerable evidence that

[14] Stock (1985).

over time, price differentials between markets decreased and fluctuations were increasingly synchronous. That is, markets became increasingly integrated, whether for capital, labor, or products, both domestically and internationally. With the spreading rail network supplementing and eventually displacing much of the river and canal traffic, midwestern farmers were brought closer to East Coast and overseas consumers. The East Coast had long depended upon midwestern farmers to supply much of its needs in grains, and the two regions became ever more closely linked as transport costs and time in transit declined. Beginning in the 1850s, however, the midwestern grain market expanded overseas as Europe increasingly turned to American farmers for their supply of wheat. Initially, as during the Crimean War, the increase in foreign demand drove prices higher, but eventually supply expanded not just in America but also in the rest of the world. This expansion of the market had a profound impact upon the midwestern economy.

In the period 1875–79 the East Coast farmers produced barely half the wheat consumed there, while Britain produced just 41 percent of its consumption needs. By 1910–13 East Coast production relative to consumption had slipped to only 23 percent, and Britain met only 27 percent of its own needs.[15] These grain deficits were met by imports from a growing number of countries, including Canada, Argentina, and Australia. Much, though, was supplied by midwestern farmers. In 1875–79 the East North Central states produced more than twice what they consumed; the West North Central states, two and a half times as much. By 1914 growing wheat specialization in the West North Central states had boosted their surplus to over 328 percent of consumption needs although in the East North Central states the replacement of wheat with corn had left that region just self-sufficient in wheat. Overall, midwestern wheat exports grew fourfold between 1870 and 1892, and agricultural exports in real 1913 dollars increased from $248 million to $986 million.

The increasing distance between producing and consuming regions would normally mean an increasing spread between the price received by the producer and the price paid by the consumer because of higher transport costs. Instead the gap narrowed dramatically and was virtually eliminated by 1890. For example, the price of No. 2 wheat in Chicago between 1852 and 1856 was less than half that in Liverpool. By 1880–85 it had risen to 84 percent of the British price, and by the eve of World War I the prices were virtually the same (Figure 15.7).

At the same time regional wheat prices within the United States also converged. In the late 1860s and early 1870s wheat prices in the midwestern wheat-growing states ranged from $1.08 per bushel in Nebraska, where settlement was just beginning, to $1.88 in Indiana, the state closest to the East Coast and European markets. This equals a price spread of 80 cents for a ho-

[15] Harley (1978, 1980).

FIGURE 15.7

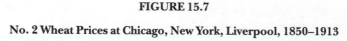

No. 2 Wheat Prices at Chicago, New York, Liverpool, 1850–1913

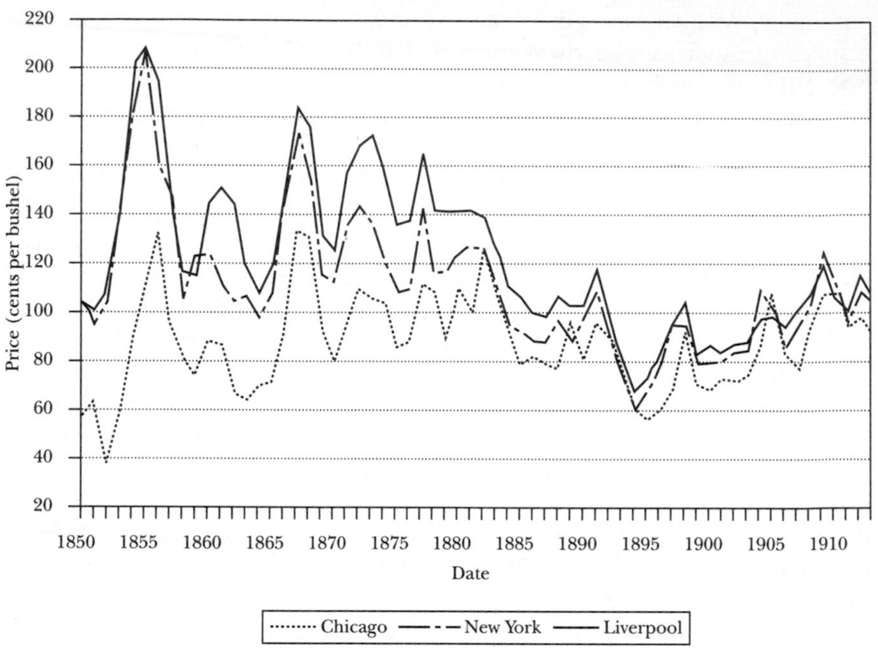

Source: Data from C. Knick Harley, "Transportation, the World Wheat Trade, and the Kuznets Cycle, 1850–1913," *Explorations in Economic History* 17 (1980): 246–47.

mogeneous, relatively inexpensive product. By the late 1880s the spread had narrowed to 37 cents, and by 1913 the spread was just 16 cents, with prices ranging from $1.49 per bushel in Indiana to $1.33 in Nebraska.[16]

The major factor underlying the dramatic reductions in price differentials was improvement in transportation. The spread of rail transportation into areas hitherto served only by wagon was accompanied by continued productivity gains in rail transportation that reduced the real cost of shipping and handling. In 1852–56 the freight cost on a bushel of wheat from Chicago to New York was 20.8 cents. By 1910–13 the cost had been cut to 5.4 cents. Moreover, the substitution of steam and iron for sail and wood reduced transatlantic shipping costs from 14.2 cents per bushel just after the Civil War to 4.9 cents by World War I (Table 15.3).

Analysis of the spatial price data by state and of the spreading rail network shows a strong supply response by farmers to both the price of wheat and the density of the rail system. Higher prices and greater railroad density

[16] Harley (1978).

TABLE 15.3

Price of Wheat, Chicago, New York, and Liverpool with Transportation and Associated Costs, Average 1868–1872, 1880–1884, 1910–1913

	Price of wheat ($)								
	1868–1872			1880–1884			1910–1913		
	Spring	Winter		Spring	Winter				
Chicago	1.02	—		1.07	1.09			0.98	
New York	1.32	1.39		1.17	1.20			1.05	
Liverpool	1.52	1.63		1.31	1.35			1.07	
Spread									
Chicago–New York	0.30	—		0.10	0.11			0.07	
New York–Liverpool	0.20	0.24		0.14	0.15			0.02	
	Transport and Costs ($)								
	Lake & Canal	Lake & Rail	All Rail	Lake & Canal	Lake & Rail	All Rail	Lake & Canal	Lake & Rail	All Rail
Chicago–New York									
Freight rate	0.176	0.212	0.287	0.086	0.117	0.157	0.054	0.062	0.095[a]
Chicago charges	0.015	0.015	0.015	0.012	0.012	0.012	0.005	0.005	0.005
Insurance	0.009	n.a.	n.a.	0.003	n.a.	n.a.	0.003	n.a.	n.a.
Buffalo charges	0.027	n.a.	n.a.	0.022	n.a.	n.a.	0.005	n.a.	n.a.
New York charges	0.020	0.020[a]	0.020[b]	0.005	0.005	0.005	0.005	0.005	0.005
Total Chicago–New York	0.247	0.247	0.322	0.128	0.134	0.174	0.072	0.072	0.106
New York–Liverpool									
Freight rate	0.142			0.086			0.049		
New York charges	0.020			0.008			0.005		
Insurance	0.020			0.012			0.010		
Liverpool charges	0.070			0.065			0.005		
Total New York–Liverpool	0.252			0.171			0.069		

[a] The rate of export reported as $0.078

[b] George G. Tunell, "The Diversion of the Flour and Grain Traffic from the Great Lakes to the Railroads," *Journal of Political Economy* 5 (1897): 345, 346, suggests those charges were higher on grain arriving by rail.

Source: C. Knick Harley, "Transportation, the World Wheat Trade, and the Kuznets Cycle, 1850–1913," *Explorations in Economic History* 17 (1980): 224–25.

led farmers to plant more acres and to do so rather quickly. Econometric estimates suggest that within six years of the advent of cheap overland transportation farmers would have expanded settlement and increased the area under cultivation by an amount sufficient to eliminate about half of any differential between actual and desired production of wheat. This pattern is consistent with the traditional explanation, which holds that falling agricultural prices in the late nineteenth century resulted from shifts in a highly elastic supply curve coupled with price inelastic demand that shifted only modestly in response to population growth and higher incomes.

Increases in supply were available at essentially constant marginal cost as farmers expanded onto new land or planted more of their old land in wheat. Supply shifted in response to transportation improvements, particularly an increasingly dense rail network that reduced the distance one had to ship by high-cost wagon transport to the nearest railhead. As a result, the gap between farm price and market price narrowed, with the bulk of the savings going to consumers by way of lower prices rather than to the farmers in terms of higher receipts for their crops. Demand plays essentially no role in this model of agricultural price determination. All the dynamics are supply-driven.

Jeffrey Williamson, however, disagrees with this characterization of the wheat market, at least for the late 1860s and early 1870s. While the price elasticity of domestic demand might have been very low because American consumers had few alternatives given the wedge of transport costs, the foreign demand for American grain was highly elastic. In the world wheat market the United States was still a small country and was a price taker rather than a price maker. Indeed, Morton Rothstein, the authority on the international grain trade, has argued that "by the mid-1880s there was almost universal acknowledgment of the crucial role of the British market in fixing prices."[17] Certainly, the British were not dependent upon American wheat, for there were times when the British must have been supplied from elsewhere because the New York price of No. 2 wheat was above the Liverpool price. As price takers midwestern wheat producers were hurt by lagging total factor productivity down on the farm and increasingly inelastic land supplies that raised their costs of production. Nevertheless, expanding, price-elastic foreign demand for American wheat prevented the collapse of domestic wheat prices and may have played a crucial role in midwestern economic development and growth.

There are other reasons to believe that supply may have played a smaller role in the dynamics of the American wheat market in the years immediately following the Civil War than later on, especially in the 1880s. Although land

[17] Rothstein (1960): 406.

entries reached a fifteen-year high in 1872, it was not until the 1880s that public land entries reached the levels achieved in the mid-1850s (see Figure 9.3 above). Similarly, while railroad construction boomed in the late 1860s and early 1870s, the principal beneficiaries were the residents of both coasts who were now linked by the transcontinentals. The railroad construction booms of the 1880s, on the other hand, were in areas already served by rail transportation (see Chapter 16). Indeed, it is precisely in this later period that the most dramatic narrowing in the price spread between the midwestern producers and consumers elsewhere takes place (see Figure 15.7). Conceivably, therefore, both Williamson and Harley are correct: Demand shifts played an important role in the determination of the price of wheat in the decade or so following the American Civil War, while supply shifts, primarily resulting from improvements in transportation, played the more important role later on.

The Late-Nineteenth-Century Farm Protest Movement

Many farmers were distinctly unhappy about many of the late-nineteenth-century agricultural developments: falling commodity prices, increased entry costs to farming, rising tenancy, and farm foreclosure, not to mention the supply uncertainties generated by harvests in other hemispheres and reliance upon markets an ocean away. Indeed, farmers were so unhappy that on December 4, 1867, Oliver Kelley, a Yankee government clerk appointed by President Andrew Johnson to investigate agricultural conditions in the southern states, organized a secret fraternal society for farmers known as the National Grange of the Patrons of Husbandry. By 1875 the Grange had more than 850,000 members and was a potent political force, particularly in the American Midwest. In Iowa in 1874 there was one grange for every seventy-five farm families; in Kansas, one for every sixty-six farm families. The Grange movement was just the first of a number of protest movements organized around disaffected farmers. Other organizations—the Greenbackers and the Alliance—soon followed, beginning a wave of protest that culminated in the Populist campaigns of the 1890s, which challenged established political parties and offered a prescription for the economic woes of farmers.

Until recently historians were inclined to take the protesters' complaints at face value, accepting the notion that farmers were trapped by relatively sluggish growth in demand for their products and by the economic power of railroads, land speculators, and banks. These traditional arguments are, alas, only weakly buttressed by evidence. Agricultural historian Theodore Saloutos probably got it right when he argued that it was the farmers' disappointment in their failure to realize the prosperity that they had expected that drove the agricultural protest movement of the late nineteenth century.

PRICES

Farm prices fell during most of the post–Civil War period. Corn that had sold for about 70 cents a bushel in the early 1870s fetched only 30 to 40 cents in the late 1880s. Wheat prices slipped from about $1 to 70 cents during the same period, and cotton prices similarly declined by 20 to 30 percent. These figures are not very useful, however, even as a first approximation of the farmers' plight, for other prices fell as well. Conservative postwar monetary policies designed to retire the national debt, interacting with enormous improvements in industrial productivity and declining transport costs, led to a long decline in wholesale and consumer prices that ended only in the late 1890s. Consequently, the important index is what happened to the purchasing power of farm products—the terms at which farm output could be traded for other commodities.

The farm terms of trade index in Figure 15.8 shows a marked upward trend from the early 1870s onward, but it is a less than perfect measure of how farmers fared. Prices used in the construction of the index were mainly sampled in New York City, not in rural areas, and farm products cannot be separated from the all-commodity index to provide a price measure for the farm/nonfarm terms of trade. Still, at the close of the century the index stood 10 percent or more above the levels reached during the Civil War. This rise probably understates the true magnitude of the gains in farm terms of trade because the rise in the quality of nonfarm goods (despite their falling prices) was almost certainly greater than the rise in quality of agricultural goods, where the principal gain was from speedier delivery to the consumer made possible by the spreading railroad network. Estimates of the real value of farm revenue emphasize the economic gains made by the farm sector. For example, in Illinois, Indiana, Iowa, and Wisconsin—states where farm protest was both loud and persistent—farm purchasing power grew at about 2 percent or more per year from 1870 to 1900.[18]

THE SQUEEZE ON FARMERS

There is no doubt that farmers perceived themselves as victims, and they had no difficulty in identifying their oppressors. Enemy number one was the railroads, which farmers were convinced stole the profits of the land by charging monopolistic freight rates.

The evidence on railroad rates is mixed. Where railroads were competitive with each other or with water routes—that is, east of Chicago—rates

[18] Bowman and Keehn (1974).

FIGURE 15.8

Indexes of Farm Prices Relative to Railroad Rates

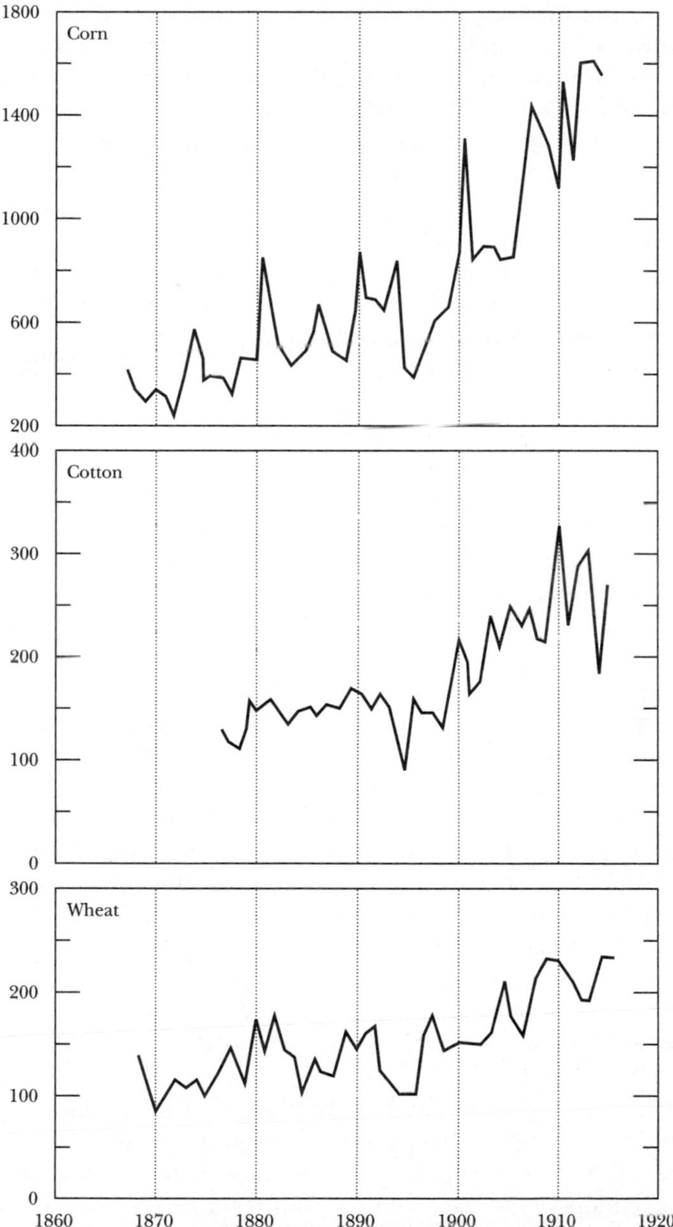

Source: Robert Higgs, "Railroad Rates and the Populist Uprising," *Agricultural History* 44 (1970): 295.

were probably no higher than the average cost of providing the service. And the special economics of the railroad industry—enormous initial investments but very low operating costs—often led to rate wars in which shipping prices fell below the levels needed to generate adequate rates of return on railroad-invested capital. Farther west, however, there was less competition and consequently greater opportunity for profitable rate discrimination against local shippers. Undoubtedly at times there were routes where the railroads earned substantial monopoly profits at the expense of struggling farmers. However, it is difficult to make a strong case for widespread victimization of farmers. For the industry as a whole, any monopoly profits earned at the expense of some farmers were apparently frittered away in rate wars since the average profits of the industry were not particularly high.

Before 1890 railroad freight rates fell at about the same rate as farm prices. Thereafter they fell much more rapidly (Figure 15.8). Moreover, the railroads were just the first link in the distribution chain that linked midwestern farmers to European consumers. Between 1870 and 1900 Atlantic freight rates fell by two-thirds. Increased competition and organizational efficiencies guaranteed that reduced international distribution costs narrowed the gap between what consumers paid and what farmers got. As a result, the case for farmers as victims of a monopolistic transportation sector fades away.

If the railroads were public enemy number one, then moneylenders and land speculators competed for the honor of runner-up. The Populists believed that the interest demanded on farm mortgages was a form of bloodsucking, that the principal goal of lenders was farm foreclosure, and that the land speculators "overpriced" land, capturing gains that "rightfully" belonged to the farmer. All these arguments are relatively easily dismissed. If mortgage lending was competitive—and the evidence suggests that it was, with large numbers of personal and institutional investors from the East in search of good mortgages—then mortgage interest rates must have approached the market rate of interest, subject only to a risk premium. Lenders faced default risk, a potentially serious risk in times of falling land values, especially since their security was an asset whose value was presumably highest in the hands of the current farmer. It was not in the lender's interest to incur foreclosure costs and potential capital losses. At the same time, though, there is a question of moral hazard. If farmers knew of these costs to the lender, they had an incentive to use the bargaining power that these costs conveyed to secure preferential terms by threatening default. What held this strategy in check was the short term of the mortgages, which made the system one of repeated games. That is, the strategy might work once, but lenders would have found a counterstrategy to negate the potential gains from threatened default to the borrowers. Finally, by definition, capital gains are unearned rents accruing as a result of secure property rights. They do not affect current resource use. The only economic question is one of distribution. Late-nineteenth-century speculators, however, seem to have earned much lower returns than the pre–Civil War land speculators.

Why, then, did farmers complain? One possibility is that generalities about price trends, railroad rates, and loan costs mask great variations in the experiences of individual farmers. It is surely plausible that the system produced large numbers of losers who had much to complain about. It was of little comfort to a North Dakota farmer that rates extorted by the local carrier would be returned to other farmers somewhere down the line through cutthroat competition. For farmers so foolish or unlucky as to become caught between expensive mortgages and declining grain prices, the general improvement of the agricultural capital market would be no comfort at all. Protest movements don't run on averages. The big losers can carry the majority, particularly when the majority consists of those near the bottom of the economic ladder.

A variety of institutional changes exposed post–Civil War family farmers to greater risks than they had faced earlier. Prior to the war most farmers tried, with varying degrees of success, to produce surpluses for market sale, but farmers were not yet dependent upon the market. When wheat prices in the local market fell, say, by 10 percent in the 1850s, an Indiana farmer's total real income might fall by 3 or 4 percent. The blow was cushioned by the fact that the farmer consumed much of his or her own output as food, clothing, and shelter. Postwar grain farmers—like the postwar cotton farmers—were compelled by economic forces to sell a far greater proportion of their output in commercial markets. For example, machinery was needed to grow grain competitively, and with machines came fixed debt obligations that required large cash flows from the sale of cash crops to service the debt. Farm incomes were subject to greater leverage by price changes under these circumstances. The quarterly mortgage payment for an encumbered western Kansas wheat farmer remained the same, and so did the railroad freight rate, when the Chicago price of wheat fell 10 percent. Under such circumstances, net farm income after these unavoidable expenses might fall by 20 or 30 percent because of specialization. The fact that both the interest rate and the freight rate were determined competitively is cold comfort for those suffering a sharp income decline. Nor does the fact that in boom times the leverage works in reverse, magnifying the impact of market gains, help much.

Instead of serving customers just beyond the farm gate in isolated markets, America's farmers increasingly supplied consumers thousands of miles distant whose wants, tastes, and habits were transmitted by an impersonal market signal: price. That price reflected global supply conditions more than the local harvest, so that farmers could no longer count on higher prices to offset locally poor crops. Income variability and price uncertainty increased.[19] Local capital markets offered little opportunity to smooth these

[19] McGuire (1981).

fluctuations by saving during prosperous times and borrowing in times of distress.[20] In rural communities the principal asset was land, and the farm mortgage was about the only debt instrument available to farmers. Consequently, they bought more land in good times and took out mortgages in bad times, with the result that mortgage risk of foreclosure simply added to farm uncertainty.

In the decades following the Civil War, agricultural output growth was largely extensive. Some labor productivity gains were realized as grain farming mechanized, but nothing on the order of the productivity achievements of the industrial sector. Transport improvements opened vast new agricultural land areas that were capable of delivering grain to market at constant real resource cost. As a result, farm goods prices did not go up sharply with demand expansion, denying established farmers the especially high profits they might otherwise have received by entering the business on the "ground floor."[21]

This line of reasoning, incidentally, can be generalized to help explain the thread of agrarian discontent that runs from the Whiskey Rebellion in 1794 to the American Agriculture Movement of 1979. In competitive labor markets wages are determined by the minimum it takes to keep the marginal worker from moving to another industry or dropping out of the labor market altogether. Farmers are often unhappy with their wages because others are willing to work the land for very little return. When farm prices go up, raising the total return to farm enterprise, one of two things happens: Other farmers move onto virgin land, driving down land and produce prices and farmers' incomes, or if more good land is unavailable (the situation today in the United States), the price of existing acreage is bid up to the point where the return to labor services is back to the competitive rate. Those fortunate enough to own property receive capital gains from land, but the returns to current productive activity are depressed to the competitive margin, and entry for the next generation of aspiring yeoman farmers is that much more difficult.

Whether farmers' complaints were real or imagined, there is no doubt that their anger was very real and had a profound impact upon the politics and economic institutions of the late nineteenth century. The two main political parties could not afford to ignore the votes received by the protest parties such as the Populists or platforms that attracted those voters. Nor did they. Unhappy farmers led the march toward the regulation of the nation's railroads and the push toward antitrust. In their distrust of banks they promoted unit banking and fatally weakened the banking system in many states. Their desire as debtors for a more inflationary money supply based upon sil-

[20] Stock (1983).
[21] North (1966).

ver generated a run against the dollar. In short, farmers stirred things up, as we shall see in some of the chapters that follow.

Bibliography

Alston, Lee J. "Farm Foreclosures in the United States during the Interwar Period." *Journal of Economic History* 43 (1983): 885–904.

Atack, Jeremy. "Tenants and Yeomen in the Nineteenth Century." *Agricultural History* 62 (1988): 6–32.

Bogue, Allan. *Money at Interest: The Farm Mortgage on the Middle Border.* Ithaca: Cornell University Press, 1955.

Bowman, John D., and Richard H. Keehn. "Agricultural Terms of Trade in Four Midwestern States, 1870–1900," *Journal of Economic History* 34 (1974): 592–609.

Fogel, Robert W., and Jack Rutner. "The Efficiency Effects of Federal Land Policy, 1850–1900." In *Dimensions of Quantitative Research in History,* ed. William Aydelotte et al. Princeton: Princeton University Press, 1972: 390–418.

Gates, Paul W. "Land Policy and Tenancy in the Prairie Counties of Indiana." *Indiana Magazine of History* 35 (1939): 1–26.

———. *Landlords and Tenants on the Prairie Frontier: Studies in American Land Policy.* (Ithaca: Cornell University Press, 1973.

Goldenweisser, E. A., and Leon E. Truesdell. *Farm Tenancy in the United States.* (Washington, D.C.: 1924).

Gregson, Mary Eschelbach. "Specialization in Late 19th Century Midwestern Agriculture: Missouri as a Test Case." *Agricultural History* 67 (1993): 16–35.

Harley, C. Knick. "Western Settlement and the Price of Wheat, 1872–1913." *Journal of Economic History* 38 (1978): 865–78.

———. "Transportation, the World Wheat Trade, and the Kuznets Cycle, 1850–1913." *Explorations in Economic History* 17 (1980): 218–50.

Hibbard, Benjamin H. *A History of the Public Land Policies.* New York: Macmillan, 1924.

Higgs, Robert. "Railroad Rates and the Populist Uprising." *Agricultural History* 44 (1970): 291–97.

Kendrick, John W., and Maude R. Pech. *Productivity Trends in the United States.* National Bureau of Economic Research General Series 71. Princeton: Princeton University Press, 1961.

Lindert, Peter. "Long-Run Trends in American Farmland Values." *Agricultural History* 62 (1988): 45–86.

Mayhew, Anne. "A Reappraisal of the Causes of Farm Protest in the United States, 1879–1900." *Journal of Economic History* 32 (1972): 464–75.

McGuire, Robert. "Economic Causes of Late Nineteenth Century Agrarian Unrest: New Evidence." *Journal of Economic History* 41 (1981): 835–52.

North, Douglass C. *Growth and Welfare in the American Past: A New Economic History.* Englewood Cliffs, N.J.: Prentice-Hall, 1966.

Parker, William N., and Judith L. V. Klein. "Productivity Growth in Grain Production in the United States, 1840–1860 and 1900–10." In National Bureau of Economic Research, *Output, Employment, and Productivity in the United States after 1800,* Studies in Income and Wealth, vol. 30. New York: Columbia University Press, 1966: 523–80.

Rothstein, Morton. "America in the International Rivalry for the British Wheat Market, 1860–1914." *Mississippi Valley Historical Review* 47 (1960): 401–18.

Saloutos, Theodore. "The Agricultural Problem and Nineteenth-Century Industrialism." *Agricultural History* 22 (1948): 156–74.

Stock, James H. "Real Estate Mortgages, Foreclosures, and Midwestern Agrarian Unrest, 1865–1920." *Journal of Economic History* 44 (1984): 89–105.

Williamson, Jeffrey G. "Greasing the Wheels of Sputtering Export Engines: Midwestern Grains and American Growth." *Explorations in Economic History* 17 (1980): 189–217.

Wright, Gavin. "American Agriculture and the Labor Market: What Happened to Proletarianization?" *Agricultural History* 62 (1988): 182–209.

Railroads and nineteenth-century american economic growth and development

16

Canals had radically reshaped trade flows in America, intercepting freight in far-distant hinterlands and diverting it to the port cities which they served. As a result, these cities grew at the expense of those that lacked such connections. In the competition for trade, more than city prestige was at stake. The very economic survival of these ports and their merchants depended upon tapping the growing trade of an expanding interior as the nation pushed westward. The merchants in those ports that lacked cheap connections to interior markets faced a choice: Either meet the competition or see their trade stagnate and possibly decline. New York, for example, gained traffic at the expense of other East Coast ports—particularly Philadelphia, Boston, and Montreal—after the Erie Canal opened. Similarly, Washington, D.C., the terminus of the Chesapeake and Ohio Canal, was in a position to tap traffic that otherwise would have gone to Baltimore. While Philadelphia sought economic salvation with the unsuccessful Pennsylvania Main Line Canal, Baltimore responded with the nation's first railroad—the Baltimore and Ohio, chartered in 1828. The B&O was to connect Baltimore with the Ohio River at Wheeling, West Virginia—about 250 miles away—tapping the growing trade of the Ohio and Mississippi river valleys. Other cities followed Baltimore's lead. Boston championed the Boston and Worcester Railroad to provide cheap transportation between Boston and Albany at the eastern end of the Erie Canal, while Charleston, South Carolina, built a rail line into the interior to draw cotton traffic away from Savannah, Georgia.

Railroads in American Historiography

The coming of the railroads has played a crucial role in explanations of American economic growth. Walt Rostow, one of the first new economic historians, has credited the railroad with causing America's takeoff into self-sustained growth. In his view:

> The railroad has been historically the most powerful single initiator of take-offs. It was decisive in the United States. . . . The railroad has had three major kinds of impact on economic growth during the take-off period. First, it has lowered internal transport costs, brought new areas and products into commercial markets and, in general, performed the Smithian function of widening the market. Second, it has been a prerequisite in many cases to the development of a major new and rapidly enlarging export sector which, in turn, has served to generate capital for internal developments as, for example, the American railroads before 1914. Third, and perhaps most important for the take-off itself, the development of railways had led to the development of modern coal, iron and engineering industries.

Rostow was neither the first nor the only economic historian to pay homage to the railroad. In a classic 1944 article Leland Jenks, summarizing the views of many others, talks of the railroad "revolution" and covers much of the same ground as Rostow. Louis Hacker, writing in 1940, cites subsidies to railroads as a crucial government initiative in the emergence of industrial capitalism. Indeed, for decades the singular importance of railroads had been one historical issue enjoying widespread agreement from the experts.

These views were substantially revised in the early 1960s with the publication of independent but parallel studies by Albert Fishlow and Robert Fogel on the quantitative contribution of the railroads to American economic growth before and after the Civil War. Fishlow's focus was upon the stimulus to economic growth and national development generated by the expansion of the railroad network between 1830 and 1860. His conclusion that the railroad was "important" *in this context* was in accord with the prevailing prejudices and thus raised few eyebrows, though his analysis, like Fogel's, was novel. Fogel's work, on the other hand, sparked a controversy startlingly like the slavery contretemps of the early 1970s (see Chapter 12). Fogel concluded that the railroads were not *indispensable* to American economic growth. That is, he argued that America could have developed without the railroad. In the howls of protest over this heretical proposition,

Fogel's central point that "no single innovation was vital for economic growth" has been lost, and his concession that if any innovation had claim to such a distinction, it would have been the railroad has been overlooked.

Railroad Expansion

When rail construction was temporarily halted by the nationwide business recession that began in 1839, some three thousand miles of track were in service. The early railroads, however, posed little threat to the major interregional water transport routes because much of the track had been laid between East Coast cities and carried passengers rather than freight. Not until 1849 did railroad freight revenues exceed those from passengers.

The East Coast intercity lines required relatively modest financial backing and quickly paid for themselves. The ambitious east-west lines, by contrast, were extremely vulnerable to financial upheaval. They were not pay-as-you-go projects. Profitable traffic depended upon completion of the original interregional design, and even with the economic upturn after 1843 construction was not immediately completed. Instead more than half the track laid in the 1840s served the densely populated parts of New England and New York. By 1850 the East Coast–Great Lakes connection had been finished and some nine thousand miles of railroad had been built (Figure 16.1).

With the completion of the New York Central to Chicago in 1853, the Midwest had direct service to the East Coast. Other trunk line connections soon followed: the Baltimore and Ohio to St. Louis and the Central Virginia to Memphis in 1858. Virtually every productive farm in the Midwest was tied into the East Coast trade. During this second railroad construction boom the South held its own. Cotton-marketing centers in the interior of Mississippi and Alabama were connected by rail to New Orleans and Mobile, and an all-southern east-west railroad hooked Memphis and Nashville to the East Coast.

By 1860 railroad mileage exceeded 30,000 miles, and America had half the world's total railroad mileage at a cost of perhaps $1 billion—five times as much as invested in America's canals. The basic railroad network was complete between the East Coast and the Midwest (Figure 16.2). But the system was not a unified, integrated whole. There existed a multiplicity of different track gauges—the distances between the rails—that made the interchange of traffic between competing lines difficult and expensive. In the 1860s, for example, there were five different gauges with at least 1,000 miles of track each. Many of the southern railroads had a five-foot gauge while in the North, four feet nine inches was the most common gauge although the New York and Erie Railroad started out with a six-foot broad gauge and the Grand Trunk used a five-foot six-inch gauge. These broad gauges were easiest to

FIGURE 16.1

Railroad Mileage in the United States, 1830–1900

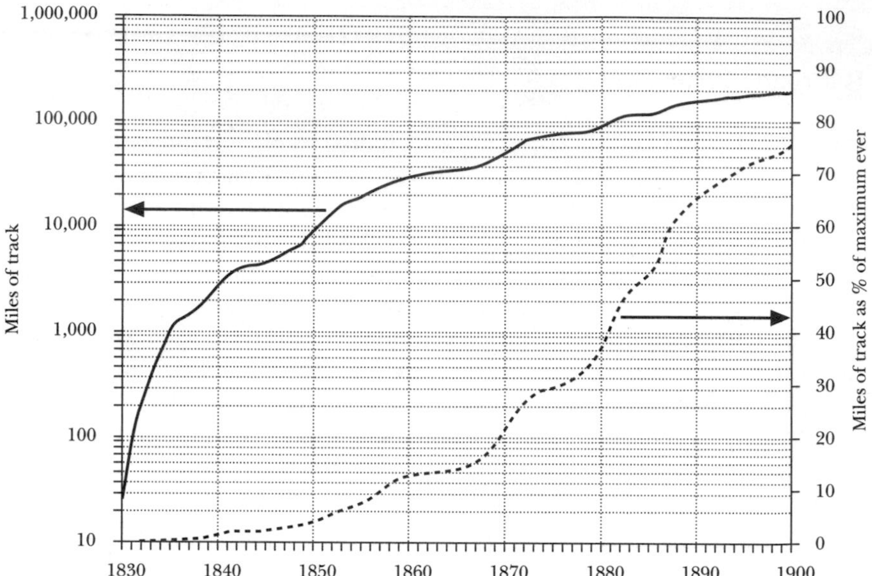

Source: U.S. Bureau of the Census, *Historical Statistics of the United States* (Washington, D.C.: Government Printing Office, 1975): Series Q321 and Q329.

adapt to the emerging four-foot-nine-inch gauge. A third rail was simply laid within the existing track, allowing both broad- and standard-gauge trains and rolling stock to run over the same track. Switching the five-foot gauge to the standard gauge was more difficult. But it could be done. On July 29, 1881, for example, the Illinois Central suspended normal operations for the day along its Chicago, St. Louis, and New Orleans line. A preplaced work crew of three thousand men moved each western line eastward, by three inches. The changeover was accomplished in that one day along the 547 miles of five-foot gauge track, and service resumed. It had, however, required careful planning and preparation that involved the removal of the inside spikes from the westernmost rail and the preplacement of the new spikes on the east side of the places where the new rails would be laid. Other southern railroads followed suit, and by the late 1880s all the railroads that served the public had adopted the standard gauge.

Railroad construction had slowed abruptly with the Civil War though heavy wartime use and destruction increased replacement demand. Growth resumed after the war and, like the prewar expansion, came in waves (Figure 16.3). These cycles are closely linked to the Kuznets (construction) cycle in American economic growth and reflected construction of branch lines and

FIGURE 16.2

Railroad Lines in Actual Operation October 1860

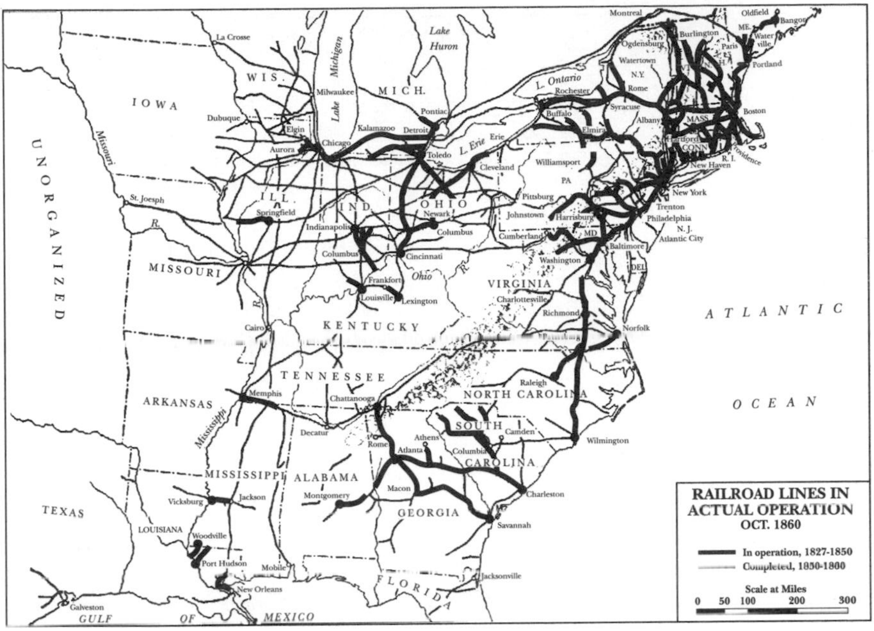

Source: Adapted from: Charles O. Paullin, *Atlas of the Historical Geography of the United States* (Washington, D.C.: Carnegie Institution, 1932): Plates 139A and B; and Richard B. Morris, *Encyclopedia of American History,* New York: Harper & Row, 1976: 605.

feeders into the main network rather than new main lines.[1] The first post–Civil War surge between 1868 and 1873 doubled the miles of track. A good portion of this growth, oddly enough, came in the Northeast and Midwest, where service was already relatively good. But the enormous northeastern regional economy easily absorbed the growth. Clearly the most impressive accomplishment of this wave of construction was the completion of the first transcontinental line in May 1869, when the Union Pacific Railroad and the Central Pacific met at Promontory Point, Utah.

The rapid western expansion of the railroads was built on a fragile financial structure of highly leveraged capital that collapsed during the cyclical decline of the national economy in the mid-1870s. With nearly one-fifth of the nation's track in bankruptcy, construction paused for a few years before climbing back up to the rates set in the early 1880s. Some eight thousand miles a year, on average, were built between 1879 and 1883, including the Southern Pacific, Northern Pacific, and Santa Fe transcontinental.

[1] Harley (1980).

FIGURE 16.3

Railroad Construction in the United States, 1830–1900

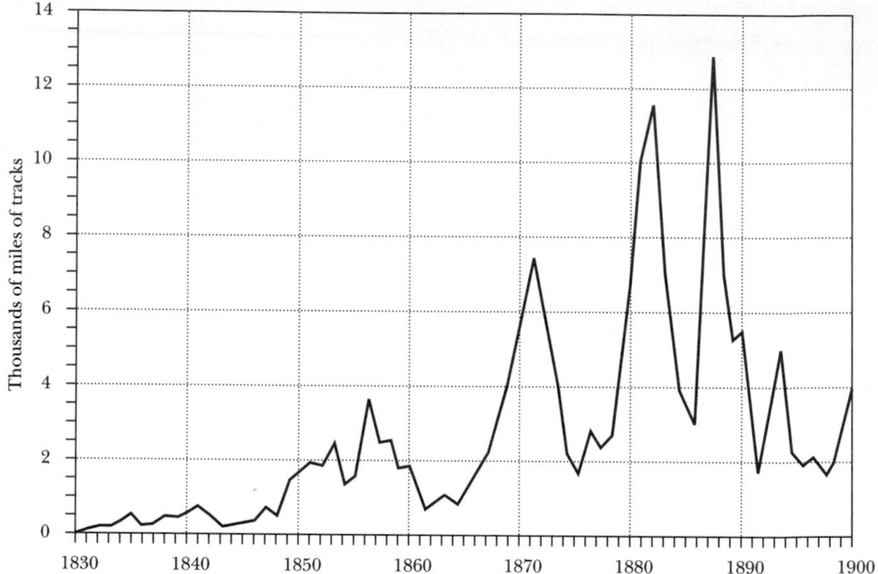

Source: U.S. Bureau of the Census, *Historical Statistics of the United States* (Washington, D.C.: Government Printing Office, 1975): Series Q329.

Another short cyclic pause occurred in the mid-1880s and was followed by a last surge (1886–92). By 1900 almost two hundred thousand miles of railroad track were in use—approximately three-quarters of the total mileage that would ever be built in the United States. The big holes in the southern and Gulf Coast systems were filled in, and another transcontinental rail line was laid to the Pacific Northwest. Traffic density also made practicable secondary connections in much of the country.

Construction Ahead of Demand

The rapid extension of the railroad between the 1850s and the 1880s led many observers, including the great political economist Joseph Schumpeter, to argue that railroads actually pulled the economy west: By building "ahead of demand" across the Midwest, Great Plains, and Rockies, they led the growth of the country. This view fits nicely, too—at least in a casual sense—with Rostow's endorsement of the railroads as the "leading" sector in the growth process.

The notion of building ahead of demand, however, is difficult to pin down. It clearly means more than that the service created its own demand. Every new product does that. Rather the notion is that railroads invested in facilities that were at first utilized at less than capacity. Some degree of building ahead of demand is almost inevitable when the construction period is very long; the future is not seen with perfect sight. Sometimes it can even be profitable, at least for a while, as many electric utility companies building nuclear power plants found in the early 1970s. But the focus on lead time between construction and full utilization can only obscure the real issue: Was rail construction the most valuable use of investment resources at the time of the investment?

One measure, whether or not the return to private investors exceeded the opportunity cost of capital by more than any alternative investment, is imperfect for projects such as railroads. Railroad construction was a collective good; society's gains from major investments like these may be greater than the gains to the investors. Some of the benefits may be classically defined "externalities," for example, the increased value of land along the right-of-way or increased engineering expertise that found use in other sectors. Others may derive from the nonmarginal aspect of a major innovation like the railroad: Market prices are determined by the value of services to those users who value it least; thus many of the benefits flow to those lucky consumers who would have been willing to pay more but didn't have to. The value of their consumer surplus may have been very large.

Depending upon the temporal pattern of returns, it is conceivable that the private return to a rail project could come so far in the future that the discounted returns would be insufficient to attract private investors although the total gains to society might have been well above the investment cost. It is also possible that private investors' aversion to risk was greater than society's as a whole, leading private investors to discount future returns at too high a rate and thereby to undervalue the income stream from a rail project.

Analysis by Albert Fishlow indicates that midwestern railroads were not built ahead of demand. Most routes were profitable almost immediately (see Table 16.1). Although the average returns were not spectacularly high, they hardly suggest that railroads were losing propositions. Railroads in the 1850s were typically built to serve established farm regions. For example, 60 percent of the railroad mileage in Illinois by 1853 was in the leading wheat and corn counties that made up just 25 percent of the state's area. Similarly, in Wisconsin, seven wheat-producing counties (plus Milwaukee), constituting only 10 percent of the state's area, had 60 percent of the track in 1856.

Fogel's investigation of the Union Pacific Railroad paints a somewhat different picture. To judge by investors' behavior before construction, the transcontinental railroad was indeed built ahead of demand. Ex post returns in 1870, 1871, and 1872 would have been too low to attract capital (Table 16.2). Thus Congress would seem to have been wise in granting public subsidies to secure what it believed were the very large total social returns that

TABLE 16.1

The Average Net Earnings of Western Railroads (percentage of construction costs)

State	1849	1855–56	1859
Ohio	7.5	6.4	3.7
Indiana	6.1	6.2	5.2
Michigan	4.2	10.2	4.6
Illinois	8.7	6.8	3.5
Wisconsin	—	12.5	3.1
Iowa	—	—	3.0
Average	5.6	7.2	3.7

Source: Albert Fishlow, *American Railroads and the Transformation of the Ante-Bellum Economy* (Cambridge: Harvard University Press, 1965): 178. Copyright © 1965 by the President and Fellows of Harvard College. Reprinted by permission.

included the "binding" of the continent although in the end the private returns were also very high.

Much of the cyclical pattern of postwar railroad construction (see Figure 16.2 above) may have been due to the periodic breakdown of informal oligopoly agreements among the railroads regarding exclusive construction rights in particular areas.[2] Such exclusive rights were not legally recognized and would have been impossible to enforce anyway in view of the strong public sentiment in the West in favor of railroad construction.

These agreements arose because building a railroad in a particular location was a once-and-for-all decision: Construction now precludes construction later. Construction later, when settlement and the demand for transportation were greater, would clearly be more profitable and thus more desirable from the railroad's standpoint than construction today. There is thus a strong incentive to delay construction, but only so long as an individual railroad could be sure that those higher profits were reserved exclusively to it.

Railroads that colluded to delay construction stood to gain, but as settlement increased, so did pressure to break ranks. First, there was the ever-present threat of outside entry that was normally held in check by the considerable costs associated with the need to provide a main line connection. However, as the present value of branch lines became positive, the relative cost of providing a new main line connection to Chicago declined. Second, as present values became positive, each individual party to the exclusive agreement would be better off if it could have built *all* the lines (in its own as well as its rival's territory) that had a positive present value, so long as

[2] Harley (1982).

TABLE 16.2

Private and Social Returns on the Construction Costs of the Union Pacific Railroad, 1870–1879

Year	Accumulated Cost (millions $)	Net Earnings	Benefits Not Captured by Investors (millions $)	Private Return (%)	Social Return (%)
1870	53.1	2.2	5.9	4.2	15.3
1871	54.0	3.6	6.8	6.7	19.4
1872	54.8	3.7	7.8	6.7	20.9
1873	55.2	5.0	8.8	9.1	25.0
1874	55.5	5.5	9.8	9.9	27.5
1875	55.6	7.0	10.7	12.6	31.9
1876	55.6	8.8	11.7	15.7	36.8
1877	59.2	8.7	12.7	14.7	36.1
1878	59.2	10.5	13.7	17.8	40.9
1879	59.2	10.4	14.7	17.5	42.2
Average	—	—	—	11.6	29.9

Source: Robert Fogel, *The Union Pacific Railroad: A Case of Premature Enterprise* (Baltimore: Johns Hopkins University Press, 1960): 106.

the others stuck to the agreement. These pressures would occasionally lead railroads to break ranks. The critical value, for Kansas at least, was when settlement achieved about 35 percent of its potential. Beyond this threshold a construction frenzy would result, although eventually the economic incentives to collude would reassert themselves.

Railroad Land Grants

Repeating a time-honored process, much of the railroad construction, particularly of the transcontinental, was encouraged and underwritten by government through a system of federal land grants. This practice dates back to the legislation that created the state of Ohio in 1802, when the federal government promised to donate 5 percent of the proceeds from public land sales in the state to help build public roads. Thereafter various grants were given for specific purposes. In 1823, for example, Ohio received a grant of more than 80,000 acres to build a road from Lake Erie to the Connecticut Western Reserve, and Indiana received more than 170,000 acres for a road from Lake Michigan to the Ohio River. Canal grants were more generous. Illinois, for example, received 324,000 acres to help with the Illinois and

Michigan Canal, while Indiana received almost 1.5 million acres for the Wabash and Erie Canal.

These grants were dwarfed by the land grants to the railroads. Whereas earlier grants had been made to states, railroad land grants were made directly to the companies themselves or transferred to the states for conveyance to the railroads. In 1850 Congress passed a bill providing for alternate sections of land for six miles on either side of the railroad line connecting Chicago to Mobile to be conveyed to the states along the right-of-way. The monies from the sale were to be used to defray construction costs, whether by a public agency or a private company. Thus was born the Illinois Central. In return U.S. troops were to be transported free and mail was to be carried at rates fixed by Congress. These general provisions were continued in all subsequent land grants. Between 1850 and 1871 the federal government gave 131 million acres of public land to the railroads. In addition, Texas—which had not ceded its public lands to the federal government when it joined the Union—donated 27 million acres. Thus a total of 158 million acres—nearly 250 million square miles of public land—was transferred to private railroad ownership.

One argument for land grants was to mitigate market failure resulting from an inadequate and poorly developed capital market. Because the railroads were given land, they could directly underwrite construction costs from cash sales. Furthermore, they would have recourse to the well-established mortgage market rather than have to rely on the nascent private bond and equity markets. Certainly the sums involved were relatively large. In 1851 the promoters of the Illinois Central estimated the cost of the seven-hundred-mile railroad to be $16.5 million, an amount that was more than double the total investment in all Illinois manufacturing industry at the time. Nevertheless, similarly large sums had been raised earlier to fund canal construction. This parallel between railroad construction and canal construction may help explain the appeal to government. Roughly three-fourths of the $190 million investment in canal construction had been made with public funds—tax monies and revenues from bonds sold by state and local authorities. The most ambitious of the canal projects, like the Pennsylvania Main Line and the Wabash and Erie, however, had been financial disasters, which made both state governments and private investors wary of similar commitments. On the other hand, the federal government had yet to be burned, and land grants avoided the moral hazards associated with either direct underwriting or profit guarantees.

More important, though, land grants were seen as a way to mediate the gulf between private and social returns from railroad construction. This was particularly the case with the transcontinental. Faced with the prospect of hundreds of miles of desolation and the expense of crossing the Rocky Mountains and the Sierra Nevada, the railroad promoters saw little prospect of earning an adequate return on capital from building a transcontinental railroad. Expected costs were high, and revenues, low. Private business was therefore reluctant to undertake the project.

A transcontinental railroad, however, offered substantial social benefits. Not only would it link East Coast to West and avoid the hazards and expense in time and money of the overland wagon trek or the journey by ship around Cape Horn or across Panama, but it also promised substantial capital gains to landowners along the way. Instead of these gains' accruing to a multitude of individual small landowners, the primary beneficiary would be the federal government since most of the land was still in the public domain. The government therefore had considerable incentive to intervene. At the same time, by giving the railroads some of this land, the government resolved a part of the free rider problem. The capital gains on land that resulted from improved accessibility to markets would accrue, in part, to those who bore the costs and risks of supplying rail service.

With some notable exceptions, the land grants were not a major source of capital for the railroads. Between 1850 and 1880 gross investment in track and equipment was about $8 billion (in 1909 dollars).[3] The value of land grants was much smaller, though there is a debate over exactly how much they were worth. It has also been argued by railroad apologist Colonel Robert Henry and others that the true subsidy value was the market value of the land in the absence of railroads. And since the government had not been able to sell the land at its reservation price of $1.25 an acre, the market value of the grants might have been as little as $1 per acre. In this view, the fact that the land was worth many times that sum after railroad construction is irrelevant because the additional value should be properly called a capital gain to the railroad and thus would be considered part of the private return to rail construction.

This approach has a clever straightforwardness about it that masks underlying ambiguities. If the government had auctioned the land to a public savvy about a potential railroad, its value would have been determined in part by expectations of the success of the transport improvement. There was no auction, of course. But the entrepreneurs who accepted the land subsidies obviously did so in the belief that a railroad would be constructed. Hence the $1 per acre figure is, as a measure of value, quite conservative.

Railroad land, when actually sold, brought an average return of $3.38 per acre, but this figure surely *overstates* the subsidy for a number of reasons. First, the land was only sold after the completion of the railroads. Even the most optimistic rail entrepreneur must have had some doubt about the success of the project and thus would not have been willing to pay full value in advance. Second, land sales occurred over many years (some of the land is still owned by the railroads today). Land that sold for $3.38 an acre in, say, 1880, was worth less in 1869. Third, present value of the obligation to trans-

[3] Fishlow (1966).

port federal troops and property at less than market rates was not known at the time of construction, but it was certainly nonnegligible.

For want of a better number, it is estimated that the land subsidy was worth about $400 million—that is, about 5 percent of the amount invested in railroads between 1850 and 1880, although these numbers are not really comparable because the periods of the subsidies and the investment are not identical.[4] The land subsidies played an important role during the shorter period of 1865–70, when they must have represented a much higher percentage of total investment.

Both at the time and since, federal land grant policy has been extremely controversial. Many railroads, notably the Union Pacific, were shady financial enterprises from which a few intelligent—but dishonest—entrepreneurs made a great deal of money. For example, the Crédit Mobilier of America—the construction company for the Union Pacific—bought congressional votes on a scale that was shocking even in that cynical age, to secure passage of favorable land grant legislation. Hence the public suspected that the land grants were giveaways—needless gifts of national treasure to begin or augment some of America's greatest fortunes. Others chafed at the apparent effect of the land-grant system on the availability of western land for settlement, although the railroads only received a narrow right-of-way through federal territory plus alternating sections of land from broad swatches of land along the right-of-way for each mile of track built. Depending upon the specific legislation, railroads received from six alternating sections within six miles of either side of the track to as many as forty alternating sections within forty miles of the track for each mile of track they built. In the event that some of these sections had otherwise been disposed of or were reserved for schools and the like, the railroad was permitted to choose a like amount of land from within a contiguous zone, known as the indemnity limits. These limits are shown in Panel A of Figure 16.4, and the actual areas taken up by the railroads are shown in Panel B. However, until the railroads were completed and took up their land grants, the federal lands within the indemnity limits—more than one-third of all land in the land-grant states—were held off the market. Moreover, when the transfers were completed, settlers found that the remaining public lands near the right-of-way commanded a premium minimum price of $2.50 an acre.

The checkerboard pattern of alternating sections of federal land and land granted to the railroads prevented the railroads from preempting the best land and ensured that any capital gains accruing to the railroad from construction of the line were shared equally by the federal Treasury. The land-grant policy permitted the railroad to capture some of the social benefits of capital gains on land, thus partially resolving the free rider problem.

[4] Fishlow (1972).

FIGURE 16.4

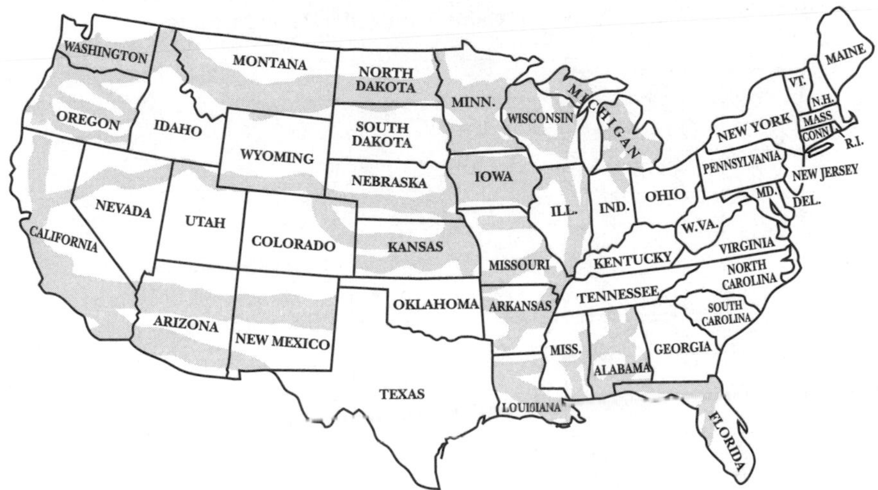

Indemnity Limits for Federal Land Grants to the Railroads

PANEL A

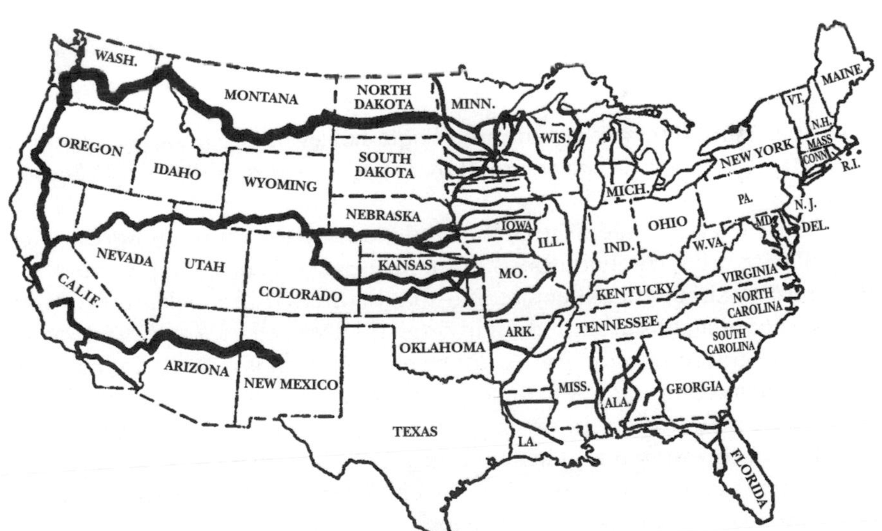

Federal Land Grants Received by the Railroads

PANEL B

Source: Robert S. Henry, "The Railroad Land Grant Legend in American History Texts," *Mississippi Valley Historical Review* 32 (1945): 180.

FIGURE 16.5

The Distribution of Gains from Federal Land Grants

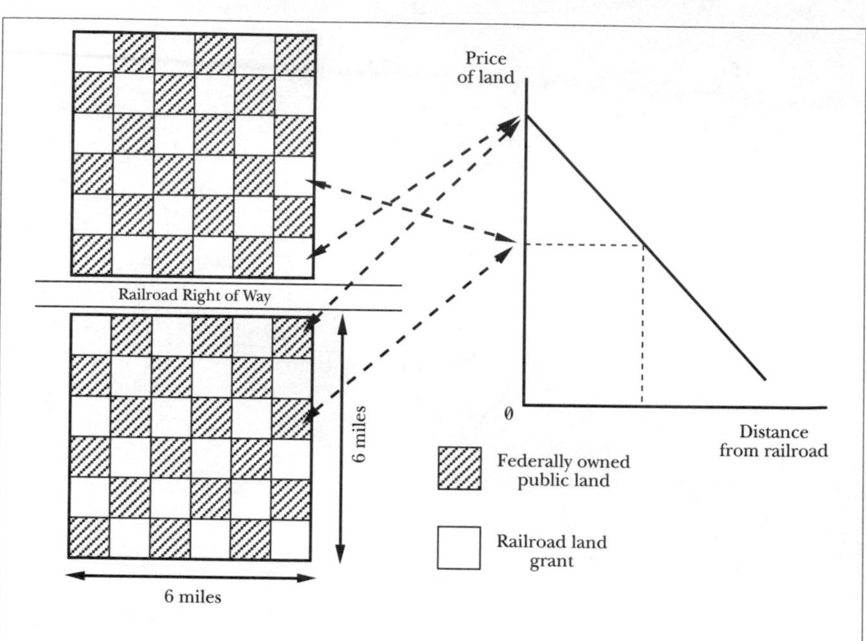

The policy simultaneously guaranteed equal or even larger capital gains to the federal Treasury, which retained ownership of most of the land (Figure 16.5).

Even so, it is still alleged that the land grants to the railroads were a give-away. There are several questions. It might be asked, for example, whether the railroads should have been built—that is, whether the social return (rail profits plus net gains to shippers and others) exceeded the opportunity cost of the invested resources. The evidence on this point is overwhelming. The social returns computed by economic historians are all well above the most reasonable measure of opportunity cost—contemporary interest rates on equally risky investments.[5] Thus there can be little debate over the fact that the nominal intent of the subsidies—to encourage construction of the western railroads—made economic sense.

This does not necessarily mean that every railroad, or every addition to the basic transportation network that received federal help, generated a superior social return. Nor does it necessarily mean that the land grants cre-

[5] Fogel (1960); Mercer (1970).

ated incentives for the optimal time path of development. Thanks to the subsidies, it is possible that some of the railroads were built a few years earlier. But the evidence is ambiguous. The Union Pacific earned a social return on investment of 15.3 percent in its first year of operation, a rate that climbed steadily to 42.3 percent in 1879. Delaying the road would have retarded the flow of benefits, reducing their present value at the beginning of construction by more than the opportunity cost of the capital invested.[6] Computations of total annual costs and benefits from the Central Pacific reveal a similar pattern,[7] and a survey of the *private* returns on six land-grant railroads shows at least one other railroad, the Great Northern, generated immense social returns immediately. For three others, however, the private returns were initially very low, leaving open the possibility that the social returns for the early years were also below that of competing uses of capital.[8]

Even if it is agreed that railroads were worthy social investments, it does not follow that subsidies were necessary to induce private parties to make the investment. The investments might have been made anyway, in which case the land grants were simply "icing on the cake" for wealthy railroad promoters. The test is whether the rail return exceeds the private competitive return. By this test, the public was clearly ripped off in some instances. In others, probably not. Estimates show that the internal rate of return on the Central Pacific, Northern Pacific, Union Pacific, and Great Northern should have been sufficient to attract investors without government aid, while the Texas Pacific, Santa Fe, and Northern Pacific needed help (Table 16.3). For some railroads, at least, the relatively modest private returns are misleading in that a few inside decision makers made far greater returns. For example, the promoters of the Union Pacific received annual rates of return of between 65 and 1,207 percent on their investment even without the land grants.[9] However, the fact that projects like the Union Pacific or Great Northern turned out to be immensely profitable does not prove that these railroads would have been built without public aid. What counts is the ex ante (or expected) rate of return on the private investment before construction began. This rate is difficult or impossible to measure. If promoters were pessimistic about the chances for profit in the Union Pacific, they would not have gone ahead without help; if the Santa Fe's backers were overly optimistic, the subsidy was unnecessary.

Enough is known about the early financing and construction of the Union Pacific to allow a highly plausible direct estimate to be made of the minimum ex ante return. Under the terms of the government's loan guarantee (separate from the land grants), the promoters received a fixed

[6] Fogel (1960).
[7] Mercer (1970).
[8] Mercer (1974).
[9] Fleisig (1975).

TABLE 16.3

Returns to Railroad Investment and the Opportunity Cost of Capital

System	Private Return (without Government Aid)	Opportunity Cost of Capital
Central Pacific	10.6	9.0
Union Pacific	11.6	9.0
Texas and Pacific	2.2	7.7
Santa Fe	6.1	7.9
Northern Pacific	6.3	7.9
Great Northern	8.7	6.3

Opportunity cost is estimated from the average earnings on common stocks on the New York Stock Exchange, adjusted for general inflation or deflation.
Source: Lloyd Mercer, "Building Ahead of Demand: Some Evidence from the Land Grant Railroads," *Journal of Economic History* 34 (1974): 499. Reprinted by permission of Cambridge University Press.

amount of government bonds and were permitted to issue a like amount of their own bonds each time they completed twenty miles of track. They were also permitted to siphon off the top a profit equal to 10 percent of construction costs as construction continued. Since the road was built on a pay-as-you-go basis, and the promoters were under no legal obligation to complete construction if they ever had difficulty covering ongoing costs out of borrowed money, the Union Pacific's managers risked very little yet earned somewhere between $3.8 and $5.4 million in construction profits. Depending upon how much they actually risked and how great the construction profits were, the minimum ex ante rate was somewhere between 15 and 541 percent. Thus aid, such as the land grants, was not needed to induce construction of the Union Pacific. Much the same can be said for the Central Pacific. Unfortunately, though, it is impossible to generalize from this evidence to other railroads.

Railroad land grants served to raise the expected private return without affecting risk very much. If the railroads turned out to be unsuccessful in generating traffic, the land the government provided along the right-of-way would have minimal value. If, on the other hand, the railroad succeeded, the land would probably be worth a great deal, and the railroad's profits would be supplemented by large profits from the sale of the land. Such a subsidy policy was therefore inappropriate if the primary purpose of government aid was to shelter private enterprise from the financial risks of pathbreaking transportation improvements.

The case against the land-grant form of public subsidy is thus obvious, and it would be decisive, too, were it not for the peculiar economics of railroad operation. Railroads are (in the jargon of economics) "natural monopolies." That means most of the cost of operating railroads are overhead costs—the burden of the enormous investment in track, rolling stock, and right-of-way needed before the first train can leave the station. To earn a profit, railroad rates must ordinarily include a large charge for this overhead, plus a small marginal charge for extra labor and use-related depreciation. The real cost of the marginal freight haul is this small cost of the variable factors (labor, wear and tear). Thus, if the railroads (or any other natural monopoly) set prices equal to the average cost (that is, earn a "normal" rate of profit), they will effectively deny service to customers who could be served at minimal cost but are unwilling to pay the higher average cost for service.

This is a classic economic dilemma: To stay in business while charging everyone the same rate, natural monopolies keep prices above marginal cost, but average cost pricing reduces output below the efficient level. Economic theory offers a number of ways out of this bind. Public operating subsidies can be used to cover the fixed cost portion of total costs. Two-part pricing—requiring customers to pay a standby charge in advance to be eligible for service (as with telephone, water, gas, or electric service) and then setting the price of the service at marginal cost—effectively produces the same result. So, too, does price discrimination, in which the natural monopoly charges a lot to people who are willing to pay and a little to those who are not.

By giving the railroads a vested interest in capital gains on land, land grants should have encouraged railroads to charge less than average cost. Agricultural land in the unpopulated West was valuable only if shipping costs were low enough to allow farmers to get the crop to market and still make a profit. If the railroads had been given all the land within wagon-haul distance from the rail line, then every dollar charged by shippers above marginal costs would have been precisely offset by a dollar reduction in the competitive rental value of the land. Add $100 to railroad profits by increasing a grain farmer's shipping bill by $100, and the return to the investment in that land automatically falls by the same $100. Owning (and leasing out) the land would thus have been analytically equivalent to perfect price discrimination—that is, charging in rent the maximum that all customers would be willing to pay for shipping. The discrimination would have been automatically built into the rental rate the land commanded in a competitive market. But since the railroads did not get all the land whose value was affected by their presence, an extra dollar earned on freight rates meant far less than a dollar lost in land rents to the railroads. Moreover, once railroads sold the land, they regained the incentive to act like old-fashioned profit-maximizing, output-restricting monopolists.

Federal land grant subsidies, then, were a proposition of dubious value. They were unnecessary incentives for some of the railroads since claims of market failure were unfounded. They were an unnecessarily expensive incentive for the others because the actual form of mitigating market failure was inefficient. The only possible saving grace of federal land grant subsidies was their value as a deterrent to inefficient monopoly pricing by the carriers. But the practical impact of that deterrent has yet to be demonstrated empirically.

Railroad Productivity Growth

The railroads were more than twice as productive in 1859 as they had been in 1839. Productivity doubled again between 1859 and 1890 (Table 16.4). In the period before the Civil War, about half the productivity growth resulted from growth in the use of an underutilized system of tracks thanks to commercial development. But the other half can be attributed to technical improvements in the construction and use of rails, locomotives, rolling stock, and terminal facilities. These sources became progressively more important after the Civil War.

The very first rail lines in the 1830s were carbon copies of British railroads. Techniques, though, were soon adapted to American relative factor endowments. In particular, less capital-intensive techniques were substituted. American railroads avoided topographic obstacles rather than level them, bridge them, or tunnel through them. Iron and wood combinations replaced all-iron tracks and ties, and wooden trestle bridges substituted for

TABLE 16.4

Total Factor Productivity Growth in American Railroads 1839–1910

Year	Output	Labor	Capital	Fuel	Total Factor Productivity
1839	0.08	0.3	0.8	0.07	16.0
1849	0.46	1.1	2.2	0.20	32.8
1859	2.21	5.0	10.1	1.5	33.5
1870	6.57	13.5	16.6	5.4	47.3
1880	13.87	24.5	31.5	11.7	53.6
1890	32.82	44.1	61.9	28.7	66.6
1900	54.84	59.9	72.3	45.9	86.7
1910	100	100	100	100	100

Source: Albert Fishlow, "Productivity and Technological Change in the Railroad Sector 1840–1910," in National Bureau of Economic Research, *Output, Employment and Productivity in the United States after 1800,* Studies in Income and Wealth, vol. 30 (New York: Columbia University Press, 1966): 626.

stone and brick arches. American railroads also improved upon European designs. For example, the T rail (named for its cross section) was adopted to increase the strength to weight ratio, and domestically manufactured locomotives incorporated flexible trucks (the frames carrying the locomotive and carriage wheels), making them capable of riding tighter curves at higher speeds.

To minimize labor-intensive maintenance and increase load capacity, steel rails gradually replaced iron after the 1860s. This was the single most important technological innovation of the railroads, resulting in direct and indirect savings of $479 million in 1910, or about 82 percent of railroad net income for that year. The first steel rails in America had been laid sometime after 1862 by the Pennsylvania Railroad, which ordered 150 tons of British steel rails for trials in an effort to combat the accelerated rail wear caused by heavy Civil War traffic. The trial was a success, and in 1867 the Cambria Iron Works in Johnstown, Pennsylvania, filled the first regular order for American-made steel rails. Although steel rails lasted about eight times longer than iron, the switch to steel was delayed by the greater initial cost of steel. In 1867, for example, iron rails cost $83.13 a ton, compared with $166 per ton for steel. Indeed, the real price difference was even greater because there existed a ready scrap market for iron rails but not for steel. Thanks, however, to rapid technological progress in the iron and steel industry, prices fell sharply. By 1880 prices had fallen to $48.25 a ton for iron and $67.50 a ton for steel, and by 1883 steel prices had fallen below those for iron. As a result, all new track was probably laid in steel. By the end of the 1880s more than 80 percent of the nation's track was steel, compared with only 30 percent at the start of the decade.[10]

Also made were various improvements that further raised railroad productivity. Locomotives increased in power without proportional cost increases, allowing the use of larger boxcars and longer trains. Automatic couplers, air brakes, and a new signaling system reduced labor requirements and permitted operation at higher speed. These technical innovations explain about half the increase in total factor productivity between 1870 and 1910. The rest can be attributed to economies of scale, organizational changes that maximized equipment operating time and reduced transshipment of freight. The average annual increase in productivity was 2.6 percent for 1839–1910, and 1.9 percent for 1870–1910.[11] By comparison, total factor productivity change for the economy as a whole was below 1 percent annually in both periods.

Much of the benefit of this increased productivity went to consumers and shippers. In terms of 1910 prices, the average cost of hauling a ton of

[10] Atack and Brueckner (1983).
[11] Fishlow (1966).

freight one mile dropped from 1.65 cents to 0.75 cent from 1870 to 1910. This works out to an average annual savings of 2 percent, slightly more than the industry's 1.9 percent productivity improvement.

The Direct Benefits of Railroads

By reducing the real cost of moving freight and passengers around the country, railroads should have contributed directly to economic growth. If we assume that water was the next best alternative means of transportation, the savings to society per ton of freight is equal to the difference between rail and water transport charges after we allow for the speed, freedom from seasonal restrictions, and safety advantages of railroads. This, multiplied by the number of tons receiving the benefit, is a measure of the so-called social savings of the railroad in freight tonnage. It is the same as the change in the consumer surplus attributable to the technological change represented by the substitution of the railroad for the canal. For passengers, the social savings calculation is based on the per mile price difference between rail and either water or stagecoach, whichever was relevant to the particular route without making any allowance for the improvement in comfort that railroads provided over land transport. Calculated in this way, the 1859 social savings were \$155 million for freight and \$70 million for passengers, with a lower-bound estimate of at least \$150 to \$175 million for the aggregate.[12]

This calculation of the direct benefits from railroads is simple enough in theory. In practice it has caused an immense amount of trouble. Consider Figure 16.6. Before the advent of the railroad, the marginal cost curve for transport services is MC_w, and the demand curve for transport services is D_0. The quantity of services P_wF is therefore purchased at price P_w. Once the railroad is built, the marginal cost curve shifts down to MC_{rr}, while the demand curve has shifted out to D_1 because of increases in national income. Now $P_{rr}B$ services are purchased at price P_{rr}. The social savings from the railroad consists of the extra rail services' value received by consumers less the opportunity cost of the extra resources devoted to transportation. This is represented by the area between the old and new cost curves and the new demand curve (P_wCBP_{rr}). But this area is difficult to measure. All that is observable is the new level of output, point B, and price P_{rr}. The observed market prices before and after the introduction of the railroad are equal to the social cost only if the transport industry is operating in competitive equilibrium. To find the point C, we would need to know what the old cost curve, MC_w, and the new demand curve, D_1, looked like or, that failing, at least some idea of the elasticities of MC_w and D_1.

Instead we have to rely upon an approximation. The difference between

[12] Fishlow (1965).

FIGURE 16.6

Measuring the Social Savings of the Railroad

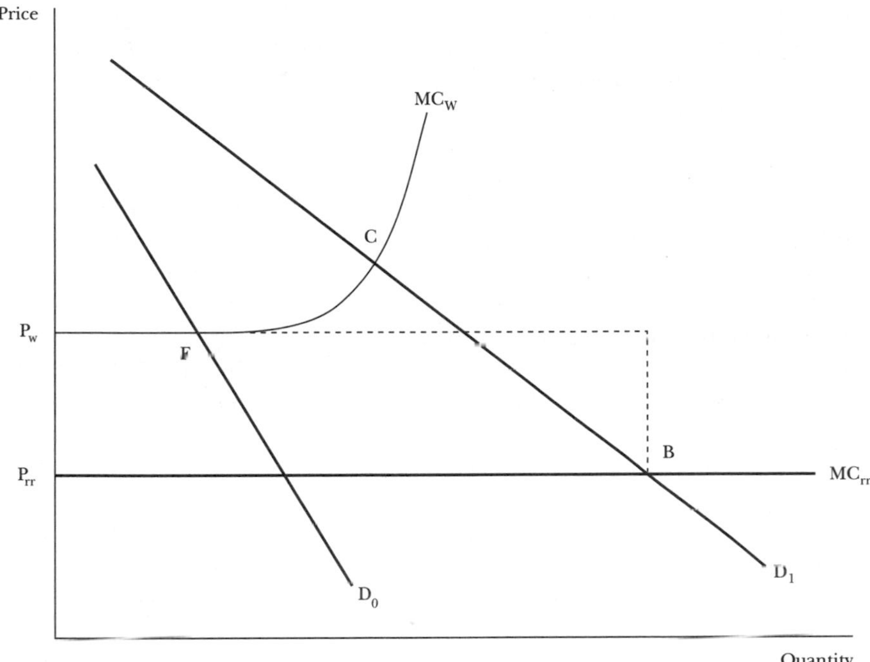

unit costs for the two transport modes—that is, $(P_w - P_{rr})$, if we assume prices equal marginal costs—is multiplied by B to approximate social savings. If P_w and P_{rr} are indeed equal to marginal costs and the elasticity of transport supply under the old technology is high, then the social savings estimate will be a true upper-bound measure of direct social savings. Unfortunately, as a number of people have observed, the railroads frequently behaved as oligopolists. As a result, it is unlikely that price equaled marginal cost.

The estimated \$150 to \$175 millions' savings in 1859 represents about 4 percent of GNP—a not inconsiderable sum, but less perhaps than many would have expected. On this basis, if the ton-mile and passenger-mile rate differences between railroad and the alternatives were the same at the end of the nineteenth century as they had been in 1859, the social savings later on would have been much larger. A reduction in freight costs of roughly 75 percent would yield \$1.5 billion annually, while the passenger gain would total \$300 million. Together they would account for about 15 percent of GNP in the late nineteenth century.[13]

Robert Fogel made an explicit set of estimates of rail social savings for

[13] Ibid.

freight traffic in 1890. He divided the problem into two parts: interregional traffic savings and intraregional traffic savings. Without taking into account the superior service provided by railroads in the form of reduced cargo losses, lower inventories, and simplified handling, Fogel's first approximation of the social savings on interregional shipment of four major agricultural commodities (pork, beef, wheat, and corn) was *negative*—rail cost more than water—but after adjustment, there was a positive net savings of about $73 million.

Estimating intraregional savings—the reduced cost of moving commodities from farms to distribution centers—is more complex. The net cost difference in hauling the goods actually produced in 1890 by wagon and by existing water routes, adjusted to account for service quality differences, was $337 million, or 2.8 percent of 1890 GNP. However, Fogel argues that this figure exaggerates the real social savings because many of the farms in 1890 were in production only because of the availability of low-cost rail service. Without cheap rail transportation the cost of shipping crops from some farms to markets by alternative means would have exceeded the total market value of the crop. Having to rely upon high-cost wagon transportation would have rendered 24 percent of the country's farmland uneconomic for market production. This land, which lay more than forty miles from an existing navigable waterway, was worth about $1.9 billion in 1890 (Figure 16.7) and generated an annual income of about $154 million (Table 16.5). Since land is a truly fixed factor, its return is the residual claimant after capital and labor have been paid their competitive, market-determined rates. This figure, therefore, captures the economic advantage of reduced transportation costs and is then added to a more conventionally derived estimate of the increased cost of hauling goods to waterways for the balance of the nation's farmland. Fogel's grand total is some $248 million annual social savings, 2.1 percent of 1890 GNP. But even this figure, Fogel argues, is an overestimate of the social savings since more land could have been opened up by additional canal construction. He suggests that a system of five thousand additional miles of canals could have made cultivation profitable on 93 percent of 1890 farmland. Combining an estimate of lost land rents on the remaining 7 percent of land with an estimate of rail versus water social savings, Fogel pares his social savings figure to just $175 million. This could have been reduced still further with additional construction of surfaced, all-weather roads.

Agricultural commodities, however, represented only a modest fraction of total freight in the 1890s—perhaps one-quarter of all ton-miles recorded. But multiplying by a factor of four would overstate the savings on all freight. Half of the nonagricultural freight by weight consisted of coal and iron ore—low-value, nonperishable bulk commodities. They stood to gain little from speedier delivery and gentler handling. The agricultural social savings, moreover, implicitly include a portion of the nonagricultural since all of the

FIGURE 16.7

Areas within 40 Miles of Water Transportation

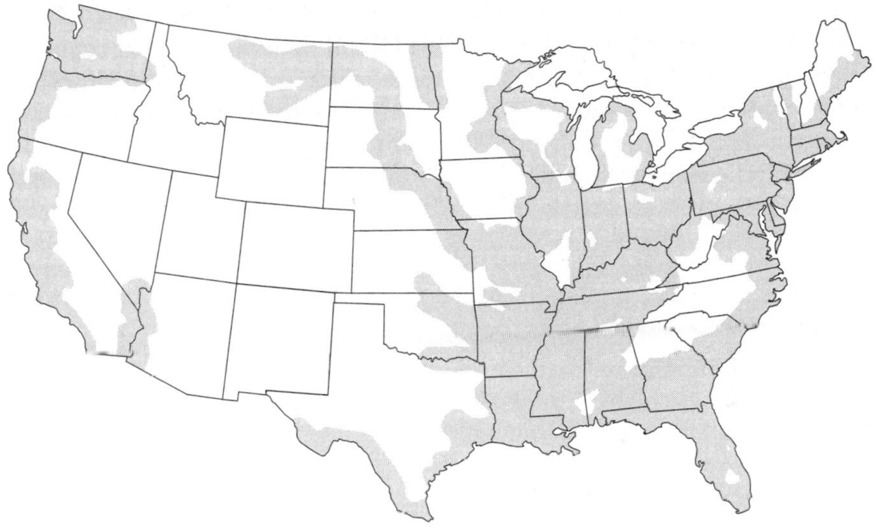

Source: Robert W. Fogel, *Railroads and American Economic Growth* (Baltimore: Johns Hopkins University Press, 1964): 81.

TABLE 16.5

Rental Losses Caused by Reductions in the Area of Feasible Commercial Agricultural Production in the Absence of the Railroad in 1890

Region	Land Value Lost (%)	Value of Lost Land (millions $)	Rental Income Lost (millions $)
North Atlantic	0.5	6	—
South Atlantic	21.1	118	8
North Central	29.2	1,442	110
South Central	21.5	159	14
Western	27.2	218	20
Total	23.9	1,943	152

Note: Column 3 is computed by multiplying the estimated mortgage interest rate prevalent in the state times the reduced value of the land.

Source: Robert W. Fogel, *Railroads and American Economic Growth* (Baltimore: Johns Hopkins University Press, 1964): 82–83.

railroad overhead cost was attributed to agriculture. Yet shipment of the two kinds of commodities often complemented each other because they went opposite directions on the same routes. Fogel therefore guesses that overall, the social savings could have been no more than $560 million, or just 4.7 percent of 1890 GNP—less than one-third of the savings projected by Fishlow.

One reason why Fogel's estimate is so much smaller than Fishlow's is that Fogel makes no allowance for passenger savings. This has been estimated at about $344 million in 1890.[14] Combined with Fogel's own figure for freight traffic savings, then the upper bound on total social savings reaches $904 million, or 7.3 percent of GNP, still short of Fishlow's estimates.

The Debate over Social Savings

Attempts to measure railroad social savings and assess their significance to the economy generated a flood of scholarly criticism. Some of the more important issues are addressed below.

THE COSTS OF TRANSPORTATION VERSUS FREIGHT RATES

Social savings measure the reduction in real resources needed to provide a given amount of transport services. The data that Fogel and Fishlow were forced to use, however, were not actually resource cost data at all but price data. Competition between transportation media, for example, should guarantee identical fares on identical routes for equal service. The lower price that canals charged reflected their inferior service, explaining why Fogel's first approximation of interregional rail savings was negative. Stanley Lebergott has tried to avoid the cost/price problem by reconstructing cost per ton-mile for typical rail and canal service. He estimates that as early as 1840 canal costs were already four times as high as railroad costs. This is roughly consistent with Fishlow's computation for 1859. Actually, Lebergott argues, this is probably an underestimate of the true social savings since rail technology improved greatly after 1840 and railroads offered greater safety and speed.

BIASES

The central proposition of Fogel's argument is that the significance of rail social savings has been overstated by others. Such estimates are, of necessity, very crude. As a result, there is an obligation to bias the results against the case one is trying to prove. Fogel tries to do this. For example, he assumes that demand for transportation is absolutely inelastic while the supply of alternative transportation is perfectly elastic. This approach embodies both upward and downward biases, and one cannot be sure that they simply

[14] Boyd and Walton (1972).

cancel out. Paul David, in particular, has raised a number of questions about Fogel's assumptions. He argues that the waterways could not have handled the 1890 freight volume at constant cost per unit. As facilities became increasingly congested, secondary, less efficient water routes would have been needed to supplement the cheapest, most direct routes. Nor were all sites along navigable waterways equally desirable as transshipment points. Furthermore, not all rivers were created equal. For example, the Red River of the North, though navigable, forms the boundary between Minnesota and the Dakotas and flows *north* to Lake Winnipeg in Canada—hardly a desirable transportation route to market! Further, David argues that Fogel seriously underestimated the size of emergency storage facilities needed to handle inventories in transit during weather interruptions on water routes. As a result, the social savings from the railroad may have been much higher than Fogel estimated.

COMPARATIVE STATICS VERSUS GENERAL EQUILIBRIUM

Fogel's counterfactual—an America in 1890 without the railroad—is a world that never was. Instead in the actual world of 1890 more than 160,000 miles of track served thousands of new communities. Would these towns and cities have been where they were in the absence of the railroad? What else would have changed? Would the internal-combustion engines of Lenoir or Otto have enjoyed earlier commercial success? We simply don't know.

This is a critical question, however, since social savings are defined as the difference between the actual cost of shipping goods in a particular year and the alternative cost of shipping *exactly the same bundle of goods between exactly the same points* without the railroad. Certainly it seems likely that things would have been relatively much more different in 1890 than in 1860 in this counterfactual world. But Fogel's model cannot capture this because it compares one static partial equilibrium solution with another. What is needed is a dynamic general equilibrium model to capture these interactions.

Jeffrey Williamson has used a computable general equilibrium model to simulate the American economy from 1870 to 1892. Assuming that transport costs were unchanged over the period (whereas, in fact, railroad freight rates from Chicago to New York declined by perhaps 60 percent), he concluded that real GNP in 1892 would have been 18 percent lower than it actually was. This calculation, however, overstates the contribution of the railroad since it measures the savings from reduced transport costs in general, including handling charges and insurance as well as marine freight charges on exports. These contributed an unknown amount to the economic gain.

IN DEFENSE OF FOGEL'S SOCIAL SAVINGS ESTIMATES

Williamson's computable general equilibrium estimates should not be accepted at their face value. Two factors seem to be critical. First, he assumed zero resource cost for additional transportation. In particular, Williamson's model assumes railroads could be built without capital at a time when rail construction was accounting for a relatively large share of gross domestic private capital formation. Second, he used 1870 prices in calculating GNP. Charles Kahn's experiments with the same model but without these assumptions yield much lower estimates of the social savings. Indeed, he finds that social savings were not too different from those suggested by Fogel: between 2.3 and 3.0 percent of 1871 GNP, 5.3 and 6.4 percent of 1880 GNP, and 3.2 to 4.2 percent of 1890 GNP, depending on whether prices reflect the change in transportation costs or not. Other dynamic effects may add a percent or so to these estimates.

Fogel has also vigorously defended both his methodology and his conclusions. For example, he dismissed Lebergott's suggestions that railroad freight rates should have been based upon minimum long-run costs (which would raise social savings by increasing the price spread) on the ground that the degree of intensity of track utilization achieved by the Philadelphia and Reading Railroad (which carried coal downhill from the Pennsylvania coalfields to Philadelphia) was infeasible for the railroad system as a whole. Similarly, Boyd and Walton's critique of Fogel's assumption of zero demand elasticity is answered by a table showing that the measurement of social savings was quite sensitive to assumptions about the elasticity of demand.

Not all questions, such as the amount of winter storage required by an 1890s' America dependent upon water and road transportation, are answered. It is clear that the debate over what Fogel calls the "axiom of indispensability"—the notion advanced by Jenks, Rostow, and others that the railroad was the critical institutional change upon which nineteenth-century economic growth depended—will never be the same. A glance at the timing of growth and the relatively late start of the railroads suggests that the two were not inextricably linked, and Fogel's counterfactual five thousand miles of canals to open the Great Plains to commercial agriculture also raises questions about the argument that railroads were crucial to the physical expansion of the frontier.

But what if the axiom is rephrased in more cautious language—that is, that railroads were extremely important to economic growth? Fogel's calculation puts the direct social savings on freight haulage from railroads at 4.7 percent of GNP in 1890, a figure that he dismisses as small. But is it? On the one hand, it presents less than three weeks' worth of production in 1890; on the other, it represents more than one year's growth in GNP and more than two years' growth in per capita income. Few, if any, other inventions have made so large a mark. Certainly the market rewarded railroading. By Fishlow's calculations the average return for all railroads in 1859 was 15 percent—at least twice the return on secure assets—while David estimates that the return in 1890 was 12 to 16 percent. Further, the social rate of return was substantially higher. Fogel, for example, estimates that the average social rate of return for the Union Pacific was 30 percent while Lloyd Mercer estimates a social return for the Central Pacific system of 24 percent.

Backward Linkages

Development economists call the demands that a growing industry creates for other industries "backward linkages." To Rostow and others, these linkages were a critical part of the case for railroads as the leading sector in the American growth process in the first half of the nineteenth century. The derived demand for coal, iron, and advanced engineering technology is thought to have given a push to the economy far beyond the direct benefits enumerated above. The quantitative evidence, however, is relatively weak, particularly earlier in the nineteenth century.

Consider, for example, the impact of the railroads upon the American iron industry. As we have seen, the railroads relied exclusively upon iron rails, weighing fifty to sixty pounds per yard in the 1840s and somewhat more later on, held in place by large iron spikes until the late 1860s, when steel began to replace iron. The impact of this demand on domestic iron production, however, was blunted by the use of imports and by the fact that rerolled scrap rails were a good substitute for virgin pig iron in the production of new rails. Fishlow calculates that from 1840 to 1850 *net* railroad iron consumption was just 7 percent of the pig iron made in America. Fogel estimates that domestic nail production in 1849 probably used twice as much iron as rail production. With the rail boom of the 1850s, though, the percentage of domestic iron used in rails rose considerably, reaching 20 percent by the last half of the decade (see Table 16.6). After the Civil War the railroad industry's economic impact on the iron and steel industries was much greater. The railroad industry used roughly 60 percent of the Bessemer process steel produced in the United States through 1880; in 1889, 29 percent of all iron and steel production was devoted to the railroad. Similarly, before the Civil War America's railroads consumed relatively little coal before coal-fired locomotives were introduced in the late 1850s and until the American iron industry switched from charcoal to coal smelting. As more coal mines opened up, however, railroad demand expanded. Nor did the nation's railroads play an important role in the development of the lumber milling industry. For although most railroad ties were wooden and were replaced frequently as they rotted out, the railroads were convinced that sawed ties were more prone to rot than those that were split. As a result, only the board lumber demand for the construction of wagons and carriages had much impact upon the lumber milling industry.

Railroads did absorb large amounts of industrial machinery—locomotives, rolling stock, switching, signaling, and coupling equipment. Hence there is the temptation to infer a strong backward linkage to the machinery

TABLE 16.6

Derived Railroad Demand for the Products of Domestic American Industry about 1840 and 1860

Industry/Product	c. 1840 (% industry output)	c. 1860 (% industry output)
Iron rails	1.3	18.0
Iron fastenings, locomotives, and rolling stock	3.0	7.2
Coal (direct and indirect)	n.a.	6.0
Sawed railroad ties	0.3	0.5
Lumber for railroad cars	0.4	0.8
Transportation equipment	n.a.	25.4
All manufacturing	n.a.	2.8

Source: Robert W. Fogel, *Railroads and American Economic Growth* (Baltimore: Johns Hopkins University Press, 1964): chap. 4–6.

industry in general and the steam engine industry in particular. Again, however, the numbers disappoint. The railroad's share of total machine production in 1859 was less than 10 percent. Locomotive production value in that year was slightly less than the value of machinery made for the textile industry. Locomotive producers were rarely brand-new firms coaxed into existence by specialized demand. Most began as producers of marine engines and textile machinery or as general machine shops. Indeed, Fishlow's estimates imply that steamboats, not railroads, were the largest purchasers of steam engines until at least the late 1850s. Moreover, in the absence of the railroad, demand from other industries, such as the steamboating industry, would have been larger making up much, if not all, of the demand attributable to the railroad.

Consequently, the backward linkages are a disappointment to those convinced that the railroad was crucial to nineteenth-century American industrial development.

Forward Linkages

Development economists are also interested in the forward railroad linkages, the impact of railroads on those who consumed rail services. There is a plausible list of many beneficiaries: farmers, miners, food processors, and the manufacturers of equipment to serve all of them. It is important, however, to distinguish the gross impact of railroads—the enormous movements in the location of economic activity—from the gain in real output. A new transportation link that creates a meat-packing industry in Chicago or

Kansas City is not a net gain to the economy unless the change also increases the productivity of the resources employed. For example, the rise of the Chicago meat-packers was partly offset by a decline in the industry in Cincinnati.

Fogel warns, moreover, that the forward linkage efficiency gains may be "double-counted." Railroads, for example, undoubtedly made it possible for some farmers in the Midwest and on the Great Plains to specialize in grain and wheat. Resources from inefficient eastern farms could thus be transferred, resulting in higher national income. But the value of efficiency gains for a competitive economy is precisely what Fogel measures in his land value calculation and in the direct calculation of social savings resulting from lowered shipping costs.

This does not mean that forward linkage gains can be dismissed entirely. At least some of the benefits may be captured as monopoly profits by the rail sector. Some of the gains were also diffused through the economy in the form of external benefits to the forward linkage industries—learning-by-doing, the training of skilled workers, and the perfection of civil and mechanical engineering techniques. However, many of these same forward linkages in the 1830s or 1840s were as strong as or stronger with canals and steamboats than railroads. But there were other benefits, too, that other transportation media might not have generated. The telegraph, for example, was essential to the safe operation of a single-track railroad system. Once installed, however, it not only notified agents and operators along the line of the progress of a particular train but also carried economic and political news at speeds that had previously been unimaginable. For once news could be news everywhere the telegraph reached. The railroad also linked the country coast to coast; "one nation indivisible" began to take on new meaning. Before the advent of the transcontinental railroad, it took more than three weeks to reach California from New York; five weeks to reach Seattle. By the end of the century travel times had been cut to fewer than four days. Moreover, the development of the late-nineteenth-century capital markets that helped finance American industry and contributed to the rise of New York as a leading financial center in the world owed much to the active market created by railroad bonds. Rhetoric aside, the railroad was important whether its contribution was less than 5 percent in 1859 or 1890. Almost certainly no other nineteenth-century innovation mattered more.

Bibliography

Atack, Jeremy, and Jan Brueckner. "Steel Rails and American Railroads, 1867–1880: A Reply to Harley." *Explorations in Economic History* 20 (1983): 258–62.

Boyd, Haydon, and Gary Walton. "The Social Savings from 19th Century Rail Passenger Services." *Explorations in Economic History* 9 (1972): 233–54.

David, Paul. "Transport Innovation and Economic Growth: Professor Fogel on and off the Rails." *Economic History Review* 32 (1969): 506–25.

Fishlow, Albert. *American Railroads and the Transformation of the Ante-Bellum Economy.* Cambridge: Harvard University Press, 1965.

———. "Productivity Change and Technological Change in the Railroad Sector 1840–1910." In National Bureau of Economic Research, *Output, Employment, and Productivity in the United States after 1800,* Studies in Income and Wealth, vol. 30. New York: Columbia University Press, 1966: 583–646.

———. "Internal Transportation." In *American Economic Growth,* ed. Lance Davis et al. New York: Harper & Row, 1972: 468–547.

Fleisig, Heywood. "The Central Pacific Railroad and the Railroad Land Grant Controversy." *Journal of Economic History* 35 (1975): 552–66.

Fogel, Robert. *The Union Pacific Railroad: A Case in Premature Enterprise.* Baltimore: Johns Hopkins University Press, 1960.

———. "A Quantitative Approach to the Study of Railroads in American Economic Growth." *Journal of Economic History* 22 (1962): 163–97.

———. *Railroads and American Economic Growth: Essays in Econometric History.* Baltimore: Johns Hopkins University Press, 1964.

———. "Notes on the Social Savings Controversy." *Journal of Economic History* 39 (1979): 1–54.

Hacker, Louis. *The Triumph of American Capitalism.* New York: Columbia University Press, 1940.

Harley, C. Knick. "Transportation, the World Wheat Trade, and the Kuznets Cycle, 1850–1913." *Explorations in Economic History* 17 (1980): 218–50.

———. "Oligopoly Strategy and the Timing of Railroad Construction." *Journal of Economic History* 42 (1982): 797–823.

Henry, Robert S. "The Railroad Land Grant Legend in American History Texts." *Mississippi Valley Historical Review* 32 (1945): 171–94.

Jenks, Leland. "Railroads as an Economic Force in American Development." In *Views of American Economic Growth, Vol. 2, The Industrial Era,* ed. Thomas Cochran and Thomas Brewer. New York: McGraw-Hill, 1966: 35–49.

Kahn, Charles. "The Use of Complicated Models as Explanations: A Re-examination of Williamson's Late Nineteenth Century America." *Research in Economic History* 11 (1988): 185–216.

Kuznets, Simon. *Modern Economic Growth.* New Haven: Yale University Press, 1966.

Lebergott, Stanley. "United States Transport Advance and Externalities." *Journal of Economic History* 26 (1966): 437–65.

McClelland, Peter. "Railroads, American Growth and the New Economic History: A Critique." *Journal of Economic History* 28 (1972): 102–23.

———. "Social Rates of Return on American Railroads in the 19th Century." *Economic History Review* 25 (1972): 471–88.

Mercer, Lloyd. "Rates of Return for Land-Grant Railroads: The Central Pacific." *Journal of Economic History* 30 (1970): 602–26.

———. "Building Ahead of Demand: Some Evidence for the Land Grant Railroads." *Journal of Economic History* 34 (1974): 492–500.

Nerlove, Mark. "Railroads and American Economic Growth." *Journal of Economic History* 26 (1966): 107–15.

Rostow, W. W. *The Stages of Economic Growth: A Non-Communist Manifesto.* Cambridge, England: Cambridge University Press, 1960.

Schumpeter, Joseph. *The Theory of Economic Development.* Cambridge: Harvard University Press, 1949.

Williamson, Jeffrey. "The Railroads and Midwestern Development, 1870–1890: A General Equilibrium History." In *Essays in 19th Century Economic History,* ed. David Klingaman and Richard Vedder. Athens: Ohio University Press, 1975: 269–352.

The changing structure of american industry

17

During the antebellum years American manufacturing grew rapidly. In 1810 only about 75,000 people worked in industry. By 1860 there were more than 1.3 million workers in manufacturing. Nevertheless, America was still far from fully industrialized. Over the next fifty years the rate of employment growth in manufacturing slowed to about 3.4 percent per year, almost half its former rate. However, since population growth also slowed, manufacturing's share of the labor force continued to increase, peaking at about 27 percent of the labor force immediately following World War I. By 1940, thanks in part to the crisis of the Great Depression, manufacturing employment had slipped to only about 20 percent of the labor force, but its share rose in the years after World War II until sometime in the 1950s. It has since fallen again as the labor force has shifted more into service occupations. In 1970, for example, manufacturing employment totaled 20.7 million (26 percent of employment) while there were 15 million in wholesale and retail trades and 20.4 million in various other service industries. By 1990, although manufacturing employment had increased slightly, its share of employment had fallen to less than 18 percent, and many more people were employed in retail and wholesale trade (24.3 million) and services (39.1 million) than in manufacturing (21.2 million).

Behind the employment statistics for the nineteenth and early twentieth centuries lies the dramatic transformation of America from an agrarian and a mercantile economy to an industrial economy. Until the 1880s agriculture was the chief source of wealth in America. By 1890 the value of manufactures was three times that of agricultural products. Industrial concerns—labor unrest, monopoly power, pollution, and occupational hazards—increasingly occupied the public's attention and dominated public policy. In 1810, and even in 1860, American industrial output had lagged behind that of Britain and France and possibly Germany as well. By 1894, however, the United States produced more manufactures than any other country in the world, and on the eve of World War I America produced as much as its three nearest competitors—Britain, France, and Germany—combined.

Within the course of a century America had gone from industrial outpost and imitator of Europe to industrial leader. American business and American business practices provided a model for the rest of the world. Moreover, American companies, such as Armour, Coca-Cola, Du Pont, Ford, General Electric, Heinz, International Harvester, Kodak, Singer, Standard Oil, Swift, Westinghouse, and many others, had expanded overseas, playing an important role shaping industrial development in other countries and helping create the international economy of today (Table 17.1). The direct investment by these large companies overseas amounted to some 7 percent of American GNP in 1914. They were an important element in the transition of the U.S. economy from net debtor to creditor and a visible sign of the nation's changing status on the world stage.

The Changing Nature of Production: The Transition from Workshop to Factory

Although large areas of the country had little or no manufacturing in 1860—for example, only 52 manufacturing establishments were enumerated in Washington Territory, which encompassed more than sixty-eight thousand square miles, and Florida had only 185 establishments—Rhode Island, parts of Massachusetts, the area around Philadelphia and New York, and a few other pockets were already quite heavily industrialized. Rhode Island—an area of only twelve hundred square miles—for example, was home to 1,191 manufacturing firms in 1860. Thousands of industrial employees worked in these industrialized pockets. While many worked in small workshops that employed only one or two workers, others worked in large factories, some of which had thousands of employees. Industrial cities, such as Fall River, Lawrence, and Lowell, were the exception rather than the rule. Only four cities outside the East Coast states had more than five thousand residents engaged in manufacturing activities in 1860—Chicago, Cincinnati, Louisville, and St. Louis—and only one southern city—Richmond, Virginia—had reached this threshold. Massachusetts and New York, on the other hand, each had five such cities.

Most American industry in 1860, however, was widely dispersed, rural, small-scale, and simple. There were, for example, almost twenty thousand sawmills nationwide—or about ten per county—producing perhaps $4,750

TABLE 17.1

American Multinationals with Two or More Overseas Plants in 1914

*Groups 20 and 21: Food and tobacco**
American Chicle
American Cotton Oil
Armour
Coca-Cola
H. J. Heinz
Quaker Oats
Swift
American Tobacco
British American Tobacco

Groups 28, 29, and 30: Chemicals and Pharmaceuticals, Oil, and Rubber
Carborundum
Parke Davis (drug)
Sherwin-Williams
Sterns & Co (drug)
United Drug (drug)
Virginia-Carolina Chemical
Du Pont
Standard Oil of N.J.
U.S. Rubber

Groups 35, 36, and 37: Machinery and Transportation Equipment
American Bicycle
American Gramophone
American Radiator
Crown Cork & Seal
Chicago Pneumatic Tool
Ford
General Electric
International Harvester
International Steam Pump (Worthington)
Mergenthaler Linotype
National Cash Register
Norton
Otis Elevator
Singer
Torrington
United Shoe Machinery
Western Electric
Westinghouse Air Brake
Westinghouse Electric

Others
Alcoa (33)*
Gillette (34)
Eastman Kodak (38)
Diamond Match (39)

*The two-digit groups used by the U.S. Bureau of the Census in its Standard Industrial Classification.

Source: Alfred D. Chandler, *The Visible Hand* (Cambridge: Belknap Press of Harvard University Press, 1977): 368.

worth of lumber each per year. Similarly, there were almost fourteen thousand flour mills, seventy-five hundred blacksmiths, and more than three thousand manufacturers of wagons and carts. Many of these industries, such as blacksmithing and flour milling, served the needs of the farm sector. Blacksmiths, for example, produced everything from nails, horseshoes, plows, and grain cradles to farm carts and reapers. Indeed, blacksmiths in some states, especially in the South, produced most of the agricultural implements and many of the wagons and carts used on farms and plantations. Of the ten leading industries in terms of value added (value of output minus value of raw materials), five—cotton, lumber, flour, leather, and woolens—produced products that were just one stage removed from the primary product (Table 17.2). Much of the rest of industry specialized in the production of goods formerly made at home, such as boots and shoes, coarse textiles, and clothing. Often the same production methods were used that had once been used in the home: a knife, a hammer and last, a handloom, a needle and thread.

Most firms had little capital. They were usually unincorporated, organized instead as sole proprietorships or partnerships. Such firms had no separate legal identity from that of their owners and were inextricably linked to the life and fortunes of the owner, disappearing—in name at least—upon the owner's death. Their labor forces were small. The average flour mill and blacksmith's shop, for example, had only two workers, one of whom was probably the owner. As a result, employee supervision posed few problems. Where the production process demanded more power than human muscles could supply, waterpower from almost any convenient river or stream typically sufficed. When the source dried up or froze up, the costs of idled plant and the opportunity cost of forgone production was minimal. Indeed, given the low volume of demand, the lack of all-weather, year-round transportation, and the competing demands for labor especially from the agricultural sector, such periodic shutdowns may have been welcomed.

The small scale and the dispersed nature of production were perfectly in keeping with the low population density, the relatively poor transportation network, and the general simplicity of antebellum production methods. Indeed, most researchers have concluded that there were few potential scale economies in early American manufacturing industry and that whatever scale economies might have existed were already being realized by the typical plant, even though it was small (see below).

Not all businesses, however, fitted this mold. There were, for example, some very large flour mills in port cities, such as Haxell Mills in Richmond, Virginia, which employed more than a hundred workers and produced more than $1 million worth of flour and meal in 1860. More significantly, there were the cotton textile mills of New England, especially in Lawrence and Lowell. Some were extremely large in 1860. Pacific Mills, for example, had a labor force of eighteen hundred and produced more than $8 million worth of cloth. The Merrimack Manufacturing Company employed twenty-four hundred workers.

Capitalized at millions of dollars—for example, Pacific Mills was capitalized at $2.4 million—these enterprises exceeded the financial resources of an individual or small group. They were therefore incorporated and organized as joint-stock companies, adopting an organizational form already widely used by banks and internal improvement companies, such as canals

TABLE 17.2

The Ten Leading Industries in America in 1860 (1914 $ millions of value added)

Rank	Industry	Value Added (in 1914 $ millions)
1	Cotton goods	$58.8
2	Lumber (sawed)	54.0
3	Boots and shoes	52.9
4	Flour and meal	43.1
5	Men's clothing	39.4
6	Machinery (including steam engines)	31.5
7	Woolen goods	26.6
8	Leather	24.5
9	Cast iron	22.7
10	Printing and publishing	19.6

Source: Computed from the 1860 census of manufacturers.

and toll roads. For example, in 1860 forty-seven different manufacturing company stocks were being traded on the Boston Stock Market. Although their shares might be publicly traded, stock prices were often high—$1,000 per share was not uncommon—and the market was extremely thin. As a result, there were relatively few stockholders, most of whom knew one another quite well, who lived in the general area around the enterprise, and who socialized together. Thus, while the day-to-day management of the mill operations might nominally be in the hands of a hired agent or mill superintendent, ownership and control remained closely linked and personal in these businesses.

Given the size of investment in plant and equipment and the high volume of production, shutdowns in these large enterprises were expensive, especially if they were unanticipated. Consequently, these firms made great efforts to minimize seasonal dependency by constructing elaborate systems of storage reservoirs and supply canals to ensure adequate waterpower. They installed steam power either for backup or as prime mover. And they located in urban areas, where labor was relatively abundant, lived in close proximity to the factory, and was more likely to regard industrial employment as its primary, if not sole, occupation. With thousands of employees performing interdependent and increasingly specialized tasks, these large firms had to institute work rules governing such things as starting, stopping, and break times and set up procedures for monitoring performance. The labor markets that resulted were hierarchical, internal, and relatively inflexible.

Moreover, during the 1850s and especially after the Civil War an increasing share of the nation's manufacturing output came from these larger, more mechanized, less seasonal plants. Mills and factories—establishments relying upon inanimate sources of power to drive increasingly specialized machinery—gradually displaced the artisan shop, the sweatshop, and the *manu*factory as the source of the nation's manufactures. For example, manuscript census data show that whereas in 1850 none of the nation's boots and shoes were made in factories, by 1870 almost a quarter were. In the furniture industry the share of output from mills and factories increased from 29 to 67 percent in the same twenty-year period. Such inanimately powered establishments were more efficient—that is to say, they would produce the same output at lower cost or, given the same quantities of labor and capital, could produce more output—than those relying solely upon animate sources of power.[1]

Even so, displacement of workshops and other nonmechanized firms was incomplete during the nineteenth century. Small firms not only survived but prospered, and new small firms continued to be established.[2] The small firms that survived were located at some physical distance from their larger, more efficient competitors, surviving by virtue of the measure of protection afforded inefficient operations by positive transport costs. Eventually, though, as transport costs continued to fall throughout the nineteenth and into the twentieth century, their survival came to depend increasingly upon their finding a market niche where they were complementary to, rather than rival with, the larger firms.

The Changing Structure of the Market

The traditional historiography of nineteenth-century industrialization views the pre-Civil War era as a time that approximated the economist's notions of perfect competition, while in the post–Civil War period large-scale enterprises emerged that enjoyed substantial market power. However, this sharp contrast between pre– and post–Civil War industrialization has been questioned by a growing number of scholars. The fundamental fallacy in the traditional argument, according to Fred Bateman and Thomas Weiss, is the equation of small size and large numbers with perfect competition. While these are generally necessary conditions, they are not sufficient conditions for perfect competition. Economists usually add the qualifiers of a homogeneous commodity so that buyers have no preferences among the sellers—a reasonable assumption in the pre–Civil War era, when most goods were unbranded—and that scale is *relative* to the size of market. It is here that the traditional argument breaks down. Most early-nineteenth-century firms

[1] Sokoloff (1984); Atack (1987).
[2] Atack (1986).

were small only if the market was considered to be geographically large, say, a region, such as the South, Midwest, or Northeast, or the entire nation. If, instead, the relevant market was much narrower, say, a state, or perhaps more realistically, an area of fifty to one hundred miles radius of the plant, then industrial concentration within this market area was quite high early in most industries. Only where firms had immediate access to navigable waterways or the ocean or produced goods of high value, but low weight and bulk, were markets likely to be large and geographically extensive. High transport costs provided protected markets for relatively inefficient or less than optimally sized firms (see Appendix A). As a result, small, high-cost producers could persist for a long time in an industry despite the presence of larger, low-cost producers, provided the two were spatially separated. We usually explain the coexistence of these firms in today's economy in terms of market niches, in which large firms supply the mass market and small firms satisfy more specialized demands over time.

One widely used measure of market power is the four-firm concentration ratio. This ratio measures the sales of the four largest suppliers relative to total market sales of the product in the relevant market. The higher this ratio, the greater is the degree of potential monopoly power. The data to calculate four-firm concentration ratios for most industries and most markets in the nineteenth century are not available, but estimates of single-firm concentration ratios, on the assumption that markets were statewide, suggest that many industries were highly concentrated in the relevant market areas (Table 17.3). Consider, for example, the estimates of the single-firm concentration ratios in iron castings. Although there were more than fourteen hundred firms producing such castings nationwide, single-firm concentration ratios at the state level averaged 14 percent, implying a four-firm ratio of more than 50 percent—ratios as high as or higher than at the end of the century or in more recent times. This, however, is an upper-bound measure of the degree of concentration. The other firms in the industry in the market area were often much smaller than the largest producer. The size distribution of firms was highly skewed toward smaller firms that produced on average perhaps one-thousandth of the output of the largest firms. Arguably the largest firm under such circumstances may have enjoyed more monopoly power in the nineteenth century because there were fewer competitors with similar market power. Even if this line of reasoning is not accepted, the data suggest that many industries in the nineteenth century were probably as concentrated as, or more concentrated than, in the twentieth century—*within the relevant market boundaries.*

The assumption that the relevant market boundary was a state is almost certainly overly restrictive for some industries, such as textiles and chemicals. At the same time it is probably too broad for flour, lumber, boots and shoes, and clothing. Thus the concentration ratios are upper-bound for those industries in which firms serve wider markets and lower-bound for

TABLE 17.3

A Comparison of Industrial Concentration in 1860, 1901, and 1963 (output share of four largest firms unless otherwise noted)

	Single-firm concentration ratios in 1860			1901	1963	
Industry	Northeast	Midwest	South	(National)	Regional	National
Agricultural implements	45	16	20	41		43
Boots and shoes	4	16	6	26		25
Chemicals	96		100	24		56
Clothing	6	15	40			8
Cotton goods	14	99	30	20		30
Flour milling	12	4	11	39		35
Furniture	13	18	10		23	11
Iron castings	32	14	66	46		28
Iron bar	29	100	37	46	71	50
Leather	7	26	11	26		18
Liquor	7	9	21	39	68	47
Lumber milling	10	6	9	0.5	18	11
Machinery	30	15	25	41		93
Meat-packing	21	32	39	39	40	16
Tobacco	17	18	9	50		59
Woolen goods	17	7	42	20		54

Sources: 1860: Fred Bateman and Thomas J. Weiss, "Comparative Regional Development in Antebellum Manufacturing," *Journal of Economic History* 35 (1975): 203. 1901: Morris A. Adelman, "Monopoly and Concentration: Comparisons in Time and Space," in *The Economics of Antitrust,* ed. Richard E. Low (Englewood Cliffs, N.J.: Prentice Hall, 1968): 48. 1963: 89th Cong., 2d sess. *Concentration Ratios in Manufacturing Industry, 1963* (Washington, D.C.: Government Printing Office, 1966): Table 2, and 90th Cong., 1st sess. *Concentration Ratios in Manufacturing Industry, 1963: Part II* (Washington, D.C.: Government Printing Office, 1967): Table 25.

those industries in which markets were narrower. Market power was perhaps most concentrated in flour and lumber milling, clothing manufacture, and other industries that are most widely thought of as perfectly competitive. For example, the four largest flour mills in a state in 1860 might produce, on average, as much as 16 to 48 percent of a state's output of flour. There was thus considerable potential for the exploitation of local monopoly power. These large firms also accounted for a large share of the total manufacturing output in the state. Not only did they therefore have the potential for some market control, but they also represented a concentration of economic power in the industrial sector.

Large, potentially monopolist firms, however, do not seem to have systematically exploited any market power that they may have had to reap higher than average profits. The average return to large firms in relatively concentrated industries was little different from that of large firms in unconcentrated industries.[3] This suggests that monopoly power—to the extent that it existed—was not used to reap extraordinarily large profits. One possible reason is that markets were contestable—that is to say, monopolistic firms were constrained in their ability to exploit consumers by fear that new firms might enter the market, turning a profitable monopoly into an unprofitable duopoly. They thus limited profits to minimize incentives to invade the market. Moreover, although large firms earned smaller profits than smaller firms, the variance of profits for large firms was much smaller, and therefore, the return was more certain, more secure. Small firms, on the other hand, earned high profits in that there was a significant probability not only of their making a loss but even of bankruptcy. Such profits thus were in part a compensation for the increased risk borne by smaller firms with less market control and influence.

The Postbellum Expansion of Manufacturing

In 1860 much of the nation's manufacturing was concentrated around New York and Philadelphia. These areas remained the nation's leading industrial centers. By 1880 the Midwest had also developed a substantial industrial sector, and Chicago, with almost eighty thousand workers in manufacturing, had surpassed Boston as an industrial city. Industrial employment in Chicago grew more than fourfold between 1860 and 1870, and it increased by almost 50 percent between 1870 and 1880. Other midwestern cities also developed substantial, rapidly growing industrial sectors. By 1880 Cincinnati had more than fifty-nine thousand workers in manufacturing, St. Louis more than forty thousand, and Milwaukee had more than twenty thousand industrial workers. In 1860 the geographic center of manufacturing was located some miles east of Pittsburgh and the Midwest was home to just 11 percent of the nation's manufacturing employees. By 1900 the Midwest's share of manufacturing employment had doubled, and by 1920 the center of manufacturing had shifted westward several hundred miles and lay between Toledo and Springfield, Ohio. The Midwest had become the industrial heartland of the United States (Figure 17.1).

The conventional wisdom emphasizes the role of the Midwest as a primary processing center serving regional markets until the advent of the railroad made supplying a national market practical. The coming of the railroad also spurred the development of midwestern heavy industry based upon its resources of coal and iron. In this story midwestern industrialization was largely supply-driven, converting low-value-to-weight and high-

[3] Bateman and Weiss (1981).

FIGURE 17.1

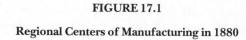

Regional Centers of Manufacturing in 1880

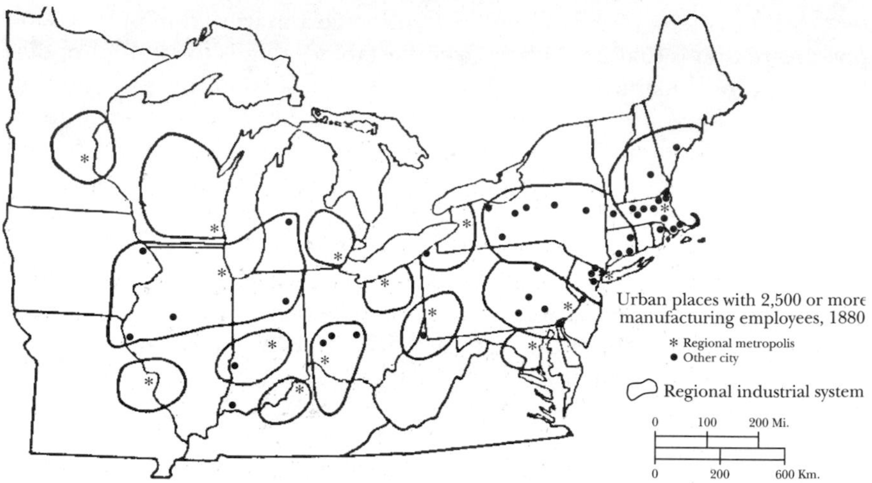

Source: David R. Meyer, "Emergence of the American Manufacturing Belt: An Interpretation," *Journal of Historical Geography* 9 (1983): 146.

processing-loss items into more easily transportable commodities for use elsewhere. Current research argues that this characterization ignores the important role played by local and regional demand within the Midwest in developing a more diversified industry mix. Demand was fed by the rapidly growing midwestern urban population while high transport costs limited the market penetration of East Coast manufacturers. Whereas processing industries employed less than a third of the urban industrial population of the Midwest, industries, such as furniture, clothing, machinery, printing, and publishing, which supplied local and regional markets, employed almost 60 percent of the Midwest's urban industrial population. The extension of the rail system into the Midwest, which eventually integrated the region into the national market, allowed these industries to expand and compete successfully with eastern manufacturers.[4]

In 1860 cotton textiles and lumber milling had ranked number one and number two nationally in terms of industrial value added. In 1880 and 1920 they still ranked number three and number four. Indeed, there was relatively little change in the makeup of the leading industries in America before 1900, except for the sudden emergence of the steel industry after the Civil War (Table 17.4). Between 1900 and 1920, however, three industries rose to

[4] Meyer (1983, 1989).

TABLE 17.4

The Ten Leading Industries in America in 1880, 1900, and 1920 (1914 $ millions of value added)

Rank	1880 Industry	Value Added	1900 Industry	Value Added	1920 Industry	Value Added
1	Machinery	111.0	Machinery	432.1	Machinery	575.6
2	Iron and steel	105.3	Iron and steel	339.2	Iron and steel	492.8
3	Cotton goods	97.2	Printing and publishing	313.5	Lumber (sawed)	393.4
4	Lumber (sawed)	87.1	Lumber (sawed)	299.9	Cotton goods	363.7
5	Boots and shoes	82.0	Clothing (men's)	262.1	Shipbuilding (steel)	348.8
6	Clothing (men's)	78.2	Liquor (Malt)	223.6	Automobile	347.3
7	Flour and grist milling	63.6	Cotton goods	196.0	General shop construction	327.7
8	Woolen goods	59.8	Masonry and brick	140.1	Printing and publishing	267.7
9	Printing and publishing	58.3	General shop construction	131.0	Electrical machinery	245.9
10	Liquor (Malt)	44.2	Meat-packing	124.6	Clothing (men's)	239.2

Source: Computed from the censuses of manufactures.

prominence. Shipbuilding, which in 1900 was not among the top twenty-five industries, ranked fifth in 1920 in terms of value added; electrical machinery, which had been a rather small industry in 1900, ranked ninth in 1920; and automobile production, which had been nonexistent in 1900, ranked sixth by 1920. By 1880 machinery and foundry products had become America's leading industry, supplying the machinery that maintained and advanced its industrial growth. It was still the leading industry in 1900 and 1920.

Between 1860 and 1880 value added (in constant dollar terms) in most of the larger industries doubled. It quadrupled between 1880 and 1900. During this period the fundamental nature of American business seems to have changed. Technological advances, such as James Bonsack's cigarette-making machine, reduction milling, fractional distillation, and the development of the disassembly system for processing animal carcasses, revolutionized production processes. The spread of electricity as a source of power and light removed physical constraints in plant layout, design, and location. Sharply falling transport costs associated with the extension of the rail system to almost every community, the adoption of a unified track gauge, and increased productivity and growing competition in the transportation industry brought about the integration of local and regional markets into a national market. The result was a profound change in the scale of plants, the organization and scope of the firm, and the structure of industry. In addition, new products, such as aniline dyes and other synthetic oil- and coal-based products and the polyphase electric motor, were developed, giving rise to whole new industries. Thereafter industry grew much more slowly between 1900 and 1920, although nominal dollar values soared in the inflation from World War I.

Consider, for example, the changes that took place in the meat-packing industry. Before the war Cincinnati was the meat-packing center of the United States, shipping pork products, especially salt pork, on steamboats down the Ohio and Mississippi rivers to southern and East Coast markets. The market for beef was small. Few farmers kept large numbers of cattle for food until the opening up of the Great Plains; retired dairy cows provided much of the beef consumed early on. Cattle were shipped live to local butchers and slaughterhouses close to the consumer, but this was expensive and inefficient. Live cattle took up more space than carcasses, and dressed meat made up less than 60 percent of the live weight of the steer.

Unrefrigerated fresh meat deteriorated rapidly, limiting the distance that it could be shipped to market. Although the development of the refrigerated rail car was crucial to the growth of the meat-packing industry in Chicago, business historian Alfred D. Chandler argues that it was not decisive to the rise of the high-volume year-round meat-packing industry. Rather, he credits Gustavus Swift's establishment of a complete distribution network for meat from the purchase of cattle on the farm and their delivery to his plant in

Chicago, through his slaughter and disassembly plants, and its speedy distribution to East Coast refrigerated storehouses for delivery to retailers with raising quality expectations while lowering price. However, it is certain that the refrigerated rail car, introduced in 1881, played a key role in assuring and maintaining the high quality of chilled dressed beef shipped from Chicago.

As volume increased, Swift increased throughput in his packing plant by increasing the division of labor in butchering and using moving "disassembly" lines to move the carcasses past men performing increasingly minute and specialized tasks on each carcass as it passed their stations. Other packers imitated Swift's methods and contributed innovations of their own. For example, Philip D. Armour was the pioneer firm in the utilization of by-products. Although only about 55 percent of the weight of a live steer represented dressed meat, another 30 percent or so of the steer's weight consisted of potentially usable and salable by-products, provided they were available in volume—that is, these products could not be used by small retail butchers/slaughterhouses, but they could be profitably recovered once capacity exceeded one hundred or so cattle per day. In 1884 Armour purchased a glue works to receive the bones and damaged hides that could not be sold to the leather tanneries. In addition, by the turn of the century the meat-packers were shipping hair to the upholstery and brush trade; bones for fertilizer, buttons, and knife handles; fats for soaps, candles, lubricants, and waterproofing preparations for leather, lard, and margarine, and various glands to the pharmaceutical industry, to name but a few of the less offensive by-products and their uses.

The Emergence of the Modern Business Enterprise

Although manufacturing industry grew more slowly after 1860 than before, Chandler argues that two forces—mass distribution and mass production—fundamentally altered industrial structure and redefined the nature of the firm in the post–Civil War period. The transformation took place first and most swiftly in the distribution system. Modern transportation—the railroad—and modern communications—the telegraph—assisted by the Great Lakes and ocean steamship and a revamped postal system, provided the means for coordinated buying and selling. In 1844, for example, Congress provided $30,000 for an experimental telegraph line between Washington and Baltimore. The test was a success, and by 1852 there were twenty-three thousand miles of telegraph and more than ten thousand miles of rail in operation. Not only was the telegraph essential for the safe and efficient operation of the nation's single-track rail system, but it also provided a real-time link between producers and consumers. These new transportation and communications systems generated almost instantaneous flows of information, increased the speed and regularity of the flow of goods, and reduced the number of transactions involved in the transfer of goods. The costs of distribution fell, and productivity rose. Indeed, Alexander Field has argued that the telegraph was absolutely essential to the success of the Chicago meat-packing industry, enabling firms to respond quickly to changing levels of demand in different markets. With this new technology, the meat-packers could even redirect refrigerated rail cars in transit as the market demanded, further reducing the two- to three-day time lag between news of an East Coast demand and delivery of new supplies.

According to Chandler, this revolution in distribution began in the marketing of wheat and cotton. The railroad not only assured cheaper and more rapid shipment to market but also facilitated the growth of terminal facilities, such as grain elevators and warehouses. Maintaining physically separated lots for each customer at these centralized storage facilities, however, became increasingly impractical. Consequently, warehouses and grain elevators began to adopt impersonal standards, weighing and grading commodities brought to them for storage and giving farmers storage receipts in exchange. Dissemination of knowledge about these standards also relieved buyers of the necessity of sampling from each lot, provided they had confidence in the integrity of the grader. These institutional changes and the advent of the telegraph stimulated the establishment of centralized markets. The Chicago Board of Trade, established in 1848, was the first commodity exchange in America. Others soon followed in cities around the nation. Eventually grading standards and weights were unified among them. These changes made practical the adoption of standardized futures contracts, specifying quantity, quality, price and delivery date and payable in cash. As a result, flour mills, for example, could contract for regular deliveries of wheat throughout the year instead of being inundated with wheat immediately after harvest.

The new means of transportation and communication also revolutionized the distribution of manufactured goods. Wholesalers became increasingly centralized, buying directly from the manufacturer and reselling to stores around the country through a network of traveling salesmen. Like the commodities dealer, wholesalers now took title to the product, reselling on their own behalf rather than accepting goods on consignment and selling on commission. They thus had a strong economic incentive to turn over the goods as quickly as possible and monitor the performance of their sales force in the field. By 1866 Chicago had fifty-nine wholesale jobbers with sales exceeding $1 million per year each, the most famous of whom was Marshall Field. Two years after he and his partner had joined with Potter Palmer in 1865, their sales reached $9.1 million, with retail sales of $1.5 million. By 1889 Field's sales were $31 million and retail sales had grown to $6 million.

Although wholesaling continued to grow, wholesalers in the nation's largest cities were increasingly challenged by large retailers, operating either as department stores or as chain stores, who contracted directly with the manufacturer for supplies. Many of them became household names—

Macy's, Bonwit Teller, Gimbel's, Wanamaker, Bergdorf Goodman, Neiman-Marcus, Marshall Field, the Great Atlantic and Pacific Tea Company (A&P), and Woolworth's—though many have recently fallen on hard times. As Chandler has put it, "mass marketers replaced merchants as distributors of goods in the American economy because they internalized a high volume of market transactions within a single large modern enterprise. They reduced the unit costs of distributing goods by making it possible for a single set of workers using a single set of facilities to handle a much greater number of transactions within a specific period . . . Economies of scale and distribution were not those of size but of speed."[5] Some economists have argued that it was the reduction in transactions costs resulting from centralization that explains the origins of the firm as an economic entity.[6]

The railroad and the telegraph provided the means for market coordination. For the first time, manufacturers were assured of a smooth and continual inflow of raw materials at the back door and outflow of finished goods through the front gate with almost instantaneous updates on demand conditions. Inventories were sharply reduced, and cash flow increased. These changes made possible unprecedented levels of production. New machinery and new processes had to be developed to take full advantage of the opportunity. Increased flow made possible the subdivision of tasks and the development of highly specialized single-purpose machines. Increased mechanization and increased emphasis upon speed of throughput led to increased energy consumption, especially when a process could be accelerated through increased temperature or pressure as in distilling, refining, furnaces, and foundries. As a result, energy consumption relative to GNP increased by almost two-thirds between 1890 and 1920 before declining as a result of improvements in thermal efficiency in power generation and the shift away from manufacturing to less power-intensive service industries (Figure 17.2, Panel A).

Wherever possible, production processes were made continuous, as in the manufacture of tobacco products, flour, canned goods, soap, animal and vegetable fats, the refining of oil, or the open-hearth process of steel manufacture. Where this was not possible, as in the Bessemer steel process, batch size was increased dramatically. As a result, the need for coordination and management increased. Manufacturing processes also became integrated. In the steel and iron industry, for example, the furnace was integrated with the foundry and the rolling mill to eliminate the need for continual reheating of the metal during its transformation from crude ore to finished product. This integration also demanded increased coordination of the flow of production within the factory and the establishment of testing procedures to monitor product quality. The result was mass production that incorporated economies of speed and economies of scale.

[5] Chandler (1977): 236.

[6] For example, Williamson (1985).

FIGURE 17.2

Some Measures of Intensified Energy Use

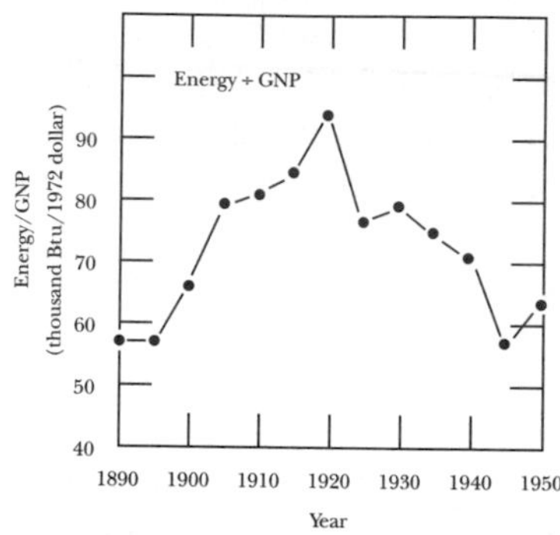

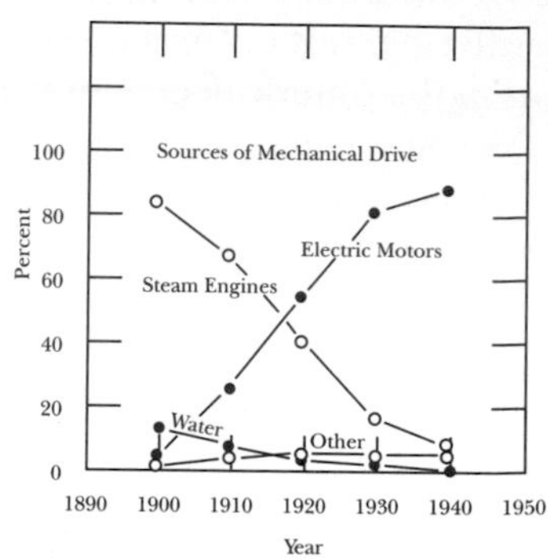

Source: Warren Devine, "From Shafts to Wires: Historical Perspectives in Electrification," *Journal of Economic History* 43 (1983): 349. Reprinted by permission of Cambridge University Press.

Consider, for example, the revolution that took place in flour milling. Other than the adoption of automated grain handling pioneered by Oliver Evans, flour mills in the mid-nineteenth century were little different from those of medieval times. Grain was still ground by a rotating stone, sifted to separate the flour from the bran, and packaged for sale. However, with the shift of wheat cultivation to the northern plains, this technology was no longer adequate. The hard kernels of spring wheat resisted grinding. Instead they scorched from the friction. As a result, millers in the northern plains were forced to adopt reduction milling, which substituted steel rollers for millstones, crushing rather than grinding the berry. This technology involved considerable investment in machinery, making seasonal shutdowns expensive, and was not easily adapted to small-scale operations. In 1880, for example, one of the Pillsbury mills in Minneapolis was using 1,475 hp from water turbines—as much power as that used by the largest integrated steel mills of the time—to mill almost $1.5 million worth of flour. By 1882 Minneapolis flour mills were producing three million bushels of flour annually. This same technology was eventually extended to the milling of other grains and led Henry P. Crowell to package and advertise his new product Quaker Oats as a breakfast cereal in order to keep his mill in continuous operation.

The integration of mass production with mass distribution allowed manufacturers to lower costs and increase productivity largely through the more effective management and coordination of production and distribution. The result was a new kind of firm—the modern business enterprise—characterized by many distinct operating units and managed by a hierarchy of salaried employees. In these firms the level of economic activity was such that administrative coordination within the firm was more efficient and profitable than coordination through the market. The visible hand of the manager had replaced the invisible hand of the market. These firms are those whose names are familiar to this day: Pillsbury, Singer, International Harvester, Armour, Swift, Standard Oil, Remington, American Tobacco, and Diamond Match, to name but a very few. Big business had arrived. It brought with it lower costs, quality control, and dependability. Unfortunately, it was often the brainchild of "robber barons" who sought to reap the profits from monopoly.

Late-Nineteenth-Century Technical Change

The modern business enterprises employed capital-intensive, energy-consuming, continuous, or large batch production methods. Their emergence and rise to dominance in the United States as well as in the rest of the world are consistent with the perception that technological change in America was faster than elsewhere and fundamentally different. As we have already seen, the labor scarcity hypothesis of H. J. Habakkuk and Edwin Rothbarth has stimulated considerable debate: Did America use "more machines"? Were American machines "better machines"? The evidence for the late nineteenth century certainly suggests that production processes in America were typically much more highly mechanized than those elsewhere: America used more machines. In part this might be explained by the sharp decline in the relative price of capital goods in the second half of the nineteenth century, which declined over 20 percent between 1860 and the 1890s. Some machines were clearly "better": American lathes—the foundation of the American machine tools industry—for example, were quickly adopted by the rest of the world. However, America continued to import technology from abroad. The Bessemer steel process was a British invention, while reduction flour milling originated in Hungary.

One distinguishing characteristic of American industrialization was the prominent role played by its natural resources. It is claimed that this characteristic has biased American manufacturing toward relatively capital-intensive production techniques and led, ultimately, to faster and more laborsaving technical change. These propositions have been tested directly by John James. His results indicate that for American manufacturing industry as a whole, labor and capital were inelastic substitutes for one another. That is, an increase in the price of labor encouraged manufacturers to substitute capital for labor, but the percentage increase in capital use was less than the percentage increase in the price of labor. However, the elasticity of substitution between capital and natural resources and between labor and natural resources was greater than unity. The results suggest that capital and natural resources were relative complements. As a result, abundant natural resources in America may have induced a higher capital-labor ratio in American manufacturing.

Others have also confirmed the existence of a pronounced laborsaving bias in American manufacturing. One study reveals evidence of a significant laborsaving bias in twelve of nineteen individual industries. This led in turn to capital-using, or resource-using, or both capital- and resource-using biased technological change. A capital-using bias was found in eleven industries while seven had a materials-using bias. Food processing, for example, had a laborsaving bias while the lumber industry had developed a laborsaving and materials-using technology. The fabricated metals industry was laborsaving and capital- and resource-using. This laborsaving technical change increased the relative marginal product of capital and led firms to adopt more capital-intensive production methods over time.[7]

Economies of Scale

These more capital-intensive production methods, in turn, increased firm size and the minimum efficient scale of operation. Although Chandler emphasizes the high-speed throughput of the modern business enterprise rather than scale per se, the adoption of continuous or large-scale batch production technologies generated a sharp increase in the size of America's manufacturing plants. There is abundant micro- and macroevidence documenting this change. Statistics on the average number of wage earners per establishment, for example, show a marked increase in plant-level employment in every industry, except printing and publishing, after 1869 (Table 17.5). In the petroleum industry the average establishment in 1869 employed fewer than thirteen wage earners while by 1919 establishments in the same industry averaged more than one hundred workers. Moreover, most of the growth in plant employment occurred in the period before 1890. Whereas employment grew more than threefold between 1869 and 1889, it little more than doubled between 1889 and 1919. Considering the general laborsaving bias in much of American industry, however, these statistics generally understate the increase in scale of output. The average men's clothing establishment produced more than four times as much output in 1920 as in 1860, while an iron and steel mill in 1920 produced more than twenty-five times the volume of output of the average iron furnace in 1860. The average boot and shoe factory produced in 1920 more than forty times the output of the average boot and shoe plant in 1860. In 1860 the average iron furnace produced less than $100,000 worth of iron a year (in 1914 dollars), while the average steelworks in 1920 averaged almost $2.5 million (1914 dollars), and meat-packing plants grew from a little under $110,000 to almost $1.4 million.

High-speed, continuous production processes were in large part re-

[7] Cain and Patterson (1981).

sponsible for this increase in the scale of production. Consider the case of cigarettes. In 1880 most tobacco was smoked in pipes or cigars, chewed, or snuffed. The market for cigarettes, a new product, was small. Four companies produced most of the nation's output, rolling the cigarettes by hand in much the same manner as cigars were produced. In 1884, however, James Buchanan Duke—a newcomer to the cigarette industry—installed two Bonsack cigarette machines. Each machine was capable of turning out 120,000 cigarettes per day, giving Duke the capacity to satisfy the entire American market. Shortly thereafter the government sharply reduced the tax on cigarettes, and prices fell, stimulating sales. Thanks to his Bonsack cigarette machines, Duke was able to meet the increased demand with high-quality, progressively cheaper cigarettes, signing an agreement with Bonsack in 1885 to use his machines exclusively in return for a lower leasing charge. To market his rapidly expanding output, Duke set up an elaborate sales and marketing organization, mounted a national advertising campaign, and contracted directly with tobacco farmers for bright leaf tobacco to assure an adequate supply at a certain price. By 1889 Duke was producing 834 million cigarettes per year.

Increased capital intensity in some industries led to sharp increases in the optimal size of firms. In distilling, flour milling, pig iron, and steel, for example, there were dramatic increases after 1870 in the optimal plant size, defined as the output necessary to achieve constant returns to scale. Before 1870 even relatively small flour mills—those producing more than a few thousand dollars' worth of output per year—experienced some diseconomies of scale and rising production costs (Figure 17.3). By 1880, though, the introduction of reduction flour milling and the availability of cheap transportation meant that only the largest firms, such as the Pillsbury mills in Minneapolis, were able to realize all the potential scale economies and produce at the minimum point on the average cost curve. Indeed, the changes in the optimum scale of establishment in some industries, including flour milling, were so large that by 1890 the optimal firm, the firm with the absolutely lowest possible unit costs—if it had existed—would have been a natural monopoly—that is, it would have supplied the entire market. Optimum scale grew somewhat more slowly for rolling mills, but even there John James estimates that four optimally sized plants might have supplied the whole market.

However, in other industries, such as chemicals and meat-packing, the optimal firm size remained small. In these industries, establishments did not have to be large to minimize average costs of production (that is, reach constant returns to scale), and thus the growing concentration in these industries was not driven by production technology. James therefore concludes that Chandler's paradigm is not appropriate for all industries.

James's analysis, however, focuses on just one aspect of Chandler's hypothesis—production—and ignores the role played by marketing and

TABLE 17.5

Average Number of Wage Earners per Establishment by Two-Digit SIC Industry, 1869–1919

Industry	1869	1879	1889	1899	1904	1909	1919
Food and kindred products (20)	5.86	8.70	8.99	8.12	8.53	7.79	10.03
				7.74	8.24	7.96	11.52
Tobacco[a] and tobacco products (21)	9.19	11.29	10.29	8.86	9.47	10.54	15.27
Textile mill products (22)	50.63	81.83	99.17	123.49	145.66	153.27	148.25
				65.35	73.28	71.76	49.68
Apparel and related products (23)	13.37	29.24	30.39	26.42	34.34	35.53	28.10
				30.23	37.71	39.14	30.49
Lumber and wood products (24)	6.31	6.94	18.00	17.43	20.38	16.94	18.50
				17.48	20.41	17.06	18.79
Furniture and fixtures (25)	8.90	11.28	36.77	46.26	43.16	39.97	42.83
				37.55	36.28	32.88	33.34
Paper and allied products (26)	24.83	33.04	41.23	52.17	62.67	66.59	86.23
				50.14	60.05	62.76	80.72
Printing and publishing (27)	17.41	17.34	14.08	11.94	12.64	11.94	11.08
				8.26	8.00	8.34	9.01
Chemicals and allied products (28)	10.12	13.70	14.34	16.72	16.14	15.19	19.98
				18.72	19.36	18.47	26.55
Petroleum and coal products (29)	12.25	43.37	46.26	59.97	65.55	68.66	107.22
				35.49	39.84	40.02	53.80
Rubber[b] and plastics products (30)				404.05	553.39	568.58	967.53
Leather and leather products (31)	5.60	8.71	20.09	32.04	39.12	40.17	46.09
				43.96	49.67	53.81	54.50

Stone, clay, and glass products (32)[a]	13.55	14.73	22.91	21.93	30.50	35.13	48.44
Primary metals products (33)	85.48	157.96	202.62	252.46	298.62	316.57	432.62
				216.38	236.17	247.23	322.31
Fabricated metals products (34)	9.01	11.14	15.06	34.40	37.30	34.67	39.95
				32.92	36.55	34.39	38.73
Machinery (35, 36)[c]	14.30	21.30	35.19	48.35	54.77	55.51	71.72
				53.64	61.96	67.65	112.16
Transportation equipment (37)	4.67	12.43	13.06	10.89	13.98	12.80	9.77
				35.97	52.98	62.14	151.50
Instruments and related products (38)	19.73	32.35	37.48	35.91	51.50	47.58	51.22
				29.12	40.81	41.04	45.17
Miscellaneous manufacturing,	13.66	16.55	18.08	22.32	28.73	27.67	27.75
including ordnance (39)				20.12	24.98	24.27	24.63

[a] No additional industries were included in the 286-industry group.

[b] No industries were included in the 171-industry group.

[c] The "nonelectrical machinery" and "electrical machinery" industries were combined.

Note: The numbers in the first line for each industry were calculated from the 171 industries for which comparable data were available in each census from 1869 to 1919. The numbers in the second line were calculated from the 286 industries for which comparable data were available in each census from 1899 to 1919.

Source: Anthony P. O'Brien, "Factory Size, Economies of Scale and the Great Merger Wave of 1898–1902," *Journal of Economic History* 48 (1988): 648. Reprinted by permission of Cambridge University Press.

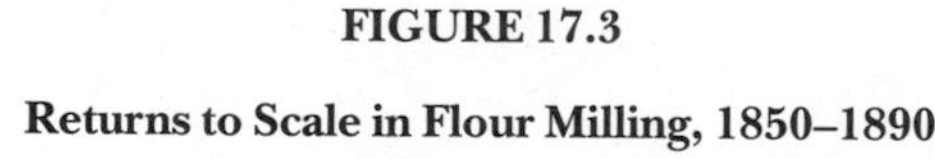

FIGURE 17.3

Returns to Scale in Flour Milling, 1850–1890

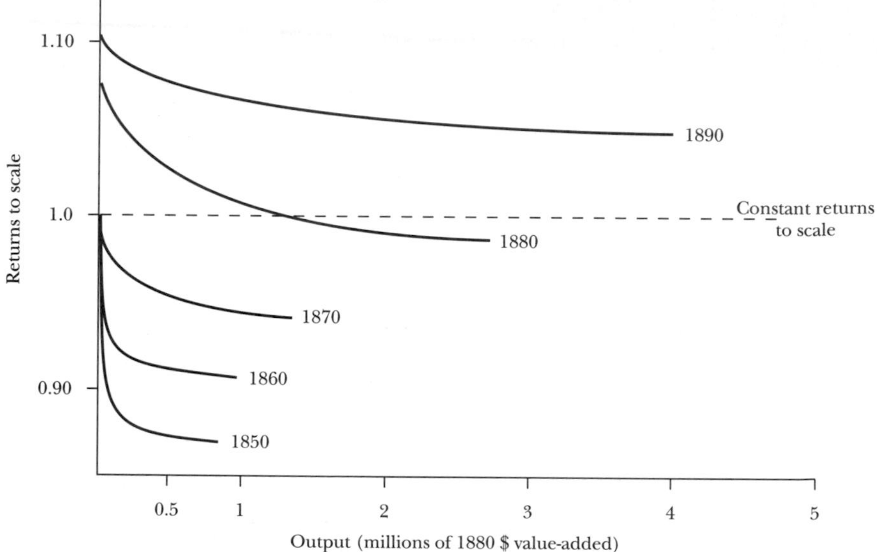

Source: John A. James, "Structural Change in American Manufacturing," *Journal of Economic History* 43 (1983): 445. Reprinted by permission of Cambridge University Press.

distribution in determining optimal plant and firm size. If larger establishments were able to realize sufficiently large-scale economies in these areas, they may have more than offset any diseconomies associated with large-scale production. Consequently, rather than estimate just how large a plant should have been if it were to realize constant returns to scale in production, Atack has extended James's analysis by examining changes in the actual distribution of plant sizes by industry over time to try to identify the scale of plants that survived the test of time. If one assumes survival of the economically fittest, and given the fundamental changes in production and distribution, one might also assume that the plants that survived to the end of the century should have been different from those that had prospered at mid-century. Not so. Surprisingly few industries exhibited a radically different industrial structure in 1900 from that which would have been expected from the long-run adjustment to conditions as they existed before 1870. The typical plant at the turn of the century was no larger than an efficient plant would have been in 1870. However, in those industries identified by Chandler as adopting mass production and mass distribution—iron and steel, distilling, malt liquors, flour milling, and tobacco—the average scale of operation in 1900 was much larger than an efficient plant in 1870 would have been (Table 17.6). For example, in 1870 meat-packing plants produc-

TABLE 17.6

The Number of Optimally Sized Plants from 1870 that Industry Output Could Have Supported in 1870 and 1900

Industry SIC	Industry	1870: Number of Potential 1870 Optimal Plants[a]	1870: Actual Number of Establishments[a]	1900: Number of Potential 1870 Optional Plants	1900: Actual Number of Establishments
2011	Meat-packing	106–212	206	3,041–6,082	1,134
2041	Flour milling	6,689–424,124	22,573	19,975–1,597,908	25,258
2057	Bread and other bakery products	633–20,270	3,550	10,209–326,503	14,917
2082	Malt liquors	63–254	1,972	833–3,335	1,509
2085	Distilled, rectified, and blended liquors	38–151	719	367–1,467	967
2100	Tobacco manufacture	1,599–12,795	5,204	20,117–160,935	14,976
2211	Cotton textiles	41–324	819	359–2,837	1,055
2231	Woolen goods	151–1,206	1,938	416–3,327	1,035
2321	Men's, youth's, boys' clothing	160–2,564	7,838	1,897–30,352	5,880
2351	Millinery	16–33	1,668	584–1,168	16,151
2421	Sawmills and planing mills	4,847–155,099	26,930	21,982–703,440	33,035
2431	Millwork	192–6,143	1,605	1,511–48,337	4,204
2511	Wood household furniture	202–809	5,423	1,669–6,678	7,972
2700	Printing, publishing, and allied industries	499–15,980	2,159	3,906–124,997	22,312
3111	Leather tanning and finishing	144–2,310	4,237	797–12,760	1,306
3131	Boots and shoes	275–4,403	23,428	737–11,798	1,600
3199	Saddlery and harness	208–26,627	7,607	960–122,829	12,934

3251	Brick and structural tile	1,743–13,945	3,114	7,081–56,649	5,423
3312	Pig iron	129–516	396	1,673–6,689	668
3321	Gray iron foundaries	217–6,954	2,328	4,260–136,317	9,324
3444	Sheet metal work	503–8,048	6,646	2,377–38,025	12,466
3511	Steam engines	313–5,009	2,400	NA	NA
3522	Farm machinery and equipment	46–713	2,076	170–2,721	715
3799	Wagons and carriages	254–1,016	11,847	487–1,947	7,632

[a] Number of potential 1870 optimal plants = (value-added [1860 dollars] at time *t*)/MES(1870) or max(survivor 1870).

[b] From U.S. Census Office (1873).

[c] From U.S. Census Office (1902).

Source: Jeremy Atack, "Industrial Structure and the Emergence of the Modern Industrial Corporation," *Explorations in Economic History* 22 (1985): 44–45.

ing between $32,000 and $64,000 of value added a year were operating under constant returns to scale. At the time the industry was producing almost $7 million in value added (in 1860 dollars). The industry therefore could have supported as many as 212 optimally sized plants, each producing about $32,000 in value added, or there could have been 106 plants, each producing $64,000 in value added in 1870. The industry actually supported 206 plants. By 1900 the industry was producing more than $190 million in value added. If the optimal size of firm had still been between $32,000 and $64,000 value added, there should have been between 3,000 and 6,000 plants. Instead there were only 1,134 plants, and the average firm produced almost three times as much value added as the largest optimally sized firm in 1870 would have produced. This suggests that there was some fundamental change in the structure of the industries arising from the changes in technology and distribution. Moreover, in three industries—meat, tobacco, and iron and steel blast furnaces—there were fewer plants operating in 1900 than predicted by the survival analysis. Each of these industries participated actively in the trust movement.

The Trust Movement and Merger Activity

The rapid growth in optimal plant sizes in those industries experiencing rapid technological change and the growth of firms reaping the benefits of mass distribution generated growing pressures for the consideration of industry capacity. The discipline of the market posed a serious threat to the growing investment in increasingly specific capital goods and human capital. As a result, firms sought to maintain or increase profits and reduce risk by controlling price or output—that is, through monopolization. Increasingly competition was viewed as "ruinous" or "cutthroat." In the post–Civil War era various industries established trade associations to foster closer cooperation. The various agreements, whether informal or formal, were difficult or impossible to enforce, and businesses sought a better way. An early solution was the "trust" (hence the concept of antitrust). Under this device, the stock of the various former competitors would be held by a trustee who would make decisions for the collective good of the trust. The device was pioneered by the Standard Oil Company although by the time the Standard Oil Trust was established in 1882, Standard Oil was already essentially a monopolist controlling 90 percent or more of the nation's oil-refining capacity.

Standard Oil's swift rise to market dominance was accomplished not so much through the exploitation of economies of scale as through the exploitation of marketing and distribution advantages. When the Standard Oil Company of Ohio was chartered in 1870, it was already the largest refiner in the country with about 10 percent of industry capacity. Part of its success can be attributed to its efficient use of distillation by-products. However, its costs of production were little different from those of its competitors (of which there were some 250), and its principal products—illuminating oil and kerosene—were indistinguishable from those of other refineries. Moreover, the refining industry was under considerable financial pressure as a result of excess capacity. Industry capacity was about twelve million barrels per year, but production was well under six million barrels per year in 1871 and 1872.

In 1871 the Pennsylvania legislature chartered a company with the uninformative name of the South Improvement Company. This business was authorized "to construct and operate any work, or works, public or private, designed to include, increase, facilitate, or develop trade, travel, or the transportation of freight, livestock, passengers and any traffic by land or water, from or to any part of the United States." It became the vehicle for Standard Oil's rise. The South Improvement Company, owned by John D. Rockefeller and a number of other oil refiners, entered into an agreement with the major railroads—the Pennsylvania, the New York Central, and the Erie—to divide oil shipments among them. Forty-five percent would go to the Pennsylvania, with the balance evenly split between the other two, in return for specific rebates off the published railroad rates. For example, the published rate on crude oil shipped to Cleveland was 80 cents per forty-five-gallon barrel, but the rate to members of the South Improvement Company was only 40 cents. On oil shipped to Boston, the published rate was $2.71 per barrel, but South Improvement Company members paid only $1.65. Similarly, while the published rate on refined oil from Cleveland, the center of Standard Oil's operations, to New York City was $2.00 a barrel, Standard Oil paid only $1.50, which was less than other refineries outside the pool paid, regardless of where they were. As a result, Standard Oil was able to undercut its competitors' prices by a cent or so a gallon which, considering the homogeneous nature of the product, was sufficient to induce customers to switch to Standard Oil's products. In addition, the South Improvement Company received kickbacks from the railroads on all petroleum shipped by nonmembers plus daily intelligence on the volume, origin, and destination of all competitors' shipments. As a result, Standard Oil was often able to buy out competitors for less than their assets were really worth and consolidate industry capacity.

Two changes prompted the creation of the Standard Oil Trust. First, the discovery of oil in Russia threatened American domination of the European market and required coordinated action to deal with the threat. Second, the success of oil pipelines undermined the South Improvement Company's deal with the railroads. Pipelines could carry oil much more cheaply than the railroads, and the Standard Oil group moved swiftly to maintain its cost advantage by setting up the National Transit Company to build and operate its pipeline system. However, efficiency demanded that some of the refineries belonging to the forty businesses in the Standard group be closed. Some centralized authority had to make the tough decisions. On January 2, 1882, shareholders of the forty companies in the Standard Oil group exchanged their stock for certificates in the new Standard Oil Trust. The trust instrument created an office of nine trustees to "exercise general supervision over the affairs of the several Standard Oil Companies." Between 1882 and 1885 the trustees reduced the number of refineries that the trust operated from fifty-three to just twenty-two, cutting the cost of refined oil from 1.5 cents per gallon to just 0.5 cent per gallon in the process.

Other trusts followed. In 1884 the American Cotton Oil Trust was established, comprising some seventy mills, mostly in the South, that manufactured and refined cottonseed oil. In 1885 the National Linseed Oil trust was formed, followed by trusts in whiskey production, sugar refining, lead, and rope and cordage. Various states mounted vigorous legal action against these trusts; some state legislatures passed laws forbidding combinations and trusts. Louisiana instituted proceedings against the Cotton Oil trust, Nebraska and Illinois attacked the Whiskey Trust, New York took on the Sugar Trust, and Ohio began proceedings against the Oil Trust. In 1889 Kansas, Maine, Michigan, North Carolina, Tennessee, and Texas all passed laws outlawing such trustee arrangements. The days of the formal trust were numbered. In May 1890 the Ohio attorney general filed suit against the Standard Oil Company of Ohio, alleging violation of state laws by placing its affairs in the hands of trustees, almost all of whom were nonresidents. In March 1892 the Ohio Supreme Court rendered its decision, affirming that "the law requires that a corporation should be controlled and managed by its directors in the interests of its own stockholders, and conformable to the purpose for which it was created by the laws of its state" and declaring that all such trustee arrangements were contrary to the laws of the state.

However, another legal device—the holding company—had already taken the place of the trust as the coordinator of consolidated enterprises. While the formal "trust" died, its spirit, the desire to control output or prices and secure the benefits of a monopoly, lived on through the New Jersey or Delaware holding company. On March 21, 1892, the holders of the Standard Oil Trust certificates met and adopted a resolution dissolving the trust and transferring the stock of sixty-four trust members to one of the remaining twenty companies. In 1889, after further litigation from Ohio for failure to comply with the court's ruling, Standard Oil was reorganized as a holding company under the laws of New Jersey. The capital of the Standard Oil Company of New Jersey was increased from $10 million to $110 million.

The idea of providing industrial corporations with a legal residence in return for incorporation fees and franchise taxes originated in New Jersey, which had long relied upon railroad taxes to fund the state. During the 1850s these taxes had made up almost all the state fund receipts and had permitted New Jersey to eliminate its state property tax. After the Civil War, however, state and local property taxes had to be reinstituted to meet the state's revenue shortfall, and the state began to look to alternative sources of income. The solution was proposed by James Brooks Dill, a corporation lawyer practicing in New York but living in New Jersey. He recognized that New Jersey's law did not require that the state attract the economic assets of corporations; simply providing them with a legal residence could generate substantial revenues under the existing tax laws. All that was needed was to regularize the process of incorporation and liberalize the corporate charter laws. To this end, he enlisted the support of the governor and the secretary of state, both of whom became directors of the Corporation Trust Company that Dix created to act as agent for companies seeking New Jersey charters.

In May 1889 New Jersey amended its corporation law to provide that the directors of any company chartered under its act of 1875 could purchase the stock of any company or companies and issue its own stock in payment thereof. In 1893 the law was further amended so that any corporation could buy and hold securities in any other corporation no matter where it might be chartered and, as owner, exercise all rights of ownership. This strategy took advantage of the federal political structure to impose a legal externality on the rest of the nation. New Jersey was open for business and businesses beat a path to its door.[8] Its first customer was the American Cotton Oil Trust, which reorganized itself in New Jersey as the American Cotton Oil Company in October 1889. Other companies quickly followed (Figure 17.4, Panel A). The American Tobacco Company, for example, was incorporated in early 1890 with a capital of $25 million and control of approximately 95 percent of the nation's cigarette production.

New Jersey's success as a corporate haven attracted competitors. Maine, Maryland, New York, and West Virginia all entered the contest, but Delaware won, adopting the New Jersey law essentially verbatim in 1899 except for a lower tax rate. In part Delaware's success reflects the smallness of the state and the importance of the franchise fees for it, which assured corporations that its government would always be receptive to their entreaties (Figure 17.4, Panel B). The state was hostage to the corporations in the exchange.[9]

The process of industrial consolidation begun by the trusts and continued by the holding company accelerated dramatically in the late 1890s. In 1895 there were 4 mergers. In 1897 there were 6. In 1898 the number jumped to 16 and then to 63 in 1899, before gradually tapering off with 19 in 1901 and 5 in 1903. These numbers, however, do not do justice to the magnitude of the change or its impact upon the nation's industrial structure. Some 1,800 firms disappeared in these consolidations, and of the 93 consolidations traced by Naomi Lamoreaux, 72 resulted in control of at least 40 percent of their respective industry outputs and 42 controlled at least 70 percent of their market (Table 17.7). The 1900 census reported that 185 industrial combinations, making up less than one-half of 1 percent of the man-

[8] Grandy (1989).
[9] Williamson (1993).

FIGURE 17.4

The Late-Nineteenth and Early-Twentieth Century Surge in Business Incorporation

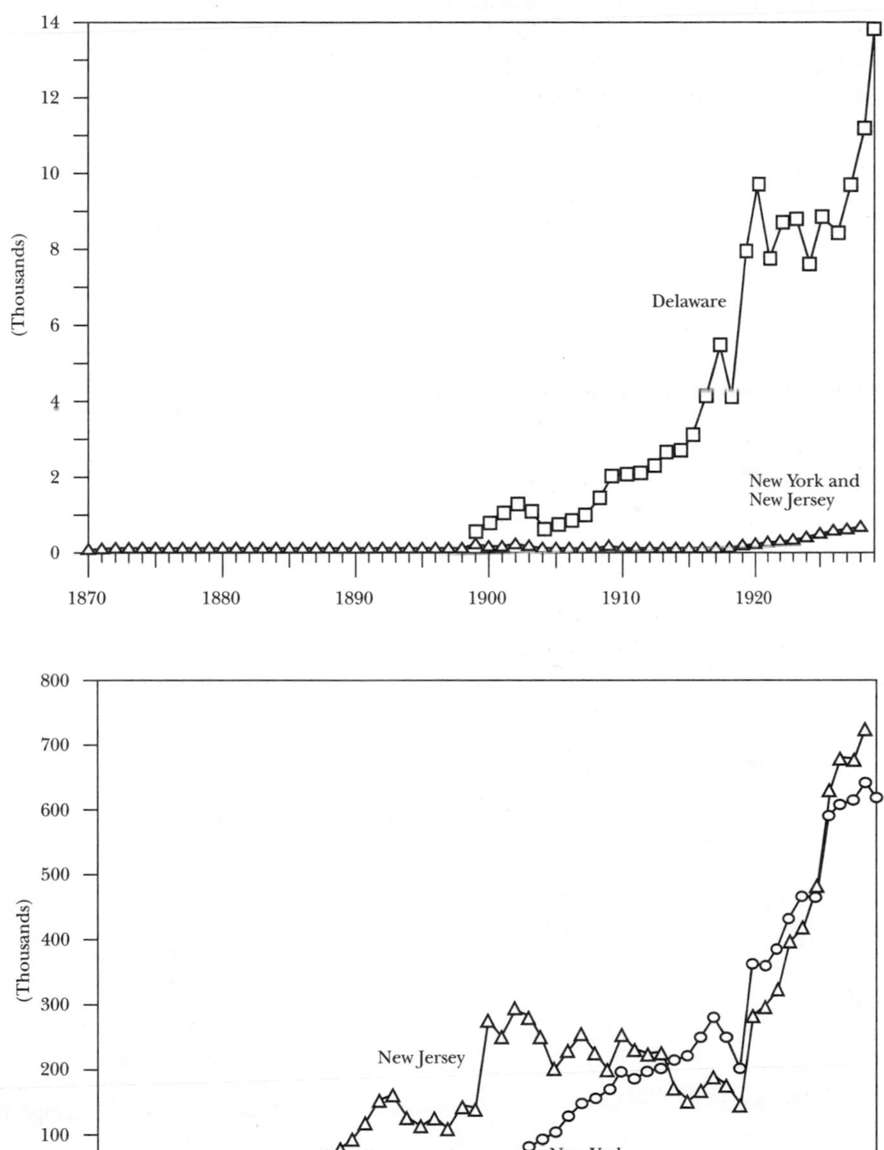

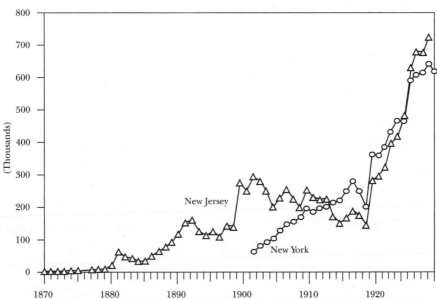

Sources: Total incorporations are from George Heberton Evans, *Business Incorporations in the United States 1800–1943* (New York: Columbia University Press for National Bureau for Economic Research, 1948), resident manufacturing firms are from U.S. Census, various years. Christopher Grandy, "New Jersey Corporate Chartermongering," *Journal of Economic History* 49 (1989): 688. Reprinted by permission of Cambridge University Press.

TABLE 17.7

Market Shares of Consolidations, 1895–1904

Consolidations with < 40%	Consolidations with ≥ 40% but < 70%	Consolidations with ≥ 70%
Amalgamated Copper	American Bicycle	American Brake Shoe & Foundry
American Cigar	American Brass	American Can
Cleveland & Sandusky Brewing Co.	American Car & Foundry	American Chicle
Dayton Breweries	American Felt	American Fork & Hoe
Empire Steel & Iron	American Fisheries	American Hide & Leather
Independent Glass	American Linseed	American Ice
Maryland Brewing	American Malting	American Locomotive
Massachusetts Breweries	American Sewer Pipe	American School Furniture
New Orleans Brewing	American Shipbuilding	American Seeding Machine
New York & Kentucky	American Smelting & Refining	American Snuff
Pacific Coast Biscuit	American Stove	American Stogie
Pennsylvania Central Brewing	American Thread	American Window Glass
Pittsburgh Brewing	American Woolen	American Writing Paper
Providence Ice	California Fruit Canners Assoc.	Casein Co. of America
Pure Oil	General Chemical	Central Foundry
Republic Iron & Steel	International Salt	Chicago Pneumatic Tool
Standard Shoe Machinery	International Silver	Continental Tobacco
Susquehanna Iron & Steel	National Biscuit	Corn Products
United Breweries	National Candy	Crucible Steel
U.S. Flour Milling	National Enameling & Stamping	Distilling Co. of America
Virginia Iron, Coal & Coke	National Fireproofing	Du Pont
	National Glass	Eastman Kodak
	New England Cotton Yarn	General Aristo
	Royal Baking Powder	Harbison-Walker Refractories
	Rubber Goods Mfg. Co.	International Harvester
	Standard Table Oil Cloth	International Paper
	United States Cotton Duck	International Steam Pump
	United States Shipbuilding	Mississippi Wire Glass
	United States Steel	National Asphalt
	Virginia-Carolina Chemical	National Carbon
		National Novelty
		Otis Elevator
		Pittsburgh Plate Glass
		Railway Steel Spring
		Standard Sanity Mfg.
		Union Bag & Paper
		United Box Board & Paper
		United Shoe Machinery
		United States Bobbin & Shuttle
		United States Cast Iron Pipe & Foundry
		United States Envelope
		United States Gypsum

Source: Naomi R. Lamoreaux, *The Great Merger Movement in American Business, 1895–1904* (New York: Cambridge University Press, 1986): 3–4. Reprinted by permission of Cambridge University Press.

ufacturing establishments in the country, owned 15 percent of the industrial capital, employed 8 percent of the industrial labor force, and produced 14 percent of industrial output of the United States. In 1904 it was estimated that 318 mergers had involved 5,300 plants across America and an investment well in excess of $7 billion.

To some, these combinations were a source of considerable concern.[10] Not only did these mergers represent a quantum shift in the extent of economic concentration and raise the specter of monopoly, but more important, they were viewed as permanently altering the industrial structure. The combinations were seen as essential for the realization of scale economies, and the rise of big business is dated from them. The mechanization of the production of chewing and pipe tobacco and snuff, for example, generated significant cost savings and stimulated the centralization of production in just a few large plants. By 1910 the *minimum* optimum scale snuff-making plant produced about 9.5 percent of total snuff production while the largest plant had a capacity of ten million pounds a year, or 32 percent of industry production.[11]

However, the evidence suggests that unexploited economies of scale were not generally that important a motivation for mergers and acquisitions.[12] Instead Lamoreaux argues that the consolidations were driven by a desire to suppress price competition in the wake of the Depression of the 1890s and the Panic of 1893. Capital-intensive mass-production firms had high fixed costs and so were particularly susceptible to pressure to cut prices to gain market share in the face of falling demand. Other events, such as the development of the New York Stock Exchange and the adoption of general incorporation laws, further facilitated the merger movement. Lamoreaux concludes that in the short run these consolidations were successful: Price competition was restricted, and the industry followed the pricing lead of the dominant firm. Indeed, the evidence of alleged predatory pricing by Standard Oil—defined as the setting of a price that is too low to maximize profits unless industrial structure changes—is also consistent with Standard Oil's behaving as the dominant firm in the industry—which it was.[13]

In the longer run, Lamoreaux argues, many of the combinations increased costs and prevented the firms from continuing to dominate the market unless they were successful in preventing entry. For example, the American Sugar Refining Company controlled 98 percent of the country's cane sugar-refining capacity in 1892, but by 1900 it controlled barely two-thirds of sugar production. By 1910 its share had fallen to just 42 percent, thanks in part to the development of a western beet sugar industry. Similarly

[10] See, for example, Moody (1904).
[11] Burns (1983).
[12] See Chandler (1977); James (1983); Atack (1985, 1987).
[13] Mariger (1978).

in 1902 International Harvester produced more than 90 percent of the nation's grain binders, more than 80 percent of the mowers, and about two-thirds of the rakes, but by 1918 its share of the binder market had slipped to 65 percent, and that of the mower market to barely 60 percent.

The Emergence of Antitrust

Although Congress passed, and the president signed, the Sherman Antitrust Act in 1890 outlawing "every contract, combination in the form of trust or otherwise, or conspiracy in restraint of trade or commerce among the several States, or with foreign nations" and declared that "every person who shall monopolize, or attempt to monopolize . . . any part of the trade or commerce" was guilty of a misdemeanor, nothing much changed immediately. True, the trust device was quickly abandoned in favor of the holding company, but that perhaps owed as much, if not more, to growing legal complications with the various states as to the entry of the Federal government into this regulatory marketplace. Certainly the law did little to hinder the dramatic wave of consolidations that took place around the turn of the century despite the degree of economic concentration many of them entailed. And it did absolutely nothing about the Chicago meat-packers whose activities motivated passage.[14]

Part of the problem was that the law was vague. "Trust" and "monopoly" were nowhere defined. Nor were the courts particularly sympathetic to the government. The first case to come before the Supreme Court under the Sherman Antitrust Act in 1895, *United States* v. *E. C. Knight Company*, was a loss for the government. The case involved the American Sugar Refining Company's acquisition of four Pennsylvania refineries that gave it control of 98 percent of the nation's sugar-refining capacity. The government charged that the acquisition of E. C. Knight and the other three companies constituted a combination in restraint of trade and sought divestment. However, the Court ruled that Congress had the authority to regulate only interstate commerce and that commerce succeeded manufacture but was not a part of it even though "the power to control the manufacture of a given thing involves in a certain sense the control of its disposition, but . . . affects it only incidentally and indirectly." As a result, the merger wave of the late 1890s went ahead unimpeded by any judicial restraint.

However, judicial sentiment began to change. In 1899 the Supreme Court declared the cast-iron pipe pool illegal in the case of *Addyston Pipe and Steel Company* v. *United States*. In 1904 the Court, in a narrow decision, ordered the Northern Securities Company—the holding company for the Northern Pacific Railway and the Great Northern Railway—dissolved as combination

[14] Libecap (1992).

in restraint of trade. And most significant of all, in 1909, the U.S. circuit court in a unanimous decision held that the Standard Oil Company was a combination in restraint of trade in violation of Section One of the Sherman Antitrust Act and a monopoly in violation of Section Two of the act. This decision was affirmed by the Supreme Court in 1911, and Standard Oil was ordered dissolved into separate, smaller companies, including Standard Oil of New Jersey, Standard Oil of Indiana, Standard Oil of Ohio, Standard Oil of California, and Atlantic Refining. Last, but not least, the meat-packers eventually succumbed in 1919 to a Federal Trade Commission investigation and signed a consent decree in 1920 agreeing to divest themselves of interests in stockyards, market journals, retail meat sales, and a wide variety of foods other than meats.[15]

In the late nineteenth century America was transformed from a predominantly rural-agrarian economy into an urban-industrial powerhouse. The structure of the firm in many industries was sometimes radically altered by the new technologies of mass production and mass distribution. Production became increasingly concentrated both industrially and geographically. By 1900 the United States was the dominant industrial power. American firms spanned the globe, and American technology and management techniques increasingly became the standard around the world. This transformation brought with it a host of new problems, such as concentrations of poverty and crime, unemployment, labor unrest and agrarian protest, and pollution. Accompanying the new problems were new challenges, such as funding these new giant enterprises, regulating their market power, and providing the means of urban transportation and recreation for their workers. Many of these problems remain unsolved, and the challenges unmet.

Appendix: Transportation and the Economics of Spatial Competition

The existence of positive transport costs can explain the persistence and growth of small, relatively inefficient producers in many industries during the late nineteenth century. Consider Figure A.1. Large firms locate in the large urban areas because of supply and demand factors—their need for labor and capital and an adequate market in the immediate vicinity to justify their scale—for example, at A. Unit production costs are relatively low, $OP = AB$. Sales to customers located away from the factory incur transport costs of \$t per mile. Thus the price of this product to a consumer located m miles from the factory is given by the equation

$$OP + mt = \text{Price}$$

[15] Aduddell and Cain (1981).

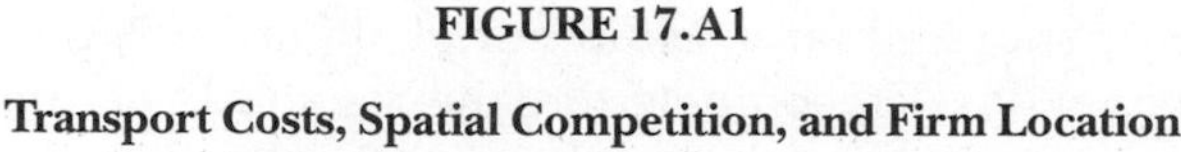

FIGURE 17.A1

Transport Costs, Spatial Competition, and Firm Location

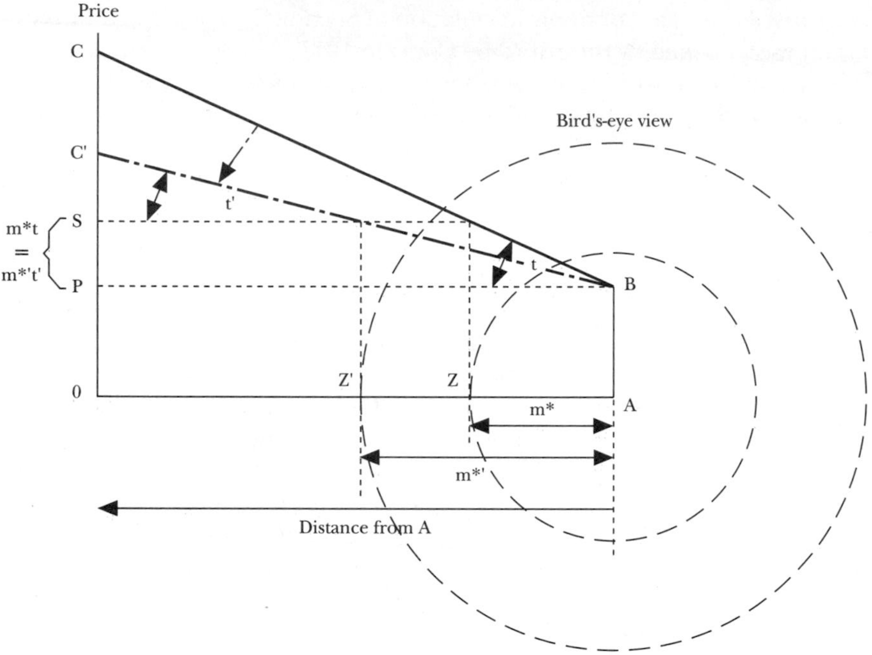

and is represented by the line BC, which has slope, t. Suppose now that small firms have unit production costs equal to \$OS. In this case, small firms can locate no closer to the large producer than

$$OS = OP + m^*t$$

where m* miles is the critical distance that prevents the high-cost producer from being undersold by the larger low-cost producer. The market thus consists of an area within the circle center A and radius m* around the city (see bird's-eye view to Figure A.1), which is the market domain of the large firm and the area beyond in which small high-cost producers operate. Within this area the large firm is a monopolist and all consumers located between A and Z buy from that firm. To the extent that market density decreases as distance from the city increases we expect small firms to cluster around the periphery m* miles from the city and their density to decrease at greater distances. Large low-cost producers thus coexist with small high-cost producers, but they sell in different markets.

Over time, declining transport costs per mile shift from BC to BC′, widening the area over which the large firm is able to sell its product and driving out of business all those small producers located between Z and Z′ and falling between the perimeters of the circles of radius m* and m*′. Natural increase and immigration lead to increasing population density so that the sales of the large firm increase even faster than the area of its market. As a result, the large firms tend to grow rapidly. At the same time, however, increasing population density also maintains the market for small high-cost producers along and beyond the market boundary m*′. Indeed, we would expect the number of small producers to increase because the market boundary, $2\,\Pi m^{*\prime} > 2\,\Pi m^{*}$, has grown.

Bibliography

Aduddell, Robert M., and Louis P. Cain. "Public Policy towards "The Greatest Trust in the World." *Business History Review* 55 (1981): 217–42.

———. "The Consent Decree in the Meatpacking Industry, 1920–1956." *Business History Review* 55 (1981): 359–78.

Atack, Jeremy. "Industrial Structure and the Emergence of the Modern Industrial Corporation." *Explorations in Economic History* 22 (1985): 29–52.

———. "Industrial Structure and the Size Distribution of Firms in American Industry in the Nineteenth Century." *Journal of Economic History* 46 (1986): 463–76.

———. "Economies of Scale and Efficiency Gains in the Rise of the Factory in America, 1820–1900." In *Quantity and Quiddity: Essays in U.S. Economic History,* ed. Peter Kilby. Middletown, Conn.: Wesleyan University Press, 1987: 286–335.

Bateman, Fred, and Thomas Weiss. "Comparative Regional Development in Antebellum Manufacturing." *Journal of Economic History* 35 (1975): 182–208.

———. *A Deplorable Scarcity: The Failure of Industrialization in the Slave Economy.* Chapel Hill: University of North Carolina Press, 1981.

Burns, Malcolm R. "Economies of Scale in Tobacco Manufacture, 1897–1910." *Journal of Economic History* 43 (1983): 461–74.

Cain, Louis P., and Donald G. Paterson. "Factor Biases and Technical Change in Manufacturing: The American System, 1850–1919." *Journal of Economic History* 41 (1981): 341–60.

Chandler, Alfred D. *The Visible Hand: The Managerial Revolution in American Business.* Cambridge: The Belknap Press of Harvard University Press, 1977.

———. *Scale and Scope: The Dynamics of Industrial Capitalism.* Cambridge: Harvard University Press, 1990.

———. "Organizational Capabilities and the Economic History of the Industrial Enterprise." *Journal of Economic Perspectives* 6 (1992): 79–100.

Devine, Warren. "From Shafts to Wires: Historical Perspective on Electrification." *Journal of Economic History* 43 (1983): 347–72.

Field, Alexander J. "The Magnetic Telegraph, Price and Quantity Data, and the New Management of Capital." *Journal of Economic History* 52 (1992): 401–13.

Grandy, Christopher. "New Jersey Corporate Chartermongering, 1875–1929." *Journal of Economic History* 49 (1989): 677–92.

Habakkuk, H. J. *American and British Technology in the Nineteenth Century.* New York: Cambridge University Press, 1962.

James, John A. "Some Evidence on Relative Labor Scarcity in 19th Century American Manufacturing." *Explorations in Economic History* 18 (1981): 376–88.

———. "Structural Change in American Manufacturing, 1850–1890." *Journal of Economic History* 43 (1983): 433–60.

Jones, Eliot. *The Trust Problem in the United States.* New York: Macmillan, 1924.

Lamoreaux, Naomi R. *The Great Merger Movement in American Business, 1895–1904.* New York: Cambridge University Press, 1986.

Libecap, Gary D. "The Rise of the Chicago Packers and the Origins of Meat Inspection and Anti-Trust." *Economic Inquiry* 30 (1992): 242–62.

Mariger, Randall. "Predatory Price Cutting: The Standard Oil of New Jersey Case Revisited." *Explorations in Economic History* 15 (1978): 341–67.

Meyer, David R. "Emergence of the American Manufacturing Belt: An Interpretation." *Journal of Historical Geography* 9 (1983): 145–74.

———. "Midwestern Industrialization and the American Manufacturing Belt in the Nineteenth Century." *Journal of Economic History* 49 (1989): 921–38.

Moody, John. *The Truth about Trusts: A Description and Analysis of the American Trust Movement.* New York: Moody Publishing Co., 1904.

O'Brien, Anthony P. "Factory Size, Economies of Scale, and the Great Merger Wave of 1898–1902." *Journal of Economic History* 48 (1988): 639–50.

Rosenberg, Nathan. "American Technology: Imported or Indigenous." *American Economic Review* 67 (1977): 21–26.

Rothbarth, Edwin. "Causes of the Superior Efficiency of U.S.A. Industry as Compared to British Industry." *Economic Journal* 56 (1946): 383–90.

Sokoloff, Kenneth L. "Was the Transition from the Artisanal Shop to the Nonmechanized Factory Associated with Gains in Efficiency? Evidence from the U.S. Manufactures Censuses of 1820 and 1850." *Explorations in Economic History* 21 (1984): 351–82.

Williamson, Harold F., and Arnold R. Daum. *The American Petroleum Industry: The Age of Illumination, 1859–1899.* Evanston, Ill.: Northwestern University Press, 1959.

Williamson, Oliver E. "Credible Commitments: Using Hostages to Support Exchange. *American Economic Review* 73 (1983): 519–40.

———. *The Economic Institutions of Capitalism: Firms, Markets and Relational Contracting.* New York: Free Press, 1985.

Structural change in america's financial markets

18

There were more than sixteen hundred state-chartered banks operating in the United States on the eve of the Civil War.[1] The majority of these banks were small, serving predominantly local clienteles, and their activities were regulated by the laws of the state that had chartered them. Each chartered bank was authorized to receive deposits and issue bank notes—of which there were some nine thousand different designs in circulation. These notes were legally convertible into lawful money—gold or silver—upon demand at the bank of issue, but they often circulated far from the bank of issue. Consequently, their conversion to lawful money was troublesome, time-consuming, expensive, and potentially risky. As a result, most notes were accepted only at a discount from their face value except in the immediate local area around the bank of issue. Moreover, there were thousands of spurious notes in circulation, fifty-four hundred by one count: counterfeits and notes with forged signatures or altered denominations, as well as issues from insolvent banks, from banks no longer in existence, and even some from banks that had never existed.

This chaotic money and banking system in America increased the costs of doing business. Trade and the smooth flow of funds were impeded despite the development of an information industry of "bank note reporters" to help merchants evaluate the probable worth of notes offered in payment.

[1] In addition to state-chartered banks, there were an unknown number of private banks operating. Private banks were not registered with, or sanctioned by, the states in which they operated. While private banks could not issue bank notes, they could issue promissory notes or certificates of deposit that may have circulated as money.

This financial system underwent a fundamental and permanent restructuring as a result of the fiscal crisis facing the Union government during the Civil War. While the restructuring began a process of rationalization in the money supply, replacing the confused mixture of discounted notes and coin with a uniform currency of full value, it increased the complexity of the American banking system and contributed to the weakness and vulnerability of American financial institutions.

Money and the Fiscal Crisis of the Civil War

Neither the Union nor the Confederate government had the tools to finance a major war efficiently. Since the adoption of the Constitution the federal government had relied upon excise taxes, the tariff, and land sales for its revenues, but these revenue sources could not be expanded overnight. Excise taxes, however, had not been levied since the 1820s, and borrowing prospects were not particularly bright. The bond market was still quite small. All the details of each loan—the amount, interest rate, and terms of sale—required congressional approval, making it difficult or impossible to adapt to rapidly changing market conditions. Efforts to deal with these problems brought about fundamental changes in America's financial markets.

In the months before secession, the federal government had mixed success in selling $21 million in bonds to fund the accumulated short-term debt. The initial sale of $10 million at 5 percent interest fell through when some nervous investors preferred to forfeit their deposits and only $7 million was actually taken up. A new authorization of $10 million was eventually placed but only at the unprecedentedly high rate (for the time) of 12 percent. Once the war began, Lincoln's treasury secretary, Salmon P. Chase (whose likeness appears on the $10,000 bill), found it increasingly difficult to borrow money, and the fiscal crisis was becoming critical. During the first three months of the war expenditure had totaled $23.5 million while receipts totaled only $5.8 million, a gap that the government met through short-term borrowing and stretching out payment of its bills.

For the fiscal year beginning July 1, 1861, Chase projected expenditures at $319 million, of which $240 million was to be borrowed, with the balance raised through taxes, some of which were new. Among these new taxes was the first U.S. tax on incomes. The rate was initially set at 3 percent on all incomes over $800 (more than five times average per capita income at the time) effective January 1, 1862. It was subsequently raised to 3 percent on incomes between $600 and $10,000 and 5 percent on incomes over $10,000. Relatively little thought, however, was devoted to the probable impact of the government borrowing on the nation's financial markets. The proposed debt increase was more than three times the entire national debt at the time. Part of it—$50 million—was authorized in non-interest-bearing Treasury notes. These so-called demand notes were redeemable upon demand in specie and acceptable in payment of all debts to the government. Although they were accepted only reluctantly by the public, the supply was soon exhausted, and the government again needed funds. Chase turned to the banks rather than try to sell directly to the public. In August 1861 a consortium of large banks agreed to lend the government $50 million immediately by purchasing three-year 7.3 percent Treasury notes with the right to take an additional $50 million in October and again in November.

The situation, however, was not quite so straightforward. The banks had only $63 million in specie on hand. They therefore expected that the Treasury would leave the funds on deposit and pay by check as needed while they resold the notes to the public. Chase demanded payment in specie, although he eventually compromised for $5 million in coin immediately with the balance to be available as needed. Unfortunately for the banks the news from the war front was not good and got worse. As a result, they were able to resell only $45 million of the first issue and none of the second. Moreover, instead of the specie's circulating and being redeposited in the banks, the bad news drove it into hoards. This shortage of specie was then further aggravated by Chase's decision to issue another $33 million in demand notes. These were quickly presented for payment in specie. By December specie was critically short—so short, in fact, that on December 30, 1861, the banks suspended specie payment. The government suspended payment in specie the following day. It was seventeen years before specie payment was resumed.

Although deposits and currency were no longer being redeemed in specie, gold remained essential for certain key transactions—notably foreign trade and the payment of customs duties and interest on the national debt. As a result, on January 13, 1862, there opened in New York a gold market where individuals and the government could buy and sell gold for paper money. Prices on this market were sensitive to advances and reverses of fortune of the Union army. For example, when Lee invaded Pennsylvania in early 1863, the paper money price of gold rose from $1.00 gold for $1.39 in paper to $1.00 gold for $1.49 in paper, and it reached a high of $2.85 in paper after Grant's defeat at Cold Harbor.

Greenbacks

Suspension of convertibility threw the money market into turmoil and raised questions about the faith and credit of the Union government. One result was that Congress determined that it would be very difficult—and expensive—to borrow more money. At the same time the prospects for new taxes yielding an immediate windfall to meet the fiscal crisis seemed remote. As an alternative, the House Ways and Means Committee proposed a new issue of non-interest-bearing Treasury notes that, unlike the earlier demand notes, would be legal tender for all debts public and private (except for payment of customs duties and interest on the national debt) despite being nonredeemable in specie. This proposal met with vigorous opposition from the banking lobby, but Congress approved the plan anyway. The Legal Tender Act of February 1862 authorized an issue of $150 million in such notes in denominations of $5 or more. These notes, known eventually as greenbacks, were quickly spent. Congress authorized two additional issues of $150 million each in mid–1862 and early 1863, some of which were in denominations of less than $5 (Figure 18.1). Eventually a total of $450 million was issued in 1862 and 1863, roughly doubling the prewar stock of money in the United States. This generated considerable inflationary pressure (Table 18.1) and depreciated the value of greenbacks in terms of gold. When first issued, a greenback dollar was worth over 99 cents in terms of gold. That is to say, someone with 99 cents in gold could buy as much as someone with a greenback dollar. In early June 1864, though, after Grant's loss at Cold Harbor, it took $2.85 in greenbacks to purchase what could be bought with $1.00 in gold. Part of the depreciation of the greenback dollar reflected the risk of repudiation should the Confederacy win, and part reflected the oversupply of paper money relative to gold and relative to the supply of goods and services. The cost of living rose 68 percent between 1860 and 1865. Not all prices rose, however, distorting relative prices and redistributing income as some prices proved more flexible than others in the short run. In particular, there is evidence that wages lagged behind the rise in the cost of living so that real wages fell while business profits surged (see Chapter 13).

Fiat money—currency whose value derived from the dictates of government—had arrived. And it stayed although Congress had originally provided for the convertibility of greenbacks into 5–20 bonds at par (bonds redeemable in five years and maturing in twenty years) assuming people would rather have interest-bearing bonds than non-interest-bearing notes. Since the bonds were then trading at less than par, however, few people availed themselves of the privilege of conversion. Instead, the provision simply placed a ceiling on the price of 5–20 bonds and a floor under interest rates of 6 percent (the yield on a 5–20 at par), and the idea of convertibility was eventually scrapped.

Efforts to redeem greenbacks after the war also failed when farmers protested the deflationary impact of this policy. Some $300 million in greenbacks are still counted as part of the money supply today. The oversupply of greenbacks, however, had produced a situation in which two prices were quoted: one for transactions in gold; the other, higher price for transactions in greenbacks. For a while the value of a dollar depended on whether it was in coin or paper. Until a 1:1 exchange rate was achieved, a return to a convertible currency was impossible. Growth in demand for money eventually began to catch up with the excess supply of paper money, and in January

FIGURE 18.1

A Greenback

Source: Robert Friedburg, *Paper Money of the United States* (New York: Coin & Currency Institute, 1962).

TABLE 18.1

Gold Prices, The Cost of Living, and Wages in Paper Money 1862–1865 (1860 = 100)

	Prices of Gold in Greenbacks			Cost of	Wage
Year	Low	Average	High	Living	Index
1862	100.5	113.3	134	112	101
1863	122.1	145.2	172.5	129	112
1864	157.5	203.3	285	156	130
1865	128.6	157.3	233.75	168	150

Source: Wesley C. Mitchell, *Gold, Prices, and Wage under the Greenback Standard* (Berkeley: University of California Press, 1908): 4, 279.

FIGURE 18.2

Civil War Fractional Currency

Source: Robert Friedburg, *Paper Money of the United States* (New York: Coin & Currency Institute), 1962.

1875 Congress passed the Resumption Act, directing the Treasury to begin redeeming in coin any greenbacks presented for payment after January 1, 1879. President Hayes's secretary of the treasury, John Sherman, upon whose shoulders the task of implementing resumption fell, believed that it would work only if the Treasury had on hand gold equal to at least 40 percent of the outstanding greenbacks, or about $130 to $140 million. At the time the Treasury had about $25 million in gold. He therefore proposed acquiring the difference through the sale of American bonds to foreign investors at rates somewhat above those currently being offered by European governments. His strategy was successful, and by late 1878 the Treasury had more than $140 million in gold. By mid-December the gold premium had disappeared, and resumption took place on schedule and without a hitch.

During the war the depreciation of the greenback caused not only the disappearance of gold from circulation but also the disappearance of subsidiary silver coinage (i.e., coins of less than $1). Under the Coinage Act of 1853, Congress, ever-mindful of the possibilities of arbitrage, had been careful to assure that $1 in subsidiary coin was worth only about 97 cents in gold. This had eliminated any incentive to convert the subsidiary coins into gold. Indeed, it had encouraged their circulation through Gresham's law. However, as greenbacks depreciated in value, the holders of half dollars, quarters, and dimes began to hoard them or ship them to Canada in exchange for gold that could be used to buy depreciated greenbacks. As a result, subsidiary coins over a penny virtually disappeared from circulation. Instead postage stamps were used for a while, but eventually Congress authorized the printing of fiat fractional notes to replace the subsidiary coinage (Figure 18.2).

The Silver Question

Subsidiary silver coinage had virtually disappeared during the Civil War, and it did not return once the war ended (Figure 18.3). In 1869, for example, circulation was less than $6 million, compared with perhaps $21 million before the war. Moreover, silver dollars had essentially disappeared from circulation after the mint ratio was changed in 1834, making silver more valuable on the bullion market than at the mint. Thus, when the Office of the Comptroller of the Currency reviewed the coinage and mint laws in 1870, it recommended dropping the silver dollar from the coinage—a change tantamount to declaring that silver was no longer usable as money since the silver dollar was the major silver coin being minted.

The proposal was adopted by Congress in the Coinage Act of 1873. Since the mint valued silver at $1.292 an ounce, compared with $1.298 an ounce in the market, nobody paid much attention to these changes at the time. Shortly thereafter, however, silver prices fell sharply as more European countries adopted the gold standard—selling off their unwanted surplus silver—and production increased as a result of some major silver discoveries in the American West. By 1874 the price of silver had fallen to $1.238 an ounce. Silver producers would thus have been overjoyed to sell their output to the mint for $1.292, but the mint wasn't buying because it had no use for silver beyond that needed for subsidiary coins. As a result, the Coinage Act of 1873 became known as the "Crime of '73" and was a rallying point for those forces opposed to the government's policy of deflation or price stability as a prelude to the resumption of specie payments. Over the ensuing years, with William Jennings Bryan and others taking up the challenge of "free silver," considerable political pressure was put on Congress and the executive to restore bimetallism through the unrestricted free coinage of both gold and silver. These pressures were resisted, but there were compromises.

In 1878 Congress overrode a presidential veto approving the purchase of between $2 million and $4 million of silver bullion per month at market prices for coinage into silver dollars at the 16:1 ratio (the Bland-Allison Act). The silver dollars so minted were to be full legal tender, but the silver certificates that were also issued were not, although they were receivable by the government. During the twelve years that this law was in force, the Treasury bought 291.3 million ounces of silver for $308.3 million and coined $378.2 million, represented by the increase in silver dollars and silver certificates in Figure 18.3. The difference between the expenditure and the value of the coinage represents the seigniorage received by the Treasury.

The resulting "limping standard" satisfied no one.[2] Silver purchases were too limited to prop up the market price—indeed, price fell from $1.20 an ounce to only 93 cents an ounce during the time the law was in effect—while the advocates of "sound money" feared the inflation that would result

[2] The phrase "limping standard" is Studenski and Krooss's (1952).

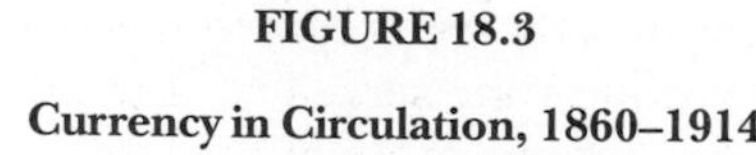
FIGURE 18.3

Currency in Circulation, 1860–1914

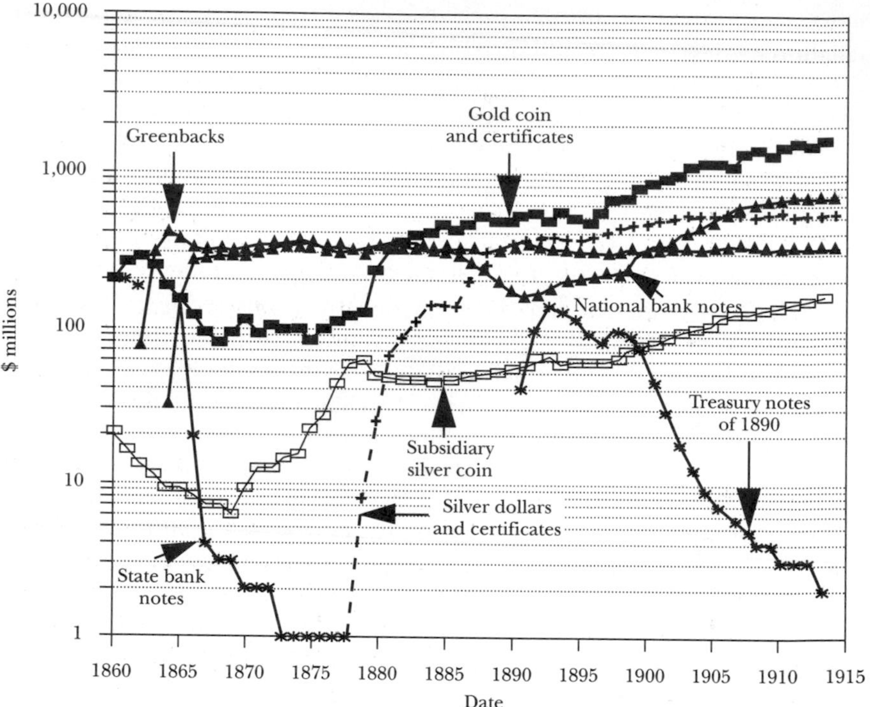

Source: U.S. Bureau of the Census, *Historical Statistics of the United States* (Washington, D.C.: Government Printing Office, 1975): Series X424–437.

from unlimited circulation of silver should the trickle of silver become a flood.

Nor was this fear totally unfounded. The peace won by the compromise with the prosilver forces was only temporary. When the balance of trade suddenly worsened in 1888 and agriculture was hard hit by declining export markets, silver agitation resumed. Once again a compromise was reached, this time through logrolling between supporters of more liberal silver legislation and supporters of the McKinley Tariff. Both pieces of legislation were passed. The McKinley Tariff raised duties to an average rate of 48 percent and was one of the most protectionist tariffs in American history. The Sherman Silver Purchase of 1890 directed the Treasury to buy 4.5 million ounces of silver a month at market prices using specially printed Treasury notes ("Treasury Notes of 1890"). These were full legal tender and redeemable in silver or gold. The only saving grace in this legislation so far as the "sound money" advocates were concerned was that redemption in gold *or* silver was at the discretion of the secretary of the treasury. So long as redemption was in gold, the de facto gold standard was preserved—that is, the United States monetary system functioned as if it were on a gold standard, even though legally it was still on a bimetallic standard (see Chapter 4). But there remained what Charles Calomiris and others have called the "silver risk": The only thing standing between the de facto gold standard and a silver standard with its attendant inflation was how long the Treasury's gold reserves would hold out. Indeed, the United States soon found itself facing a run on gold. In early 1890 the Treasury's gold balance had been almost $200 million, but by June 1891 the Treasury's gold stock had fallen to only $117.6 million. Furthermore, the Populist party committed itself to increased coinage of silver for its 1892 campaign, and the Senate passed a free silver coinage bill that died in the House.

During fiscal 1893, $72.3 million in gold was exported to satisfy nervous foreign investors. On April 22, 1893, the gold reserves dipped below $100 million for the first time since payment in specie had been resumed in 1879. Thereafter the situation only worsened with a full-blown financial panic beginning in May. In August President Cleveland called Congress back for a special session at which he pleaded for the repeal of the Sherman Silver Purchase Act, warning that it jeopardized gold as the de facto monetary standard, reinforcing fears of the "silver risk." The House quickly voted to support the president, but the issue dragged on in the Senate until October, a period during which the nation's gold reserves were further eroded.

Despite repeal of the Sherman Silver Purchase, the "silver risk" was not finally laid to rest until 1900, when Congress passed the Gold Standard Act. This officially scrapped the bimetallic standard adopted in 1791, establishing gold as the sole monetary standard and legalizing what had been a fact of life since 1879. However, all these changes had hardly resulted in a simpler, more coherent currency.

The Spread of Clearinghouses

In the years before 1853 banks everywhere in America had settled accounts, principally bank notes, with one another in full in specie at periodic intervals. In New York City, for example, Friday was settlement day, and runners were dispatched around town to settle accounts, virtually bringing normal banking activities to a standstill and forcing the calling of loans to meet the temporary demand for specie. In an effort to facilitate settlement, it was not uncommon for the larger banks to maintain deposits of $2,000 to $3,000 with as many as thirty other banks. But this was an expensive and inefficient solution to the problem.

As an alternative, 52 of the largest New York City banks established the nation's first clearinghouse in 1853, providing for the daily settlement of interbank balances. Boston banks followed suit in 1855, with Baltimore, Cleveland, and Philadelphia banks forming their own clearinghouses in 1858. By 1913 there were 162 clearinghouses nationwide, clearing over $170 billion. Most of them were small in comparison with New York's, which cleared almost $100 billion, compared with only $16 billion by the next largest clearinghouse, Chicago's. Their functions were taken over thereafter by the newly established Federal Reserve System, which ultimately achieved what the clearinghouses had failed to realize: universal clearing at par—that is, the acceptance of bank money, including checks, at full face value.

Besides speeding up the process of interbank settlement and reducing transactions costs, the clearinghouse banks, especially those in New York, assumed a leadership role in the banking community, trading upon their unimpeached reputation for financial integrity and probity to stabilize the banking system. Indeed, Gary Gorton credits the New York Clearinghouse with originating central banking in America. In the Panic of 1857, when banks in upstate New York were unable to redeem their notes in lawful money after the failure of the Ohio Life Insurance and Trust Company, the New York Clearinghouse accepted short-term certificates secured by the country banks' loan portfolios and paying 6 percent interest rather than force the banks into insolvency. Thereafter this practice became regularized and spread to the other clearinghouses around the country. By issuing certificates secured by bank assets, the clearinghouses, in effect, offered banks the opportunity to rediscount their assets in times of need although the liquidity created in this way could be used only within the clearinghouse.

These certificates saw frequent, and sometimes large-scale, use during the various financial panics that assaulted the banking system later in the nineteenth and twentieth centuries, for example, in 1860, 1861, 1863, and 1864. They were used more widely in the Panic of 1873, when at least $42 million in such certificates were issued by clearinghouses across the country. In the Panic of 1893 the New York Clearinghouse alone issued over $41 million, and at least twelve clearinghouses issued over $68 million. Some of these certificates were issued in small denominations and circulated outside the clearinghouse without the sanction of law. Their use as money simply emphasizes the high repute in which the clearinghouses were held.

The National Banking Act

As early as December 1861—before payment in specie was suspended—Treasury Secretary Chase had proposed the establishment of a national banking system. The system would be chartered and regulated by the federal government to create a uniform currency replacing the plethora of state bank notes and to provide a market for government bonds since the national banks would be required to invest their capital in government bonds. The proposal was quickly sidetracked by the tide of economic and military crises afflicting the Union government. It was revived and adopted by Congress in February 1863, but it failed to achieve its goals. Bankers proved reluctant to relinquish their state charters to operate under untried, but seemingly more restrictive, federal charters. As of October 1863, only sixty-three national banks had been established. Most of them were new banks rather than conversions from state charters, and most were located in the Midwest. Their combined note circulation was less than $4 million, compared with a circulation of state bank notes of about $239 million.

In the competition for member banks, the national banking system was found wanting. Rather than see the fledgling system wither and die, Congress liberalized the law in June 1864 and imposed a 2 percent tax on state bank notes. But even this failed to achieve its desired goal of forcing conversion from state to federal charter. As of October 1864, there were still only 508 national banks with a note circulation of less than $46 million, and the national banking system had bought up only $108 million of government debt. Stronger measures were called for, and in March 1865 Congress raised the tax on state bank notes to 10 percent. The high tax made it unprofitable for state banks to continue to issue notes, and they were finally coerced into the national banking system. By October 1865 there were 1,513 national banks with a note circulation of $171 million. A year later national bank note circulation had increased to $280 million, and the number of national banks had increased to 1,644. During the same period the number of state-chartered banks fell from 1,466 in 1863 to 1,089 in 1864 to only 349 in 1865, after the 10 percent tax went into effect. By 1866 there were only 297 state-chartered banks left, and they reached their nadir in 1868, when only 247 remained (Figure 18.4).

The National Banking Act of 1864, like state free banking legislation earlier, allowed any group of five or more persons to obtain a national banking charter. Unlike the free banking legislation, it also tried to impose a homogeneous structure upon the banking system despite the heterogeneity of needs. National banks in cities of fifty thousand or more were required to be capitalized at $200,000 or more. In cities between six thousand and fifty thousand, $100,000 was required, and in towns of under six thousand, a minimum of $50,000 capital was required. One-third of this capital (but not less than $30,000) had to be in government bonds and deposited with the comptroller of the currency. In exchange, the banks received national bank notes equal to the lesser of 90 percent of par or the market value of the bonds.

The national banks were also required to keep minimum reserve ratios. Banks in so-called reserve cities—the major metropolitan areas—were required to maintain a 25 percent reserve ratio in lawful money in vault cash against their deposits. Those in other cities were also required to maintain a 25 percent reserve ratio, but half of it could be in the form of a deposit with

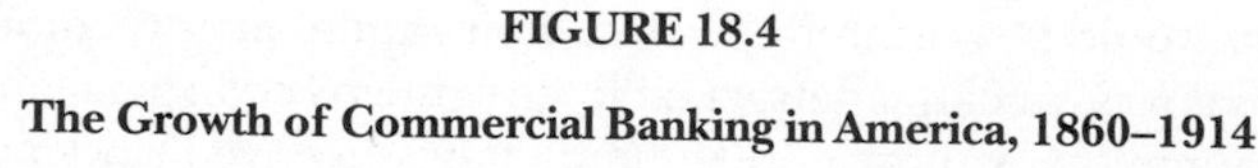

FIGURE 18.4

The Growth of Commercial Banking in America, 1860–1914

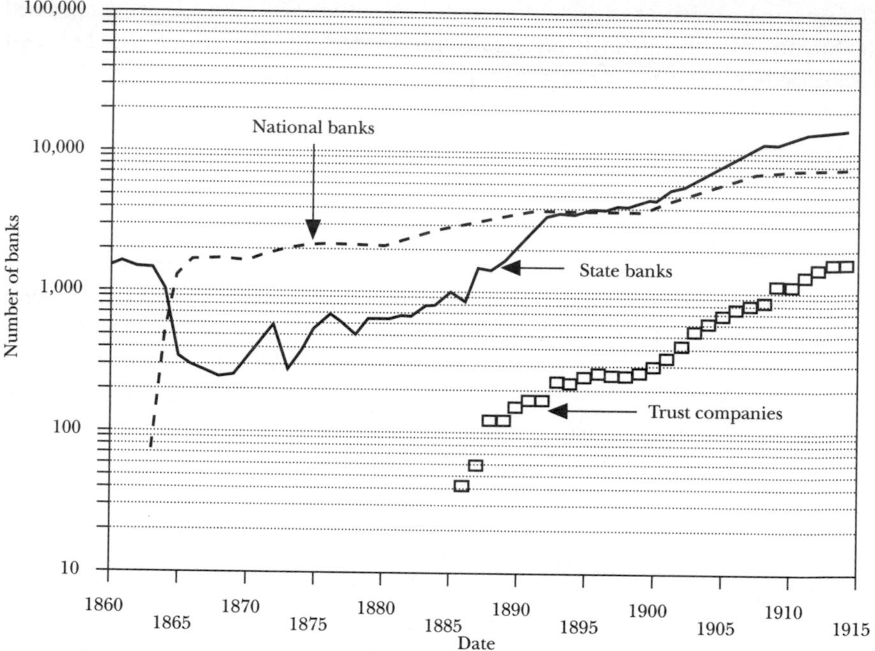

Source: Eugene N. White, *The Regulation and Reform of the American Banking System, 1900–1929* (Princeton: Princeton University Press, 1983): 12–13, 39.

one of the New York City (called the central reserve city) national banks. Country banks got by with a 15 percent reserve ratio, three-fifths of which could be a deposit with a city bank. These capital and reserve requirements were considerably more restrictive than required under many state banking charters; that explains why banks were so reluctant to convert from state to federal charters until they were forced to do so. Congress imposed such high minimum capital and reserve requirements in an effort to minimize the risk of bank failure and illiquidity. Moreover, Congress imposed various limits on the kinds of business that national banks could conduct. For example, national banks were originally prohibited from owning real estate other than their bank building unless it had been acquired through foreclosure.

Unlike the notes of state banks, which they were intended to replace, the national bank notes were receivable at par—that is, for their face value—in all parts of the country and marked the first giant step toward establishing a homogeneous currency. However, rather than let the market decide how many notes were needed, Congress imposed an initial ceiling of $300 million on the circulation. Of this, one-half was distributed among the states according to population with the balance distributed according to bank demand. This restriction produced some anomalies. For example, Connecticut had a larger circulation than Michigan, Iowa, Minnesota, Kansas, Missouri, Kentucky, and Tennessee combined, and while the per capita circulation of national bank notes in Rhode Island was $77, it was only 13 cents in Arkansas.

The Resurgence of State Banking

After 1870 state bank membership began to recover. By 1895 state banks once again outnumbered national banks, although the value of their assets was only a fraction of those of the national banks (see Figure 18.4, above). The principal explanation for this new lease on life for state banking was the substitution of the personal check for the bank note as a means of payment, thus avoiding the tax penalty on noncongressionally sanctioned bank notes. However, restrictions upon branching also meant that much of the increased demand for banking services had to be met by opening new banks rather than opening new offices of existing banks.

Densely settled areas were served first (Figure 18.5, Panel A), and banks there tended to be relatively large. The smaller communities and rural areas were served later by smaller banks. Much of the growth in banking in the late nineteenth and early twentieth centuries was represented by extension of banking services to precisely these areas (Figures 18.5, Panels B and C). However, the minimum capital required for a national banking charter was often larger than that required to obtain a state charter, and national banks were required to maintain higher reserve ratios than most state banks. In 1895 at least twenty-two states chartered banks, the minimum capital requirement of which for country banks was smaller than the federal requirement. In California, for example, the minimum was $25,000. In others, such as Arkansas, Mississippi, Oklahoma, and South Carolina, it was effectively zero. Similarly, while national banks were required to maintain reserves of between 15 percent and 25 percent as late as 1887, reserve requirements were written into the law in only three states. This eventually changed, but in 1895 thirty-one states still had no specific reserve requirements. Moreover, national banks were prohibited from making mortgage loans, yet real estate was the principal asset in rural areas. As a result, a majority of the new banks adopted state, rather than federal, charters, and the two systems became locked in competition for membership.

In the Gold Standard Act of 1900, the federal government reduced the minimum capital requirement for national banks in towns under three thousand to $25,000. Nine states—Alabama, Colorado, Georgia, Louisiana, Maryland, Pennsylvania, Utah, Washington, and Wisconsin—that in 1895 had minimum capital requirements at or below national banking levels re-

FIGURE 18.5

Geographic Distribution of Banks

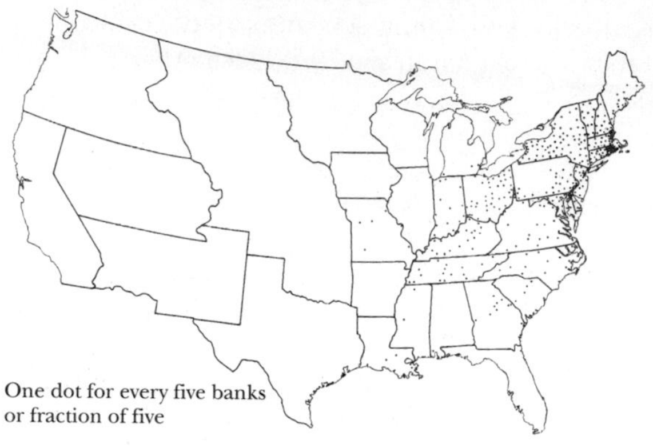

PANEL A: 1850

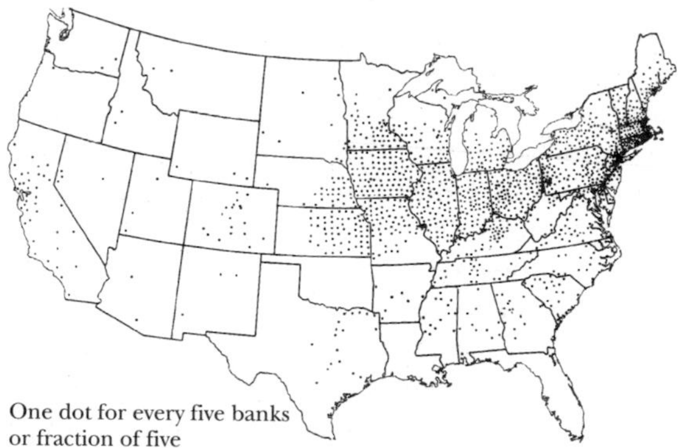

PANEL B: 1880

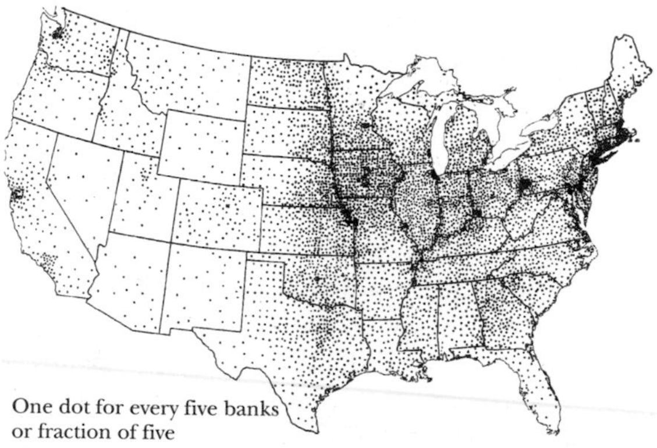

PANEL C: 1910

Source: Charles O. Paullin, *Atlas of the Historical Geography of the United States* (Washington, D.C.: Carnegie Institution, 1932): Plates 154E, 154G and 154J.

sponded by lowering them to maintain their advantage. Ten other states passed "free banking" legislation that had capital requirements of from $5,000 to $15,000. Similarly, although the number of states with no reserve requirements had dwindled to only thirteen by 1909 and most states had reserve requirements equal to those required of national banks, the terms of what constituted reserves was generally much more liberal for state than national banks. As a result, Eugene White argues that the competition between state and federal regulatory systems had the effect of weakening banking regulation to the point where entry was virtually unrestricted. Competition also probably played a role in the increasing rate of bank failures and suspensions in the 1890s, the late 1900s, and especially the 1920s, culminating in the debacle of the 1930s.

The Growth of Other Financial Instruments and Intermediaries

Also emerging in the post–Civil War period were various other financial markets and financial intermediaries, among them life insurance companies, trust companies, mortgage brokers and mortgage banks, investment banks, the securities market, and various futures markets. Until recently they have received relatively little attention from economic historians, but they played an important role in mobilizing savings and serving as intermediaries between creditors and debtors.

One early and very popular financial instrument was tontine insurance. It was introduced in 1868 by the Equitable Life Assurance Company as a combination life insurance and old-age savings plan. Tontine policies proved extremely popular, and similar policies were introduced by virtually every life insurance company. By 1905 more than 60 percent of the policies—about nine million policies worth $6 million—in force from thirty-four large insurers was tontine insurance.[3] Under a standard life insurance contract, the insured pays fixed premiums. These are initially much higher than warranted by the risk assumed by the company, but as the policyholder ages, the risk of death increases. Eventually the annual premiums no longer cover the risk, and additional insurance costs are met instead out of the excess premiums paid in earlier. However, to provide a measure of added security and to generate an adequate contingent reserve, premiums are set at a level substantially higher than those necessary to meet these expected costs. The excess accumulated reserves are normally rebated to policyholders (in the case of mutual life insurance companies) or paid out to stockholders. In tontine insurance contracts, on the other hand, policyholders deferred the receipt of these dividends for a fixed period of time during which the monies were invested by the company on behalf of the policyholders. At the end of the contract period the resulting fund was divided

[3] Ransom and Sutch (1987).

among the surviving policyholders. The advantage of this type of insurance is that while those dying before the end of the contract received the promised death benefit, those who survived received the accumulated deferred dividends of the deceased policyholders and those whose policies had lapsed. Although the rate of return on the tontine fell short of that advertised, the typical return to survivors exceeded that on savings bank deposits—a plausible alternative for the small saver. Despite the popularity of tontine insurance with the public, it was outlawed by New York State in 1905. Other states subsequently followed suit.

The demise of the tontine insurance industry was the result of a turn-of-the-century muckraking exposé on the insurance industry that prompted a congressional investigation. The congressional committee's report recommended a number of reforms, including the prohibition of tontine insurance, apparently on the grounds that it encouraged gambling, that the tontine policies were misrepresented by the insurance companies, and that the policies were immensely profitable for the insurance industry. Whatever the truth of these allegations, though, tontine insurance was equivalent, or superior, to the alternatives for the small saver then available, and it had one major plus in its favor: It avoided moral hazard. The insured had a strong financial incentive to live a longer life than the others in the pool and thus collect the dividends on those policies.

Large savers had a much wider choice of financial instruments in which to invest. One such opportunity that was of growing importance in the late nineteenth century was the stock market. Although the New York Stock Exchange was not formally organized until 1817, it had operated informally since 1792. Similar exchanges existed in other major cities, such as Boston, but New York's was the largest. Early on the principal securities traded on these exchanges were government bonds, bank stocks, and the bonds of various state-sponsored internal improvement projects. Indeed, trading in bonds dominated the market throughout the nineteenth century although railroad and industrial stocks became increasingly numerous and active, particularly once states had started passing general limited liability and incorporation laws. As late as 1898, though, there were only twenty industrial issues officially listed on the New York exchange, but there was a very large and rapidly growing trade in unlisted industrial stocks after about 1885. In the late 1850s average turnover was about seventy thousand shares per day; in 1886 the market had its first million-share trading day. Despite the absence of any federal regulation requiring full and complete disclosure of all relevant information simultaneously to all investors, this market seems to have functioned "rationally"—that is to say, stock prices were approximately equal to the present discounted value of the infinite stream of dividends that the stock was expected to pay. Where deviations occurred, they were relatively short-lived and may be explained by specific institutional factors. There is little evidence that stock watering, price manipulations, and insider

FIGURE 18.6

Cumulative Inflation-Adjusted Total Return on Different Investments Assuming an Initial Investment of $1 in 1871 and the Reinvestment of All Proceeds

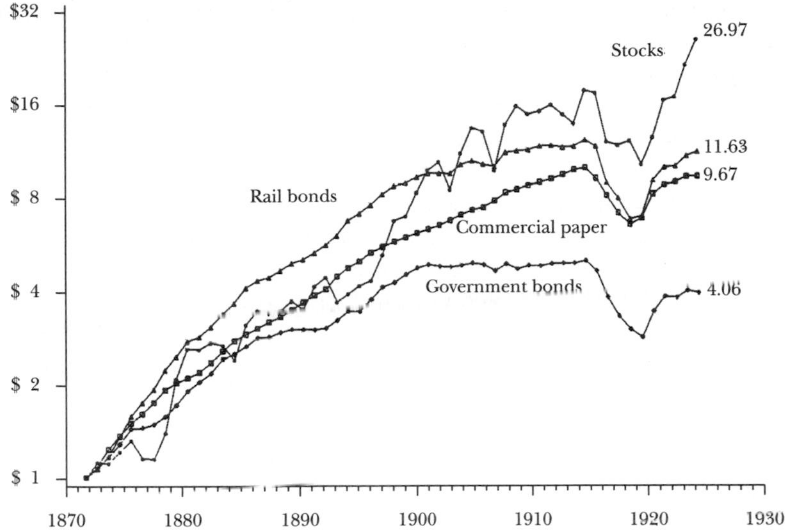

Source: Kenneth Snowden, "Historical Returns and Security Market Development, 1872–1925." *Explorations in Economic History* 27 (1990): 393.

trading prevented investors from earning a "fair" return. Inflation-adjusted stock returns over the period from 1872 to 1925 compare favorably with those since then, and bond returns were generally higher than in more recent times (Figure 18.6). Before 1900, however, stocks were outperformed by railroad bonds and did no better than commercial paper. Around 1900 two changes occurred: Real interest rates declined, and stock volatility increased. Thereafter stocks outperformed other assets, as they have continued to do since.[4]

Not all the financial intermediaries that emerged after the Civil War were new, but their function and structure changed fundamentally during this period. For example, trust companies were originally chartered as corporations serving the wealthy with power to receive deposits and purchase securities "in trust" for their customers as well as to provide life and fire insurance, fidelity and title insurance, and safe deposits. However, they soon expanded into the banking business, competing with banks for deposits, col-

[4] Snowden (1987, 1990).

lateralized lending, and buying commercial paper. Once they made this switch, trust companies became the key factor underlying the merger movement at the end of the nineteenth century that transformed the face of American industry and transportation as well as the crucial catalyst of structural change in the banking industry.[5] States had to scramble to bring trust companies under their banking regulations, particularly once their numbers began to grow rapidly beginning in the late 1880s (see Figure 18.4). This growth often came at the expense of state banks. For example, in the decade before the creation of the Fed, no new state banks were chartered in Massachusetts, Maine, or Vermont; instead trust companies supplied the commercial banking services. Although trust companies emerged first in New England and were concentrated along the East Coast, they expanded everywhere and were a part of the challenge to the hegemony of the national banking system. Increased competition from trust companies was a major factor prompting mergers among New England's unit banks in the late nineteenth century.[6]

The Existence and Persistence of Regional Interest Rate Differentials

Throughout much of American history there has been a deep and abiding mistrust of bankers and a widespread fear of a "money monopoly"—a fear that those needing to borrow would be taken advantage of by those able to lend. Such questions had figured prominently in the debates over the fates of the First Bank and Second Bank of the United States, and they played a role in the popular support of free banking legislation. They had also led to the almost universal adoption of usury ceilings on interest rates (typically 6 percent) that were more honored in name than reality. These concerns were the subject of congressional inquiries, the most famous of which were the Pujo hearings into the Money Trust in the wake of the 1907 Panic. During the hearings J. P. Morgan was the subject of protracted and vigorous cross-examination by the House Banking and Currency Committee counsel Samuel Untermyer. This event was unremarkable in itself but was one that is alleged to have played a key role in the failure of the banking system and the Federal Reserve rescue of the Bank of United States in 1930 (see Chapter 21).

One reason why these concerns about the Money Trust endured is the persistence of substantial regional interest rate differentials from the Civil War to the outbreak of World War I. For example, an 1898 study found that the average discount rate on prime, two-name commercial paper (that is, a

[5] Neal (1971).
[6] Lamoreaux (1991).

bill drawn to finance trade or production and endorsed by two different parties) between 1893 and 1897 ranged from 3.83 percent in Boston and 4.41 percent in New York to 5.01 percent in Cincinnati, 7.98 percent in Omaha, 5.85 percent in New Orleans, and 8.34 percent in Dallas to 6.22 percent in San Francisco but 10 percent in Denver. The study attributed these differences to the "disinclination of capital to migrate." Over time, however, there is evidence that the rates tended to converge. This took place first and most completely among reserve city banks, but the same trend was also apparent in the data from nonreserve city banks (Figure 18.7). In the early 1870s, for example, the average net return for midwestern reserve city banks (banks in Chicago, St. Louis, etc.) was almost 6.5 percent. The rate of return for San Francisco banks was over 7.5 percent, while the return on New York City banks was less than 3.5 percent. The spread was over 2:1, with a gap of three percentage points or more. By the early 1890s the spread between New York city banks and midwestern reserve city banks had narrowed to about 3:2 with a gap of about one percentage point. By the first decade of the twentieth century even western interest rates had converged toward those in the rest of the country, and the interregional interest rate differential was less than one percentage point. Among the nonreserve city banks, the interregional interest rate gap remained a little wider than among reserve city banks.

Since national banks were prohibited from investing in real estate mortgages prior to 1913, Lance Davis attributed the convergence to the spread of a market in short-term commercial paper—what we might call the segmented market hypothesis—while the absolute interest rate differential captured monopoly power in areas less well served by banks and other financial intermediaries. Richard Sylla, however, has argued that the differential regional interest rates reflected differential rates of monopoly power in banking arising from the National Banking Act. This act restricted entry into the banking industry in small towns through setting an overly high minimum capital requirement of $50,000 in cities of less than six thousand. Not until these capital requirements were halved by the Gold Standard Act of 1900 were there increased bank entry and competition. As a result, regional interest rates converged thereafter. But most of the convergence took place before 1900—especially if we ignore the far West (region VI).[7] Even if minimum capital requirements had restricted market entry by national banks, requirements were much less restrictive, and in some cases nonexistent, for state banks. Indeed, state banking grew by leaps and bounds from the 1880s (see Figures 18.4, 18.7, and 18.8). It thus seems more likely that the competition from and between state banks, reinforced by increasingly close correspondent banking arrangements, was more responsible for the decline in and convergence of regional interest rates. Certainly, work on San Francisco and the West Coast clearly shows that correspondent banking arrangements

[7] James (1978).

FIGURE 18.7

The Convergence of Regional Interest Rates 1870–1914

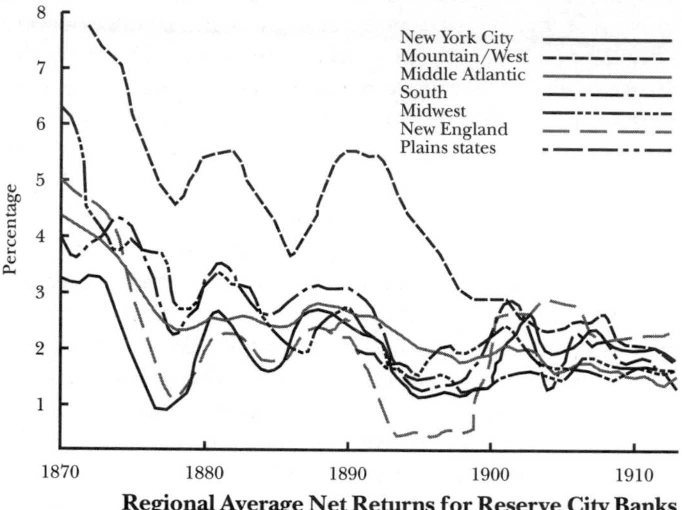

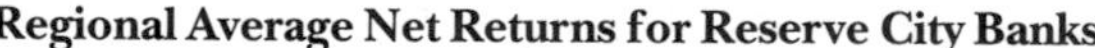

Regional Average Net Returns for Reserve City Banks

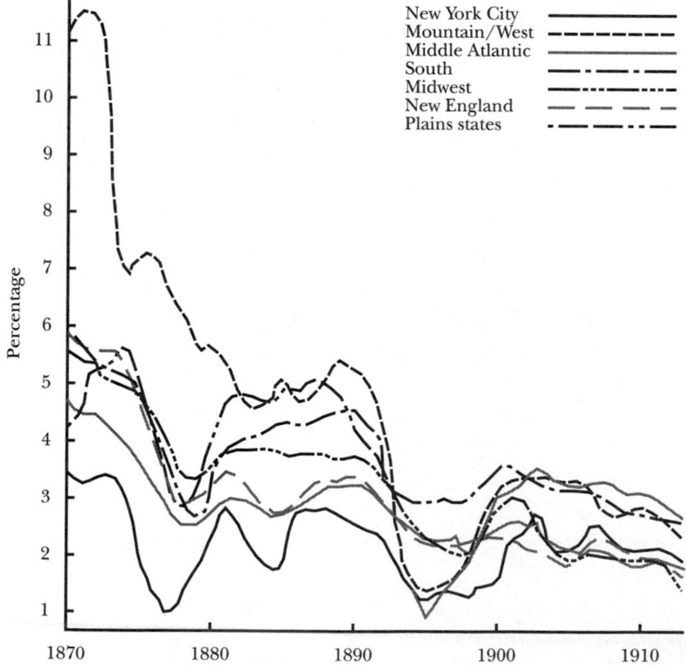

Regional Average Net Returns for Nonreserve City Banks

Source: Lance E. Davis, "The Investment Market, 1870–1914: The Emergence of a National Market," *Journal of Economic History* 25 (1965): 369. Reprinted by permission of Cambridge University Press.

were largely responsible for the development of capital markets within that region and their integration with the rest of the country.[8] Changes in the structure of the banking industry may not have been the only factor eroding local bank monopoly power. For example, the rise of a substitute equity financing market in New York and its extension to unlisted stocks in the 1880s allowed businesses to choose between debt and equity financing and freed them from dependence upon local banks.[9]

Not everyone has accepted a bank monopoly power explanation for the existence of regional interest rate differentials and the eventual convergence in those rates. Some have pointed to differences in the riskiness of bank loans and the risk of bank failure as explanations of differences.[10] The same explanation seems to account for similar differences in state and regional long-term mortgage rates in the farm mortgage market that disappear after adjustment for the risk of foreclosure.[11] In the residential mortgage market, however, while default risk explains some of the differences in interest rates, there remain substantial regional variations that are consistent with the segmented market hypothesis.[12] That is, the interest rate differentials reflected the cost of moving funds between regions and the uneven diffusion of financial innovations, whether these were correspondent banking arrangements or the spread of specialized institutions such as mortgage banks and life insurance companies that specialized in mortgages. Others have pointed out that the data show no systematic positive relationship between bank assets and bank returns, as one would expect if banks were able to exercise any degree of monopoly power to exact rents from their customers, emphasizing instead changes in restrictions on branching and the activities of private banks and differential changes in regional agricultural returns.[13] Yet others have focused on the demand for loanable funds rather than on supply conditions. For example, with the completion of the major rail links in the Midwest by the early 1880s, stable demand for midwestern grain, and the cessation of population redistribution to the Midwest, increasing demand for loanable funds no longer drove up midwestern interest rates relative to the East Coast.[14] Though plausible, this explanation unfortunately cannot explain a similar convergence between West Coast and other regional interest rates at about the same time.

One inference from Davis's work is that capital market imperfections must have been greater before the Civil War, when there were fewer banks, transportation costs were higher, communications less speedy, and slavery

[8] Odell (1989).
[9] Sushka and Barrett (1984).
[10] Rockoff (1977) and Smiley (1975).
[11] Eichengreen (1984).
[12] Snowden (1987).
[13] Binder and Brown (1991).
[14] Williamson (1974).

impeded the flow of labor. Recent research, however, suggests that antebellum financial markets were rather well integrated.[15] If so, then it seems likely that the postwar convergence was a product of the disruption of the nation's financial markets by the Civil War. Markets that were once integrated became segmented. Indeed, much of the perceived postbellum convergence comes from movements in southern and far western interest rates. In the South the war destroyed what little banking there was, and it took time to rebuild. In South Carolina, for example, only the Bank of Charleston survived the war and Reconstruction. For the West the explanation is different. After 1861 the West found itself on a different monetary standard from the rest of the country. In the East the suspension of specie payment had made the greenback dollar the unit of account, and gold sold for a substantial premium on the New York gold market. In the West, on the other hand, the gold dollar—thanks to the continued output of western gold mines—remained the unit of account, and greenbacks traded at a discount. The exchange rate between gold and greenbacks and fluctuations in that rate thus affected any decision to move funds between the two regions. In particular, after the war greenbacks appreciated steadily relative to gold, reducing the attractiveness of higher nominal interest rates in the West. Resumption of payment in specie upon demand in 1879 eliminated this exchange rate risk, coinciding with the elimination of much of the gap between interest rates in the far West and other relatively isolated parts of the country.

Although the evidence in favor of monopoly banking is weak, there are good reasons to suppose that banking did become much more competitive over the course of the nineteenth century. In 1860 there was approximately one bank for every 10,000 inhabitants. This ratio decreased during the Civil War decade to about one bank for every 20,500 inhabitants, but thereafter it rose dramatically. By 1890 there was one bank for every 7,700 residents, and by 1914 there was one bank for every 3,500 people. When this rise in number of banks is coupled with improvements in transportation—the interurban railroad, the tramway, and the beginnings of the automobile age—and communications—the telegraph, the telephone, and the print media—it seems eminently plausible that more customers, whether at the deposit window or the loan desk, had a choice of banks.

The Flawed American Banking System

The American banking system suffered from a number of serious flaws that, though not fatal, made it especially vulnerable to financial panics. Many of those flaws arose from the National Banking Act. The act created a tiered

[15] Bodenhorn and Rockoff (1992).

banking structure, consisting of country banks on the bottom, then city banks and reserve city banks, with central reserve city banks constituting the top tier. Each tier was subject to different capital and reserve requirements. The objective was twofold. First, the legislature recognized that the repercussions from the failure of a large, highly visible bank were likely to be much more serious than if a small, isolated bank failed. They therefore tried to minimize the probability of a large bank's failing by setting higher reserve requirements for reserve city banks, demanding that they have a greater percentage of reserves available immediately as cash on hand, and by requiring banks in large urban areas to have more capital. This policy limited the ability of the national banking system to compete with the state system. Growing competition between the federal and state banking systems for member banks led to the progressive weakening of the regulatory structure governing banking through, for example, the lowering of capital requirements and the easing of loan restrictions. Second, Congress believed that the "pooling" of reserves would create a bigger pool from which legal tender could be drawn in times of need. However, by providing that a part of country and nonreserve city bank reserves could be held in the form of deposits with New York City banks, the system resulted in the concentration of system reserves in a few New York City banks. In 1912, for example, eight New York City banks held about 60 percent of the city's interbank deposits, or about one-third of all interbank deposits. Moreover, while the reserve pool might be large, there was no provision for the creation of additional legal tender in times of crisis; there was no lender in last resort to whom the New York City banks might turn. This problem came to be known as "the problem of the inelastic currency"—in the short run the quantity of legal tender was essentially fixed—though this problem was not confined solely to the national banking era.

Indeed, banks had recognized the problem well before the National Banking Act and had found a solution, albeit one not sanctioned by law: the use of clearinghouse certificates to satisfy claims within the clearinghouse. The National Banking Act made the system weaker and more vulnerable because it placed the New York City banks in a profits squeeze. By law the New York City national banks were required to keep a 25 percent reserve ratio in vault cash, and therefore, they had to derive their entire income from just 75 percent of their assets. At the same time the largest banks competed among themselves for the reserves of city and country banks by paying interest on these deposits despite repeated efforts by the New York Clearinghouse to discourage the practice. Thus the New York City banks had to earn higher returns from their loan portfolios to earn a rate of return on total assets comparable to that earned by other banks. They could do this by accepting higher risk assets. In particular, the New York City banks became accustomed to placing money at call with the stock market, thereby linking the fortunes of the banking system with other financial markets. The dangers of this became all too apparent in 1907, when stock speculation, especially in copper, spread from the stock market and jeopardized the banking system.

The Panic of 1907: Catalyst for Reform

Although there is no clear, single cause of the financial panic that began in Europe in 1906 and spread to the United States in 1907, the event shook the American financial system to its foundations, prompting fundamental legal changes in the American banking system. Some blame the San Francisco earthquake, others, the Russian-Japanese War, but whatever the proximate cause, European central banks reacted to a persistent gold outflow from their countries by raising their interest rates. The Bank of England, for example, raised its discount rate in several stages from 3.5 percent in September 1906 to 6 percent by mid-October. This reversed the flow of gold to the United States. The Bank of England also pressured London financial houses to repatriate their American loans. As a result, American stock prices, particularly those of some of the more popular companies, such as the Union Pacific, fell sharply in early 1907, dropping 30 percent in less than two weeks. Two months later, in May 1907, the business cycle in America peaked. With reserves at New York City banks close to the legal minimum, interest rates tightened just when the country banks began a part of their seasonal drawdown of deposits to meet harvest needs.

In mid-October panic broke out with runs on eight banks, five of them members of the New York Clearinghouse. The runs were prompted by the banks' involvement in copper speculation that had soured. The clearinghouse bailed them out, but the financial crisis worsened when the Knickerbocker Trust Company—the third-largest trust company in New York with seventeen thousand depositors and more than $50 million in deposits—was unable to meet demands for repayment and closed its doors. Milton Friedman and Anna Schwartz suggest that if the Knickerbocker Trust had been a member of the clearinghouse, it, too, might have been helped and the panic halted. Instead other runs began on Trust Company of America and the Lincoln Trust Company, threatening confidence in the entire credit system. The clearinghouse once again rendered assistance and averted closure, but this failed to allay fears outside New York. Loans contracted, call money rates soared to more than 100 percent, and stock prices collapsed despite the organization of money pools by J. P. Morgan to support the market. Clearinghouse banks were forced once again to issue scrip. According to contemporary estimates, at least $238 million in large-denomination clearinghouse certificates were issued. Also issued were various smaller certificates and checks "payable in clearinghouse funds" that circulated outside the clearinghouses. Some estimates suggest that as much as $500 million in clearinghouse certificates and drafts may have been issued. Even so, the system came perilously close to collapse as the reserves of the New York banks fell from a surplus of $11 million to a deficit of $54 million.

Shaken by these events, Congress passed the Aldrich-Vreeland Act in May 1908, authorizing groups of at least ten national banks with at least $5 million in capital to form national currency associations. In the event of a financial emergency, these currency associations could apply for emergency currency backed by their bank assets. To prevent abuse and encourage retirement of the emergency currency once the crisis had passed, any notes issued under the act were subject to a tax of 5 percent per year in the first month, increasing 1 percent per month up to a maximum of 10 percent. In effect, Aldrich-Vreeland authorized what the clearinghouses had already been doing all along but widened coverage to include nonclearinghouse members while providing a means of ensuring that this privilege would not be abused.

In addition, the Aldrich-Vreeland Act provided for the creation of a National Monetary Commission to study the banking and monetary systems and make recommendations for their improvement. The key recommendation was for the creation of a central bank controlled by the bankers themselves with voluntary membership, organized around a national reserve association with fifteen regional associations. But the plan was not adopted after the Democrats gained control of the House in 1910. When the Democrats also captured the Senate and the presidency in 1912, the problem of banking reform fell squarely in their lap. The new plan that emerged owed much to Aldrich's original proposal, although under the Democrats' plan, which became law, the government had more power over the central agency while bankers retained control over the regional banks. The Federal Reserve Act was approved and signed into law in December 1913.

The Federal Reserve System

The Federal Reserve Act provided for the creation of a Federal Reserve Board (known as the Board of Governors of the Federal Reserve since 1935) in Washington, D.C. The board was composed of five presidential appointees serving ten-year terms (terms were staggered to preserve the figment of their independence from the executive branch). In addition, the secretary of the treasury and comptroller of the currency served as ex officio members of the board (their participation on the board was terminated in 1935). The board's role was to determine policy to achieve the goals of the Fed and to supervise a network of twelve district banks (Figure 18.8).

Each district bank had nine directors. Three (Class A) represented the banking community; three (Class B) represented business, commerce, and agriculture. Though elected by the member banks, no Class B director could

FIGURE 18.8

Federal Reserve Districts, Banks, and Branches in 1919

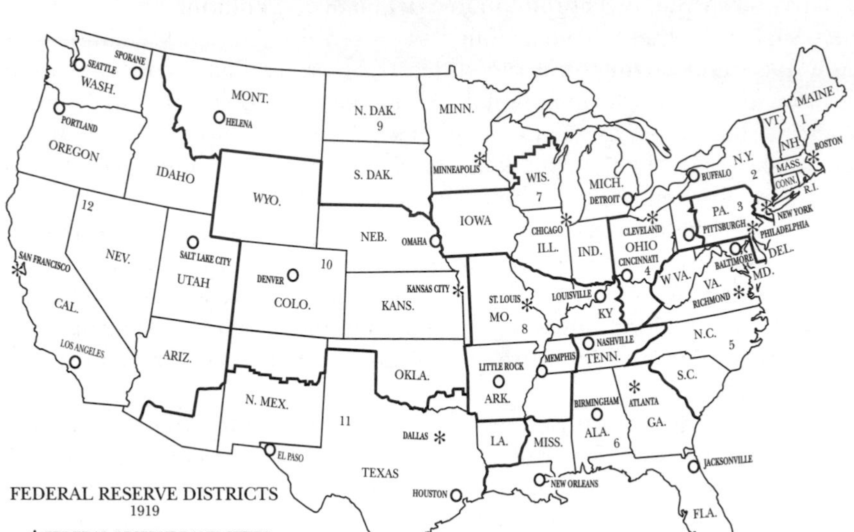

be an employee or stockholder in a bank. The last three directors (Class C) represented the public and were appointed by the Federal Reserve Board. One of their number was designated Federal Reserve agent and was expected to direct the district bank as its CEO, coordinating local policy with the board in Washington. But it did not work out this way. Instead the directors of each district bank elected their own chairman of the board, to be styled the "Governor" of the bank, rather than accept the Federal Reserve agent. The governor, not the Federal Reserve agent, quickly came to be recognized as the real source of power within the district bank, breaking the chain of command between Washington and the district. If the governor of the local Federal Reserve district bank was king, the governor of the Federal Reserve District Bank of New York, Benjamin Strong, was the king among kings. Strong played a central role in the development of domestic monetary policy after World War I and represented the Fed in its dealings with central banks around the world.

All national banks were required to become members of the Federal Reserve System, while state banks that met federal requirements were permitted to become members. The district banks themselves were owned by the member banks, which were required to buy stock in the Federal Reserve System equal to 3 percent of their capital with an additional 3 percent on call. Member banks receive dividends on this stock, limited by law to 6 percent, with the excess going to the federal government as a franchise tax and to the Federal Reserve surplus account. The system has proved immensely successful, paying dividends from the start and contributing millions of dollars in excess profits to the federal budget.

Each district bank issues its own Federal Reserve notes. Under the terms of the original legislation, these were to be secured by 100 percent two-name commercial paper and a 40 percent gold reserve. The banks were permitted to rediscount commercial paper of up to ninety days maturity for their members—that is, the Fed stood ready, at a price, to buy commercial paper that the member banks had purchased from their customers. The district banks were allowed to buy agricultural loans of up to six months' maturity and could buy and sell gold, government obligations, and foreign currency. They were also to serve as fiscal agents for the government, and they were to establish a system for clearing checks without cost to payee or the payer.

The intent of the Federal Reserve Act was summarized in its full title: "An Act to provide for the establishment of Federal Reserve banks, to furnish an elastic currency, to afford means of rediscounting commercial paper, to establish a more effective supervision of banking in the United States, and for other purposes." Only two of these goals were realized before the disaster of the Great Depression overtook the nation's financial institutions, beginning in late 1929. A system of Federal Reserve district banks was established, and the Fed did provide member banks with a market for rediscounting commercial paper. The Fed, however, failed to solve the problem of creating an elastic currency, and it failed to gain regulatory control over the banking system. So long as the United States remained committed to the gold standard, the Fed lacked complete control over the supply of currency, and its ability to act as "lender in last resort" was compromised. Similarly, supervision of the nation's banks could never be truly effective as long as only a third or so of the banks were members of the Federal Reserve System and thus subject to the Fed's rules and regulations.

The problems of an inelastic currency and of bank supervision, however, were hardly new ones. The commercial banks themselves had done much to solve the currency question, although their solution—issuance of clearinghouse certificates in times of financial crisis—lacked legal authority before adoption of the Aldrich-Vreeland Act. Once the Fed was operational, though, commercial banks lost this remedy. The rapid growth of financial intermediation, particularly beginning in the 1880s, simply exacerbated an almost impossible regulatory problem. State and federal banking systems were locked in competition for member banks and for customers. The battle for customers squeezed bank margins and reduced interest rate differentials for an increasingly mobile and better-informed clientele. The battle for member banks was fought by easing capital and reserve requirements and lending restrictions. The price was the financial soundness of the banks on the margin. At the same time banks faced growing competition for customers from other financial intermediaries, including trust companies, mortgage banks, insurance companies, the stock market, and, after 1910, the federal government through the U.S. Postal Savings System. These competitive pressures drove the financial system toward the lowest common denominator and ultimately to the shake-out and survival of the fittest (or the most fortunate) in the 1920s and 1930s.

Bibliography

Baskin, J. "The Development of Corporate Financial Markets in Britain and the United States, 1600–1914: Overcoming Assymetric Information." *Business History Review* 62 (1988): 199–237.

Binder, John J., and Anthony T. Brown. "Bank Rates of Return and Entry Restrictions, 1869–1914." *Journal of Economic History* 51 (1991): 47–66.

Bodenhorn, Howard, and Hugh Rockoff. "Regional Interest Rates in Antebellum America." In *Strategic Factors in Nineteenth Century American Economic History*, ed. Claudia Goldin and Hugh Rockoff. Chicago: University of Chicago Press, 1992: 159–87.

Breckenridge, R. M. "Discount Rates in the United States." *Political Science Quarterly* 13 (1898): 119–42.

Calomiris, Charles. "Price and Exchange Rate Determination during the Greenback Suspension." *Oxford Economic Papers* 40 (1988): 719–50.

———. "Greenback Resumption and Silver Risk: The Economics and Politics of Monetary Regime Change in the United States, 1862–1900." University of Illinois Working Paper, July 1992.

Carosso, Vincent J. *Investment Banking in America.* Cambridge: Harvard University Press, 1970.

Davis, Lance E. "Capital Immobilities and Finance Capitalism: A Study of Economic Evolution in the United States, 1820–1920." *Explorations in Entrepreneurial History* 1 (1963): 88–105.

———. "The Investment Market, 1870–1914: The Evolution of a National Market." *Journal of Economic History* 25 (1965): 355–93.

Eichengreen, Barry. "Mortgage Interest Rates in the Populist Era." *American Economic Review* 74 (1984): 995-1015.

Friedman, Milton, and Anna Schwartz. *A Monetary History of the United States, 1867–1960.* Princeton: Princeton University Press, 1963.

Gorton, Gary. "Clearing Houses and the Origin of Central Banking in the U.S." *Journal of Economic History* 45 (1985): 277–84.

Hammond, Bray. *Sovereignty and an Empty Purse: Banks and Politics in the Civil War.* Princeton: Princeton University Press, 1970.

James, John A. "Banking Market Structure, Risk, and the Pattern of Local Interest Rates in the United States, 1893–1911." *Review of Economics and Statistics* 58 (1976): 453–62.

———. "The Development of the National Money Market, 1893–1911." *Journal of Economic History* 36 (1976): 878–97.

———. *Money and Capital Markets in Postbellum America.* Princeton: Princeton University Press, 1978.

Kindleberger, Charles P. *Manias, Panics and Crashes: A History of Financial Crises.* New York: Basic Books, 1978.

Lamoreaux, Naomi. "Bank Mergers in Late Nineteenth-Century New England: The Contingent Nature of Structural Change." *Journal of Economic History* 51 (1991): 537–58.

Mitchell, Wesley C. *Gold, Prices, and Wage under the Greenback Standard.* Berkeley: University of California Press, 1908.

Neal, Larry. "Trust Companies and Financial Innovation." *Business History Review* 45 (1971): 35–51.

Odell, Kerry A. "The Integration of Regional and Interregional Capital Markets: Evidence from the Pacific Coast States, 1883–1913." *Journal of Economic History* 49 (1989): 297–310.

Ransom, Roger, and Richard Sutch. "Tontine Insurance and the Armstrong Investigation: A Case of Stifled Innovation, 1868–1905." *Journal of Economic History* 47 (1987): 379–90.

Rockoff, Hugh. "Regional Interest Rates and Bank Failures." *Explorations in Economic History* 14 (1977): 90–95.

Schweikart, Larry. *Banking in the American South from the Age of Jackson to Reconstruction.* Baton Rouge: LSU Press, 1988.

Smiley, Gene. "Interest Rate Movements in the United States, 1888–1913." *Journal of Economic History* 35 (1975): 591–620.

Snowden, Kenneth. "Mortgage Rates and American Capital Market Development in the Late Nineteenth Century." *Journal of Economic History* 47 (1987): 671–92.

———. "American Stock Market Development and Performance, 1871–1929." *Explorations in Economic History* 24 (1987): 327–53.

———. "Historical Returns and Security Market Development, 1872–1925." *Explorations in Economic History* 27 (1990): 381–420.

Studenski, Paul, and Herman Krooss. *A Financial History of the United States.* New York: McGraw-Hill, 1952.

Sushka, Marie E., and W. Brian Barrett. "Banking Structure and the National Capital Market, 1869-1914." *Journal of Economic History* 44 (1984): 463–78.

Sylla, Richard. "Federal Policy, Banking Market Structure and Capital Mobilization in the United States, 1863–1913." *Journal of Economic History* 29 (1969): 657–86.

Weiner, Robert J. "Origins of Futures Trading: The Oil Exchanges in the Nineteenth Century." Brandeis University Working Paper 301 (1991).

White, Eugene. "The Membership Problem of the National Banking System." *Explorations in Economic History* 19 (1982): 110–27.

———. *Regulation and Reform of the American Banking System, 1900–1929.* Princeton: Princeton University Press, 1983.

Williamson, Jeffrey G. *Late Nineteenth Century American Development: A General Equilibrium History.* New York: Academic Press, 1974.

The market for labor in historical perspective

19

A wide variety of labor-related topics have already been addressed, including the "price" (in years) of an indentured servant, the transition from indentured labor to slavery, how slave work effort responded to the threat of punishment compared with the promise of reward, and the propensity to migrate in response to differential economic opportunities. This chapter, on the other hand, examines the general question of how—and how well—the market for labor functioned in America. Quantitative labor history has flowered in recent years, moving the field far beyond the traditional preoccupation of labor history with labor unions. The studies dealt with here document the evolution of labor markets and the subtle but important differences in the way in which historical labor markets operated from the way in which they operate today.

The growth of the labor force, defined as persons age ten and older (today age sixteen is taken as the age of potential entry into the labor force), mirrors the growth of population. Defined in this way, the labor force grew from 1.9 million in 1800 to 8.25 million in 1850 and to more than 29 million in 1900 (Table 19.1). As population growth slowed in the twentieth century, so, too, has the growth of the labor force. Behind these aggregate statistics, there are some important trends.

First, until the Civil War ended slavery in the United States, a large but declining fraction of the labor force was enslaved. Whereas in 1800, 28 percent of the labor force was slave, by 1860 the proportion of slaves in the labor force had slipped to 21 percent. Labor force participation among slaves was probably close to 100 percent. They had no choice whether or not to work. Indeed, the evidence in Chapter 12 suggests that they were a part of the labor force well before age ten. After emancipation, however, labor force

TABLE 19.1

The Labor Force 1800–1990

	LABOR FORCE (Age 10 and older)			EMPLOYMENT (Persons with occupation [including unpaid family members] age 10 and over)											
							Manufacturing					Transport			Services
Year	Total	Free	Slave	Agri-culture	Fishing	Mining	Con-struction	TOTAL MFG.	Cotton Textiles	Iron & Steel	Trade	Ocean Shipping	Railroads	Teachers	Domestics
1800	1,900	1,370	530	1,400	5	10			1	1		40		5	40
1810	2,330	1,590	740	1,950	6	11		75	10	5		60		12	70
1820	3,135	2,185	950	2,470	14	13			12	5		50		20	110
1830	4,200	3,020	1,180	2,965	15	22			55	20		70		30	160
1840	5,660	4,180	1,480	3,570	24	32	290	500	72	24	350	95	7	45	240
1850	8,250	6,280	1,970	4,520	30	102	410	1,200	92	35	530	135	20	80	350
1860	11,110	8,770	2,340	5,880	31	176	520	1,530	122	43	890	145	80	115	600
1870	12,930			6,790	28	180	780	2,470	135	78	1,310	135	160	170	1,000
1880	17,390			8,920	41	280	900	3,290	175	130	1,930	125	415	230	1,130
1890	23,320			9,960	60	440	1,510	4,390	222	149	2,960	120	750	350	1,580
1900	29,070			11,680	69	637	1,665	5,895	303	222	3,970	105	1,040	436	1,800
1910	37,480			11,770	68	1,068	1,949	8,332	370	306	5,320	150	1,855	595	2,090
1920	41,610			10,790	53	1,180	1,233	11,190	450	460	5,845	205	2,236	752	1,660
1930	48,830			10,560	73	1,009	1,988	9,884	372	375	8,122	160	1,659	1,044	2,270
1940	56,290			9,575	60	925	1,876	11,309	400	485	9,328	150	1,160	1,086	2,300
1950	65,470			7,870	77	901	3,029	15,648	350	550	12,152	130	1,373	1,270	1,995
1960	74,060			5,970	45	709	3,640	17,145	300	530	14,051	135	883	1,850	2,489
1970				3,463		516	4,818	20,746			15,008			6,126	1,782
1980				3,364		979	6,215	21,942			20,191			7,654	1,257
1990				3,186		730	7,696	21,184			24,269			8,637	1,023

Sources: Stanley Lebergott, *Manpower in Economic Growth* (New York: McGraw-Hill, 1964): 510. Data for 1970–1990 from various issues of U.S. Bureau of the Census *U.S. Statistical Abstract* (Washington, D.C.: Government Printing Office).

participation rates among African-Americans became more like those for the white population, except that black women, especially black married women, were much more likely to be in the labor force than their white counterparts.[1]

Second, in the nineteenth century at least, men entered the labor force early and worked until death. Women, on the other hand, had much lower labor force participation rates, being occupied instead with household chores and child rearing. In particular, women tended to exit the labor force at marriage. This has been the greatest change in recent times. Today not only are a majority of married women in the labor force, but they are much more likely to remain in the labor force through child bearing and child rearing.[2] Indeed, the latest data for 1991 show a labor force participation rate of 59.9 percent among married women with children under age six, compared with only 18.8 percent thirty years ago.

Third, over time workers have spent progressively fewer years in the labor force. This has been the result of two separate and distinct phenomena. Increased emphasis on education, both as a consumption good and as an investment, has delayed entry into the labor force, especially since World War II. Higher incomes (with associated savings), the development of new financial instruments (retirement annuities and insurance), and the passage of the Social Security Act (in 1935), on the other hand, have made it easier to retire from the labor force rather than to exit through death.

Employment—those persons in the labor force with occupations—was dominated by agriculture throughout the nineteenth century, although industrial employment was growing much more rapidly, especially during the early phase of industrialization before the Civil War. The number of persons employed in farming peaked in 1910, and industrial employment surpassed agricultural employment during World War I. In recent decades, though, industrial employment has been essentially constant. By 1910 service sector employment, in a hodgepodge of activities, was approximately equal to manufacturing employment. The service sector has since surpassed industry as the leading sector in terms of employment.

The Agricultural Labor Market

Most slaves worked in agriculture, but they were not the only agricultural workers who were not free to sell their labor to the highest bidder. Members of the farm family, particularly older sons, "were bound to the entrepreneur by ties of custom, law, fear and affection."[3] Their father—the farmer—was

[1] Goldin (1990).
[2] Ibid.
[3] Parker (1972), 395.

not above holding out the promise of a future inheritance to secure labor from family members at less than the current market wage rate. To the extent that this strategy was successful, marginal farms remained profitable. But resources that should have been allocated elsewhere remained in agriculture, reducing potential output while the artificially low price of family labor did little to encourage its efficient and productive use on the farm. This may have been a factor retarding farm productivity growth before the Civil War.

The relative decline of agricultural employment during the early nineteenth century, according to Paul David, was the most important single source of growth in per capita income (see Chapter 1). However, there now seem good reasons to question the existing estimates of the size of the early agricultural labor force. The estimates in Table 19.1 depend critically upon distributing workers described as "laborers" among agriculture, manufacturing, and transportation. The procedure used by Stanley Lebergott was to allocate laborers between agriculture and other activities during the first half of the nineteenth century on the basis of the ratio of "farm laborers" to "laborers" at the 1860 census since this was the first census to distinguish between these different kinds of laborers. Such a procedure seems to be eminently reasonable, but analysis of the 1860 census data by Thomas Weiss reveals that many of those whom the census described as "laborers" lived in rural areas, far removed from sources of employment other than agriculture. Presumably, therefore, many of them must have worked in agriculture at least part-time. Many of them even lived on farms. Consequently, it seems very likely that many of them were farm laborers.

Weiss's adjustments in the size of the agricultural labor force—decreasing it by between 15 and 20 percent before 1820 and by 5 to 10 percent after the Civil War, while increasing the size of the agricultural labor force by between 5 and 9 percent between 1840 and 1860—have a dramatic impact upon estimates of the pattern and timing of productivity growth in the agricultural sector by lowering the denominator in the earlier period and raising it in later periods. These adjustments reduce the rate of agricultural productivity growth (and overall economic growth) before the Civil War and increase the rate of growth thereafter. They resolve a puzzle implicit in Lebergott's original estimates that implied that productivity grew marginally faster before the war than afterward. Instead the revised estimates imply rates of labor productivity after the war that were three or four times higher than those before the war. This pattern is also more consistent with data on wage rates.

Relatively little is known about the *extent* of the wage labor market in agriculture at the start of the nineteenth century. Entries in farm account books suggest that farmers frequently exchanged labor services and kept a rough accounting of these trades even though money wages were probably not paid. Rather, reciprocal goods or services, such as crops, use of workstock, or the services of a bull, would be exchanged. Indeed, many historians argue that there was no market mentality in much of rural America until sometime around the middle of the nineteenth century. Instead they talk of a "moral economy" in which exchanges were governed by "use" or "need" rather than the dictates of supply and demand.

Economists, however, tend to be skeptical about the alleged absence of markets. Certainly, the evidence clearly shows that there was a formal market for wage labor. There existed a pool of landless people who had no alternative but to offer themselves for hire, and even those with land sometimes hired out. Rather than there being one market for agricultural labor, though, it has been argued that there were at least two separate agricultural labor markets. One market was for casual day laborers; the other for longer-term workers hired by the month.[4] The larger market was for day labor, although the total quantity of labor supplied by monthly contract laborers (whose contracts averaged about five months) far exceeded that of day laborers.

Few workers switched between these markets despite a substantial wage premium paid to day workers. Day wages in Massachusetts, for example, were about 80 to 90 percent higher than the implicit daily wage paid to monthly contract workers. About the time of the Revolution an agricultural day laborer earned 39 cents per day in nonharvest work and could earn as much as 48 cents per day at harvesttime. A monthly worker during the same period, however, earned only the equivalent of 21 cents per day. Nominal wages rose in the nineteenth century, but the ratio remained essentially unchanged. In the 1850s Massachusetts farm day laborers earned 87 cents per day, and $1.15 at harvesttime, while workers hired by the month earned an average of only 45 cents per day.

One explanation for the significant wage differential between day and monthly contract workers is that the highly seasonal demand for agricultural labor—concentrated especially around harvesttime—inevitably bid up spot rates (the wage paid to day laborers) in local markets where the labor supply was relatively inelastic. Thus an unexpectedly bountiful harvest might lead to day harvest labor's receiving a considerable wage premium over the daily wage of monthly workers. Indeed, the harvest premium for day workers averaged about 30 percent. Part of the differential wage between day and monthly workers also represented compensation for unemployment risk, which fell disproportionately on the day labor force.

Moreover, the two groups received fundamentally different total compensation packages. While day laborers might receive a midday meal and dinner (especially during harvest), monthly labor typically boarded with the farm family (Table 19.2). In addition, contract labor also probably received additional, oftentimes undocumented compensation, such as laundry and

[4] Rothenberg (1992).

TABLE 19.2

Wage Rates for Farm Work, 1866–1909

	Monthly (with room and board)	Monthly (room only)	Daily (with room and board)	Daily (no room or board)
1866	$10.00	$15.50	$0.65	$0.90
1869	10.00	15.50	0.65	0.85
1874–75	11.00	17.00	0.70	0.95
1877	11.00	17.00	0.60	0.85
1879–80	11.50	17.50	0.65	0.90
1880–81	12.50	18.50	0.65	0.90
1881–82	13.00	19.00	0.70	0.95
1884–85	13.00	19.00	0.70	0.95
1887–88	13.50	19.50	0.70	1.00
1889–90	13.50	19.50	0.70	0.95
1891–92	13.50	20.00	0.75	1.00
1893	14.00	20.00	0.70	0.90
1894	12.50	18.50	0.65	0.85
1895	12.50	18.50	0.65	0.85
1898	13.50	19.00	0.70	0.95
1899	14.00	20.00	0.75	1.00
1902	15.50	22.00	0.85	1.10
1906	18.50	26.00	1.05	1.30
1909	22.00	28.00	1.00	1.25

Source: U.S. Bureau of the Census, *Historical Statistics of the United States* (Washington, D.C.: Government Printing Office, 1975): Series K174–83.

the mending of clothes, or other "perks," such as use of a horse to visit friends. A complete accounting for such perks and benefits can do much to close any nominal wage gap between day and monthly contract labor and between rural-agricultural workers and urban-industrial workers. Indeed, during the 1920s perks were valued at about 60 percent of the agricultural wage and closed about half of the nominal wage gap between agriculture and manufacturing.[5]

This dual agricultural labor market differed fundamentally from the modern primary and secondary labor markets. In the labor market now the better jobs tend to be held by the longer-term workers (the primary market) while the short-term workers—the casual day laborers—are often less desirable for one reason or another and make up the secondary market. By contrast, in the early nineteenth century at least, day agricultural laborers were

[5] Alston and Hatton (1991).

typically young (in their mid–twenties) and single with roots in the local community. They were the upwardly mobile, saving perhaps for marriage and farms of their own. On the other hand, the monthly farm workers were typically much older (late thirties or early forties), often married, and geographically mobile. They may have been individuals who had failed for whatever reason to buy farms of their own or who had lost their farms. Certainly such workers, especially if they "lived in," could be closely monitored. Although the two groups occupied the same position on the agricultural ladder (see Chapter 15), the day workers may have been on their way up the ladder to some form of tenancy and eventually perhaps to ownership, while the monthly workers were locked into the wage labor system.

Reliance upon wage labor in agriculture varied regionally and temporally, reflecting changes in family structure, farm size, and crop mix as well as other institutional changes. These differences also show up in local and regional wage differentials (Table 19.3) that may only have been partially offset by differences in the cost of living. Although labor was mobile and the

TABLE 19.3

Monthly Farm Wages with Board, 1818–1860

	1818	1826	1830	1850	1860
New England					
Maine	$12.43	$12.43	$12.43	$13.12	$14.34
New Hampshire	10.16	10.16	11.66	12.12	14.34
Vermont	10.00	10.00	10.00	13.00	14.14
Massachusetts	13.50	13.50	12.00	13.55	15.34
Rhode Island	11.93	11.93	11.93	13.52	16.04
Connecticut	13.11	11.61	11.61	12.72	15.11
Middle Atlantic					
New York	10.00	8.00	8.00	11.50	13.19
New Jersey	8.50	8.50	8.50	10.18	11.91
Pennsylvania	11.00	9.00	9.50	10.82	12.24
North-Central					
Ohio	9.00	9.00	9.00	11.10	13.11
Indiana	9.00	9.00	9.00	10.50	13.71
Illinois	12.00	10.00	10.00	12.55	13.72
Michigan				12.00	15.27
Wisconsin				12.69	13.69
Minnesota				17.00	14.10
Iowa				11.80	13.18

Source: Stanley Lebergott, *Manpower in Economic Growth* (New York: McGraw-Hill, 1964): 539, Table A-23.

evidence is consistent with labor moving in response to real wage differentials, there is little evidence that gaps were totally eliminated through internal migration. Indeed, as we shall see, there is considerable evidence to suggest that labor markets in the nineteenth century and even into the early twentieth century were regionally segregated, especially between North and South.

The census estimated that there were about eight hundred thousand farm laborers in 1860 nationwide (not counting slaves). New England farms were most reliant upon hired labor, with about one farm laborer in the Northeast for every two farms. Dependence upon hired labor in the Northeast reflects lower farm family fertility and the switch to more labor-intensive crops, such as dairy products and market gardens, where northeastern farmers still enjoyed a comparative advantage, thanks to proximity to a rapidly growing urban-industrial population. In the Midwest, on the other hand, there were only about two laborers to every five farms.

In the South, free white labor eschewed the occupation of farm laborer, especially in the cotton-growing areas, where it was closely identified with African-Americans, whether slave or free. Emancipation, as might be expected, had an immediate and dramatic impact upon the southern agricultural labor market. Lacking both land and capital, ex-slaves who stayed in agriculture were forced to become wage laborers in the short run. According to data assembled by Gavin Wright, in the South Atlantic states where crop mix was more varied and where farms and plantations were subdivided more slowly, the number of wage laborers per farm jumped from 0.35 in 1860 to 2.17 in 1870 (Figure 19.1). In the South-Central states, where cotton was more prevalent and sharecropping was more quickly adopted, laborers per farm increased from 0.15 in 1860 to 1.10 in 1870. Thereafter, as southern farm owners adjusted the scale of farming to southern labor market conditions, switching to smaller and smaller operating units farmed by family labor almost everywhere except Texas, the number of wage laborers per farm declined. Outside the South the number of wage laborers per farm also grew after 1860, but there it did not peak until 1910. This paralleled modest increases in average farm size in the Midwest, reduced reliance upon family members as farm fertility declined, and the switch to more labor-intensive crops, such as vegetables and dairy, in the East. However, wage labor returned to the South during the 1930s as landlords consolidated tenant farms and sharecropper lots into larger operating units, apparently so that southern landowners rather than the tenant or cropper would receive payments under the Agricultural Adjustment Act. The incentives were considerable and increased over time. On good cotton land the expected return to the landlord from displacing a sharecropper was $1.75 per acre in 1934 and $16.78 per acre by 1939. The returns from displacing share tenants were even higher: $2.62 per acre in 1934 and $19.16 in 1939. Not surprisingly,

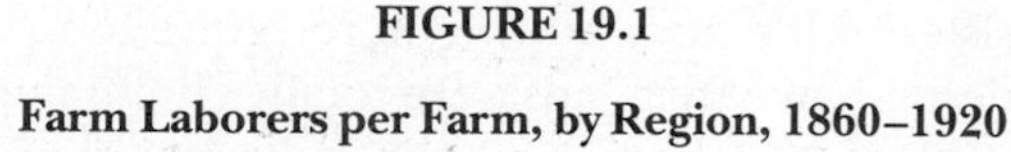

FIGURE 19.1

Farm Laborers per Farm, by Region, 1860–1920

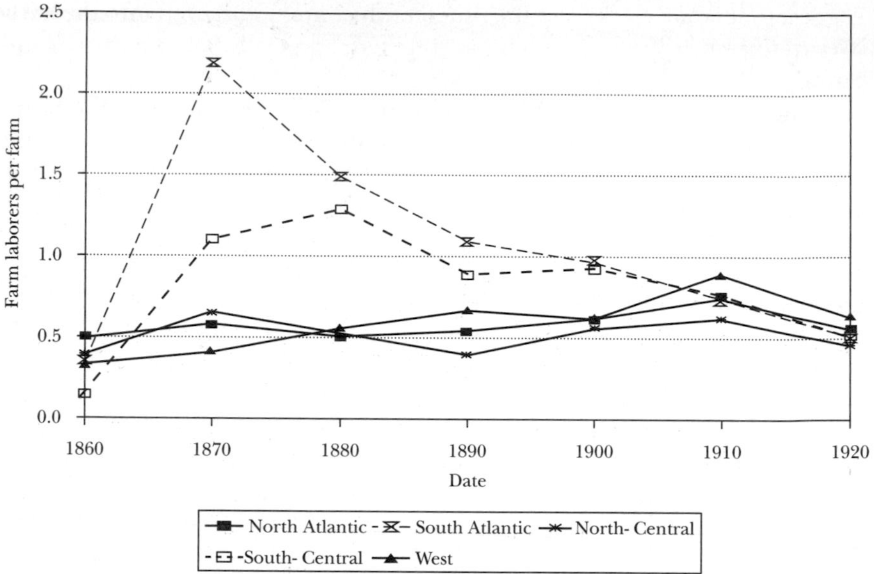

Source: Data from Gavin Wright, "American Agriculture and the Labor Market: What Happened to Proletarianization," *Agricultural History* 62 (1988): 194: Table 6.

even higher: $2.62 per acre in 1934 and $19.16 in 1939. Not surprisingly, whereas tenants had cropped over 35 percent of delta land in 1930, they accounted for only 8 percent of Mississippi delta land cropped in 1940, while land farmed with wage labor increased from 18 percent to 42 percent between 1930 and 1940.[6]

The Industrial Labor Market

At the start of the nineteenth century a significant group worked outside agriculture as craftsmen: blacksmiths, who were the jacks-of-all-trade in the local economy, chandlers, boot and shoemakers, coopers, and lumber and flour millers. They formed the nucleus of an industrial labor force although many of them probably still worked part-time in agriculture. For example, midwestern meat-packers before the Civil War packed only during the late

[6] Whatley (1983).

fall and winter months, working in agriculture during the spring and summer. Industrial employment, like agricultural work, was seasonal. Demand in localized markets may not have been sufficient to sustain year-round production. Production was often at the mercy of the seasons. Moreover, high harvest day wages compared favorably with those offered by manufacturers.

WOMEN IN INDUSTRY

Alexander Hamilton had championed early manufacturing as the complement to agriculture, providing employment to women and children who could not find as productive an employment on the farm or in the home. The New England textile mills were especially quick to take advantage of the growing pool of underemployed single farm women in the region. Around 1815, for example, a woman working in Massachusetts agriculture could earn only about 29 percent of the average male wage, whereas in manufacturing the differential was somewhat less with women earning as much as 30 to 37 percent of the average male wage. By 1832 women were earning about 40 to 45 percent of the prevailing male wage in industry; by 1850 women received perhaps half the male wage by 1850 (Figure 19.2). Subsequent gains in the relative wages of women have come much more slowly. Not until the 1920s did the ratio of female to male wages exceed 60 percent; it is still only about 70 percent today.[7]

This relative pay differential between manufacturing and agriculture drew thousands of farmers' daughters into the Massachusetts textile industry and other New England industries, where they played an important role in early industrialization. To induce farmers to allow their daughters to enter industrial employment, the mills took great pains to assuage parental fears over the moral welfare of their unmarried daughters. Wages were often paid directly to the farmer, or a regularized system of remittances was set up, and the women were required to live in closely supervised dormitories or lodging houses, working long hours (averaging eleven and one-half hours a day around 1830), six days a week, with Sunday school attendance expected on Sundays. This regimen left no time, energy, or means for socializing much beyond their (female) co-workers.

With the new employment opportunities, female labor force participation in the industrial economy rose from essentially zero in 1810 to about 10 percent by 1832 among women aged ten to twenty-nine in the less industrial northeastern states, such as Connecticut and New Hampshire. In Massachusetts and Rhode Island the labor force participation rate of women grew to 25 percent or more by 1832. The rapid growth of the textile industry, however, strained the supply of Yankee farm girls at a time when New England agriculture was becoming increasingly labor-intensive and

[7] Goldin and Sokoloff (1982); Goldin (1990).

FIGURE 19.2

Ratio of Female to Male Earnings, 1815–1987

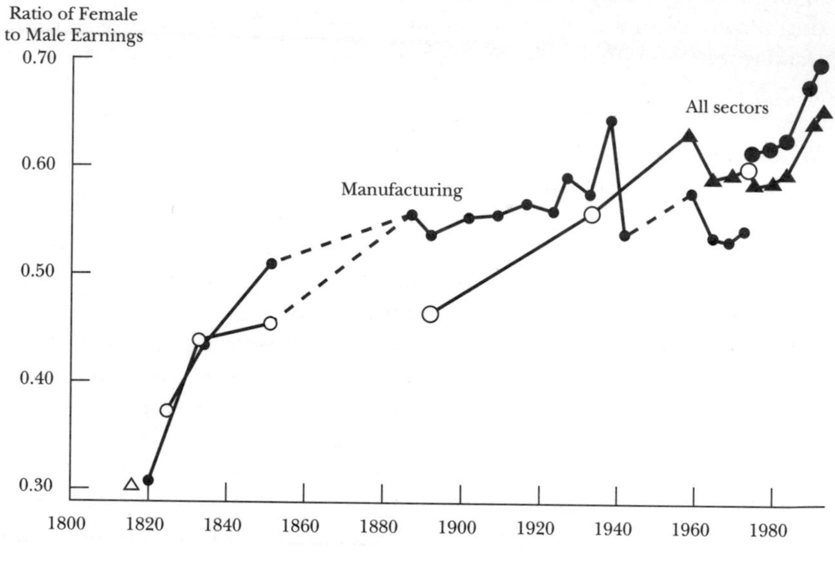

△ Agriculture
● Manufacturing, New England to 1850 and U.S. after 1850
○ Manufacturing, Middle Atlantic
○ Weighted average of six sectors
▲ Current Population Survey, median year-round
● Current Population Survey, median weekly

Source: Claudia Goldin, *Understanding the Gender Gap* (New York: Oxford University Press, 1990): 62.

other, possibly more attractive, employment opportunities were opening up. Between 1835 and 1847, for example, the number of mills more than doubled, and the number of spindles and looms increased even further. To close this gap between labor demand and their traditional labor supply, the mills turned increasingly to a new source of labor—recently arrived Irish immigrants—in the late 1840s.

The changeover was remarkably rapid. Before about 1845 (when the flood of Irish began reaching American shores), the mill weaving rooms had been more than 95 percent Yankee. By 1850 they were only about 60 percent Yankee, and by 1855 they were more than 60 percent Irish. This switch to immigrant labor wrought fundamental changes in how the labor market functioned. Yankee farm girls always had the option to "exit"—i.e., quit—

whether to return to the family farm or to move on to some other job if working conditions became too onerous. The Irish, however, had few alternative opportunities, and increased emphasis was placed upon "voice"—that is to say, organized labor demanding change rather than seeking alternatives. Certainly there is evidence that working conditions did indeed change as the mills began using Irish labor. The intensity of labor increased as millowners increased the number of looms each mill hand tended from two—the norm for Yankee farm girls—to three just prior to the "exit" of the Yankee farm girls and then to four looms in 1857.[8] Moreover, the same period marks the onset of a secular decline in real wages in the industry.

Although most of the women who took jobs in manufacturing in the early nineteenth century were single, data assembled by Claudia Goldin suggest that female labor force participation rates for both single and married women probably fell sometime after mid-century, reaching a nadir about the 1890s. Since then participation rates have risen, particularly among married women. In 1890 less than 3 percent of white married women were in the labor force, compared with more than 20 percent participation among nonwhite married women and more than a third among widowed or divorced women. By 1980 more than half of the married white women were in the labor force, and labor force participation rates among nonwhite and among widowed women exceeded 60 percent (Figure 19.3).

Two reasons have been suggested for the decline in female labor force participation in the late nineteenth century. One explanation blames the change on changed perceptions of the status of female workers. Prior to the influx of immigrant labor, millwork was seen as highly desirable. However, the extreme poverty of immigrant women forever tainted female workers so that only those forced by economic circumstances to participate in the labor force did so.[9] The other, more likely explanation is that the change reflected a shift in public opinion about the desirability of women's working induced by periodic bouts of mass industrial unemployment first during the 1870s and again in the 1890s. This, it is claimed, caused many to question women's right to work although it is doubtful that many men were actually displaced from work by women.[10]

Competition between men and women for jobs is a fairly recent phenomenon. Occupations in the nineteenth and even into the twentieth century were rigidly segregated by gender. There was men's work, there was women's work, and rarely did the twain meet (Table 19.4). For the most part these distinctions were broken down only slowly, though clerical work—particularly the job of secretary—changed quickly from a male to a female job in the early twentieth century with the adoption of the typewriter. The

[8] Lazonick and Brush (1985).
[9] Lerner (1979).
[10] Abbott (1906).

FIGURE 19.3

Labor Force Participation Rates by Cohort and Race for Married Women, 1890–1980, for Cohorts Born 1866–1965

PANEL A

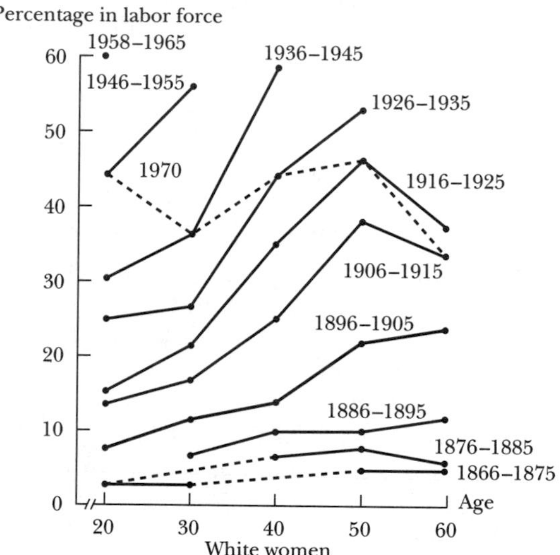

PANEL B

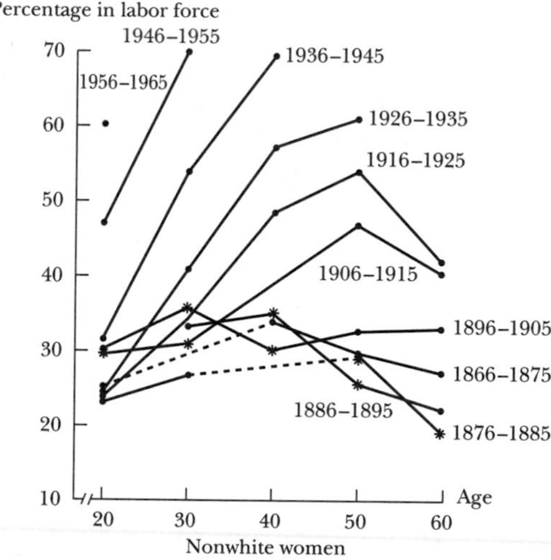

Note: Observations are the midpoints of five age-groups: 15–24, 25–34, 35–44, 45–54, and 55–64. Dashed lines denote missing data. Asterisks for nonwhite cohorts denote depression period, 1930 to 1940. Dotted line is the 1970 cross section.

Source: Claudia Goldin, *Understanding the Gender Gap* (New York: Oxford University Press, 1990): 22–23.

TABLE 19.4

Male- and Female-Intensive Industries, 1890

Male-Intensive Industry		Female-Intensive Industry	
Industry	Percent Male	Industry	Percent Female
Agricultural implements	98	Boots and shoes (factory)	29
Blacksmithing	100	Boxes	65
Boots and shoes (custom)	98	Carpets	45
Brick and tile	94	Clothing (men's)	49
Carpentering	100	Clothing (women's)	63
Carriages and wagons	99	Confectionary	39
Cooperage	98	Corsets	81
Flour milling	99	Cotton goods	52
Foundry and machine shops	99	Dressmaking	97
Furniture (factory)	95	Fruit and vegetable canning	48
Iron and steel	99	Gloves and mittens	59
Leather	98	Hats and caps	34
Liquor (malt)	98	Hosiery and knit goods	67
Lumber milling	98	Men's accessories	74
Painting and wallpapering	100	Millinery and lace	73
Plumbing	98	Millinery (custom)	98
Saddlery and harness	95	Shirts	79
Shipbuilding	100	Silk	57
Slaughtering/Meat-Packing	96	Woolen goods	38
Tin and copperware	94	Worsted goods	46
"Mixed" Industry		"Mixed" Industry	
Clothing (men's custom)	77	Paper	23
Printing (book and job)	83	Printing (newspaper)	11
Tobacco	73		

Source: Adapted from Claudia Goldin, *Understanding the Gender Gap* (New York: Oxford University Press, 1990): Table 3.4.

biggest change, however, came when "Rosie the Riveter," who appeared on World War II posters, convincingly demonstrated to even the most skeptical employers the feasibility of replacing men with women. Even so, many jobs today remain essentially single-sex occupations.

WAGE TRENDS

Most studies of wage trends before the Civil War are based upon extant business records and have focused upon specific locations and industries. Examples include a description and analysis of the wages paid to skilled and unskilled labor (represented by carpenters and common laborers) by the Erie Canal between 1828 and 1881 or wages in Philadelphia and the surrounding area after the Revolution.[11] More recently Robert Margo and Georgia Villaflor have published estimates covering all regions of the country from 1820 to 1856 for a variety of occupations, both skilled and unskilled. Their data are drawn from the records of army quartermasters who engaged civilian employees for specific tasks at the forts scattered around the country. Though some were in East Coast urban areas, most were closer to the frontier. The data include when and where each worker was hired (virtually all were men), receipt of perks (such as army rations), occupation, and legal status (some slaves were hired in the South). Although their results accord with expectations about how the labor market worked—for example, they find that wages were systematically higher in urban areas and on the frontier than in rural areas, and skilled workers were paid more than the unskilled—their estimates provide the widest coverage of wage trends for so early a period. Nominal wage rates grew at from a low of 0.1 percent per year for laborers in the South Atlantic states to as much as 1.9 percent per year for clerks in the Midwest (Table 19.5). The army wage data also suggest that regional labor markets were incompletely integrated in the first half of the nineteenth century although migration did have an impact upon local wages.

More data are available from 1860 onward from which to chart the course of wages. These suggest that wages grew somewhat more rapidly after 1860 than before. For example, between 1860 and 1890 the annual rate of growth of money wages in manufacturing was between 1.3 and 1.4 percent per year (Figure 19.4).[12] The rate of growth of money wages accelerated fur-

TABLE 19.5

Average Annual Rate of Growth of Nominal Wages by Occupation and Region, 1820–1856

Occupation	Northeast	Midwest	South Atlantic	South–Central
Artisan	0.8	0.8	0.5	0.4
Clerks	1.5	1.9	0.9	1.6
Laborers	1.1	1.1	0.1	0.7

Source: Claudia Goldin and Robert Margo, "Wages, Prices, and Labor Markets before the Civil War," in *Strategic Factors in Nineteenth Century American Economic History,* ed. Claudia Goldin and Hugh Rockoff (Chicago: University of Chicago Press, 1992): Tables 2A.1, 2A.2, and 2A.3.

[11] Walter Smith and Donald Adams.
[12] Long (1960).

FIGURE 19.4

Daily Money and Real Wages in Manufacturing, Annually, 1860–1930

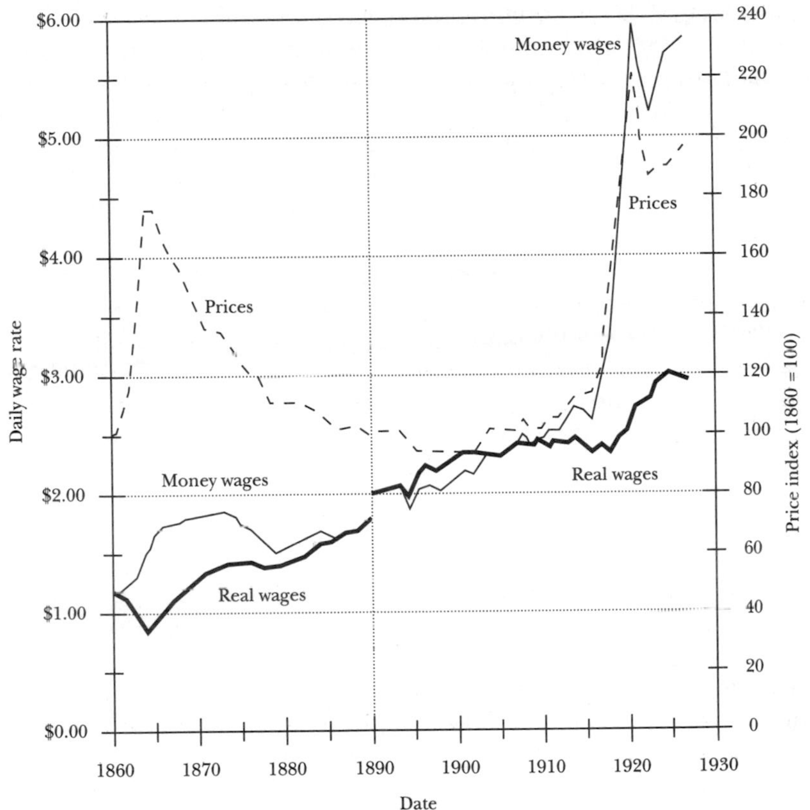

Sources: 1860–1890: Clarence D. Long, *Wages and Earnings in the United States,* 1860–1890 (Princeton: Princeton University Press, 1960): Table A-10. 1890–1926: Paul Douglas, *Real Wages in the United States, 1890–1926* (Boston: Houghton Mifflin, 1930), as reproduced in U.S. Bureau of the Census, *Historical Statistics of the United States* (Washington, D.C.: Government Printing Office, 1975): Series D766.

ther thereafter: between 1890 and 1926 wages approximately tripled—a growth rate of a little over 3 percent per year.[13]

A number of considerations complicate these comparisons of wage trends between regions, occupations, and over time. If we leave aside for the

[13] Douglas (1930).

moment issues of possible discrimination based upon race, ethnicity, sex, or marital status, a wide variety of factors impinge upon wage determination. Occupations may serve as a proxy for skill levels, but there is often little or no evidence about worker experience that is embodied in such factors as educational attainment, age, or number of years on the job. Indeed, age is particularly important in light of persistent evidence of a life cycle in earnings between job market entry and exit.

There is also abundant evidence that supply might be "thin" (that is, few persons have the necessary skills, aptitudes, and attitudes) in local labor markets and that demand might be "thick" (that is, employers could substitute factors and reorganize production, essentially shifting their demand for labor over some range). While we like to think of the wages being determined by the ebb and flow of labor supply and demand, the evidence points to considerable price rigidity in the labor market. Wages for specific occupations or tasks changed only infrequently. This was particularly true of the labor market before the Civil War. A specific wage rate might be quoted for years, suggesting that norms and customs played a role in setting wages. One consequence of this is that short-run labor market adjustment often took place through changes in employment rather than changes in wages, with workers switching between "low-wage" agriculture and "high-wage" industry depending upon the state of trade even if in the long run the wage was ultimately determined by productivity.[14] If so, then rising real wages during deflations benefited only those who remained employed at their customary wage.

A variation on this theme is the emergence of so-called efficiency wages, exemplified by Henry Ford's decision to institute the $5 day on his newly developed assembly line in 1914. This wage was above the prevailing market wage for unskilled labor. One interpretation for such a wage is that it was necessary to compensate workers for the drudgery and intensity of assembly line work. Efficiency wage explanations, on the other hand, rationalize the payment of wages above the worker's marginal product in terms of discouraging labor turnover because of high training costs, trying to ensure that the employer has the choice of workers from a large labor pool (a variation on adverse selection in the labor market), or moral hazard—that its purpose was to discourage shirking by increasing the worker's opportunity cost of being fired, thus economizing on supervision costs. These explanations, however, are found wanting in Ford's decision to pay an efficiency wage of $5 a day. Instead it has been suggested that Ford was willing to pay this wage as the price for peace.[15]

The intensification of work effort and falling real wages that accompa-

[14] Goldin and Margo (1992).

[15] Raff (1988).

nied the mass immigrations into this country during the nineteenth century—in particular, the Irish in the 1840s and 1850s and southern and eastern Europeans toward the end of the century—suggest that the "immigrant was an exploited unskilled laborer."[16] Certainly, labor groups felt threatened by immigrants and generally opposed uncontrolled immigration into this country while manufacturers' associations were in favor of continued immigration. One explanation for labor's opposition, of course, is simply that an increase in the supply of labor, other things equal, will drive down the equilibrium wage rate. However, a variety of other factors also help explain lower wages for immigrants. Immigrants often had lower human capital, as measured by such factors as literacy and ability to speak English. As a result, they might be expected to be less productive. Even after taking account of human capital factors, though, there is strong evidence that the Irish and those from southern and eastern Europe were paid about 10 percent less than the native-born (or immigrants from northern and western Europe, other than Ireland). This margin may represent discrimination against the immigrants, who were paid less than the value of their marginal products.

Throughout much of the nineteenth century, manufacturing wages were quoted by the "day" even if they were paid by the piece, with the "stint"—i.e., expected output—determining the daily norm. This method is problematic. Not only does the length of the day vary between winter and summer, but it varies between North and South. For example, at the winter solstice there are just over nine hours of daylight in Boston, compared with over ten hours in New Orleans, while at midsummer there are more than fifteen hours of daylight in Boston but only fourteen hours in New Orleans. A "day" was therefore a very flexible concept, and what constituted a day of work varied differentially between agriculture and manufacturing. Whereas in agriculture the hours of daylight tended to remain the determining factor in the length of the working day, manufacturing moved toward set hours, which may have differed between summer and winter but which were generally less than the hours of daylight.[17]

Unless workers suffered from a money illusion—that is to say, they considered only the number of dollars in their pay packet—their interest was not so much in the nominal wage as in the real wage, which is adjusted for differences in the cost of living.[18] This introduces myriad complexities. Consumption bundles certainly differed by region and perhaps between town and country (at least with respect to expenditure on rent). They also

[16] Handlin (1973): 195.

[17] Atack and Bateman (1992).

[18] There is, however, evidence of a ratchet that created strong labor resistance to reductions in nominal wages.

differed over time. In addition, prices show considerable regional variation. Moreover, as the transportation network improved and as industrial firms realized scale economies, urban prices fell relative to rural. As a result, there is no universally accepted cost of living deflator.[19] The choice of price index proves to be crucially important. Although most of the indexes move together, indicating some degree of market integration or subjection to much the same set of common influences, rates of change can differ markedly between indexes.[20] Moreover, considering the relative rigidity of nominal wages, fluctuations in prices generate most of the variation in the real wage over time and across space.[21]

SKILL PREMIUMS

Skilled workers received higher wages than unskilled workers. This premium reflects greater productivity and provides workers with a return to their increased investment in human capital—education and training. Among workers employed by army quartermasters, the skill premium was as high as 48 to 65 percent for a master craftsman over a journeyman's pay. Distinctions were also made among skilled workers so that masons, painters, and blacksmiths were paid 2 to 13 percent more than carpenters. Williamson and Lindert have argued that the skill differential, measured by the gap between skilled and unskilled wages, increased during industrialization (Figure 19.5). In 1830, for example, skilled workers earned 40 to 60 percent more than unskilled workers, but by 1850 they earned 60 to 80 percent more. This widening skill premium was a major factor underlying rising inequality in America since there were fewer skilled individuals than unskilled workers. Their argument is that the skill premium increased because of an increase in demand for skilled workers owing to the complementarity between capital goods (whose prices were falling) and skilled labor (whose wages were thus rising). Such complementarity has been documented repeatedly.[22]

This story, however, is at odds with the traditional argument that attributes the capital deepening of the American system to the scarcity of skilled labor and the substitution of embodied human skills in machine for operative skills. Certainly no broad secular trend in skill differences appears in the wage data from army forts. True, there were periods, such as 1838–40, when the differential increased quite sharply, but there were also periods, such as

[19] See, for example, Rothenberg (1979), Williamson and Lindert (1980), Margo and Villaflor (1987), Sokoloff and Villaflor (1992), and Goldin and Margo (1992).
[20] As demonstrated by Sokoloff and Villaflor (1992).
[21] Coehlo and Shepherd (1976).
[22] See, for example, Griliches and Mason (1972) for the modern economy and Smith (1963) for the nineteenth century.

FIGURE 19.5

Ratio of Wages for Skilled Workers to Those of Unskilled Workers, 1771–1890

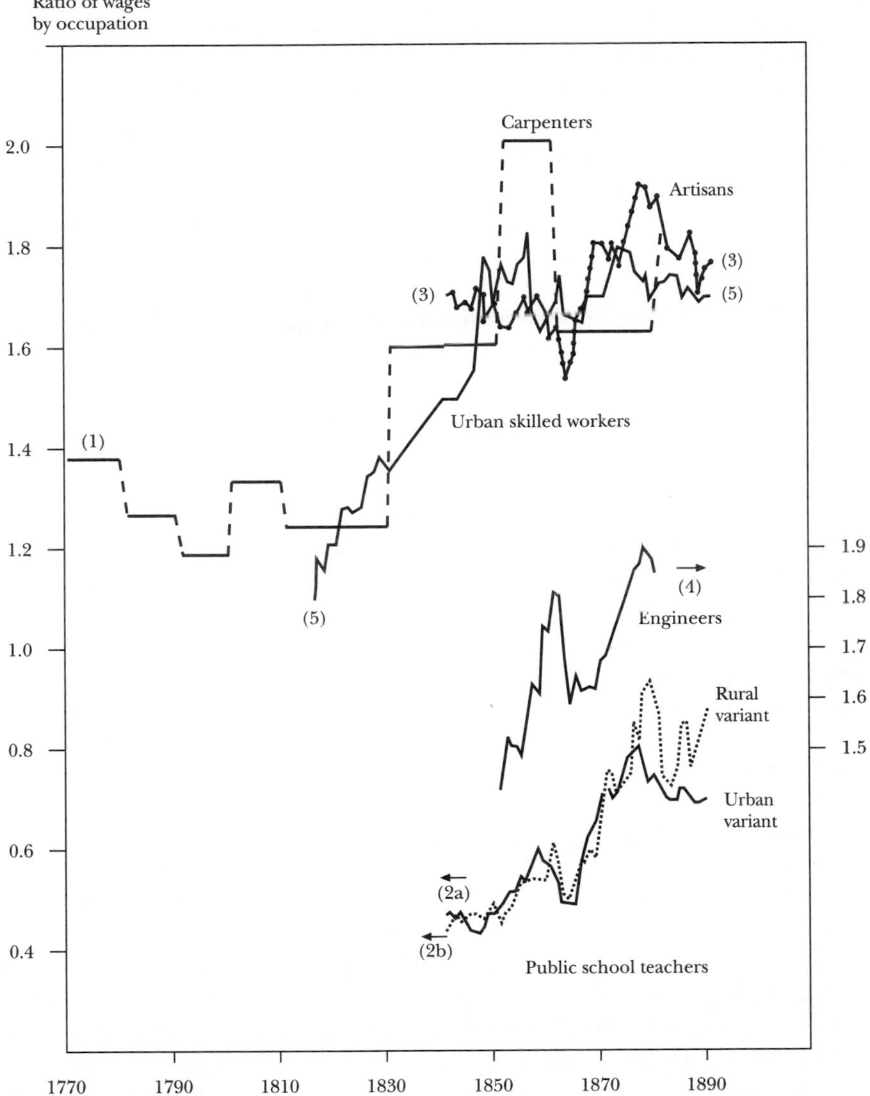

Source: Jeffrey G. Williamson and Peter Lindert, *American Inequality* (New York: Academic Press, 1980): 69.

the early 1850s, when the differential narrowed. This pattern fits a model where manufacturers held on to scarce skilled labor during economic downturns but competed with agriculture for unskilled labor during upswings in the business cycle.

CONDITIONS OF WORK

Wage rates describe only one aspect of the labor contract. Other conditions of work, such as the length of the working day, occupational safety, security of job tenure, and unemployment risk, lead to provision of side payments affecting the value of the overall wage package to compensate for these various workplace disamenities.[23] Thus, for example, if one assumes that the pay period implicitly describes the labor contract period, then day workers received somewhat higher pay per day than workers with equivalent skill levels, experience, and so on who were paid by the week. They in turn received a higher daily rate than workers paid by the month.

Many early manufactories provided little more than a rented workshop for workers as their place of business. In such establishments, working hours seem to have been flexible and workers were free to come and go as they chose, often working in frenzied bursts toward the end of the week to catch up lost output caused by absences earlier in the week. However, as production processes became more integrated and as fixed investment increased, firms increasingly moved toward fixed hours of work. Around 1830 the average working day in manufacturing was about eleven and a half hours, with somewhat longer hours in summer and shorter hours in winter. By 1860 the working day had fallen to between ten and a half and eleven hours, and by 1880 workers had achieved the ten-hour day—a rallying cry of labor since the 1830s.[24] Further cuts to eight-hours were made during World War I; the eight-hour day was adopted as the norm in the Fair Labor Standards Act of 1938.[25]

Long hours of work were frequently the cause of labor unrest, particularly after the Civil War. For the most part, however, shorter hours seem to have come about as a result of legislation rather than workplace collective bargaining. The reduction to ten hours a day, for example, coincided with adoption of laws limiting hours of work for women.[26] Given relatively rigid gender segregation by occupation and the need for various groups to cooperate to produce the final product, such laws had the effect of reducing hours of work for both men and women. Indeed, it is suggested that male-dominated trade unions championed these laws for precisely this reason, rather than as a part of an overall rent-seeking strategy to exclude low wage competition from women. Similarly, partial credit for the decline to eight

[23] See, for example, Williamson and Hatton (1991) and Fishback and Kantor (1991).
[24] Attack and Bateman (1992).
[25] Whaples (1988, 1990); Hunnicut (1988).
[26] Goldin (1988, 1990).

hours has to go to state and federal legislation during World War I, though increasingly tight labor markets and such factors as electrification of the workplace may have been much more important than changes in the law.[27]

Other work rules frequently accompanied the transition to fixed hours. Factory gates restricted the ability of workers to come and go as they chose. Attendance became mandatory; unexcused or excessive absences or tardiness were punished by fines or dismissal. Social interactions, such as talking, were restricted in the workplace. Employers put increasing emphasis upon supervision and monitoring to maintain discipline. It remains unclear to what extent these changes were prompted by a desire to intensify work effort and how much was due to the employment of an untrained and undisciplined work force unaccustomed to punctuality, precision, and cooperative work habits.

The custom of quoting wage rates by the day has led to the perception that the industrial labor market of the nineteenth century was dominated by short-term casual workers. Certainly there is evidence that labor market adjustments overwhelmingly took place through quantity, not price, adjustments. Nominal wages were sticky, resistant to downward pressure even during business recessions and periods of falling prices. One implication is that unemployment rates must have been quite volatile, and unemployment, common.[28] Data on California wage earners in the 1890s, however, suggest quite long-term job tenures among California workers, averaging about thirteen years. Fewer than 7 percent of workers had job tenures shorter than three years. Work might be interrupted by periods of unemployment, but workers did not "float" between employers.[29] Long job tenures also suggest the emergence of what labor economists call an "internal labor market," which is a hierarchical, bureaucratic system of internal job promotion. Certainly these, along with the personnel departments that administered them increasingly appeared about the turn of the century.[30]

How Many Labor Markets?

Despite the extraordinary American experience with internal migration and mass immigration, the evidence strongly suggests that there was no single market for labor in America in the nineteenth century. Rather labor markets were regionally segmented, with relatively free flow within regions and between Northeast and Midwest but little interchange between North and South. Although there is considerable evidence of long-run convergence in wages and earnings,[31] large wage and earning gaps remained in the late

[27] Whaples (1990).
[28] Goldin and Margo (1992); Sundstrom (1990).
[29] Carter and Savoca (1990).
[30] Jacoby (1985).
[31] Easterlin (1968); Lebergott (1964); Margo and Villaflor (1987).

nineteenth century between regions, between towns and the countryside, and between agricultural and industrial employment. There is evidence of wage gaps on the order of 10 to 20 percent between cities within two regions and a gap of 20–25 percent between midwestern wages and the East Coast, in favor of the Midwest (Table 19.6).[32] Moreover, between agriculture and manufacturing the wage gap may even have grown from about 29 percent in the antebellum North to 41 percent in the postbellum period, reaching 50 percent by the mid-1890s and peaking at about 65 percent in the 1930s. Even after adjustment for cost of living differences, disamenities, in-kind payments, and seasonal differences, the gap remains.[33]

TABLE 19.6

Relative Real Wage Levels, 1870–1898

	1870–74	1875–79	1880–84	1885–89	1890–94	1895–98
CITIES						
Northeast						
New York	100.0	100.0	100.0	100.0	100.0	100.0
Boston	92.2	89.8	88.0	91.3	92.8	93.7
Baltimore	84.6	91.6	88.5	91.1	91.9	92.3
Philadelphia	94.7	92.0	84.4	86.1	85.9	86.2
Pittsburgh	94.3	88.9	92.1	95.1	99.0	97.7
Midwest						
Cincinnati	120.8	117.7	106.5	102.1	101.1	95.6
Chicago	123.1	118.7	117.5	120.0	123.0	126.9
St. Louis	100.9	112.8	110.4	109.3	112.4	112.6
St. Paul	110.2	122.4	120.8	119.4	117.5	119.1
West						
San Francisco	135.6	136.0	118.5	119.4	114.3	114.7
South						
Richmond	85.6	87.9	81.2	81.0	81.7	80.6
New Orleans	97.2	102.4	95.5	98.2	100.1	100.3
REGIONS						
Northeast	100.0	100.0	100.0	100.0	100.0	100.0
Midwest	122.5	128.0	126.3	121.8	121.2	120.5
West	146.2	147.5	131.8	129.6	122.6	122.9
South	97.2	102.0	97.2	96.5	96.9	96.3

Source: Joshua Rosenbloom, "One Market or Many? Labor Market Integration in the Nineteenth-Century United States," *Journal of Economic History* 50 (1990): 95. Reprinted by permission of Cambridge University Press.

[32] Rosenbloom (1990).
[33] Williamson and Hatton (1991).

Rather than treat this gap simply as a disequilibrium distortion, Jeffrey Williamson and Timothy Hatton explain it in terms of sticky industrial wages, flexible farm wages, and urban unemployment. Their argument is that the industrial wage was sticky (that is, not determined by the instantaneous interaction of market supply and demand) as a result of institutional factors, such as unions. As a result, firms may have paid efficiency wages to their workers so that they might exert greater control over their work forces which feared the loss of such high-paying jobs, while giving employers a pool of labor from which to select their employees. These high manufacturing wages induced farm workers to migrate to the city in hopes of obtaining one of the high-paying industrial jobs, driving up the agricultural wage, while in the cities there was persistent unemployment among hopeful job seekers who were reluctant to return to the countryside. Certainly the evidence is consistent with this model. Unemployment seems to have been more common in cities than the countryside, and workers migrated from the countryside, to cities and towns in search of higher-paying jobs.

Perhaps the most dramatic evidence on labor market segmentation is provided for the South. Robert Higgs has characterized the operation of southern labor markets after the war as a struggle between the forces of competition and coercion. Efforts to restrict job opportunities for African-Americans through law or custom and exploit their labor by paying less than the value of their marginal product were increasingly challenged by the new job opportunities created by economic growth and development. As a result, labor gravitated to where its returns were highest, and those southerners with a taste for discrimination paid an increasingly high price.

Gavin Wright in *Old South, New South* paints a somewhat different picture. In his model, labor markets *within* the South are integrated (economically, if not racially) but separate from the rest of the country, and the South developed as a low-wage enclave in a high-wage country. The wage gap between North and South in 1866 (Figure 19.6) widened in *absolute* terms down to at least World War I despite declines in the cost of transportation and improvements in information flows over the period. At the same time, wages *within regions* between high-wage and low-wage states converged as factor price equalization requires.

The key question, of course, is, Why didn't factor price equalization work between the regions especially since it seems to have been working within each region? Migration is traditionally the dominant force in factor price equalization; labor migrates from low-wage areas to high-wage areas. Clearly this failed. But it did not fail because debt peonage and crop liens immobilized southern labor.[34] On the contrary, there was considerable migration within the South, but too few southern workers moved from South to North to close the gap. One explanation for the failure of South-North mi-

[34] See Chapter 14.

FIGURE 19.6

Farm Labor Wage Rates per Day without Board (Deflated by WPI) in Selected States, 1866–1942

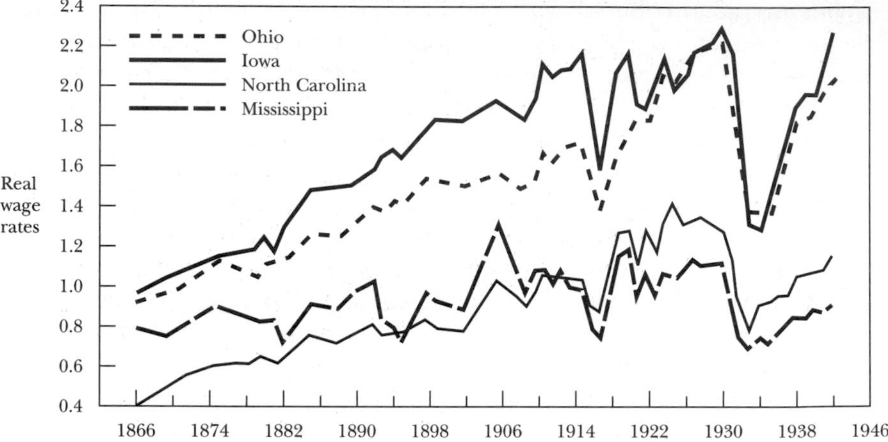

Sources: Gavin Wright, *Old South, New South* (New York: Basic Books, 1986): 66. Data from U.S. Department of Agriculture, *Crops and Markets* 19 (1942): 150–55; U.S. Bureau of the Census, *Historical Statistics of the United States,* part 1 (Washington, D.C.: Government Printing Office, 1975): 200–02.

gration is the distinct cultural identity in the South. The alternative to labor outflow, capital inflow, also failed because of the difficulty of fitting northern technology to the southern resource base, although some industry, notably textiles, did migrate to the South to take advantage of lower wages, lax state regulations on hours and child labor, and absence of unions.

A major factor discouraging labor outflow from the South and discouraging capital inflow was the low level of spending on public schooling in the South.[35] To the extent that public education was financed by property taxes and increased the earnings potential and opportunity set of the person being educated, white southern landowners had little incentive to provide education to their African-American tenants and sharecroppers, whose children might find superior opportunities elsewhere. Nor did private industry have the incentive to provide this public good when they could not capture the benefits and when a more educated labor force existed elsewhere.

Agriculture dominated the southern economy, and African-Americans were overwhelmingly concentrated in the agricultural sector as wage labor-

[35] Margo (1990).

ers, croppers, tenants, and even owners. In some states, such as Mississippi, a majority of all farms in the state were operated by African-Americans. The concentration of African-Americans in agriculture did not imply their absence from other industries. Indeed, they made up almost half the employees of saw and planing mills and more than half the workers in the southern tobacco and iron and steel industries (Table 19.7). Nevertheless, there were few African-Americans employed in the southern textile mills.

Wright explains the strong African-American attachment to agriculture in terms of the opportunities for economic advancement that agriculture afforded them. Elsewhere racial prejudice limited the upward mobility of African-Americans. In 1890, for example, 61 percent of African-American men and 91 percent of African-American women in the southern labor force were employed in menial jobs, as opposed to just 31 percent and 54 percent for whites whose parents were born in the United States.[36] Similarly,

TABLE 19.7

Black Workers by Occupation in Southern Industry, 1910 and 1930

Industry Occupation	Percentage of Black Workers 1910	 1930
Cotton textiles		
Laborer	23.4	30.8
Operative	0.01	0.01
Loom fixer	0.00	0.00
Iron and steel		
Laborer	74.0	81.8
Semiskilled	n.a.	41.4
Molder	24.2	30.5
Saw and planing mills		
Laborer	62.8	61.9
Semiskilled	39.9	35.1
Sawyer	23.6	23.7
Tobacco		
Laborer	75.2	76.6
Operative	59.2	61.0

[36] Ransom and Sutch (1973).

while 63 percent of the laborers in the lumber industry in 1910 were African-American, only 40 percent of the semiskilled workers and just 24 percent of the skilled sawyers were African-American. Much the same pattern was to be found in West Virginia coal mines, which were a stopping-off point for many African-Americans in their northward migration.[37] African-Americans were disproportionately concentrated in the more menial and less desirable tasks, although they were not excluded from the highest-paying and best jobs. Those who achieved such status, however, frequently found more attractive positions elsewhere. Few African-Americans rose to supervisory positions because of the reluctance of white workers to tolerate such arrangements.

It was relatively easier for an African-American to ascend the agricultural ladder from laborer to sharecropper to tenant with the acquisition of workstock (i.e., mule or horse) and on to owner than for an African-American to ascend the industrial job hierarchy. To be sure, African-American farmers probably faced more obstacles than Caucasians along the way, but significant numbers were able to advance along this course. Within agriculture there existed two interrelated markets. One, for wage laborers, operated over a wide geographic area. The other, for tenants and sharecroppers, operated more locally. Although movement between the markets was possible, wage laborers tended to be younger and single while tenants and croppers were older, married, and had children.

The dominance of agriculture meant that the agricultural wage set the base market wage in the southern economy (Figure 19.7). This was true even in the cotton textile industry, which employed virtually no African-Americans. As the contemporary vernacular held, millowners could hire white labor at blacks' wages. Indeed, the emergence of night work in southern cotton mills is attributed to the excess supply of labor in the presence of a rigid money wage in agriculture that led millowners to require that families supply night workers as a condition of employment.[38]

Another measure of labor market integration is the distribution of wages (Figure 19.8). The modal wage for African-American and white workers was the same: $8.00. Indeed, there seem to have been relatively few instances where African-Americans and whites were paid different wages for the same job. At the same time it is clear that whites had access to many more high-paying jobs than African-Americans, so that the average or median wages differed substantially between the two groups. African-Americans could get the market wage for unskilled jobs, but they found it difficult to progress beyond that level to higher-paying, more skilled work, perhaps because of lack of education but more likely because of prejudice and outright exclusion.

Wright explains the "whiteness" of the southern textile industry in terms

[37] Fishback (1984).
[38] Shiells and Wright (1983).

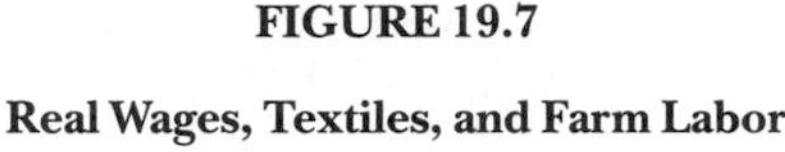

FIGURE 19.7

Real Wages, Textiles, and Farm Labor

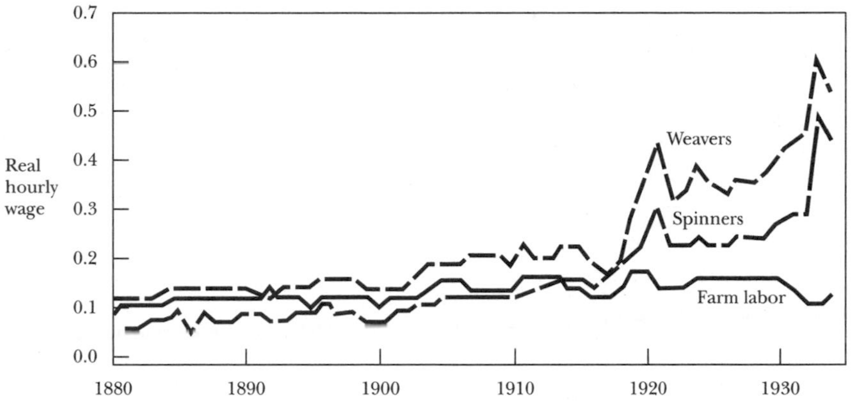

Sources: Gavin Wright, *Old South, New South* (New York: Basic Books, 1986): 137. Data from U.S. Bureau of Labor Statistics, *Wages and Hours of Labor,* Bulletin nos. 65, 71, 77, 128, 150, 190, 239, 262, 288, 345, 371, 446, 492, 539 (Washington, D.C.: Government Printing Office, 1906–31); U.S. Department of Agriculture, *Crops and Markets* 19 (1942): 150–55; U.S. Commissioner of Labor, *Seventh Annual Report: Wages and Hours of Labor* (Washington, D.C.: Government Printing Office, 1904).

of segregation-based learning-by-doing. By historical accident, whites were first employed in the southern textile industry and passed on their skills to their children, who went to work in the same mills. African-Americans could not compete because they had no opportunity to acquire these skills. Moreover, they had no incentive to work for less since the textile wage was linked to the agricultural wage, which was always open to African-Americans. Thus the white textile workers and millowners could satisfy their racial prejudices at little or no cost, and this industry remained segregated until well into the twentieth century.

This picture of economically integrated, but socially segregated, markets in the South begins to break down after World War I. Increasingly, "black jobs" became synonymous with "low wage" while "white jobs" were associated with "high wage." Wright offers no new explanation for this phenomenon other than to note the growing racial exclusivity of labor unions and the decline of public schooling (primarily African-American) in the 1890s. As a result, the nature of southern dualism changed to one in which African-Americans and whites had not only different jobs but noncompeting jobs at different base pay rates. Market development thus brought divergence and increasing inequality.

FIGURE 19.8

Aggregate Wage Distributions in Virginia, 1907

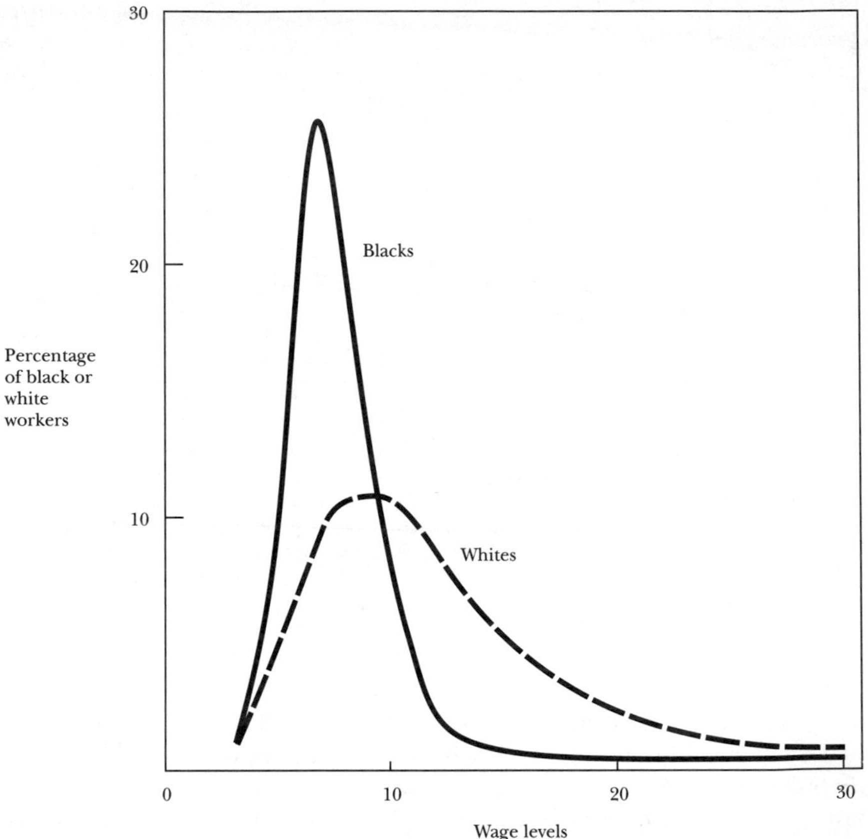

Sources: Gavin Wright, *Old South, New South* (New York: Basic Books, 1986): 184. Data from Bureau of Labor and Industrial Statistics for the State of Virginia, *Eleventh Annual Report* (Richmond, Va.: Davis Bottom Superintendent of Public Printing, 1908).

Nonfarm occupational skills were even more difficult for African-Americans to acquire since training usually came through apprenticeship. The majority of white artisans were, it is presumed, prejudiced against using African-American helpers. Those who might otherwise have been attracted to hiring African-American apprentices because they could be had for less pay than whites were deterred by the general racial climate. If customers would not patronize a shop with African-American labor because they thought African-American work was inferior or job integration was wrong, it did not pay to hire African-Americans no matter how competent they might be. As a result, nineteenth-century labor markets remained separate, segregated by race, gender, and location.

Many of these same characteristics are to be found in today's labor markets. Despite equal opportunity employment, discrimination and job segregation have not disappeared. The educated and the skilled still receive premiums. Those in less desirable occupations receive compensating payments. Women are paid less than men, and those with no voice, such as the illegal immigrant, have only a choice between exit or silence.

Bibliography

Abbott, Edith. "The History of Industrial Employment of Women in the United States: An Introductory Study." *Journal of Political Economy.* (1906): 461–501.

Adams, Donald R. "Wage Rates in the Early National Period: Philadelphia, 1785–1830." *Journal of Economic History* 28 (1968): 404–26.

Alston, Lee, and Timothy Hatton. "The Earnings Gap between Agricultural and Manufacturing Laborers, 1925–1941." *Journal of Economic History* 51 (1991): 83–100.

Atack, Jeremy, and Fred Bateman. "How Long Was the Workday in 1880?" *Journal of Economic History* 52 (1992): 129–60.

Carter, Susan B., and Elizabeth Savoca. "Gender Differences and Earning in Nineteenth-Century America: The Role of Expected Job and Career Attachment." *Explorations in Economic History* 28 (1991): 323–43.

Coehlo, Philip, and James Shepherd. "Regional Differences in Real Wages: The United States 1851–1880." *Explorations in Economic History* 13 (1976): 203–30.

David, Paul A. "The Growth of Real Product in the United States before 1840: New Evidence, Controlled Conjectures." *Journal of Economic History* 27 (1967): 151–97.

Douglas, Paul. *Real Wages in the United States 1890–1926.* Boston: Houghton Mifflin, 1930.

Easterlin, Richard. *Population, Labor Force, and Long Swings in Economic Growth: The American Experience.* New York: Columbia University Press, 1968.

Fishback, Price. "Segregation in Job Hierarchies: West Virginia Coal Mining 1906–32." *Journal of Economic History* 44 (1984): 755–74.

———."Did Coal Miners 'Owe Their Souls to the Company Store?' Theory and Evidence from the Early 1900s." *Journal of Economic History* 46 (1986): 1011–30.

———, and Shawn Kantor. "The Good, the Bad, and the Paycheck: Compensating Differentials in Labor Markets, 1884–1903." Paper presented at the Kansas Conference on Historical Labor Statistics, Lawrence, Kansas, June 1991.

Goldin, Claudia. "Maximum Hours Legislation and Female Employment: A Reassessment." *Journal of Political Economy* 96 (1988): 189–205.

———. *Understanding the Gender Gap: An Economic History of American Women.* New York: Oxford University Press, 1990.

———, and Robert Margo. "Wages, Prices, and Labor Markets before the Civil War." In *Strategic Factors in Nineteenth Century American Economic Growth: A Volume to Honor Robert W. Fogel,* ed. Claudia Goldin and Hugh Rockoff. Chicago: University of Chicago Press, 1992: 67–104.

———, and Kenneth Sokoloff. "Women, Children, and Industrialization in the Early Republic." *Journal of Economic History* 42 (1982): 741–74.

Griliches, Zvi, and William Mason. "Employment, Income and Ability." *Journal of Political Economy* 80 (1972): S74–S103.

Handlin, Oscar. *The Uprooted,* 2d ed. Boston: Little, Brown, 1973.

Hatton, Timothy, and Jeffrey Williamson. "Wage Gaps between Farm and City: Michigan in the 1890s." *Explorations in Economic History* 28 (1991): 381–408.

Higgs, Robert. *Competition and Coercion: Blacks in the American Economy, 1865–1914.* New York: Cambridge University Press, 1977.

Hunnicutt, Benjamin. *Work without End: Abandoning Shorter Hours for the Right to Work.* Philadelphia: Temple University Press, 1988.

Jacoby, Sanford. *Employing Bureaucracy: Managers, Unions and the Transformation of Work in American Industry, 1900–1945.* New York: Columbia University Press, 1985.

Lazonick, William, and Thomas Brush. "The 'Horndal Effect' in Early U.S. Manufacturing." *Explorations in Economic History* 22 (1985): 53–96.

Lebergott, Stanley. *Manpower in Economic Growth.* New York: McGraw-Hill, 1964.

Lerner, Gerda. "The Lady and the Mill Girl: Changes in the Status of Women in the Age of Jackson." *Midcontinent American Studies Journal* 10 (1969): 5–14. Reprinted in Nancy Cott and Elizabeth Pleck, eds., *A Heritage of Her Own.* New York: Simon and Schuster, 1979.

Long, Clarence. *Wages and Earnings in the United States, 1860–1890.* Princeton: Princeton University Press, 1960.

Margo, Robert. *Race and Schooling in the South, 1880–1950.* Chicago: University of Chicago Press, 1990.

———, and Georgia Villaflor. "The Growth of Wages in Antebellum America: New Evidence." *Journal of Economic History* 47 (1987): 873–96.

Parker, William N. "Agriculture." In *American Economic Growth,* ed. Lance Davis et al. New York: Harper & Row, 1972: 369–417.

Raff, Daniel M. G. "Wage Determination Theory and the Five-Dollar Day at Ford." *Journal of Economic History* 48 (1988): 387–400.

Ransom, Roger, and Richard Sutch. "The Ex-Slave in the Post-Bellum South: A Study of the Economic Impact of Racism in a Market Environment." *Journal of Economic History* 33 (1973): 131–48.

Rosenbloom, Joshua. "One Market or Many? Labor Market Integration in the Nineteenth-Century United States." *Journal of Economic History* 50 (1990): 85–108.

Rothenberg, Winifred. "A Price Index for Rural Massachusetts, 1750–1855." *Journal of Economic History* 39 (1979): 975–1001.

———. "The Emergence of Farm Labor Markets and the Transformation of the Rural Economy: Massachusetts 1750–1855." *Journal of Economic History* 48 (1988): 537–66.

———. *From Market-Places to a Market Economy.* Chicago: University of Chicago Press, 1992.

Shiells, Martha, and Gavin Wright. "Night Work as a Labor Market Phenomenon: Southern Textiles in the Interwar Period. *Explorations in Economic History* 20 (1983): 331–50.

Smith, Walter. "Wage Rates on the Erie Canal." *Journal of Economic History* 23 (1963): 298–311.

Sokoloff, Kenneth, and Georgia C. Villaflor. "The Market for Manufacturing Workers during Early Industrialization: The American Northeast, 1820 to 1860." In *Strategic Factors in Nineteenth Century American Economic Growth: A Volume to Honor Robert W. Fogel,* ed. Claudia Goldin and Hugh Rockoff. Chicago: University of Chicago Press, 1992: 29–65.

Sundstrom, William. "Was There a Golden Age of Flexible Wages? Evidence from Ohio Manufacturing, 1892–1910." *Journal of Economic History* 50 (1990): 309–20.

Weiss, Thomas. "Long Term Changes in U.S. Agricultural Output per Worker, 1800 to 1900." NBER Working Paper Series on Historical Factors in Long Run Growth, 23, 1991.

Whaples, Robert. "The Great Decline in the Length of the Workweek." Working paper, University of Wisconsin, Milwaukee, 1988.

———. "Winning the Eight-Hour Day, 1909–1919." *Journal of Economic History* 50 (1990): 393–406.

Whatley, Warren. "Labor for the Picking: The New Deal in the South." *Journal of Economic History* 43 (1983): 905–30.

Williamson, Jeffrey. "American Prices and Urban Inequality." *Journal of Economic History* 36 (1976): 303–33.

———, and Peter Lindert. *American Inequality: A Macroeconomic Perspective.* New York: Academic Press, 1980.

Wright, Gavin. *Old South, New South: Revolutions in the Southern Economy since the Civil War.* New York: Basic Books, 1986.

———. "Labor History and Labor Economics." In *The Future of Economic History,* ed. Alex Field. Boston: Kluwer-Nijhoff, 1987: 313–48.

———. "American Agriculture and the Labor Market: What Happened to Proletarianization?" *Agricultural History* 62 (1988): 182–209.

America comes of age: 1914–29

20

World War I broke out in August 1914 and ended with an armistice on November 11, 1918. For the United States, however, World War I ended almost before it had begun. Despite a gradual policy tilt in favor of the Allied side (Britain, France, Belgium, Italy, Russia, and other countries) after 1915, America did not officially enter the war on the Allied side until April 6, 1917. Consequently, the U.S. economy had barely achieved conversion to a wartime footing and full mobilization before the command economy apparatus that had made it all possible was abruptly dismantled. Nonetheless, the war brought about fundamental changes in the domestic economy, in the role of government, and in America's position in the world economy. These changes complicated and sometimes frustrated the American quest for ever-rising prosperity for all its people, but most of them are still with us today. For the first time it became possible to talk about a deliberate economic policy to promote domestic equilibrium, national prosperity, and international stability.

The American Economy in World War I

The suspension of gold convertibility of the major European currencies at the end of July 1914, and the outbreak of war in early August prompted a short-term speculative run against the dollar. Since the Federal Reserve banking system was not yet fully operational, the sudden withdrawal of bank reserves by country banks from city banks—especially those in New York—strained the ability of these city banks to make payment in legal tender. As an alternative, city banks issued clearinghouse loan certificates to their correspondent country banks, while nervous country and city bank depositors reacted by withdrawing their deposits in legal tender and precipitating bank runs. Rather than suspend payment entirely, the banks met this demand for cash with National Currency Association money issued under authority of the Aldrich-Vreeland Act. By the end of November about $400 million—or about one-eighth of the stock of legal tender—had been issued. Most of it was held by the public.

On the basis of this single experience, Milton Friedman and Anna Schwartz suggest that had the same institutional arrangement been in place in 1930, the banking system would not have tottered on the edge of total collapse and the course of events in the business contraction that we now call the Great Depression might have been very different. Instead the Aldrich-Vreeland Act and national currency associations passed into history at the end of June 1915.[1]

The war in Europe, however, quickly proved a boon for the American economy. Foreign demand for "neutral" America's foodstuffs, raw materials, finished products, and ocean transportation reached record highs. Suddenly America's visible exports regularly began to exceed its imports. Shipments of wheat to the Allied countries, for example, were seven times what they had been immediately before the war. Sales of zinc increased thirty-seven-fold. Gold, in search of a safe haven, flowed into American banks. As a result, the money supply grew rapidly and prices rose sharply (Figure 20.1).

Neither Great Britain nor Germany respected American neutrality. Whereas British action was largely limited to the interdiction and seizure of American cargoes bound for the Axis powers, indiscriminate submarine warfare by Germany—especially the sinking of the liner *Lusitania* with the loss of 1,198 lives, including 128 Americans—slowly but inexorably led the United States into the war on the Allied side. American democracy and the free enterprise system, though, were ill suited to the needs of modern warfare, which required the massive mobilization of resources for public, rather than private, benefit. The sudden, unexpected increase in demand and the competing priorities of government and the private sector wreaked havoc on the system. The solution was "a totally planned economy run largely by big-business interests through the instrumentality of the central government which served as the model . . . for state corporate capitalism for the remainder of the twentieth century.[2]" To this end the federal government seized control of vital sectors of the economy. Some preliminary planning had been done before America's formal entry into the war through the public-private Council for National Defense, which included cabinet officers and corporate executives. The first director, for example, was Walter

[1] Authority for the Aldrich-Vreeland Act was supposed to expire June 30, 1914, but was extended to June 30, 1915, under the Federal Reserve Act of 1913.
[2] Rothbard (1963).

FIGURE 20.1

Wholesale Prices, 1913–1922

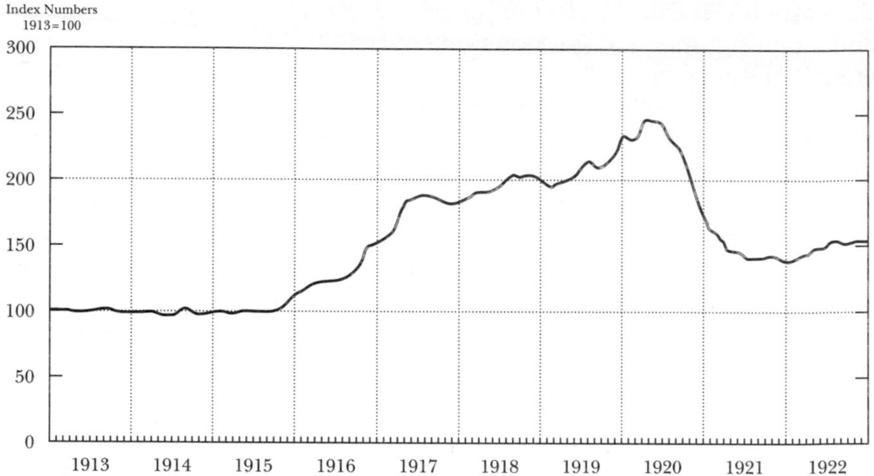

Source: Paul A. Samuelson and Everett E. Hagen, *After the War, 1918–20* (Washington, D.C.: U.S. National Resources Planning Board, 1943): 13.

Gifford, the chief statistician for AT&T. Other members included the president of Sears, Roebuck & Company and the president of the B&O Railroad. The council discussed such issues as conscription, price controls, and the government take-over of private industry and formed the nucleus of the command mechanism that emerged after war was declared.

Shortly after war was declared, the council created the War Industries Board. It was charged with determining priorities, fixing prices, converting plants to meet war needs, and purchasing—requisitioning if and when necessary—supplies for the United States and the Allies. Other directives were to follow (see Table 23.1 below). The Lever Food and Fuel Control Act, for example, empowered the president to make regulations and issue orders to stimulate production and control the distribution of food and fuel; the Trading with the Enemy Act imposed new controls on foreign commerce and authorized the seizure and sale of assets (including patent rights) owned by residents of those countries with which the United States was at war; the nation's railroads were placed under the control of the U.S. Railroad Administration; and the Capital Issues Committee restricted private access to the capital market if such borrowing competed with government borrowing.

With the creation of this command economy, the size of the federal budget mushroomed. Whereas before 1915 federal expenditures had never exceeded $760 million a *year, monthly* expenditures exceeded that level from April 1917 until August 1919. In the period from 1900 to the outbreak of war government receipts averaged $634 million and expenditures averaged $628 million. During the 1920s receipts averaged $4.318 million and expenditures $3.556 million. Even after allowance is made for price changes, though, the federal budget in the 1920s was some three times what it had been before the war. The war not only increased the scale of government but also permanently increased its scope.[3] Some of the changes in scale and scope are shown in Table 20.1, which compares receipts and expenditures in 1913 with those for 1927. About 80 percent of the increase in receipts between 1913 and 1927 came from the individual income tax and the expanded corporate tax. On the expenditure side, the sharp rise in the fraction devoted to paying interest on the national debt is particularly noticeable. In 1913 this represented less than 2.5 percent of the federal expenditures, but by 1927 it was diverting almost 22 percent. The government also adopted responsibility for some roads and greatly expanded its role in hospitals and law enforcement.

The Department of Commerce GNP estimates for this period suggest that the command economy created for World War I was a success, wringing an additional 18 percent output from the economy in 1917 and 1918. If true, these statistics imply that the newly created wartime command economy was more efficient than the free enterprise system—a surprising conclusion in the wake of the recent collapse of centrally planned economies around the world—unless there were substantial unemployed resources available. Unemployment, though, seems to have been fairly low in 1917—under 5 percent—and while it fell sharply as a result of the war effort, it is hard to imagine that unemployed resources could be so productive. Indeed, labor productivity should have fallen as men joined the armed forces and were replaced by less experienced workers.

There is, however, reason to question these GNP estimates. Systematic, contemporaneous estimates of GNP only date from the 1930s. Estimates for earlier dates were instead constructed by scholars such as Simon Kuznets and John Kendrick in the 1950s by piecing together various, often incomplete and sometimes inconsistent, component series. At least one scholar, Christina Romer, has suggested that the way in which these early estimates of GNP, unemployment, and the like were assembled exaggerates cyclical volatility.[4] Her revised GNP estimates dramatically reduce the magnitude of the World War I boom. Instead of GNP growing by 18 percent between 1917 and 1918, she estimates that it rose only 5 percent—a figure that is consis-

[3] This is the phenomenon referred to as the ratchet effect by Robert Higgs (1987). See Chapter 23.

[4] One implication of Romer's procedures is that the apparent post–World War II macroeconomic stability relative to earlier periods is a product of the statistical procedures generating the numbers rather than genuine economic change.

TABLE 20.1

Federal Government Receipts and Expenditures, 1913 and 1927 ($m)

	Receipts				Expenditures		
Source	1913	1927	1927 (in 1913 $)	Function	1913	1927	1927 (in 1913 $)
Individual income tax	—	879	529	Intergovernmental			
Corporate income tax	35	1,259	758	Education	3	10	6
Customs duties	310	585	352	Highways	0	83	50
Alcoholic beverages	223	20	12	Public welfare	2	1	.6
Tobacco products	77	376	26	Other	7	29	17
Death and gift tax	—	90	54	General expenditure			
Other taxes	17	154	93	National defense	250	616	371
Postal receipts	267	683	411	Postal service	270	711	428
Miscellaneous receipts	33	349	210	Education	5	8	5
Veteran life insurance				Highways	0	10	6
trust revenue	—	48	29	Public welfare	5	10	6
Employee retirement				Hospitals	1	68	41
insurance trust revenue	—	25	15	Health	4	8	5
				Police	3	20	12
				Natural resources	30	112	67
				Housing	—	1	.6
				Veteran services	177	579	349
				Financial administration	45	114	69
				Interest on debt	23	764	460
				Transportation	90	254	153
				Other	55	105	63
				Insurance trust expenditure			
				Employee retirement	—	14	8
				Veterans life insurance	—	16	10
Receipts							
Net of borrowing	**962**	**4,469**	**2,690**	**Total expenditures**	**970**	**3,533**	**2,127**

Note: 0 = less than $500,000; — = zero.

Source: U.S. Department of the Treasury, *Annual Report, 1970: Statistical Appendix,* Washington, D.C.: Government Printing Office, 1970. U.S. Department of the Treasury, *Annual Report, 1946,* Washington, D.C.: Government Printing Office, 1946.

tent with the relatively high level of employment in 1917 and the decline in unemployment in 1917 and 1918 (Figure 20.2). Similarly, the Department of Commerce Real GNP series shows a decline of over 37 percent from the preceding year in each of 1919, 1920, and 1921. Yet by all accounts, production (surely a large part of the economy) boomed for most of 1919 and the first half of 1920. Romer's series, on the other hand, shows growth in 1918 and 1919, a modest decline in 1919 and 1920, and a sharper decline in 1920 and 1921. Her pattern is more consistent with the qualitative evidence.

Romer's revisions themselves, however, remain extremely controversial. David Weir, for example, has raised serious questions about Romer's claim that post–Second World War stabilization is a statistical illusion. Others have reached similar conclusions, and in this respect her conclusion may well be wrong.[5] Similarly, both Weir and Stanley Lebergott find fault with Romer's revised unemployment estimates on both technical and methodological grounds. However, her revisions to the GNP and unemployment series for

FIGURE 20.2

Percentage Change in Real GNP, 1914–1929

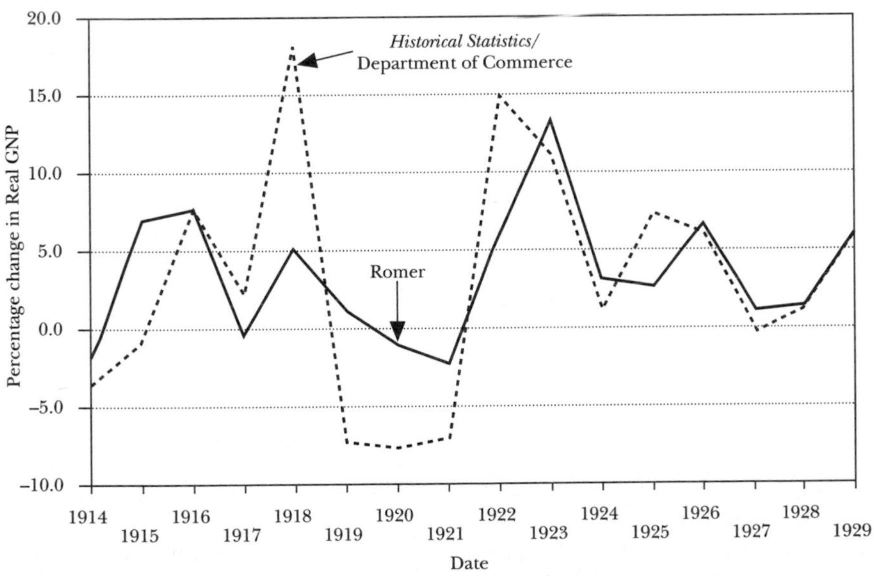

Source: Christina Romer, "World War I and the Postwar Depression," *Journal of Monetary Economics* 22 (1988): 106.

[5] For example, Diebold and Rudebusch (1992).

World War I and its immediate aftermath have not drawn specific criticism, and these remain credible. They dispense with two puzzles that are not otherwise easily explained: the amazingly good economic performance of the command economy and the dramatic swings in unemployment between 1919 and 1923 as depicted in the official and semiofficial statistical series.

Demobilization and the Postwar Boom

The signing of the armistice on November 11, 1918, brought about an abrupt reversal of federal government policy. The dollar-a-year executives who had been seconded to Washington to help run the government during the war rose from their desks, locked their offices, and went to Florida for short vacations before returning to their permanent corporate jobs. Although the story may be apocryphal, some Washington offices reportedly were closed so abruptly that stenographers had to borrow money to get home.[6] Certainly, though, wartime contracts and controls were ended abruptly. Calls canceling War Department contracts reportedly jammed the lines out of Washington the day after the armistice, and of the $6 billion in contracts outstanding, $2.5 billion were canceled within a month. Relief to the suppliers was limited to one month's production. A day later the War Industries Board started dismantling price controls.

Discharges from the armed forces also began almost immediately. In December 1918 six hundred thousand men who had not yet embarked for Europe were discharged. By April 1919 almost two million servicemen had been demobilized, and within a year four million had returned to the civilian labor market. But the market was ill prepared for their return. In January 1919 Congress had cut the appropriation for the U.S. Employment Service by 80 percent although 490 of the original 750 offices nationwide managed to remain open with volunteers or through private contributions. Boy Scouts reportedly were delegated to solicit promises from employers to rehire veterans. In the patriotic fervor that engulfed the country much of the burden of labor market readjustment fell on the shoulders of those who had recently been drawn into the labor force, particularly women and retirees.

Despite these shocks to the economic system and the federal government's feeble efforts to prop up aggregate demand through a "Build-Your-Own-Home" publicity campaign, the downturn in the economy following the armistice was brief and mild. By April 1919 the economy had recovered, and America entered a brief boom, ending in an equally brief but intense depression (Figure 20.3). Between March 1919 and February 1920, when the index peaked, the Federal Reserve's index of industrial production rose 25 percent, from 76 to 95 (1923–25 = 100). By November 1920 it had fallen

[6] Samuelson and Hagen (1943).

FIGURE 20.3

Federal Reserve Seasonally Adjusted Index of Industrial Production

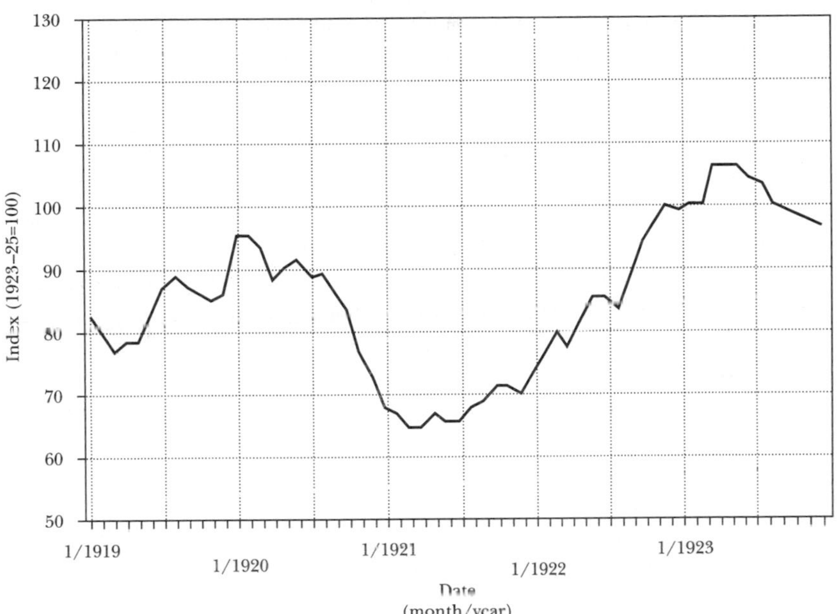

Source: Federal Reserve Board, *Bulletin* (Washington, D.C.: Federal Reserve Board: various issues).

back to its March 1919 level. The index fell another 15 percent, to 64, in April 1921 before industrial production began to recover. Thus, from the business cycle peak in early 1920 to the trough in early 1921, the index of industrial production fell more than 30 percent.

Economists explain a similar boom after World War II in terms of deferred wartime consumption expenditures. This explanation cannot be used for the post–World War I boom. Regulations curtailing consumer goods production did not go into effect, for the most part, until September and October 1918. Few expenditures appear to have been cut despite appeals from the president and the secretary of the treasury for "moral restraint" in consumer goods purchases. Automobile production—one of the first industries to be affected—soared in 1917 to 1.75 million units before falling to 1 million in 1918. In 1919 production recovered to 1.65 million vehicles. Deferred demand was therefore likely to have been relatively small, especially for durable goods (those products with life expectancies of at least three years). Furthermore, when the war ended, the patriotism of Americans was measured by how much they had saved and invested in Liberty bonds. Twenty-one million people subscribed to the Fourth Liberty Loan, and of the $21 billion of Liberty bonds outstanding in 1919, only $4 billion was in the hands of financial institutions and businesses. As a result, the savings rate was at a historically high level. In 1919 and 1920 individuals on average spent only 91.6 percent of their income, compared with 94.4 percent of higher incomes spent between 1922 and 1929.

Instead the boom was fueled by high levels of demand from the government and the foreign trade sectors, rather than by consumption expenditures. Although the government had been quick to cancel war orders after the armistice and had rapidly demobilized the armed forces, the level of government demand still remained high. With more than twelve million men under arms, the $60-plus-transportation bonus paid to discharged service personnel represented a large expenditure. Government acceptance of one month's production at current rates on canceled war orders was often spread over a number of months as overtime and multiple shifts were cut. Furthermore, after the armistice the federal government advanced the Allies $2 billion in loans, almost all of which they spent in America because their domestic economies were much slower than ours in reconverting to a peacetime footing. Thus, although the budget deficit peaked in December 1918 at $1.9 billion, the budget remained in deficit until the last quarter of 1919 (Figure 20.4).

FIGURE 20.4

The Federal Budget, 1916–1921

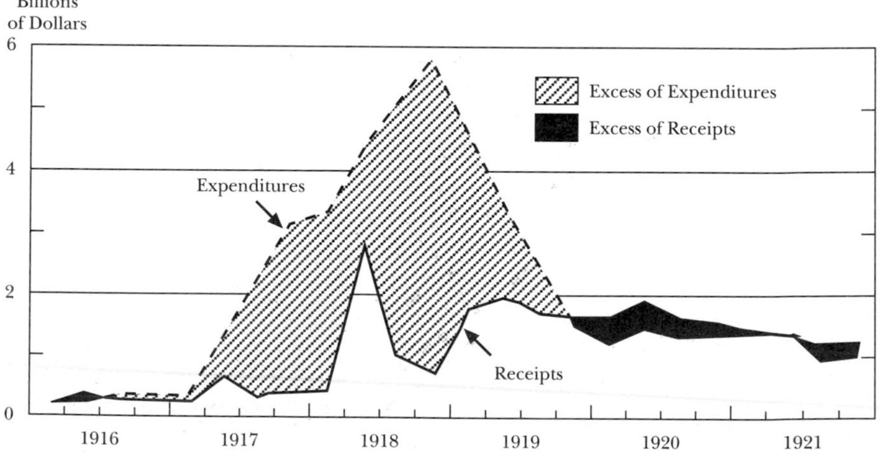

Source: Paul A. Samuelson and Everett E. Hagen, *After the War, 1918–20* (Washington, D.C.: U.S. National Resources Planning Board, 1943): 22.

European demand for American goods, especially food, also helped bolster the American economy. When the war ended, much of Europe was close to starvation. Central Europe, in particular, was devastated. The diversion of nitrate fertilizers into munitions production had lowered soil fertility and crop yields; manpower shortages and transportation dislocations made harvesting and distribution difficult or impossible, and in Russia, the bread basket of Europe, war, revolution, and civil strife had reduced agricultural output in 1920 to just 54 percent of its prewar level. As a result, the American trade balance on goods and services was \$4.9 billion in surplus in 1919 and \$3.5 billion in surplus in 1920.

The economic stimulus from high levels of government expenditure and the substantial trade surplus was reinforced by historic highs in new plant and equipment expenditures. In 1920 business investment exceeded \$3 billion, a total not equaled again until just before World War II. Much of this investment went into plant and equipment for the new products of the age: the automobile, electric power, and electrical appliances (see the following pages).

FIGURE 20.5

Earning Assets of Federal Reserve Banks, 1914–1919

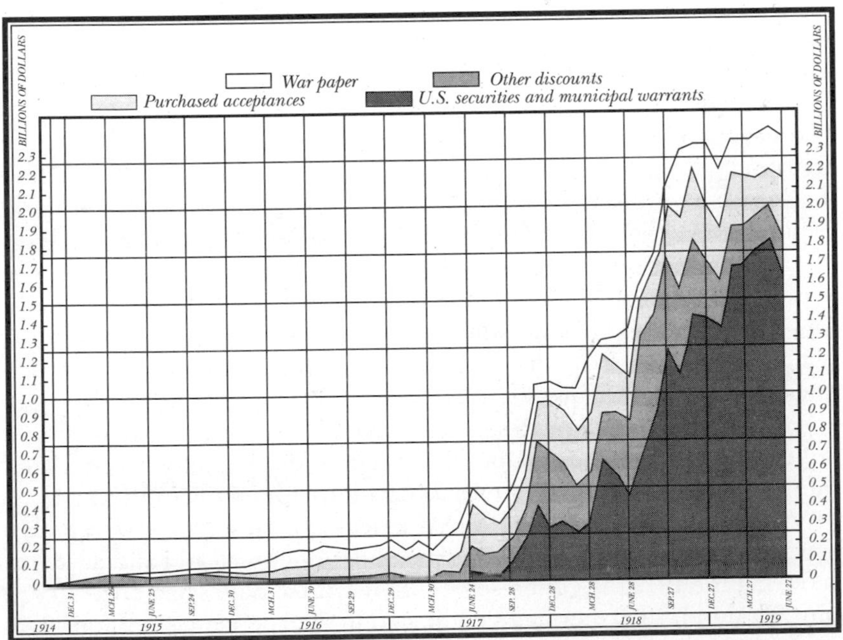

Source: Federal Reserve Board, *Bulletin* (Washington, D.C.: Federal Reserve Board, 1919): 772.

By 1920 manufacturing employment and industrial production were again at their wartime highs, and with worldwide shortages caused by transportation disruptions from the war, prices rose rapidly after price controls were removed. The Bureau of Labor's wholesale price index, which had been at 206 (1913 = 100) in November 1918, when the armistice was signed, stood at 272 by May 1920. Indeed, from March to April 1920, prices rose at an average annual rate of more than 70 percent—faster than at any time since the Revolution (see Figure 20.1).

These inflationary pressures were reinforced by monetary forces. During the war the monetary base expanded rapidly as gold flowed into the country to escape war-torn Europe and to pay for America's large trade surplus. Federal Reserve policy further aggravated the situation. As late as October 1917 Federal Reserve notes in circulation amounted to less than $1 billion, but by December 1918 almost $2.8 billion was in circulation. Much of this increase resulted from the monetization of federal debt (Figure 20.5).

During the war and immediately afterward the Fed tried to keep interest rates low to facilitate Treasury borrowing to pay for the war. Indeed, for a while the Fed offered member banks loans at rates below the coupon rate on government bonds to encourage them to buy these bonds, crowding out private-sector lending. This policy was so successful that the Fed found itself compelled to keep interest rates low to avoid depressing bond prices and jeopardizing bank portfolios.

The Depression of 1920–21

The economic stimulus from large government deficits ended in the last quarter of 1919, when the government had a surplus of $154 million. During the first six months of 1920 the federal budget surplus amounted to $831 million as expenditures were sharply curtailed (see Figure 20.4). Export markets also abruptly disappeared as financially strapped European countries were no longer able to buy American products with the proceeds of American government loans, and American invisible earnings from the carrying trade evaporated as the worldwide shipping shortage eased and freight rates declined (see Figure 20.5).

Moreover, the Federal Reserve, which had been pursuing an easy money policy to keep interest rates low and facilitate the Treasury's conversion of short-term war debt to longer-term obligations, found not only that this policy was no longer needed but that America's gold reserves were rapidly approaching the legal minimum of 40 percent under the Gold Standard Act of 1900. In June 1919 the gold reserves of the United States had been 50.6 percent. By March 1920 they had shrunk to only 40.6 percent—perilously close to the minimum. Beginning in January 1920, the Fed started raising the discount rate from the 4 to 4.5 percent range up to 6 to 7 percent by May. The Federal Reserve also eliminated the preferential rates on government paper. Member banks were holding $3 billion in government bonds and were in debt to the Fed to the tune of $2.5 billion (an all-time record). Some have criticized the Fed's new policy as "too much, too late."[7] Others argue that in the early stages of the downturn, the Fed behaved in a manner entirely consistent with nineteenth-century English economist and central bank expert Walter Bagehot's dictum to lend freely but at a high rate in times of panic.[8] Although the Federal Reserve had stressed the need for an "orderly liquidation" of commercial bank holdings of U.S. government bonds, what resulted was far from orderly. Banks recalled loans, bonds were dumped on the market depressing bond prices and bank asset values, and banks failed. Whereas in 1919 only 63 banks had failed, in 1920, 155 banks failed, and in 1921, 506 banks went under. The money supply contracted sharply, falling by 9.4 percent—the largest single-year decline ever and exceeded in cumulative magnitude only by the decline during the great contraction from 1929 to 1933. The level of consumer and wholesale prices fell sharply.

What had begun as a relatively mild downturn became increasingly severe with an unprecedented decline in prices. Real GNP, as measured by the Commerce Department, declined sharply beginning in 1919, falling almost 21 percent from 1918 to 1921. Christina Romer's GNP series shows a much more modest fluctuation, peaking in 1919 and falling just over 3 percent between 1919 and 1921 (Figure 20.2 above). Similarly, whereas Lebergott's series has unemployment increasing from only 1.4 percent in 1919 to 11.7 percent in 1921—about 4.9 million persons—before dropping back to 6.7 percent in 1922, Romer estimates that unemployment increased from 3 percent to only 8.7 percent in 1921—substantial but not calamitous—and declined more modestly to 6.9 percent in 1922 (Figure 20.6). The burden of unemployment was extremely unequally distributed. While man-hours in iron and steel fell by 76 percent, total hours in cotton textiles fell only 7 percent. Boots and shoes posted a modest increase.

What is most remarkable during the depression of 1920–21, however, is the degree of price flexibility. The Bureau of Labor Statistics index of wholesale prices, for example, fell by 46 percent, while Romer's GNP deflator falls "only" 16 percent, reflecting differential price flexibility for primary products and raw materials compared with final production.

As the nation's most recent serious recession the 1920–21 episode led most economists and policy makers in the late 1920s and early 1930s to underestimate the seriousness of the downturn that began a little more than

[7] For example, Friedman and Schwartz (1963).
[8] Wicker (1966a, 1966b).

FIGURE 20.6

Unemployment, 1915–1930

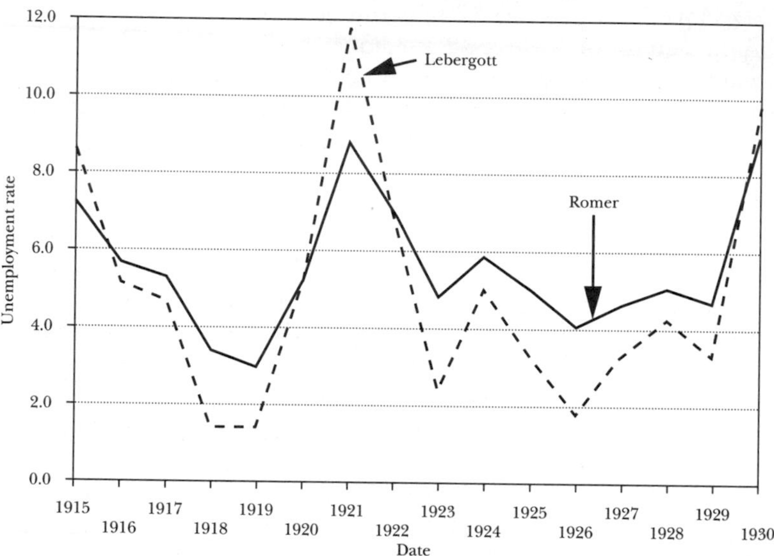

Source: Christina Romer, "Spurious Volatility in Historical Unemployment Data," *Journal of Political Economy* 94 (1986): 31, Table 9.

eight years later and became the Great Depression. The declines in key economic variables, such as price and industrial production, and the rise in unemployment in 1929 and 1930 looked modest by comparison with the declines from 1920 to 1921. Thus pundits confidently reassured the public that recovery was just around the corner, as the economy slipped deeper into depression in early 1930.

The Evolution of Federal Reserve Monetary Policy

The Federal Reserve reversed its policy of credit restraint in the spring of 1921 and the discount rate was gradually lowered to its previous levels of 4 to 4.5 percent. In addition, the Federal Reserve purchased $400 million of government securities in early 1922. This open market operation was not, however, part of a deliberate policy of money management by generating additional liquidity. That was to come later. Rather it reflected the low volume of rediscounts received by the Fed at the current high rates, which had depleted the Fed's income-earning assets. However, as the Fed was quick to note, this bond purchase provided some monetary stimulus. The yield on short-term Treasury bills, for example, fell from 4.8 percent in December 1921 to 3.2 percent by April 1922, prompting the Treasury to complain that Fed policy was making it difficult for it to price new issues and requesting that the Fed consult with the Treasury on future occasions.

Responding to Treasury criticism of Fed policy, the governors of five East Coast Federal Reserve Banks established a coordinating committee for open market sales and purchases operating out of the Federal Reserve Bank of New York in May 1922. This informal group was superseded in April 1923 by the Open Market Investment Committee (OMIC), a five-member committee under the chairmanship of the influential Governor Benjamin Strong of the New York Fed. The OMIC operated under the general authority of the Federal Reserve Board, although the Fed never fully established control over the committee. According to Friedman and Schwartz, the establishment of the OMIC marked the start of the federal government's assumption of responsibility for promoting and maintaining economic stability, both domestically and internationally.

The Federal Reserve Act of 1913 had given the Fed the power to set reserve ratios and the rediscount rate. It was envisaged that the setting of reserve ratios (or the threat to exercise that power) would be the "stick," while variations in the rediscount rate—which affect the ex post profitability of particular kinds of bank loans—would be the "carrot" for regulating member bank activities. Indeed, the sale to the Fed of what came to be called eligible paper, such as bankers' acceptances and commercial or industrial paper, was the only way until 1917 that member banks were *eligible* to borrow money from the Fed. In addition, the Fed was authorized to buy and sell U.S. government debt. Such activity was envisaged as providing the Fed with a reliable source of revenue and assisting it in its capacity as Treasury agent.

The emphasis upon eligible paper reflected the prominence of the Real Bills doctrine in banking circles at the time and provided the theoretical underpinnings for central bank activities in the Federal Reserve Act of 1913. The conventional wisdom was that financial crises were the result of "inelasticity" in the supply of currency and bank credit—that is to say, there was a shortage of legal tender and credit in financial crises. One solution—the Real Bills doctrine—was to allow the Fed to rediscount for its member banks commercial, agricultural, and industrial paper and bankers' acceptances (originally just those arising from foreign trade but including those from domestic trade after 1916) since such loans were self-liquidating and of short maturity and originated in some productive, socially useful activity. The supply of such paper would ebb and flow with the level of business activity and according to seasonal needs. In such a system the Fed's role was passive in the sense that its only obligation was to stand ready to buy all eligible acceptances offered to it at set rates, although the rates that it set were supposed to signal Federal Reserve policy to the member banks.

World War I, however, had disrupted this plan. The pressing needs of wartime finance coerced the Fed into cooperating with the Treasury to keep borrowing costs low, and after the war the Fed acquiesced to Treasury wishes to keep interest rates low while the short-term war debt was converted to longer-term obligations. Consequently, it was 1920 before the discount rate really served as a signal for Fed policy.

Within three years, however, attitudes within the Fed had changed, and monetary policy had been revolutionized. According to Lester Chandler, while Benjamin Strong (along with most other Fed officials) had believed that price deflation and credit contraction were both necessary and desirable in 1921, Strong's attitude had completely changed by 1924. Instead of doing nothing or, worse yet, tightening credit to protect the Fed's position during the downturn in 1924, he advocated an aggressive open market option to buy government bonds, thereby putting money in people's hands and providing liquidity. He recommended an open market policy be used together with reduction in the discount rate to stimulate domestic borrowing and foreign lending. Almost overnight open market operations had become the principal tool of monetary policy, while discount rate variations played only a supporting role.

Friedman and Schwartz refer to the period 1921 to 1929 as the "High Tide of the Reserve System." They view Fed policy as if the Fed were solely committed to domestic prosperity and cared nothing about the international economy. For example, when $200 million in gold flowed into the country on the heels of recovery from the 1920–21 depression and threatened to generate renewed inflationary pressures, the Fed sold $525 million in government debt, completely offsetting its potential impact upon the domestic money supply. Similarly, when economic growth paused in early 1927 and prices eased, the Fed reacted by buying $230 million in government securities and reducing the buying rate on banker acceptances and the discount rate on commercial paper.

True, the Fed did occasionally make mistakes, especially early on. For example, between June and September 1923, the Fed's own Index of Production in Basic Industries declined 10 percent, wholesale prices fell about 5 percent, interest rates eased, and the Index of Factory Employment fell, yet the Fed *sold* $127 million of government securities in June. However, it reversed its policy at the end of 1923, buying $510 million in government securities. Despite such temporary lapses, Friedman and Schwartz imply that the Fed, with Benjamin Strong at the helm of the New York Fed providing leadership to the entire system, was so successful in minimizing economic fluctuations that those same policies, if they had been continued, might have prevented the economic downturn in the second half of 1929 from ballooning into the Great Depression.

The Fed, however, was not necessarily committed solely to domestic economic stability. Indeed, Elmus Wicker and others argue that international considerations were often dominant in determining Fed policy rather than an almost exclusively domestic focus as Friedman and Schwartz claim.[9] Wicker attributes the reversal of Fed policy at the end of 1923, when the Fed decided to purchase $510 million in government securities, not to the dawning realization that given the signs of domestic recession, Fed policy was wrong but rather to the Fed's desire to rebuild its investment portfolio. Moreover, as the Fed wished to aid Britain's return to gold, an easy money policy would discourage gold inflows into the U.S. and also facilitate the sale of the Dawes loan[10] on Wall Street to provide the gold and foreign exchange backing for the newly created German reichsmark, replacing the old mark at a rate of 1 new reichsmark per 1 trillion old marks. Similarly, in 1927 the Fed was more concerned with continued European currency weakness than with the growing stock market speculation. As a result, the Fed eased credit, reducing the discount rate from 4 to 3.5 percent and buying $230 million of government bonds, only to reverse itself abruptly in early 1928, selling $405 million and raising the discount rate to 5 percent, actions that John Maynard Keynes and others argue played a role in the economic downturn that began in 1929.

Nor was there necessarily any change in Federal Reserve policy between the 1920s and the 1930s, as Friedman and Schwartz suppose. David Wheelock finds that instead of pursuing a countercyclical monetary policy—that is, a monetary policy designed to offset changes in economic activity—as Friedman and Schwartz claim, Fed policy was actually procyclical. Using the so-called scissors rule, Fed officials relied upon the volume of member bank borrowing as the key indicator to determine the ultimate volume of open market operations. Such borrowing was positively correlated with economic activity. According to this rule, spelled out in the Fed's Tenth Annual Report, credit was adequate once member bank borrowing matched open market sales on a dollar-for-dollar basis. However, during recessions, member bank borrowing tended to decline, in part because of declining loan demand, signaling monetary ease to the Fed. Moreover, the worse the recession, as in 1930 and 1931, the less vigorously the Fed would respond under its own policy guidelines.

Even if the Fed's policy goals had been clearly articulated and even if it had perfectly understood the means of achieving them, determination of the appropriate monetary policy during the 1920s was far from straightforward. Although hindsight usually gives twenty-twenty vision, the economic information available to the Fed at the time was often patchy, imperfect, and incomplete. Many of the familiar statistics that are collected today by state

[9] Wicker (1966); Wheelock (1989; 1991) and Toma (1989).

[10] Charles Dawes was appointed the first director of the newly created U.S. Bureau of the Budget in 1921. He headed the Allied Reparations Committee in 1923 and 1924, charged with putting German finances on a sound footing after the hyperinflation of 1922 and 1923. His contribution to the post–World War I peace process was recognized when he was awarded the Nobel Peace Prize (jointly with Sir Austen Chamberlain) in 1925.

and federal bureaucracies did not exist in the 1920s. While there were indexes of factory output and estimates of crop production, there were no estimates of gross national product. Perhaps even more shocking is that despite the passage of almost forty years since the establishment of the Bureau of Labor Statistics, the United States had indexes of factory employment but no estimates of unemployment. Even if such information had existed, the theory of central banking and the principles of a managed money supply were not yet fully worked out. The multivariate techniques necessary for modeling the complex causal relationships and the time lags between policy action and economic reaction had yet to be developed. Moreover, there was an inherent policy contradiction between a managed domestic money supply and the gold standard. But even if this contradiction had not existed, the requirements of the domestic and international economies were frequently at odds, and the needs of business and agriculture often conflicted with Fed attempts to control speculation, as in 1927. Such problems, at best, led to mixed signals, and at times they confounded Fed policy.

America: The Unwilling Leader of the World Economy

The 1920s witnessed a dramatic change in America's role in the world. During the First World War the European nations had fought themselves into a stalemate that was resolved only by the addition of American soldiers and American production to the Allied side. This permanently changed America's position vis à vis the other nations, although for a long time the United States was unwilling to acknowledge this change and accept the responsibilities that it brought.

America's new role was embodied in the armistice that ended the war. This agreement was based on President Wilson's fourteen-point plan and required that Germany pay compensation for civilian casualties and property damage. Wilson's plan, however, expressly excluded compensation for Allied military casualties or their opportunity cost in prosecuting the war. But no sooner had Germany laid down its arms than the other Allies altered the terms of the peace, in part because of a spirit of vindictiveness toward Germany in France and Great Britain. Fullest indemnities, for indirect as well as direct costs arising from the war for the military as well as for the civilian population, were now to be demanded. Although America detached itself diplomatically from these demands, it was unable to divorce itself from them economically. The economic stability of Europe depended upon American actions.

During the war Britain, France, and the other Allied powers had liquidated most of their American investments, which they had built up over the preceding 125 years, to purchase food and war matériel from the United States. Britain, for example, liquidated about 70 percent of its holdings of bonds and stocks. Since this was insufficient to purchase all that the Allies needed, the British borrowed the difference from the U.S. government. By the end of 1919 the net intergovernmental debt owed the federal government was $9.6 billion—about one-sixth of the American GNP at the time (see Figure 20.7). Although Great Britain was the largest single debtor, owing the U.S. government about $4 billion, Britain itself was a net creditor owed more by France, Italy, Russia, and the other Allied nations than it owed the United States. The international payments picture was further clouded by the Bolshevik repudiation of the Russian war debt, totaling $4 billion.

None of this inter-Allied governmental debt had existed before the war. In the view of the European allies, this debt existed only because of the unbridled aggression of the Central Powers (Germany, the Austro-Hungarian Empire, and the Ottoman Empire). It was therefore the Allies' view that the

FIGURE 20.7

Inter-Allied Governmental War Debt and the Question of Reparations

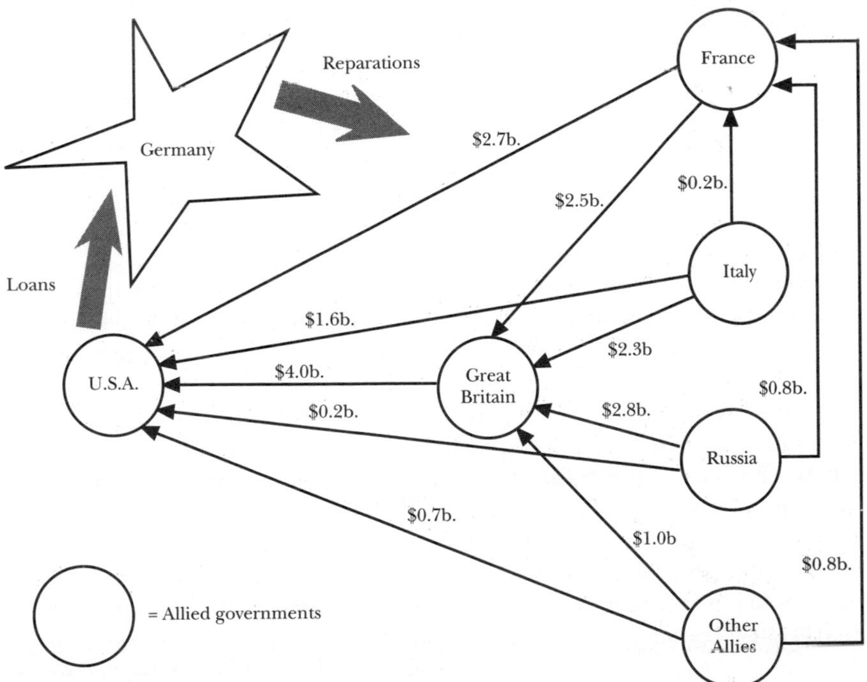

Source: Adapted from John Maynard Keynes, *The Economic Consequences of the Peace* (London: Macmillan, 1920).

Central Powers should be held responsible for the debt. The U.S. government, on the other hand, viewed this debt as a normal "commercial" transaction, freely entered into by the Allied governments and separate from the question of reparations. John Maynard Keynes, the renowned British economist who represented his country at the Versailles peace talks, was later to express the paradox:

> America's contribution for some time after she came into the war was mainly financial, because she was not yet ready to help in any other way. So long as America was sending materials and munitions to be used by Allied soldiers, she charged us for them, and these charges are the origin of what we now owe her. But when later on she sent men too, to use the munitions themselves, then we were charged nothing. Evidently there is not much logic in a system which causes us to owe money to America, not because she was able to help us so much, but because at first she was able to help us, so far at least as man power was concerned, so little.[11]

The European Allies ultimately agreed upon a reparations obligation from Germany of $33 billion, payable at the rate of $375 million a year until 1925 and $900 million thereafter in *interest alone.* Keynes argued that this was far beyond Germany's capacity to pay. Others have concluded that the burden was actually well within Germany's economic capacity to pay.[12] The reparations burden upon Germany (whether measured as a percent of GDP or a share of trade) was far less than that which Germany had imposed upon France after the Franco-Prussian War in 1871 and somewhat less than that which Britain transferred to its Allies during the Napoleonic Wars or the United States transferred to Europe in the Marshal Plan after the Second World War. However, reparations certainly proved to be beyond Germany's willingness to pay.

One result of the Allied reparations demand was the collapse of the German monetary system in 1923 after a spectacular inflationary episode that totally destroyed the value of the mark. On July 31, 1914, the German money supply had amounted to 6 billion marks convertible upon demand into gold. By November 1923, the money supply consisted of 92.8 quintillion (1 quintillion = 10^{18}) marks convertible into virtually nothing. For example, a newspaper sold for 200 billion marks, a loaf of bread for 428 billion marks, and a postage stamp for a domestic letter, 100 billion marks. In 1913 the dollar-mark exchange rate had been $1 = 4.2 marks; by July 1919 it was $1 = 229 marks; but by November 13, 1923, it was $1 = 4.2 billion marks. The currency was stabilized at this point by the introduction of a new currency, the rentenmark, on November 20, 1923, with an exchange rate of 1 trillion paper

[11] Keynes (1928).
[12] For example, Maclup (1975).

marks to 1 rentenmark. Thus the exchange rate became $1 = 4.2 rentenmarks, or the same relationship as had existed before the war.

However, the rentenmark was not freely convertible; convertibility awaited acceptance of the Dawes Plan negotiated by the United States. This plan reduced the reparation payments, linking them to Germany's recovery and capacity to pay, and provided $800 million as the reserves backing the newly convertible reichsmark (RM) at $1 = 4.2 RM. The loan was floated on Wall Street with the assistance of the Federal Reserve by pursuing an easy money policy.

Thus America provided Germany with the basis to pay the reparation demands so that the European Allies could meet their debt obligations to the U.S. government. In effect the private sector in America paid the foreign obligations to the federal government. Even this plan eventually broke down. After an abortive attempt to restructure debt payments in the Young Plan (1929), America was ultimately forced to accept a moratorium on intergovernmental debt payments and their cancellation by default.

The war fundamentally changed America's role in the world economy from a debtor nation, owing some $3.7 billion in 1914, to a creditor nation, owed almost $12.6 billion in 1920. Before the war the surplus on the visible trade account had just about balanced immigrant remittances and interest and dividend payments on foreign investment in America. After the war not only did the United States have an excess of exports over imports (averaging about $3.5 billion between 1916 and 1920), but U.S. citizens and businesses began to receive investment income of $0.5 billion or more, compared with American payments to foreigners of $100 million or so. One result was that foreigners could no longer buy American goods unless the United States bought more foreign goods or unless the Americans lent foreigners the money. There was a dollar shortage, of which the 1920–21 depression was just one manifestation. Onetime creditor nations, such as Britain, found it difficult or impossible to adjust to their new debtor status. Indeed, Britain's problems were compounded by its decision to return to the gold standard at the prewar exchange rate, £1 = $4.86, although it overvalued the pound sterling by perhaps 10 percent and placed British goods at a competitive disadvantage.

To bring things into balance, America needed to buy more and sell less. But this it proved unwilling to do. Angered by European restrictions on American imports (especially food), and with the "infant" wartime industries of dyes and chemicals threatened by renewed European competition, Congress passed an emergency tariff in 1921 that was regularized by the Fordney-McCumber Tariff Act of 1922.

Although America lent money overseas, its balance of payment surplus on the visible trade account and surplus on interest and debt payments resulted in an inflow of gold into the United States, not all of which was reloaned to foreigners. Indeed, U.S. official reserves increased by $1.149

million during the decade. Under the strict gold standard this should have expanded the money supply in the United States sufficiently to raise prices, choking off the export surplus. But this did not happen. Gold reserves rose by more than 50 percent during the decade, but the money supply (M1) increased by only 12 percent, and prices, as we have seen, hardly at all. As a result, the burden of adjustment was thrown wholly upon the debtor nation rather than shared between the debtor and creditor nations. Britain, with its overvalued currency after 1925, was particularly harmed by this policy. To attract short-term investment funds, London had to maintain interest rates above the levels in New York or Paris. These high interest rates reduced British domestic investment and plant modernization so that Great Britain fell progressively farther behind the rest of the developed world.

Hard Times down on the Farm

The very sharp decline in wholesale prices in 1920 and 1921 relative to the GNP deflator reflected the collapse of American farm prices in the wake of bountiful harvests and the evaporation of European demand for American farm produce. Agricultural prices had begun rising as early as 1914, and had risen more rapidly than other prices as export demand boomed. The farm sector had responded by expanding its scale using marginal lands and increasing debt through mechanization. The collapse of agricultural prices, coupled with the sudden unexpected credit tightness resulting from Fed policy, caused a serious liquidity crisis for many farmers. Wheat that once sold for $2.58 a bushel fetched as little as 92 cents in 1921. Corn prices fell from $1.85 a bushel to just 41 cents, and hog prices fell from 19 cents a pound to 6 ½ cents. As a result, the average net farm income declined from $1,395 to $517 per farm.

Prices did not recover very much once the recession had ended. They did not regain their World War I highs until after 1945, yet the prices of the inputs purchased by farmers did not fall by comparable amounts. The result was a shift in the farm terms of trade (called the parity ratio) against the farmer. This ratio assumes greater importance in the face of the growing cash needs of the American farmer, who increasingly depended upon the market to supply essential inputs for production and foodstuffs for home farm consumption. Instead the 1920s began a period of painful readjustment for American farmers and their creditors.

The farm sector found itself in a serious economic bind. Farm overexpansion had raised costs and reduced productivity. Restricted markets for agricultural commodities had reduced farm gate prices and the value of farmland. Low-income elasticity of demand for farm products and slower population growth reduced farm incomes at a time when farm cash flow demands were rising because of increased use of purchased inputs. The result was a sharp increase in farm foreclosure rates as prices fell relative to mortgage payments fixed in nominal dollars. Nationwide, the farm foreclosure rate had averaged just 3.2 per 1,000 between 1913 and 1920. Between 1921 and 1925 it more than tripled to 10.7 per 1,000. In the depression of 1920–21, 453,000 farmers lost their farms. The foreclosure rate rose even more between 1926 and 1930 to 16.7, peaking in 1933 at 38.8 per 1,000.[13] The agricultural distress was very unevenly distributed across the country. In Montana, for example, 280 of every 1,000 farmers lost their farms between 1920 and 1923. Distress was particularly concentrated in those areas specializing in wheat, corn, livestock, and cotton, which had expanded their scale of operation the most in response to high prices. Thus, for example, in 1926 the foreclosure rate in Minnesota was 60.8 per 1,000 farms and 52.5 per 1,000 in South Dakota, but only 9.3 per 1,000 in Texas and 5.5 per 1,000 in Massachusetts.

The 1920s mark the end of the dream for rural farm life. Farm population declined throughout the decade from almost 32 million people on 6.5 million farms to 30.5 million on 6.3 million farms, while the U.S. population grew by more than 8 million to 62 million. This decrease in farm population reflected the declining economic opportunities during the 1920s. Although both the number of farms and the farm population rose again during the 1930s, that simply represented a shift of population to a source of food during the depression.

The substitution of the tractor for the horse seemed to offer salvation to the individual farmer by reducing costs, reducing the drudgery, and decreasing dependency on hired labor. However, it only compounded the farmers' problems. Fuel and spare parts had to be purchased, while horse feed could be grown, and spare parts (shoes) were often fitted by the farmer. Horses could be a self-perpetuating or growing stock, but tractors depreciated. In addition, the replacement of the horse by the tractor released twenty-five million acres from hay and oats during the 1920s, and ultimately put ninety million acres of intramarginal lands back into market production. It also increased the debt burden of the farmer at a time of declining income and prices.

Because of the low price elasticity of demand for virtually all farm products—particularly in their raw states—farm income declined with the falling prices of farm products. Moreover, most of the cereals and raw material produced on the farm had low income elasticities, so farmers failed to gain from the rising affluence of consumers during the 1920s. Consequently, while the average earning for all employees rose from $1,236 in 1920 to $1,356 in 1929, farm income fell from an average of $1,196 to $945 in 1929. The decline in farm income also produced a precipitous decline in land values. In 1920 the average value per acre of land and buildings was $69.31. By

[13] Foreclosure rates from Alston (1983); number of farmers losing farms from Soule (1947).

1929 this value had fallen to $49.25 an acre. Land values fell an average of 51 percent between 1920 and 1940, with a range from 77 percent in South Dakota to just a 7 percent decline in Rhode Island. Farmers lost equity value in their farms, and the farm debt ratio rose during the same period from 13 percent to 20 percent. The collapse in land values also hurt the balance sheets of many of the farmers' creditors, especially the small rural banks, many of which failed.

"Supply-Side" Tax Cuts: Andrew Mellon's Tax Policy

The federal government in the 1920s did not have a fiscal policy—defined as the deliberate manipulation of government income and expenditures to achieve specific policy goals. Fiscal policy first began to emerge under Hoover as the Great Depression took hold. During the 1920s, however, the federal government did experiment with tax rates in an effort to improve the yield from the income tax. The author of this policy was Andrew Mellon, the longest-serving secretary of the treasury in American history. He became treasury secretary in 1921 under Harding and continued with Coolidge and Hoover until his "promotion" to ambassador to the Court of St. James's (that is, Great Britain) in 1932.

During his tenure Mellon instigated three separate tax cuts on the argument that the tax rates had already passed the point where they could be collected and that "by cutting the surtaxes in half, the Government, when the full effect of the reduction is felt, will receive more revenue from the owners of large incomes at the lower rates of tax than it would have received at the higher rates."[14] At the time (1921) single taxpayers had a personal exemption of $1,000 and the tax rate was 4 percent on the first $4,000 of taxable income with the rates peaking out at 73 percent on incomes over $1 million. By way of contrast, in 1981, before the Reagan tax cuts were enacted and with the dollar worth less than 20 percent of its 1921 value, the personal exemption was $2,000 for a single taxpayer—less than half the personal exemption in 1921. The minimum tax rate was 14 percent on the first $1,100—more than three times the rate in 1921 on an income incapable of supporting a person even in poverty. The top tax rate in 1981 was 70 percent on income over $108,300.

The first Mellon tax cut in November 1921 repealed the World War I excess profits tax and reduced the maximum surtax rate from 65 percent to 50 percent. In November 1923 Mellon again appeared before the House and told it that "wealthy men will not pay one half of their income to the government, therefore it is better to tax them at a rate they will pay."[15] His plan called for a reduction in the minimum tax rate to 3 percent on taxable in-

[14] Mellon (1924): 17.
[15] O'Connor (1933): 131.

comes under $4,000 and a cut from 8 percent to 6 percent on incomes under $8,000. In addition, the surtax rate was cut to 40 percent. In 1926 the last tax cut measure was passed, reducing surtax rates to 20 percent and also cutting inheritance taxes by half to 20 percent.

As a result of Mellon's tax cuts, someone with $1 million income saw his tax bill dwindle from $663,000 in 1921 to under $200,000. Despite this, income tax receipts rose during the 1920s, in part because incomes rose but also because it was no longer worth avoiding taxes. In 1921 the income tax yielded $719 million from 6.6 million returns; in 1929 the tax yield was $1 billion from 4 million returns, having risen by about the same percentage as the increase in nominal GNP. As in the 1980s, however, income inequality increased sharply. Whereas in 1921 the top 1 percent of the population had received 14.2 percent of the disposable income, in 1929 it received 19.1 percent of the income, or about the same as in 1990. There is, however, one important difference. Whereas in the 1980s government debt soared, in the 1920s the size of the national debt was sharply reduced from $24 billion to $16 billion, thanks to persistent budget surpluses—a performance unequaled since the 1880s and never repeated.

Electric Power in Industry and the Home

The 1920s also witnessed a dramatic change in the source of power in both the home and the factory in America. In 1919 55 percent of the power in manufacturing was supplied by electricity. By 1929 electricity supplied 82 percent of the power. This statistic obscures the dramatic increase in electric power use in small workshops and among other small power users as a result of the perfection of the fractional horsepower electric motor. The switch to electric power gave manufacturers complete freedom of location. They were no longer tied to a fixed site by direct-drive waterpower, nor were they forced to balance their location decisions between consumers and raw materials, one of which—fuel—lost all mass and volume in the production of output. One result of this switch from direct-drive waterpower to electricity was the migration of the cotton textile industry from the New England fall line, where waterpower was cheap, to the South, where labor was cheap.

The adoption of electric power and use of the fractional horsepower electric motor also brought with it complete flexibility in the location of pieces of machinery and equipment within the factory. As a result, scientific management techniques could be exploited to their fullest. This was an element in the extraordinary pace of productivity growth during the 1920s. By rendering obsolete so much plant and equipment, the switch to electric power further increased productivity by reducing the average age of plant and equipment and moving the country closer toward universal use of best practice methods. It also provided stimulus to the construction industry.

Electric power revolutionized the home. With its installation came small and large electrical appliances: refrigerators, fans, washing machines, ranges, toasters, and radios. During the 1920s as many as two million home refrigerators were sold, revolutionizing the food shopping habits of about 10 percent of the population. In 1924 one-third of all the money that households spent on furniture was spent on radios; there were some fourteen hundred radio stations broadcasting nationwide. By 1929 the radio had found its way into more than ten million households (more than a third of all households), where it brought a new source of entertainment, reduced provincialism, and brought new social attitudes and awareness.

The Automobile and American Life in the 1920s

Another consumer durable that found its way into more household budgets during the 1920s was the automobile. In 1920, 1.9 million automobiles rolled off the assembly line. There were 8.1 million passenger cars registered, or 1 car to every 3 households. When the decade ended, there were 23.1 million registered automobiles (almost 4.5 million of which had been produced in 1929), or 1 car per 1.29 households. In addition, there were 3.5 million trucks registered in 1929, triple the number at the start of the decade.

The automobile revolutionized life-styles. The migration of population from the central city, which had first been made possible by the streetcar, accelerated. Automobiles and trucks needed surfaced roads both within and between cities (Figure 20.8). The mileage of such rural and municipal roads increased from 369,000 miles in 1920 to 662,000 miles by 1929, supplemented by almost 190,000 miles of federally supported highway connecting principal centers of population. Expenditure for the construction and maintenance of these roads in 1929 was over $2 billion by federal, state, and local authorities, or about 2 percent of GNP, having more than doubled over the decade. This expenditure was vigorously opposed by the railroads, which faced new competition from the truck and the automobile. The railroads argued (unconvincingly in view of their own hand in the public purse with land grants) that expenditure on road improvements was an unfair public subsidy of a competing transportation medium.

The automobile industry quickly established itself as a major industry in the United States. In 1929 the industry, which had hardly existed thirty years earlier, produced 12.7 percent of manufacturing output, employed 7.1 percent of manufacturing wage earners, and paid 8.7 percent of the total industrial wages. The automobile brought with it traffic accidents, deaths, and the problems of urban congestion and pollution. It was also an important contributor to growing consumer indebtedness during the 1920s, as the majority of the millions of new cars sold during the 1920s were bought on credit. In 1919 perhaps 5 percent of households bought a car on credit, but by 1929, when almost a quarter of all American households bought a car,

FIGURE 20.8

A RURAL "ROAD" BEFORE IMPROVEMENT

A RURAL HIGHWAY AFTER IMPROVEMENT

Source: George Soule, *The Prosperity Decade* (New York: Holt, Rinehart and Winston, 1947): 248. Photo credit: Brown Brothers.

more than half were buying on credit. Indeed, in 1925, 68.2 percent of new cars were credit-financed, a percentage that was not exceeded until 1968. Moreover, credit was expensive. In this era before truth-in-lending laws, interest rates of 30 percent or more were not uncommon.[16]

The Construction Boom

The spread of electric power and the automobile generated a major construction boom in the 1920s. All indexes of construction activity show a dramatic increase after the First World War, peaking in 1925. For example, the index of the value of new building permits stood at 24.1 in 1918 (1930 = 100). By 1920 it had risen to 87.6, and in 1925 it peaked at 252.3. New construction was not, however, confined to transportation and industry. Residential construction also boomed as the automobile allowed the population to move out from the central city and away from workplaces into what became known as the suburbs. In 1920 work began on 247,000 new houses. The number of housing starts rose each year (including the depression of 1920–21) until it peaked in 1925 at 937,000 units, then declined to 509,000 in 1929. The 1925 peak was not reached again until 1946.

The Speculative Mania

One less productive development during the 1920s was the emergence of speculation as a major preoccupation for Americans. The Florida land boom, beginning soon after the war, was a portent of things to come. Prospective customers—many of them from the Snow Belt—were given free bus trips around the state by real estate promoters before being sold their lots from blueprints. Few customers actually saw their lots, which, as often as not, were swampland awaiting landfill. The Florida land boom collapsed when a hurricane on September 19, 1926, exposed the vulnerability of people's purchases. Thereafter speculation began in earnest on the stock market.

The end of the construction boom, the growing speculative mania that gripped the country, and the depressed conditions in the farm sector and among the rural banks that served its needs all threatened America's continued prosperity. Some even viewed a short-lived recession as desirable to bring values back into line with their fundamentals and to shake out the weak, thereby ultimately strengthening the economy. Few, if any, however, anticipated the economic crisis that was to overtake the economy and persist for more than a decade. Moreover, the continuation of shortsighted 1920s

[16] Olney (1991).

international economic policies worsened the depression when it came and, according to some, was a major reason why America's depression became a worldwide depression. It is to a consideration of these factors that we now turn.

Bibliography

Alston, Lee. "Farm Foreclosures in the United States During the Interwar Period," *Journal of Economic History* 43 (1983): 885–904.

Chandler, Lester V. *Benjamin Strong, Central Banker.* Washington, D.C.: Brookings Institution, 1958.

Diebold, Francis X., and Glenn D. Rudebusch. "Have Postwar Economic Fluctuations Been Stabilized?" *American Economic Review* 82 (1992): 993–1005.

Eichengreen, Barry. *Golden Fetters: The Gold Standard and the Great Depression 1919–1939.* New York: Oxford University Press, 1992.

Friedman, Milton, and Anna Schwartz. *A Monetary History of the United States, 1867–1960.* Princeton: Princeton University Press, 1963.

Hicks, John D. *Republican Ascendancy, 1921–1933.* New York: Harper & Row, 1960.

Higgs, Robert. "Crisis, Bigger Government, and Ideological Change: Two Hypotheses on the Rachet Phenomenon." *Explorations in Economic History* 22 (1985): 1–28.

———. *Crisis and Leviathan.* New York: Oxford University Press, 1987.

Kendrick, John W. *Productivity Trends in the United States.* Princeton: Princeton University Press, 1961.

Keynes, John Maynard. *Economic Consequences of the Peace* . London: Macmillan, 1920.

———. *Essays in Persuasion, Part I: Cancellation.* London: Macmillan, 1932.

Kindleberger, Charles. *The World in Depression, 1929–1939,* rev. ed. Berkeley: University of California Press, 1986.

Kuznets, Simon. *National Income and Its Composition, 1919–1938.* New York: Columbia University Press, 1941.

Lebergott, Stanley. "Discussion." *Journal of Economic History* 46 (1986): 367–71.

Machlup, Fritz. "The Transfer Problem: Theme and Four Variations," in *International Payments, Debts and Gold.* New York: New York University Press, 1975: 374–95.

Mellon, Andrew. *Taxation: The People's Business.* New York: Macmillan, 1924.

O'Connor, Harvey. *Mellon's Millions: The Biography of a Fortune.* New York: John Day, 1933.

Olney, Martha. *Buy Now, Pay Later.* Chapel Hill: University of North Carolina Press, 1991.

Romer, Christina D. "Is Stabilization of the Postwar Economy a Figment of the Data?" *American Economic Review* 76 (1986): 314–34.

———."New Estimates of Prewar Gross National Product and Unemployment." *Journal of Economic History* 47 (1986): 341–52.

———. "Spurious Volatility in Historical Unemployment Data." *Journal of Political Economy* 94 (1986): 1–37.

———. "World War I and the Postwar Depression: A Reinterpretation Based upon Alternative Estimates of GNP." *Journal of Monetary Economics* 22 (1988): 91–116.

———. "The Prewar Business Cycle Reconsidered: New Estimates of Gross National Product, 1869–1908. *Journal of Political Economy* 97 (1989): 1–37.

Rothbard, Murray. *America's Greatest Depression.* Princeton: Princeton University Press, 1963.

Samuelson, Paul A., and Everett E. Hagen. *After the War, 1918–20.* Washington, D.C.: U.S. National Resources Planning Board, 1943.

Soule, George. *The Prosperity Decade, 1917–1929.* New York: Holt, Rinehart and Winston, 1947.

Toma, Mark. "The Policy Effectiveness of Open Market Operations in the 1920s." *Explorations in Economic History* (1989): 99–116.

Weir, David. "The Reliability of Historical Macroeconomic Data for Comparing Cyclical Stability." *Journal of Economic History* 46 (1986): 353–65.

Wheelock, David. "The Strategy, Effectiveness, and Consistency of Federal Reserve Monetary Policy, 1919–1933. *Explorations in Economic History* 26 (1989): 453–76.

———. *The Strategy and Consistency of Federal Reserve Monetary Policy, 1924 to 1932–33.* Cambridge: Cambridge University Press, 1991.

Wicker, Elmus. "Federal Reserve Monetary Policy, 1922–23: A Reinterpretation." *Journal of Political Economy* 73 (1965): 325–43.

———. "A Reconsideration of Federal Reserve Policy during the 1920–1921 Depression." *Journal of Economic History* 26 (1966): 223–38.

———. *Federal Reserve Monetary Policy, 1917–1933.* New York: Random House, 1966.

The great depression: explaining the contraction

21

For many people the prosperity of the 1920s ended, symbolically at least, with the stock market crash of October 1929. Just fourteen months earlier Herbert Hoover, accepting his party's nomination for the presidency of the United States, had declared, "We in America today are nearer to the final triumph over poverty than ever before in the history of any land."[1] He won, carried to victory on the promise to apply business management skills and engineering efficiency to government and to put "a chicken in every pot and two cars in every garage." When he was voted out of office just four years later, shantytowns known as Hoovervilles dotted the countryside (Figure 21.1); Chicago, the manufacturing center of the United States, had some seven hundred thousand unemployed, or about 40 percent of those who reported gainful occupations; bread lines stretched around blocks (Figure 21.2). The U. S. Army, with bayonets fixed, sabers drawn, and supported by tanks, had dispersed the so-called Bonus Army of unemployed veterans from World War I who had gathered on Anacostia Flats just outside Washington, D.C., to petition the government peacefully for redress of their grievances. Clearly something had gone dreadfully wrong. Nor was normalcy quickly restored. Indeed, it was a decade before some economic indicators had returned to the levels they had achieved in 1929. This period quickly displaced the 1890s in American historiography as the Great Depression—a time still vividly remembered by many of our parents and certainly by our grandparents. Its legacy is enshrined in so many of our political, economic, and social institutions and thought.

[1] *New York Times* (August 12, 1928): 1.

FIGURE 21.1

A "Hooverville" in New York's Central Park

Source: Ross M. Robertson and Gary M. Walton, *History of the American Economy,* 4th ed. (New York: Harcourt Brace Jovanovich, 1979): 413. Photo credit: Bettmann Archives.

Despite its pervasive impact, there are few events on which there is less consensus about the issues, the data, the relevant hypotheses, or the appropriate tests than the Great Depression. Among the key questions are whether or not a different economic policy, particularly by the Federal Reserve, would have avoided the collapse and what role the international power vacuum left by World War I might have played in the worldwide crisis. The origins of the crisis are as heatedly debated as is the question of what led to eventual recovery. This chapter examines the events and explanations associated with the downturn, the period lasting until 1932 or 1933. Consideration of the recovery is deferred to Chapter 22.

Some Facts

Between 1929 and 1933 real output fell by 29 percent (Figure 21.3). It then took five years to inch back to predepression levels. Gross investment fell from about 15 percent of GNP—approximately the long-run historical average—to less than 1 percent in 1932 and 1933 and remained below the

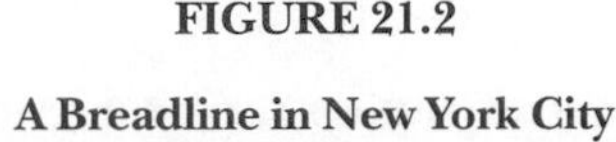

FIGURE 21.2

A Breadline in New York City

Source: Broadus Mitchell, *The Depression Decade* (White Plains: M. E. Sharpe, 1947): facing 110. Photo credit: Acme.

long-term trend until World War II rearmament. Net investment (gross investment less wear and tear) was probably negative between 1932 and 1934 — that is, the capital stock of the country was allowed to shrink.

Behind these economic aggregates, however, hides the appalling toll that the depression had upon the lives of so many Americans. Millions lost their livelihoods—and eventually their self-respect. In 1929 only 3.2 percent (1.5 million persons) of the labor force was unemployed. Many, if not most, of them were in the normal process of switching jobs. By 1933 the situation had changed dramatically. Well over 10 million Americans were pounding the pavement looking for work, and another 2.2 million had make-work emergency jobs (at low pay) from state, local, and federal governments. That adds up to 21 or 25 percent of the labor force unemployed, depending on whether those employed in government make-work programs are counted among the unemployed (Figure 21.4).

Even these figures mask the true trauma of the events because they fail to measure the unequal burden of the economic collapse. Although hard numbers are difficult to come by, there is little question that urban blacks and other racial minorities living in cities were more severely affected than the population as a whole. In early 1930, before the depression's grip had re-

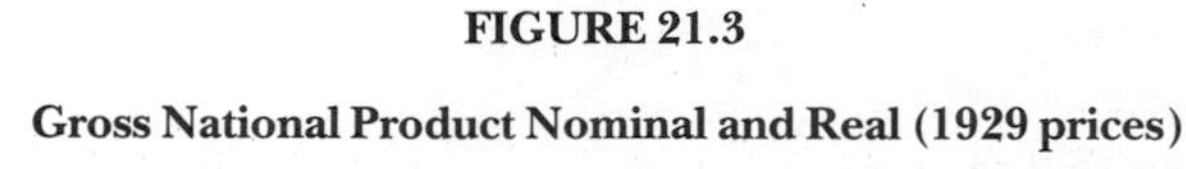

FIGURE 21.3

Gross National Product Nominal and Real (1929 prices)

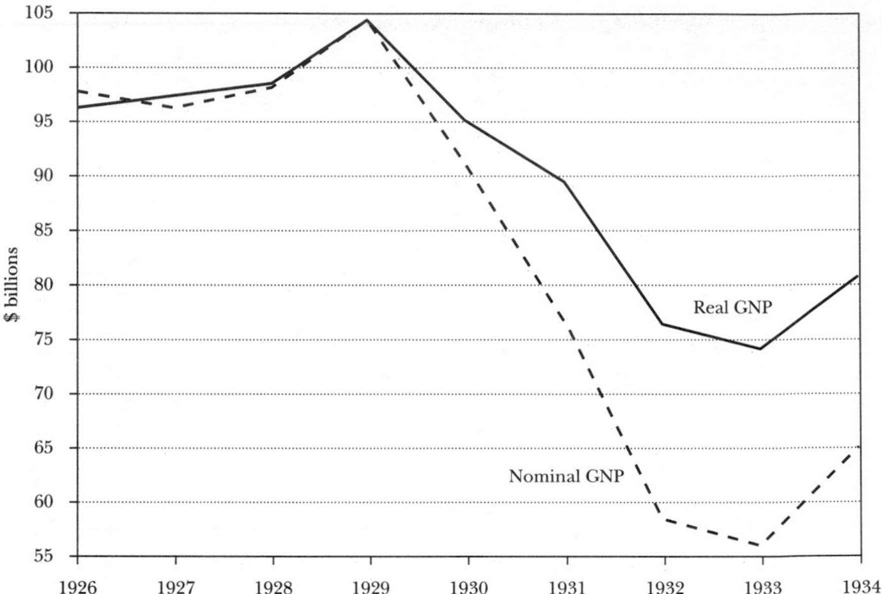

Source: U.S. Bureau of the Census, *Historical Statistics of the United States* (Washington, D.C.: Government Printing Office, 1975): Series F1 and F5.

ally tightened, unemployment among African-Americans was similar to that among the white population—between 6 and 7 percent nationwide—but only because most of the black population lived in the South, where unemployment rates were lower (because of the relative importance of agriculture). By early 1931, in ten surveyed cities, African-American unemployment rates were at least 50 percent higher than among white workers. Among African-American females, unemployment rates were more than two and half times higher than among white females. Black men and women were fired first both because of discrimination and because a disproportionate number worked in the particularly hard-hit service sectors: household domestics, restaurant and hotel workers, and so on. Indeed, African-American unemployment rates would have been even higher but for their relative concentration in agriculture and the South.[2]

Then, too, the overall unemployment rate does not distinguish between the unpleasantness of a month or two out of work and the catastrophe of a year or two without work. In good times most unemployment is transitory in

[2] Sundstrom (1992).

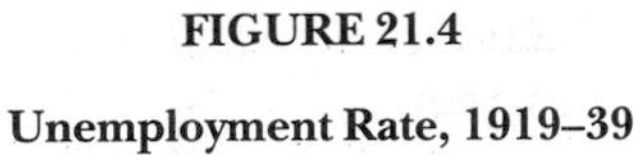

FIGURE 21.4

Unemployment Rate, 1919–39

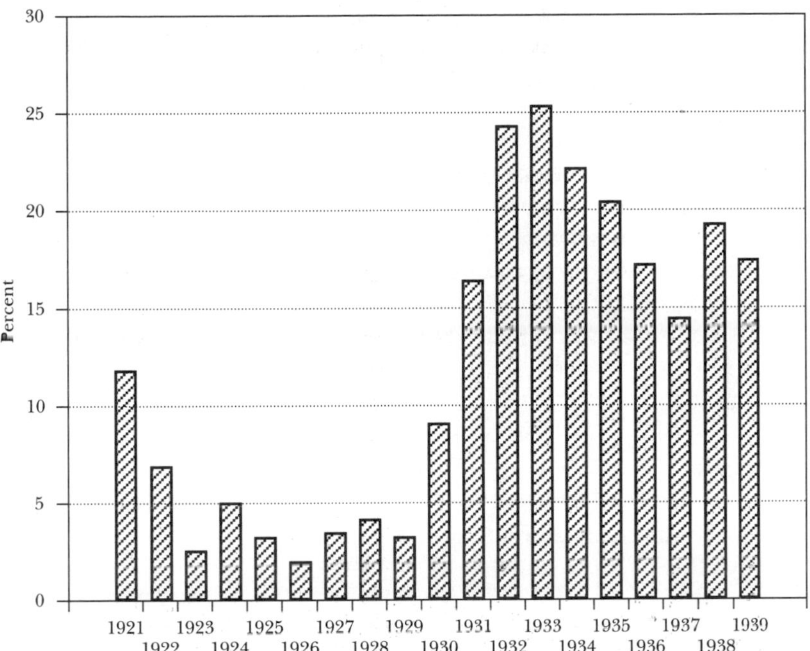

Source: U.S. Bureau of the Census. *Historical Statistics of the United States* (Washington, D.C.: Government Printing Office, 1975): Series D86.

nature with people finding themselves between jobs. During the depression, when unemployment remained at least double the 1929 rate for ten straight years, a large fraction of the unemployed had no reasonable prospect of ever again making a living without government aid. In retrospect, then, it is no wonder that the depression produced the most serious challenge to the established political and social order in America since the Civil War.

Early Course of Events, 1929–30

It was the stock market crash that brought the economic situation to the attention of most Americans, but this was not the first indication of impending trouble, and nothing prepared anyone for what was to follow. Nor was the crash itself all that sudden. Signs of a recession appeared in the summer of 1929, when the Federal Reserve's index of industrial production turned down after growing 5 percent during the first half of the year (Figure 21.5). The great British economist John Maynard Keynes and others have attributed this slowdown to an abrupt change in Federal Reserve policy begun in January 1928.

In an effort to curb stock market speculation and rising prices during the upswing of the business cycle, the Fed moved to restrict growth in the money supply by selling government bonds and raising interest rates. From 1921 through 1927 the money supply defined as currency plus bank deposits grew at an average annual rate of 4.5 percent. During 1928 and 1929, however, the rate slowed abruptly to 0.6 percent per year as the Fed sold $405 million of government bonds, raised the buying rate on banker's acceptances, and raised the discount rate from 3.5 percent to 5 percent in three steps. In August 1929 the buying rate on acceptances was lowered to help seasonal demand in trade and agriculture while the New York Fed raised its

FIGURE 21.5

Federal Reserve Seasonally Adjusted Index of Industrial Production

Source: Federal Reserve Board. *Annual Report, 1937* (Washington, D.C.: Federal Reserve Board, 1937).

discount rate another percentage point to 6 percent to discourage further stock market speculation.

One consequence of rising interest rates was higher rates on call loans—money lent overnight and subject to daily renewal—which stood at 12 percent in March 1929, and rose to 20 percent before declining during the summer as new money poured into the market. The Standard & Poor's Composite Stock Index peaked on September 7, 1929 (Figure 21.6). During the rest of the month and on into early October the market drifted lower, falling about 10 percent, without any panic, before rallying.

Among the factors underlying the September break in the market were revelations of fraud on the London Stock Market and a sharp rise in London interest rates as the Bank of England sought to discourage an outflow of gold and maintain the gold exchange standard. At their September 24 meeting, members of the Open Market Investment Committee, the Fed's chief policy

FIGURE 21.6

Standard & Poor's Composite Daily Stock Price Index (1941–43 = 100)

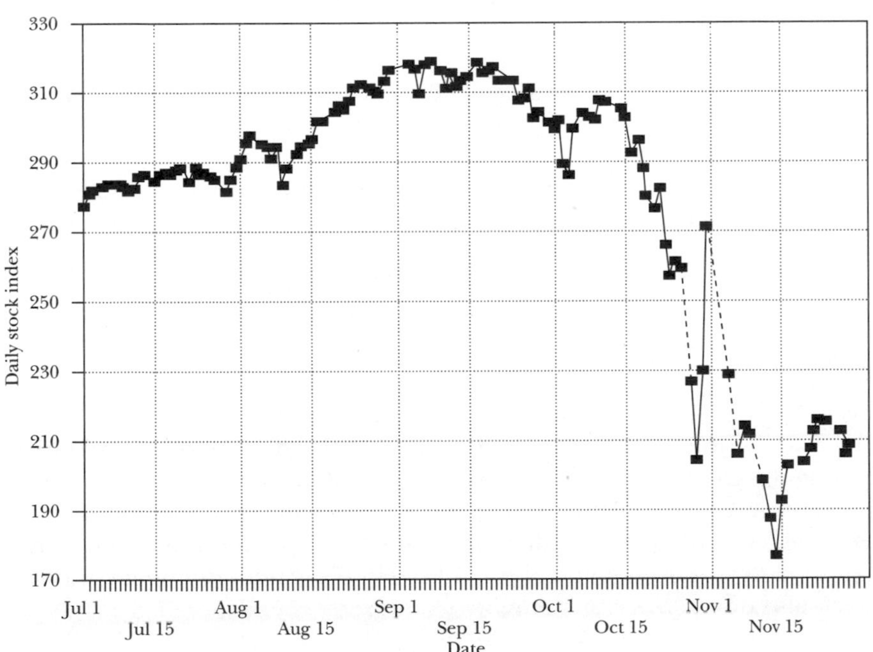

Source: Data from Standard & Poor's. Trade and Securities Statistics, *Security Price Index Record* (New York: Standard & Poor's, 1971).

arm, determining their open market policy for the following month, expressed concern about the fall in industrial production and signs of weakness in the stock market and authorized a modest relaxation of then-tight monetary policy by buying $25 million per week of government bonds. In early October the New York Stock Exchange rallied somewhat, rising about 8 percent. The return to higher prices led one widely respected economist, Irving Fisher of Yale University, to pronounce that the stock market stood on "what looks like a permanently high plateau" and could expect to be "a good deal higher than it is today within a few months."[3] The same day his words were uttered, October 15, Standard & Poor's index fell 3.5 percent, and selling continued in the days that followed. By Monday, October 21, volume had reached six million shares, but Fisher declared that the breaks in the market had "driven stocks down to hard rock."[4] After a slight rally on Tuesday the market lost $4 billion on Wednesday, and brokers clogged telephone and telegraph lines with margin calls to customers to increase their down payments securing their stock holdings. For many investors it was the third such call within a few days, and many were sold out before they could reply.

Panic selling hit the market the next day, October 24: "Black Thursday." By the time the market closed, almost thirteen million shares had changed hands, overwhelming the technology of the day. At 1:00 P.M. the ticker was running an hour and a half late. Sellers no longer knew the prices received on their trades, nor would they know until 7:00 that night, when the tape recorded the last of the day's exchanges. The decline in prices might have been worse but for a conspicuous meeting of the leading bankers at the offices of J. P. Morgan & Company. Their word that they would support the market, however, was hardly unselfish and disinterested. The banks themselves had a major stake in the market quite apart from any concern they may have felt about the liquidity positions of some of their major customers.

The shock wave from Wall Street rippled around the world, precipitating crashes, first in the London exchange, then in Paris and Berlin, and eventually in Tokyo. On Friday President Hoover tried to reassure the market that the "fundamental business of the country—that is, the production and distribution of goods and services—is on a sound and prosperous basis," and prices stabilized temporarily. The market was in trouble, however. Although call loan rates had fallen, stock dividends covered only one-third of the interest on borrowed funds and the stockholder's continued willingness to hold stock bought on margin depended upon some prospect for short-term capital gains. Instead more bad economic news followed. The Fed's index of industrial production for the third quarter showed a decline, particularly in automobiles, tires, and steel production. Building contracts were also down. Nor was the news from overseas encouraging: Prices on

[3] Hirst (1931): 18–19.
[4] Ibid.: 21.

Brazil's coffee exchange had collapsed, threatening Brazil's ability to meet its foreign debt obligations.

The market opened lower and on Monday and Tuesday, October 28–29, fell 23 percent, erasing the capital gains for the entire year on a volume of more than sixteen million shares (Figure 21.7). Unlike Black Thursday, however, the stocks that fell belonged to the major corporations AT&T, U.S. Steel, and General Electric. U.S. Steel, for example, was down $17\frac{1}{2}$ points on Monday, and General Electric fell $47\frac{1}{2}$ points. Again the bankers met, but this time no action was forthcoming. Except for minor, short-lived rallies the market continued to drift lower. On November 13, 1929, AT&T, which had sold at 304 on September 3, traded at $197\frac{1}{4}$; General Electric traded at 168.125 down from $396\frac{1}{4}$, and stock in U.S. Steel, which had sold for $261\frac{3}{4}$, sold at 150. Prices continued to drift lower until mid-1932. Other indexes also declined. By December 1929 industrial production was only 82 percent of its June 1929 level. Residential building contracts were only 64 percent of

FIGURE 21.7

Change in Stock Index from Trading Day to Trading Day and Cumulative Gains

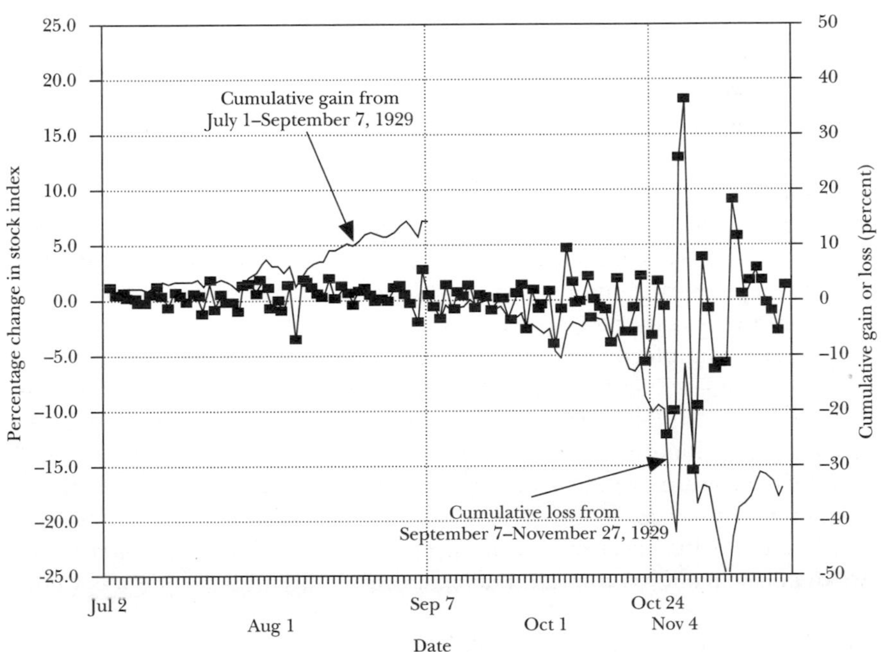

Source: Computed from Figure 21.6.

their June level. By March 1933, the economy's low point by most indexes, the index of industrial production stood at 47 percent, residential building contracts were at 8 percent, and factory employment was only 57 percent of the June 1929 levels.

Explaining the Depression

There is remarkably little unanimity among economists about the issues, explanations, or tests of the theories concerning the Great Depression. For example, writing in 1976, MIT economist Peter Temin argued that monetary forces were not the cause of the depression, which he attributes primarily to an unanticipated and unexplained decline in consumption expenditures. John Maynard Keynes in the early 1930s attributed the crisis to the impact of changes in Federal Reserve monetary policy but later, in his influential book *The General Theory of Interest, Money, and Employment* in 1936, blamed the decline upon the loss of business confidence that undermined investment spending. Nobel Laureate and University of Chicago emeritus economist Milton Friedman and his collaborator, Anna Schwartz, in *A Monetary History of the United States, 1867–1960* also emphasize the role of Federal Reserve policy and the impact of specific monetary shocks to the financial system. More recently Schwartz has emphasized nonmonetary forces as well as monetary forces in the onset of the depression. Others, now labeled "neo-Austrians"—identifying them primarily as followers of the great Austrian economist Friedrich von Hayek—also emphasize the role of monetary forces but take a view diametrically opposed to that of Friedman and Schwartz.[5] While Friedman and Schwartz criticize the Federal Reserve for doing too little too late, the neo-Austrians argue that the Federal Reserve did too much: Its actions inhibited the free market's adjustment to a new equilibrium, intensifying and prolonging the depression. Furthermore, a large number of scholars, both at the time and more recently, have given a central role in their interpretations to international trade and finance.[6] In short, there are many competing explanations, not all of which are mutually exclusive. For example, one can accept Temin's hypothesis of an unexpectedly large, unexplained shift in consumption expenditures as the explanation for the onset of the depression without rejecting Friedman and Schwartz's monetary explanation. Temin focuses his attention upon the events of 1929 and 1930; Friedman and Schwartz place greater emphasis upon the events from late 1930 onward.

The following sections elaborate upon these various explanations for the depression and try to present a balanced picture of the evidence. In the

[5] For example, Rothbard (1972). For earlier proponents of this argument, see Robbins (1934).
[6] For example, Eichengreen (1992); Kindleberger (1986), and Lewis (1949).

final analysis, though, there are more explanations for the events than events to be explained. The Great Depression was probably the product of many different causes.

Aggregate Demand-Based Explanations

Perhaps the simplest way to look at some of the factors underlying the depression is to use a simple Keynesian formulation of the identity between aggregate supply (*GNP*) and aggregate demand where aggregate demand is the sum of consumption expenditures (C), investment expenditures (I), net exports (X-M), and government purchases (G):

$$\text{aggregate supply} = \text{aggregate demand}$$
$$GNP = C + I + (X - M) + G$$
$$\Delta GNP = \text{multiplier} \times (\Delta C + \Delta I + \Delta(X - M) + \Delta G)$$

that is to say, the change in GNP is a multiple of the changes in the spending components of aggregate demand.

Let us consider each of the possible sources of change in aggregate demand in turn.

CONSUMPTION

In 1929 consumption expenditures totaled $77.2 billion; in 1933 they totaled just $45.8 billion. Even when one allows for declining prices, real consumption expenditures declined over 23 percent to $59 billion. A variety of explanations have been offered for this decrease.

Economists have found it both convenient and plausible to model consumption as an increasing function of wealth and income where income consists of both "permanent" income (i.e., long-term income), which determines customary consumption habits given tastes, habit, prices, and so on, and "transitory" income, which consists of short-term fluctuations in income about the permanent level. They generally argue that consumption is relatively insensitive to reductions in income that are viewed as temporary but that individuals consume a relatively higher proportion of transitory increases in income to purchase luxury items.

Joseph Schumpeter, the Harvard economist perhaps best remembered for his work on business cycles, and others have suggested that the Great Depression was the result of "underconsumption"—the corollary to "overproduction"—as a result of structural changes in the American economy during the 1920s. The argument is as follows: During the 1920s labor productivity grew rapidly as a result of technological advances (many of them related to electrification) and managerial improvements, but this increase was not fully reflected in rising real wages. As a result, the ability to produce goods outstripped the means to buy them, and a fundamental readjustment to this new reality was eventually required.

There is some evidence consistent with this hypothesis. The number of labor hours needed to produce a unit of output in manufacturing, for example, fell 40 percent during the decade, but nominal wages changed very little, and prices fell only by about 20 percent.[7] The difference was reflected in a rise in corporate profits (which helped fuel the rise in stock prices to the extent that those prices measured the net worth of corporate assets or the present discounted value of future dividends) and an increase in the inequality in the distribution of income, which was further reinforced by the 1920s tax reforms of Secretary of the Treasury Andrew Mellon. These changes in the distribution of income favored those who saved over those who consumed. Consumption thus failed to keep pace with production, and the marginal propensity to consume may have fallen.

There are, however, many problems with the underconsumption thesis that make it a less than satisfactory explanation for events between 1929 and 1933. First, there is the question of timing. Even if one accepts all the assumptions implicit in the hypothesis, nothing explains why consumption collapsed only after 1929 in virtually every sector of the economy, well after economic downturn had begun. Second, in its most extreme form, the underconsumption hypothesis presupposes rigid prices though little in American history down to that time, nor the events of 1929–33, give much support to such a claim. Between 1929 and 1933 prices fell an average of about 25 percent, with agricultural prices falling somewhat more and manufactured goods' prices falling less rapidly. Third, the development of consumer credit for durable goods purchases did much to maintain and even build demand for "big ticket" items despite lagging current income levels.[8]

Income for one group, farmers (who made up perhaps a quarter of the population at the time), declined particularly quickly. Farm income fell some 30 percent, from $6.2 billion in 1929 to $4.3 billion in 1930, under the combined effects of bountiful harvests (the 1930 wheat crop, for example, was 10 percent larger than the 1929 crop) and shrinking markets, particularly overseas. Farm prices collapsed. Wheat, which in 1929 had sold for $1.05 per bushel, fetched only 67 cents a bushel in 1930, and cotton prices declined 43 percent. Indeed, wheat was so cheap that many farmers substituted wheat for corn in livestock feed. As a result of this sharp decline in their income, many farmers, particularly those who had borrowed money to expand farm operations or to buy new implements such as tractors, faced a severe cash flow crisis. Moreover, their financial difficulties hurt their creditors, the nation's small rural banks, but this gets us ahead of our story. The impact of reduced farm income and consumption levels, however, was at

[7] U.S. Bureau of Census (1975): Series D802, E135, and W4.[8] Olney (1991).

least partially offset by the rise in real income purchasing power among the rest of the population as food prices dropped, making it possible for the nonfarm population to spend more money on other goods.

No such offsetting gains resulted from the loss of paper wealth from the stock market crash, which knocked billions of dollars off the market value of stocks. Between September 1929 and the start of 1930, capital losses totaled $57 billion, and between September 1929 and June 1932, when the market finally turned around, about $179 billion of value was lost on the nation's thirty-four exchanges. Perhaps half this loss occurred on the New York Stock Exchange alone (Table 21.1). How great the impact of this wealth loss—whether realized or not—was upon consumption is unclear. Two factors would suggest that the initial effect may not have been too great. First, stock ownership was quite limited despite the myth of almost universal stock speculation in the late 1920s. Only about five million people owned any stock, and perhaps five hundred thousand of these owned 75 to 85 percent of the outstanding stock. Second, the effect upon consumption depends in large part on whether the loss in wealth is viewed as permanent. On the other hand, for many Americans the bull market of the 1920s had been a symbol of unbridled economic prosperity, and its collapse must have caused them to reassess their expectations pessimistically.

The conventional wisdom today suggests that for every $1 change in net worth, consumption changes by 6 cents.[9] If we assume that this relationship also held during the Great Depression, a third or more of the decline in consumption between September 1929 and June 1932 might be attributed to the wealth effects of the capital losses suffered on the nation's exchange. Indeed, if we suppose that monthly consumption expenditures tracked the same pattern as industrial production in 1929 (which peaked in June of that year), then capital losses from September 1929 to the end of the year should have reduced consumption by perhaps double the observed decline in consumption. Perhaps during that year consumer expenditures were temporarily buoyed by other considerations, such as the losses' being thought temporary rather than permanent. A similar but more plausible calculation for 1930 and 1931 estimates that at least one-third of the observed decline in consumption expenditure might be attributed to continued capital losses in the market. Further, perhaps a quarter of the decline in consumption between January and June 1932 might be attributed to continued losses on the stock market before the market finally turned around.

Not only did households suffer realized or paper losses in financial wealth, but the real value of their liabilities increased as prices fell and they were compelled to repay their debts with increasingly valuable (and scarce) dollars. Between 1929 and 1930, for example, the real value of household li-

[9] Ando and Modigliani (1963).

TABLE 21. 1

Estimated Capital Losses on Common and Preferred Stock Held by Nonfarm Households and Their Possible Impact Upon Consumption Expenditures, September 1929–June 1932

Date (Year end unless otherwise noted)	Stock Prices[a] ($ billions) (1)	Change in Stock Prices[a] ($ billions) (2)	Estimated Capital Loss[a] ($ billions) (3)	Predicted Impact of Losses on Consumption[b] ($ billions) (4)	Change in Consumption Expenditures[c] ($ billions) (5)	Predicted / Actual (percent) (4)/(5)
Sept. 1929	237.8					
1929	163.7	−74.1	−57.0	−3.42	−1.78	192
1930	117.0	−46.7	−44.6	−2.68	−7.34	37
1931	61.2	−55.8	−53.3	−3.20	−9.42	34
June 1932	35.9	−25.3	−24.1	−1.45	−5.94	24
Cumulative		−201.9	−179.0	−10.74	−24.48	44

[a] Source: George Green, "The Economic Impact of the Stock Market Boom and Crash of 1929," in Federal Reserve Bank of Boston, *Consumer Spending and Monetary Policy: The Linkages* (Boston: Federal Reserve Bank of Boston, 1971): Table 21.4.

[b] Estimated capital loss * 0.06.

[c] U.S. Bureau of the Census. *Historical Statistics of the United States* (Washington, D.C.: Government Printing Office, 1975): Series F48. Consumption decline in the last third of 1929 estimated by distributing actual consumption over the year in same pattern as monthly index of industrial production. One-half of the consumption decline in 1932 is allocated to the first half of the year.

abilities—loans to buy stocks, mortgages, consumer credit, and so on—increased by 20 percent. As a result, the balance sheet for the average American household took a dramatic turn for the worse with declining net worth and an increasing debt burden, placing households in increasingly unfavorable liquidity positions and discouraging expenditures on durable goods and large-ticket illiquid assets such as houses.[10]

When the recession began, few, if any, recognized that it would become the longest and most severe depression in American history. As a result, although unemployment more than doubled between 1929 and 1930, rising from 3.2 percent to 8.7 percent of the labor force, it probably had relatively little effect upon current consumption patterns since consumers viewed it as a purely transitory loss of expected income. At some point the realization began to sink in that the income loss might be more permanent, and spending habits were drastically revised. Such a change in perceptions may well account for the inexplicably large drop in consumption that Temin finds in 1930. However, it is not clear why consumers should have so quickly rejected recent experience such as the depression of 1920–21 as their best model for the situation in which they found themselves, particularly since most economists at the time confidently predicted that recovery was just around the corner.

The unexpectedly large decline in autonomous consumption expenditures in 1930 occupies a central role in Temin's explanation of the Great Depression. In his words "the fall in consumption was unusually large in 1929. . . . Goods that could not be sold were not produced. The fall in aggregate demand spread throughout the economy. And as the fall of 1930 wore on and business did not recover . . . businessmen lost the confidence that underlies private investment. The economy continued to decline."[11] Temin thus offers a Keynesian style of aggregate demand explanation for the depression, but one markedly different from that of Keynes himself, who explained the event in terms of the collapse of business confidence underlying gross private domestic investment.

GROSS PRIVATE DOMESTIC INVESTMENT

Keynes was among the first economists to assign an important role to investment in the downturn. He wrote: "I attribute the slump of 1930 primarily to the deterrent effects on investment of the long period of clear money which preceded the collapse itself. But the collapse having occurred, it greatly aggravated matters, especially in the United States, by causing a disinvestment in working capital."[12] By the time he was writing his *General Theory*, however, he had modified this view to the notion that the marginal efficiency

[10] Mishkin (1978).
[11] Temin (1976): 172.
[12] Keynes (1930): II, 196.

of investment curve (then called the marginal efficiency of capital) had shifted in toward the origin because of the volume of prior investment, which had averaged 16 percent of GNP during much of the 1920s.[13]

During the 1923–33 downswing, however, not only did gross investment fall, but the period was actually characterized by disinvestment. Not only was excess capacity mothballed, but total capacity was reduced as businesses opted not to replace the wear and tear on what investment was kept in operation (Table 21.2). Indeed, the changes in investment during the early years of the depression are of such magnitude that they can plausibly explain the entire change in aggregate demand between 1929 and 1933—just as the Keynesians argue.

Investment, however, had begun to decline well before the onset of the depression, having peaked in 1926. Much of the change in investment spending in both the 1920s and the 1930s can be traced to variations in construction activity, particularly residential construction. The housing industry, in particular, had boomed in the mid-twenties. In each of the years between 1924 and 1927 the ratio of real residential construction to GNP was

TABLE 21.2

Gross Private Domestic Investment and Its Components 1929–1939 ($ billions)

Date	Gross Private Domestic Investment	Change in GPDI	Net Change in Inventories	Residential Construction	Net Private Domestic Investment
1929	16.2		1.7	4.0	8.7
1930	10.3	−5.9	−0.4	2.3	2.8
1931	5.6	−4.7	−1.1	1.7	−1.3
1932	1.0	−4.6	−2.5	0.7	−5.1
1933	1.4	0.4	−1.6	0.6	−4.3
1934	3.3	1.9	−0.7	0.9	−2.5
1935	6.4	3.1	1.1	1.2	0.6
1936	8.5	2.1	1.3	1.6	2.6
1937	11.8	3.3	2.5	1.9	5.3
1938	6.5	−5.3	−0.9	2.0	−0.1
1939	9.3	2.8	0.4	2.9	2.8

Source: U.S. Bureau of the Census, *Historical Statistics of the United States* (Washington, D.C.: Government Printing Office, 1975).

[13] See also Hansen (1951) and Gordon (1974).

at record levels—in excess of 8 percent of GNP—and it represented about half of gross private domestic investment. That level, however, could not be sustained or justified, and by 1929 residential construction was less than half its mid-decade peak. In part the decrease stemmed from declining demand for housing. Population growth was slowing down as fewer families were formed and fewer immigrants landed on these shores. Indeed, it has been estimated that the demographic slump of the 1920s and 1930s can account for about 28 percent of the decline in housing starts by 1933 and 39 percent by 1940.[14] Hence it is doubtful whether the level of building activity could have been maintained in the face of demographic forces. Moreover, even if household growth had continued at its level of the early 1920s and income had been maintained, predicted housing starts would still have fallen by 35 percent between 1925 and 1930. The actual decline in housing starts was 65 percent. Allowing for the reduced rate of household formation over the period raises the predicted decline in housing starts to 49 percent. America's builders overbuilt but the deflationary economic impact of the decline in residential construction was delayed and disguised by the buoyancy of consumer expenditure and stock market speculative fever until these collapsed in 1930.

NET EXPORTS

In 1928 net exports were at their highest level since 1921; American imported goods were valued at $4 billion, and exported goods worth $5 billion. As a result, foreign trade injected $1 billion into the circular flow of income in 1928. Net exports generally declined thereafter and reached their nadir in 1936, when exports exceeded imports by a mere $33 million on a trade volume that was less than half that of 1928–29.

In 1929 America exported more than in 1928, but net exports declined because of the rapid growth of imports brought about by the boom conditions and domestic industry's inability to satisfy demand. The increase in exports, however, disguised a weakening of demand for American products from some major trading partners, particularly in western Europe. The economic downturn began early in western Europe, limiting its demand for American exports. Moreover, Europeans' ability to purchase imports was compromised by their international payments difficulties. Great Britain, for example, in 1925, had returned to the gold standard at the prewar parity level, which overvalued the pound sterling by 10 percent or so. As a result, British exports were too expensive to be very attractive to foreign customers while imports in Britain competed vigorously with domestic products. Nonetheless, Britain remained a source of long-term foreign investment, fi-

[14] Hickman (1973).

nancing it and the British trade deficit by short-term borrowing. Britain's ability to do this depended upon low interest rates in New York making London's relatively more attractive. The rise in American interest rates beginning in 1928, however, compromised Britain's ability to continue this policy. Similarly, Germany's ability to maintain a high rate of domestic investment, to purchase imports, and to meet the reparation payments depended upon American willingness to lend money to Germany. But the well ran dry in 1928, as the boom on Wall Street eclipsed the returns to be made on foreign loans. Nor was the Fed willing to allow international capital flows into the United States to determine the American price level as required under a true gold standard. Instead the Fed deliberately tried to neutralize the effects of gold inflows through the sale of government bonds to mop up the surplus funds. This policy forced the entire burden of adjustment upon the debtor countries—particularly Britain and Germany but also much of Latin America and Asia—and they eventually broke under the strain. The result, as in the title of Charles Kindleberger's book, was a world in depression.

The other force affecting foreign trade was a renewed spirit of economic nationalism. Initial agitation for tariff protection came from the ailing U.S. farm sector, but as the Smoot-Hawley Tariff legislation moved through the House and the Senate, its coverage was widened, and the level of protection increased. The duty on raw sugar from Cuba was, for example, raised from 1.76 cents a pound to 2 cents a pound, which exceeded the difference in costs of production between Cuban cane sugar and western beet sugar. The duty on wheat was raised from 32 cents a bushel to 40 cents, to the disadvantage of Canada. In manufacturing the duty on cotton textiles was raised from 40.27 percent to 46.42 percent, notwithstanding the fact that the current troubles in the industry were the result of competition between New England and southern mills rather than between domestic and foreign. As a result of the new legislation, average ad valorem rates on dutiable imports rose from 25.9 percent over the period 1921–25 to 50.02 percent between 1931 and 1935. A contemporary British economist at the time described ratification of the tariff as "a turning point in world history," for it brought with it the collapse of the international gold standard.[15] Primary product prices were driven down, and primary producers, such as Australia and Argentina, were the first to be forced to abandon the gold standard. For the United States it brought temporary relief, but at a very high price. The U.S. balance of payments shifted from deficit to surplus, the stock of monetary gold increased, the trade balance did not decline very much, and prices in the United States fell less in 1930 than in other countries. Not until the following year did prices in the United States fall faster than those abroad.[16]

Retaliation by other countries to the Smoot-Hawley Tariff followed al-

[15] Mitchell (1947): 73; Saltzer (1932): 173.
[16] Meltzer (1976).

most immediately upon its adoption[17] and brought with it the collapse of world trade (Figure 21.8). American exports fell faster than imports as the rest of the world jockeyed for a competitive edge via tariffs or other trade restrictions. Whereas in 1929 U.S. net exports had amounted to $842 million, by 1933 they were only $225 million on about one-third of the pre–tariff war, predepression levels of trade. These declines are, however, modest by comparison with the changes in consumption and investment expenditures that have already been discussed.

GOVERNMENT PURCHASE OF GOODS AND SERVICES

A Keynesian would find little to fault in federal government actions in 1929, 1930, and 1931, except perhaps that the policy was not pursued with sufficient vigor to overcome the decline in the other autonomous spending components. The year 1929—a year of full employment despite the ominous signs—found the federal budget in surplus; receipts exceeded disbursements by $1.3 billion. Indeed, during the fiscal year (July 1, 1929–June 30, 1930) the national debt was reduced by $746 million. It was not to decrease again until 1947. After 1929, however, rather than depress aggregate demand, government spending offset some of the decline in consumption, gross domestic private investment, and net exports. For example, in January 1930 President Hoover submitted requests for increased public works expenditures—$500 million for public buildings, $150 million for rivers and harbors, $75 million for roads, and $60 million to start work on the Boulder Dam—and a $160 million income tax decrease. During 1930 new public construction (in 1929 constant dollars) amounted to $2.8 billion, an increase of 22 percent over the 1929 level. The fiscal year ended with a $1 billion deficit, much to the embarrassment of Treasury Secretary Mellon, who as late as December 1930 had predicted a deficit no greater than $180 million. Much of the deficit was met by borrowing, and the public debt increased by $616 million. Outlays were one-third higher than they had been during fiscal 1930, but individual and corporate income taxes, the principal sources of revenue, were down 23 percent—in part a result of the tax cut.

The deficit increased in fiscal 1932 to $2.7 billion as receipts slumped to less than half their level of fiscal 1930 and expenditures soared. With the passage of a massive tax increase on June 6, 1932, however, federal government policy changed from being countercyclical—whether by accident or design—to procyclical. This ultimately played a role in converting what was by then a most severe depression into the Great Depression. Note, though, that government fiscal policy from the Keynesian perspective of aggregate demand played no role in the onset of the depression itself or its intensification before the finale of the contraction in late 1932, by which time there were some small signs of recovery in the reversal of the declining stock market

[17] Jones (1934).

FIGURE 21.8

The Contracting Spiral of World Trade, January 1929–March 1933: Total Imports of 75 Countries (Monthly Values in Terms of Old U.S. Gold Dollars [millions])

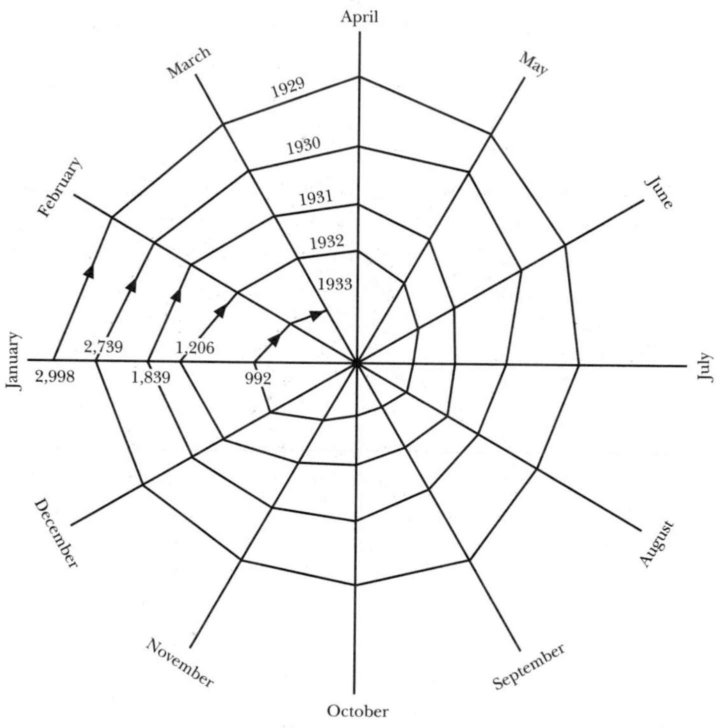

(in millions of dollars)

	1929	1930	1931	1932	1933
I	2,997.7	2,738.9	1,838.9	1,206.0	992.4
II	2,630.3	2,454.6	1,700.5	1,186.7	944.0
III	2,814.8	2,563.9	1,889.1	1,230.4	1,056.9
IV	3,039.1	2,449.9	1,796.4	1,212.8	
V	2,967.6	2,447.0	1,764.3	1,150.5	
VI	2,791.0	2,325.7	1,732.3	1,144.7	
VII	2,813.9	2,189.5	1,679.6	993.7	
VIII	2,818.5	2,137.7	1,585.9	1,004.6	
IX	2,773.9	2,164.8	1,572.1	1,029.6	
X	2,966.8	2,300.8	1,556.3	1,090.4	
XI	2,888.8	2,051.3	1,470.0	1,093.3	
XII	2,793.9	2,095.9	1,426.9	1,121.2	
Average:	2,858.0	2,326.7	1,667.7	1,122.0	

Source: Charles Kindleberger, *The World in Depression* (Berkeley: University of California Press, 1986): 170. Data from League of Nations, *Monthly Bulletin of Statistics* (February 1934): 51.

and an easing in the free fall in prices, industrial production, and factory employment.

Monetarist Explanations for the Great Depression

Just as there are a variety of aggregate demand explanations of the Great Depression, such as Temin's emphasis upon an unexplained decline in autonomous consumption expenditure and Keynes's explanation in terms of the loss of business confidence causing a collapse in investment expenditure, there are divergent monetarist explanations. One, advanced by Milton Friedman and Anna Schwartz, blames the Federal Reserve for not doing enough to ease the liquidity crisis among the nation's banks. Another, championed by followers of Hayek, also blames the Fed, but instead of being blamed for doing too little, the Fed is criticized for intervening and thus interrupting the economy's readjustment to a new equilibrium.

THE FRIEDMAN-SCHWARTZ VIEW

Friedman and Schwartz devote nearly one-sixth of their *Monetary History of the United States 1867–1960* to the analysis of the four-year period 1929–33, but they give virtually no consideration to the factors that produced the initial downturn in 1929. More recently, Anna Schwartz has clarified their position: "The period 1929–33 began as a cyclical contraction much like others, this time in response to the immoderate concern of the Federal Reserve Board about speculation in the Stock Market." This concern led the Federal Reserve to curtail the rate of growth of the money supply through the sale of bonds and, by raising the discount rate, to discourage member bank borrowing. As a result, the money supply (defined as currency plus checking and time deposits, otherwise known as M2 money), which had grown by 3.8 percent from 1927 to 1928, grew by only 0.4 percent from 1928 to 1929. Indeed, between April 1928 and November 1929 (when the Federal Reserve entered the market to supply liquidity in the wake of the stock market crash) the money supply fell at a rate of more than 1 percent per year. To the extent that this sudden reversal of policy was unanticipated, it may have been sufficient to precipitate the pause in business activity in the summer of 1929. This view of the origins of the depression is surprisingly close to that first articulated by Keynes early in the Great Depression.

Once the depression had begun, however, Friedman and Schwartz argue, it was made much worse by a series of serious exogenous monetary shocks that disrupted the financial markets and impeded the functioning of the "real" economy. These were further compounded by the failure of the Fed to deal adequately with, or respond appropriately to, either the shocks themselves or the consequences that followed from them. As a result, Friedman and Schwartz describe the contraction as "a tragic testimonial to the importance of monetary forces. . . . [D]ifferent and feasible actions by the monetary authorities could have prevented the decline in the stock of money [and such action] would have reduced the contraction's severity and almost certainly its duration."[18]

MONETARY SHOCKS

Friedman and Schwartz identify five separate financial shocks to the system: the stock market crash, October 1929; the first banking crisis, October 1930–February 1931; the second banking crisis, March 1931–August 1931; Britain's abandonment of the gold standard, September 1931; and the final banking crisis, October 1932–March 1933. Following each monetary shock, bank failures soared, and public confidence in the banking system—represented by the ratio of bank deposits to currency held by the public—declined. Despite increases in the quantity of high-powered money, the stock of money declined, especially in the months following Britain's abandonment of the gold standard. The sections that follow take up each of the shocks in turn.

The Great Crash (October 1929)

In his book *The Great Crash* John Kenneth Galbraith explains the stock market crash of October 1929 as the inevitable consequence of financial innovations and changes in how the unregulated market operated. The major financial innovation was the investment trust. This had originated in Great Britain as a device to pool the monies of many small investors who in the normal way might not have been able to buy stock in even one company. Those monies were then used to purchase a large diversified portfolio of stocks, spreading risk and bringing to the small investor the benefits of diversification enjoyed by the large investor. As investment funds evolved in Britain, they were what we would today call mutual funds. In America, however, new wrinkles were added to this form by the aggressive use of margin buying to multiply the stock held and by selling a large amount of fixed interest bonds relative to common stock. This increased financial leverage but at the cost of increased volatility. The bondholders were promised a fixed interest payment and given first claim on the trust assets in the event of default. The equity holders, on the other hand, stood to benefit from any capital gains on the full value of the portfolio even though most of the funds used to buy the portfolio were borrowed. The United States and Foreign Securities Corporation, set up in 1924 by the investment bankers Dillon, Read & Company, was one such investment trust. It issued three classes of stock: first preferred, second preferred, and common. Dividends on the preferred

[18] Friedman and Schwartz (1963): 300–01.

stock were limited to 6 percent—1 to 2 percent above the rate on corporate, municipal, state, or U.S. government bonds. The first preferred was sold to the public for $25 million, and the lucky purchasers received as a reward an allocation of one-fourth of the common stock (which initially had a negative value). Dillon, Read retained the remaining common stock and the second preferred with an investment of $5 million. In 1928, after meeting the interest obligations to the preferred stockholders, this trust had a cash surplus of $10 million, and at one time its common stock sold for $72 a share. It is estimated that the final return to Dillon, Read on its investment of $5 million was on the order of $50 to $60 million.[19] An even more spectacular example was the American Founders Group, begun in 1922 with an investment of $500, yet by 1929 holding more than $1 billion in securities.[20] In 1921 there were 40 investment trusts in America; by 1929 there were more than 750.

Turning to changes in how the financial markets operated, Galbraith cites increased buying on low margins as the main culprit, since it provided additional financial leverage. In the unregulated market of the 1920s creditworthy customers could buy stock with as little as 10 percent down (though 20 percent was perhaps more typical), borrowing the balance from their brokers with the stocks themselves serving as collateral for the loan. Since the dividends alone typically exceeded the rate on margin loans from the brokers, margin borrowing made sense so long as the market was expected to remain stable or increase in value. For example, in 1927 the broker loan rate averaged 4.35 percent, while corporate dividends averaged 4.77 percent. Investors were, in effect, being paid to take a market risk. Moreover, this market risk paid off handsomely for many years. In the twelve months of 1927, for example, the fortunate purchaser of a "representative market portfolio" reaped a capital gain of almost 30 percent, while in 1928 the value of a similar portfolio rose by more than 30 percent. Indeed, even as late as the beginning of 1929, with the market up over 20 percent for the year, substantial gains were to be made although the gradual rise in margin requirements beginning in October 1928 dampened investor leverage.[21] Such capital gains, though substantial, have been equaled or surpassed by modern-day success stories such as Fidelity's Magellan Fund. The real difference lies in the ability to buy on low margin and capture the capital gains on the entire value of the portfolio.

The growing demand for credit to buy stocks pulled new funds into the market. This brought about a major reallocation of credit. Corporate treasurers, for example, discovered that call money loans were far more lucrative for short-term surplus funds than the corporate bank account or buying short-term bonds. Thus, nonbank loans to brokers increased from $550 mil-

[19] Pecora (1938).
[20] Galbraith (1972).
[21] Smiley and Keehn (1988).

lion in 1924 (about 25 percent of the total loan volume) to $3.885 million in 1928 (60 percent of the total), and according to Galbraith, Standard Oil of New Jersey in 1929 averaged $69 million per day in call money loans to brokers, while Electric Bond and Share averaged $100 million. This high volume of nonbank loans to the market helped frustrate Federal Reserve efforts to limit market speculation.

There is considerable debate about whether the rise in stock prices during the 1920s was justified or represented a speculative bubble. Evidence suggests that until the start of the second quarter of 1928, stock prices rose more or less in line with rising dividends, and only from about March or April 1928 is there a marked divergence between dividends—which continued to increase—and stock prices—which soared (Figure 21.9). This period then may mark the onset of a speculative bubble, destined sooner or later to "pop."

But what was the pin that burst the bubble? No single explanation seems to suffice. Rather, a number of factors—all occurring more or less together—cumulatively served to deflate the speculative mania. Adverse eco-

FIGURE 21.9

Stock Price and Dividend Indexes

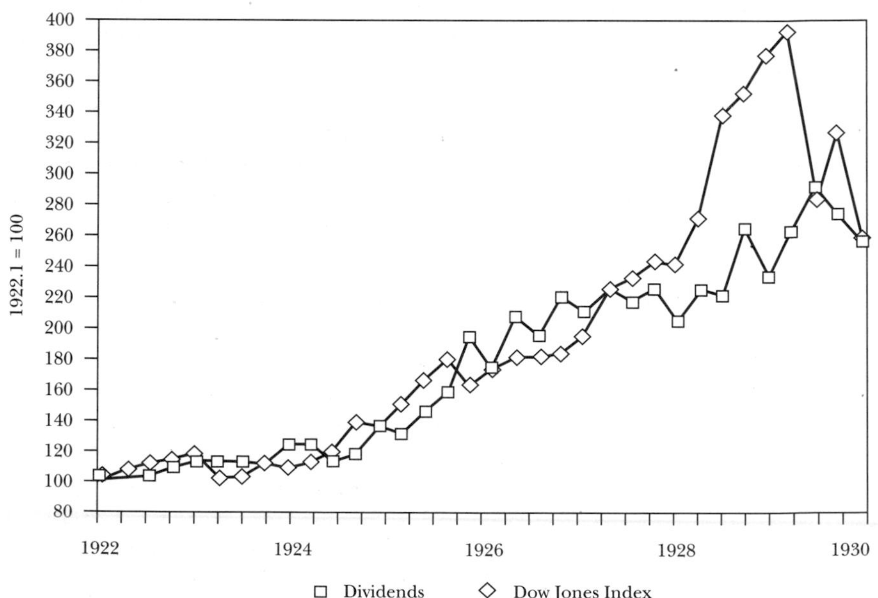

Source: Eugene N. White, "The Stock Market Boom and Crash of 1929 Revisited," *Journal of Economic Perspectives* 4 (1990): 73.

nomic news began to appear in August 1929: Industrial production had peaked and was falling. The tight monetary policy instituted by the Federal Reserve in 1928 began to bite in 1929, raising the cost of borrowing and making it less profitable to bear the market risks on margin purchases. Market experts also became increasingly pessimistic. For example, on the day the Standard & Poor's stock index peaked, September 7, 1929, the *Commercial and Financial Chronicle* carried a speech by the well-known stock guru Roger Babson before the annual National Business Conference in which he warned that "sooner or later a crash is coming and it may be terrific . . . factories will shut down . . . men will be thrown out of work . . . the vicious circle will get in full swing and the result will be a serious business depression." In addition, a number of people have linked the price break on the stock market to the abrupt revision of investor expectations about the future profitability of major U.S. exporters if the Smoot-Hawley Tariff passed and provoked the expected retaliatory response from the rest of the world.[22]

The First Banking Crisis (October 1930–February 1931)

Friedman and Schwartz assign a special significance to this first banking crisis in the contraction of the 1930s, arguing that "the monetary character of the contraction changed dramatically. . . . A contagion of fear spread among depositors, starting from the agricultural areas. . . . But such contagion knows no geographic limits"[23] as the public lost confidence in the banking system and converted bank deposits into currency. Research by Eugene White confirms the importance of both real (for example, the agricultural crisis) and monetary factors (such as the condition of a bank's balance sheet) in contributing to the crisis, although little distinguishes 1930 as a whole from other years in the late 1920s. Until October 1930 deposits in suspended banks were no higher than levels during the 1920s. In November, though, deposits in suspended banks were more than double any previously recorded monthly peak. They doubled again in December. Federal Reserve data list 236 banks as failing in November. In December 328 banks failed, among them a large New York City bank, the Bank of United States, which failed on December 11 with more than $200 million in deposits.[24] At the time it was the largest bank ever to have failed. Moreover, Friedman and Schwartz claim that its unusual name led many to assume an official connection. As a result, the failure was of "especial importance"—to use Friedman and Schwartz's own words—and has been the subject of a heated debate.

In a lengthy footnote to their book Friedman and Schwartz describe the

[22] Including Brunner (1981) and Wanniski (1978).
[23] Friedman and Schwartz (1963): 308.
[24] Use of the definite article in the bank's title was not allowed by the banking authorities so as to avoid confusion with the First or Second Banks of the United States (see Chapter 4).

various attempts by the New York superintendent of banks, Joseph A. Broderick, and the New York Federal Reserve Bank to organize a rescue of the Bank of United States by the clearinghouse banks, but these plans all collapsed, and the bank failed. Broderick was later indicted by a New York grand jury for neglect of duty, his first trial ended in mistrial, his second in acquittal. Friedman and Schwartz's position is that the bank should not have failed because it was fundamentally sound. As evidence, they cite its eventual repayment of little over 83 cents on the dollar to its depositors despite the fire sale price of the bank's assets in the depths of the depression. Instead they explain the failure as the result of a colossal miscalculation by all parties (particularly the Federal Reserve) and suggest that anti-Semitism by J. P. Morgan, Jr., of the firm of J. P. Morgan & Company—a key player in the New York Clearinghouse—may have played a role in the failure of the rescue efforts since the Bank of United States was a Jewish-owned bank serving customers in New York's garment district.

Both Peter Temin and Joseph Lucia take exception to Friedman and Schwartz's characterization of the Bank of United States as a sound bank. Following the death of the bank's founder, Joseph S. Marcus, in late 1928 his son, Bernard Marcus, succeeded to the presidency of the bank and launched an ambitious expansion program that took the bank from $6 million in capital and six branches to $25 million in capital and fifty-nine branches by the time it failed. Along the way the bank invested heavily in relatively illiquid real estate loans. Whereas the average New York City bank had about 12 percent of total loans in real estate, the Bank of United States had 45 percent. When bank examiners made their report on the financial condition of the bank in mid-1930, they noted that nonperforming, impaired, and questionable loans exceeded the bank's surplus and undistributed profits. As the financial condition of the bank weakened in a weakening market, the bank tried to disguise the true nature of its portfolio by exchanging real estate loans for short-term debt with its holding company affiliates. As a result of this attempted deception, Marcus and two other bank officers were eventually convicted of fraud and jailed. It is not too surprising, then, that given this financial picture, the clearinghouse banks might be less than enthusiastic about taking over the "assets" of the bank. Moreover, the Bank of United States had pledged to maintain the price of its stock. This proved a serious drain upon the bank's cash as it struggled to maintain price on a falling market. Lastly, even if depositors did eventually receive 83 cents on the dollar, this was worth considerably less than that sum since the final distribution was not made until 1944. If the payouts are discounted back to 1930 at the prevailing annual rate on Aaa bonds (a low discount rate), the present discounted value of the payments was only about 76 cents on the dollar.

Despite the prominent role given to the Bank of United States by Friedman and Schwartz, Elmus Wicker argues that the initial cause of the banking crisis was the failure of Caldwell and Company, a Nashville-based holding company for the South's largest chain of banks with assets in excess of $200 million. Caldwell had controlling interests in insurance companies, manufacturing plants, publishing enterprises, and investment trusts as well as banks with combined assets of about $500 million. But it was in a precarious financial position when the depression hit, with only a small cushion of liquid assets relative to notes payable and deposits. Withdrawals quickly eliminated this reserve, and Caldwell was insolvent—that is, unable to liquidate assets quickly enough to meet claims against it. Within two weeks of the failure of Caldwell and Company, more than 120 banks in four states (70 of them in Arkansas alone), almost all of them affiliated with Caldwell, suspended payments. For example, depositors withdrew $4 million of $15 million on deposit with the American Exchange Trust before it suspended payments. Indeed, the entire banking crisis may have originated in the failure of Caldwell and Company. Of 236 bank failures in November 1930, 141 occurred in the St. Louis Federal Reserve District, and 20 in the Richmond District—the areas in which Caldwell operated. These same two districts recorded 159 of the 328 bank failures in December 1930. In contrast, while no banks failed in the Boston, New York, or Philadelphia regions in November, Boston recorded 5 failures in December, and there were only 6 each in the other two districts, lending support to the proposition that Caldwell and Company, rather than depressed conditions in general and the failure of the Bank of United States in particular, was responsible for many of the bank failures during the first banking crisis.

The Second Banking Crisis (March 1931–August 1931)

Friedman and Schwartz give no reason why public confidence in banks eroded further in March 1931, but the public renewed its conversion of deposits into currency, and banks for their part sold assets both to meet this demand and to build up excess reserves. In early May, however, the revelation of unexpectedly large losses by the Creditanstalt, the largest private bank in Austria, led to a run against the bank that the government tried to stem. But the bank failed anyway, and the Austrian government was itself forced to borrow money to meet the demand for conversion of Austrian shillings into gold, ultimately exhausting its credit. The Bank for International Settlements arranged credits from the largest central banks, including the Reichsbank, the Federal Reserve, and the Bank of England. Each subsequently came under selling pressure against its own currency.

The international crisis deepened in the wake of President Hoover's moratorium on intergovernmental debt repayment and pressure on commercial banks not to seek repayment of short-term credits, the revelation that the Reichsbank's reserve ratio had fallen below 40 percent, and massive commercial losses by the Danatbank in Germany. Given the large-scale foreign lending by America's banks in the 1920s, particularly to Germany, this news generated considerable concern about the financial security of many of America's largest banks.

Indeed, a number of authors, particularly Charles Kindleberger and Barry Eichengreen, see the Great Depression primarily as an international crisis caused by the breakdown of international financial relations. The breakdown was created by the enormous debt burden from World War I and by the failure of various countries to play the game by the rules of the classical gold or gold-exchange standard. What Barry Eichengreen has termed the "golden fetters" of the international gold standard imposed burdens upon both debtor and creditor countries: Debtor countries were supposed to experience a declining money supply, diminished economic activity, falling prices, and rising export demand while in creditor countries the money supply was supposed to grow, economic activity accelerate, prices rise, and imports increase until equilibrium was restored at the fixed exchange rates. These fixed exchange rates thus played a key role in the international transmission of shocks, and international factors played a major role in the last three of the five monetary shocks that Friedman and Schwartz identify.

Britain's Abandonment of the Gold Standard (September 1931)

Britain, which had returned to the gold standard in 1925 at its prewar exchange rate—a rate that overvalued the pound sterling by perhaps 10 percent—was particularly vulnerable to an external drain of gold as foreigners redeemed pounds for gold. Britain had been able to maintain this position only at the expense of domestic growth and by short-term borrowing. On September 21, 1931, the British government yielded to the inevitable and suspended convertibility of the pound into gold following a massive run on sterling precipitated in part by the Bank of France.[25] Pressure then switched from the pound sterling to the dollar. Between September 16 and the end of the month, the U.S. gold stock declined by $275 million; it fell another $450 million in October, offsetting all inflows during the preceding two years. Nor was this lack of confidence entirely mistaken. The secretary of the treasury, Ogden Mills, later commented that the United States was within two or three weeks of being forced off the gold standard. By the end of September nine countries, including most of Scandinavia and Canada—areas with close trading ties to Britain—had also left gold, and others were to follow. According to Eichengreen, at the height of the gold standard in 1931, forty-seven countries had currencies defined in terms of a fixed quantity of gold; by the end of 1932 the only major countries still on gold were Belgium, France, Italy, the Netherlands, Poland, Switzerland, and the United States. The loss of so many members from the gold standard club contributed to general uncertainty about the continued commitment of the

[25] New evidence by Pierre Sicsic now casts doubt upon any key role played by the Bank of France.

rest to stick with the gold standard—or their ability to do so. Moreover, short-term currency risk and uncertainty generated by floating exchange rates only further disrupted world trade.

The loss of external confidence in the dollar intensified domestic concern about the safety of the nation's banks, which was reinforced by the Federal Reserve's reaction to the external drain—the sharpest increase in the rediscount rate in the system's history—further reducing the value of bank assets and making it much more expensive for banks to borrow from the Fed. In October 1931, 522 banks closed, and in the six-month period from August 1931, 1,860 banks with deposits totaling almost $1.5 trillion suspended operations.

The Final Banking Crisis (October 1932–March 1933)

Friedman and Schwartz describe the final banking crisis as beginning in the last quarter of 1932, particularly in the Midwest and Far West, but widening in scope and increasing in volume in January 1933, as more states suspended state banking operations within their borders. Nevada was the first on October 31, 1932. Iowa was next on January 20, 1933, followed by Louisiana and Michigan. By March 3 about half the states had declared bank holidays. Bank holidays, however, hardly increased depositor confidence in banks; instead they increased pressure upon those that remained open. Recognizing this, in February Congress relieved the nation's national banks of their obligation to remain open in states that had declared bank holidays, adding to speculative runs against those banks unfortunate enough to remain open. New York City banks, in particular, experienced massive withdrawals, losing, for example, $760 million during February.

Friedman and Schwartz are a little vague in providing an immediate cause for this final banking crisis other than to ascribe it to the loss of domestic confidence in the nation's banks and the Federal Reserve's failure to create sufficient liquidity through open market purchases to meet that demand. One factor precipitating this loss of confidence (besides the all-too-recent history of bank failures) was the naming of banks that had received emergency loans from the Reconstruction Finance Corporation (RFC). This was prima facie evidence of weakness.

More recently, however, a growing number of scholars have emphasized the central role played by the gold standard in the final banking crisis.[26] The advantage of this explanation is that it not only explains the panic leading up to the nationwide bank holiday of March 6, 1933, but also explains the calm that followed.

Doubts about America's willingness and ability to continue to exchange dollars for gold had been growing, certainly since Britain left the gold standard in September 1931, if not before. Passage of the Glass-Steagall Act in

[26] For example, Barry Eichengreen, Charles Kindleberger, Peter Temin, and Barrie Wigmore.

February 1932 had further weakened the credibility of America's commitment to gold by allowing government bonds to serve as collateral for Federal Reserve notes. More damaging, though, to both domestic and international confidence were word that President-elect Roosevelt had held numerous meetings at which devaluation was discussed and his refusal to give firm assurances that the United States would meet all of its obligations in gold. Even President Hoover added to these concerns with a speech in Des Moines on October 4, 1932, in which he described how close the United States had come to leaving gold the previous year. It is therefore hardly surprising that holders of dollars at home and abroad should doubt the ability and willingness of government to maintain convertibility of the dollar into gold at the rate of $20.67 per troy ounce of gold and seek to convert those dollars for gold.

From the beginning of February to early March 1933 the Federal Reserve of New York lost 61 percent of its gold holdings and, by March 3, had on hand only $381 million in gold while the Bank of England had more than $240 million in dollar assets that it wished to reduce because of growing exchange rate uncertainty. Moreover, foreign deposits in the city's banks exceeded $600 million. As the Federal Reserve of New York board minutes for March 3 were to record, "we could not pay out gold and currency much longer at the rate of the past few days." Fortunately the New York Fed did not have to. On Saturday, March 4, 1933—inauguration day—New York joined the list of states with bank holidays, and on Monday morning, March 6, 1933, President Roosevelt invoked the Trading with the Enemy Act to suspend all banking operations in the United States for a four-day period. Before the banks reopened, regulations went into effect requiring member banks to relinquish all gold and gold certificates to the Federal Reserve and supply lists of all persons who had withdrawn gold or gold certificates, since February 1 and prohibiting the export of gold and dealing in foreign exchange. One month later individuals were prohibited from holding gold or gold certificates, and the price of gold was gradually raised to $35 per ounce, effectively devaluing the dollar by almost 70 percent against gold and by smaller amounts against foreign currency, where the "official" price of gold stayed until 1971.

THE ROLE OF BANK FAILURES

Bank failures play a pivotal role in Friedman and Schwartz's explanation of the cause of the Great Depression and its unique nature. The public lost confidence in the ability of the banking system to repay deposits upon demand and chose to substitute currency for deposits. The failure of one bank had a domino effect, spreading what Friedman and Schwartz describe as a "contagion of fear." The resulting uncertainty caused runs on other banks, which failed in turn. The money supply contracted as legal tender went to satisfy the public's demand for currency rather than serve as bank reserves and support an expansion of bank credit and money. Between 1930 and 1933 more than nine thousand banks closed—more than a third of all banks in the United States at the end of 1929 (Figure 21.10).

Part of Temin's case against Friedman and Schwartz's argument is based upon work he did estimating the supply of money as a function of interest rates, bank reserves, and the percentage of total deposits in suspended banks. His estimates suggest that while bank failures might have decreased the supply of money, the statistical importance was small. However, Temin is at pains to make clear that this does not constitute a definitive test and grounds for dismissing their hypothesis. As Figure 21.10 makes clear, the bank failure rate was low in the 1920s, high between 1930 and 1933, and essentially zero thereafter. It is therefore not too surprising that this general lack of variation fails to "explain" (statistically) the year-to-year variations in the supply of money. Moreover, there is a statistical risk that one might reject as "false" a hypothesis that is "true." Indeed, if one were to ignore statistical significance testing altogether and simply ask, "How large was the effect of

FIGURE 21.10

Bank Failures and the Bank Failure Rate 1920–1939

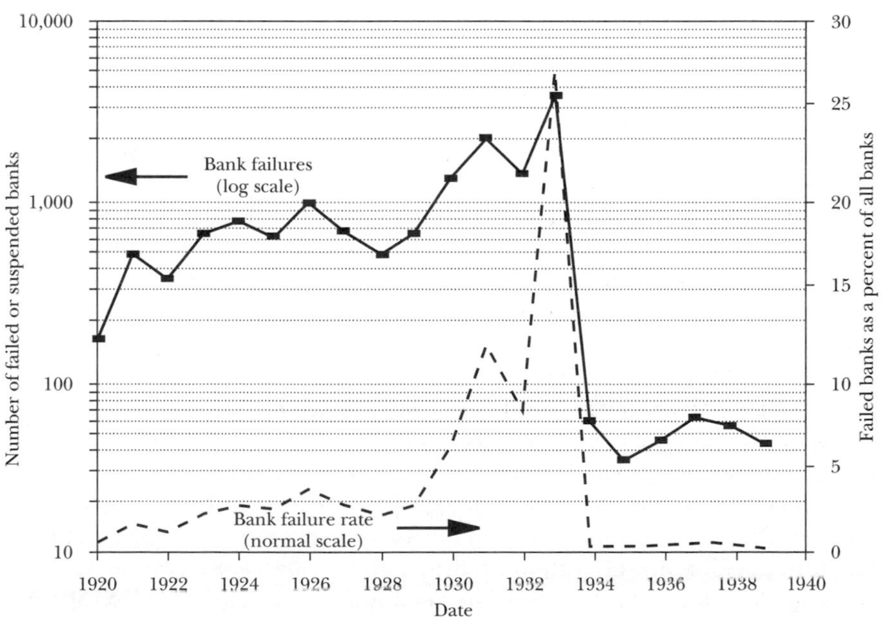

Source: Board of Governors of the Federal Reserve System, *Banking and Monetary Statistics* (Washington, D.C.: Board of Governors of the Federal Reserve System, 1943).

bank failures on the supply of money?" then by Temin's own estimate, bank failures could have accounted for the entire change in the stock of money.

THE AUSTRIAN VIEW

Although the Austrian view (so named after the Austrian economist Hayek) is not strictly a monetarist interpretation since it places emphasis upon the "real" business cycle, it makes sense to include it under this general heading since the Austrian view, like Friedman and Schwartz, blames the Federal Reserve for the depression *but for precisely the opposite reason.* Instead of monetary policy's being too tight, the Austrians, or "liquidationists," argued that monetary policy was in fact too easy and that by intervening in the market, the Federal Reserve disrupted and prolonged economic adjustment to a new equilibrium. Such beliefs were widely held at the time and have received renewed attention in recent years. President Hoover, for example, complained bitterly that Secretary of the Treasury Andrew Mellon's only advice was to "[l]iquidate labor, liquidate stocks, liquidate the farmers, liquidate real estate, liquidate banks, liquidate businesses," whereas Hoover's natural inclination (despite his being a Republican), as an engineer and a successful post-World War I European relief administrator, was to intervene. Others in positions of power shared Mellon's views—for example, Adolph Miller, a member of the Federal Reserve Board, George Norris, governor of the Federal Reserve of Philadelphia, and Lynn Talley of the Dallas Fed. Indeed, Norris vigorously criticized Fed interference "with the operation of the natural law of supply and demand in the money market."

Early in the depression Hayek argued that "the present crisis is marked by the first attempt on a large scale to revive the economy . . . by a systematic policy of lowering the interest rate accompanied by all other possible measures for preventing the *normal process of liquidation,* and that as a result the depression has assumed more devastating forms and lasted longer than ever before [Emphasis added]."[27] Unanswered in this condemnation of government interference, however, is the question of whether intervention might be justified in the face of panic that threatens the sound banks and businesses as well as the unsound.

THE DEBATE OVER FEDERAL RESERVE POLICY

Friedman and Schwartz describe Federal Reserve monetary policy taken as a whole during the contraction as "inept." In their view, the monetary system was allowed to collapse when different policies, already well known to Fed officials, who had used them successfully during the 1920s, could have saved it. Open market operations to buy U.S. government debt and put dollars into circulation were often too little and too late. For example, during the second banking crisis in 1931, the Fed limited purchases to just $130 mil-

[27] Hayek (1984): 130.

lion—little more than it had bought in the first two days following the stock market crash—at a time when hundreds of the nation's banks were failing (Table 21.3), and it did nothing to generate new liquidity during the final crisis of 1932–33. At other times, such as when Britain left gold and at the beginning of March 1933, the Federal Reserve actually pursued a "tight" monetary policy, raising the cost of borrowing. Yet when no crisis demanded its urgent and immediate attention, as in the first half of 1932, the Fed entered the market vigorously, buying more than $1 billion in government bonds.

Over the period as a whole the Fed added $1.8 billion to the stock of currency. Perhaps two-thirds of this went to satisfy the public's increased taste for legal tender rather than serve as new bank reserves. And much of that which did go into bank reserves simply provided a cushion for the banks that survived—"excess reserves"—rather than support new loans and deposits.

Friedman and Schwartz attribute much of the Fed's policy failure to the death in 1928 of Benjamin Strong, the governor of the Federal Reserve Bank of New York and pioneer of open market operations, which left the Fed leaderless at a crucial juncture: "If Strong had still been alive and head of the New York Bank in the fall of 1930, he would very likely have recognized the oncoming liquidity crisis for what it was, would have been prepared by experience and conviction to take strenuous and appropriate measure to head it

TABLE 21. 3

Principal Policy Actions of the Federal Reserve, October 1929–March 1933

Date	Open Market Operations	Discount Rate	Critical Events
Oct. 1929	Bought $120 m	6% ¼ 2% in New York 5% ¼ 3–3½% elsewhere	Stock market crash
Nov. 1929- Dec 1930	Bought $440 m	—	First banking crisis
Jan. 1931- Aug. 1931	Bought $130 m	2–3½% ¼ 1½–3%	Second banking crisis
Oct. 1931- Nov. 1931	—	**RAISED** 1½–3% ¼ 3½–4%	Britain leaves gold standard
Jan. 1932- Aug. 1932	Bought $1.110 m	4–3½% ¼ 3½–2½	No crisis (Glass-Steagall Act)
March 1933	—	**RAISED** 2½ ¼ 3½	Final banking crisis (end)

Source: David P. Eastburn, *The Federal Reserve on Record* (Philadelphia: Federal Reserve Bank of Philadelphia, 1965): 69–70.

off, and would have had the standing to carry the system with him."[28] As a result, Friedman and Schwartz argue, there was a policy shift within the Federal Reserve away from a countercyclical monetary policy and away from a policy of isolating the domestic economy from the ebb and flow of gold across national borders. However, there is sufficient ambiguity in Strong's statements and policies during the 1920s to make it difficult to infer conclusively how he would have acted if faced by the crises of 1929–33.[29] Although he offset gold inflows in 1922 and 1923 by selling government debt and raising the discount rate, Strong might not have felt able to counter the outflow in October and November 1931 by open market purchases and reductions in the discount rate. Indeed, David Wheelock finds little empirical evidence of a policy shift by the Federal Reserve even though it held far fewer government securities during the early 1930s than one would predict on the basis of Fed behavior in the 1920s. He explains this apparent contradiction by emphasizing that the Federal Reserve, both during Strong's tenure and after his death, used member bank borrowing as the key indicator of monetary ease or tightness. If member banks were borrowing, money was "tight"; if they were not borrowing, money was easy. During the early 1930s member banks did little borrowing; therefore, concluded the Fed, money was easy.

While Friedman and Schwartz characterize the Fed's policy as inept, Federal Reserve policy is entirely consistent with the Fed's having multiple goals that were sometimes contradictory. In particular, if we accept the proposition that the Fed saw defense of the gold standard as its principal charge and serving as lender in last resort to the banking system as subordinate to that, then all incongruities in the Fed's behavior disappear. So long as the Fed had "free gold"—that is, gold above and beyond that which it believed necessary to give credibility to its promise to redeem Federal Reserve dollars for gold upon demand—the Fed stood ready and willing to supply additional liquidity to the system. However, when the Fed faced an outflow of gold as in October and November 1931 and again in early 1933, it felt obliged instead not only to act to conserve what gold it had rather than create new obligations against gold but also to endeavor to attract additional gold to these shores by offering higher interest rates. Friedman and Schwartz dismiss this "free gold" argument, but it forms a central theme in Eichengreen's recent study. Moreover, such a commitment is consistent with Fed behavior from its founding to its being relieved of that obligation in 1933.

Gerald Epstein and Thomas Ferguson have analyzed the motivation and timing behind the Federal Reserve's massive open market operation in 1932. They argue that the Federal Reserve had deliberately delayed inter-

[28] Friedman and Schwartz (1963): 412–13.

[29] See, for example, Wheelock (1989, 1991).

vening much earlier, say, in 1930 or early 1931, because the liquidationist view of the business cycle was dominant among its officials but that intervention was further delayed by the lack of "free gold" during the last quarter of 1931, when rising interest rates drove down bond prices and threatened the solvency of many banks. In this interpretation, support of the bond market was thus a major goal of the 1932 open market operation. The policy succeeded in driving down interest rates; indeed, the policy may have succeeded too well, driving short-term Treasury rates under 1 percent and jeopardizing bank earnings. As a result, the Fed faced increasing pressure to halt purchases, especially when the sharp increase in dollar claims against gold began to threaten convertibility.

An alternative, public choice interpretation of Federal Reserve behavior during the contraction holds that rent-seeking member banks seized the opportunity to rid themselves of their troublesome nonmember competitors.[30] Some circumstantial evidence supports this argument: More than 75 percent of the banks failing between 1929 and 1933 were nonmember. Moreover, the Fed had argued since its inception that the dual system was unworkable. But this hardly constitutes proof. First, the failure rate among *member* banks during the depression was much higher than it had been during the 1920s. Of banks failing in 1931 and 1932, 23 percent were members of the system, and in the final wave of banking failures member banks made up 32 percent of the total, whereas in the 1920s member banks made up less than 20 percent of the failing banks. Second, instead of implementing this policy (if such it was) directly through capture of the Fed, the pressure came through the House and Senate Banking committees since states with representatives on these committees had higher rates of nonmember bank failures although why representatives and senators should have been more responsive to the pressure of member banks than the much more numerous nonmember banks is not clear. Third, it is not clear how the Fed selectively targeted nonmember banks. Lastly, the alleged ulterior motive—increased bank profits (the "rent" that the member banks were supposedly seeking)—failed to materialize. Share prices of the large New York member banks declined relative to other price indexes and was unaffected by changes in the money supply.[31]

Concluding Remarks

As was pointed out at the outset, there is no single tidy, universally accepted explanation for the economic decline between 1929 and 1933. Recovery began with Roosevelt's inauguration on March 4. Indeed, some indexes—

[30] See Anderson, Shughart, and Tollison (1988, 1990).
[31] Santoni and Van Cott (1990).

notably the stock market index—turned around in mid-1932 shortly after Roosevelt's selection as the Democratic candidate for president and in anticipation of a new administration. The question, however, is how much of this recovery was attributable to the specific policies put in place during the Roosevelt administrations, especially those embodied in the New Deal, and it is to that task that we now turn.

Appendix: The Hicks-Hansen Synthesis of Income Equilibrium Models

The two principal hypotheses for the sharp economic decline between 1929 and 1933—spending and monetary—can best be understood with the help of the graphical synthesis first offered by John Hicks and Alvin Hansen. The Hicks-Hansen, or IS-LM, synthesis applies equally well to Keynesian and monetarist views of macroeconomic relationships and events. We develop the bare bones of the Hicks-Hansen model and then show how spending and monetary explanations of the depression fit.

Hicks-Hansen focuses in turn on the conditions for income equilibrium requiring (1) that intended investment equal intended savings and (2) that the desired quantity of money assets held by the private sector equal the amount of money actually available. First, consider the investment-savings (IS) equilibrium condition. As Figure 21.A1 suggests, the amount of investment spending is related to interest rates on loans. The lower the interest rate, the higher the rate of investment.

Figure 21.A2 shows the relationship between savings and income: The more income people have, the more they wish to save. Now, in order for national income to be in equilibrium, it is necessary that the amount investors wish to invest equals the amount of income left over after income recipients decide how much they wish to consume. Hence Figures 21.A1 and 21.A2 indirectly reveal what interest rate (and therefore investment rate) is consistent with what level of national income (and therefore savings rate). The so-called IS relationship is shown in Figure 21.A3. It slopes downward because high interest rates mean little investment and thus a low equilibrium level of income.

Now consider the other condition that must be met if national income is to be in equilibrium. The demand for money is determined by both the level of business activity and interest rates. The more business, the more money individuals and firms think they must hold to meet day-to-day expenses. By the same token, the higher the interest rate on securities, the more income they give up by holding their assets as non-interest-bearing money. The higher interest rates are, the greater the motive to pare down non-interest-bearing cash balances.

Suppose the supply of money is fixed independently; it is usually a con-

FIGURE 21.A1 **FIGURE 21.A2**

The Relationship between Investment and Interest Rates and Savings and GNP

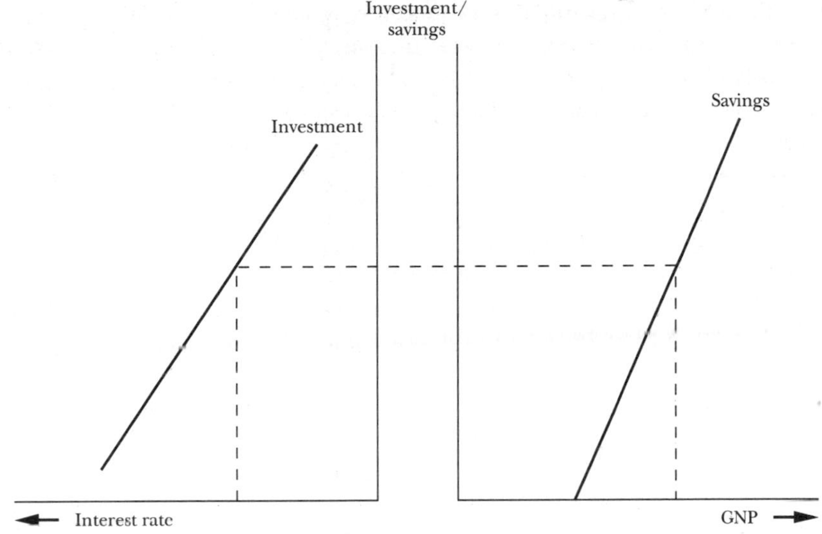

FIGURE 21.A3

The Investment-Savings (IS) Relationship

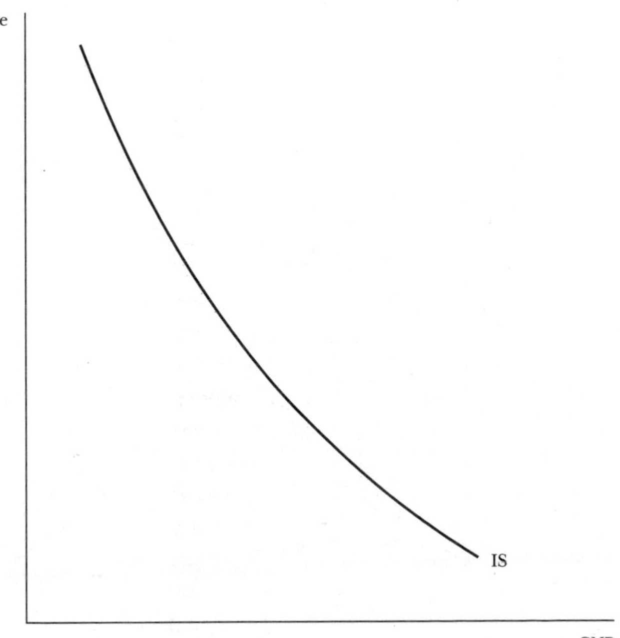

venient simplification to think of the Federal Reserve as controlling the money supply completely. Suppose, too, that at current income and interest rates there is just enough money to go around to satisfy cash holders. The only way this fixed quantity of money will be able to accommodate a higher income (and higher rate of business transactions) is for interest rates to go up. This will give cash holders an incentive to economize by switching into interest-bearing securities and freeing the cash for use by others. Hence, for a fixed money supply, higher interest rates will be consistent with a higher level of national income. The so-called LM relationship is shown in Figure 21.A4.

Only one point, the intersection of the IS and LM curves, satisfies both equilibrium conditions, and thus the intersection represents the equilibrium interest rate and income for the economy. Note that expansionary fiscal policy works to increase equilibrium income by lowering the amount of private investment needed to support a given level of income. Increased government expenditures or reduced taxes tend to shift the IS curve to the right. Equilibrium income goes up, and interest rates rise to accommodate the LM side of the system (see Figure 21.A5).

Expansionary monetary policy works by increasing the quantity of

FIGURE 21.A4

Equilibrium in the IS-LM Model

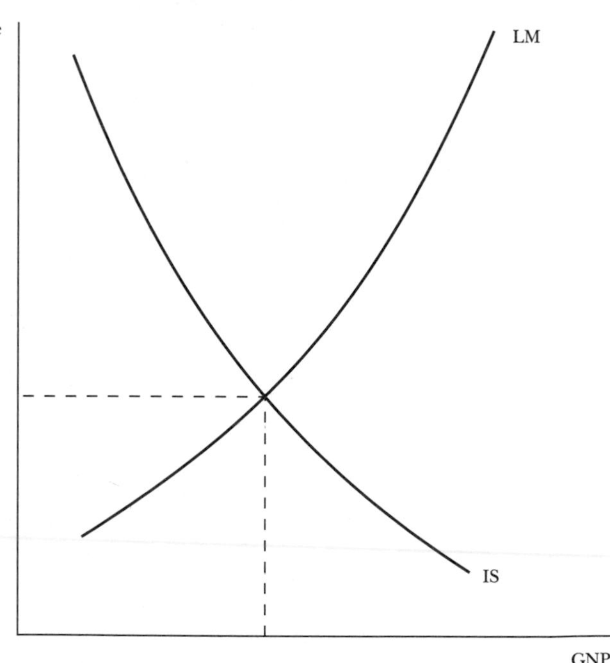

money available for cash users, thereby raising the level of national income supportable at any given interest rate. All other factors being equal, an increase in the supply of money raises equilibrium income. But it also *lowers* equilibrium interest rates, as investors must be given an incentive to invest more (see Figure 21.A5).

Now we are ready to see how the depression theories may be classified. Spending theories, in one form or another, translate into backward shifts of the IS curve:

- Reduced investment opportunities, resulting from the saturation of the housing or auto markets, mean that investors will invest less at any given interest rate; thus a lower rate of interest will be needed to equilibrate the same level of investment and savings.

- A stock market crash reduces the wealth of individuals and makes them more conservative consumers. This means that savings will be higher at any given level of income, and investment will have to be higher also to use up the economic resources left over after desired consumption rates. The higher investment level will be attainable only at lower interest rates; thus the backward shift in the IS curve. The

FIGURE 21.A5

Monetary and Fiscal Policy in the IS-LM Model

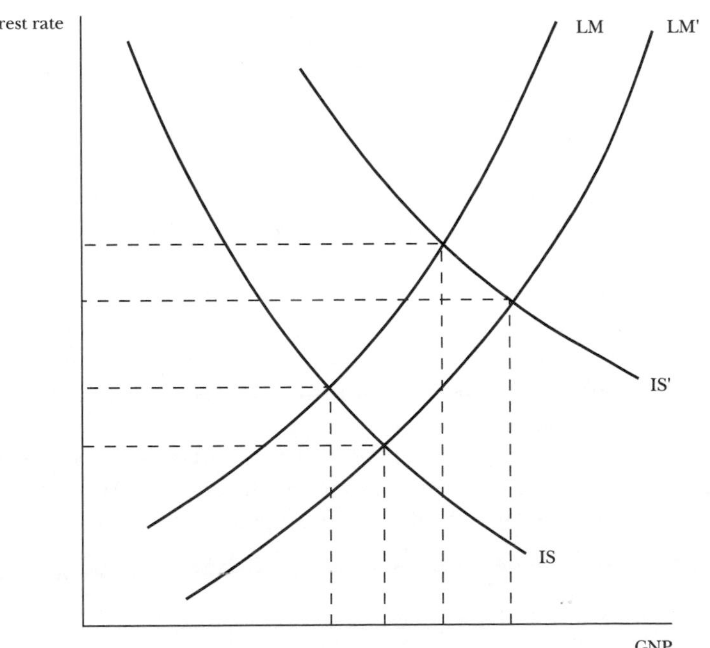

stock market crash could also reflect changing expectations about the profitability of corporate investment. Analytically, this would have the same effect on the IS curve as housing market saturation or any other perceived reduction in investment opportunity.

Monetary theories, on the other hand, work by shifting the LM curve to the left:

- Bank failures reduce confidence in the banking system, leading depositors to turn their funds into currency and leading banks to call in loans. Both actions reduce the money supply and thus make it necessary to have a higher level of interest rates to keep money holders satisfied with their balances at a given level of income—that is, the LM curve shifts backward.

- If one wishes to emphasize the role of the Federal Reserve, the same basic analysis applies. The Fed can prevent the money supply from shrinking by compensatory open market operations, trading Fed cash for publicly held government securities. Or it can lend reserves to the banks directly, encouraging them to borrow from the Fed by charging a low "rediscount" rate on Fed-to-bank loans and then putting the borrowed reserves to work in business loans. The Fed's failure to do either may have allowed destabilizing forces to contract the money supply, shifting back the LM curve and lowering equilibrium income.

Does the Hicks-Hansen synthesis provide a means of choosing between spending and monetary hypotheses? Yes and no. Yes, because of the difference in the predicted effect of each on interest rates. A reduction in aggregate demand shifting the IS curve to the left should lower interest rates, while an autonomous contraction in the money supply should raise interest rates. Temin's research supports the spending side since he finds that interest rates fell sharply in 1930.

No, because the test is not definitive. The Hicks-Hansen structure is too simple to accommodate the complexities of the real world. As noted in the text, real interest rates are not observable because they depend upon private expectations of future price changes. There is not a single interest rate to measure, moreover, but a whole series of interest rates that may not move together. Hence the somewhat contorted monetarist explanation that falling interest rates on some securities may not reflect the scarcity of loanable funds. In short, the Hicks-Hansen synthesis can only be used on the first step in analyzing the macroeconomics of the depression. And as Peter Temin explains in great detail, the subsequent steps are exceedingly difficult to make.

Bibliography

Anderson, Gary M., William F. Shugart II, and Robert D. Tollison. "A Public Choice Theory of the Great Contraction." *Public Choice* (1988): 3–24.

———. "A Public Choice Theory of the Great Contraction: Further Evidence." *Public Choice* (1990): 277–84.

Ando, Albert, and Franco Modigliani. "The 'Life Cycle' Hypothesis of Saving: Aggregate Implications and Tests." *American Economic Review* 53 (1963): 55–84.

Brunner, Karl, ed. *The Great Depression Revisited.* Boston: Martinus Nijhoff, 1981.

———, and Allan H. Meltzer. "What Did We Learn from the Monetary Experience of the United States in the Great Depression?" *Canadian Journal of Economics* (1968): 334–48.

Eichengreen, Barry. *Golden Fetters: The Gold Standard and the Great Depression 1919–1939.* New York: Oxford University Press, 1992.

Epstein, Gerald, and Thomas Ferguson. "Monetary Policy, Loan Liquidation, and Industrial Conflict: The Federal Reserve and the Open Market Operations of 1932." *Journal of Economic History* (1984): 957–84.

———. "Answers to Stock Questions: Fed Targets, Stock Prices, and the Gold Standard in the Great Depression." *Journal of Economic History* 51 (1991): 190–200.

Fabricant, Solomon. "The Changing Industrial Distribution of Gainful Workers: Comments on the Decennial Statistics 1820–1940." In Studies in Income and Wealth, vol. 11 (New York: NBER): 1–49.

Friedman, Milton, and Anna Schwartz. *A Monetary History of the United States, 1867–1960.* Princeton: Princeton University Press, 1963.

———. *The Great Contraction 1929–1933.* Princeton: Princeton University Press. 1965.

Galbraith, John Kenneth. *The Great Crash.* Boston: Houghton Mifflin, 1972.

Gordon, Robert A. "Investment Behavior and Business Cycles." *Review of Economics and Statistics* 37 (1955): 23–34.

———. *Economic Instability and Growth: The American Record.* New York: Harper & Row, 1974.

Green, George. "The Economic Impact of the Stock Market Boom and Crash of 1929." In Federal Reserve Bank of Boston, *Consumer Spending and Monetary Policy: The Linkages.* Boston: Federal Reserve Bank of Boston, 1971: 189–220.

Hansen, Alvin H. *Business Cycles and National Income.* New York: W. W. Norton, 1951.

Hayek, Friedrich A. von."The Fate of the Gold Standard." In *Money, Capital and Fluctuations, Early Essays of Friedrich A. von Hayek,* ed. Roy McCloughry. London: Routledge, 1984: 118–35.

Hickman, Bert G. "What Became of the Building Cycle?" In *Nations and Households in Economic Growth: Essays in Honor of Moses Abramovitz,* ed. Paul David and Melvin Reden. New York: Academic Press, 1973.

Hoover, Herbert H. *The Memoirs of Herbert Hoover.* New York: Macmillan, 1952.

Jones, Joseph M. *Tariff Retaliation.* London: H. Milford, 1934.

Keynes, John Maynard. *Treatise on Money.* New York: Harcourt Brace, 1930.

———. *The General Theory of Employment, Interest, and Money.* New York: Harcourt Brace, 1936.

Kindleberger, Charles. *The World in Depression, 1929–1939,* rev. ed. Berkeley: University of California Press, 1986.

Lewis, William Arthur. *Economic Survey, 1919–1939.* London: Allen and Unwin, 1949.

Lucia, Joseph. "The Failure of the Bank of United States: A Reappraisal." *Explorations in Economic History* 22 (1985): 402–16.

Meltzer, Allen. "Monetary and Other Explanations of the Start of the Great Depression." *Journal of Monetary Economics* 2 (1976): 455–71.

Mishkin, Frederic S. "The Household Balance Sheet and the Great Depression." *Journal of Economic History* 38 (1978): 918–37.

Mitchell, Broadus. *The Depression Decade: From New Era through New Deal, 1929–1941.* White Plains: M.E. Sharpe, 1947.

Olney, Martha. *Buy Now, Pay Later.* Chapel Hill: University of North Carolina Press, 1991.

Pecora, Ferdinand. *Wall Street under Oath.* New York: Simon and Schuster, 1939.

Robbins, Lionel. *The Great Depression.* London: Macmillan, 1934.

Rothbard, Murray, *America's Great Depression.* Princeton: Van Nostrand, 1972.

Salter, Sir Arthur. *Recovery: The Second Effort.* New York: New Century Company, 1932.

Santoni, Gary, and Norman Van Cott. "The Rutheless Fed: A Critique of the AST Hypothesis." *Public Choice* 67 (1990): 269–76.

Schumpeter, Joseph. *Business Cycles.* New York: McGraw-Hill, 1939.

Schwartz, Anna J. "Understanding 1929–1933." In *The Great Depression Revisited,* ed. Karl Brunner. Boston: Kluwer-Nijihoff, 1981: 5–48.

Smiley, Gene, and Richard H. Keehn. "Margin Purchases, Brokers' Loans, and the Bull Market of the Twenties." *Business and Economic History* 17 (1988): 129–42.

Soule, George. *The Prosperity Decade: From War to Depression, 1917–1929.* White Plains: M. E. Sharpe, 1947.

Stein, Herbert. *The Fiscal Revolution in America,* rev. ed. Washington, D.C.: American Enterprise Institute, 1990.

Sundstrom, William A. "Last Hired, First Fired? Unemployment and Urban Black Workers during the Great Depression." *Journal of Economic History* 52 (1992): 415–29.

Temin, Peter. *Did Monetary Forces Cause the Great Depression?* New York: W. W. Norton, 1976.

———. *Lessons from the Great Depression.* Cambridge: MIT Press, 1989.

Wanniski, Jude. *The Way the World Works.* New York: Touchstone, 1978.

Wheelock, David. *The Strategy and Consistency of Federal Reserve Monetary Policy, 1924 to 1932–33.* New York: Cambridge University Press, 1991.

White, Eugene. "When the Ticker Ran Late: The Stock Market Boom and Crash of 1929." In *Crashes and Panics: The Lessons from History,* ed. Eugene White. Homewood, IL: Dow Jones/Irwin, 1990a: 143–87.

———. "The Stock Market Boom and Crash of 1929 Revisited." *Journal of Economic Perspectives* 4 (1990b): 67–84.

Wigmore, Barrie. "Was the Bank Holiday of 1933 Caused by a Run on the Dollar?" *Journal of Economic History* 47 (1987): 739–56.

Wicker, Elmus R. *Federal Reserve and Monetary Policy 1917–1933.* New York: Random House, 1966.

The great depression, 1933–39: the recovery?

22

In his speech accepting the Democratic party's nomination for the presidency on July 2, 1932, Franklin Delano Roosevelt pledged "a new deal for the American people." When he was sworn into office as the thirty-second president of the United States on March 4, 1932, he was expected to make good on that promise. The details of the various policies are discussed in Chapter 23. Here we focus upon the macroeconomic question of recovery and the role, if any, that government policy may have played in that recovery.

When Roosevelt took office, the nation was in turmoil, racked by almost four years of economic decline that had revealed numerous flaws in the structure of the American economy and cracks in the veneer of society. At least a quarter of the population was classified as unemployed; countless others had long since abandoned the search for work where none was to be found; thousands had lost their homes and farms; millions had lost at least part of their savings in the successive waves of bank failures that in four years had claimed more than nine thousand banks, a third of all banks in the country; the nation was living off its invested capital, no longer even replacing wear and tear on capital goods; the real value of domestic production was little more than 70 percent of its 1929 peak; and world trade had been seriously impeded by a storm of competitive devaluations and protective tariffs.

The contraction had also done immense structural damage to the economy that was exceedingly difficult to repair. It had destroyed institutions as well as income. Capital markets were unraveled by disintermediation: People, with good reason, distrusted banks after 1931 and were reluctant to use them again. Bankrupt corporations—including many banks—were immersed in legal proceedings that made it difficult to use their underlying assets productively. And the stock market crash brought home to many investors the inherent risks in equity investments, as well as exposed the degree to which the market was vulnerable to stock price manipulation and securities fraud. All this increased the cost of raising capital for businesses that wanted to increase production. Moreover, the burden was not borne equally. Experiences during the depression were often radically different across industries. Such industries as iron and steel and lumber experienced much sharper declines and slower recovery than industry as a whole. Other industries, notably petroleum and tobacco, which were doing much better than average before the onset of the depression, continued to do much better, as a result of differences in the rate of technical change and the nature of demand for their products (Figure 22.1).[1]

The Recovery

A glance at almost any of the statistical data covering the period, such as unemployment, GNP, the money supply, or prices, shows that no matter how kindly disposed one may be to Roosevelt's policies, recovery did not come with the New Deal. The economy clawed its way back to levels achieved in the late 1920s only very slowly. By most standards, recovery was far from complete when war broke out in Europe in 1939, providing a much-needed stimulus. Not until after the Japanese attack on Pearl Harbor in 1941 can recovery be considered complete in terms of economic indicators, such as unemployment and real GNP. Even then, one must question whether or not the exigencies of a wartime economy constitute recovery and a return to normality.[2] Thus, although recovery was one of the goals of the New Deal, on this score it can hardly be considered a resounding success.

Unemployment, for example, remained stubbornly high—above 14 percent until after 1940. Moreover, unemployment increased sharply between 1937 and 1938 as the economy entered a recession within the midst of the Great Depression. One might even argue that the government contributed to the unemployment problem through its emergency relief make-work projects, such as the Civilian Conservation Corps and the Works Progress Administration. Those holding such relief jobs, who numbered among the millions at times—the WPA, for example, had 3.4 million on its payroll by March 1936—are officially classified as unemployed, apparently on the ground that participation in these programs was of limited duration, sometimes part-time, and at annual wages that were often far below those in the rest of the economy.

[1] Bernstein (1987).
[2] Higgs (1992).

FIGURE 22.1

Industrial Production, 1927–1941

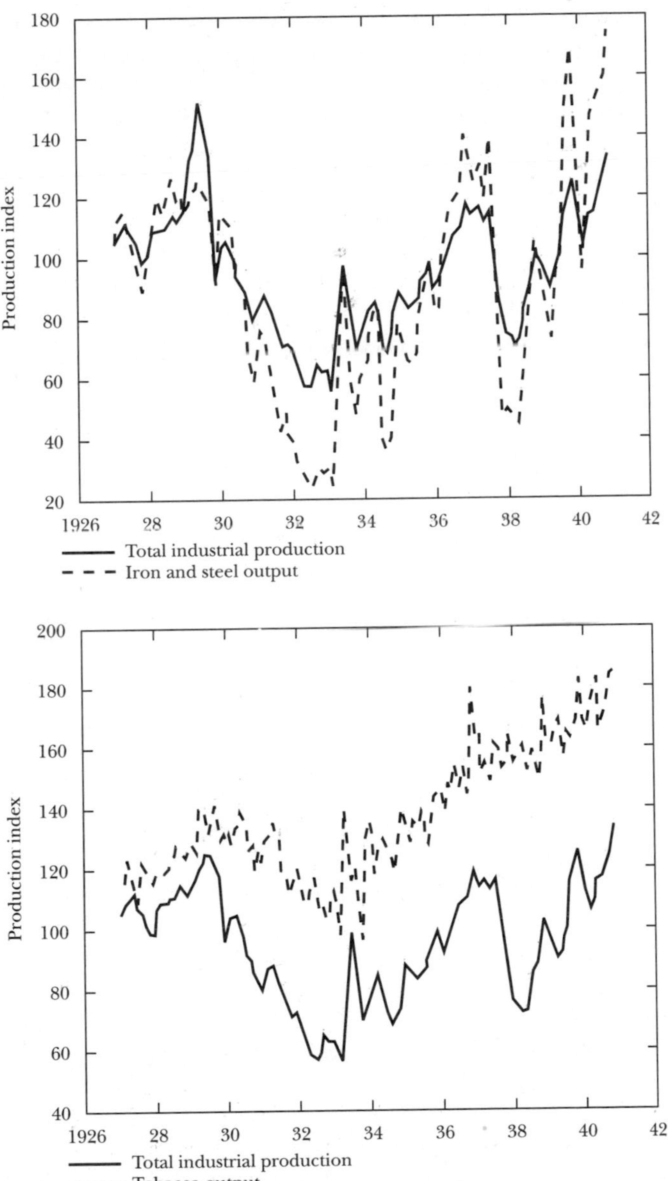

Source: Michael A. Bernstein, *The Great Depression: Delayed Recovery and Economic Change in America, 1929–1939* (New York: Cambridge University Press. 1987): 9.

On the other hand, participants in these programs often created things of lasting value: national forests, lodges in national parks, the Blue Ridge Parkway, and buildings on university campuses around the country. One might therefore reasonably argue that these emergency workers fitted the definition of someone who was gainfully employed. Consequently, Michael Darby has proposed an alternative unemployment series that treats emergency workers as employed since they were no longer searching for jobs. Public make-work projects seen from this perspective were substitutes for the search for private employment. The result is to reduce the unemployment rate by 4 to 7 percentage points and the number of employed by 2 to 3.5 million at the depths of the depression (Figure 22.2). Even with such an adjustment to the unemployment estimates, unemployment remained above 9 percent until after 1940—far in excess of the natural rate, although Darby argues that had it not been for the recession of 1937–38, the economy might have achieved its "natural" rate (i.e., where unemployment reflects job switching rather than structural or cyclical factors) of around 5 percent.

FIGURE 22.2

Unemployment during the Great Depression

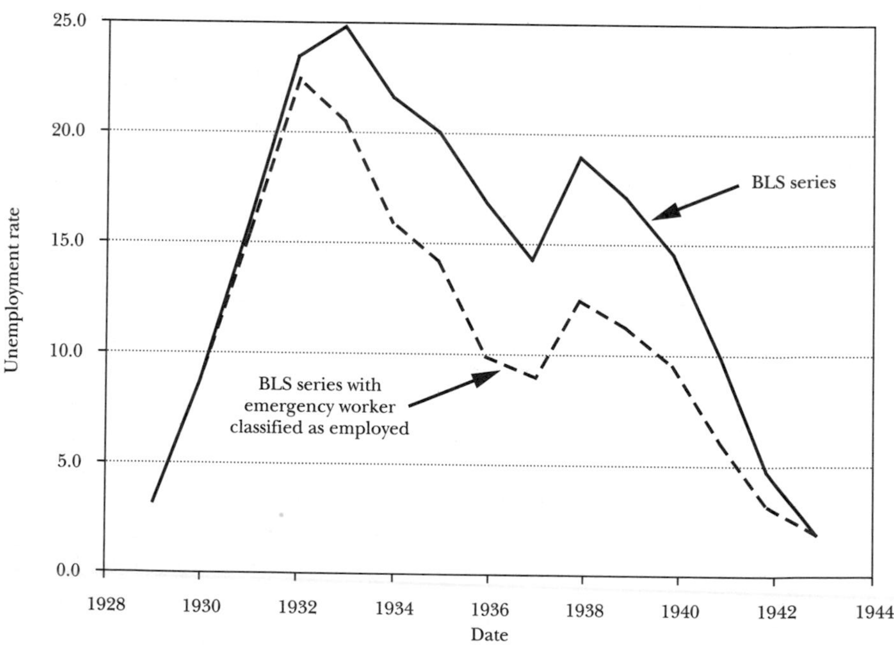

Michael Darby, "Three and a Half Million U.S. Employees Have Been Mislaid: Or, an Explanation of Unemployment, 1934–41," *Journal of Political Economy* 84 (1976): 8.

Employment in nonmanufacturing activities held up much better than employment in manufacturing. Nationally employment in nonmanufacturing declined between 1929 and 1933, bottoming out at 81 percent of its 1929 level and recovering to almost 90 percent of its 1929 level by 1935, and had essentially fully recovered by 1937. Manufacturing employment, on the other hand, fell to only 67 percent of its 1929 level in 1933 and did not fully recover until 1940. Moreover, employment in the South, particularly in the South Atlantic region, held up much better than elsewhere. In the South Atlantic region employment declined only 14 percent between 1929 and 1932, was actually recovering by 1933, and by 1940 was 26 percent above its 1929 level. The rest of the South didn't do quite as well, but it recovered quickly. Two factors may account for the South's relatively good employment record during the depression. First, southern industry was heavily concentrated in light industry, which maintained production and employment levels much better than heavy industry. Second, fewer southern workers were covered by Social Security and unemployment insurance taxes that raised the cost of labor and had a negative impact on employment.[3]

State-level employment estimates are probably not as robust as the regional estimates, but they present intriguing contrasts between experiences in different states during the Great Depression. Manufacturing employment in Arizona, for example, apparently declined by more than 50 percent between 1929 and 1933. Arizona, of course, was hardly an industrialized state, but neither was Florida, where employment dropped by less than 24 percent. Experiences differed sharply among the industrialized states. In Illinois employment declined almost 48 percent between 1929 and 1933, whereas in Massachusetts it declined "only" 35 percent.[4]

Work by Robert Margo shows that unemployment experiences also differed widely by occupational group, industry, and age. Unemployment rates followed a U-shaped pattern with respect to age; young and old had much higher incidences of unemployment than the middle-aged. Blue-collar workers were also much more likely to be unemployed than white-collar workers or professionals. In Philadelphia in 1936 (when recovery was supposedly well under way), for example, the unemployment rate among the unskilled was 44 percent, compared with 21 percent among clerical workers and only 12 percent among professionals and managerial workers. Unemployment was particularly high among construction workers—hardly surprising in view of the fact that the Federal Reserve construction index fell to less than one-tenth of its 1929 level by 1933. In March 1933, for example, the unemployment rate among construction workers was 73 percent, compared with 40 percent in manufacturing and "only" 14.5 percent in agriculture.

[3] Wallis (1987; 1989).
[4] Wallis (1989).

Ironically, those on work relief were much more likely to suffer long-term unemployment than those who did not secure work relief jobs. Indeed, more than half of those on work relief had been unemployed for more than a year, compared with less than a third of those not on relief. Being unemployed was, of course, a prerequisite for a work relief job, and those receiving relief were still officially counted as unemployed, but people who had received work relief were much less likely to find gainful private employment than those who had not received work relief. People on work relief differed from the other unemployed: They were more likely to be young, married, nonwhite, native-born, and rural and to live outside the Northeast. These data suggest a need to reinterpret the Keynesian interpretation that high unemployment resulted from sticky wages that would not adjust downward. Instead long-term relief work provided security and an alternative to a potentially fruitless job search, reducing the downward pressure on nominal wages; the unemployed on relief stopped looking for work. Participation in relief work may also have stigmatized workers, screening out the more complacent, risk-averse individuals for public, rather than private, sector employment. Thus relief may have compromised recovery if recovery is measured by reductions in the unemployment rate and increases in employment.[5]

With the onset of the depression real GNP fell, bottoming out in 1933. It was not until 1937 that real GNP exceeded its 1929 level. If real GNP had instead continued to grow after 1929 at the same rate as from 1921 to 1929, when it grew at an average annual rate of 4.4 percent, then by 1939 real GNP would have been about $165 billion (Figure 22.3). Its actual level was only $111 billion (in 1929 prices). Actual real GNP during the 1930s totaled $932 billion, whereas if the rate of growth during the 1920s had been maintained, it would have been about $1.365 billion—a shortfall of over $400 billion, or almost a third.

Although the economy began to recover after 1933, the rate of growth during that recovery was little different from what it had been during the days of full employment in the 1920s, despite the existence of considerable unemployed and underemployed resources. There was no real "rebound" in the economy. Sluggish as the recovery in America was, it was faster than in most other countries, except Germany and Japan, which were embarking on their militaristic expansion that resulted in World War II. Given the magnitude of the United States' decline, though, one might reasonably have expected a much stronger recovery than actually occurred.

Following the debacle of the final banking crisis that ended with the bank holiday of March 1933, monetary growth resumed, growing at annual rates of 9.5 percent, 14 percent, and 13 percent from June 1933 through June 1936. Milton Friedman and Anna Schwartz attribute this rapid recovery

[5] Margo (1991).

FIGURE 22.3

Real Gross National Product, 1919–1939
(1929 prices)

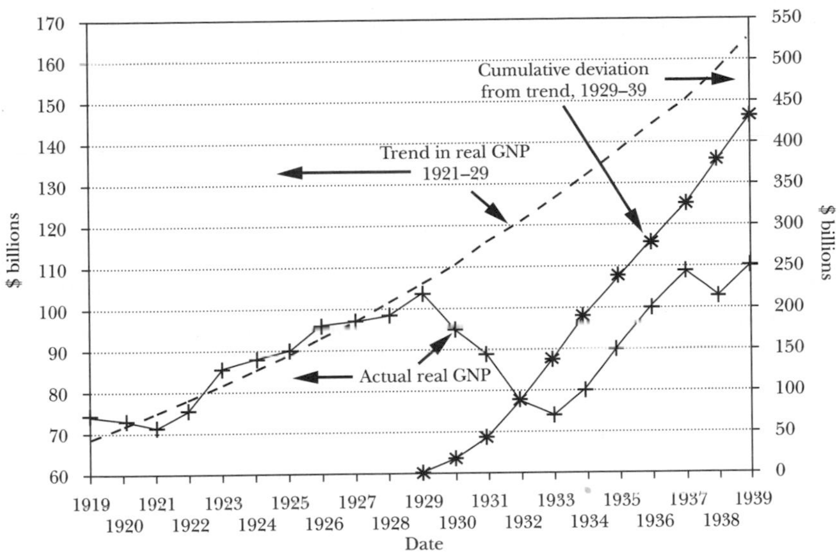

Source: Peter Temin, *Did Monetary Forces Cause the Great Depression?* (New York: W. W. Norton, 1976): 4. Trend calculated as a simple growth trend 1921–29 extrapolated over the period. Cumulative deviation calculated as the difference between actual real GNP and the trend cumulated from 1929 on.

to the inflow of gold stimulated by devaluation—gold would buy 67 percent more dollars after devaluation than before ($35 per ounce, compared with $20.67 prior to 1933)—and capital flight (particularly from Germany) rather than the recovery of business. Prices also showed some recovery, though the price index remained far below its levels of the 1920s throughout the 1930s (Figure 22.4).

Recession in the Midst of Recovery, 1937–38

Unemployment rose again from1937 to 1938, and real GNP declined. Some argue that this setback to recovery resulted from a reversal of the government's fiscal policy in response to mounting federal deficits, but other factors were also at work. First, other countries, notably Britain, France, and Canada, also experienced economic decline about the same time, the ex-

FIGURE 22.4

Inflation and the Consumer Price Level 1919–1939

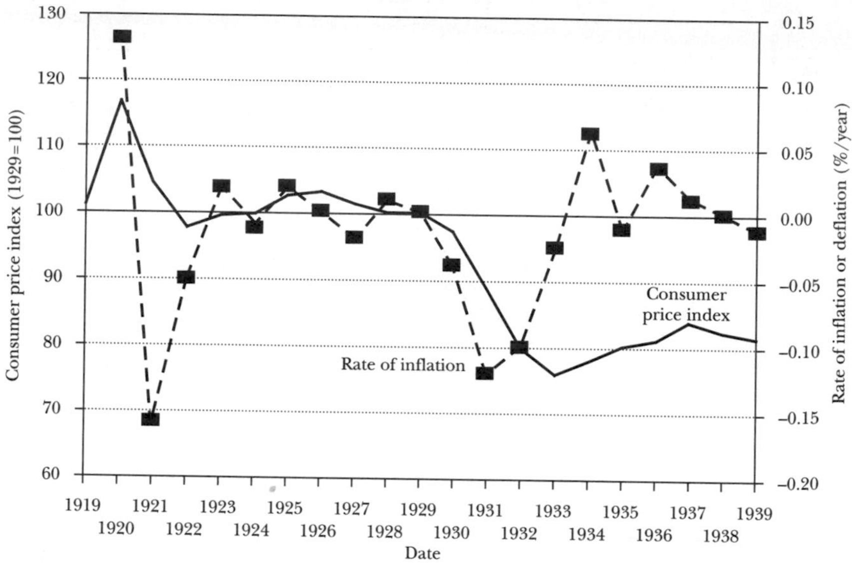

Source: U.S. Bureau of the Census, *Historical Statistics of the United States* (Washington, D.C.: Government Printing Office, 1975): Series E135 (reindexed).

ceptions being those nations on a war footing and where national socialism was dominant (Figure 22.5). Second, there was an abrupt reversal of domestic monetary policy in the United States. Money, which had grown by 14 and 13 percent in the preceding two years, grew only 4.2 percent between June 1936 and June 1937, and it fell 2.4 percent the following year.

Friedman and Schwartz argue that it was this abrupt change that precipitated the recession from May 1937 to June 1938. The money supply had peaked in March 1937; it turned around in May 1938. These reversals reflected policy changes by the Fed. Prompted by concern about the inflationary potential of the large volume of excess reserves held by the banks, the rapid growth of the money stock, and the modest increase in prices, the Fed had increased reserve requirements. As a result, interest rates rose and business confidence collapsed while banks wanted to maintain a cushion of excess reserves. The Fed returned to its policy of sterilizing gold inflows that underlay the rapid expansion of the money supply from 1933. The result was the third-largest recorded decline in the money supply, exceeded only by the declines in 1920–21 and 1929–33. This explanation is all the more credible

FIGURE 22.5

Changes in Industrial Production in Selected Countries, 1924–29, 1932–37, 1929–30, and 1937–38 (index numbers with specified bases)

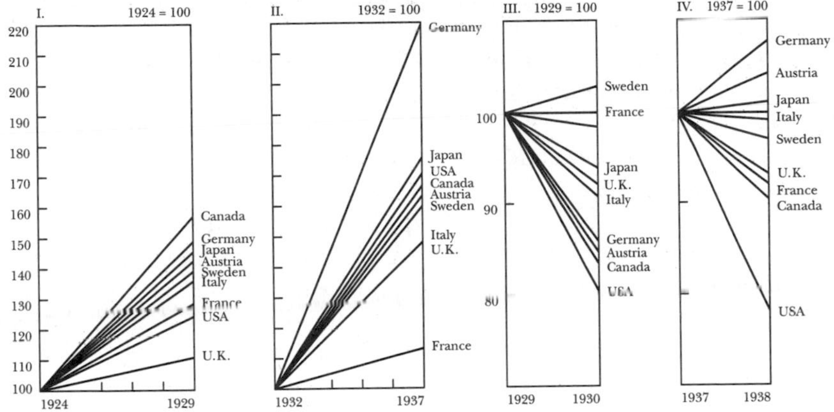

Source: Charles P. Kindleberger, *The World in Depression* (Berkeley: University of California Press, 1986): 278.

since recovery and monetary growth resumed once the Fed reduced reserve requirements, lowered the discount rate, and made some modest open market purchases.

Explaining Recovery from 1933

Many explanations have been offered for the turnaround of the economy in 1933. Friedman and Schwartz credit the halt of the collapse of the financial system and the resumption of growth in the money supply. One might argue that considering the magnitude of the decline, sooner or later things had to turn around.[6] Subsistence placed a floor beneath the economy; thereafter the only way out was up. For liquidationists—the Austrian school—recovery came when the unsound businesses had finally been put out of their protracted misery.[7] The Keynesian interpretation is that recovery resulted from New Deal spending and the massive government deficits that accrued as the government substituted public spending for inadequate private spending—a view that will be discussed in more detail later.[8]

More recently the recovery has been attributed to the shock of Roosevelt's new policy regime (but not the spending associated with it),

[6] Kindleberger (1986).
[7] Robbins (1934); Hayek (1984).
[8] Keynes (1936); Hansen (1984).

which altered expectations and stimulated renewed investment.[9] Specifically, Peter Temin and Barrie Wigmore identify the devaluation of the dollar and the subsequent rise in farm prices and incomes as crucial. Devaluation broke the iron grip of the gold standard that tied America to the rest of the world and the rest of the world to America. This explanation is appealing. It provides a better—that is, more timely—explanation of the turning point than Friedman and Schwartz's claim that recovery was sparked by expectations of higher prices resulting from the National Industrial Recovery Act (NIRA), which was passed some two months after devaluation was a fait accompli, and codes of fair competition took a number of additional months to be drawn up and implemented. Others have also linked devaluation to recovery in the rest of the world.[10] On the other hand, the market anticipated devaluation long before Roosevelt was sworn in as president. Indeed, the run on gold that led up to the bank holiday reflected those expectations and, it might be argued, left policy makers with no choice but to devalue. Furthermore, since foreign trade was relatively small, this explanation makes international trade the tail that wags the dog. Still, as Temin and Wigmore point out, while other factors such as the NIRA and the Agricultural Adjustment Act (AAA) may have affected prices independently of devaluation, the prices of internationally traded agricultural commodities, such as wheat and cotton, changed by more and responded much more quickly than domestically traded commodities, such as soft fruits, milk, and vegetables.

As plausible as these explanations may be, and despite the considerable evidence in support of them, many still believe that recovery was a direct result of the fiscal stimulus supplied by Roosevelt's New Deal. Consequently, it is worthwhile reviewing the evidence for and against this hypothesis in greater detail.

FISCAL POLICY

The federal government had the weapons with which to fight the depression: fiscal and monetary policy. Monetary policy, however, was in the hands of the same individuals—the Board of Governors of the Federal Reserve—who had never smelled the smoke in 1930 and then refused to help put out the fire in 1932. They did virtually nothing from 1933 to 1937 that could be construed as policy of any sort. This left fiscal policy. Did Roosevelt play an aggressive role, adopting the new interventionist approach called for by John Maynard Keynes and his crowd? Probably not.

Keynes, Cambridge University's premier economic theorist and the controversial adviser to several British governments, did meet Franklin Roosevelt—once. But that meeting came off badly—neither found his audience sufficiently respectful—and there is not a hint that Roosevelt was in-

[9] Temin (1989); Temin and Wigmore (1990).
[10] Eichengreen (1992); Eichengreen and Sachs (1985).

fluenced by Keynes. However, it took the analysis of E. Cary Brown, writing in 1956, to bury the myth that Roosevelt was the first American Keynesian.

In Keynes's analysis, the depression was the result of a decline in aggregate demand (defined as the sum of consumption expenditures, investment expenditures, net exports, and net government spending) sparked by a reduction in the level of desired business investment arising from less optimistic business expectations. The decline in aggregate demand led in turn to a reduction in aggregate supply below the level at which resources were fully employed. As reductions in aggregate supply rippled through the economy, people were thrown out of work. The unemployed had little choice but to reduce their consumption expenditures. Even those who were still employed may have felt compelled to increase their savings at the expense of current consumption just in case they were next on the layoff list. With rising inventories of unsold goods, businesses had no incentive to invest in new plants and equipment to maintain existing output levels, let alone expand production.

Government, however, had within its power the means to counter the decline in private aggregate demand. If private-sector expenditure fell short of that necessary to attain and maintain full employment, the public sector could make good, increasing its expenditures relative to its income and borrowing if need be. Public spending could be substituted for private spending. Government expenditure (G in Figure 22.6) and taxes (T) are viewed as discretionary variables; to be set at whatever levels the government deems necessary to achieve its policy objective. The way it's supposed to work is as follows:

For each level of aggregate demand, there is an equilibrium level of GNP, Y*, where aggregate demand is equal to aggregate supply, represented by the 45° line in Panel A of Figure 22.6. If prices are inflexible, especially if they are sticky downward, then the economy may be in equilibrium (defined as the income level where aggregate supply equals aggregate demand) at less than full employment. Suppose, however, that the government is committed to full employment, represented by $\overline{Y}$, and that resources are currently unemployed ($Y^* < \overline{Y}$). Under such circumstances, Keynes suggested that by increasing government expenditures relative to taxes by ΔG, the government could increase aggregate demand and the equilibrium level of GNP by a sufficient amount to reach the goal of full employment—provided the private sector does not react so as to offset the increased aggregate demand arising from increased government spending.

Budget deficits represent injections of cash into the circular flow of income, increasing the demand for goods and services. They are expansionary and potentially inflationary. Budget surpluses, on the other hand, represent withdrawals from the circular flow of income. They are contractionary or deflationary. Politicians are fond of using the size of the budget deficit as a gauge of fiscal impact. But there is a problem here. Since taxes also tend to

FIGURE 22.6

Fiscal Policy

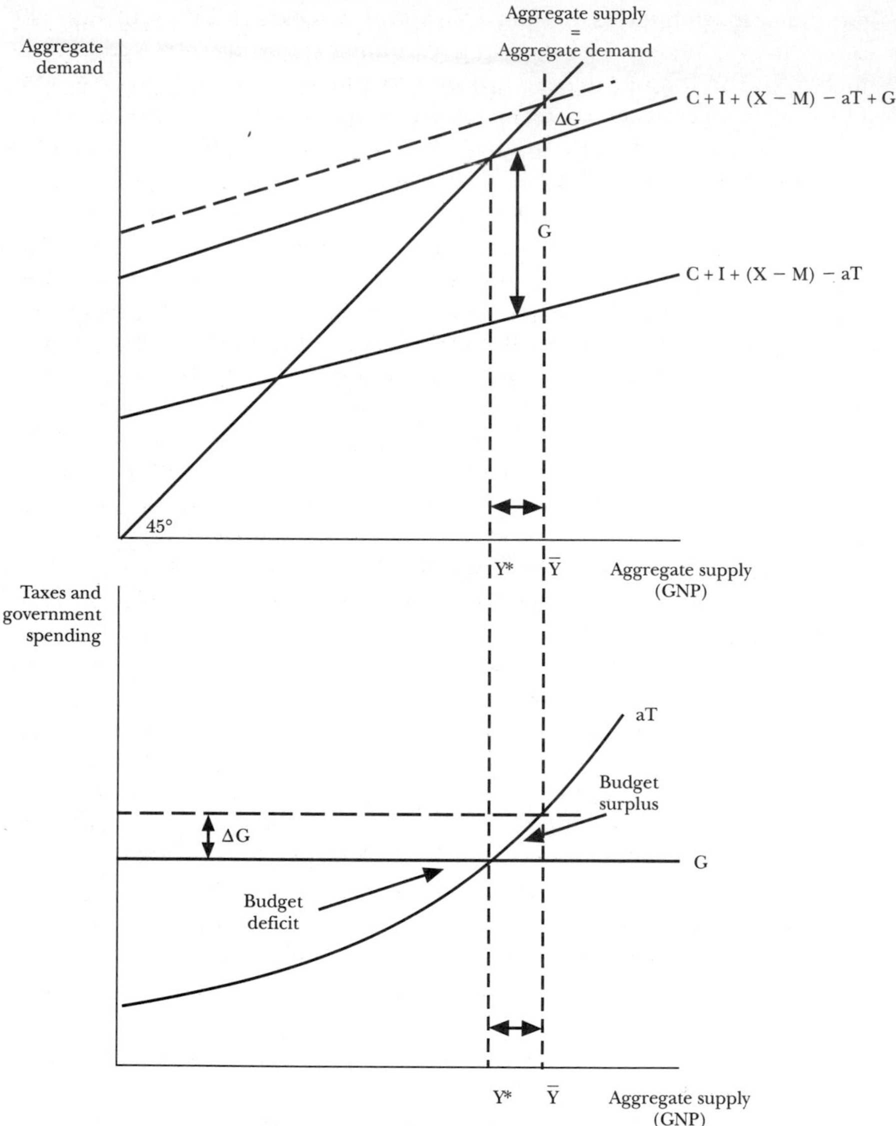

rise as GNP increases, the fiscal stimulus provided by a given level of government spending at any moment of time depends upon the level of GNP. The same set of tax rates and government spending programs may generate either a budget surplus or a budget deficit depending on the vigor of the private sector. If businesses and individuals spend aggressively on their own, tax collections go up. Moreover, government spending tends to fall as the need for welfare, unemployment benefits, and jobs programs disappears. As a result, the federal budget could be in surplus. If, on the other hand, private spending is slack, then tax revenues fall and government social spending accelerates and the federal budget is in the red. This explains why economically conservative governments, like the Eisenhower administration, could run up big deficits without even trying. During the 1958–59 recession President Eisenhower's advisers were horrified to find that federal expenditures exceeded federal revenues by 16 percent, the largest deficit since the crisis years of World War II.

One must be extremely cautious about judging the fiscal stimulus of a particular combination of taxes and government spending programs by the magnitude of the current budget deficit or surplus. The current budget surplus or deficit merely indicates the direction in which fiscal policy is driving the economy. Instead Brown measured the relative impact of fiscal policy on aggregate demand at full employment income—that is to say, the GNP that would be produced if all resources were to be fully and efficiently employed. Brown's question was, Would the economy have ever reached full employment if the government had maintained a particular year's fiscal policy for long enough? That is, given the levels of expenditure and taxation, and if we assume that these levels didn't change, would the economy have expanded to full employment, or would recovery have stopped short of that goal? The question is an important one because the fiscal stimulus from any given tax and spending program diminishes as GNP increases—a phenomenon referred to as fiscal drag. Moreover, fiscal stimulus ceases once the budget is balanced. Thus, if the budget is balanced at less than full employment GNP, fiscal policy will never move the economy to full employment GNP, and recovery will stop short. On the other hand, if full employment GNP is less than the balanced budget GNP, then recovery may be complete, but inflationary pressures are likely to cause other problems.

Brown, of course, did not know exactly how large the government deficit or surplus would have been at full employment. However, by assuming that (1) government expenditures were virtually unaffected by income levels, (2) tax collections were roughly proportional to increases in income above actual income levels, and (3) full employment income was growing at 3 percent a year, he was able to construct counterfactual full employment budgets (Table 22.1).

By these estimates, federal fiscal policy was, on balance, expansionary during six of the seven Roosevelt administration years shown (1933 on). Only in 1937 would there have been a budget surplus at full employment, amounting to a reduction in full employment GNP of about 0.7 percent. But that should be cold comfort, indeed, for Roosevelt partisans. On closer inspection, it becomes clear that the expansionary stimulus of fiscal policy was very modest. At the trough of the depression, when Brown calculates that ac-

TABLE 22.1

Impact of Federal Fiscal Policy on Aggregate Demand
($ billions)

Year	Government Spending (current dollars)	Taxes (current dollars)	Current Budget Deficit (−) Surplus (+)	Real Spending	Real Full Employment Taxes	Full Employment Budget Deficit (−) Surplus (+)	Full Employment Budget as % of Full Employment GNP
1929	1.4	2.6	1.2	2.5	3.4	0.9	−0.6
1930	1.5	1.8	0.3	2.9	3.0	−0.1	+0.1
1931	1.8	−0.3	−2.1	3.4	0.3	−3.1	+2.1
1932	1.6	0.1	−1.5	3.2	1.5	−1.7	+1.0
1933	2.5	1.2	−1.3	5.2	4.7	−0.5	+0.3
1934	4.6	1.8	−2.8	8.4	5.6	−2.8	+1.6
1935	4.6	2.1	−2.5	8.3	5.5	−2.8	+1.6
1936	5.4	2.0	−3.4	9.3	5.4	−3.9	+2.1
1937	5.1	4.9	−0.2	8.8	10.2	1.4	−0.7
1938	5.9	3.9	−2.0	10.6	9.4	−1.2	+0.6
1939	5.8	3.6	−2.2	10.2	8.5	−1.7	+0.8

Source: Adapted from E. Cary Brown, "Fiscal Policy in the Thirties," *American Economic Review* 46 (1956): 864–65, Table 1.

tual output was 39 percent below full employment capacity, the full employment deficit would have been only 0.3 percent of GNP. In 1936 the Roosevelt budget reached its expansionary peak (2.1 percent of GNP)—but only because Congress, over White House objections, sweetened the veterans' compensation program. And the following year political pressures to balance the budget pushed fiscal policy into its most conservative stance since the late 1920s.

Note, too, that the extremely moderate stimulus of the Roosevelt budgets was offset by increasingly conservative financial policies of state and local governments that were up to their capitol domes in debt. During the last three disastrous years of the Hoover administration (1930–32), state and local governments maintained a slightly positive fiscal stance, raising the net simulative impact of all government activity. But after 1932, efforts to stem growing deficits made nonfederal government budgets a net deflationary force, fully offsetting Roosevelt's cautious expansion. As a result, the net impact of all government on aggregate demand was negative in four out of seven Roosevelt years and was surely less expansionary overall from 1933 to 1939 than it had been from 1930 to 1932 (Table 22.2)! By Brown's standard, then, Herbert Hoover was a better Keynesian than FDR.

Larry Peppers's reworking of Brown's computations puts depression fiscal policy in an even worse light. Peppers adjusted Brown's estimates of full employment income and made more sophisticated projections of tax revenues and expenditures at the full employment level. He discovered that the federal budget would have been in full employment *surplus* in every depression year, with the exception of 1931 and 1936 (see Table 22.3).

Why was fiscal policy so perversely practiced during the depression? The simple—and nearly complete—answer is that policy makers did not know any better. To be fair, ignorance was a perfectly reasonable excuse in the early 1930s. Monetary policy makers at least had intuition working in their favor: Saving the banks by pumping liquidity into the system seems sensible if the banks were caught by a panic caused by a general crisis of confidence rather than the result of their own unwise lending policies, speculation, or fraud. Fiscal planners, by contrast, had only classical macroeconomic theory, which prescribed nothing but increased labor market competition as the answer to unemployment, and the false analogies with private business and the household budget to guide fiscal planning.

Government budget deficits were seen as a threat to stability in the same way operating deficits were seen as a threat to the stability of the corporation. The only proper course, it appeared, was to batten the hatches and head into the wind. It could be said, too, that government was hostage to these homilies even if policy makers were not fully taken in by them. Radical departures from accepted policies could have further weakened confidence in the economy and thereby defeated their own purpose. All in all, however, Herbert Hoover comes out looking a tad better than Franklin Roosevelt as

TABLE 22.2

Fiscal Impact of Federal, State, and Local Government Taxes and Spending ($ billions)

Year	Actual Federal Budget Deficit (−)	Actual State & Local Budget Deficit (−)	Full Employment Federal Budget	Full Employment State & Local Budget	Aggregate Full Employment Budget (Federal+State+Local)	Aggregate Full Employment Budget as a Percent of Full Employment GNP
1929	1.2	−0.2	0.9	−2.0	−1.1	+0.7
1930	0.3	−0.6	−0.1	−2.3	−2.4	+1.6
1931	−2.1	−0.7	−3.1	−1.7	−4.8	+3.2
1932	−1.5	0.3	−1.7	0.3	−1.4	+0.9
1933	−1.3	0.0	−0.5	2.2	1.7	−1.0
1934	−2.8	0.4	−2.8	3.0	0.2	−0.1
1935	−2.5	0.5	−2.8	2.8	0.0	0.0
1936	−3.4	0.5	−3.9	1.9	−2.0	+1.1
1937	−0.2	0.7	1.4	2.2	3.6	−1.9
1938	−2.0	0.5	−1.2	2.4	1.2	−0.6
1939	−2.2	0.1	−1.7	1.4	−0.3	+0.1

Source: Adapted from E. Cary Brown, "Fiscal Policy in the Thirties," *American Economic Review* 46 (1956): 864–65, Table 1.

TABLE 22.3

Peppers's Full Employment Budget Calculations, 1929–39

Year	Potential Budget Surplus (+) in billion ($)	Potential Taxes (% GNP)	Potential Expenditures (% GNP)	Full Employment Surplus (% GNP)
1929	1.3	3.75	2.55	1.20
1930	0.9	3.57	2.67	0.90
1931	−0.5	3.78	4.32	−0.54
1932	0.8	4.43	3.56	0.87
1933	1.7	6.34	4.44	1.90
1934	0.1	6.59	6.45	0.14
1935	0.8	7.10	6.34	0.76
1936	−0.7	7.57	8.14	0.57
1937	3.2	9.31	6.50	2.82
1938	3.4	10.09	7.17	2.92
1939	2.6	9.53	7.32	2.21

Source: Larry Peppers, "Full Employment Surplus Analysis and Structural Change: The 1930's," *Explorations in Economic History* 10 (1973): 203.

an economic leader. It was Hoover who embarked upon ambitious public works projects to put people to work. It was Hoover who established the Reconstruction Finance Corporation to lend money to private businesses and banks in financial difficulties. It was Hoover who ran the largest budget deficits relative to GNP. But as historian (and fiscal planner under the Nixon administration) Herbert Stein argues, Hoover had no hope of breaking with conventional policies that had yet to be demonstrated ineffective to the business and financial communities. Instead much of his energies seemingly went into increasingly inane speeches about prosperity being just around the corner when everything all around seemed to be falling apart. The philosophy was that business confidence needed bolstering to encourage private investment. Arguably Hoover had a point: Private investment was much larger than government spending at the time, and thus any given percentage increase in private investment would have increased aggregate demand by more than the same percentage increase in government spending.

Roosevelt had the advantage of some hindsight: The policies he inherited obviously had not worked at all. But he resisted an expansionary approach out of the conviction that the economy's problems were structural, rather than fiscal. In the short run budget deficits might be tolerated in order to provide emergency relief for the unemployed. But Roosevelt believed—or at least acted as though he believed—that the country could not spend its way out of the depression. Salvation could be had only through structural reform.

This goes a long way toward explaining the passions of Roosevelt's economic advisers in defending the New Deal's emphasis on structural change. Nor is it clear that this New Deal emphasis upon structural change was misplaced. The depression revealed fundamental flaws in some basic institutions. Private charities, for example, were completely overwhelmed. However, liberal economists today get a painful surprise when they look back and see what the first modern liberal attempted. For while New Dealers of the 1930s and mainstream liberal economists of the 1970s share a common commitment toward income redistribution, contemporary liberal economists have far greater respect for the value of competitive market mechanisms in making sure there is something to redistribute.

The Objectives of New Deal Spending

By the standard of the times, enormous resources were invested in New Deal programs. This investment seems reasonable as part of the Roosevelt administration's attempt to cope with the impact of the depression on real incomes. But what seems less reasonable is the great variations in per capita allotments of funds among the states (Table 22.4); Nevada residents averaged $1,499 per person, while North Carolinians managed only $228.

Don Reading argues that the New Deal's goals were more specifically defined by the president as first relief and recovery and then reform. For Reading, relief and recovery meant repairing the immediate economic damage done by business failure and unemployment. Reform meant dealing with a failed Federal Reserve System, an uncontrolled stock market, falling wages and prices, and the farm crisis. Reform also meant attacking the structural causes of poverty: low productivity, racial discrimination, unequal wealth distribution. To measure the New Deal's goals in practice, Reading chose variables that showed the states' relative relief needs (such as percent decline in income and level of unemployment) and the state's relative reform needs (such as per capita income, percentage of tenant farmers and percentage of African-Americans). He then statistically regressed these variables (plus others to allow for the practical problems of setting up aid programs) against per capita New Deal aid to see if they explained state-by-state variations in spending.

His results show a much deeper dollar commitment to relief than to reform. Expenditures were greatest where, other factors being equal, unemployment and the rate of decline of income were greatest. Loan dollars appear to be related to income declines but not to unemployment. This

TABLE 22.4

New Deal Outlays per Capita, by State, 1933–1939

Region/State	Rank	Allocation ($)	Region/State	Rank	Allocation ($)
Northeast	6	301	Indiana	34	333
Connecticut	47	237	Iowa	15	467
Delaware	36	310	Michigan	21	389
Maine	32	336	Minnesota	17	426
Massachusetts	39	286	Missouri	31	340
New Hampshire	45	248	Ohio	22	383
New Jersey	35	330	Wisconsin	20	290
New York	33	335	*Great Plains*	3	424
Pennsylvania	42	261	Kansas	16	434
Rhode Island	46	247	North Dakota	6	708
Vermont	19	390	Oklahoma	30	343
Southeast	5	306	South Dakota	7	702
Alabama	37	310	Texas	216	362
Arkansas	18	396	*Pacific*	2	536
Florida	23	377	California	10	538
Georgia	40	273	Oregon	12	536
Kentucky	44	251	Washington	13	528
Louisiana	23	370	*Mountain*	1	716
Maryland	28	345	Arizona	4	791
Mississippi	27	358	Colorado	14	506
North Carolina	48	228	Idaho	5	744
South Carolina	38	306	Montana	2	986
Tennessee	29	344	Nevada	1	1,499
Virginia	43	255	New Mexico	8	690
West Virginia	41	265	Utah	9	569
Midwest	4	380	Wyoming	3	897
Illinois	25	365			

Source: Don Reading, "New Deal Activity and the States, 1933–39," *Journal of Economic History* 33 (1973): 794–95. Reprinted by permission of Cambridge University Press.

follows, Reading argues, from the fact that all the programs specifically targeted against unemployment—welfare, public works—were grant programs.

Surely the most striking result from the study is the apparent failure of New Deal administrators to pass out funds according to the single clearest measure of need: per capita income. It also explains why Congress was so interested in discovering Harry Hopkins's secret formula. The poorest region of the country, the South, got relatively little, while the richest, the Pacific states, averaged 75 percent more per capita. In a sense, this fits the recovery versus reform dichotomy; the New Deal simply never got as far as reform. But it also adds weight to the argument that Roosevelt was most concerned with defusing political and social unrest. Within bounds, it is logical that people would react more strongly to changes in income than to their absolute level of purchasing power. Thus an Oregon orchard owner, who had lost half of his or her substantial income, would be a better candidate for aid than a dirt-poor North Carolina sharecropper, whose income had fallen only marginally during the contraction and who did not vote.

It has been suggested that Roosevelt may have had something more prosaic—more Machiavellian—in mind, too: getting himself and other Democrats reelected.[11] This idea is elegantly developed by Gavin Wright, who econometrically tests several alternative models of spending for votes. A smart politician with limited resources to offer does not simply reward loyalty; a dollar spent on a sure vote is a dollar wasted. Rather, the politician tries to maximize the clout of expenditures, spending where the money is most likely to change the course of an election. This implies that more should be spent in states where, other factors being equal, (1) the voting is expected to be close and (2) there have been substantial swings in voter sentiment, suggesting that voters can be persuaded to switch party allegiance in return for favors.

Even without formal statistical testing, the predictive power of this approach is clear. The South, ever-loyal to the Democratic party, seemingly got little, while western states that switched allegiance frequently were heavily courted with dollars. Wright's regression analysis bears out the intuitive: Adjusting for the "ruralness" of states—the combination of electoral votes per capita, variability in previous elections, and the closeness of the 1932 election vote—explains 80 percent of state-to-state variations in New Deal spending.

These three variables dominate the statistical analysis so completely that plausible alternatives—like Reading's relief hypothesis—wash out. When the percentage decline in per capita income, the percentage of families on government relief, and the unemployment rate are added to the basic "political" model, they have no statistical impact on the spending equation. Wright's political explanation works differently, however, in accounting for one important component of New Deal spending, public jobs. Here the political variables all make some difference in 1936 but even in that year collectively explain just 37 percent of state-to-state variations in how the administration apportioned some 2.5 million Works Progress Administration jobs.

[11] Arrington (1969; 1970).

John Wallis's state-level employment estimates, however, suggest a need to temper this interpretation somewhat. After taking account of the simultaneous determination of grants to states and state employment, Wallis finds that grants and per capita income were positively related: Richer states got more grants because they tended to spend more of their own money on relief and hence qualified for larger matching federal grants. Moreover, he concludes that economic as well as political factors were important in explaining the interstate variations in grants per person. Indeed, a one standard deviation decrease in employment would raise the annual per capita grant by $6.70 (grants averaged $44 per person per year) whereas a one standard deviation increase in political productivity would raise the per capita grant by only $3.20.

Furthermore, the South did get something out of the New Deal. The Agricultural Adjustment Act, for example, was particularly favorable to the South in terms both of the support given tobacco and cotton and of how the benefit payments were to be distributed. The favorable treatment accorded southern planter interests is hardly surprising since the chairman and ten of the twenty-four House Agriculture Committee members were from the South. Similarly, farm labor was excluded from the minimum wage legislation and exempted from unemployment insurance taxes and Social Security. True, lip service was paid to the problems of race, of tenancy, of poverty, but relatively little was done about them. In the 1930s African-Americans, sharecroppers, and the poor did not vote.

Did Roosevelt's political spending strategy work? It is not enough to show that he was reelected three times. It is necessary to demonstrate that New Deal funds changed the share of Democratic votes in the states. Here Wright's statistical analysis produced more ambiguous results. Improvements in income raise the percentage of Democratic votes, all right, but the effect of government spending per se is barely visible in the 1936 election and disappears entirely in the 1938 and 1940 elections. It can be argued that government spending raised incomes, so that the indirect effect of spending was still there to be seen. But that isn't very persuasive because the link between government spending and per capita income is not tight. Clearly a more complex model of voting behavior is needed—or, as likely, a different model for each election. Wright notes that the European war probably dominated other issues in the 1940 election. Indeed, the single variable with the most power to explain votes is the percentage of German-Americans in the state population.

Roosevelt, then, probably tried to use, and less probably succeeded in using, New Deal spending to keep Democrats in office. Economic goals either were secondary or did not figure in decisions on how to allocate funds. Roosevelt need not be judged harshly for this preoccupation with politics, though. It would take an unreconstructed cynic to claim that FDR did not believe that his reelection and the election of New Deal Democrats to

Congress would help the economy. However the New Deal is judged, there was certainly more to it than the maximization of Franklin Roosevelt's political power.

Bibliography

Arrington, Leonard. "The New Deal in the West: A Preliminary Statistical Inquiry." *Pacific Historical Review* 38 (1969): 311–16.

———. "Western Agriculture and the New Deal." *Agricultural History* 49 (1970): 337–51.

Bernstein, Michael A. *The Great Depression: Delayed Recovery and Economic Change in America, 1929–1939.* New York: Cambridge University Press, 1987.

Brown, E. Cary. "Fiscal Policy in the Thirties: A Reappraisal." *American Economic Review* 46 (1956): 857–79.

Darby, Michael. "Three and a Half Million U.S. Employees Have Been Mislaid: Or, an Explanation of Unemployment, 1934–41." *Journal of Political Economy* 84 (1976): 1–16.

Eichengreen, Barry. *Golden Fetters: The Gold Standard and the Great Depression 1919–1939.* New York: Oxford University Press, 1992.

———, and Jeffrey, Sachs. "Exchange Rates and Economic Recovery in the 1930s." *Journal of Economic History* 45 (1985): 925–46.

Friedman, Milton, and Anna Schwartz. *A Monetary History of the United States, 1867–1960.* Princeton: Princeton University Press, 1963.

Hansen, Alvin H. *Business Cycles and National Income.* New York: W. W. Norton, 1951.

Hayek, Friedrich A. von. "The Fate of the Gold Standard." In *Money, Capital and Fluctuations, Early Essays of Friedrich A. von Hayek,* ed. Roy McCloughry. London: Routledge, 1984: 118–35.

Higgs, Robert. "Wartime Prosperity? A Reassessment of the U.S. Economy in the 1940s." *Journal of Economic History* 52 (1992): 41–60.

Kesselman, J., and N. E. Savin. "Three and a Half Million Workers Never Were Lost." *Economic Inquiry* 16 (1978): 205–25.

Keynes, John Maynard. *The General Theory of Employment, Interest, and Money.* New York: Harcourt Brace, 1936.

Kindleberger, Charles. *The World in Depression, 1929–1939,* rev. ed. Berkeley: University of California Press, 1986.

Margo, Robert A. "The Microeconomics of Depression Unemployment." *Journal of Economic History* 51 (1991): 333–42.

Peppers, Larry. "Full Employment Surplus Analysis and Structural Change: The 1930s." *Explorations in Economic History* 10 (1973): 197–210.

Reading, Don. "New Deal Activity and the States, 1933 to 1939." *Journal of Economic History* 33 (1973): 792–810.

Robbins, Lionel. *The Great Depression.* London: Macmillan, 1934.

Temin, Peter. *Lessons from the Great Depression.* Cambridge: MIT Press, 1989.

———, and Barry Wigmore. "The End of One Big Deflation." *Explorations in Economic History* 27 (1990): 483–502.

Wallis, John J. "The Birth of the Old Federalism: Financing the New Deal. *Journal of Economic History* 47 (1984): 139–60.

———. "Employment, Politics and Economic Recovery during the Great Depression." *Review of Economics and Statistics* 69 (1987): 516–20.

———. "Employment in the Great Depression: New Data and Hypotheses."

Explorations in Economic History 26 (1989): 45–72.

———. "The Political Economy of New Deal Fiscal Federalism." *Economic Inquiry* 29 (1991): 510–24.

———, and Daniel K. Benjamin. "Public Relief and Private Employment in the Great Depression." *Journal of Economic History* 41 (1981): 97–102.

Weinstein, Michael M. *Recovery and Redistribution under the NIRA*. Amsterdam: North-Holland, 1980.

———. "Some Macroeconomic Impacts of the National Industrial Recovery Act, 1933–1935." In *The Great Depression Revisited,* ed. Karl Brunner. Boston: Kluwer-Nijihoff, 1981.

Wright, Gavin. "The Political Economy of New Deal Spending: An Econometric Analysis." *Review of Economics and Statistics* 56 (1974): 262–81.

———. *Old South, New South.* New York: Basic Books, 1986.

The extension of government intervention: from the price of bread to the price of wheat

23

Despite politicians' promises to "get government out of our lives," the role of government in the late twentieth century is all-pervasive. For all the lip service paid to free enterprise, private markets today are typically partners—and often junior partners at that—of government. For example, nowadays the price of beef, the crash-worthiness of cars, the design of ladders, the purity of streams and the air, the gender of employees, the wages of construction workers, the job prospects for teenagers, the number of lines on our television screens, the vocabulary of media entertainers, and the decoration and language in the workplace all are subject to government influence, if not outright regulation. It wasn't always so. But it also didn't begin with Franklin D. Roosevelt and the New Deal. Rather it began with the earliest English settlements.

The Origin: Our Colonial Past

English common law and English customs, embodying centuries of tradition, crossed the Atlantic with Captain John Smith to Virginia and with the *Mayflower* to Massachusetts. The laws of colonial America were essentially the laws of England, and this legal heritage was preserved despite the Revolution. Colonial government at all levels, acting in the public interest, could set the "just" price for milling and the price of bread, regulate the purity of beer, establish reasonable charges for essential services, such as ferry charges, and grant monopoly franchises. Government was even free to set wages and to require work. Established custom—which had the force of law— even included holdovers from medieval guilds' regulations, permitting the establishment of minimum quality and maximum quantity regulations on products as diverse as preserved fish and meat or shoes and clothing. This whole complex set of rules and regulations was then enforced by a wide variety of government functionaries, including constables, wardens, and gaugers.

The problems that the colonial governments faced were not so different from those facing governments in more modern times. For example, the famous agricultural historian Lewis C. Gray, writing in the late 1920s, drew attention to the parallels between the problems facing colonial tobacco farmers and those facing farmers in the 1920s and to the similarity in various nonmarket solutions proposed by the respective governments. In colonial times Spanish tobacco was a luxury good in London, commanding a very high price—perhaps 216 pence per pound (between 10 and 15 percent of per capita income) as late as 1619. Virginia's early attempts to compete with the Spanish tobacco produced an inferior product that the British valued at 120 pence a pound for the purposes of customs duty but that actually sold for about half that price. Given these prices, agents of the Virginia Company offered 36 pence per pound for the best grades and 18 pence per pound on inferior, second-growth (seconds) tobacco in 1619 at their warehouse in Virginia. The difference between prices in the colonies and London represented transport costs, handling charges, and expected profit. Such prices stimulated production and the export trade boomed. By 1622, 60,000 pounds of tobacco were being exported. Six years later exports exceeded 500,000 pounds, and they reached almost 1.4 million pounds a year between 1637 and 1640.

The boom in production led to a rapid collapse in prices. By 1630 tobacco in Virginia fetched less than 1 pence per pound (see Figure 2.2). Thereafter prices never returned to their original high levels despite the best efforts of producers and government. Instead, price fluctuated between ½ pence and 3 pence per pound until the Revolution. Farmers were bitterly disappointed by this collapse in prices and the evaporation of their expected supernormal returns. At times this disappointment spilled over into violence. In 1682, for example, disgruntled farmers reportedly destroyed about 10,000 hogsheads (about 750,000 pounds) of tobacco (presumably belonging to others, though considered the inelastic demand, all collectively stood to gain from a reduction in supply). In an effort to appease them, the colonial governments in Virginia and Maryland tried various legislative solutions. For example, in 1632, 1633, 1639, and 1640, the legislature passed laws establishing minimum prices for tobacco and prohibiting exchange at lower prices. These laws could not be enforced since such trade was beneficial to both buyer and seller. In other legislative action, the packing of ground leaves, suckers, or second growths was prohibited, sometimes requiring inspection of the fields after harvest to ensure destruction of the plants, thereby limiting supply. Legislatures also passed regulations regarding the size and shape of hogsheads. Bulk shipment was prohibited. Viewers were employed to inspect the product. Informers were rewarded. Warehouses, though privately owned, were declared public utilities, and their rates and conditions of storage set by law. Tobacco even occasionally served as a medium of exchange and store of value — as money. Yes, at one time, money did grow on plants, if not on trees! However, as economic theory would predict, only inferior tobacco was used as money; the prime tobacco was sold for export.

Government in the American Economy

Although many of the colonial regulations had disappeared by the time of the American Revolution, the Revolution itself did very little to interrupt institutional continuity. Legal authority was preserved. English common law remained the foundation of American law, as the Supreme Court repeatedly affirmed. The Revolution thus changed the form but not the nature of government. Government "of the people, by the people, for the people" sought to use its power to shape and influence economic growth and development from the framing of the Constitution onward.

Nor was the government shy about exercising its powers. Alexander Hamilton, for example, spoke of the necessity for the "extraordinary aid and protection of the government" in the development of domestic manufactures as a justification for the tariff. In transportation and internal improvements, Albert Gallatin, President Jefferson's secretary of the treasury, proposed an ambitious plan for federally funded projects, and while it didn't fly, the federal government underwrote snag removal and harbor improvement on the western rivers and built post roads and bridges. However, federal intervention in purely intrastate projects was temporarily curbed by President Andrew Jackson's veto of the Maysville Road in 1830.

Governments other than the federal government were also active. Beginning with New York State's underwriting of the construction of the Erie Canal, most canals constructed in the 1820s and 1830s were built with government resources. Similarly, continuing colonial practices, governments kept on granting rights and privileges to petitioners. For example, in 1785 the Massachusetts legislature authorized the Charles River Bridge

Company to construct and operate a toll bridge over the Charles River. In 1792 it extended the company's charter to seventy years. In 1828, however, a charter was granted for the construction of the Warren Bridge across the Charles River just a short distance from the Charles Bridge. Like the Charles Bridge, the Warren Bridge charged tolls, but the charter stipulated that the bridge was to be turned over to the state after recovery of the construction costs. The Charles River Bridge Company sued, arguing that competition would impair the obligation of its contract with the state. In 1837 the Supreme Court rejected this claim, ruling that the charter contained no implied contract granting exclusive rights and that where there was uncertainty, that uncertainty must favor public, not private, interests.

The government was a potent force in the economy. Nowhere was this more clearly demonstrated than in the history of banking. As we have seen, the federal government established the First and Second Banks of the United States as central banks with effective power to regulate commercial banks chartered and licensed by state governments, notwithstanding Jeffersonian opposition to the creation of a "money monopoly." States did not always take kindly to this. Maryland, for example, passed a law requiring that all banks in the state that were not created by the authority of the state were to comply with restrictions on note issue or pay an annual $15,000 tax. The Second Bank refused to comply, and its Baltimore cashier was sued by the state. In the landmark Supreme Court ruling *McCulloch v. Maryland* (1819), Chief Justice Marshall in his decision against Maryland observed that "the power to tax involves the power to destroy" and that "the power to destroy may defeat and render useless the power to create. . . ." As an illustration of Marshall's point, in 1865 Congress imposed a 10 percent tax on state bank notes. As a result, the number of banks with state charters fell from 1,089 in 1864 to 349 in 1865 and 247 by 1868 while the number of national banks chartered by the federal government increased from 467 to 1,294 to 1,640 in 1868.

The Changing Scale and Scope of Government

These examples of government intervention from early in America's history should serve to illustrate the tradition of government involvement in the economy, notwithstanding the perception— or misconception—that there existed a period of laissez faire in the late eighteenth and early nineteenth centuries and that the government intervention of the late nineteenth and early twentieth centuries was new. However, we need to distinguish between the scale and scope of government. Big government—scale—begins with the founding of this country. Almost from the very first budget the federal government has grown faster than the economy (Figure 23.1). State and

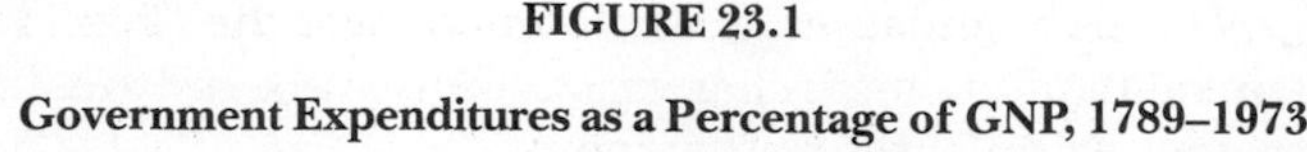

FIGURE 23.1

Government Expenditures as a Percentage of GNP, 1789–1973

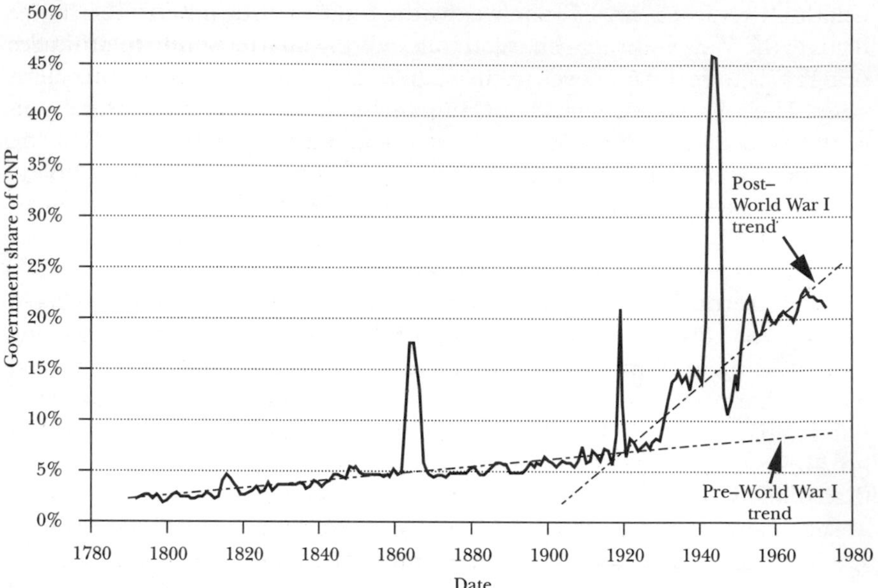

Sources: Thomas S. Berry, "Production and Population since 1789," Bostwick Paper No. 6 (1988), and U.S. Bureau of the Census, *Historical Statistics of the United States.* (Washington, D.C.: Government Printing Office, 1975): Series F1 and Y457.

local governments also undoubtedly grew right alongside the federal government but much less is currently known about their fiscal activities.[1]

One reason for the expanding scale of government is the very nature of the democratic process in our political system. Legislators are expected by their constituents to "bring home the bacon," but to do so, they must make common cause with other legislators to form a majority coalition (if necessary, a coalition sufficiently large to guarantee congressional override of any presidential veto). Such coalitions are most easily formed through the trading of votes on individually favored projects, so-called logrolling and pork-barrel politics. The benefits of such legislation are disproportionately concentrated upon a few favored constituents while the costs are dispersed across all taxpayers so that no individual taxpayer has much of a compelling economic interest in opposing a specific legislative proposal. Today the

[1] Ongoing research by John Legler, Richard Sylla, and John Wallis promises to close this major gap in our statistical knowledge by producing the first comprehensive consolidated accounts for state and local governments before 1902, when the first official statistics become available.

"bacon" is roads and recreation areas. A century ago the "logs" were land grants to the railroads, urban waterworks, and sewage systems. Two centuries ago the "pork" was roads and harbors.

It is easy to understand the increasing scale of government. The more interesting question is at what share of GNP will government expenditures stabilize. The scale of government is finite. It cannot increase to the point where government accounts for 100 percent of GNP because government itself produces little beyond national defense and the supply of law and order. Indeed, by its very nature, government's share must fall well short of 100 percent of GNP since governmental activities are primarily redistributive and incur bureaucratic losses (costs of administration) with the result that those "giving" give more than the recipients receive.

In 1789 the federal government controlled about 2 percent of GNP. On the eve of the Civil War this had grown to perhaps 5 percent. During the war the government's share of GNP expanded dramatically, but it contracted sharply with war's end to the level it would have achieved in the absence of the war. About the end of the nineteenth century, however, the rate of growth of the federal government appears to have accelerated. True, World War I added a sharp spike, pushing the federal government's share beyond 20 percent, but the trend had been sharply upward from about the 1890s. It retreated somewhat in the 1920s before pushing higher in the Great Depression and soaring in World War II, when the government accounted for more than 45 percent of GNP.

Government hasn't just gotten bigger in terms of scale; it has gotten bigger in terms of scope —what Robert Higgs calls "Big Government" as opposed to "big government." New services and activities are constantly added by government. For example, few states had adopted compulsory public schooling before the Civil War, but most passed such laws after the war, and educational expenditures expanded rapidly. The federal government also entered the educational arena during the war with the Morrill Act, which made land grants to each loyal state to help establish agricultural colleges. With the passage of time, government, particularly the federal government, has assumed new roles; it has gotten Bigger as well as bigger.

Higgs explains this tendency for the scope of government to increase by the ratchet effect: Periodically, specific challenges and crises arise that demand a political response —Bigger Government— represented by an extension of the scope of government's effective authority and an expansion of the authority itself to deal with the problem (Table 23.1). Examples include the farm protest movement of the late nineteenth century, wherein the Populists threatened the hegemony of the two-party system; the waves of industrial unrest in the late 1880s that threatened law and order; World War I; the Great Depression; World War II; *Sputnik* and the first man in space (Yuri Gagarin). The shock from each of these events generated political pressure to seek a solution: the Interstate Commerce Commission; the Sherman

TABLE 23.1

The Expanded Role of Government in Six Areas during Three Crises

World War I	Great Depression	World War II
Transportation		
Shipping Board; Emergency Fleet Corp.; Adamson Act. Railroad Administration (nationalization of ocean shipping and railroads	Emergency Railroad Transportation Act (extended regulation); Railway Labor Act of 1934	War Shipping Administration; Office of Defense Transportation; emergency powers of Interstate Commerce Commission (assignment of priorities; extended regulation; price-fixing)
Labor		
Military conscription; War Labor Board; War Labor Policies Board (selective deferrals; interventions and plant seizures in labor disputes)	Labor provisions of the National Industrial Recovery Act; Wagner Act (promotion of labor cartels); Fair Labor Standards Act (regulation of wages and hours)	Military conscription; National War Labor Board; War Manpower Commission (selective deferrals; allocation of labor; intervention and plant seizures in labor disputes)
Agriculture		
Lever Act; Food Administration (price-fixing and assignment of priorities)	Agricultural Adjustment Act of 1933; Soil Conservation and Domestic Allotment Act; Agricultural Adjustment Act of 1938 (price-fixing, loans, marketing orders, acreage restrictions)	War Food Administration (food rationing); Office of Price Administration (price-fixing, subsidies)
Industry		
War Industries Board (allocations of materials; assignment of priorities; selective price-fixing)	Reconstruction Finance Corp. (loans and investments); National Recovery Administration (promotion of product sellers' cartels)	War Production Board (assignment of priorities; restrictions on civilian production); Defense Plant Corp. (plant construction); Office of Price Administration (price-fixing)
Credit		
War Finance Corp. (loans); Capital Issues Committee (regulation of securities issues; allocation of credit)	Reconstruction Finance Corp. (loans); Securities and Exchange Commission (regulation of securities issues); Farm Credit Administration (loans); Home Owners Loan Corp. (loans); Banking Act of 1935 (more centralized government control of money and banking)	Reconstruction Finance Corp. (loans); Federal Reserve System (allocation of credit; control of interest rates)
International trade		
Trading with the Enemy Act; War Trade Board (licensing and regulation of traders; seizure and administration of enemy property)	Presidential Proclamation of March 6, 1933; Gold Reserve Act (control of all transactions in gold and foreign exchange; abandonment of gold standard)	Board (later office) of Economic Warfare; Foreign Economic Administration (control of and direct participation in international trade); War Production Board (import licensing)

Source: Robert Higgs, "Crisis, Bigger Government, and Ideological Change: Two Hypotheses on the Ratchet Phenomenon," *Explorations in Economic History* 22 (1985): 20–21.

Antitrust Act; the federal take-over of the nation's railroads and other trappings of a command economy; the New Deal; the Office of Price Administration and the Manhattan Project; and NASA. Once in place, however, each solution created an entrenched constituency—whether of voters or bureaucrats—that prevented a return to normality even after the crisis has passed. As a result, each crisis has led to both an increase in scope and an increase in the scale of government even if it has had no lasting impact upon the long-term rate of growth of government.

The phenomenon is illustrated in Figure 23.2. Prior to the crisis, the size of government is increasing as shown by the positive slope of the line segment AB. The appearance of a crisis at time T_1, however, calls forth a special response that leads government to explore the boundaries of its traditional authority. Spending accelerates rapidly, as shown by the line segment BC. In

FIGURE 23.2

The Ratchet Effect

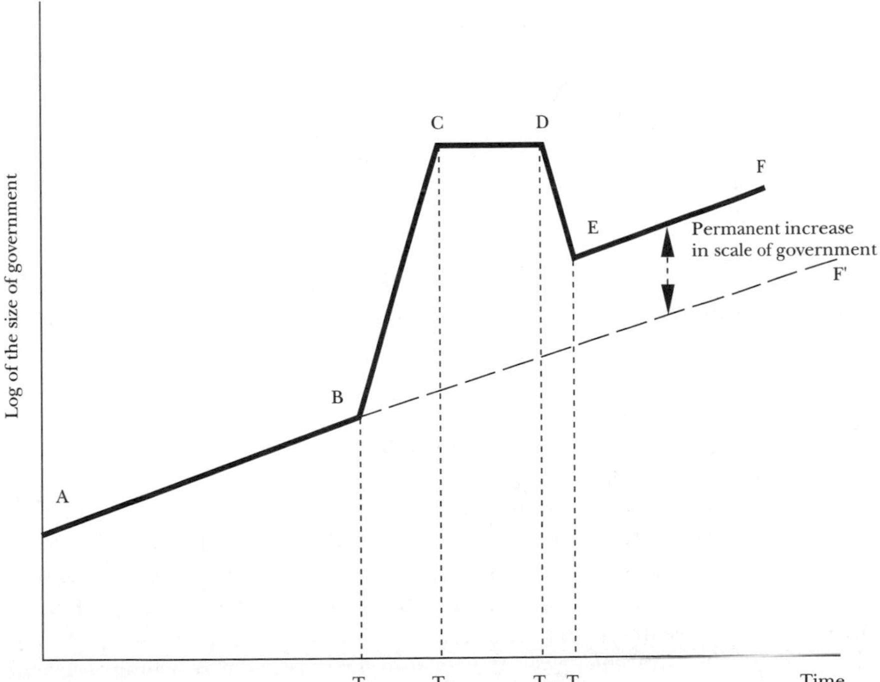

Source: Robert Higgs, "Crisis, Bigger Government and Ideological Change: Two Hypotheses on the Ratchet Phenomenon," *Explorations in Economic History* 22 (1985): 4.

part this is possible because the associated costs are disguised. Expenditures may occur off budget or out of special appropriations; sometimes, too, the funds are drawn from several agencies and budgets since by definition no specialized agency for that particular problem as yet exists. There is a wedge between actual and perceived costs which the government exploits. As the immediate crisis fades—time T_2—spending first stabilizes (line segment CD) and then may retrench, beginning at time T_3, in the "return to normalcy" (line segment DE). However, the return to normalcy is incomplete in the sense that spending does not return to the level it would have achieved in the absence of the crisis. It remains permanently elevated at EF even if it resumes its normal long-term growth rate. This is in part because the new bureaucratic services generate constituencies that oppose their liquidation and in part because Congress lacks the political will to force deep cuts. But the change also reflects a shift in ideological stance. Crises affect attitudes. People accept the proposition that something drastic should be done and the government is the appropriate agency to do it. Opposition to World War II controls, for example, would be regarded as unpatriotic; opponents of cold war expenditures risked being labeled "Communists" or "soft on communism."

Governments, particularly democratic governments, respond to political pressure from their constituencies. We can identify three broad motives that drive constituencies to seek government aid: They may need help (1) to capture and preserve rents, (2) to mediate market failure, or (3) to attain private goals that have proved impossible through private action. In the process, however, governments constrain future courses of action and create interest groups both within and without government.

The following sections will focus on three specific events that illustrate the motivation and consequences, both intended and unintended, of government intervention: (1) regulation of the railroads as a response to the farm protest movement, (2) bank deposit insurance as a solution to periodic banking panics, and (3) Franklin D. Roosevelt's New Deal as an answer to the Great Depression.

Railroads and Government Regulation

Liberal opinion about the proper role of government regulation has changed enormously in recent years. Where it was once assumed that federal regulation defended the "public interest" against the antisocial tendencies of unleashed capitalists, there is increasing uncertainty about what the public interest really is and whether regulators are likely to serve it. The sheer cost and ineffectiveness of government control and oversight create obvious targets for the new critics of regulation. For example, the federal Occupational Safety and Health Administration (OSHA) has written thousands of rules about such questions as the proper distance between ladder rungs and the paint color on factory warning signs, none of which has had a noticeable impact on industrial accident rates. Food and Drug Administration (FDA) testing requirements are so onerous that lifesaving medications take decades to be readied for distribution. Some never make it at all. However, sometimes in response to national crises, such as the AIDS epidemic, the bureaucracy can be forced to rewrite the rules. For example, the benefits of the drug AZT were so overwhelming in early testing that experimental double-blind testing was abandoned and the drug approved for wider use.

A less intuitively understood charge leveled against regulators is that they inevitably become the captives of the businesses they are empowered to regulate. Capture can be overt: An industry employee may simply switch to the public payroll without really changing bosses, or ex-regulators can find comfortable jobs with the regulated. Or it can be subtle: Dedicated, honest regulators may be overwhelmed by persuasive arguments from well-paid lobbyists representing the regulated. Either way, the end result may be to shield the business from the discipline of the marketplace or, ironically, from the discipline of more effective forms of legal regulation, such as antitrust laws.

The number one offending regulatory agency, in the view of many economists (both liberal and conservative), is the Interstate Commerce Commission (ICC). Charged with the responsibility of ensuring safe, efficient, reasonably priced interstate transportation, the commission has in recent decades watched helplessly as railroad freight service collapsed. Its major accomplishment, apparently, has been to guard the monopoly profits of licensed trucking firms at the expense of truckers without licenses and, of course, the public. One economist has estimated that ICC regulation costs the economy as much as $10 billion a year in wasted transportation services. No surprise, then, that economic historians have turned a jaundiced eye on the events leading to the establishment of this first and most important regulatory commission and doubt that the ICC has ever served the interest of the shipping public.[2]

The conventional tale—a tale that hardly anyone still unqualifiedly accepts—goes as follows. By virtue of their monopoly position in the farmlands of the Midwest and the Great Plains, the railroads were able to exploit farmers, drawing off the profits of productive agriculture through high shipping rates. Certainly the railroads did little to dispel this image of themselves as monopolists. Instead they organized numerous cartels and pooling arrangements. For example, the roads between Council Bluffs, Iowa, and Chicago combined in 1869 in the so-called Iowa Pool. The major railroads

[2] The work on the ICC is but the first of many reappraisals of federal regulatory agencies that includes Gary Libecap's work on the first federal meat inspection laws in the United States (Libecap, 1992) and the operation of the Texas Railroad Commission (Libecap, 1989) and Peter Temin's work on telecommunications (Temin, 1989).

south of the Ohio and east of the Mississippi organized as the Southern Railway and Steamship Association, incorporating, as the name implies, western river and coastwise steamboats. Where shippers were very large, they were able to fight back and even use rate discrimination to their own advantage. The Standard Oil Company, for example, played off the Erie, the New York Central, and the Pennsylvania railroads against one another, extracting secret rebates on published petroleum transport rates. But the only hope for small farmers was to take collective political action to convince the government to intervene. In so doing, they threatened the two-party structure that dominated American politics, with the creation first of the National Grange, the Farmers' Alliance, the Greenback party, and eventually the Populist party.

That political action eventually paid off in the early 1870s, when Illinois passed a series of laws designed to regulate the storage and shipment of grain. These laws specified maximum freight rates for railroads, regulated the transportation of grain, and established an oversight commission, the Illinois Commerce Commission. They also provided, among other things, for the licensing and inspection of grain elevators and established maximum rates for grain storage. Although these were not the first laws regulating the marketing of agricultural crops (see, for example, the case of colonial tobacco farming above), the Granger laws were the most encompassing, and they became the model for the federal Act to Regulate Commerce of 1887 establishing the Interstate Commerce Commission. Not only was Illinois a major grain producer, but by virtue of its location it was the leading grain collection point for shipment east. Within three years, Iowa, Wisconsin, and Minnesota had also passed similar laws.

In 1871 the Illinois state's attorney for Cook County brought suit against the Chicago grain elevator of Ira Y. Munn and George L. Scott for failure to obtain the prescribed license. This action was eventually consolidated with other legal challenges (such as *Chicago, Burlington and Quincy Railroad v. Iowa*) to the Granger laws in the other states and found its way to the U.S. Supreme Court on the ground that the laws involved the taking of property without due process—a violation of Fourteenth Amendment rights.

The Supreme Court decision, rendered in 1877 as *Munn v. Illinois*, upheld the Illinois law on the common law ground that such regulation of private property "affected with a public interest" had been customary in England from time immemorial and in America since colonization for ferries, common carriers, hackmen, bakers, millers, and so on. *Munn* was thus viewed as legitimating any and all regulation. Indeed, as dissenting Associate Justice Stephen Field noted, "if this be sound law . . . all property and all business in the state are held at the mercy of a majority of the legislature."

Ironically, by the time the Supreme Court decision was rendered, only Illinois still clung to its Granger laws. In the wake of the decision, though, states nationwide scrambled to enact their own railroad regulations, and by the time a second legal challenge to the Illinois laws was mounted in 1886, there were twenty-five state railroad commissions nationwide. In 1886, however, the Supreme Court decision *Wabash, St. Louis and Pacific Railroad v. Illinois,* struck down the Illinois law prohibiting freight rate discrimination between the long haul and the short haul whenever the shipments involved interstate transportation. Since most shipments were out of state, the ruling gutted the Illinois regulations. The stage was set to shift power from the states to the federal government, which, it seemed, was the only remaining potential source of countervailing power. Indeed, precisely this expansion of the role of government to the federal level had been recommended by the Cullom Committee, chaired by Senator Shelby Cullom (Illinois), in 1885.

In 1887, according to the traditional story, farmers acting in concert with other small shippers who also found themselves at the mercy of the railroads secured passage of the Act to Regulate Commerce. The act prohibited rate discrimination among rail shippers buying the identical service; no longer could Standard Oil get cheaper rates than other oil companies shipping heating oil from Cleveland to Toledo and so forth. It also forbade rate discrimination between long and short hauls unless a specific exemption was granted, and it established the Interstate Commerce Commission to ensure enforcement.

However, the ICC was unable to exert much pressure on the railroads because the courts remained obdurate. Judicial interpretations of the vague Commerce Act language all seemed to end up on the side of the carriers—so much so that in 1897 the commissioners wrote that "the people should no longer look to this Commission for a protection it is powerless to extend."

Congress once more came to the aid of "the people" by passing a series of laws between 1903 and 1913—especially the Elkins Act, the Hepburn Act, and the Mann-Elkins Act—that considerably broadened the ICC's statutory authority. The commission could now approve rates submitted jointly by several railroads and prescribe rates themselves rather than bear the obligation to challenge railroad policies after the fact. The legislation did not end all abuses by the railroads but provided some countervailing power to that of private business.

The biggest problem with this tale is that the facts do not quite fit.

Organized farmers and shippers were surely instrumental in securing federal regulation over the railroads as they had been in promoting state regulation. But the railroads themselves were not always averse to federal intervention. The most eloquent general reinterpretation of the railroads and regulation is by historian Gabriel Kolko. In Kolko's view, federal regulation was initially viewed by the carriers as a means of outflanking more threatening state regulation. Eventually, though, federal regulation evolved into a powerful protector of railroad privilege, enforcing anticompetitive collusion among the carriers where the railroads themselves had been unsuccessful.

Kolko is certainly correct in writing that railroads lent tacit support to federal railroad legislation efforts, and he is probably correct that the overall strategy of the railroads was to capture the ICC for their own use. This latter hypothesis should be qualified because the historical record is inconsistent; some railroads, some of the time, feared federal intervention. But there is little doubt that at the very least, the industry landed on its feet, quickly adjusting to the concept of bargaining effectively with the government rather than with shippers in the marketplace.

Did, in fact, the railroads benefit from federal regulation before the First World War? Kolko argues that they did. Predatory price-cutting on competitive, long-haul service was ended by ICC control. Rebates used by powerful shippers to best established rates were outlawed, and the law was enforced by the federal government. The establishment of formal federal authority, Kolko believes, also put the Congress and the president in the position of being responsible for the industry. Neither Theodore Roosevelt nor Woodrow Wilson ever "used regulation to attack the essential interests of the railroads. . . ." This is not a universal view, however. At least one prominent student of railroad history, Albro Martin, sees in early federal railroad policies the origins of the eclipse of railroads by other forms of long-distance transportation.

What do economists say? Paul MacAvoy has analyzed the role of regulation in enforcing group conformity to a cartel pricing scheme. He examined railroad price behavior on the potentially most competitive railroad routes where cartel pricing was attempted before regulation—eastbound transport from the Hog and Corn Belts of the Midwest to the East Coast. He concluded that a voluntary cartel did operate successfully from 1871 to 1874. Prices were stable. But with the entry of the Baltimore and Ohio into the Chicago market in 1875, agreements to keep prices high and limit capacity proved unworkable (see Appendix A). Although numerous formal agreements were signed, none lasted very long because of strong incentives for individual railroads to cheat and reduce rates. Price volatility increased. For example, in August 1884 the Chicago Board of Trade reported that the rate on freight between Chicago and New York was 35 cents per hundred pounds. By June 1885 freight rates had fallen by almost two-thirds to 13 cents, which probably just covered variable costs (see Appendix B). They recovered by August to 25 cents but collapsed again in September.

By contrast, MacAvoy found that between the creation of the ICC in 1887 and 1893 the cartel seemed to work pretty well: Posted prices served as actual prices to shippers. For example, between 1891 and mid-1893 the rate on freight between Chicago and New York fell only twice and then only in the narrow band from 30 to 25 cents per hundred pounds. Only in the 1890s, when the Supreme Court denied the ICC the authority to enforce rebate prohibitions, did the cartel again break down.

MacAvoy's statistical analysis is not in itself compelling.[3] He tests (in a rough-and-ready fashion) the proposition that the *actual* price movements as reported by shippers' trade organizations (or inferred from the difference in the price of grain in New York and Chicago) reflected movements in the posted prices. That is not the same as testing the success of the cartel, where success is defined as keeping the actual prices near the joint profit-maximizing monopoly price. A very weak, unsuccessful cartel, after all, could "succeed" by posting very low prices that provided no particular incentive for members to cheat.

Even so, MacAvoy's study has much value. It shows that before the ICC, the actual prices were unstable and sometimes extremely low while after the commission was formed, overt signs of competition were successfully suppressed. This does not prove Kolko's point; proof would be too strong a word. Certainly, however, the burden of proof shifts to those who believe that the ICC was the natural enemy of the railroads.

Thomas S. Ulen's analysis of the operation of one railroad cartel—the Joint Executive Committee (JEC)—which organized the trunk lines and feeder roads from the Midwest to eastern seaboard ports north of Baltimore, casts doubt upon the revisionist views of Kolko and MacAvoy that federal regulation simply served to promote cartel interests and make its operations more efficient. Taking price stability and adherence to the principle of joint profit maximization as his criterion of cartel efficiency, Ulen found that between 1879, when the cartel was finally established, and the creation of the ICC in 1887, there were suggestions (but not necessarily proof) of cheating in fewer than one-quarter of the 328 weeks of cartel operation that he studied. As one might expect, such cheating was most likely during a downturn in the business cycle or when actual and promised market share diverged markedly. Even so, Ulen believes that considering the incentives to cheat by the railroads and the incentive of suppliers to destabilize the cartel by false allegations of price-cutting, the evidence shows a surprisingly high degree of cartel cohesion. Why?

The answer, he concludes, lies in the unique enforcement policies adopted by the cartel. These included the posting of performance bonds, the appointment of a distinguished arbitration board on generous retainer, and the employment of cartel agents to monitor and police compliance with the agreement. In addition, the JEC arranged for the weekly publication of data on the freight carried by each road in the financial press. These data were certified by the Chicago Board of Trade and permitted short-run comparisons between promised and actual market shares. And deviations between promised and actual market shares—a frequent source of cartel friction and breakdown—could be quickly eliminated because the Joint

[3] See Wright (1990).

Executive Committee had the authority to reassign freight between the roads.

When cheating was detected, cartel members were authorized to match the cuts and jointly agreed to refuse to interchange freight with the violator. This latter action could effectively exclude the cartel cheater from certain markets and was a severe penalty.

So successful were these enforcement provisions that Ulen argues the JEC had no need to resort to co-opting the police powers of the state to enforce agreement. Furthermore, Ulen notes, the ICC outlawed activities, such as the reassignment of freight, that had aided cartel effectiveness and maintained cohesion. The ICC was thus not only unnecessary but disruptive as well to existing arrangements. Ulen's unpublished work also shows that the same factors explaining price stability before the establishment of the ICC explain price stability *after* its creation, casting doubt upon the contribution of this federal regulatory agency.

These results suggest a third interpretation of the persistence of the ICC: Rather than serve the public interest (i.e., consumers) or the interests of the regulated, the ICC came to serve the regulator interest. It became a bureaucratic sinecure, a permanent employment act for civil servants, lawyers, economists, and the cronies of their political bosses.

There is one ironic footnote to the story of railroad capture of federal regulation. After World War I the railroads lost much of their passenger traffic and most of the potential growth of their freight traffic to alternative transport modes. In part this decline in rail use was inevitable — the railroad could not compete across the board for business with pipelines, cars, buses, trucks, and airplanes — but some economists believe that ICC regulation accelerated the decline by adopting price structures that made trucking far more attractive to shippers than railroads. The trucking companies, at least by this interpretation, played the railroads' game with federal regulation, only they played it better.

Not all regulation moved from the state to the federal level after 1887. The Texas Railroad Commission, for instance, played a key role in regulating the domestic oil industry from the 1930s until the emergence of OPEC as the dominant force in 1973. This was possible because of the dominant position of Texas oil reserves and production and had the effect of supporting high-cost, small-producer stripper wells.[4]

Bank Deposit Insurance

The savings and loan debacle of the 1980s has raised many questions about the perversity of bank deposit insurance. On the one hand, failure to price

[4] Libecap (1989).

insurance commensurately with risk encouraged excessive risk taking by the thrifts. This was especially true where earlier losses on bad loans had already depleted reserves, leaving little to risk from playing the very long shot, or where entrepreneurs, such as Charles Keating, were able to enter the savings and loan business and use it to underwrite their own risky ventures. On the other hand, depositor faith in the insurance system eliminated market discipline by removing any incentive for depositors to monitor the activities of their bankers. Indeed, large numbers of new depositors were attracted to precisely those institutions most at risk by the offer of higher rates of interest even when those rates further jeopardized the financial integrity of the institution. The resulting cost to society as a whole, thanks to the pledge of the full faith and credit of the United States, will be with us for a very long time. Likewise, it doubtless came as a shock to savers in Rhode Island—as it was to many Ohioans before them—to find that their deposits with privately insured savings and loans were only as secure as their insecure insurers.

Despite these problems, which date back to the very earliest bank insurance scheme in this country, New York's Safety Fund (see Chapter 4), the idea of deposit insurance as the solution to bank runs in times of crisis has never died. There were numerous formal and informal attempts to revive deposit insurance during the antebellum period.[5] For example, Vermont set up a short-lived voluntary system that survived just two bank failures—one through fraud, the other, a bank already weak when it joined the system—before its clientele fled. But a mutual guarantee system in Indiana, later copied by Iowa and Ohio, proved a success. During its thirty years of operation beginning in 1834, no mutually guaranteed bank in Indiana failed. While Indiana banks temporarily suspended convertibility in 1837 and 1839, they weathered the Panic of 1857 without interruption. As with the more successful railroad cartels, the key to success was the institutional form: the rules by which the game was played and the means by which the rules were enforced. For the Indiana mutual guarantee system, mutual aid and unlimited liability guaranteed mutual monitoring of the activities of all members. Regulation was internal. Members decided whom to admit, whom to exclude, and when a bank should be closed for the good of all. This system was subsequently adopted, also with a high degree of success, by the various clearinghouses (see Chapter 18).

The various antebellum state insurance schemes were effectively ended by the National Banking Act of 1864. The subsequent tax on state bank notes decimated the ranks of state banks until the state banking system revived with the development of deposit banking in the 1880s. Each periodic banking crisis in the postbellum period, however, revived interest in deposit insurance. In the wake of the Panic of 1893, for example, politician, lawyer, and orator William Jennings Bryan presented a bill to Congress for deposit

[5] Calomiris (1990).

insurance, and legislatures in Populist western states, such as Nebraska, also debated the issue, but nothing came of it.

Popular sentiment, however, changed with the Panic of 1907. At the height of the panic the Oklahoma legislature passed a law requiring bank membership in a state-sponsored deposit insurance system. This scheme was supposed to apply to all banks, both state-chartered and national, but the U.S. attorney general in 1908 prohibited national banks from joining the scheme. The scheme proved immensely popular with both the banks and their depositors. Between March 1908, when the law went into effect, and November 1909 the number of state banks in Oklahoma increased more than 40 percent to 662 banks, and deposits rose from $18 million to $50 million. During this same period the number of national banks in Oklahoma declined from 312 to 220 as banks switched from national to state charters. Oklahoma's law sparked a period of destabilizing competition between state banking systems and the national banking system that weakened the entire banking system of this country, culminating in the collapse of banking in the Great Depression.[6]

The Oklahoma law, however, failed to appreciate the lessons of history. Regulation and supervision were lax, all deposits were insured and payable immediately upon bank closure, and banks could advertise their insured status to attract customers. Trouble began almost immediately when the largest bank in the state, the Columbia Bank and Trust Company, failed. Between September 1908 and September 1909 its deposits had grown from $365,000 to more than $2.8 million, and its failure immediately jeopardized the insurance fund, which at the time contained only about $400,000. A special levy on all member banks was required to pay off Columbia's depositors. Even so, other states—Texas, Kansas, Nebraska, South Dakota, Mississippi, North Dakota, and Washington—followed Oklahoma's lead and adopted deposit insurance. None of the schemes survived the 1920s.

World War I was the high tide of American agricultural prosperity. Small, thinly capitalized rural banks grew fat on commissions from real estate mortgages in the burgeoning land boom that gripped the country, particularly many of the nation's farmers. The collapse of agricultural prices in 1920–21, however, burst the bubble. Farm foreclosures soared. So, too, did nonperforming loans. Faced with rising bank insolvency and failures, state bank insurance funds found themselves in trouble. In Washington State, where membership was voluntary, onetime members fled the system rather than face rising assessments. By the end of 1923 the insurance fund was exhausted, and depositors who were caught late received only a fraction of the value of their deposits. Where membership was compulsory, banks fiercely resisted special assessments. One by one the funds were wound up. For example, by 1929, when it was dissolved by the state legislature, South Dakota's

[6] White (1987).

fund contained just $1 million to meet more than $37 million in claims. It paid out less than 1 cent on the dollar after administrative expenses.

Econometric analysis by Eugene White and by Charles Calomiris reveals that branch banking might have been a viable alternative to insurance. By giving banks direct access to a wider pool of potential debtors, the establishment of bank branches permitted banks to diversify the risk in their loan portfolios. Banks in states that permitted branching were on average much larger than those in states that allowed only unit banks—that is, where a bank could have only one office. Bank failure rates and branch banking were inversely correlated. Similarly, states with restrictive banking regulations—capital requirements meeting or exceeding those required for national banking charters and high reserve ratios—had little incentive, or need, to adopt bank deposit insurance. According to Calomiris, between 1921 and 1929 only thirty-seven branching banks failed in the United States, most of them with only one or two branches, whereas almost fifty-seven hundred unit banks closed their doors. Even in those states hit hard by the agricultural depression of the 1920s, the failure rate among branch banks was only about one-fourth that among unit banks. In the wake of the banking crises of the 1930s, a number of states—Mississippi, North Carolina, South Dakota, and Washington—moved to some form of branch banking. It remains to be seen whether unit banking holdouts, such as Illinois, will survive the latest crisis.

It is not clear—certainly with the problems of Federal Savings and Loan Insurance Corporation (FSLIC) fresh in our minds—that the adoption of federally guaranteed deposit insurance has resolved the moral hazard and adverse selection problems inherent in all but the mutual guarantee insurance schemes. While it may still be true that "no depositor has ever lost a penny at a federally insured deposit institution" (subject, of course, to the individual insurance limit, currently $100,000 per person), the same cannot be said for the taxpayers whose credit—taxes—are pledged.

The New Deal

On Saturday afternoon, March 4, 1933, Franklin Delano Roosevelt delivered the first of his four inaugural addresses to the nation, declaring, "The only thing we have to fear is fear itself" and acknowledging that "This Nation asks for action, and action now." Should Congress prove unwilling, continued the president, he would "ask . . . for the broad Executive power to wage a war against the emergency, as great as the power that would be given me if we were in fact invaded by a foreign foe. . . . The people of the United States have not failed. In their need they have registered a mandate that they want direct, vigorous action." They got it. Within days the scope of government was suddenly and dramatically expanded.

Two days after assuming office, on March 6, Roosevelt declared a four-day bank holiday, suspending all banking functions, citing the World War I Trading with the Enemy Act as his legal authority. (The holiday continued until March 15, when about half of the nation's banks with about 90 percent of total deposits were allowed to reopen.) On March 7 the secretary of the treasury issued a regulation requiring all member banks in the Federal Reserve system to deliver all gold and gold certificates that they held to the Federal Reserve. The next day the Federal Reserve Board directed all members to deliver lists of the names and addresses of all those who had withdrawn gold or gold certificates since February 1.

Rule by executive order, however, was just a stopgap measure. On March 9 Congress was called back into special session. The same day it passed (unanimously in the House) the Emergency Banking Act, authorizing ex post the president's declaration of a bank holiday, allowing the Reconstruction Finance Corporation (RFC) to subscribe to the stock of distressed banks, allowing the Federal Reserve to lend to nonmember banks and businesses, and providing a plan for the eventual reopening of those of the nation's banks that could be saved. The following day, March 10, the president prohibited the export of gold and trade in foreign currency except under license from the Treasury. This, together with earlier actions limiting access to gold, effectively terminated the gold standard, the demise of which was formally announced on April 19, 1933. But this was only the beginning.

Roosevelt's solution to the crisis challenge of the Great Depression was a veritable blizzard of "alphabet-soup" legislation (Table 23.2). By the time the special session of Congress recessed on June 16 (during the so-called First Hundred Days), it had passed comprehensive legislation affecting the nation's banking, industry, agriculture, and labor, though, as sketched below, additional important legislation was also passed by later Congresses.

In light of the range of laws and regulations adopted during the period, it is convenient to think of specific legislative initiatives as directed primarily toward one of three goals: recovery, reform, or relief. For example, two of the major legislative efforts were directed at promoting recovery: the National Industrial Recovery Act (NIRA) and the Agricultural Adjustment Act (AAA). On the other hand, the Civilian Conservation Corps (CCC) and the Federal Emergency Relief Administration (FERA) relieved the suffering of the unemployed and destitute, while legislation, such as the Glass-Steagall Act of 1933 and the Securities and Exchange Act of 1934, attempted to reform institutions viewed as having "failed."

1. THE FIRST 100 DAYS: MARCH 9–JULY 16, 1933

The Emergency Banking Relief Act of March 9, 1933, authorized the emergency steps taken to halt the banking crisis since Roosevelt's inauguration. Among its provisions, gold hoarding and gold export were prohibited under pain of up to a $10,000 fine and ten years in jail; the secretary of the treasury was authorized to call all gold and gold certificates; sound banks could reopen only under license from the Treasury Department; and the comptroller was directed to appoint conservators for the insolvent national banks. At the end of March the Civilian Conservation Corps Reforestation Relief Act was passed, establishing the CCC as an unemployment relief agency for 250,000 *male citizens* aged eighteen to twenty-five to work on reforestation, road construction, national parks, soil erosion, and other projects under the direction of army officers. Successful applicants were paid $30 per month, part of which went directly to dependents. At one time the CCC had 500,000 on its rolls, and by 1941 it had employed some two million men.

In April Congress took a "breather." In May the legislative whirlwind was renewed. On May 12 the Federal Emergency Relief Act created the Federal Emergency Relief Administration (FERA) to distribute $500 million in relief funds to the states. Half was designated for federal matching grants on the basis of $1 federal for every $3 of state and local relief aid; the balance was for discretionary grants based upon a state's need and fiscal effort to deal with its problems. The same day Congress passed the Agricultural Adjustment Act to restore farm purchasing power by eliminating surpluses through reductions in the production of basic commodities and the establishment of "parity" prices. On May 18, the Tennessee Valley Authority (TVA) was established to revitalize the area, and at the end of the month the Federal Securities Act mandated registration and full disclosure of new stock offerings.

FERA marks the beginnings of a switch in government expenditure from the local level to the national level: the new federalism. Whereas in 1930 the average American received more than half the government services from local government and less than 20 percent from the federal government, by 1940 about 50 percent were supplied by the federal government and only 30 percent by local governments (Figure 23.3). Today the federal government accounts for more than 60 percent of all spending by government in the United States. The most important element underlying this switch was the implementation of national relief programs under the New Deal. Between 1932 and 1940 direct relief expenditures accounted for about 45 percent of the growth in federal expenditures from $4.7 billion to $9.1 billion.

FERA also marks the beginnings of the federal policy of matching grants to state and local governments that continues to this day. This policy change plays a role in the new federalism, since the monies went to the state, not the local, government although they might ultimately be disbursed by local government. Such matching grant programs are traditionally viewed as ensuring federal control of state relief efforts, but during the New Deal they developed as a means of escaping close federal control that neither the states nor Congress wished to confer upon the executive branch of govern-

TABLE 23.2

Legislative Initiatives during Roosevelt's First 100 Days: March 9, 1933–June 16, 1933

Date	Legislation	Abbreviation	Action
March 9	Emergency Banking Relief Act		Authorized bank holidays; gave RFC authority to invest in banks and Fed authority to lend to nonmember and businesses; gave broad powers over transactions in gold, silver, or foreign exchange.
March 31	Civilian Conservation Corps Reforestation Relief Act	CCC	Authorized employment of 250,000 males for reforestation, road construction, national parks, flood and soil erosion control.
May 12	Federal Emergency Relief Act	FERA	Appropriated $500 million for relief. Half given directly to the states, rest on a $1 federal for each $3 state relief.
May 12	Agricultural Adjustment Act	AAA	Established parity prices returning farmers to pre–World War I purchasing power. Subsidized voluntary reduction of acreage or crops. Provided for refinancing of farm mortgages through federal land banks. Authorized the president to reflate the currency through devaluation of gold content, coinage of silver, or printing of $3 billion paper currency.
May 18	Tennessee Valley Authority	TVA	Created the TVA with authority to construct dams and power plants along the Tennessee River and develop programs for the social and economic well-being of the region.

May 27	Federal Securities Act		Required full disclosure to investors on all public stock offerings or sales through the mail or interstate (incorporated into SEC in 1934).
June 6	National Employment System Act		Authorized creation of U.S. Employment Service.
June 13	Home Owners Refinancing Act	HOLC	Created Home Owners Loan Corporation with $200 million capital and authorized bonding authority of $2 billion to refinance home mortgages and furnish cash advances for taxes, repairs, and home maintenance.
June 16	Banking Act of 1933 (Glass-Steagall)		Created FDIC for deposit insurance; widened Fed membership. Permitted branch banking.
June 16	Farm Credit Act	FCA	Provided for short- and medium-term credits for agricultural production and marketing; long-term farm mortgage loans.
June 16	Emergency Railroad Transportation Act		Prohibited "unnecessary" duplication of services; promoted reorganization and consolidation; placed railroad holding companies under the ICC.
June 16	National Industrial Recovery Act	NIRA	Authorized "Fair Trade" codes under the National Recovery Administration (NRA) and granted exemptions from antitrust. Authorized National Labor Board with rights to enforce collective bargaining. Authorized $3.3 billion for the Public Works Administration (PWA) to build roads, bridges, and public buildings.

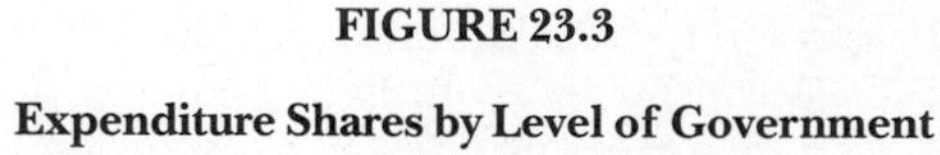

FIGURE 23.3

Expenditure Shares by Level of Government

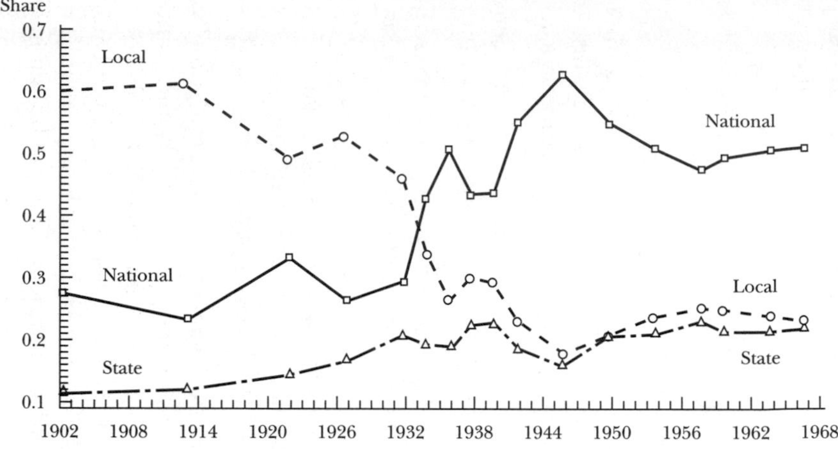

Source: John J. Wallis, "The Political Economy of New Deal Fiscal Federalism," *Economic Inquiry* 29 (1991): 511.

ment.[7] With approximately 150,000 administrative jobs at stake, in addition to the relief jobs themselves, FERA offered significant opportunities for political patronage, "honest graft," or outright corruption. Deciding what jobs would be done and where provided extraordinarily lucrative opportunities that politicians were reluctant to pass up. Certainly, tight federal control over FERA had proved something of a problem to many states and politicians. For example, despite protracted testimony by the FERA administrator Harry Hopkins, Congress was unable to determine how the agency determined a state's relief needs and fiscal effort for discretionary grants, Governor Martin Davey of Ohio had a arrest warrant sworn out for Hopkins should he set foot in the state, and a number of politicians, the most notable being Governor William Langer of North Dakota, were convicted of misusing funds and served time in jail. As a result, Congress made sure that subsequent relief programs were on a strict matching-funds basis with control over patronage and any other political benefits residing with the state rather than the executive.

Farmers had been hit especially hard by declining prices and incomes during the contraction. In 1929 the gross farm product was valued at $13.8

[7] Wallis (1984, 1991).

billion; by 1932 it had fallen to $6.5 billion. Corn, which in 1929 had sold at 77 cents per bushel, was selling for as little as 19 cents per bushel in early 1933, and wheat, which had fetched $1.08 per bushel, was selling for only 33 cents a bushel. At country grain elevators prices were probably even lower. Parity prices, on the other hand, promised a return to the heyday of American farming, restoring the purchasing power of the farmers' dollar to 1909–14 levels for corn, cotton, wheat, rice, hogs, and dairy products and in 1919–20 for tobacco (with additional crops included in 1934).

The AAA perceived the problem of low prices as one of excess supply in the face of reduced domestic and international demand. Individual responses simply compounded the problem since farmers reasonably viewed themselves as perfect competitors and hence incapable of affecting market price through individual action. Each therefore sought to offset low prices through increased production to try to maintain farm income, thereby exacerbating the problem. Instead the Agricultural Adjustment Administration assumed responsibility for calculating the crop size (taking account of any carryover) needed to achieve the parity price, given projected demand, and converting that crop into an acreage (or herd size) estimate. This was then allocated among the various states on the basis of each state's share of total production between 1928 and 1932, and each state's allotment was then allocated among the individual farmers within the state on the same basis. Farmers who voluntarily reduced acreage or production to the target levels were to be directly compensated by the government, using the proceeds of levies upon the processors of the agricultural commodities. These levies and production controls were subsequently ruled unconstitutional in 1936 (*United States v. Butler*). In addition, the AAA provided funds to refinance farm mortgage through the federal land banks (established 1916).

Unlike the later National Industrial Recovery Act (see below), however, the AAA made no provision for raising agricultural wages although such plans had been included in early drafts of the legislation. Lee Alston and Joseph Ferrie argue that efforts to include wages in the AAA were successfully thwarted by southern Democrats since it would have disproportionately affected southern agriculture, which relied much more heavily upon wage labor (primarily supplied by African-Americans) and weakened white planter paternalistic control over their labor force.

Other, even more far-reaching legislation followed in June. Early in the month (June 5) Congress abrogated gold clauses in any and all contracts. Henceforth debts (other than intergovernmental) would be payable only in current legal tender. The next day Congress authorized a national employment system in cooperation with the states. The Home Owners Refinancing Act (June 13) established the Home Owners Loan Corporation (HOLC) to refinance nonfarm home mortgage debts and give loans for maintenance, repairs, and taxes. By the time the HOLC was wound up three years later, it had made more than one million mortgages.

These legislative accomplishments, however, paled by comparison with those of the final day of the special session, June 16, 1933. On that one day four legislative acts were passed. Two were relatively minor: The Farm Credit Act consolidated short- and medium-term agricultural credits for production and marketing under a single agency, the Farm Credit Administration (FCA), while the Emergency Railroad Transportation Act put railroad holding companies under the Interstate Commerce Commission and tried to avoid the duplication of facilities and services. The other two acts were of more importance. The Glass-Steagall Act of 1933 created the Federal Deposit Insurance Corporation (FDIC), guaranteeing individual bank accounts up to $5,000 (equivalent to about $75,000 today), minimizing the risk of runs pushing marginal banks into insolvency. However, as recent history has shown, it failed to resolve the issue of moral hazard implicit in all such insurance schemes, and its real contribution to bank stability has been questioned.[8] The last legislative initiative of the special session of the seventy-third Congress was perhaps the most important: the National Industrial Recovery Act. Indeed, according to historian Arthur Schlesinger, the NIRA was "the most important and far-reaching legislation ever enacted by the American Congress." Its goal was to revive industrial production and business activity and reduce unemployment by dealing directly with the vicious cycle of price deflation set in motion by the great contraction through "fair" competition as opposed to "ruinous" competition.

Rapidly falling prices had done considerable damage to the economy. Like inflation, deflation is an uneven process since some prices go down faster than others. Food prices, for example, fell about 37 percent between 1929 and 1933, while clothing prices fell only 24 percent. The uncertainty created by unpredictable changes in relative prices made investment and production decisions extremely difficult. If changing prices were poorly anticipated, businesses exposed themselves to great risks; costs could exceed revenues by the time a contract was completed. The only predictable result of deflation is inefficiency: a tendency for business to pass by investment opportunities with high expected returns, allowing some firms that produce poorly but guess right to survive and bankrupting other firms that produce efficiently but guess wrong.

The NIRA was the industrial analogue of the AAA and suffered a similar fate, being ruled unconstitutional in 1935 (*Schechter Poultry Corporation v. United States*). Like the AAA, it sought to raise prices by restricting output. Whereas the government set the parameters under the AAA, the NIRA delegated control to the businesses themselves; indeed, this was the crux of the constitutional challenge to the law. The NIRA, in effect, suspended antitrust laws and mandated the formation of planning boards, staffed by representatives from business and labor, to draw up "codes of fair competition." In

[8] Most recently by Calomiris (1990) and by Wigmore (1987).

short, the NIRA was an order to cartelize. Once approved by the executive branch, these codes were legally enforceable. What better way, the New Dealers asserted, to fight the spiral of deflation that had lowered prices and wages? It seemed to provide the freedom from uncertainty offered by state socialism but without public ownership or direct government control of business. At best it should be viewed as the product of misguided economic theory. At worst it can be seen as part of America's flirtation with the rigid antilibertarian national socialism sweeping Germany, Italy, and Spain in the thirties.

Many of the contemporary complaints about the NRA concerned its impact on income distribution. It was suspected (perhaps correctly) that business could dominate the boards and increase capital's share of the pie. But for those who respect the allocative advantages of competitive markets, there were other, perhaps deeper problems. The codes were supposed to raise wages and profits by raising prices and reducing output. However, if only some sectors of the economy are allowed to cartelize, then their members will be better off at the expense of the rest of the economy. On the other hand, if everybody joins a cartel, then two results are possible. Suppose everyone's prices go up by the same percentage; this leaves relative prices unchanged and has no effect on resource allocation or the real income of those working. It is much more likely, however, that some cartels will be more successful than others, and relative prices will change. That leaves some firms (and perhaps workers) better off but distorts resource allocation. The successful cartels will produce too little, and real national income will fall.

Nevertheless, within the first year, codes had been adopted in 450 industries covering about twenty-three million workers. By January 1, 1934, NRA regulations covered about 90 percent of the industrial work force. By the time the law was declared unconstitutional in 1935 there were more than 550 codes covering virtually the entire private, nonagricultural sector.

Despite its brief history, there is some evidence that the NRA did succeed in raising prices. Estimates suggest that the adoption of codes of fair competition increased nominal wages by 2.15 percent per month and prices by 1.17 percent per month while their nullification by the Supreme Court decreased wages 1.15 percent per month and prices by 0.55 percent per month from the levels achieved under the codes.[9] As a result, about half the increase in wages and almost a third of the recovery in prices before the *Schechter* decision may be attributed to the codes. In the absence of the codes, the hourly wage in manufacturing in May 1935 might have been only 35 cents, compared with its actual level of almost 60 cents per hour, and prices might have been as low as 62 (1926 = 100), compared with their actual level of 80.2. These results, however, place a heavy burden upon the data,

[9] Weinstein (1980).

which come from a discontinuous sample from the early 1920s and the period December 1931 through December 1935.

2. OTHER LEGISLATIVE INITIATIVES OF THE SEVENTY-THIRD CONGRESS

As active as the legislative agenda was during the first one hundred days, it does not represent the New Deal in its entirety. Other important legislative initiatives were passed in later sessions and by other Congresses. When Congress returned to session in October 1933, it established the Commodity Credit Corporation under the AAA to extend loans to farmers secured by their crops. Cotton farmers in particular were early beneficiaries, and the program was expanded over the years from an initial capital of only $3 million to $100 million in 1936. In November the Civil Works Administration (CWA) was established as an emergency employment program, putting the jobless to work on make-work projects. The program ended in March 1934, and its functions were transferred to FERA. In the interim, though, it spent $933 million ($740 million in wages and salaries) on 180,000 projects around the country. Relief efforts were further expanded in early 1934 with passage of the Civil Works Emergency Relief Act with a budget of $950 million for civil works and direct relief through FERA, and by 1935 some 2.5 million were in the program.

Three other pieces of legislation by the Seventy-third Congress are particularly noteworthy. On June 6, 1934, the Securities Exchange Act provided for federal regulation of the securities market through the Securities and Exchange Commission to eliminate various abuses, such as insider trading and stock price manipulation, brought to light during the Senate Committee on Banking and Currency hearings on stock exchange practices. The Senate counsel for those hearings, Ferdinand Pecora, became the first commissioner. In addition, the law gave the Fed the power to set margin requirements for stock purchases. In mid-June the Communications Act established the Federal Communications Commission (FCC) to regulate interstate and international radio, telegraphic, and cable communications. In late June the Federal Farm Bankruptcy Act was adopted to prevent farm foreclosures. Under this legislation farmers could repurchase foreclosed farm property at newly appraised (lower) values over a six-year period at an interest rate of only 1 percent. Where creditors objected, bankruptcy proceedings were to be suspended for a five-year period, during which the farmer could retain use and possession on reasonable terms.

3. THE SECOND NEW DEAL

In his address to the Seventy-fourth Congress, January 4, 1935, Roosevelt outlined a program of social reforms organized around the themes of security of livelihood, security against old age, unemployment, or dependency, and improved housing, marking the start of the second New

Deal with a narrower focus upon smaller farmers and labor. In August 1935 Congress passed the Social Security Act, establishing the federal-state program of unemployment compensation and imposing a tax levied equally upon employers and employees to provide for old age and survivors' insurance beginning in 1942 that are still with us today.

The Emergency Relief Appropriation Act in April 1935 marked the federal government's withdrawal from providing direct relief and the establishment of a massive works program directed by the Works Progress Administration for the able-bodied, who were required to pass a means test before being accepted into the program. By March 1936, the WPA had 3.4 million men and women on the federal payroll, averaging 120 to 140 hours per month at the prevailing hourly wage rate. By the time the program was terminated in 1943, more than 8.5 million had worked for the agency on about 1.5 million projects, which included construction of more than 650,000 miles of roadway, work on 124,000 bridges, 125,000 public buildings, more than 8,000 parks, and more than 850 airports at a cost of $11 billion. In an effort to improve the quality of rural life and bring it into the twentieth century, the Rural Electrification Administration was created to bring power to those areas not served by private utilities.

Following the Supreme Court's action overturning the NIRA, Congress moved swiftly with the National Labor Relations Act, creating the National Labor Relations Board, to restore the right to join a trade union and bargain collectively and restricting employer activities to discourage unions. This was followed in 1938 by the Fair Labor Standards Act, which applied to all enterprises engaged in interstate commerce *except* farm workers (thanks once again to the voting strength of southern Democrats), establishing a minimum wage of forty cents an hour, a maximum workweek of forty-four hours, and prohibiting the employment of children under sixteen.

Similarly, when the Court overturned the AAA, Congress quickly substituted the Soil Conservation and Domestic Allotment Act (February 1936), paying farmers to turn land over to soil-conserving crops instead of paying them to limit production of such soil-depleting crops as corn, cotton, oats, wheat, or tobacco — that is, much the same range of crops as originally covered under the AAA. This legislation was subsequently incorporated into the Agricultural Adjustment Act of 1938, which established marketing quotas and provided for nonrecourse crop loans through the Commodity Credit Corporation. These loans in effect established a floor under agricultural prices, allowing farmers to borrow against their crops on the basis of parity prices rather than the current market price and to default without penalty or recourse if the market price fell below the loan price. In the event that market prices were higher, farmers could simply liquidate their loans, redeem the crops, and sell them at the market prices.

The one glaring exception to the social reform bias of legislation during the second New Deal was the Banking Act of 1935. This reformed what was viewed as the flawed structure of the Fed. Henceforth authority was to be concentrated in an expanded seven-member Board of Governors of the Federal Reserve (replacing the Federal Reserve Board) while the comptroller of the currency and the secretary of the treasury were removed as ex officio members to guarantee further the independence of the board. Open market operations, while still conducted through the New York Fed, were now to be directed by the Federal Open Market Committee (FOMC), consisting of the members of the Board of Governors plus five of the twelve Fed district bank presidents. The board was also given authority to set reserve requirements for member banks.

Many of New Deal structural reforms were misguided or inefficient. For instance, minimum wages eliminated jobs for some unskilled workers. Farm programs have led to the ludicrous situation where there are more employees of the Department of Agriculture today than there are full-time farmers, and farming has still not contracted sufficiently to bring supply and demand into equilibrium. Pork-barrel politics led to an oversupply of public works and to expensive and inefficient regulations that plague private business. These reforms may even have slowed America's growth relative to that of many of its competitors.

Although the flurry of New Deal legislative activity built upon the foundation of the command economy laid down during World War I, its goal was nothing short of a complete restructuring of the American economy, a complete reform of its institutions.[10] Whereas the law had once prohibited "conspiracies in restraint of trade," collective bargaining was now not only sanctioned but enforced; firms once fearful of talking to one another in the wake of the infamous "Gary dinners" hosted between 1907 and 1911 by Judge Elbert Gary (chairman of the board of directors of U.S. Steel) at which the nation's steel producers had colluded to set prices were now encouraged to set minimum "fair trade" prices; contracts specifying repayment in gold were nullified; caveat emptor no longer held in stock purchases. No longer would the nation's farmers be subject to the market discipline. The farmstead received protection from foreclosure; farm prices were guaranteed by the state, and efforts undertaken to alleviate price-depressing surplus production. Moreover, the federal government now accepted responsibility for the relief of poverty and unemployment, and a new government agency undertook to develop one of the more backward areas of the country.

Much of this legislation was conceived in haste and repented at leisure. Both the Agricultural Adjustment Act and key provisions of the National Industrial Recovery Act were struck down by the Supreme Court. On May 27, 1935, in the case of *Schechter Poultry Corporation v. United States*, the Court unanimously ruled that the Congress in the NIRA had unconstitutionally delegated legislative powers to the executive branch in its grant of control

[10] Higgs (1987).

over wages and hours in the poultry industry, especially where that business was purely intrastate. Seven months later (January 6, 1936), the Court by six to three ruled in the case of *U.S. v. Butler* that the tax on agricultural commodity processors used to finance acreage or crop reductions was constitutionally indefensible. Much of the legislative activity of the special session of the Seventy-third Congress survived, however, and the nature of government in the American economy was never the same again. The scope of government was forever increased, and this trend has not reversed to this day. Once government came in, it has proved very difficult to get it to leave.

Appendix A: Cartels and the Incentive to Cheat

A cartel serves the interest of its members by allowing the group to maximize industry profits like a true monopoly. If members compete openly, the price would tend to fall to P_o and output rise to Q_o, where industry cost equals price (Figure 23A.1). If the members collude to limit output to Q_m (where marginal cost equals marginal revenue), they can maximize profits

FIGURE 23.A1

Cartel Pricing

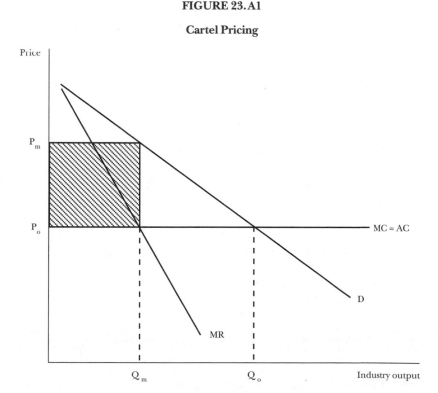

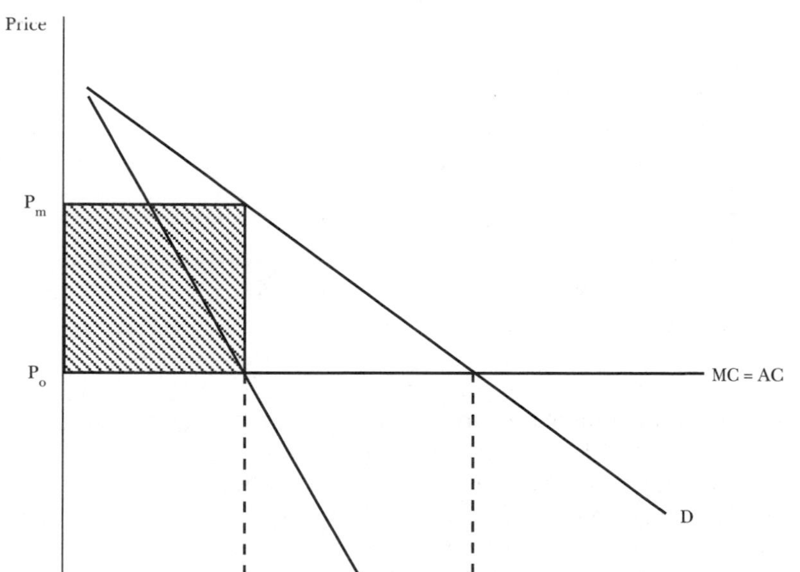

by charging P_m; excess profits are earned equal to the crosshatched portion under the demand curve. Naturally the cartel agreement must somehow apportion the limited output among member firms; this in turn determines how the profits will be apportioned.

The more potential competitors there are, the greater the tendency for the market to move toward the competitive output level and the greater the collective interest in collusion. Unfortunately (for the firms anyway) the more members, the greater the incentive for any individual member to cheat. Figure 23A.2 shows why. With many members, the cartel output share is very small for any one member, yet the demand curve for that member considering lowering the price below P_m is very elastic (flat). That means a small cut in price will increase the cheater's sales (and therefore profits) enormously. Excess profits for the profit-maximizing cheater increase from area ABCE to area FGHE in Figure 23A.2. Note, too, that in a very large cartel in which some members produce only a small fraction of total output, it may even be difficult for the honest cartel members to notice marginal cheaters. OPEC's experience illustrates this point: a few small hungry oil producers cheated regularly whenever their output fell below capacity.

In the case of railroads in the nineteenth century, the perceived need for a cartel (and the incentives to cheat) would be particularly great. These railroads were probably natural monopolies (see above). Thus without col-

FIGURE 23.A2

Cartel Cheating

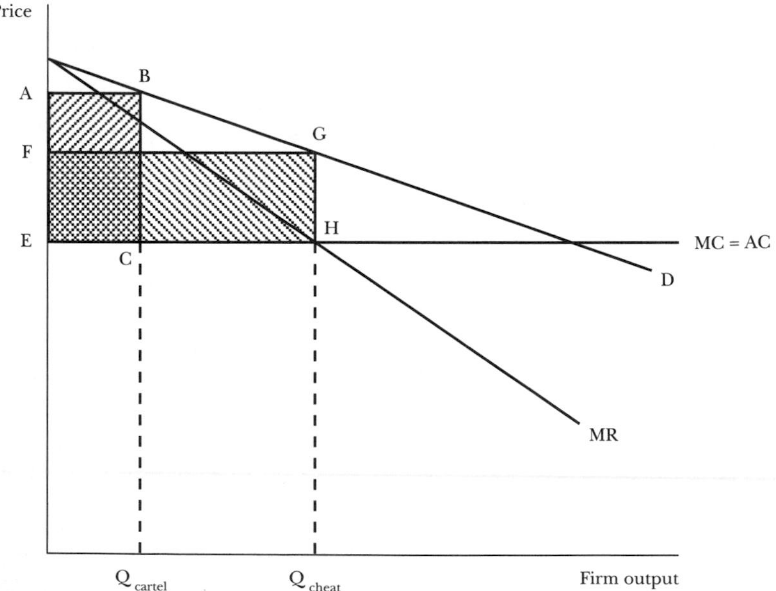

lusion there would be a tendency for prices to fall toward marginal cost, well below even the long-run break-even price. On the other hand, the alternatives to rail transport were limited on many routes, so the industry's demand curve is thought to have been inelastic and the possibilities for earning excess profits are thought to have been very large.

Appendix B: The Simple Economics of Natural Monopolies

A natural monopoly is an enterprise whose marginal production costs remain below average costs at practical output levels. Public utilities—telephone companies, power distribution, railroads—often fit the description because they must have great amounts of capital invested to open shop but can then accommodate users at relatively small cost.

From the viewpoint of efficiency we would like the natural monopoly to produce at output level A (see Figure 23B.1), where marginal cost just equals the value of the service to the marginal purchaser. If the enterprise produces

FIGURE 23.B1

Natural Monopolies and Efficiency

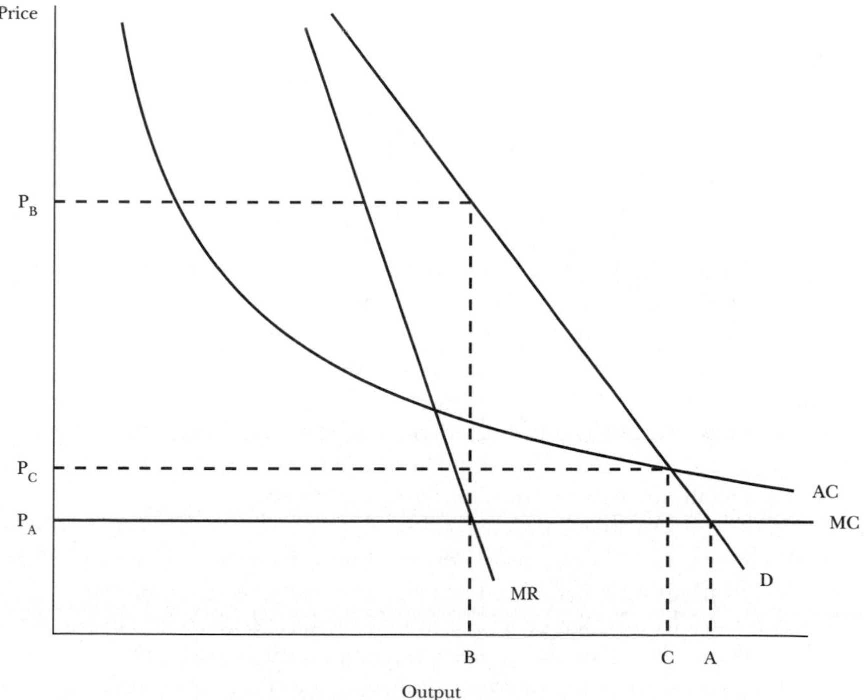

less than A, some potential purchaser who values the service more than it cost to create will be shut out; if it produces more, the additional resources employed could have generated more value used in other ways. Unfortunately this efficient output and price combination cannot be sustained without subsidy, since the utility will be unable to recover its costs in the long run; average cost exceeds price. The owner of the utility would most prefer to produce at output B, where marginal revenue equals marginal cost, and profits are maximized. Regulators often take a middle ground, requiring output C (Price = Average Cost), where prices are high enough to insure a fair return to the enterprise's investment but lower than the profit-maximizing monopoly price.

Is there any way to reconcile the demand for efficiency with the need to pay fair return on capital in order to keep the firm in business? Society as a whole (or the utility's customers, if they are a well-defined group) may underwrite the initial capital costs in return for a guarantee of a marginal cost pricing policy. This is effectively what happens when a town uses property taxes on residents to build roads and then opens the roads to general use at no extra charge. But it is rarely practical when the enterprise is privately owned.

The natural monopoly may be given the right to "price discriminate" on the condition that total revenues do not exceed total costs. This is often done in regulated transportation. Airlines, for example, charge business travelers more than average cost (because they will fly anyway) and charge vacationers less than average cost (because otherwise they will drive or stay home). Railroads charge shippers of valuable freight, like machinery, more per ton-mile than they charge coal or gravel shippers, who have access to alternative barge transport. Price discrimination allows output levels closer to A without forcing profits below zero. But its use is often limited by popular opposition to market discrimination in any form.

Here is where the land grants fit in. Any agricultural shipper who would be able to pay a higher price than the railroad charges must be making a profit greater than the return needed to stay in business. And we can expect these profits to be capitalized in the value of the farmland. If the railroad owns the land, leasing it or selling it at a price contingent on guaranteed shipping fees, the profit-maximizing output of the railroad will change from the monopoly output (B) to the efficient output (A). Were the railroad to produce less than A, the competitively determined rent collected from the land would fall more than shipping costs would rise.

The obvious problem with this solution is that it is inequitable: Under all but the most unusual circumstances, the total profits earned by a perfectly price discriminating railroad will be excessive. We know that was the case for the western railroads as a group because Fogel's and Mercer's estimates of social rate of return are far above the opportunity cost of the capital invested. The social return from direct railroad benefits—the sum of railroad profits and net gains to shippers—really represents a lower bound on the potential return to a perfect price discriminator. Since railroads charged much more than marginal cost to their customers, output was surely below the efficient level. Hence the actual social returns measured by economic historians are below the private return that could, in theory, have been earned by a profit-maximizing railroad conglomerate.

Bibliography

Alston, Lee J., and Joseph P. Ferrie. "Paternalism in Agricultural Labor Contrasts in the U.S. South: Implications for the Growth of the Welfare State." *American Economic Review* (forthcoming, 1993).

Benson, Lee. *Merchants, Farmers and Railroads.* Cambridge: Harvard University Press, 1955.

Calomiris, Charles. "Is Deposit Insurance Necessary: A Historical Perspective." *Journal of Economic History* 50 (1990): 283–96.

Fogel, Robert. *The Union Pacific Railroad: A Case in Premature Enterprise.* Baltimore: Johns Hopkins University Press, 1960.

Gray, Lewis C. "The Market Surplus Problems of Colonial Tobacco." *Agricultural History* 2 (1928):1–34.

Higgs, Robert. "Crisis, Bigger Government, and Ideological Change: Two Hypotheses on the Ratchet Phenomenon." *Explorations in Economic History* 22 (1985): 1–28.

———. *Crisis and Leviathan.* New York: Oxford University Press, 1987.

Hughes, Jonathan R. T. *The Governmental Habit: Economic Control from Colonial Times to the Present.* New York: Basic Books, 1977.

———. *The Governmental Habit Redux*. Princeton: Princeton University Press, 1991.

Kolko, Gabriel. *Railroads and Regulation.* Princeton: Princeton University Press, 1965.

Libecap, Gary. "The Political Economy of Crude Oil Cartelization in the United States, 1933–1972." *Journal of Economic History* 49 (1989): 833–55.

———. "The Rise of the Chicago Packers and the Origins of Meat Inspection and Anti-Trust." *Economic Inquiry* 30 (1992): 242–62.

———, and S. N. Wiggans. "The Influence of Private Contractual Failure on Regulation: The Case of Oil Field Unitization." *Journal of Political Economy* 93 (1985): 690–714.

MacAvoy, Paul. *The Economic Effects of Regulation.* Cambridge: MIT Press, 1965.

Martin, Albro, *Enterprise Denied.* New York: Columbia University Press, 1971.

———. *Railroads Triumphant.* New York: Oxford University Press, 1992.

Mercer, Lloyd. "Rates of Return for Land-Grant Railroads: The Central Pacific." *Journal of Economic History* 30 (1970): 602–26.

Temin, Peter. *The Fall of the Bell System: A Study in Prices and Politics.* New York: Cambridge University Press, 1989.

Ulen, Thomas S. "The Market for Regulation: The ICC from 1887 to 1920." *American Economic Review, Papers and Proceedings* 70 (1980): 306–10.

———. "Railroad Cartels before 1887: The Effectiveness of Private Enforcement of Collusion." *Research in Economic History* 8 (1983): 125–44.

Wallis, John J. "The Birth of the Old Federalism: Financing the New Deal." *Journal of Economic History* 47 (1984): 97–102.

———. "The Political Economy of New Deal Fiscal Federalism." *Economic Inquiry* 29 (1991): 510–24.

White, Eugene. "The Membership Problem of the National Banking System." *Explorations in Economic History* 19 (1982): 110–27.

———. *The Regulation and Reform of the American Banking System, 1900–1929.* Princeton: Princeton University Press, 1983.

———. "State-Sponsored Insurance of Bank Deposits in the United States, 1907–1929." *Journal of Economic History* 41 (1987): 537–58.

Weinstein, Michael M. *Recovery and Redistribution under the NIRA*. Amsterdam: North-Holland, 1980.

Wigmore, Barrie A. "Was the Bank Holiday of 1933 Caused by a Run on the Dollar?" *Journal of Economic History* 47 (1987): 739–55.

Wright, Gavin. "The Origins of American Industrial Success, 1879–1940." *American Economic Review* 80 (1990): 651–68.

Glossary

Ad valorem duties: Import duties whose dollar value is based upon the value of the product. **Specific duties,** on the other hand, are a fixed sum of money regardless of the value of the imported good.

Adverse selection: Situations in which the sellers have better information than buyers about the quality of goods offered for sale and thus have an incentive to mix the bad with the good and sell all at one (higher) price since the proportion of defective products is unknown to the buyer.

Agency theory: The study of the implicit or explicit contractual relationship between one or more persons (the **principals**) who engage others (the **agents**) to act on their behalf. Differences in preferences, motives, and goals between the principals and their agents lead agents to act in a manner inconsistent with the best interests of the principals unless agent actions are constrained and monitored. For example, in a representative democracy, such as the United States, voters (the principals) elect representatives (their agents) to represent their interests, but representatives after election have some discretion in how they vote and may not always act in the interests of their electorates. Similarly, employees may be regarded as agents of their employers, who may in turn be agents of the company's stockholders.

Agglomeration: The benefits that arise from the concentration of economic activities in cities, such as the availability of highly specialized services; economies of scope; positive **externalities**; external economies.

Aggregate demand: The dollar value of all goods and services in final consumption, usually broken down between personal consumption expenditures, investment, net exports, and government expenditure.

Agricultural ladder: A metaphor for the socioeconomic status of agricultural workers which views agricultural laborers as standing on the lowest rungs of a ladder with **sharecroppers**, share tenant and cash tenants on the ladder rungs above them, and the mortgage-free, owner-occupier farmer (a **yeoman** farmer) standing on the topmost rung of the ladder. Successively higher rungs represent higher economic and social status.

American system: The embodiment of scarce human skills into sophisticated machines for use by less skilled labor in producing products with interchangeable parts.

Amortized loan: A loan in which the principal and interest are paid off in a given number of equal installments.

Arbitrage: Taking advantage of price differences in two different markets by buying in the lower-priced market and selling in the higher.

Autonomous spending: Expenditure not based upon the level of income. In the income expenditure model of national income determination, investment expenditure (which depends upon interest rates), government spending (which depends upon policy decisions), and exports (which depend upon foreign, not domestic, demand) are the prime examples.

Backward linkages: The relationship between an industry and its sources of supply, the demand for which is derived from the demand for the industry's final product.

Balance of payments: An accounting of the external transactions of a country during a given period of time. The balance of payments accounts are usually divided between the **current account,** which are payments for goods and services, and the **capital account,** which is an accounting of money flows, including borrowing and lending and repatriated profits and interest. The current account in turn is frequently split between **visible trade,** which involves tangible products, and the **invisible account,** which involves payment for such services as shipping and insurance.

Bank reserves: Funds set aside to meet bank liabilities. Historically these were held in the form of cash in the vault. Today banks hold reserves as a combination of vault cash plus deposits with the local Federal Reserve district bank, and banking laws specify minimum reserve ratios for banks under their jurisdiction: **required reserves** = deposit liabilities × reserve ratio. Banks may have higher reserves than required by law, forgoing some potential interest income on loans. In such cases the differences between a bank's actual reserves and its required reserves are known as **excess reserves.**

Banker's acceptances: Drafts or bills of exchange that banks have "accepted" as their own liabilities. In effect, banks substitute their credit for that of their customers to increase acceptability.

Bimetallic standard: Coinage defined in terms of specific quantities of both gold and silver, thereby defining a fixed rate of exchange between gold and silver.

Bonds: A fixed-interest marketable debt. Failure to pay the interest on time may result in bankruptcy proceedings to force the sale of assets to meet the debt. The face value (**par**) is repaid upon maturity. In the case of bonds with no maturity date, known as consols, the current selling price is the interest payment on the par value divided by the current rate of interest.

Bubble (speculative): A sharp rise in the price of an asset unassociated with a rise in the earnings potential of the asset that generates expectations about the potential for additional price rises in the future.

Capital asset pricing model: Equilibrium pricing of a capital asset. A willing buyer would pay a price for an income-producing asset just equal to the present value of the discounted future stream of net earnings over the life of the asset. The seller would be indifferent toward owning the asset or having that sum of money.

Capital deepening: The process of accumulating capital at a faster rate than the rate of growth of the labor force so that the capital-labor ratio is rising.

Capital widening: The process of accumulating capital at the same rate as the rate of growth of the labor force. As a result, the capital-labor ratio is constant.

Capture (theory of): Theory of economic regulation developed by George Stigler (University of Chicago) in which the industry benefits from regulation by "capturing" the regulatory agency. Capture may take place through political influence, the exchange of employees between the regulatory agency and the regulated industry, the need to rely upon the highly technical advice of insiders in the regulated industry, or the need for industry cooperation.

Cartel: A formal agreement between firms in an industry to divide the market between them and maintain a uniform market price.

Chattel: An article of personal (as opposed to real) property. The distinctive feature is mobility. Thus slaves were chattels.

CIF (cost, insurance and freight): The price of a product delivered to the final consumer reflecting all production and transactions costs, including handling and shipping charges.

Circular flow of income: The flow of payments between domestic households and domestic firms for goods and services. This is the fundamental principle of national income accounting: Income received by households (including labor income, rental income, interest payments, profits and losses) must equal the value of goods and services produced by firms. Foreign trade and government then represent injections into or withdrawals from this circular flow.

Clearinghouse: A financial institution organized by banks to settle mutual indebtedness, taking advantage of the reduced transactions costs and scale economies from offsetting debits and credits and settling net balances rather than settling each debit and credit separately. These functions are now performed by the Federal Reserve, but originally membership was restricted to the largest and most creditworthy banks, which monitored the activities of the other members.

Cohort: A group sharing some characteristic in common—for example, a year of birth. Cohort analysis substitutes the study of different cohorts at a moment in time for the study of a particular cohort over time.

Compensating differences: The notion that if markets are perfect and in equilibrium, then the advantages and disadvantages of a particular job are fully reflected in the compensation package. For example, workers in hazardous occupations should receive higher wages to compensate them for their increased risk while workers in attractive jobs are willing to work for less than the market wage for their skills.

Complements: Goods are said to be complements when a change in the price of one leads to a shift in demand in the opposite direction for that good's complement. For example, milk and cereal are complements if an increase in the price of milk (that is, a movement along the demand curve for milk) leads to a reduction in the demand for cereal (that is, the demand curve for cereal shifts to the left). Technically the **cross-elasticity of demand** for complements is negative.

Computable general equilibrium: A mathematical model of the economy determining the equilibrium course of prices, outputs, and allocations over time. Defines the values at which all markets are simultaneously in equilibrium given initial distributions and relationships.

Concentration ratio: A measure of market power. Traditionally defined in terms of the share of industry output produced by the largest four firms in the industry. Hence, the **four-firm concentration ratio**.

Constant returns to scale: Constant marginal cost of production; minimum long-run average cost. Under constant returns to scale, a simultaneous 1 percent increase in all factor inputs will increase a firm's output by exactly 1 percent. See also **diseconomies/economies of scale** and **decreasing/increasing returns to scale**.

Consumer surplus: The difference between what a consumer was willing and able to pay to consume a product and the price that he or she actually paid. This is the area under the demand curve less the amount the consumer spent to purchase the product.

Contestable markets: Markets are said to be contestable when there are no barriers to entry and the competitive pressures from potential entrants constrain the behavior of those already in the market.

Counterfactual: What if?

Credible commitment: Whatever it takes to make a promise believable. Borrowers, for example, try to make their promises to repay loans more credible by offering some collateral to the lenders that is worth at least as much as the loans.

Crowding out: When the economy is at full employment, increased government expenditures replace or displace—that is, crowd-out—private investment or consumption expenditures through higher interest rates and prices. Conversely, it has been suggested that decreased government expenditures lower interest rates. They may stimulate—that is, "**crowd in**"—private investment.

Currency ratio: The proportion of monetary assets that the public chooses to hold in the form of legal tender. It is a measure of the public's confidence in bank money. The ratio rises in times of financial crisis and instability.

Current account: That portion of the balance of payments accounts of a country dealing with trade in currently produced goods and currently rendered services.

Decreasing return to scale: Increasing marginal costs of production and rising long-run average cost. Under decreasing returns to scale, a simultaneous, 1 percent increase in all factor inputs increase a firm's output by less than 1 percent. Also known as **diseconomies of scale.**

Deflation: A decline in the average price level.

Depreciation: Depending upon the context, either a reduction in the value of a nation's currency through **inflation** or **devaluation** or a reduction in the value of an asset as a result of wear and tear or technological change.

Depression: A *sustained* reduction in the level of economic activity. The bottom—trough—of the business cycle, characterized by unemployment, plant shutdowns, reduced production, and falling prices. A severe, relatively long-lived recession.

Derived demand: Demand for a good or service whose consumption is the means to an end rather than an end in itself. Firms, for example, demand labor not for the satisfaction of having people work for them but rather to produce goods for which there is a demand.

Devaluation: A reduction, or **depreciation,** in the value of a nation's currency relative to the currencies of other countries or gold under a regime of fixed exchange rates. For example, while under the Gold Standard Act of 1900, $1 had been worth 0.0484 of an ounce of gold (1 oz gold = $20.68), under the Gold Reserve Act of 1934, President Roosevelt devalued the dollar, fixing its value at 0.0286 of an ounce of gold (1 oz gold = $35).

Discount rate: A market-determined rate of interest on a loan granted by means of a discount. Instead of receiving the principal and repaying principal plus interest, as with a conventional loan, on a discount one receives the principal less the interest due over the life of the loan and repays the principal. The true rate of interest on a discount is thus fractionally higher than on a conventional loan at the same interest rate.

Discrimination: Unequal treatment of specifically targeted and identifiable groups, such as women or African-Americans. In the labor market, discrimination is usually explained in terms of the power of one group over another (that is, its ability to benefit at the expense of those being discriminated against), the tastes of the discriminators (which imposes costs upon both groups), or informational imperfections that result in individuals being judged by stereotype or group statistical averages rather than individual characteristics.

Diseconomies of scale: See **decreasing returns to scale.**

Disintermediation: Decreased reliance upon financial intermediaries, such as banks to link savers and investors.

Disinvestment: Reduction in the capital stock. Additions to the capital stock are less than **depreciation**.

Dumping: The selling of goods for less than the costs of production. Done either to drive out the competition and generate future monopoly profits or to secure economies of scale in production and exploit monopoly power in another market. Often in the context of foreign trade, dumping refers to the sale of goods in export markets for less than the price in the domestic market.

Duopoly: A market in which there are only two producers. Such a situation generates considerable opportunities for strategic behavior and encourages collusion.

Economies of scale: Decreasing long-run average cost. Firms producing larger outputs have lower unit production costs. Synonymous with **increasing returns to scale**.

Efficiency: Used alone, efficiency is synonymous with productivity defined as output per unit of input.

Efficiency wage: Wages paid in excess of the marginal product of labor. By definition such wages are non-market-clearing—there are more persons willing to work for these wages than there are jobs—allowing employers to select workers from the available pool and increasing employee opportunity costs of being fired. The payment of efficiency wages is supposed to produce a higher-quality, more motivated labor force with less labor turnover.

Efficient markets: A market is said to be efficient if the current price fully reflects all information. If so, then there exist no **arbitrage** possibilities and any profits from trade are random.

Elasticity (price/income/cross): A measure of the responsiveness of one variable with respect to a change in another variable. Thus **price elasticity** measures the response of the quantity consumed to a change in the price of the product, **income elasticity** measures the change in the quantity consumed as a result of a change in income, and **cross-elasticity** measures the responsiveness of the quantity of good N consumed as a result of a change in the price of good M. A product is said to be income- or price-**elastic** if the percentage change in quantity is greater than the percentage change in income or price.

Enumerated goods: Colonial products specifically listed in British parliamentary legislation regulating their production and disposition as a part of British **mercantilist** trade policy.

Exploitation: Paying a factor of production less than the value of its marginal product. In the case of labor, paying wages less than the value of the worker's marginal product.

Extensive growth: Growth of aggregate output keeping output per person (the same as income per capita) constant.

Externalities: Situation in which my economic consumption or production affects your well-being. Otherwise known as spillover or neighborhood effects or external economies and diseconomies. They arise because markets fail to exist, often as a result of a failure or inability to define and enforce property rights. They may be positive, as in the case of the plant fertilization services provided by honeybees incidental to their production of honey, or negative, as in the case of water or air pollution generated by certain industrial processes.

Factor price equalization: The theory that mobile factors of production gravitate toward their highest valued uses and locations until the price differential is eliminated by raising their marginal value in the activities they migrate from and driving down marginal values in those activities to which they migrate. When factors are immobile, trade flows may substitute generating shifts in the **derived demand** for the relatively low-valued factor of production.

Factors of production: Land, capital, labor, and entrepreneurship.

Fecundity: The ability to reproduce.

Fertility rate: Reproduction rate, generally measured as the number of births per thousand women of childbearing age.

FOB (free on board): The price of a good at the point of production, such as the factory or farm gate. Does not include the various handling charges and transportation costs associated with delivery to the consumer. See **CIF.**

Fractional reserve system: The banking principle that it is very unlikely that all customers will simultaneously demand repayment of their deposits in legal tender. Therefore, banks need have on hand only a certain fraction in legal tender of the deposits that they have received in order to make their promise to repay customers upon demand credible. See **bank reserves** and **credible commitment**. The smaller this faction of deposits held as reserves against the demands of their customers, the more money a bank can lend and the greater its ability to create money.

Free banking: Legislation granting individuals a general right to start a bank, provided they meet certain conditions, such as a minimum capitalization and a minimum reserve ratio.

Free rider: Someone who derives a benefit without paying his or her share of the costs. The free rider problem arises particularly in the provision of **public goods** where individuals cannot be excluded from receiving benefits that will be supplied regardless. Free riders have a strong incentive to understate their willingness to pay. As a result, where there are many free riders public goods will be undersupplied.

Frontier: Those areas of the country where the population density was between two and six persons per square mile. Those areas where population density was less than two were considered unsettled and beyond the frontier. Those areas where population density exceeded six were considered settled.

Game theory: The study of activities in which strategic behavior generates different outcomes and rewards for the participants.

GDP (gross domestic product): The aggregate value of factor incomes from productive (that is, income-generating) activities in the domestic economy or the aggregate value added for all domestically produced goods and services.

GNP (gross national product): **GDP** plus net income from abroad.

GNP deflator: Price index used to adjust **GNP** for changes in the prices of goods and services.

Horndal effect, or Learning-by-Doing: The principle that experience leads to better, more efficient (that is, lower-cost) ways of performing tasks.

Human capital: Investments embodied in human beings, such as education and skills, that enhance productivity.

Hyperinflation: An unspecified but very rapid and accelerating rate of **inflation,** typically at least 15 percent or so per month.

Illiquid: Not easily or cheaply converted into cash.

Increasing returns to scale: Decreasing long-run average cost. Under increasing returns to scale, a simultaneous, 1 percent increase in all factor inputs increase a firm's output by more than 1 percent. Synonymous with **economies of scale**.

Index number: A number used to measure changes in prices, wages, and so forth, relative to an arbitrary base of 100.

Inelastic: A product is said to be income- or price-**inelastic** if the percentage change in quantity in response to a change in income or price is less than the percentage change in income or price. See **elasticity**.

Infant industry: A newly established industry that has not yet had a chance to expand its scale of operation to reach its minimum long-run average cost.

Inflation: A rise in the average price level.

Infrastructure: Elements of the economy that facilitate growth (but do not necessarily contribute to growth directly), such as public waterworks and sanitation systems, or that facilitate the flow of goods and services from supplier to consumer, such as transportation and communications.

Innovation: The process of adopting, or bringing into general use, a new invention.

Insolvent: A situation in which liabilities exceed assets.

Institution: The rules of the game in a society that structure incentives and govern relationships. These rules may be formal (as in the case of laws) or informal (customary).

Intensive growth: Growth of output per unit of input. Otherwise known as total factor productivity (or more simply just as **productivity**) growth.

Invisible trade: Trade in intangibles, such as insurance and shipping services.

Keynesians: Followers of the English economist John Maynard Keynes (pronounced Kānz) who argue that government spending can substitute for inadequate private consumption or investment expenditure to stimulate economic activity and increase the level of employment.

Learning-by-doing: The principle that repeated and extended experience leads to more efficient and lower-cost ways of performing specific tasks. Sometimes referred to as the **Horndal effect**.

Legal tender: Money that the government declares must be accepted in payment of all debts, public and private. The Federal Reserve dollars in your pocket are so designated, as the statement of their face side declares; your checks and credit cards, on the other hand, are not legal tender.

Liquidationists: A descriptive name for the followers of the Austrian economist Friedrich von Hayek and others who argue that market forces cannot be circumvented by government action. They deny the propositions of Keynesians or monetarists who would have the government or the central bank intervene in the economy to stimulate growth and maintain high levels of economic activity and employment. In the liquidationist view, such intervention merely prolongs the period of adjustment from one equilibrium to a new equilibrium.

Liquidity: Low **transactions costs** for converting an asset into **legal tender**.

Margin, buying on: Buying stock by paying a small fraction of the purchase price and borrowing the balance against the security of the stocks being purchased. Margin today is typically 50 percent down. In the early 1920s it could be as low as 10 percent down.

Marginal product: The increment to total product from the employment of one more factor of production. Thus the marginal product of labor is the increase in output resulting from the employment of one more worker.

Market integration: Markets are said to be integrated if prices in two or more markets are driven by a common set of forces. The more closely linked the movement of prices in separate markets, the more closely integrated are those markets.

Mercantilism: A discredited economic theory of the sixteenth to the nineteenth centuries that equated the wealth and power of a nation to the country's stock of gold and silver and encouraged active government intervention in the economy to promote the growth of the stock of gold and silver through trade policies.

Monetize: To cause to function as money.

Money: Anything acceptable as a medium of exchange. In addition, money may serve as a store of value and as the unit of account.

Monopoly: The sole supplier of a product for which there is no close substitute.

Moral hazard: Moral hazard refers to situations and actions which increase the likelihood of an unfortunate outcome. For example, when the provision of insurance increases the likelihood of the insured event's happening. Thus, bank deposit insurance benefits risk-taking banks by removing the depositor's incentive to monitor bank activities because of a divergence between private costs and private benefits.

Morbidity: The risk of falling sick.

National bank: A bank chartered by the federal government under the terms of the National Banking Act of 1864.

Oligopoly: A market in which there are just a few (more than two) producers of a relatively homogeneous product.

Opportunity cost: The value of the best forgone alternative.

Optimal tariff: The national income maximizing tariff rate.

Par: Face value.

Peonage, debt: Debt slavery or servitude. When a creditor dictates the activities of the debtor to guarantee repayment of the debt.

Perfect competition: Large number of small producers of a homogeneous product who are unable to influence market price through their individual actions.

Pool: A group of firms that agree to pool their revenues and divide them among members according to an agreed formula. The purpose of a pool is to limit the incentive for individual firms to cut price so as to gain market share at the expense of their rivals.

Populists: Members of a political party of the late nineteenth century with an agenda calling for, among other things, government ownership of transportation and communications facilities, restrictions on immigration, shorter hours of work, unlimited minting of silver coinage, and the elimination of banks.

Principal-agent problem: The principal is the person or persons who engage others—the agent or agents—through an explicit or implicit contract to act on his behalf. The problem arises because of differences in the goals and preferences of principal and agents and is solved through monitoring performance and the structure of incentives for the agent to engage in the behavior desired by the principal. See also **agency theory.**

Producer surplus: The difference between the value of output and the resource cost of producing that output that is measured by the area under the supply curve. It is thus the area above the supply curve and below the price line.

Production function: A mathematical representation of the relationship between factor inputs and output. The most widely used production function is the Cobb-Douglas production function. See the Appendix to Chapter 1.

Productivity: Output per unit of input. If inputs are measured as a composite bundle of labor, land, and capital, then the productivity measure is known as total factor productivity. Otherwise, if the input is just land, labor, or capital, then the productivity measure is land productivity (that is, yield per acre), labor productivity, or capital productivity.

Property rights: Rights governing the ownership, use, and disposal of resources. Market efficiency requires secure, clearly defined property rights.

Protectionism: The economic policy of limiting foreign competition with domestic producers through either the imposition of tariffs or the establishment of import quotas.

Public goods: A good or service that, if supplied to one person, can be made available to others at no extra cost and from which others cannot be excluded. Examples include justice, national defense, fresh air, and beautiful sights and sounds. The inability to exclude consumption by others generates **free rider** problems.

Quantity theory (of money): Relates the effective supply of money to the level of prices and economic activity in the country.

Ratchet effect: The principle that government expenditures are easy to increase and difficult to reduce since they create political constituencies of beneficiaries. In particular, government expenditures rise sharply during times of crisis but fail to return to precrisis levels after the crisis has passed.

Rational expectations: Rational individuals do not make systematic forecasting errors.

Real bills doctrine: The view that so long as the Federal Reserve restricted its activities to rediscounting commercial paper, its activities would neither be inflationary nor deflationary and that the legitimate cash needs of the economy would be just satisfied.

Recession: A reduction in the level of economic activity and employment. Compared with a **depression**, a recession is relatively mild and short-lived.

Rediscount: The purchase of discounted commercial paper from member banks by the Federal Reserve. The rediscount rate is not a market-determined rate of interest but rather is set by the Fed at a level consistent with its policy objectives and influences other market interest rates.

Repeated games: Strategic interactions repeated between the same parties in which each has the opportunity to learn from past interactions.

Reserve ratio: The fraction of deposit liabilities held by banks to meet customer demand for immediate repayment. Banking laws often prescribe some minimum ratio, but banks are free to hold reserves in excess of those required by law. See also **bank reserves.**

Returns to scale: See **economies of scale.**

Risk: The *probability* of a particular event's occurring.

Section: One mile square of land containing 640 acres. This was the basic land survey unit defined in the Land Ordinance of 1785.

Segmented markets: Two or more distinct and separate markets for the same factor or product. Limited or nonexistent factor mobility or arbitrage possibilities prevent the equalization of prices between the markets.

Sharecropper: Legally an agricultural wage laborer who sells his or her labor for a mechanic's lien against the crop on which he or she works in lieu of wages. A share tenant, on the other hand, is a tenant whose rent was specified as a particular share of the crop or crops.

Snag: A sunken tree posing a hazard to navigation.

Social choice: The application of economic analysis to "nonmarket" decision making, as, for example, decision making by governments.

Social saving: Aggregate **consumer surplus** accruing in an economy as the result of an **innovation.**

Specie: Gold and silver, whether as coin or unminted metal (bullion).

Specific duties: Import duties of a specific dollar amount regardless of the price of the imported product.

Speculator: Someone who engages in buying purely for the purpose of reselling in the *same market* at a profit.

Substitutes: Products with a negative **cross-elasticity of demand**.

Technique: The factor proportions chosen by a firm to produce a given product, typically thought of in terms of the capital-labor ratio.

Technology: The process underlying production. The "black box" that converts hours of labor and machine time and acres of land into goods and services.

Terms of trade: A rate of exchange. Generally the terms of trade refer to the ratio of export prices to import prices, but we sometimes also speak of the farm terms of trade defined as the ratio of prices received by farmers for their crops to prices paid by farmers.

Transactions costs: Those costs other than price incurred in making an exchange. They include information costs, the costs of protecting **property rights,** and the costs of negotiating and enforcing contracts. See also **agency theory.**

Uncertainty: A situation in which no probability can be attached to the likelihood of an event's occurring, whereas probabilities can be assigned in the case of **risk.**

Underemployment: Employment less than full-time or in a manner that fails to take advantage of specific valuable skills or other human capital.

Value Added = value of output − value of raw materials: Value added is the increase in value generated by the production process.

Visible trade: Trade in tangible goods.

Wildcat banks: Banks with excessively low reserve ratios deliberately located in remote areas to discourage noteholders from attempting to redeem the bank's notes in specie upon demand.

Yeoman: A small farmer who owns the land that he or she farms. A freeholder.

Index